CHICAGO PUBLIC LIBRARY

R03130 59281

D1033951

BUSINESS/SCIENCE/TECHNOLOGY DIVISION
CHICAGO PUBLIC LIBRARY
400 SOUTH STATE STREET
CHICAGO, IL 60605

BUSINESS/SCIENCE/TECHNOLOGY DIVISION
CHICAGO PUBLIC LIBRARY
400 SOUTH STATE STREET
CHICAGO, IL 60605

BUSINESS/SCIENCE/TECHNOLOGY DIVISION
CHICAGO PUBLIC LIBRARY

HANDBOOK
OF ADVOCACY
ADVERTISING

Ballinger Series in
BUSINESS IN A GLOBAL ENVIRONMENT

S. Prakash Sethi, *Series Editor*

Center for Management
Baruch College
The City University of New York

R03130 59281

BUSINESS/SCIENCE/TECHNOLOGY DIVISION
CHICAGO PUBLIC LIBRARY
400 SOUTH STATE STREET
CHICAGO, IL 60605

S. PRAKASH SETHI

HANDBOOK OF ADVOCACY ADVERTISING

CONCEPTS, STRATEGIES, AND APPLICATIONS

Cambridge
Massachusetts

Ballinger Publishing Company
a subsidiary of
Harper & Row, Publishers, Inc.

INFORMATION CENTER
AMERICAN MARKETING ASSOCIATIO
250 South Wacker Drive
Chicago, Illinois 60606

Ballinger Publishing Company
Cambridge, Massachusetts
A Subsidiary of Harper & Row, Publishers, Inc.

© 1987 S. Prakash Sethi

Library of Congress Cataloging-in-Publication Data

Sethi, S. Prakash.
   Advocacy advertising.

   Includes index.
   1. Advocacy advertising—Case studies.   I. Title.
II. Series.
HD59.3.S44   1985   659.1'13   85-16954

ISBN 0-88730-163-0

All rights reserved. No part of this publication may be reproduced, stored in a
retrieval system, or transmitted in any form or by any means, electronics,
mechanical, photocopying, recording and/or otherwise without the prior
written permission of the publishers.

Manufactured in the United States of America

10   9   8   7   6   5   4   3   2   1

HD
59
3
.344

CONTENTS

Contents

Contents

Contents

FOREWORD

More and more, business is speaking out. It has always advertised to inform the public about the products and services it sells. Now business is running ads to convey its ideas as well. This is a switch from conventional practice.

For all their involvement and aggressiveness in the product marketplace, companies have traditionally shied away from the marketplace of ideas. They have tended, in the public policy arena, to cede turf to the antibusiness activists, those people and organizations that are hostile to free enterprise, especially big business, and bent on reshaping our society more to their leanings.

Confronted by their critics, many companies have reacted by hunkering down in silence or, perhaps, by vocalizing a pained whimper or two. Or they have responded to their attackers with defensive, platitudinous statements lacking credibility and force.

That's all changing. Gone is the low profile and supine posture of the past, at least among growing numbers of corporations and industry associations, such as the ones covered in the case studies in this book.

At last, business is going on the offensive in the marketplace of ideas. It is asserting its viewpoint on issues. It is presenting its case directly to the public in an effort to raise awareness, inform, illuminate, and build support. It is speaking out on behalf of our system of competitive capitalism, individual initiative and responsibility, and risk-and-reward enterprise.

Business is stepping up its communication in many forms, among them speeches, seminars, house organs, community and governmental programs, and publications of all sorts. One of the forms is advocacy-issue advertising, both in print and broadcast media. This is a rising genre of advertising in which such organizations as corporations and trade associations take out ads not to promote wares but to voice views. Because opinion leaders and decision-makers are the primary audience, advocacy ads often appear in newspapers on the page opposite editorials and in modest-circulation journals and magazines dealing with issues and ideas.

In the new activism of business, advocacy-issue advertising has become a potent vehicle of communication. Companies are adopting it to make themselves heard on a broad range of social, economic, and legislative issues.

And why not? Why shouldn't business, just as much as antibusiness advocates, exercise its constitutional right to take part in the dialogue that contributes to the making of public policy through our laws and regulations? Business has as vital a stake as anyone in societal progress, economic growth, and the quality of life. The well-being of hundreds of thousands of individuals is linked to the viability of any of America's largest corporations: employees and their families, shareholders, customers, suppliers, and residents of plant communities.

We at United Technologies Corporation, with more than 250,000 employees and shareowners, are avid adherents of advocacy-issue advertising. We've been running such ads since 1977, addressing issues such as technology, trade, education, defense, taxation, and numerous other subjects being debated and discussed in the policy-making councils and by concerned people everywhere. It's a healthy sign in our free society that more business organizations are becoming advocacy-issue advertisers. How some of them are speaking out, and why, and with what effect—that is the subject of this relevant and well-researched volume.

Harry J. Gray
Former Chairman and
* Chief Executive Officer*
United Technologies Corporation
Hartford, Connecticut

ACKNOWLEDGMENTS

This book would not have been possible without the active cooperation of a large number of people from the business community, labor unions, government agencies, state-owned enterprises, and public interest groups. They willingly shared information on their campaign objectives and execution strategies, even where their campaigns were less than totally successful. They have my gratitude for their cooperation. I am, however, solely responsible for any errors of omission and commission.

For their support of the overall concept of the book and their willingness to read various parts of the manuscript, I am grateful to Harry Darling, vice-president, Association of National Advertisers; William P. Mullane, corporate vice-president, Information Services, AT&T; Robert L. Dilenschneider, president and chief operating officer, national operations, Hill & Knowlton, Inc.; Julian Scheer, senior vice-president—corporate affairs, and John W. Johnson, vice-president—corporate public affairs and advertising, The LTV Corporation; Kalman B. Druck, public relations counselor; Raymond D'Argenio, senior vice-president, United Technologies; H. J. Young, senior vice-president, Edison Electric Institute; Ronald Rhody, senior vice-president—Communications, Bank of America; Philip Lesly, president, The Philip Lesly Company; Stephen B. Elliott, director—corporate advertising, W. R. Grace & Co.; William Latshaw, manager, corporate affairs division, Bethlehem Steel Corporation; Ken Colby, vice-president—corporate affairs, NORCEN Energy, Canada; Trey Taylor, manager of marketing services, ITT-Dialcom; and Linda Cheeseman, accounts supervisor, Ogilvy & Mather Advertising.

For their assistance and cooperation in the preparation of case studies of their respective organizations' advocacy campaigns, or their perspectives on the campaigns with which they have been associated, I am grateful to Michael Ivens, AIMS of Industry, United Kingdom; Philip

Sparks, The American Federation of State, County and Municipal Employees (AFSCME); John McGill, American Trucking Association; James Keyser, Association of American Railroads; Grant Woodruff, British Railways Board, United Kingdom; Jamie Deacy and Ian R. Smyth, Canadian Petroleum Association; James Sites, Richard L. Wilson, and Priscilla Moore, Chemical Manufacturers Association; A. R. Eovine, Commercial Union; Alan Gray, Decima Research, Ltd., Canada; Edward R. Luter, Dresser Industries, Inc.; Hon. Michael Forsyth, Member of Parliament, United Kingdom; Antonio Navarro, W. R. Grace & Co.; Graham Mather, Institute of Corporate Directors, United Kingdom; Theodore Price, Lone Star Industries; Calvin McLauchlan, McLauchlan, Mohr, Massey, Ltd., Canada; Robert Rodale, Rodale Press; Shirley Kaiden, Ruder Finn & Rotman; Michael Stevenson, Savings and Loan Foundation; William Grala and Andrew Gillinson, SmithKline Beckman Corporation; James Knox, *Spectator*, United Kingdom; and Virginia McGrath, VanSant Dugdale Advertising.

For giving me permission to use their advertisements in the book, I am grateful to the following organizations: Association of Metropolitan Authorities (United Kingdom); Association of Metropolitan County Councils (United Kingdom); British Airport Authority; BiPartisan Budget Coalition; Catholics for a Free Choice; Church League of America; Coalition for a New Foreign and Military Policy; Common Cause; Friends of Animals; International Program Organization, Austria; Internorth; International Society for Animal Rights; International Fund for Animal Welfare; Izaak Walton League; League of Voluntary Hospitals and Homes of New York; Metropolitan County Council, United Kingdom; Moral Majority, Inc.; Planned Parenthood; R. J. Reynolds Tobacco Co.; Todd Shipyards; United Steel Workers of America; United Federation of Teachers; and Zenchu—The Central Union of Agricultural Cooperatives, Japan.

During the course of the three years in which this book was in preparation, a number of graduate students assisted me in the research on various case studies. Professor Carl L. Swanson coauthored the study on the National Maritime Association. I gratefully acknowledge the work of Mohamed Nabil Allam, Josette Quiniou, and Ingrid Schwindt, who carried a large part of this burden. In addition, Minoo Mortazavi, Abbas Alkhafaji, F. Mohmoud Elfekey, Jeannie Kee, and Alan Rosenberg worked on individual case studies, and their assistance is appreciated and recognized.

The logistical and secretarial support was provided by the Center for Research in Business and Social Policy, The University of Texas, Dallas; Research Program in Business and Public Policy at the Center for the Study of Business and Government, Center for Management Development and Organization Research, and Department of Management at Baruch College, The City University of New York. I am thankful to all these organizations for their assistance and cooperation.

No amount of thanks could recompense Mame Chambers, my secretary at the University of Texas at Dallas, who undertook the major burden of typing the numerous drafts of large segments of the book. Additional typing and secretarial assistance was provided at Baruch by Frances G. Krull, Bettye R. Steinberg, Jean Cracchiolo, Sandy Kane, and Anthony Rivera. I am grateful to all of them for their cheerful and uncomplaining support under extreme time pressure and often difficult working conditions.

And last, but not least, I wish to express my appreciation to my wife Donna and my two sons, Amit and Ravi, for their love and affection, which makes research and writing a pleasant avocation.

Great Neck, New York
April 1986

Part I   PERSPECTIVES

ON ADVOCACY

ADVERTISING:

EVOLUTION AND

GROWTH,

1975–1985

Chapter 1   INTRODUCTION

In 1977, when I first published *Advocacy Advertising and Large Corporations,* the subject of advocacy, or idea-issue, advertising had just begun to rise in the American consciousness. No doubt it was spurred in large measure by a spate of advocacy campaigns launched by oil companies, notably Mobil Oil, to explain and defend their large profits following the Arab oil boycott and the resultant skyrocketing of oil prices. The late 1960s and early 1970s also constituted the period when corporations were faced with broad public attacks and more intensive government regulation because of increased national concern for a cleaner environment, health and safety, and a better quality of life. It is not surprising that early entrants into the fracas, in addition to oil, were companies from such industries as chemicals, minerals, heavy (smoke-stack) industries, and forestry products.[1]

Advocacy Advertising and Large Corporations received considerable media and scholarly attention, as it raised serious issues of public policy. An equally important consideration, from the business community's viewpoint, was my conclusion, based on an extensive analysis of a large number of advocacy campaigns then underway, that advocacy advertising as it was being practiced by major corporations and industry groups, with some notable exceptions, was of largely questionable value and doubtful effectiveness on economic, sociopolitical, and legal grounds.

I had also argued that, when properly conceived and executed, advocacy advertising could serve a vital function in broadening the scope of public debate on issues that were socially important but hitherto had not been adequately understood by the public or sufficiently explored and discussed in the marketplace of ideas. It was suggested that advocacy advertising could become a cutting edge in further opening up the process of informing the public. It could also be an effective tool by which business could create a better public understanding of what could be reasonably expected of business in fulfilling society's expectations.

A great deal has happened since the publication of *Advocacy Advertising and Large Corporations*. The sociopolitical environment of business in the United States has become far more receptive to the concept of paid political advertising by large corporations. There has been a tremendous increase in both the magnitude and the growth of advocacy advertising. The phenomenon has spread to many other countries, notably Canada, Great Britain, and to a lesser extent, the nations of Western Europe. The diversity of sponsorship has also increased and is no longer confined to large corporations and industry groups. It now includes trade unions, ideologically oriented public interest groups, religious organizations, political parties and candidates, and even state-owned corporations and government agencies. The types of issues covered have also become more varied. This has had the unusual effect of creating combined sponsorship on specific issues among groups who otherwise do not share common goals and objectives.

An equally important element of change has been in the practice of advocacy advertising. Having analyzed over a hundred advocacy campaigns in depth, I have discerned a noticeable process of maturation. Sponsors have become more realistic about their expectations of what advocacy advertising can accomplish. They have also become more sophisticated about the use of this tool as an instrument for modifying public opinion and attitudes and effecting change in national agendas and public policies.

A number of these elements have had a positive effect on the growing public acceptance of advocacy advertising. However, not all the changes have been constructive or in the right direction. Therefore, what we do with this important communication tool will influence not only the activities of its sponsors—notably the private corporate sector—but also the nature of public policy debate. One has only to look at the onslaught of political commercials during an election campaign to appreciate how they have irrevocably changed the character of the electoral process, and indeed the political process, in the United States.

In the last analysis, advocacy advertising will not be judged solely or even primarily for its effectiveness as a communication tool in achieving its sponsor's objectives. Advocacy advertising, ultimately, is an educational tool and a political tool designed to play an active role in influencing a society's priorities. Therefore, its legitimacy and effectiveness will also be judged in political terms—by the public's perception that its practitioners are using it responsibly and, in addition to their self-interest, also serving some larger public purpose.

WHAT IS ADVOCACY ADVERTISING?

Considerable confusion and misunderstanding exist as to what constitutes advocacy advertising, because in a sense all advertising is advocacy. Moreover, even when we narrow the scope of advocacy advertising by excluding messages that promote a sponsor's products and services, there remains a vast area of institutional advertising where it must be distinguished from traditional public relations—goodwill advertising, public service messages, and public interest "educational" advertising.

This ambiguity, however, is not unexpected, given the evolving nature of the phenomenon, the predilections of different practitioners, and the legal and tax considerations that influence how certain ad messages are categorized. A more precise definition must await the passage of time and broad public acceptance of the scope of advocacy advertising. Nevertheless, we can define advocacy advertising in fairly explicit terms, based on its objectives and manner of execution.

Advocacy advertising, including idea-issue advertising, is part of that genre of advertising known as corporate image or institutional advertising. It is concerned with the propagation of ideas and the elucidation of controversial social issues deemed important by its sponsor in terms of public policy. The managerial context of advocacy advertising is that of defending or promoting the sponsor's activities, modus operandi, and position on controversial issues of public policy. The behavioral and social context of advocacy advertising is that of changing public perception of the sponsor's actions and performance from skepticism and hostility to trust and acceptance—and/or to a more neutral position. The political context of advocacy advertising is that of the constitutional safeguards for freedom of speech; a sponsor is asserting its right to speak out on issues of public importance without any regulation or censorship on the part of other private groups or government agencies.[2] The political context of advocacy advertising would thus encompass even otherwise allegedly purely educational messages where the issues raised involve important matters of public policy, may be of a controversial nature, and the sponsor's objective is to heighten public awareness of those issues or some preferred options for their resolution. Thus LTV's 1984 campaign publicizing the views of the presidential candidates on major economic and defense issues [Exhibit 1] and W. R. Grace's recent campaign to highlight waste and mismanagement in federal government spending [Exhibit 2] would be classified as advocacy advertising.

A NORMATIVE FRAMEWORK FOR UNDERSTANDING THE ROLE OF ADVOCACY ADVERTISING

In a democratic society the primary tasks of the nation are carried out by the major private and public social institutions. The society at large exercises control over these institutions and holds them accountable through an evaluation of their activities. Effective control is based on three elements: (1) the quality of the information provided by the institutions; (2) the capability of the news media to manage the "public communications space" to ensure adequate access for various viewpoints; and (3) the ability of the people to sift various ideas and select those that meet their expectations. The first two elements are thus critical to the notion of adequate public control. One of the assumptions behind issue-advocacy advertising by business institutions is their belief

Exhibit 1

THE LTV 1984 LEADERSHIP SERIES

THE ELECTION

REAGAN VS. MONDALE:

How will you provide jobs for Americans?

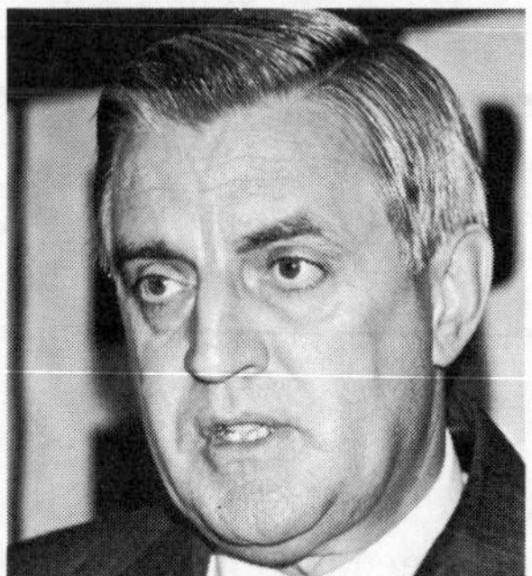

Baruch College asked the leading candidates the following questions: How will you improve employment opportunities: job programs, retraining, opportunities for minority groups? What should the Federal government's role be?

Ronald Reagan
Republican, California

Four years ago, America was in the grip of stagflation. Growth had stalled, and unemployment had climbed from under 6 percent in 1979 to 7.5 percent. And with double-digit inflation and record interest rates wrecking the economy, unemployment was bound to increase further.

The previous Administration, ill-prepared to tackle stagflation, took refuge behind the myth of the "no-growth society." A Carter-Mondale adviser said, "We can't avoid a decline in our standard of living. All we can do is adapt."

But the no-growth society actually resulted from their no-growth policies. Productivity plummeted as overspending, high taxes and overregulation dried up investment. We fell farther behind our competitors—and lost jobs.

Over nine years, though nearly $60 billion had been expended on the scandal-ridden, make-work Comprehensive Employment Training Act (CETA) program, only 18 percent of that money went to job training. Only 30 percent of CETA participants found permanent jobs—and only half of those were private-sector jobs. In two decades, unemployment among young people increased over 50 percent and the rate for black male teenagers more than doubled.

Today, those no-growth days are over. Our policies have opened new vistas of opportunity.

We cut spending growth by two-thirds, reduced taxes to encourage business and boost productivity and reduced regulation.

In fact, three words describe our recovery program: jobs, jobs and jobs. Over six million jobs have been created by our recovery. In late 1982, liberals in Congress pushed for legislation they claimed would have created 300,000 make-work jobs—at a cost of over $3 billion. Our recovery has produced an average of nearly 300,000 every *month* since then—900,000 in May alone. Today, almost 107 million American men and women are at work. In fact, there are more Americans working in 1984 than ever in our history.

And everyone has benefited. Unemployment has dropped for men and women, blacks and Hispanics.

But our efforts have gone beyond economic recovery. Our Jobs Training Partnership Act (JTPA) is an innovative partnership among Federal, state and local government and the private sector to provide permanent employment in the private sector.

JTPA annually provides 1.25 million disadvantaged and handicapped individuals, offenders, displaced homemakers, older workers, and teenage parents with remedial education, basic skills and on-the-job training. JTPA also provides dislocated workers job search assistance, retraining, prelayoff assistance and relocation expenses.

Under JTPA, unlike CETA, 70 percent of funds go directly to job training; make-work "public service employment" has been eliminated. Ninety percent of funds go to economically disadvantaged persons. And the private sector—which knows best the training necessary for productive, career-building jobs—helps develop jobs training plans.

But expanding employment is not enough. We must protect the growing work force on the job. And 1982 saw the lowest total job injury rate ever recorded. In fact, nearly every job safety indicator improved during our first two years.

Still, we intend to build on our successes by recovery and promoting innovative programs to expand opportunity.

One initiative is a youth summer minimum wage for teenage workers. Mandating $3.35 an hour for start-up jobs just guarantees that fewer teenagers will be hired.

The bill protects the jobs of adult workers and wages of teenagers already on the job, and limits the lower wage to summer months. Still, Democratic leaders and organized labor have blocked the bill despite the fact that it could provide up to 400,000 summer jobs, and has been endorsed by the National Conference of Black Mayors. We have also worked to extend the targeted job tax credit for disadvantaged youths, which provided 300,000 jobs in 1983.

And we have proposed enterprise zones—which would revitalize depressed areas by reducing tax and regulatory barriers to business growth and job creation. Local versions of our urban enterprise zones proposal—which has been blocked by House Democrats—have proved successful in moving jobs and investment to depressed inner-city areas.

Our opponents would reverse the policies which produced recovery and enhanced opportunity. They have already promised to raise taxes. They even want to tear apart our program of tax indexing—allowing inflation to push the working men and women of America into higher tax brackets.

And they would reverse our philosophy of faith in people that has produced sustained recovery. Instead, they would resort to intervention into the free market and more make-work jobs programs. This defeatist "era of limits" thinking implies that Americans cannot outinnovate, outproduce, and outsell anyone on their own.

But we know we can—if only government will give us the room to reach as high as our vision and God-given talents take us. With your help and support, we can keep America's great job-creating engine revving—and produce a future of prosperity and full employment for all Americans.

Walter Mondale
Democrat, Minnesota

One of America's greatest strengths is our profound belief in the importance of work. Work means more than merely making a living. It provides us with dignity and with the satisfaction of making a contribution to society. It gives meaning to our lives.

Little wonder, then, that unemployment is so devastating to our society and to the people it touches. The Reagan recession cost us nearly $700 billion in lost income, unbuilt housing, and unmade investment. Its human cost was far higher.

In a nation that believes in work, it is intolerable to accept an economic policy that consciously condemns millions of Americans to the profound humiliation of joblessness. To accept unemployment of 6 or 7 percent as "full" or "normal" means more than 7 million Americans without jobs. It means continued misery for families, and continued decline for hard-hit communities. It is socially indecent and economically self-defeating.

Our goal must be a job for every American who wants or needs one. To achieve this goal, we must take two steps: We must create sustainable, long-term economic growth; and we must ensure that our economy includes people who are shut out today.

First, economic growth. A sensible economic program starts by chopping down this massive deficit which has sent real interest rates to record highs, made our exports uncompetitive in the world market, choked our economy, and mortgaged our future for generations to come.

We must scale the defense budget to reality. I favor steady spending increases for a sound, sensible defense, but our defense budget must make choices, not hand a blank check to the Pentagon.

We must deal with entitlements. Health care costs are rising much faster than overall inflation. We must have a tough program of health care cost containment and increase competition in the health industry.

We must shape a sensible, long-term farm policy. Today, American farmers are in their worst shape in decades—despite farm programs whose costs last year were the highest ever. Our farm policy must increase farm income, bring production in line with demand, and boost exports in a sensible and effective way.

And we must reform our tax code so that wealthy individuals and large corporations join the rest of us in paying their fair share. In the longer run, I will work toward a simpler, fairer system that restores progressivity and promotes savings and productive investments—not tax shuffles of paper assets.

Shrinking the budget deficit will help produce long-term, sustainable growth with civilized interest rates, and reduce the $125 billion commercial trade deficit—saving nearly 3 million American jobs.

But growth alone is not enough. I want economic growth that includes all Americans.

We must enforce our civil rights laws, and extend entrepreneurial opportunities to minorities, women, and others for whom such opportunities have been beyond reach. The Federal government—through the Small Business Administration, the 8(a) program, contracting, set-aside programs, and across the board—can be a tremendously powerful instrument in this area.

We must work toward pay equity to bridge the chasm between women's and men's earnings. Women are more than half our population and head an increasing number of our households. They must be fairly compensated for the work they do.

As President, I will enforce the laws prohibiting discrimination against predominantly female jobs and direct the EEOC to establish clear guidelines and open its administrative process for review of sex-based wage complaints. I will make sure the Federal government gets its house in order, with a review of the Civil Service classification system for sex bias. I will establish a Federal pay equity clearinghouse. And I will use the Presidency as a place of moral leadership, to speak out on the significance of pay equity.

We must also encourage businesses to invest in people and equipment, not in wasteful mergers and shuffles of paper assets. One way to encourage productive investment is through carefully targeted tax cuts. Specifically, I propose eliminating the capital gains tax for long-term new investment in smaller businesses or for gains that are rolled over into new smaller businesses; making the 25 percent research and development tax cut permanent; and expanding the investment tax credit to include added worker training and education.

We must invest more in our country. We should be revitalizing our basic industries—instead of letting our best jobs disappear overseas. We should be encouraging our emerging, high-tech industries—instead of allowing our foreign competitors to dominate the industries that will provide tomorrow's jobs. And we should be repairing our crumbling roads, ports, bridges, and cities—instead of letting youth and minority unemployment persist at tragic levels.

Finally, we must invest more in our people, to help them get the skills they need. We cannot compete effectively unless we regain our edge in science and research. We cannot protect our nation's security unless we are at the frontiers of technology. We cannot meet the economic challenges of the future unless we prepare our children with tomorrow's skills today.

I have proposed a major new Federal investment in education so our students can learn the skills they will need in the future. I favor a much more systematic effort to address specific shortages of skilled personnel. And I believe we must invest more in vocational training and retraining for displaced workers. To perform the jobs of the future, this generation of Americans must be the best trained, best educated generation in history. As President, I will work to make sure they are.

We are now in the final phase of The LTV Corporation's 1984 *Leadership Series.* Earlier in the year, we presented a forum for all the Presidential candidates to express their views on a variety of topics. Now, we focus on comprehensive statements by President Reagan and former Vice President Mondale on six vital election issues.

The nominees' statements were obtained by Baruch College of the City University of New York.

To provide a broader perspective, LTV commissioned Opinion Research Corporation to poll a sampling of opinion leaders on these same issues. Leaders from business, labor, academics, the media, government, and public interest groups were queried in March of 1984.

Opinion leaders' attitudes about employment

On the subject of employment, 80% of the opinion leaders felt that the best way to provide jobs for the unemployed was through the growth of private enterprise, not through the expansion of the public sector. At the same time, however, 77% favored government retraining programs for displaced workers as well as improving education criteria, and 60% recommended more special programs for minorities and women.

A public service of LTV

LTV endorses no candidate or political position; we are sponsoring *The Leadership Series* and a number of other programs as a public service during this election year.

We are also publishing a booklet containing comprehensive statements from President Reagan and former Vice President Mondale on each of the issues featured in *The Leadership Series:* the deficit, defense strategy, employment, education, the environment, industrial policy, and foreign trade. For your free copy of "The Candidates 1984," mail requests on your letterhead to: The Candidates, The LTV Corporation, P.O. Box 225003-W22, Dallas, TX 75265.

On behalf of The LTV Corporation, I hope you will find this useful and informative as you decide whom you will support in the upcoming election.

Raymond A. Hay

Raymond A. Hay
Chairman and Chief Executive Officer

LTV: Looking Ahead

The LTV Corporation
AEROSPACE/DEFENSE·ENERGY·STEEL

These statements were obtained by Baruch College of the City University of New York and its School of Business and Public Administration, a leading national center for education, research and policy studies in business and administrative sciences.

Exhibit 2

SHE'S GOT HER MOTHER'S EYES, HER FATHER'S NOSE AND HER UNCLE'S DEFICIT.

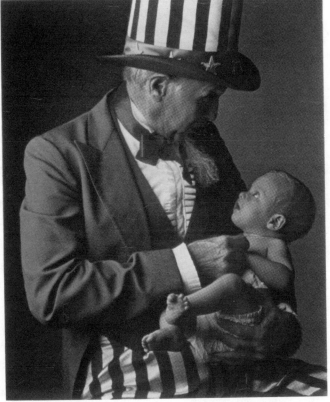

It's quite a legacy her uncle has handed her. (Her favorite uncle, at that.) Annual federal deficits approaching $200 billion. A current national debt of $1.6 trillion. Potentially, $13 trillion by the year 2000.

When the numbers get this big, they tend to get meaningless. Until you look at it this way. If federal deficits continue at their current rate, it's as if every baby born in 1985 will have a $50,000 debt strapped to its back.

The great debate over deficits, of course, no longer centers on whether or not they should be reduced, but how.

One side favors raising taxes. But whose? 90% of all personal taxable income already comes from tax brackets of $35,000 and below. Does anyone seriously suggest increasing the tax burden of lower and middle income families?

Well then, the argument follows, tax the rich. But, if the federal government took every penny of every dollar over the $75,000 tax bracket that isn't already taxed—not a surcharge, mind you, but took it all—it would only collect enough to run the country for a week. Besides, there's no guarantee that Congress would spend less money if we all gave them more.

The alternative seems clear. Cut spending. But, again, the question is how.

We're W.R. Grace & Co. While our business interests in chemicals, natural resources and consumer services are worldwide, our primary interest is in the future of America's economy. That's where any corporation's best interest lies.

To that end, our chairman headed a presidential commission that identified ways to end abuses in federal spending. It found 2,478 ways. Specific ways.

The President has seen the report. So has Congress. We think you should know what they know. There's a booklet that summarizes it all. For your free copy, write to this address: USA DEBT, Dept. U, P.O. Box 3190, Ogden, Utah 84409.

Unfortunately, almost 75% of the commission's recommendations won't be implemented unless Congress acts on them. And, sometimes, the words "Congressional action" are mutually exclusive. That's why we all have to take action first.

Read the booklet. If it gets you angry, it's up to you to get things changed. Write to Congress. If you don't think that'll do it, run for Congress.

Our children and grandchildren don't deserve to pay for our mistakes. We should be passing on to them a healthy economy and a high standard of living. That should be their inheritance. That should be their birthright.

GRACE
One step ahead of a changing world.

W.R. Grace & Co., 1114 Avenue of the Americas, New York, N.Y. 10036

7

that their access to the public communication space is limited. The conflict between the two institutions has to do with their relative perceptions of what is adequate entry. The objective is to make a better case for the legitimacy of an institution and its control over a share of society's physical and human resources.

Freedom of speech, while fundamental to the notion of a free and democratic society, is not absolute. To operate in a reasonable, socially equitable, and politically acceptable manner, some restrictions are inevitable to curb the access of one group while facilitating greater expression for other groups that would otherwise be squeezed out of the marketplace of ideas. For example, the courts have attempted to make distinctions among various categories of speech, such as political and commercial, and afforded them varying degrees of protection.[3] Regulatory agencies promulgate the rules to ensure adequate access to opposing viewpoints on the nation's airwaves or to protect individuals or groups from receiving misleading information.[4] The news media serve a similar purpose by exercising judgment and presenting balanced news stories and expressing alternate positions through editorials. Individuals and groups also must exercise self-restraint and use the right of free speech in a responsible manner so that the rights of other individuals and groups are not violated and the need for external constraints is avoided or minimized. Exhibit 3 provides a scheme for understanding these relationships.

It should be apparent that access to the public communication space is not unlimited and is constrained by a variety of factors. In general, monitors 1 and 2 are more flexible and offer substitution choices to the communicator in developing an effective entry into the public communication mix. Monitor 3 is much more rigid in character: It defines the boundaries of a communication and also prescribes the exclusions in terms of the message and the medium that are proscribed. The constraints under monitor 3 are likely to be more onerous and penalties for noncompliance more burdensome, to the extent that monitors 1 and 2 are not used or a particular communicator can circumvent their working to the detriment of other groups so that the smooth working of the system is impeded.

The reception and interpretation of a communication by its recipient is subject to a variety of constraints, including source credibility, previously held beliefs, and peer group and opinion leader influences. The information is communicated back to different groups who then interact based on the intensity of beliefs expressed by the public and the likely effect on the future viability of the group if it does not conform to the wishes of the people.

ISSUE-ADVOCACY ADVERTISING: SOME UNRESOLVED ISSUES OF PUBLIC POLICY

It was not surprising that the surge in advocacy advertising, compressed as it was over a relatively short time following the Arab oil boycott, evoked strong public criticism and concern. Moreover, since early advocacy campaigns were conducted primarily by large corporations, notably oil companies, there was widespread public skepticism as to the

Exhibit 3

Social Information Processing and Public Communication Space

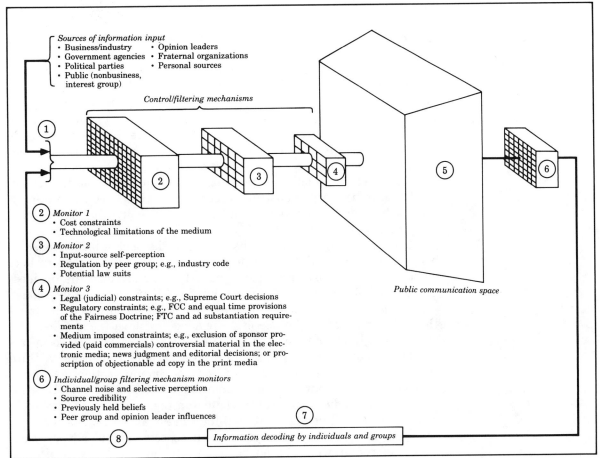

Sources of information input
- Business/industry
- Government agencies
- Political parties
- Public (nonbusiness, interest group)
- Opinion leaders
- Fraternal organizations
- Personal sources

Control/filtering mechanisms

Public communication space

(2) Monitor 1
- Cost constraints
- Technological limitations of the medium

(3) Monitor 2
- Input-source self-perception
- Regulation by peer group; e.g., industry code
- Potential law suits

(4) Monitor 3
- Legal (judicial) constraints; e.g., Supreme Court decisions
- Regulatory constraints; e.g., FCC and equal time provisions of the Fairness Doctrine; FTC and ad substantiation requirements
- Medium imposed constraints; e.g., exclusion of sponsor provided (paid commercials) controversial material in the electronic media; news judgment and editorial decisions; or proscription of objectionable ad copy in the print media

(6) Individual/group filtering mechanism monitors
- Channel noise and selective perception
- Source credibility
- Previously held beliefs
- Peer group and opinion leader influences

Information decoding by individuals and groups

truthfulness of these messages and the credibility of their sponsors. There were demands for control of such advertising from a number of political leaders and public interest groups.

The growth of issue-advocacy advertising during the last ten years has muted some of the earlier social policy concerns. A host of other concerns, however, remain unresolved and will continue to vex public mind and fuel controversy. Their resolution will come about through debate and discussion in the public arena and its influence on public opinion. They will also be affected by any evidence of abuse on the part of practitioners, and any potential harm perceived by the nation's leaders and public opinion.

Until now, the debate in the political context has revolved around the issue of the public's need to be exposed to different ideas and viewpoints. Many a sponsor of advocacy advertising has argued that paid communication is the only way to gain reasonable access to the marketplace of ideas—an access that sponsors feel is denied them because of unfair and unequal exposition of their positions and viewpoints in the news media. This is equally true of pure idea-issue advertising dealing with business and economic issues that allegedly receive scant attention in the mass media.

The business community's aggressive posture and the need to resort to advocacy advertising is founded on the belief that the traditional corporate response of ignoring unwarranted and uninformed attacks, or defending one's own position only when called for, has been ineffective. There is also a commonly shared belief among businesspeople that the prevailing low credibility of business is more a consequence of exaggerated expectations on the part of the public of what business can do than an indication of poor performance. The problem is further aggravated by groups who do not share any responsibility for the fulfillment of societal expectations but are quick to demand more and more from the business community. Corporate critics and social activists, on the other hand, were concerned with providing some mechanism that would ensure them adequate public expression of opposing viewpoints, not encumbered by financial constraints, especially when business interests could determine the debate agenda through the choice of issues selected for advocacy campaigns.

It is surprising how much the nature of the debate has changed in a few short years. Most of the legal issues concerning a corporation's right to engage in political speech have been resolved in the business community's favor by the Supreme Court in *Bellotti* and other decisions.[5] Another important change has been in the number and diversity of groups that have resorted to the use of issue-advocacy advertising. These include not only labor unions, but also public interest groups, social activists, religious organizations, and even government agencies. A third important element has been the diversity of communication media employed in advocacy advertising. In addition to mass media, mostly print, issue-advocacy advertising can be found on television, radio, cable TV, and in direct mail and "educational-informational" films. Not only has the total number of dollars spent on all aspects of issue-advocacy advertising been growing at a phenomenal rate, but the diversity of sponsors and multiplicity of communication channels has exacerbated many of the existing issues while giving rise to some new ones.

The Concept of Legitimacy

Propagation of ideas and promotion of preferred positions on public policy issues is inextricably linked with the interests of the sponsor. For an individual, the link is direct and unambiguous. For institutions, this link is not so clear, and in many cases is deliberately disguised. For example, the Supreme Court has held that a commercial advertisement is protected not so much because it pertains to a seller's business, but because it furthers society's interest in the "free flow of commercial information." As the Court considered the right of the corporation to speak on public issues, it noted that:

> The Court below framed the principal question in this case as whether and to what extent corporations have First Amendment rights. We believe that the Court posed the wrong question. The Constitution often protects interests broader than those of the party seeking their vindication. The First Amendment, in particular, serves significant societal interests. The proper

question, therefore, is not whether corporations "have" significant First Amendment rights and, if so, whether they are coextensive with those of natural persons. Instead, the question must be whether (the Massachusetts statute) abridges expression that the First Amendment was meant to protect.[6]

Without a clear identification of the sponsor, or his/her right to speak on behalf of a constituent group, the public's right to know is seriously jeopardized. Under these conditions, the line between education and dissemination of information on the one hand, and misleading propaganda and an attempt to brainwash the public on the other, becomes increasingly blurred. Moreover, it is not clear whether it is the right to free speech that is being protected, or that someone is being granted the privilege of deliberately misleading the public.

Although the corporation's right to speak publicly on controversial issues of public policy has been largely resolved, there still remains the larger issue of how this right is exercised. Since this right is invariably exercised by the corporate management, one needs to ask, for whom does the management speak? The stockholders are a diverse group, and while they may all have a common interest in a corporation's economic performance, they may not share similar political views. Therefore, without a specific mandate, the management cannot claim an implied right or superior knowledge about either *all* stockholder preferences, or those of other stakeholders in the corporation. Without such a mandate, a management's right to speak on public issues or advocate policy positions stands on shaky grounds.[7]

The legitimacy issue is no less pertinent and potent for more recent entrants into issue-advocacy advertising, notably labor unions and public interest groups. In the case of established groups such as labor unions and religious institutions, their right to speak on behalf of their constituents on issues that lie outside the areas for which these institutions were organized is equally contentious and disturbing. Like the corporate managers, there is no evidence that union or church leaders have ever sought a specific mandate from their memberships to espouse positions on controversial issues of public policy where a heterogeneous membership may hold divergent views, and has clearly not authorized the leadership to speak on its behalf.

The situation is even worse in the case of the new social activist groups that are not formed on the basis of a constituency. Instead, a small group of individuals organizes itself as a self-perpetuating, nonprofit public interest group, purporting to represent a constituency of ideas or issues. These groups do not have a constituency in the sense that they receive a mandate from the body politic. Instead, they claim a constituency by asserting to speak on behalf of those who are adversely affected by a particular issue and whose interests they have chosen to represent. Fearing charges of the nonrepresentational character of their organizations, many public interest groups and social activists have been playing down the lack of legitimacy argument.

The Role of the News Media

One of the most frequently offered arguments in support of advocacy advertising by its practitioners has to do with the alleged inadequacy or bias on the part of the news media in devoting sufficient time and space to explaining complex economic and social issues, or in fairly presenting the views of a group that is under attack or whose position is considered antithetical to that of important segments of the press.[8] The advocacy campaigns of W. R. Grace and Kaiser Aluminum illustrate these concerns.[9] Many other campaigns—e.g., United Technologies, Smith-Kline—although not completely devoted to this issue, have nevertheless devoted an ad hoc ad to the topic. A more recent ad by the House of Seagram complains about the refusal of certain newspapers and television networks to accept its ads [Exhibit 4]. And, of course, Mobil Oil has devoted a considerable part of its advocacy campaign to pointing a finger at the shortcomings of the news media. Mobil's advertisements are easily found with some regularity on the Op-Ed page of the *New York Times* and other leading national newspapers.

Apparently, the groups making these assertions would not need to resort to advocacy advertising if the news media had been doing a good job in the first place. It is quite possible, and indeed reasonable, to expect that at times a particular news medium or individual reporter/editor would be found wanting in meeting the high standards of the journalism profession. At the institutional level, the news media may be subjected to similar concerns of commercial viability, profitability, and a need for satisfying the immediate interests of their readers, rather than serving the long-term needs of society. As "going business concerns," they may display shortcomings in their operations and behavior akin to those of most other businesses or institutions. One could also argue that while the heterogeneity of the news media may dissipate some of these bad effects, it alone may not be enough to correct the situation. There is a constant need for self-examination not only on the part of the news media, but also on the part of the body politic to see how the role of news media can be further strengthened in order to create a greater and less biased flow of information and ideas and thereby improve the quality of public discussion and debate on issues that pertain to society's long-term interests.

However, like all complex social issues, the question of the appropriate role of the news media and an evaluation of news media performance is more involved, and the solution less obvious, than what is presented by critics of the media. A careful analysis of the specific charges made against the news media would lead one to conclude that this concern for adequacy and fairness is somewhat exaggerated and can be explained in terms of reasons that are not entirely inherent to the news media, but are embedded in the self-interest of those making the assertions.[10]

- The questions of inadequacy and inaccuracy of coverage necessarily involve issues of judgment, and the rights and obligations of editors and publishers to make those decisions. "Inadequate" coverage of a particular issue may be a reflection of the judgment by editors and

Exhibit 4

IT'S TIME AMERICA KNEW THE FACTS ABOUT DRINKING.

12 oz. of beer, 5 oz. of wine and 1 ¼ oz. of liquor all have the same alcohol content.

It's time ABC, CBS and NBC let the facts be heard.

We submitted TV commercials to the networks which simply stated the facts of alcohol equivalency, and they have refused to put them on the air. Network policy bars advertising for distilled spirits. But these announcements are not commercials for products...ours or anyone else's. The message here is the fact of equivalence. A fact people have a right to know. A fact we want to tell.

It's Time All Of Us Were Heard.

We share the concern of other public spirited groups who believe that the popular misconceptions about beverage alcohol can be dangerous. The National Institute on Alcohol Abuse and Alcoholism urges every American to know the facts of equivalency.

The American Automobile Association incorporates the facts of equivalence in its driver safety and alcohol education programs.

The Motor Vehicle Departments of California, New Jersey and Maryland explain the facts of equivalence in their drivers' manuals.

The Insurance Information Institute and Citizens for Highway Safety, are also publicizing the facts.

This message is *that* important.

The facts are, there is the same amount of alcohol in a 12 ounce can of beer, a 5 ounce glass of wine, and a 1¼ ounce serving of 80 proof whiskey, vodka, gin or rum. To be exact, the typical serving of beer contains 0.54 ounces of alcohol. The typical serving of wine contains 0.55 ounces of alcohol. The typical serving of spirits contains 0.50 ounces of alcohol.

THE HOUSE OF SEAGRAM

© 1985, THE HOUSE OF SEAGRAM, N.Y.

13

publishers as to the importance of that news event relative to the interests and needs of their readers, and also relative to other news items that vie for accommodation within limited time and space constraints.

- The issue of fairness is also highly subjective. Clearly, those who are under attack are likely to feel that their viewpoints and positions have not received a fair hearing. However, to give every person who feels aggrieved an automatic right to reply would be to reduce a particular news medium to the level of a common carrier—an untenable situation.

- The concern for accuracy is a genuine one and is a valid complaint to the extent that it goes beyond an occasional lapse of discipline or human error. However, its recurrence to any significant degree is likely to cause a newspaper to lose its credibility, and a journalist professional standing and pride. Therefore, they are contrary to the best interests of the reporters and institutions, and should be self-correcting in a free and competitive marketplace.

- Those who criticize the news media for unfair and biased treatment of news are often guilty of the practices they denounce in others. Corporations present their ideas and views disguised as information and cloaked in news formats similar to those of well-known network news programs—and use familiar news personalities—to present programs on many cable and independent television stations. Canned promotional pieces supplied to many television and radio stations, and press releases furnished to newspapers, are then fed into regular news programs without the news medium identifying the source of that information. The fact that a broadcast station or a newspaper reporter or editor was remiss in his/her responsibility does not absolve the suppliers of these deceptions—for they will be the first one to scream foul should a similar deception be discovered where their interests were adversely affected.

Media Access for Opposing Viewpoints

Users of advocacy advertising frequently justify their use of this medium on the ground that their organization's "message" has not been fairly treated by the media. The news media's alleged antibusiness or anti-whatever bias prevents it from presenting an accurate assessment of a sponsor's viewpoint. An added concern is related to the frustration of many corporate sponsors because of their inability to buy air time to present their side of the story on television because of the latter's unwillingness to accept commercials on issues of a controversial nature that are properly considered the domain of news programming. Companies like Mobil Oil have been quite vocal in their complaints against the three television networks for the latter's refusal to accept issue-advocacy commercials without prior editing.[11]

Of late, however, this concern has been greatly ameliorated. There has been considerable expansion in the availability, both paid and unpaid, of mass media channels for the public expression of multiple viewpoints. Although television networks continue to restrict advocacy commercials, their definition of advocacy has been considerably narrowed.

Furthermore, a sponsor who is so inclined can effectively reach all its targeted audiences across the nation through a combination of independent stations, network affiliates, and cable television.

The increasing incidence of paid issue-advocacy advertising in the print and electronic media has raised the specter of business using its "deep pockets" to clog the communication channels with one-sided messages in a manner that overwhelms and squeezes out the expression of alternative viewpoints. So corporate critics, while seeking free access to news media, have also undertaken paid advocacy campaigns.

The business community does not accept the logic of the "deep pocket theory" and instead suggests the alternative explanation of a "bigger soapbox." Corporate critics' relatively unrestricted media access compels business to use paid communications in order to have its viewpoint placed before the public (see Kaiser Aluminum's advocacy campaign).[12] Moreover, a number of business-sponsored idea-issue campaigns do not necessarily aim at advocating a narrow viewpoint, but instead attempt to refocus public attention on issues these businesses consider important for the public to be informed about and understand. The notion of advocacy is embedded in the selection of issues themselves (see the advocacy campaigns of W. R. Grace, SmithKline Beckman, LTV, United Technologies, and AIMS of Industry).[13]

Nor are all the campaigns by corporate critics aimed at refuting the messages of corporate sponsors. Instead, many such campaigns seek to build a constituency for the issue advocated by particular groups and thereby create a legitimacy for their sponsors that had not existed before. These campaigns also seek to raise funds to enable their sponsors to expand their activities. They may also use exaggerated claims of the purported harm inflicted upon an unwary public and the potential benefits that would accrue from support of the sponsors of these campaigns.

Nevertheless, the issue of inundating the news media with equally biased and self-serving messages, from whatever source, is quite disturbing and should be of concern to all of us. To the extent that it results in simply raising the level of noise and increasing public cynicism, its potential for harm may be constrained. Moreover, the news media may be able to counteract some of the effects of these partisan messages through regular news programming. However, it is also possible that once advocacy campaigns become significant revenue producers, they may inhibit the use of independent news judgment on the part of more timid or financially weak news publications. At this stage, the question remains largely unanswered.

Our present and future concern, therefore, is not primarily the business community's, and other private groups', right to speak or become politically involved. Instead, we are concerned about corporate America and other economic and private voluntary groups exercising this right and with what political effect. Ultimately the issue will be resolved in terms of the ground rules that determine the role the business community or any other major special interest group can play in the determination of a nation's policy choices.

PUBLIC PERCEPTION OF AND ATTITUDES TOWARD ADVOCACY ADVERTISING

One of the most important factors influencing the future growth and direction of issue-advocacy advertising is likely to be the attitude of large segments of the public toward the use of such advertising as a communication form by the business community and other private voluntary groups. An added element is the operating conditions or "rules of the game" that are considered acceptable by the public. This is important, because the receptivity of the sociopolitical environment and the public's predisposition to receive such messages in an attitudinally neutral, if not positive, state of mind will greatly influence the effectiveness of advocacy advertising in general, and the success or failure of individual campaigns in particular.

Unfortunately, there is an extreme paucity of publicly reported survey research or public opinion data pertaining to advocacy advertising. The three major studies known to the author were conducted by the Opinion Research Corporation in 1980,[14] and the Roper Organization in 1982 and 1984.[15] These studies show some significant changes, even over a short period of four years, in people's awareness of advocacy advertising, acceptance of the business community's right to engage in such advertising, and the impact of advocacy advertising in changing people's attitudes toward the issues raised in such campaigns.

The ORC Study

In a nationwide survey of public attitudes, the ORC study found that 60 percent of those questioned favored companies using paid advertising to present their points of view on controversial public policy issues. The study was based on telephone interviews with a sample of 1,010 people. The findings were based on a scientifically selected, and statistically valid, representative sample of the U.S. population aged 18 years and over. A remarkably high segment—90 percent—reported having read or heard of corporate advocacy ads in the previous two years. Of that group, 70 percent cited television as the primary source of such ads, 38 percent newspapers, 28 percent magazines, and 13 percent radio.

Over two-thirds of the 90 percent who were aware of advocacy ads declared them to be at least fairly believable, and nearly the same number believed the advocacy ads helped them better understand the issues involved. Sixty percent of the respondents endorsed the concept of corporate advocacy advertising, even though 64 percent acknowledged that companies using such advertising might have an unfair advantage over public interest groups because the latter would have less money to spend. Fifty-seven percent of those who said they had been aware of issue advertising reported that the ads had caused them to change their minds about an issue. And what they learned from the ads had prompted 84 percent to vote for or against a candidate; 40 percent to attempt to change someone else's mind about an issue; 25 percent to write to public officials, and 12 percent to write letters to the editor.

The findings, although quite encouraging, leave a number of questions unanswered and raise a host of other issues. For example:

- The findings pertain to one time period only. Since the public's perception of and attitudes toward emerging and emotionally charged social issues take some time before they are stabilized, more information is necessary to see how these attitudes are changing over time.
- People's recall of where they might have seen or read about a particular news item or advertisement is notoriously weak and has been known to decline rapidly. Moreover, recollection of a message in a particular medium is likely to be more related to the proportion of time devoted to viewing or reading that particular medium than to the actual appearance of a particular message in that medium. A superficial examination of the ORC data would indicate this to be the case. While 70 percent of the people cited television the primary source of such ads, the number of advocacy commercials appearing on television is minuscule compared with those appearing in the print media. Furthermore, proportionately more people from upper socioeconomic strata indicated having seen these ads, yet this is also the group that has the lowest ratings for extent of television viewing. The 70 percent figure is closer to the number of people who indicate television as their primary source of information and news.
- The only relationship between data and respondents is in terms of socioeconomic characteristics. However, no tests of significance were undertaken to find out if different socioeconomic groups were indeed different in their attitudes toward issue-advocacy advertising.
- Studies of certain other major sociopolitical issues show that demographic and socioeconomic variables alone are insufficient to explain attitudes toward an issue.[16] One possible explanation is that the availability of mass communication and information has reduced class-based perceptual differences, while accentuating differences based on some other intervening constructs, such as an individual's personal philosophy or beliefs, his/her attitude toward large corporations and the proper roles of business and government, and his/her awareness and concern for environmental or other social issues. Since this sophistication is not restricted to certain socioeconomic groups, the relationship between perception of advocacy advertising as a phenomenon and socioeconomic characteristics is neither simple nor direct.

The Roper Studies

The Roper studies were undertaken during the month of October in 1982 and in 1984. They were based on a scientifically selected, and statistically valid, sample of 2,000 men and women, 18 years of age and over, and represented a cross section of the U.S. population in all socioeconomic and demographic classifications, and all geographical regions. Personal face-to-face interviews were conducted by professional interviewers in respondents' homes.

In contrast to the ORC study, which reported 90 percent as having read or heard corporate advocacy ads, the 1984 Roper study reported a much smaller segment—only 38 percent—as having seen advocacy ads, with 51 percent reported as having not seen any advocacy ads. Females showed slightly less positive awareness (34 percent in 1984 and 32 percent in 1982), as opposed to males (43 percent in 1984 and 41 percent in 1982). The age group of 30 to 44 reported the highest seen rate (44 percent in 1984 and 42 percent in 1982), while the over-60 group seemed to be least aware of these ads (30 percent in both 1984 and 1982). Awareness increased with household income: the highest percentage (52 percent in 1984 and 50 percent in 1982) was found in people with annual incomes of over $30,000.

College graduates also showed the highest level of awareness of advocacy advertisements (54 percent in 1984 and 52 percent in 1982), while in the case of non–high-school graduates, it was only 21 percent (24 percent in 1982). People in professional occupations recorded a high degree of awareness (52 percent in 1984 and 54 percent in 1982). For blue-collar workers, on the other hand, only 37 percent reported having seen advocacy ads (33 percent in 1982).

There was a small increase between 1982 and 1984 among people's acceptance of corporations using advocacy advertising in all media [Table 1]. Moreover, as Table 2 shows, an increasing plurality of people felt that for television equal time provisions should apply for both commercials and programs (36 percent in 1982 and 41 percent in 1984).

Exposure to advocacy advertisements, however, had a positive effect on willingness to let business do advocacy advertising [Table 3], with 58 percent expressing such approval after having seen such ads, compared to 32 percent of the people who had not seen advocacy ads. Finally, respondents were asked whether television should be required to give free time to people on the opposite side to express their views. The findings are presented in Table 4.

The most critical finding was that a large positive feeling toward application of the equal time requirement (50 percent) was found among respondents who had seen advocacy advertisements, compared with 41 percent for all people and only 38 percent for those who had not seen advocacy ads. Thus one is led to conclude that those who had been exposed to advocacy advertising, and believed in the right of business to engage in such advertising, were also those most likely to support regulation that guaranteed equal time to opposing viewpoints. Recall that people who had seen such ads and supported business' right to engage in advocacy advertising came from highly educated, upper-income, professional and managerial groups. It raises two important points:

- There is a strong concern among influential and well-informed people that advocacy messages by corporations might squeeze out the public expression of alternative viewpoints, which needs to be protected.
- Current business-sponsored advocacy campaigns have not been persuasive enough in convincing people that business was merely correcting an imbalance that already existed in the public's mind about business' viewpoint.

The latter point was confirmed by the findings of another study conducted by the American Association of Railroads in 1979 as part of its research to measure the effectiveness of that industry's advocacy campaign.[17] Although this research was conducted on a nationwide sample of randomly selected people, its findings may not be easily generalizable because of the specific context within which the questions were asked. Almost 40 percent of the American public (and over 67 percent of the

Table 1   **Attitudes toward Corporations Using Advocacy Advertising**

Corporate Use of Advocacy Advertising	1984	1982
Is all right	41%	38%
Should not use advertising that way	46	51
Don't know	13	11

Table 2   **Application of Equal Time Rule on Television for the Expression of Opposing Viewpoints**

Equal Time Rule Should Apply	1984	1982
Commercials and programs	41%	36%
Programs only	28	30
Commercials only	5	5
No rule for either	10	12
Don't know	17	18

Table 3   **Exposure to Advocacy Advertisements and Attitudes toward Corporations Using Advocacy Advertising**

Corporate Use of Advocacy advertising	Total		Yes, Have Seen Ads		No, Have Not Seen Ads		Don't Know/ No Answer	
	1984	1982	1984	1982	1984	1982	1984	1982
Is all right	41%	38%	58%	54%	32%	29%	24%	21%
Should not use advocacy advertising this way	46	51	40	43	53	60	33	39
Don't know	13	11	2	2	15	11	43	40

Table 4   **Public Attitudes toward Provision of Equal Time for Opposing Viewpoints**

| Equal Time Rule Should Apply To | Total | | Have Seen Ads | | | | Don't Know | |
			Yes		No			
	1984	1982	1984	1982	1984	1982	1984	1982
Commercials and programs	41%	36%	50%	42%	38%	34%	21%	21%
Programs only	28	30	29	31	30	31	17	16
Commercials only	5	5	6	4	4	5	3	3
No rule for either	10	12	10	12	9	10	13	14
Don't know	17	18	6	10	17	19	46	44

community leaders) said they were familiar with advocacy or issue advertisements sponsored by companies and industry groups, especially those of oil companies. Among this group, a majority (53 percent) considered advocacy advertising to be either uninformative or unbelievable. Twenty-six percent categorized such advertising as not at all informative, and 27 percent as not very believable. Only one-fourth admitted that such advertising had altered their opinion toward an issue.

GROWTH OF ADVOCACY ADVERTISING

Precise dollar estimates for advocacy advertising expenditures are not possible because of a lack of a clear-cut definition. In the legal area, advocacy advertising falls in the category of grassroots lobbying. Unfortunately, corporate tax returns do not provide adequate and systematic information on grassroots lobbying expenditures. The situation is further aggravated by the Internal Revenue Service's lack of precise guidelines and inadequate enforcement in the audit of business expenses for grassroots lobbying.[18]

Advocacy commercials in the mass media—both print and electronic—are only part of the effort by the business community to reach the public. A variety of other means are also being used, including employee newsletters, shareholder communications, and management presentations to customers, suppliers, and dealers. Furthermore, businesses are using direct mail techniques, with sophisticated computer programs, to organize their special constituencies and reach finely targeted market segments.

Millions of dollars are being spent in the production and distribution of educational films to thousands of college campuses across the country. Corporations are also producing informational films advocating pro-industry positions on such issues as nuclear power, oil exploration, and steel imports. Quite often the identity of the sponsoring group is carefully concealed behind public-spirited-sounding organizational names. This technique is used even more frequently by many public interest groups, where the choice of name plays an important role in creating a positive public image for the organization and in raising funds to support activities. Lacking adequate financial resources, many small and independent stations across the country use such information in their news programs, in many cases without identifying the source of information to the viewing audience.

Another significant element of advocacy campaigns, and one that is not yet recognized as such, includes participation in initiatives and referendums. This type of corporate political involvement is increasing even more rapidly than general advocacy campaigns. Traditionally these campaigns have been waged against passage of certain initiatives deemed to be against corporate interests, such as nuclear power plants or returnable bottles. However, more recently corporations have supported business-sponsored initiatives. Even more interestingly, there have been instances where different corporations and industry groups have campaigned on different sides of an initiative.

Notwithstanding the lack of accurate data, some educated guesses as to the amounts spent by business on advocacy advertising are possible. Surveys conducted by the Association of National Advertisers show that total corporate institutional advertising increased from $330.7 million in 1974 to $403.2 million in 1983.[19] A 1981 survey by ANA found that about 20 percent of the corporate sponsors listed direct advocacy of corporate viewpoints and education on issues of public interest as the objectives of their corporate advertising.[20] This was a decline of 2 percentage points from 1979. The latest data for 1983 showed this figure to have declined to 12 percent.[21] Commenting on these figures, an executive of ANA speculated that the steep decline of 1983 may be an aberration and not necessarily indicative of any trend. Oil companies, except for Mobil, have been generally pulling back from advocacy campaigns, and no other industry as a whole has stepped into the vacuum. Moreover, the pro-business environment of the Reagan administration may have reduced the perceived need for advocacy campaigns on the part of many businesses.

ANA data, however, need careful interpretation in terms of what they suggest about the magnitude of business advocacy campaigns. They do not say anything about advocacy campaigns by labor organizations or the increasing multitude of private voluntary organizations of different ideological orientations and political leanings. ANA data pertain to corporate advertising only and exclude industry or association advertising, which accounts for almost 50 percent of all institutional advertising. It is possible that some corporations may have reduced their own advocacy campaigns in favor of enlarged campaigns by their industry associations.

Another problem with the data has to do with their self-reporting nature. Each respondent is responsible for classifying its institutional advertising into various categories, so it is not possible to have total consistency in reporting. The reported data may also be subject to respondent bias; corporations may use narrow or different definitions of advocacy for tax or other legal purposes, thereby underreporting the amounts spent on advocacy advertising.

Lastly, the ANA survey does not cover corporate and trade association spending on initiatives and referendums.[22] Nor does it account for expenses incurred in direct mail campaigns through dividend and other mail stuffers, and distribution of educational films, booklets, and pamphlets by corporations and trade associations.

Total advertising expenditures and grassroots lobbying by the business community were estimated by this author to be about $1 billion per year in 1978. These estimates were arrived at through an extensive analysis of advocacy campaigns then underway, and supplemented by information collected by Common Cause,[23] the General Accounting Office, and the testimony of various experts before Senator Philip Hart's Subcommittee on Environment, part of the Senate Commerce Committee, and testimony before Representative Benjamin Rosenthal's subcommittee on Commerce, Consumer, and Monetary Affairs, of the House Government Operations Committee.

Note too that grassroots efforts were undertaken in connection with attempts to influence the general public or special segments of the public with respect to legislative matters, elections, and referendums.[24] Advocacy advertising in the mass media is only part of the broad range of grassroots lobbying. Even communications aimed at stockholders and employees, for example, legally would be considered grassroots lobbying when they concern legislative matters. Assuming a conservative growth rate of 10 percent per year, I would estimate current business expenditures on all types of advocacy to have been approximately $1.6 billion in 1984.

DIVERSITY OF SPONSORSHIP

Another notable change in the last decade has been in the variety of new groups that have begun to use advocacy advertising. These include organized labor: voluntary private groups of all types and persuasions; governments and governmental agencies; and last but not least, foreign governments and groups advertising in the United States to influence public opinion and political leaders.

Organized Labor

Organized labor unions have been taking tentative and somewhat cautious steps in the use of advocacy advertising. The longest running of the current campaigns is by the United Federation of Teachers. It is also one of the more sophisticated advocacy campaigns by trade unions in the United States. The ads feature commentaries by the UFT's President Albert Shanker under the headline "Where We Stand," and appear every Sunday in the *New York Times*. A variety of education-related issues are discussed. The ad copy follows an editorial format and is crammed with facts and figures. It attempts both to inform and to educate the general public on the issues and to present the UFT's viewpoint in a reasoned and low-key manner [Exhibit 5].

Another leading user of advocacy advertising has been the American Federation of State, County and Municipal Employees (AFSCME). In addition to occasional advertisements on labor-related issues, AFSCME launched a major campaign in 1981 against Reaganomics and the new Republican administration's attempts to cut federal budgets dealing with social spending on such matters as education, Medicare, and social security. Like many business campaigns, this campaign was designed to influence the outcome of specific legislation and was not aimed at long-term change in public opinion.

In 1984 organized labor entered the advocacy arena in a big way. In August, the United Auto Workers (UAW) broadcast TV commercials proclaiming that the UAW's goal in forthcoming contract negotiations with the auto industry was to protect American jobs. The campaign was estimated to have cost $2 million.

In September 1984, the AFL-CIO unveiled a nationwide $1 million television campaign on issues affecting American society. Despite the nearness of the presidential election, AFL-CIO's President Lane Kirkland stated that the campaign had "no relationship to the election or to advance the cause of any particular candidate." The three-week cam-

Exhibit 5

Where We Stand

by Albert Shanker President, United Federation of Teachers.

Couple Could Owe $76,000 for College

Plan Saddles Student With High Debt

Last week I gave this space to guest columnist Denis P. Doyle of the American Enterprise Institute, who made two important points. First, he argued that proposed cutbacks in higher education (I would have added elementary and secondary education as well) were very unwise national policy. Our country will need engineers, doctors, physicists, mathematicians. Failure to invest in education today will mean that these skills will not be there when we need them in the years to come. Said Doyle, "It takes 20 years to train the next generation of engineers, scientists, linguists,"

But that's not the only point Doyle made. His second dealt with the question of how to pay for college education. Right now students nationally pay about a third of the cost of college. Two-thirds is paid for by previous generations, in the form of tax-supported public colleges and universities, government aid to higher education, student grants and loans and private contributions. We do this because we consider higher education for our people an investment in the future of our country.

Doyle would replace all this with a proposal originally made by John Silber. Under the plan, the federal government would set up a $15 billion fund. All but the wealthiest students would borrow what they needed to get through school and, after graduation, would repay the principal plus interest over a period of years. College graduates who agreed to serve in areas of national need—Doyle gave as examples rural health care or inner-city teaching—would not have to fully repay their loans; they could "work off" all or part of their obligation.

The others, of course, would have to repay the loan—and Doyle fudged the question of interest. He wrote of "an income tax surcharge of several percentage points" when the former student starts working in order for the government to "recover costs." Or, said Doyle, "students could be expected to repay an amount greater than the original advance." But there is clearly going to be interest at a fairly high rate, because Doyle noted that the $15 billion fund would be for the "first five years" and was thereafter expected to become "self-sustaining." In a period of inflation and over a number of years, high interest rates would be necessary in order to sustain the fund and make future loans available.

I received a letter from John P. Mallan, vice president for governmental relations of the American Association of State Colleges and Universities. Mallan points out that AASCU and almost every other higher education group have opposed this college funding idea and a number of variations on it which were promoted by Milton Friedman and Christopher Jencks. It was opposed because it would saddle most college graduates with very high long-term debts from the time of their graduation forward. Buying a college education would be something like buying a house. Mallan wrote:

"Here are some estimates of what the plan might cost at current college prices. A public college student might need $16,000 for four years of undergraduate college. When he pays this back, depending on the interest charged and the period of repaying, his total debt could amount to $38,000—at the age of 22. If he marries [and his wife had also been a student who had borrowed similarly], he and his spouse could begin their married lives with a debt of $76,000!"

(Guaranteed student loans are now at 9% and widely expected to go up; the federal government subsidizes the difference between the 9% and the bank's going rate. Auxiliary loans to assist undergraduates are at an unsubsidized 14%, with repayment to begin at graduation. Checking with a local bank, we learned that if a student takes a $16,000 loan at an interest rate of 14% and expects to repay it over 15 years, he would face payments of $213.09 per month for that time period; if both partners in a marriage were saddled with the same loans from their student days, the monthly tab for 15 years would be $426.18. Each would wind up repaying $38,356.20, or $76,712.40 for the couple.)

Mallan continued: "A private college student might owe $40,000 for four years, plus $30,000 in interest—$70,000 at the age of 22, or twice that if he marries [a classmate].

"Those who went on to graduate or professional school would acquire debts approaching those of smaller Third World nations." (The March 24 *Chronicle of Higher Education* reports a survey by the American Association of Dental Schools showing that 56.1% of last year's graduates had accumulated more than $20,000 in debt by graduation, with the average among those who had debts at $24,700. Dental school officials said they thought that cumulative debts for a new dental school graduate might soon reach $50,000.)

A second important objection to the Silber plan, according to Mallan, is that it would "almost certainly encourage states, institutions, and profit-making schools to raise tuition and other charges, since the lifetime repayment system would be available to pay for it.

"Most important," Mallan wrote, "it would be a radical break with the principle of low tuition and the idea that each generation should pay the costs of college—like elementary and secondary education—for the next generation. At present, students and their families pay about one-third of all college costs and the public much of the rest. Most of us would like to keep it that way. This arrangement has given the United States what is universally recognized as the world's most outstanding and also democratic system of higher education. There is no reason, after two hundred years, to abandon it."

Mr. Shanker's comments appear in this section every Sunday. Reader Correspondence is invited. Address your letters to Mr. Shanker at United Federation of Teachers, 260 Park Avenue South, New York, N.Y. 10010. ©1982 by Albert Shanker.

paign consisted of 14 30-second TV spots on six issues: education, jobs, affordable health, trade policy, taxation, and equal rights. It ran on 42 television stations in 24 metropolitan markets around the country, with a potential audience of 38.6 million households, including 8 million union members. In announcing the campaign, Kirkland said the AFL-CIO hoped to reach its own members with the message that it cared about issues affecting everyone, and the general public with the goal of improving attitudes toward organized labor.

Some of the reasons for organized labor's engaging in advocacy advertising are similar to those of the business community—for example, loss of public trust. However, my analysis of most of the labor campaigns leads me to conclude that they lack a coherent long-term strategy and are not likely to be effective.

- The overwhelming emphasis is on rhetorical and emotional appeals delivered through 30- and 60-second TV commercials. These commercials may warm the hearts of union members but are likely to do little to improve their understanding of the issues involved or prepare them to discuss these issues with nonunion members or the general public.
- These short TV commercials are inappropriate as educational devices that could inform an increasingly skeptical public about the complexity of the issues, the shortcomings seen by the unions' detractors, and the substance of the unions' arguments. Though they may give instant gratification to their sponsors, they are unlikely to have any lasting impact on the public.

In addition to these campaigns, other unions, notably the United Steel Workers of America, the Postal Workers, the Amalgamated Clothing & Textile Workers, and the International Ladies Garment Workers, have run occasional print ads and television and radio commercials. USW ads have run the gamut of issues confronting the union and the U.S. steel industry and address topics that are part of the nation's political agenda. Some of these advertisements criticize U.S. Steel Corporation's demand for work rule changes and also oppose that company's plans to import semifinished steel from foreign countries. They also support the industry's position for greater protection against foreign imports [Exhibits 6–10]. Most of the ads by trade unions, however, have been either one-shot or of extremely short duration, with low frequency and reach. Their impact is not likely to be significant.

Governments and Governmental Agencies

The use of advocacy advertising by a national government to persuade the populace to accept certain policies raises serious issues that may affect the very foundations of a democracy. In a free society, a nation's government and its elected officials have ample opportunities to explain their policies and programs to the people through free access to the news media. In fact, one of the major arguments made by private groups in their use of advocacy advertising is their inability to compete with governmental bodies and their unequal access to free press coverage.

Exhibit 6

BULLSEYE

Brazil is the latest country to propose sending hundreds of thousands of tons of subsidized steel slabs to the United States for finishing into steel products. The slabs would replace steel made in America, further reduce the steelmaking capacity of this country, and throw additional thousands of steelworkers out of work.

The Brazilian deal, being promoted by the Wheeling-Pittsburgh Steel Corporation, mirrors the one new being negotiated between the British Steel Corporation and U.S. Steel.

In each case, a foreign, government-owned steel company would ship huge quantities of subsidized, semi-finished steel to companies in the U.S. American companies would close down steel making facilities and concentrate on turning the foreign steel into finished products.

Wheeling-Pittsburgh proposes to deal with a Brazilian military dictatorship which has "targeted" steel as a loss leader in an effort to tap foreign trade markets. Brazil itself is in the midst of a massive debt crisis—owing $90 billion, more than any other nation.

The government-owned British Steel Corporation is faced with huge financial losses, and the proposed deal with U.S. Steel is widely described in Britain as a "bail-out".

If either or both of these deals should be finalized, we can expect a flood of similar schemes between other American steel companies and foreign governments.

Our country would lose its basic steel-making capacity and become dependent on foreign suppliers. This would seriously jeopardize our national security.

What is happening in the steel industry is a dramatic example of the problem of international targeting of selected industries.

Through targeting, a government gives preferred treatment to a chosen industry—subsidizing its development in many ways until its products can be dumped on foreign markets at prices which do not reflect the true cost of production.

Because of our high consumption and lack of a national industrial policy, the United States is a sitting duck for these practices. Look at what has happened in some other industries which have been targeted:

COMPUTERIZED MACHINE TOOLS: Japan's share of this market in the United States has increased from 5% to 50% since 1976. 24,000 American jobs have been lost.

COLOR TELEVISION: Japan targeted this industry in the 1960's. Since then, 13 American color television producers have dropped out, leaving only five. 27,364 American jobs have been lost. A total of 63,000 have been lost in related consumer electronics industries including radios, tape decks and phonographs.

AIRBUS: Western European countries targeted the world commercial aircraft market in the early 1970's with the creation of a joint venture called Airbus Industries—which now accounts for half of the free world market for widebodied aircraft. This rapid market penetration contributed to Lockheed's decision to stop production of the L1011, with a loss of 4,000 jobs.

This country, its industries, workers and stockholders suffer because of targeting by foreign governments. This situation will continue, and worsen, until we understand targeting and develop a national industrial policy to deal with it.

USA

Brazil Joins Britain In Attack On USA's Steel Independence

UNITED STEELWORKERS OF AMERICA
Lloyd McBride, President
Five Gateway Center
Pittsburgh, Pennsylvania 15222

25

Exhibit 7

ENOUGH IS ENOUGH!

U.S. STEEL HAS RIPPED OFF THE AMERICAN TAXPAYER, THE STATE OF ILLINOIS, THE CITY OF CHICAGO AND THE UNITED STEELWORKERS OF AMERICA!

On December 27, 1983, United States Steel Corporation announced that it had scrapped plans to build a rail mill at Chicago's South Works and would close much of South Works itself, thereby eliminating thousands of jobs. The company blamed the United Steelworkers of America and its members at Local Union 65 for the decision not to build the rail mill.

U.S. Steel has publicly stated that the union did not cooperate to help make construction of the rail mill a reality. *That is completely false.* But no one should be surprised because U.S. Steel is well known for its deceptions.

Here are the facts: In promising to build the rail mill, U.S. Steel made two demands, and much later a third.

U.S. STEEL'S DEMANDS	THE USWA'S RESPONSE
1. A new manning agreement with major labor changes to make the mill economically competitive.	Negotiated a new agreement satisfactory to U.S. Steel, which was ratified by the members of Local Union 65.
2. Repeal of a state sales tax on rails produced in Illinois for sale out of state.	Lobbied the Illinois Legislature and Governor James Thompson. Won repeal of the tax to help U.S. Steel.
3. Overturning of an Environmental Protection Agency consent decree requiring the company to install $33 million worth of pollution control equipment at Gary Works.	Worked closely with Attorney General Neil Hartigan and other public officials in developing a solution to protect the environment and still help U.S. Steel.

In addition, U.S. Steel was the major beneficiary of contract adjustments worth more than $3 billion negotiated between the union and the steel industry last March.

Given the facts, any objective person can only conclude that the USWA and its members at Local Union 65 have done more than their fair share to help U.S. Steel.

The union wanted the mill to be constructed.

What did U.S. Steel do? It kept demanding More! It demanded more from the union . . . more from the taxpayers . . . more from the state . . . more from Congress. Well, when a greedy wolf with bared fangs is at your door, threatening your life, you must defend yourself.

U.S. Steel has been deceiving the USWA, the American taxpayer, the City of Chicago, the State of Illinois and the entire nation for too long.

U.S. Steel's deceptions and its slick public relations campaign to discredit the union is a slap in the face to its workers, the union and the nation. Isn't it a shame that at the same time U.S. Steel was demanding sacrifices from its workers, the company found $6.2 billion to purchase Marathon Oil Company. Why didn't U.S. Steel use these $6.2 billion to modernize their entire steel operations? Does U.S. Steel have no allegiance to this country anymore?

U.S. Steel's arrogance and greed, like that of many other corporations, makes it important that this country develop an industrial policy addressing questions such as federal plant shutdown legislation, overseas investment and corporate responsibility to the communities in which they are located.

THESE AREN'T QUESTIONS JUST FOR STEELWORKERS BUT FOR ALL WORKERS . . . ALL AMERICANS.

We are all in this together. We must all help. Here's what you should do to help. Call for a Congressional investigation resulting from the use of the Tax Code in U.S. Steel's shutdown announcement and decision not to build the rail mill at South Works. Fill out the coupon with this ad and send it today to U.S. Representative Daniel Rostenkowski (D-ILL.) as shown. He is Chairman of the House Ways and Means Committee, where all tax legislation begins.

UNITED STEELWORKERS OF AMERICA

Five Gateway Center   Pittsburgh, PA 15222

Lynn R. Williams

Lynn Williams
Temporary Acting President

Jack Parton

Jack Parton
Director, District 31
East Chicago, IN

TO: U.S. REP. DANIEL ROSTENKOWSKI
CHAIRMAN, COMMITTEE ON WAYS & MEANS
U.S. HOUSE OF REPRESENTATIVES
ROOM 1102, LONGWORTH BLDG.
WASHINGTON, DC 20515

Dear Congressman Rostenkowski:

I have had enough! U.S. Steel is getting a $1.2 billion tax write-off for putting people out of work, but I know of your concern for working people and appreciate everything you have done on the South Works matter.

Please schedule a full congressional investigation into the impact of tax code advantages from U.S. Steel's shutdown announcement and the decision not to build a rail mill at South Works in Chicago.

Sincerely,

NAME:_____

ADDRESS:_____

CITY/STATE/ZIP_____

Exhibit 8

"The British Are Coming, The British Are Coming"

AND AMERICA'S STEEL INDEPENDENCE IS GOING

A Message Especially for Stockholders Of American Steel Companies

As Independence Day approaches this year, Paul Revere's warning takes on a new and dangerous meaning.

If a deal struck by the U.S. Steel Corporation and the government-owned British Steel Corporation goes through as planned, it could be the beginning of the end for America's steel independence. As the union representing America's steelworkers, we find that prospect extremely disturbing, and for reasons that go beyond our self-interest. It is, for example, contrary to the best interests of stockholders of other American steel companies.

Here's what is involved.

U.S. Steel wants to quit making steel at its Fairless Hills plant in Pennsylvania, but continue to operate the Fairless finishing facilities. It wants to accomplish this by importing millions of tons of semi-finished steel "slabs" from the British Steel Corporation's Ravenscraig plant in Scotland.

U.S. Steel says it would be cheaper to do this than to modernize the steel-making facilities at Fairless. To make the deal more palatable for Americans, the British say they will create a so-called "private corporation" just to operate Ravenscraig.

That's supposed to take the sting out of U.S. Steel's importation of subsidized foreign steel. Of course it ignores the fact that the Ravenscraig technology is a direct result of subsidized investment. The same is true for the entire money-losing British steel operation.

The fact is that Ravenscraig would not exist but for this subsidy.

It is indeed ironic that in the past, even U.S. Steel has charged that government subsidies saved British steel from bankruptcy and allowed it to install new technology while encountering huge operating losses.

The logical, fair and reasonable thing for U.S. Steel to do is to forget the British deal and modernize Fairless. Earlier this year, our union negotiated a new contract that will save the steel industry some $3 billion. As the largest steel company, U.S. Steel will realize the largest share of those savings. Our one condition was that these savings be plowed back into existing facilities.

Certainly this is consistent with the industry's long-stated objective of modernizing its facilities to sharpen its competitive edge.

If U.S. Steel is allowed to consummate this unlikely match, it can make other deals with the Europeans, Brazilians, Nigerians, Taiwanese and others who have the capacity to flood the American market with subsidized steel. Then, one by one, other American steel companies will be forced to follow suit to remain competitive. If they don't, they'll be priced out of the marketplace.

The losers in such a scenario would be the thousands of new unemployed American steelworkers, the stockholders of other, smaller American steel companies, and the American people, who would find themselves dependent on foreign producers for our steel needs, including steel for defense purposes.

Smaller steel companies are especially vulnerable. One half or more of their investment in steel properties is tied up in iron and coal mines, and the ovens and furnaces that produce steel. If these facilities are made useless by a national shift to imported raw steel, all of that will have to be written off. The effect on balance sheets and the market value of investments is obvious.

The United Steelworkers of America is determined that this will not happen. We have committed the resources of our union to this total effort. We will employ every legal means at our disposal to block this dangerous precedent.

★ Within recent days, we have engaged counsel to file on our behalf a petition charging that the proposed transaction is illegal under U.S. trade laws.

★ We will press fully our rights under existing collective bargaining agreements with U.S. Steel, as well as our rights under the National Labor Relations Act.

★ We will call for a Congressional investigation of the entire proposed U.S. Steel-British Steel arrangement—including the issuance of subpoenas to examine all documents and notes exchanged by the parties and the relative costs of producing steel at Ravenscraig and the extent of subsidization.

★ We will carry out an extensive information program to provide the public with the facts about this important case.

On April 28, the President of our union, Lloyd McBride, testified before the Steel Caucus of the U.S. House of Representatives about this matter. He closed with these words:

"We may be witnessing here the beginning—for the U.S.—of the internationalization of American steel production. And when steel companies engage in what is essentially unfair trade for the purpose of shifting their production base out of steel for the advantage of their shareholders, then our union and its members are being severely injured and sorely used. Our steel communities are severely impacted. And, I submit to you, our nation is the worse for it. When private decisions have such widespread, devastating consequences on the private and public sectors, those decisions should not be made unilaterally without a thorough investigation of the consequences."

The consequences of U.S. Steel's proposed joint venture with the British Steel Corporation are indeed great. An entire industry as we have come to know it is at stake. U.S. Steel is single-handedly attempting to forge a new national steel policy for America.

The Steelworkers of America are prepared to fight this dangerous proposal at every juncture. And we want your help.

We invite others who share our views on this important matter—especially steel company stockholders—to join us. We'll be glad to provide you with additional information.

United Steelworkers of America
Lloyd McBride, President
Five Gateway Center
Pittsburgh, Pennsylvania 15222

Exhibit 9

"...And Then There Were None"

Blast furnaces being demolished last year after U.S. Steel closed its huge Youngstown Works in Ohio.

THE ADMINISTRATION MUST ACT NOW TO SAVE AMERICA'S BASIC STEEL INDUSTRY

Because of the crisis which exists within the American steel industry, we believe it is important to share the following message with the American public.

Our country's basic steel industry is face to face with the greatest crisis in its history. Unless the Reagan administration takes immediate action, the industry will be severely damaged and could disappear.

When Jimmy Carter became President seven years ago, there were 46 large, ore-based steel mills operating in the U.S., capable of producing 145 million tons of raw steel a year. During the Carter years, six of them were closed. Under the current administration, nine have been closed permanently. Two others have been closed for a year. More may close soon, leaving our country dangerously dependent on foreign steel producers.

The national interest is clear. At stake is the loss of hundreds of thousands of jobs connected with the steel industry, the investment of countless steel company shareholders, and the security of our country.

The immediate threat lies in a deal being pressed by the U.S. Steel Corporation and the highly-subsidized, government-owned British Steel Corporation. If this agreement is carried out, U.S. Steel would abandon its steel-making facilities at its Fairless Hills plant in Pennsylvania but continue to operate the steel-finishing plant at the same location.

U.S. Steel would then buy millions of tons of semi-finished steel "slabs" from two government-owned British plants and finish them at Fairless. U.S. Steel says this would be cheaper than modernizing its own steel-making facilities at Fairless.

This may be true because of the huge subsidies the British government has poured into these plants. Last fall, the Department of Commerce determined that this subsidy amounted to 20.33% of the price of imported British steel.

Since the U.S. Steel deal was announced, Brazil and other countries have rushed to make their own proposals for dumping subsidized steel on the American market. We believe all of these schemes are in clear violation of domestic trade laws, but laws are meaningless without enforcement.

Executives of other American steel companies have said they will be compelled by competitive pressure to import subsidized raw steel if U.S. Steel gets away with its British Steel plan. This would destroy the American basic steel industry. During a time of national emergency, dependence on foreign steel would be as disastrous as dependence on foreign oil.

During the presidential campaign, Mr. Reagan often demonstrated an awareness of steel industry problems and made several promises which have not been kept by officials in his administration.

Here are some of them.

• On October 2, 1980, at the Cyclops Mill in Bridgeville, Pa., he promised to do three things which, if carried out, would go far toward resolving the steel industry's problems. He said he would:

1) Enforce anti-dumping steel laws to ensure fair trade in steel;
2) Reinstate the Trigger Price Mechanism for steel;
3) Act vigorously to negotiate reductions in foreign subsidies and trade barriers whenever possible.

These things are not being done. The Trigger Price Mechanism provides a formula for setting fair minimum price for imported steel. It has not been enforced since early 1982. This has encouraged foreign countries to flood our market with subsidized steel.

• In that same speech at Cyclops, he promised to reduce the 13% unemployment rate in the steel industry. Six days later, in Youngstown, Ohio, he said he would do whatever it took to get jobless steelworkers back to work. Since then the steelworker unemployment rate has jumped from 13% to 46%.

Layoffs of a few months have stretched out to continuous years of unemployment for many iron and coal miners, steelworkers and others. Whole communities are being wiped out. Family life is being destroyed for hundreds of thousands of hard-working Americans.

Steel-related unemployment will be much higher if the deal between U.S. Steel and British Steel becomes a reality and sets a precedent for similar schemes with other subsidized foreign producers. They, too, are eager to unload raw steel at prices below the cost of production, thus exporting their unemployment to us.

The President has the power and authority to protect the national interest in this crisis. We ask the President and officials of his administration to understand the urgency of the problem and set in motion the administrative actions which are now so desperately needed.

Specifically, we ask the President to act in these areas:

1) Direct Commerce Secretary Baldrige and Trade Ambassador Brock to launch an immediate investigation to determine if the U.S. Steel-British Steel proposal would violate our domestic trade laws or the United States-European Economic Community Arrangement. This is not a difficult investigation and should be completed within 30 days.

2) Direct Secretary Baldrige to invoke the procedures set forth in the 1982 EEC Arrangement and call for an immediate consultation with the European Coal and Steel Community on the extent and implications of semi-finished steel imports in this country.

3) If consultations do not resolve the problem, the administration should use existing procedures of the federal trade laws to promptly prohibit imports of subsidized steel.

4) Direct the appropriate officials within his administration to carry out the promises he made to steelworkers and the steel industry during the presidential campaign.

Time is short. The powers of the President of the United States are great. The time to act is now. *AMERICAN STEELWORKERS AND THEIR INDUSTRY CANNOT COMPETE WITH FOREIGN GOVERNMENTS.*

United Steelworkers of America
Lloyd McBride, President
Five Gateway Center
Pittsburgh, Pennsylvania 15222

Exhibit 10

UNCONTROLLED IMPORTS

They have taken nearly a million American jobs in apparel & textiles. They threaten the two million jobs that remain. We have one last chance. And it's in the Congress now.

S680/HR1562:

An urgent, rational bill that will put an end to uncontrolled imports of apparel & textiles, stop the erosion of our industry, save two million American jobs. And still give the nations of the world, poorer ones especially, legitimate access to our market.

THESE AREN'T JUST JOBS. WE'RE TALKING ABOUT TWO MILLION PEOPLE.

And look who they are: 7 out of 10, women. Sitting at sewing machines, standing on their feet in the mills. Supporting their families alone, or making the difference so that the family can live a little better, the kids get a little better chance.

These are people who desperately need work, they want to work and they don't have much choice about where they work.

When their plants close, they can't find jobs in other industries. The lucky ones may find a service job at the minimum wage, if you call it lucky to make about $134 a week with a couple of kids to take care of.

More often, it's welfare. And bitterness. For them, dignity, pride, faith in America are wrapped up in paying their own way.

Two million jobs are slipping away. It's not too late to save them.

WE'RE TALKING ABOUT TOWNS.

There are small towns all over this country where there's only one mill or one garment factory. The people depend on it for a living. And everything else in that town depends on those people: the local department store, the drug store, the movie house, the grocery, the gas station, the garage, the schools and services.

When the plant goes, the town goes. The other businesses fail, taxes disappear, the life of the town crumbles. A little bit of America dies.

It's already happening in many towns. And many more are hanging by a thread. We think that's urgent. Don't you?

WHY WE NEED THIS BILL RIGHT NOW.

The way things are going, by 1990 we won't have an apparel & textile industry in America at all. It's all here for everybody to see: today 1 out of every 2 garments sold in this country—men's, women's & kids'—is an import. Ten years ago, it was 1 out of 5. In category after category, imports up, up, up. And snowballing.

A FEW HORRENDOUS FACTS.

The Growth of Clothing Imports as a Percentage of the U.S. Market.

	1974	1979	1984
Women's & Children's Coats	22%	38%	52%
Men's & Boys' Shirts (woven, man-made fiber)	19%	42%	55%
Bras	29%	49%	58%
Sweaters (all)	44%	55%	68%

Imports have increased 123% in the past 10 years, 25% in 1983 alone, and a terrifying 32% over that just last year.

YOU CAN SEE WHAT'S HAPPENING WITH YOUR OWN EYES.

In the stores, for example, look for a woman's blouse made here. Instead of there. See how long and hard you have to look. If you find it at all.

Or in those beautiful mail-order catalogs: page after page, see how much is import. How little, USA.

It ought to make us mad.

We are literally being imported out of existence—our mills, our fiber plants, our garment factories, and all the workers who depend on them for a living.

In the last 10 years: nearly a million jobs we had and could have had. Gone.

In state after state, hundreds of garment factories. Gone.

In just one year, February '83-February '84, 50,000 jobs in apparel & knitting. Gone.

In 1984, in North & South Carolina alone: at least 61 textile plants. Gone.

Plant after plant, closing, and among them, just this year: our last remaining manufacturer of corduroy & velveteen, one of the oldest and most prestigious of our mills. Gone.

That's 1 out of 10 manufacturing jobs, more than steel & automobiles combined. And it's frightening.

THIS BILL IS NOT A BAIL-OUT.

Nobody's asking the government to foot the bills for us. Our American apparel & textile industry has become the most modern and productive in the world. It has spent on average a billion dollars a year on new plants and equipment. And it could hold its own against all comers, if those competitors were, like us, competing on their own.

But they're not. Our companies must compete with their governments. And their governments support them with financing, subsidies, tax-relief, and by keeping our goods out. And with workers at wages Americans find hard to believe: 16-cents-an-hour workers, 38-cents-an-hour workers, 63-cents-an-hour workers, $1.18-cents-an-hour workers. Could you live on that? Neither could we.

We can compete in productivity, we can compete in quality. But there is no way American workers can compete with those pitifully, indecently low wages. And there is nobody who thinks we should.

NOT "PROTECTIONISM," FAIRNESS.

Since 1974 we've had a trade agreement, the Multi-Fiber Arrangement (MFA), which was supposed to keep imports in balance. But it's painfully obvious now that the loopholes are big enough to bring down our entire industry.

That's what this bill is all about. Plugging the loopholes which have distorted the MFA, bringing the MFA back to its objectives of an open, orderly market fairly shared by everyone, and giving it the teeth to make it work.

S680/HR1562 doesn't break any new ground. It simply moves to correct the flaws that have damn near destroyed us.

THIS BILL IS EXTRAORDINARILY FAIR.

We're not saying, no more imports. We are saying, give us import levels we can deal with. Make it possible again for American industry and American workers to get a fair share of our own American market.

That's what this bill does. But it's not one-sided.

It recognizes the needs of the struggling economies, the impoverished peoples beyond our borders.

It says to the big exporting countries, you can come in, you can grow as we grow, but you can no longer flood us.

At the same time, it gives the smaller, poorer nations a greater opportunity in our market: more room for their goods, more room to grow.

This is a bill that is not just fair, it is compassionate. A bill every American in good conscience can support.

AND THE SPONSORS SPAN THE POLITICAL SPECTRUM.

They are Republicans and Democrats, conservatives and liberals, moderates on both sides. In the Senate and in the House, they have rallied to this bill.

They have joined forces in common agreement that America cannot afford to lose another great industry, American workers cannot afford to lose one more job.

To date 227 representatives and senators have put their names on the bill.

Even so, we can't take passage for granted. Beyond that, we want the bill to do more than squeak through. We want overwhelming congressional support that will tell the world that we are determined to defend our home markets: they are welcome to come and trade with us, but we are no longer going to sit idly by while our industries are destroyed, our workers deprived of their right to earn a living at a decent American wage.

YOU CAN HELP. BACK S680/HR1562

Write your representative. Write your senator. Let them know you want this bill. If they're sponsors, they'll know you support them. If they're undecided, they'll know how you want them to decide. If they oppose it, they'll know there is good reason to switch.

America needs this bill. We need this bill.

We're fighting for a fighting chance.

Amalgamated Clothing & Textile Workers' Union

International Ladies' Garment Workers' Union

RALLY: 12 NOON today, Wednesday, April 10, Herald Square.

(34th Street and Broadway)

Because a democratic government is elected by the people to carry out certain policies, people do not have to be sold on those policies through use of their own tax dollars. This is tantamount to propaganda and brainwashing, in its most insidious sense, by the government in power. When a party in power is using public funds to advocate its program to the public, it is in fact engaging in a political campaign and abusing its office. It also denies the opposition the equal right to present its viewpoint to the people using public funds.[25]

Fortunately, in the United States government bodies have not resorted to direct advertising campaigns that use public funds to advocate public acceptance of government's preferred programs and policies. The only exception I'm aware of is the National Maritime Council, a government-affiliated private trade organization, which engaged in a campaign in 1977 using taxpayer funds. It advocated public subsidies for U.S. flagships. The campaign was the subject of a congressional hearing in which it was sharply criticized for its use of public funds. The campaign was discontinued soon thereafter.[26]

Although political leaders of all persuasions use free news media to advocate their positions, they do not dictate the terms under which their viewpoints will be presented, if at all, by those media. It is left to journalists to report the leader's utterances, and equally important, to interpret and analyze them for audiences. There is considerable doubt about the legality of the U.S. government's use of advocacy campaigns to sell a government policy to the public. There is also little support for it in the United States, among the general public or among leaders of the major parties. In the United States, government use of paid advertising is almost exclusively devoted to promoting public health and safety; to campaigns to inform people about the availability of various services, or new laws and regulations; and for recruitment drives for the armed forces or for other jobs such as police.

In sharp contrast, the Canadian government has a long history of engaging in all forms of advertising, a role that has made it the largest advertiser in the country.[27] Ironically, the rationale for the Canadian government's use of advocacy advertising is presented in terms similar to those used by private groups, notably the business community: The news media do not do a good job of explaining complex issues to the public. Justifying the government use of advocacy advertising, a 1970 study of Canadian government advertising states:

> This then is the challenge that faces a modern government. How to achieve a greater balance in the public's attitude toward the role of the government in economic and social affairs of the nation. In answering that question, and in formulating an appropriate program of action, governments in the future may wish to rely increasingly on information services and on advertising to achieve a continuing dialogue with the people of Canada.[28]

Other Canadian government spokespersons have justified advocacy advertising by saying that "Government is too complex nowadays to rely on 'policy by press release.' Programs must be explained—not by reporters but by people who created them."[29]

The most persistent and expanded use of advocacy advertising in Canada took place in 1980–1982, during the regime of Pierre Trudeau and the Liberal party, which has advocated a larger government role in that country's industrial and economic affairs. One of the well-known advocacy campaigns in Canada pertained to the national debate over the new Constitution. As would be expected, some press coverage was favorable, and some was not. A number of provincial governments, especially those in the western provinces and/or controlled by the Conservative party, were opposed to some of the provisions of the new Constitution, which purportedly altered the balance of power between the provinces and the federal government. Therefore, it was not a question of explaining the provisions of the new Constitution to the public, but of selling the Liberal party program to the public at the taxpayers' expense.

Moreover, even if we were to accept the Canadian government's arguments at face value, the government's implementation of its advocacy campaigns makes a shambles of its protestations. The campaign under review largely used 30- and 60-second radio and TV spots that were full of jingles and exhortations. Little time was devoted to "explaining" the complex issues that a free press had "failed" to explain.

The United Kingdom presents a different approach to government use of paid advocacy advertising. The only advocacy campaign supported by the central government involved Britain's admission to the Common Market. The government had promised a referendum on the issue and had agreed to abide by its verdict. It provided public funds for campaigning to both sides, those who supported joining the Common Market and those who opposed it.

Advocacy advertising by state bodies and public agencies in the UK has taken two forms. In one case, local municipal bodies, often controlled by the opposition Labour party, have used taxpayers' money to campaign against laws advocated by the central government. An example is The Association of Metropolitan County Councils' opposition to Prime Minister Thatcher's legal initiatives to abolish the metropolitan county councils. Similarly, the Association of Metropolitan Authorities (local municipal governments) has engaged in heavy media campaigns against the central government because of the latter's attempt to restrict local government's allegedly excessive spending, paid for by the central government, on local subsidized services beyond those paid for by the local taxpayers or approved by the central government. In both cases, the party in power was using public funds to promote a program that was distinctly political [Exhibits 11–12].

Another form of advocacy advertising in the United Kingdom has been undertaken by state-owned corporations, notably British Rail[30] and British Gas. In the case of British Rail, the company was campaigning against cuts in its capital budget proposed by the British government. In the case of British Gas, the campaign was aimed against privatization. More recently, British Airways [Exhibit 13] and London airports [Exhibit 14] have also launched similar campaigns against the central government's plans to sell them to the public.

The case for state-owned companies engaging in advocacy campaigns is akin to a management campaigning against its stockholders,

Exhibit 11

THEY BELIEVE IN FREE SPEECH.
BUT NOT FAIR HEARINGS.

"The Probation Service is not a part of local government and certainly has not been taken into consideration on the abolition question. Yet if the proposals go ahead we are clearly going to suffer gratuitous harm and cost for no ostensible benefit whatever." (ASSOCIATION OF CHIEF OFFICERS OF PROBATION)

"The prospect of individual Councils preparing structure plans... is appalling." (HOUSE BUILDERS FEDERATION)

"A recipe for delay, indecision, confusion and waste... the measures which the Government wishes to introduce will make matters worse not better." (TOWN AND COUNTY PLANNING ASSOCIATION)

"The improvements (under the metropolitan county councils) have been dramatic... with great improvements in performance and standards... naive to think that authorities of widely different political outlook will work together." (INSTITUTE OF WASTE MANAGEMENT)

Since publishing its proposals for the abolition of the metropolitan county councils, the Government has received literally thousands of responses. From industry and commerce, professional and academic institutions, the Church, voluntary organisations and numerous individuals.

The majority are highly critical, in part or in whole, of the Government's plans.

Many have demanded that at the very least an inquiry should be held, before such an important constitutional change is enacted.

But the protests, however significant, are falling on deaf ears.

It seems the Government's mind is made up, and that it is determined to get its Bill through Parliament with as little public debate as possible.

BEWARE CONSERVATIVE ESTIMATES.

The 1983 White Paper 'Streamlining the Cities' is the blueprint for abolition. Its architect is Mr. Patrick Jenkin, the Environment Secretary.

Its main platform was that metropolitan county councils were wasteful, unnecessary and should be abolished.

And although Mr. Jenkin originally estimated that savings of up to £120 million a year could be made, no concrete facts or figures to support the claim were produced.

This vagueness was fortuitous for the Environment Secretary, particularly in the light of two damning analyses of the Government's abolition proposals by Coopers and Lybrand Associates, a top independent management and financial consultancy.

They drew the conclusion that "There are unlikely to be any net savings as a result of the Government's proposed changes, and there could be significant extra costs... up to £61 million pounds a year."

Now, Mr. Jenkin has changed his tune, by saying: "Expenditure issues are not central to the case for abolition."

SOMETHING TO SHOUT ABOUT.

Against this conflict between Government claims and independent assessment, voices of disquiet are being raised higher and higher.

The scale of concern is demonstrated by the wide cross section of respondents to the White Paper. Including the Probation Service, the Countryside Commission, Chambers of Commerce, the Civic Trust, the Arts Council, the National Union of Ratepayers and the Law Society.

"The proposals in the White Paper are ill thought out, uncosted and unworkable. If implemented they would quickly lead to a chaotic fragmentation of services, with corresponding reduction in quality." (UNITED KINGDOM ASSOCIATION OF PROFESSIONAL ENGINEERS)

"...in the White Paper neither the case for reorganisation nor the merits of the particular proposals put forward are adequately substantiated. Indeed, by any objective judgement, the White Paper falls short of the standards to be expected of a document intended to stimulate and inform public debate on the constitutional, administrative and economic implications of a major change in the structure of Government as it operates in the main cities." (SCHOOL FOR ADVANCED URBAN STUDIES, UNIVERSITY OF BRISTOL)

"The service hopes that the impressive progress in the field of consumer protection made by the Metropolitan Counties is not lost, but developed." (NATIONAL ASSOCIATION OF CITIZENS ADVICE BUREAUX)

"Our support for the proposed abolition is given on the assumption that it will lead to substantial savings." (CBI)

"We argue that the proposed structure will lead to less effective management than at present, and will lead to higher rather than lower costs... we have no doubt that efficiency will suffer." (THE CHARTERED INSTITUTE OF PUBLIC FINANCE AND ACCOUNTANCY)

"Before any fundamental alterations are embarked upon, evidence should be produced to show that these hopes (savings and better value for money) have every chance of being realised in the future. The onus is on the Government to prove that its re-organisation plans will give... ratepayers a better deal." (NATIONAL UNION OF RATEPAYERS ASSOCIATIONS)

Concern is growing in all quarters that re-organisation will lead to a reduction in the level and quality of services.

That costs will escalate dramatically. And that direct responsibility to the electorate for countywide services will be all but eliminated.

Analysis of the Government's plans show these fears to be well founded.

But what may not be so well known, is the willingness of the metropolitan county councils to participate in any full and independent review of local government structure and finance.

The metropolitan county councils have never claimed that the present system is perfect, or that it should be above change. However, they have always sought to provide the greatest possible benefits to the 11 million people they serve.

Which is why an inquiry is essential; before the Government embarks upon a hasty and costly upheaval of local government.

A view also held by a great many other people.

Unfortunately, it appears that this Government believes people should be seen, but not heard.

ISSUED BY THE METROPOLITAN COUNTY COUNCILS OF GREATER MANCHESTER, MERSEYSIDE, SOUTH YORKSHIRE, TYNE AND WEAR, WEST MIDLANDS AND WEST YORKSHIRE.
FOR FURTHER INFORMATION, WRITE TO THE CHIEF EXECUTIVE, GMC, COUNTY HALL, MANCHESTER M60 3HP.

Exhibit 12

Watch out. Whitehall has plans for your local elections.

There's some very worrying legislation about to creep in and out of Parliament.

The idea is to take away your Local Authority's power to levy rates.

If you hate rates (and who doesn't), you could be fooled into believing it's good news.

That's what Whitehall is relying on.

But think. Without money your council is also without power.

It can't make decisions. It can't go against Whitehall. Even if you want it to on certain issues.

That's the value of your local council.

It can check excessive control of local affairs by any Government.

Remember, after an election the Government does not have to be nice for five years.

When you come to us with your problems our hands will be tied.

We'll both come up against this innocent looking law. And like all laws, just try arguing with it.

It won't matter if your local councillor agrees the roads are bad (he lives there too).

It won't matter if classes at the local school are too big (he'll probably have children there).

It won't matter if there's no room at the old people's home for our senior citizens.

There will be no point in appealing to us.

In fact there will be no real point in electing councillors at all.

As things are, our doors are open. Whitehall's will stay closed.

Governments ask you to give them your vote when it suits them.

Make no mistake. With this legislation, as far as local elections are concerned, they might as well take your right to vote away.

KEEP IT local

THIS ADVERTISEMENT HAS BEEN SPONSORED BY THE ASSOCIATION OF METROPOLITAN AUTHORITIES, REPRESENTING A LARGE NUMBER OF ENGLISH LOCAL AUTHORITIES, IN THE BELIEF THAT YOU SHOULD BE KEPT INFORMED.

Exhibit 13

And may the best airline win.

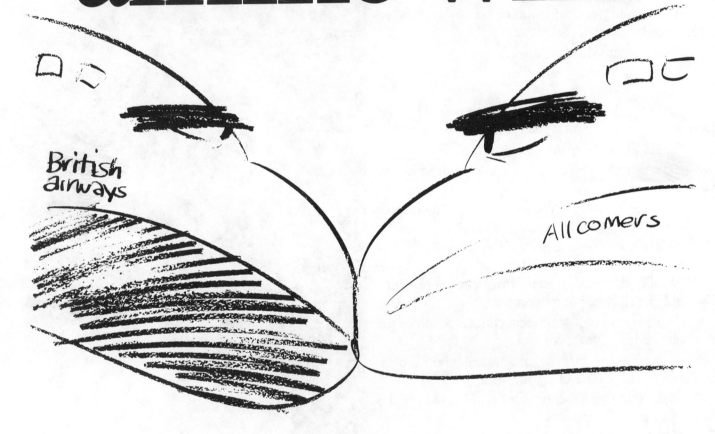

The Civil Aviation Authority airline proposals recommend handing over 30 major routes that British Airways currently operate to other British airlines on a plate.

This would simply substitute another airline for British Airways on a route, and would give no additional choice at all to the British fare paying passenger.

It does nothing to stimulate a better service since there's no extra competition.

And it will greatly damage our airline industry as a whole, and benefit major foreign airlines. First, because the foreigners will no longer have to compete with the strongest national carrier.

And second, because there's no guarantee that passengers who would normally choose British Airways would be happy to switch to other British airlines.

Particularly in overseas markets where they might well be unknown.

Wouldn't a more sensible way of maintaining Britain's share in this fiercely competitive market be to allow other British airlines to fly *in competition* with us on the routes they choose?

Not *instead* of us.

Indeed, with a bit of healthy competition we should build on Britain's share between us.

Let's put it to the test, and may the best airline win.

British airways
The world's favourite airline.

35

Exhibit 14

TRUE OR FALSE?

1. DOVER IS BRITAIN'S BUSIEST PORT.
   True ☐ False ☐

2. HEATHROW, GATWICK, STANSTED DON'T COST THE BRITISH TAXPAYER A PENNY.
   True ☐ False ☐

3. HEATHROW HANDLES MORE INTERNATIONAL PASSENGERS THAN ANY OTHER AIRPORT.
   True ☐ False ☐

4. LOS ANGELES IS THE WORLD'S BUSIEST INTERNATIONAL HELIPORT.
   True ☐ False ☐

5. HEATHROW IS THIS COUNTRY'S LARGEST RETAILER OF PERFUME.
   True ☐ False ☐

6. THE WORLD'S 5TH BUSIEST INTER-NATIONAL AIRPORT IS GATWICK.
   True ☐ False ☐

7. ALL NATIONALISED INDUSTRIES RUN AT THE PUBLIC'S EXPENSE.
   True ☐ False ☐

Take a couple of minutes and complete this questionnaire.

Then check the answers at the bottom of the page.

If you learn something about us in the process, these questions have served their purpose.

But we'll be flabbergasted if you answer all seven correctly.

Not, we hasten to add, because we imagine you to be stupid.

But because we're not the sort of nationalised industry you're likely to read about in the papers.

We're not plagued by labour relations problems. We don't make a loss.

And we don't go to the government cap in hand for some money every time we have to fork out for something like a new terminal.

In fact, we don't cost you a penny. How many nationalised industries can say that?

British Airports

ANSWERS: 1. FALSE—HEATHROW IS BRITAIN'S BUSIEST PORT LAST YEAR 16 BILLION POUNDS WORTH OF IMPORTS AND EXPORTS—1 BILLION MORE THAN DOVER. 2. TRUE. 3. TRUE—MORE THAN KENNEDY IN NEW YORK OR CHICAGO'S O'HARE. 4. FALSE—ABERDEEN IS THE WORLD'S BUSIEST INTERNATIONAL HELIPORT. 5. TRUE. 6. TRUE. 7. FALSE—BRITISH AIRPORTS AUTHORITY DOES NOT COST THE TAXPAYER A PENNY.

THE WORLD'S MOST SUCCESSFUL INTERNATIONAL AIRPORT SYSTEM
HEATHROW—GATWICK—STANSTED—GLASGOW—EDINBURGH—PRESTWICK—ABERDEEN

in this instance the government, and paying for the campaign from the corporate treasury or stockholders' money. The management of British Rail, however, offers an interesting rationale for its campaign. British Rail makes a distinction between a state-owned company engaged in commercial activities and a government department organized to perform a government function. Observes a British Rail spokesperson:

> We are not part of the Government. We are a national industry that has its shareholder in the Government—the shareholder is also the banker. We have a public charter. It is vitally important for us to swing public opinion—of which the Government in power is only a part—in favor of railways. There would be an enormous conflict if we were a government department because in that case we would exist to perform a government function assigned to us.[31]

British Rail's campaign was quite successful in achieving its objective. However, if we accept British Rail's logic for advocacy advertising, it would follow that in the United States, federal agencies—which are created by Congress and are independent of the executive branch—might consider engaging in advocacy campaigns when their mandate is threatened by budget restrictions or the appointment of commissioners by an administration not sympathetic to their programs and activities.

Campaigns by Foreign Governments and Groups in the United States

The most prevalent form of advocacy campaigns by foreign governments in the United States are those of special advertising supplements that appear regularly in major national magazines and leading newspapers. They extol the stable political environment in these countries, the incentives for direct investment, the availability of a dedicated workforce, and the existence of a strong social and economic infrastructure. Quite often, the countries that engage in these campaigns have not received a good press in the United States. In most cases, these countries are trying to attract American investment.

A different approach to advocacy advertising campaigns is taken by nongovernmental foreign groups. Their aim is to reach the American public with their viewpoint on U.S. government policies they consider contrary to their interests. They want to reach the targeted groups with the message that these policies would also be against the long-term interests of the United States. Such ads are generally one-time affairs, directed at a very specific group and are timed to coincide with a specific legislative or public policy debate. Because of their ad hoc nature and poor reach and frequency, their effectiveness is questionable. Nevertheless, this type of advertising is on the increase and may become a significant phenomenon in the future.

Two recent examples of these ads are presented in Exhibits 15 and 16. Exhibit 15 is an ad sponsored by a Japanese cooperative suggesting that Americans should not pressure the Japanese government to relax its import restrictions against American citrus and beef. The second ad,

Exhibit 15

A MESSAGE FROM THE FARMERS OF JAPAN TO THE PEOPLE OF THE UNITED STATES

urrent US-Japan agricultural talks aimed at import expansion will not ease the real problems in US-Japan trade relations. However, they could very well endanger the basis of farm life in Japan. Here's why.

DID YOU KNOW *that Japan is already the largest single importer of US agricultural products?*
Japan is the #1 market for US produced agricultural goods. Japan buys more than $10 billion worth of farm and fishery products annually.

DID YOU KNOW *that increasing beef and citrus imports will not significantly reduce the US-Japan trade imbalance?*
Expanding beef and citrus imports represent *at the most* an additional $500 million, but there is *no guarantee* that these imports will come from the US, since lower priced commodities from Australia, Argentina, Brazil and Israel are waiting to enter the market.

DID YOU KNOW *that beef and citrus represent major sources of income for Japan's small farmers?*
Beef and citrus imports have already reached 40% and 10% of its domestic production respectively. Japan is about the size of the state of Montana, with only 17% of its land arable. The average Japanese farm is 1/150th the size of the average US farm. If imports are allowed to increase, they will drive out domestically produced beef and citrus, which will mean the end of many small family farms in Japan.

DID YOU KNOW *that Japan's food self-sufficiency is the lowest of all the industrial countries—less than one-third its total requirements?*
Japan is the largest importer of agricultural and fishery products—a very risky situation for any country. A country should produce as much food at home as possible, relying on imports to meet unsatisfied demand. Japan learned this bitter lesson in 1973 when the US embargoed soybeans (for political reasons having nothing to do with Japan) and created tremendous economic difficulties.

DID YOU KNOW *that there are those in the US and Japan who seek a "cure" for trade problems in the industrial sector at the expense of the farmer?*
Increasing agricultural imports *cannot* erase the US trade deficit, which is due primarily to industrial goods (automobiles, steel and consumer products). This "quick fix" idea is a meaningless political gesture aimed at diverting attention from more basic economic difficulties.

DID YOU KNOW *that Japan has already established very liberal import policies on many agricultural products?*
Japan imposes no tariffs on imported feed grain, soybeans and wheat and has expanded imports of many other items. But no country can allow absolute free trade in its agricultural sector. As an example, the US protects its sugar, beef, dairy products and tobacco with import restrictions and subsidies. The farmer is an important part of the entire economic and social fabric of all countries, and must be protected.

We, the farmers of Japan, with our tradition of the family based farm, are the heart of our nation, just as the American farmer is the heart of your country. The Japanese farmer is not to blame for the current US-Japan trade frictions.

We must resist efforts on the part of any government, American or Japanese, to sacrifice the farmer for short term political goals.

The real answer to the current US-Japan trade issue lies in the economic revitalization of the US and a lessening of Japan's dependency on export growth—not in undermining the Japanese farmer.

This advertisement is sponsored by: **ZENCHU** **THE CENTRAL UNION OF AGRICULTURAL COOPERATIVES**
Representing 6 million Japanese farming households.
8-3 Ohtemachi 1-chome, Chiyoda-ku, Tokyo 100, Japan
For further information write: ZENCHU, 1523 17th St. NW, Washington, DC 20036

IPO

INTERNATIONAL PROGRESS ORGANIZATION

CONCLUSIONS AND JUDGEMENT OF THE BRUSSELS TRIBUNAL ON REAGAN'S FOREIGN POLICY

The International Conference on the Reagan Administration's Foreign Policy convened in Brussels from 28-30 September, 1984 under the auspices of the International Progress Organization. Reports were submitted by international jurists and foreign policy specialists on various aspects of the Reagan Administration's foreign policy. Among the participants of the conference were Seán MacBride (Nobel Laureate, Ireland), Prof. George Wald (Nobel Laureate, Harvard University), General Edgardo Mercado Jarrin (Peru), General Nino Pasti (former Deputy Supreme Commander of NATO) and Hortensia Bussi de Allende (Chile). The reports were presented before a Panel of Jurists consisting of Hon. Farouk Abu-Eissa (Sudan) Attorney, former Foreign Minister, Secretary-General of the Arab Lawyers Union; Prof. Francis A. Boyle (U.S.A.), Professor of International Law from the University of Illinois, Chairman; Dr. Hans Goeran Franck (Sweden), Attorney, Member of the Swedish Parliament; Hon. Mirza Gholam Hafiz (Bangladesh), Former Speaker of the Bangladesh Parliament and currently a Senior Advocate of the Bangladesh Supreme Court; Hon. Mary M. Kaufman (U.S.A.), Attorney-at-Law, prosecuting attorney at the Nuremberg War Crimes trial against I. G. Farben; Dr. Jean-Claude Njem (Cameroun), Assistant-Professor at the Faculty of Law, Uppsala University, and a Consultant of the Government; Prof. Alberto Ruiz-Eldredge (Peru), Professor of Law, former President of the National Council of Justice; and Dr. Muemtaz Soysal (Turkey), Professor of Constitutional Law, University of Ankara. An accusation against the international legality of the Reagan Administration's foreign policy was delivered by the Honorable Ramsey Clark, former U.S. Attorney General. The defense was presented by a legal expert of the Reagan Administration.

Based upon all the reports and documents submitted and the arguments by the advocates, the Brussels Panel of Jurists hereby renders the following conclusions concerning the compatibility of the Reagan Administration's foreign policy with the requirements of international law.

A. Introduction

1. General Introduction. The Reagan Administration's foreign policy constitutes a gross violation of the fundamental principles of international law enshrined in the Charter of the United Nations Organization, as well as of the basic rules of customary international law set forth in the U.N. General Assembly's Declaration on the Inadmissibility of Intervention in the Domestic Affairs of States and the Protection of Their Independence and Sovereignty (1965), its Declaration on Principles of International Law Concerning Friendly Relations and Co-operation Among States in Accordance with the Charter of the United Nations (1970), and its Definition of Aggression (1974), among others. In addition, the Reagan Administration is responsible for complicity in the commission of Crimes Against Peace, Crimes Against Humanity, War Crimes and Grave Breaches of the Third and Fourth Geneva Conventions of 1949.

B. Western Hemisphere

2. Grenada. The Reagan Administration's 1983 invasion of Grenada was a clearcut violation of U.N. Charter articles 2 (3), 2 (4), and 33 as well as of articles 18, 20 and 21 of the Revised OAS Charter for which there was no valid excuse or justification under international law. As such, it constituted an act of aggression within the meaning of article 39 of the United Nations Charter.

3. Threat of U.S. Intervention. In direct violation of the basic requirement of international law mandating the peaceful settlement of international disputes, the Reagan Administration has implemented a foreign policy towards Central America that constitutes a great danger of escalation in military hostilities to the point of precipitating armed intervention by U.S. troops into combat against both the insurgents in El Salvador and the legitimate government of Nicaragua.

4. El Salvador. The Reagan Administration's illegal intervention into El Salvador's civil war contravenes the international legal right of self-determination of peoples as recognized by article 1 (2) of the United Nations Charter. The Reagan Administration has provided enormous amounts of military assistance to an oppressive regime that has used it to perpetrate a gross and consistent pattern of violations of the most fundamental human rights of the people of El Salvador.

5. Nicaragua. The Reagan Administration's policy of organizing and participating in military operations by opposition *contra* groups for the purpose of overthrowing the legitimate government of Nicaragua violates the terms of both the U.N. and O.A.S. Charters prohibiting the threat or use of force against the political independence of a state. The Reagan Administration has flouted its obligation to terminate immedately its support for the opposition *contra* groups in accordance with the Interim Order of Protection issued by the International Court of Justice on 10 May 1984.

6. International Court of Justice. The Panel denounces the patently bogus attempt by the Reagan Administration to withdraw from the compulsory jurisdiction of the International Court of Justice in the suit brought against it by Nicaragua for the purpose of avoiding a peaceful settlement of this dispute by the World Court in order to pursue instead a policy based upon military intervention, lawless violence and destabilization of the legitimate government of Nicaragua.

7. Mining Nicaraguan Harbors. The Reagan Administration's mining of Nicaraguan harbors violates the rules of international law set forth in the 1907 Hague Convention on the Laying of Submarine Mines, to which both Nicaragua and the United States are parties.

Nobel Laureate Seán MacBride addressing the international conference on Reagan's Foreign Policy in Brussels (28 September 1984)

C. Nuclear Weapons Policies

8. Arms Control Treaties. The Reagan Administration has refused to support the ratification of the Threshold Test Ban Treaty of 1974, the Peaceful Nuclear Explosions Treaty of 1976, and the SALT II Treaty of 1979, in addition to renouncing the longstanding objective of the U.S. government to negotiate a comprehensive test ban treaty. As such the Reagan Administration has failed to pursue negotiations in good faith on effective measures relating to cessation of the nuclear arms race at an early date and to nuclear disarmament as required by article 6 of the Nuclear Non-Proliferation Treaty of 1968. Similarly, the Reagan Administration's "Strategic Defense Initiative" of 1983 threatens to breach the Anti-Ballistic Missile Systems Treaty of 1972.

9. Pershing 2 Missiles. The deployment of the offensive, first-strike, counterforce strategic nuclear weapons system known as the Pershing 2 missile in the Federal Republic of Germany violates the Non-Circumvention Clause found in article 12 of the SALT II Treaty. The Reagan Administration is bound to obey this prohibition pursuant to the rule of customary international law enunciated in article 18 of the 1969 Vienna Convention on the Law of Treaties to the effect that a signatory to a treaty is obliged to refrain from acts that would defeat the object and purpose of a treaty until it has made its intention clear not to become a party.

10. The MX missile. The MX missile is an offensive, first-strike, counterforce strategic nuclear weapons system that can serve no legitimate defensive purpose under U.N. Charter article 51 and the international laws of humanitarian armed conflict.

11. No-first-use. In accordance with U.N. General Assembly Resolution 1553 of 24 November 1961, the panel denounces the refusal by the Reagan Administration to adopt a policy mandating the no-first-use of nuclear weapons in the event of a conventional attack as required by the basic rule of international law dictating proportionality in the use of force even for the purposes of legitimate self-defense.

12. ASAT Treaty. The Panel calls upon both the United States and the Soviet Union to negotiate unconditionally over the conclusion of an anti-satellite weapons treaty.

D. Middle East

13. Lebanon. For the part it played in the planning, preparation and initiation of the 1982 Israeli invasion of Lebanon, the Reagan Administration has committed a Crime against Peace as defined by the Nuremberg Principles. Likewise, under the Nuremberg principles, the Reagan Administration becomes an accomplice to the Crimes against Humanity, War Crimes and Grave Breaches of the Third and Fourth Geneva Conventions of 1949 that have been committed or condoned by Israel and its allied Phalange and Haddad militia forces in Lebanon. Such complicity includes the savage massacre of genocidal character of hundreds of innocent Palestinian and Lebanese civilians by organized units of the Phalangist militia at the Sabra and Shatila refugee camps located in West Beirut that were then subject to the control of the occupying Israeli army. The Reagan Administration has totally failed to discharge its obligation to obtain Israel's immediate and unconditional withdrawal from all parts of Lebanon as required by U.N. Security Council Resolutions 508 and 509 (1982), both of which are legally binding on Israel and the United States under U.N. Charter article 25. This includes Israeli evacuation of Southern Lebanon.

14. The Palestinian Question. The Reagan Administration's policy towards the Palestinian people as well as the Reagan "Peace Plan" of 1 September 1982 violates the international legal right of the Palestinian people to self-determination as recognized by U.N. Charter article 1(2). As recognized by numerous General Assembly Resolutions, the Palestinian people have an international legal right to create an independent and sovereign state. The Palestine Liberation Organization has been recognized as the legitimate representative of the Palestinian people by both the United Nations General Assembly and the League of Arab States. The Reagan Administration's non-recognition of the PLO and its attempt to brand the PLO a "terrorist" group contravene the Palestinian people's right to liberation. The panel denounces the negative attitude of the Reagan Administration towards the call by the United Nations' Secretary General for the convocation of an international conference under the auspices of the United Nations, with the United States and the Soviet Union as co-chairmen, and with the participation of all parties involved in the conflict including the PLO, for the purpose of obtaining a just and lasting peace in the Middle East.

15. Israeli Settlements. The Reagan Administration's declared position that Israeli settlements in the Occupied Territories are "not illegal" is a violation of U.S. obligations under article 1 of the Fourth Geneva Convention of 1949 to ensure respect for the terms of the Convention (here article 49) by other High Contracting Parties such as Israel.

16. Libya. The Reagan Administration's dispatch of the U.S. Sixth Fleet into the Gulf of Sidra for the purpose of precipitating armed conflict with the Libyan government constitutes a breach of the peace under article 39 of the U.N. Charter. The Reagan Administration's policy to attempt to destabilize the government of Libya violates the terms of the United Nations Charter article 2 (4) prohibiting the threat or use of force directed against the political independence of a state.

E. Africa, Asia and the Indian Ocean

17. Apartheid. The Panel denounces the Reagan Administration's so-called policy of "constructive engagement" towards the **apartheid** regime in South Africa. This specious policy encourages discrimination and oppression against the majority of the people of South Africa; it hampers effective action by the international community against apartheid, and facilitates aggressive conduct by the South African apartheid regime against neighbour states in violation of the U.N. Charter. As such, the Reagan Administration has become an accomplice to the commission of the international crime of apartheid as recognized by the universally accepted International Convention on the Suppression and Punishment of the Crime of Apartheid of 1973. The Panel also denounces the cooperation between the Reagan Administration and South Africa in military and nuclear matters.

18. Namibia. The Reagan Administration has refused to carry out its obligations under Security Council Resolution 435 (1978) providing for the independence of Namibia, as required by article 25 of the U.N. Charter. The right of the Namibian people to self-determination had been firmly established under international law long before the outbreak of the Angolan civil war. The Reagan Administration has no right to obstruct the achievement of Namibian Independence by conditioning it upon or "linking" it to the withdrawal of Cuban troops from Angola in any way. Both the U.N. General Assembly and the Organization of the African Unity have recognized SWAPO as the legitimate representative of the Namibian people and the Reagan Administration is obligated to negotiate with it as such.

19. Angola. Cuban troops are in Angola at the request of the legitimate government of Angola in order to protect it from overt and covert aggression mounted by the South African **apartheid** regime from Namibia. There is absolutely no international legal justification for South African aggression against Angola in order to maintain and consolidate its reprehensible occupation of Namibia. The Angolan government has repeatedly stated that when South Africa leaves Namibia it will request the withdrawal of Cuban troops, and Cuba has agreed to withdraw its troops whenever so requested by Angola. According to the relevant rules of international law, that is the proper sequence of events to be followed. The Reagan Administration's "linkage" of the presence of the Cuban troops in Angola with the independence of Namibia encourages South African aggression against Angola, and thus it must share in the responsibility for South Africa's genocidal acts against the people of Angola.

20. Indian Ocean. The Reagan Administration's continued military occupation of the Island of Diego Garcia violates the international legal right of self-determination for the people of Mauritius as recognized by the United Nations Charter. The Reagan Administration has accelerated the rapid militarization of the U.S. naval base on Diego Garcia as part of its plan to create a jumping -off point for intervention by the Rapid Deployment Force into the Persian Gulf. As such the Reagan Administration's foreign policy towards the Indian Ocean has violated the terms of the U.N. General Assembly's Declaration of the Indian Ocean as a Zone of Peace (1971).

F. Conclusion

21. United Nations Action. From the foregoing, it is clear that the Reagan Administration has substituted force for the rule of international law in its conduct of foreign policy around the world. It has thus created a serious threat to the maintenance of international peace and security under article 39 of the United Nations Charter that calls for the imposition of enforcement measures by the U.N. Security Council under articles 41 and 42. In the event the Reagan Administration exercises its veto power against the adoption of such measures by the Security Council, the matter should be turned over to the U.N. General Assembly for action in accordance with the procedures set forth in the Uniting for Peace Resolution of 1950. In this way the Reagan Administration's grievous international transgressions could be effectively opposed by all members of the world community in a manner consistent with the requirements of international law.

Both the Security Council and the General Assembly should also take into account the numerous interventionist measures taken by the Reagan Administration, whether direct or indirect, seeking to impose financial and economic policies which are contrary to the sovereign independence of states, especially in the developing world, which severely damage the quality of life for all peoples.

Farouk Abu-Eissa
Mary Kaufman
Francis A. Boyle, Chairman
Jean-Claude Njem
Hans Goeran Franck
Alberto Ruiz-Eldredge
Mirza Gholam Hafiz
Muemtaz Soysal

Brussels, Belgium

30 September 1984

For more information please write to:

International Progress Organization A-1150 Vienna, Austria
Reindorfgasse 5, phone (222) 85 6112 Telex 136553.

entitled "Conclusions and Judgements of the Brussel Tribunal on Reagan's Foreign Policy," proclaimed that the Reagan administration's foreign policy constituted a gross violation of the fundamental principles of international law and that the Reagan administration had substituted force for international law in its conduct of foreign policy around the world. The sponsor of the advertisement, the International Progress Organization, based in Vienna, Austria, did not provide enough information in the advertisement to enable the U.S. reader to judge its credentials and become informed about its representational character.

Voluntary Private Organizations

Advocacy advertisements sponsored by voluntary private organizations have been one of the fastest growing segments of this genre of advertising; yet as a group, they have received little attention and their overall influence on public opinion remains largely undetermined. The sponsoring organizations can be classified into five groups:

1. Established nonsectarian organizations that engage in long-term advocacy campaigns on particular issues that are part of their organizational mandate, such as Planned Parenthood, the National Rifle Association, and Friends of Animals [Exhibits 17–20].

2. Established nonsectarian groups that use advocacy advertisements on an ad hoc basis, such as the National Organization of Women (NOW), the Izaak Walton League, the International Society for Animal Rights, the Animal Welfare Institute, the International Fund for Animal Welfare, and The Union of Concerned Scientists [Exhibits 21–25].

3. Established sectarian groups that use advocacy advertising to promote their long-term policy positions, and also to speak out on current public controversies on an ad hoc basis. Examples are the Moral Majority, the Church League of America, Catholics for a Free Choice, and the Catholic Health Association [Exhibits 26–29].

4. Ad hoc groups composed of well-known public personalities that join together to advocate public policy positions on specific issues, such as the Coalition for a New Foreign and Military Policy, the Bipartisan Budget Coalition, and Joan B. Kroc [Exhibits 30–32].

5. New advocacy groups that use advocacy advertisements to establish their identity, to espouse their cause, and also to raise funds from the public, such as the Infant Formula Action Coalition (INFACT) and Common Cause [Exhibit 33]. (Groups classified in other categories may also make fundraising appeals as part of their advocacy advertisements.)

Exhibit 17

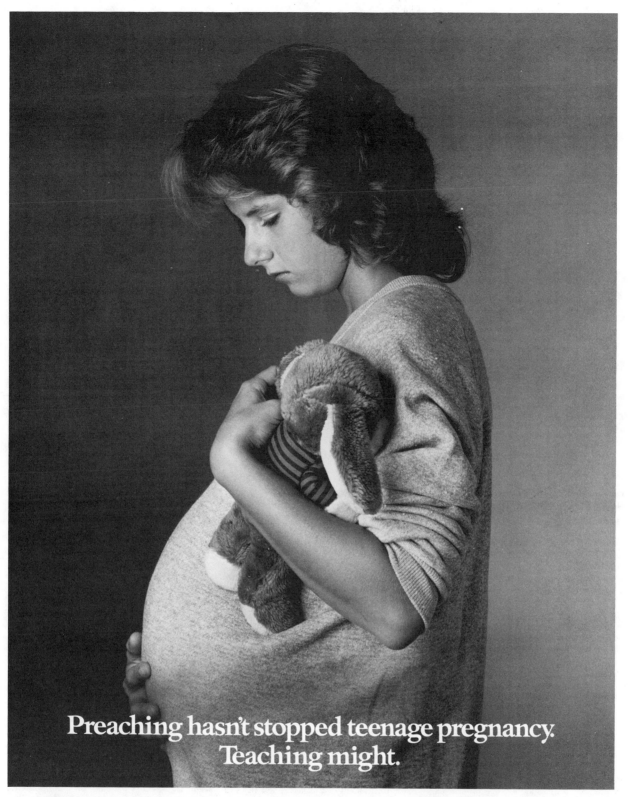

Preaching hasn't stopped teenage pregnancy. Teaching might.

She's fourteen years old, pregnant, and she could be your own daughter.

That's the personal tragedy. Now look at the national tragedy. 40% of all girls turning 14 this year will get pregnant before they turn 20.

If a teenager has a baby, the outlook for both is bleak. The baby has a higher risk of poor health. Chances are the mother will never finish school or hold a job. The odds are she will end up on welfare within 18 months. In most cases she will be raising a child alone. To complete the cycle, her daughter will probably become a teenage mother too.

Warnings and threats haven't solved the problem. Isn't it time we tried something else? Like putting sex education in the schools and helping parents educate their children at home; providing information on birth control and abortion; organizing community programs that train teenagers to counsel other teens.

These are all important points in the Planned Parenthood program. They reflect our belief that every child should be a wanted child, a child born of choice, not ignorance.

That's why we have spent the better part of the century supporting and fighting for everyone's

Planned Parenthood of New York City, Inc.
380 Second Ave., New York, N.Y. 10010 (212) 777-2002

☐ I believe in Planned Parenthood's objectives and I want to help. Here is my tax-deductible contribution of $_____ .
☐ I agree with your objectives and I'd like more facts. Please send your brochure.

Name _____

Address _____

City/State/Zip _____

Phone (H) _____ Phone (O) _____

This advertisement has been paid for with private contributions. A copy of our most recent financial report can be obtained from us or from the New York State Board of Social Welfare, Office Tower, Empire State Plaza, Albany, N.Y. 12223. © 1984 Planned Parenthood of New York City, Inc.

PLANNED PARENTHOOD
FOR THE LOVE OF CHILDREN

freedom to make their own decisions about having children.

Today, most Americans share Planned Parenthood's commitment. If you do, there are two ways you can show it.

First, you can give us your help, with money that helps us reach others.

Second, you can make the political process work for your beliefs. Speak out. Tell public officials and candidates how you stand on these key birth control issues:

• I'm in favor of sex education programs in the public schools.
• I support public funding to make birth control available to all people who want it but can't afford it.
• I believe in a woman's right to safe, legal abortion.
• I'm in favor of increased funds to find better birth control methods.

Your opinions count, so express them – in writing. Don't sit on the sidelines and then complain about the final score.

Exhibit 18

PARENTAL NOTIFICATION? OR PARENTAL INVOLVEMENT?

FROM OUR PERSPECTIVE

Art work by Ann Grifalconi.

On February 22, 1982, the Department of Health and Human Services published proposed regulations to govern family planning services funded under Title X of the Public Health Service Act. The regulations would require family planning providers to notify both parents of unemancipated minors under 18 who receive prescription birth control drugs and devices.

There is a 60-day comment period, ending April 23, during which individuals and organizations may make known their views on the proposed regulations and their potential effects. Comments should be submitted to Marjory Mecklenburg, Acting Deputy Assistant Secretary for Population Affairs, Room 725H, 200 Independence Avenue SW, Washington, D.C. 20201.

The obvious intent of the parental notification regulations proposed by the Secretary of Health and Human Services is to 1) reduce teenage pregnancies, 2) inhibit sexual activity among our nation's youth, 3) protect teenagers from the potential medical consequences of prescription contraceptives, and 4) increase the involvement of parents in young people's decisions about sexual activity.

First, the number of teenage pregnancies would increase, not decrease. One in four young people would stop attending family planning clinics if their parents had to be informed. A great majority would use "drugstore" methods or would use no birth control methods at all, greatly increasing the risk of unintended pregnancy. Fear of parental notification already is the most important reason teenagers delay obtaining contraceptives and is the cause of a large percentage of the more than one million teenage pregnancies that occur each year.

Second, sexual activity among teenagers would not decrease, primarily because most teenagers are sexually active for almost a year before they even seek contraception. In addition, only two percent of teenagers who attend family planning clinics would stop having sex if their parents had to be informed that they had received prescription contraceptives.

Third, the health risks for teenagers associated with pregnancy and childbirth are five times greater than the health risks associated with use of prescription contraceptives. In addition to the increased risks of mortality and morbidity among teenage mothers, their babies are much more likely to die in the first year of life than babies born to older women.

Fourth, rather than encouraging free and open discussion between parents and teenagers about sexuality and reproduction, the regulations would merely inform parents, after the fact, that their daughters had received prescription contraceptives. Parental notification by mail, which may well result in recriminations and arguments, is a far cry from encouraging parental involvement in a teenager's decision-making about sexual behavior.

Government should not be allowed to intrude into the privacy of family relationships and the privacy of confidential relationships between doctor and patient. When such intrusion would worsen an already serious problem, it is even more reprehensible.

There are alternatives to government mandating parental *notification* as a means of reducing the problems outlined above, and they have proven to be effective in establishing parental *involvement* in teenage decisions about sexual activity.

With common sense, with realistic goals and programs, and with a 66-year history of service, Planned Parenthood helps parents and teenagers find a level of understanding and discussion. We provide the facts. We offer guidance in bridging the generation gap. We offer programs parents and teenagers can attend together. And we provide information through publications. So that when teenagers are ready with the questions, their parents are ready with the answers.

The work of Planned Parenthood and other family planning service providers has helped parents and their teenagers voluntarily overcome the difficulty of talking together about personal matters. Right now, more than half of young teenagers who attend family planning clinics do so with the knowledge of their parents; one-fifth attend at their parents' suggestion. And the younger the teenager, the more likely the parent is to know about the visit.

All of this has been accomplished through parental involvement, not parental notification.

The statistics given were compiled by The Alan Guttmacher Institute, an independent corporation for research, policy analysis, and public education in family planning and population, and a special affiliate of the Planned Parenthood Federation of America.

 Planned Parenthood
Federation of America, Inc. ®

810 Seventh Avenue
New York, New York 10019
212/541-7800

This advertisement paid for by private contributions.

Exhibit 19

BRYAN HARDIN: 8 years old. Second grade student and a member of the National Rifle Association.

"I like to play football best. But I like my dog and I like my new BB gun. When I got it, I wanted to shoot that night, but my Dad said I had to learn the rules first. He taught me about safety and to always remember a gun is not a toy.

"We made a target out of a box in the back yard, and my Dad showed me how to aim. I didn't hit it the first time, but then I started doing better. I just need to practice more so I can go hunting with my Grandfather. He said he'd take me when I got older and after I learned some more rules.

"My Dad's a member of the NRA and so am I because he says they need kids like me to grow up and keep shooting a safe sport." **I'm the NRA.**

Each year, NRA members teach thousands of young people safe gun handling and basic marksmanship skills. If you would like to join the NRA and want more information about our programs and benefits, write Harlon Carter, Executive Vice President, P.O. Box 37484, Dept. BH-9, Washington, D.C. 20066.

Paid for by the members of the National Rifle Association of America.

Exhibit 20

$3,OOO REWARD

For Information Leading To the Conviction Of People Who Violate the Endangered Species Act

Want to protect endangered species and earn a handsome reward for your efforts?

The U.S. Fish and Wildlife Service has approved the issuing of rewards, up to $2,500 per violation, to citizens who furnish "information which leads to a finding of civil violation or a conviction of a criminal violation of any provision of this (Endangered Species) Act or any regulation or permit issued thereunder."

To this, Friends of Animals is adding another $500 which will be paid to the person that FoA believes has made the most meaningful citizen contribution to enforcement of the Endangered Species Act from now through December 31, 1979.

According to the Department of the Interior's Office of the Solicitor, when a citizen finds a violation of the Endangered Species Act, he or she should notify the nearest office of the U.S. Fish and Wildlife Service, Law Enforcement Division, and report the violation. The person reporting the violation should also promptly request the reward.

The reward is issued by the Department of the Interior after an investigation and prosecution. The person who reported the violation is eligible to receive half of any fine levied against the violator.

If you are issued a reward for helping to enforce the Endangered Species Act, contact Friends of Animals and tell us about your effort. At the end of 1979, we will select the person we judge to have made the most meaningful contribution to enforcement of the law, and add another $500 to that person's well-earned reward.

To participate, obtain a copy of the Endangered Species Act and a copy of 50 CFR 17 (that's the official list of endangered and threatened species), and become thoroughly familiar with these documents. They are available from most Fish and Wildlife offices, or write the Service's main office at Washington, D.C. 20240.

Generally, the Act protects all animals listed on 50 CFR 17. Unless someone has a special permit, it is illegal to import, export, hunt, sell, transport or possess any protected animal, alive or dead. It is even illegal to attempt, or to encourage someone else to attempt, hunting, sale or possession of a protected animal.

This means, if a person finds a business offering leopard skin coats for sale, or alligator shoes, or if they learn of someone hunting an animal protected by the law, or even keeping one as a pet without the necessary permits, they should contact the Fish and Wildlife Service at once.

Protecting wildlife is everybody's business. Indeed, the law of the land has invited general public participation in the protection of this rare and irreplaceable treasure. We at Friends of Animals want to encourage public participation. That's why we're offering the reward, and that's why we offer FoA membership to readers of this notice. Those who send us a $10 tax-deductible contribution will also be offered the opportunity to work in many other animal-protection projects with us. And we'll send along our 'Extinct Is Forever' poster with your membership package.

Get involved! Animals have carried man's burden for too long. Now it's time for us to carry their greatest burden — the threat of extinction.

friends of animals

Endangered Species Reward Program
11 West 60th Street
New York, New York 10023

Exhibit 21

Victims of the Cosmetic Industry

*The cosmetic industry is **not** required to test its products on animals. The Food and Drug Administration, which regulates the industry, has made that fact very clear.*

The industry itself elected to use animals.

Its methods, for which many species of animals are used, include:

- The LD/50 (Lethal Dose/50) test which means that 50 percent of the animals are deliberately fed (usually by force) a lethal dose of any given substance. Death is not gentle.
- Forcing the animals to inhale fumes in an exposure chamber.
- Scraping skin from bodies and then applying substances to the raw flesh.
- The Draize test, for which rabbits are used because, unlike humans, they have no tear ducts to wash away the products and ingredients poured into their eyes. The eyes become grotesquely ulcerated and swollen.

When the public several years ago demanded an end to the cosmetic industry's use of animals, the industry decided to make grants to research laboratories to find "alternatives" to its animals tests. Years are passing. Reports of the work being done in the search for "alternatives," however, show that the researchers are testing modification of some of the tests on animals; reducing the numbers of animals and using parts of animals. None of which will end the industry's use of animals.

The animals cannot protest. Only an enlightened, caring public can stop the cosmetic industry from continuing to cause the suffering and death of its animal victims.

Write today to the Cosmetic, Toiletry & Fragrance Association (CTFA), the trade association of the powerful industry, 1110 Vermont Avenue, NW, Suite 800, Washington, DC 20005. Tell CTFA that you are *not* impressed by the industry's grants to search for "alternatives." Demand that the use of animals for the testing of cosmetic products and ingredients be stopped *now.*

International Society for Animal Rights, Inc.
421 South State St., Clarks Summit, PA 18411

My tax deductible gift of $ _____ is enclosed to help you reach more people in your effort to stop the suffering and death of animals for cosmetic testing.

Name _____

Address _____

City, State, Zip _____

Exhibit 22

President Reagan:
Don't Appease the Japanese!
Save the Whales!

Japan has violated a ban on sperm whaling voted by the International Whaling Commission (IWC). Four hundred of these endangered whales were massacred to make chicken feed and lubricating oil.

And Japan has declared it will continue to massacre three species of endangered whale—sperm, Bryde's and minke—for several years to come in total defiance of the IWC's moratorium on all commercial whaling, which is set to begin at the end of this year.

Mr. President, your administration is *supporting* Japan's outlaw whaling! The spineless bureaucrats at the State Department are attempting to reverse 13 years of U.S. leadership in whale conservation.

Caving in to Japanese pressure, these Administration officials are seeking to subvert the International Whaling Commission's decision to shut down the whalers. They even worked out a bilateral deal with Japan that totally circumvents the IWC and makes a mockery of U.S. obligations to support the decisions of that 40-nation treaty organization.

On 5 March 1985, U.S. District Court Judge Charles Richey declared that the U.S. sell-out of the whales was illegal. Finding in favor of twelve conservation and animal welfare groups, the federal court ruled:

"The Secretary of Commerce may not unilaterally, or even bilaterally with the Japanese, dismiss the mandate of the IWC so as to proceed with his own particular vision of whale preservation. Congress has not given him that authority, and has, in fact, explicitly created an automatic sanction to prevent this very situation."

Sanctions Against Japan Required by U.S. Law

Mr. President, the federal court has ordered your Administration to obey the Packwood-Magnuson Amendment, which requires that outlaw whaling nations lose half of their fishing allocations within the U.S. 200-mile zone. Japan must face the consequences of its violation of the ban on sperm whaling, which was voted 25 to 1 by the IWC. The U.S. strongly supported the ban when it was adopted.

Why is your Administration now seeking to allow Japan to have at least four extra years of sperm whaling? Why is your Administration seeking to subvert the moratorium on all commercial whaling, the basic goal of U.S. policy since 1972, by condoning Japan's intention to violate it?

Six other whaling nations have already agreed to end their hunt this year. What will you do, Mr. President, if they decide they want a "special deal" to continue the massacre of the last of the whales?

Your Administration recently enforced the Packwood-Magnuson Amendment against the Soviet Union, Mr. President. The Soviets exceeded their quota of minke whales by more than 700, so they lost half of their fish allocations in the U.S. zone. They may give up whaling as a consequence.

Japan has committed an even greater violation of whaling regulations: killing "protected" species. Yet the Japanese are getting a pat on their backs from the Administration while all the other whaling nations face heavy sanctions for any violations.

Mr. President, why appease the Japanese? Please don't sacrifice the great whales for political expediency.

What the Public Can Do

If you are outraged by Japan's defiance of the whaling bans and by the attempted sell-out of the great whales by the Administration, please help the international conservation community in its campaign to bring a halt to the slaughter that has driven these extraordinary creatures to the brink of extinction:

1) Write to your two U.S. Senators and your Representative. Ask them to *demand* that the Administration impose sanctions against Japan and any other nations that defy the regulations of the International Whaling Commission.

2) Join the boycott of Japan Air Lines and all Japanese fish products. Ask your travel agent to avoid booking clients on the government-controlled air carrier. Ask your local markets and restaurants to stop selling fish from the industry that is defying the whaling bans. Particularly avoid Japanese surimi, the fish paste that is made into artificial crab legs and other morsels.

3) Make a tax-deductible contribution to the save-the-whales campaign. Your support is important. The Japanese government and whaling industry are spending millions to fight the whaling ban. Please be generous.

The Animal Welfare Institute is a non-profit, educational organization established in 1951 to reduce animal suffering and to protect endangered species. A copy of AWI's annual report is available on written request to AWI or to the New York State Dept. of State, Office of Charities Registration, Albany, N.Y. 12231.

Animal Welfare Institute
P.O. Box 3650
Washington, D.C. 20007

Exhibit 23

Do you really know what can go into a simple fish sandwich?

Fish caught by Canadian Fishermen who also kill the baby seals. Your purchase of a McDonald's or Burger King Fish Sandwich could help buy the boats, hard wooden clubs, and guns used by the seal hunters as they turn from fishing to the cruelty of killing adult and baby seals.

If you made a pledge today not to buy fish sandwiches from McDonald's or Burger King unless you were assured by the companies that no Canadian fish was used...your decision would save the seals. Canadian fishermen would have to stop sealing since they are totally dependent on their fish sales, with seal hunting a tiny sideline in comparison.

Canadian Globe and Mail of 13 March 1984, had this to say of IFAW's call for a worldwide boycott of Canadian fish: *"...But what really has the officials spooked is the U.S. market. (There) The International Fund for*

Animal Welfare (IFAW), which spearheads the anti-sealing protest worldwide, has started pressing U.S. purchasers not to take Canadian fish. The U.S. market is worth $1-billion a year to Canadian fishermen and the fast-food business in the United States is about a fifth of that market. Canada fears that, if one U.S. fast-food chain caves in to the protestors, all will surrender."

Over 15,000 seals, mostly babies just 2-4 weeks old, have been clubbed or shot over the last 28 days...and yet the Canadian Minister of Fisheries says there is no baby seal hunt.

You have it in your hands to save the baby seals today.

Please write or telephone one or both of the companies listed below and seek an assurance that they will not purchase Canadian fish until the Canadian Government passes a law banning the seal hunt forever.

Mr Fred L Turner,
Chairman of the Board,
McDonald's Corporation,
McDonald's Plaza, Oak Brook, Illinois,
IL 60521
Tel: 312/887-3200

Mr J Jeffrey Campbell, Chairman,
Burger King Corporation,
7360 North Kendall Drive,
Miami,
Florida FL 33156
Tel: 305/596-7277

SAVE THE SEALS
NO TO CANADIAN FISH

To the International Fund for Animal Welfare
I'll put animals first ... I'll do my part to help you fight the baby seal hunters.
Enclosed is my tax-exempt contribution to IFAW in the amount of:

☐ $10 ☐ $15 ☐ $25 ☐ $35 ☐ $50 ☐ $100 ☐ $500 Other $ _____
We need hundreds of gifts this size to save the baby seals forever.

Name _____
(please print)
Address _____
_____
_____ Zip Code _____

International Fund for Animal Welfare
169 Main Street, Yarmouth Port,
Massachusetts 02675 U.S.A.
Our financial statement is available to contributors. **IFAW**

Our boycott campaign needs your support. We cannot succeed without your funds, to carry our boycott to every community in America.

A copy of the last financial report filed with the Department of State may be obtained by writing to: N.Y. State Department of State, Office of Charities Registration, Albany, N.Y. 12231 or IFAW.

Exhibit 24

THE FISH WON'T BE BITING IN TWITCHELL CREEK TODAY,

OR TOMORROW, EITHER.

There was a time when with a little luck and a little patience, you could pull a fair-sized fish out of Twitchell Creek on Woods Lake in the Adirondacks.

But no more.

The fish are gone, along with the salamanders, ospreys, mayflies, swallows and myriad other creatures who once lived along the cool river banks.

They've been run off, or killed off by the rain, of all things. A deadly poisonous acid rain which has contaminated the water, choked the life out of the stream . . . . and broken the delicate food chain on water and (we're finding out) <u>on land</u> as well.

All rain contains some acid, of course. But acid precipitation is different. And far more dangerous. Acid rain contains two killers: nitric acid and sulfuric acid which form when sulfur dioxide and nitrogen oxide mix with rain water. These two chemicals are being spewed <u>by the ton-load</u> into our air every day . . . emissions from the coal-burning power plants and industrial boilers our nation uses to keep going.

Fortunately, some lakes contain "buffers" . . . neutralizing agents which help lessen acid damage. But what of the others . . . in the Adirondack Mountains, in western Virginia, in the Great Smoky Mountains, throughout New England . . .

Who Will Stop The Rain?

The Izaak Walton League is working to do just that right now. The League was formed in 1922 by a handful of sportsmen who wanted to combat water pollution. And it endures today as a grassroots conservation organization composed of 50,000 fishermen, hikers, hunters and campers who speak out—and work hard —to protect wild America.

Congress passed a Clean Air Act in 1970— soon up for renewal—which set allowable limits for sulfur dioxide emissions from power plants. Some would like to relax those laws now . . . asserting the regulations will retard energy development. We disagree. We want <u>stricter</u> regulations to reduce these emissions still further. And we'll get them. Once and for all. Because there's something at stake here far greater than fishing. And that's life itself.

For more information on our activities, write:

THE IZAAK WALTON LEAGUE OF AMERICA INCORPORATED

Izaak Walton League
1800 North Kent Street
Arlington, Virginia 22209

Exhibit 25

Whirlpool Galaxy

Nagasaki 1945

STAR WARS WILL COST TAXPAYERS A TRILLION DOLLARS OR SO.

AND LOOK WHAT YOU GET FOR YOUR MONEY.

When President Reagan first proposed his Star Wars scheme in 1983, some of us in the scientific community thought it was just another political gimmick, or some romantic vision by advisers who know nothing of scientific or military reality, and care nothing about economic reality.

But now we know that the President and the Pentagon are serious about Star Wars. Deadly serious.

In fact, they are already spending the first billions in the most dangerous and expensive escalation of the arms race ever conceived.

Star Wars must be stopped now – and we urgently need your help. We ask you to join the 100,000 people nationwide who support our work. We ask you to join with scientists across the country – including 53 Nobel Laureates and 700 members of the National Academy of Science – who are calling on the President to stop Star Wars and adhere to existing treaties that ban weapons in space.

Here are four fundamental reasons why any concerned, knowledgeable citizen should join the fight against Star Wars:

1. STAR WARS IS TECHNOLOGICALLY NAIVE.
There is not a shred of scientific evidence that it will work. Only the wildest coincidence of miracles would permit all of the Buck Rogers components of Star Wars – particle beams, geosynchronous relay space mirrors, laser battle stations, kinetic energy weapons, etc. – to work together to provide an impenetrable shield against a multiple warhead attack.

2. STAR WARS IS MILITARILY FOOLHARDY. The very existence of a Star Wars plan automatically escalates the arms race and brings us closer to nuclear war. If we put weapons in space, the Soviets will put weapons in space. And that is not all they will do. For they will also build more weapons on earth to gain the means to overwhelm any defensive system we try to put into orbit. Moreover, if they should intend to launch a first strike, their first step would be to eliminate our Star Wars space stations with space mines or other easily deployed weapons.

3. STAR WARS IS ECONOMICALLY RUINOUS.
Defense analysts say Star Wars will cost hundreds of billions of dollars, possibly a trillion dollars, or more. In terms of the Federal budget, this means deficits so large that the country could be ruined without a war. And it means the government will be left with only one tax simplification option: to demand from the average taxpayer an extra $10,000 to $15,000 as his or her share of Star Wars. Economic growth in the civilian economy will also have to be sacrificed to Star Wars, which will siphon from other industries the scientific and technical resources that are critical to improving their productivity and competitive position.

4. STAR WARS IS MORALLY REPUGNANT. Star Wars is a clear notice of intent to violate existing international treaties, signed by this country, that prohibit weapons in space. It is a direct repudiation of President Kennedy's goal for the peaceful exploration of space. It is a program that will pollute the heavens with weapons that can plunge us into war.

We urgently need your help. Please complete the coupon and put it in the mail now.

THE UNION OF CONCERNED SCIENTISTS

The Union of Concerned Scientists is a nationwide coalition of scientists, engineers, and other professionals. UCS was founded in 1969 as a faculty group at the Massachusetts Institute of Technology, and its purpose is to carry out independent studies on the impact of advanced technology on society. A major UCS study, *The Fallacy of Star Wars*, has been published by Random House and is available in book stores and libraries.

I want to join the fight to stop Star Wars and to ban weapons in space. I want the Union of Concerned Scientists to continue its independent research, and to keep speaking out. Enclosed is my contribution:

☐ $20 ☐ $30 ☐ $50 ☐ $100 ☐ $_____
PLEASE PRINT CLEARLY: ATAS

Name: _____

Address: _____ Apt: _____

City: _____ St: _____ Zip: _____
☐ Check here if you are already a UCS Sponsor or have donated to UCS in the past.
Mail Coupon and Check to:
Union of Concerned Scientists   26 Church Street
Cambridge, MA 02238   Attn: Dr. J.S. Wager

The heavens are for wonder, not for war.

Exhibit 26

"They have labeled Moral Majority the Extreme Right because we speak out against Extreme Wrong!"

Jerry Falwell, President
Moral Majority Inc.

HERE IS HOW MORAL MAJORITY INC. STANDS ON TODAY'S VITAL ISSUES:

1. We believe in the separation of church and state.
Moral Majority Inc. is a political organization providing a platform for religious and non-religious Americans, who share moral values, to address their concerns in these areas. Members of Moral Majority Inc. have no common theological premise. We are **Americans** who are proud to be conservative in our approach to moral, social, and political concerns.

2. We are pro-life.
We believe that life begins at fertilization. We strongly oppose the massive "biological holocaust" which is resulting in the abortion of 1½ million babies each year in America. Some of us believe this from a theological perspective. Other Moral Majority Inc. members believe this from a medical perspective. Regardless, we agree that unborn babies have the right to life as much as babies that have been born. We are providing a voice and a defense for the human and civil rights of millions of unborn babies.

3. We are pro-traditional family.
We believe that the only acceptable family form begins with the legal marriage of a man to a woman. We feel that homosexual marriages and common-law marriages should not be accepted as traditional families. We oppose legislation that favors these kinds of "diverse family forms," thereby penalizing the traditional family unit. We oppose legislation that might promote homosexuals as a "bonafide minority" like women, blacks, Hispanics, etc. We do not oppose civil rights for homosexuals. We do oppose "special rights" for homosexuals who have chosen a perverted lifestyle rather than a traditional lifestyle.

4. We oppose the illegal drug traffic in America.
The youth in America are presently in the midst of a drug epidemic. Through education, legislation, and other means, we want to do our part to save our young people from death on the installment plan.

5. We oppose pornography.
While we do not advocate censorship, we do believe that education and legislation can help stem the tide of pornography and obscenity that is poisoning the American spirit today. Economic boycotts are a proper way in America's free-enterprise system to help persuade the media to move back to a sensible and reasonable moral stance. We most certainly believe in and are willing to fight for First Amendment rights for **everyone**. We are **not** willing to sit back while many television programs create cesspools of obscenity and vulgarity in America's living rooms.

6. We support the state of Israel and Jewish people everywhere.
It is impossible to separate the state of Israel from the Jewish family internationally. Many Moral Majority Inc. members, because of their theological convictions, are committed to the Jewish people. Others stand upon the human and civil rights of all persons as a premise for support of the state of Israel. Others support Israel because of historical and legal arguments. Regardless, one cannot belong to Moral Majority Inc. without making the commitment to support the state of Israel in its battle for survival and to support the human and civil rights of Jewish people everywhere. **No anti-semitic influence is allowed in Moral Majority Inc.** Further, Moral Majority Inc. is committed to the human and civil rights of all persons everywhere.

7. We believe that a strong national defense is the best deterrent to war.
We believe that liberty is the basic moral issue of all moral issues. No one in Afghanistan is discussing abortion today. The only way America can remain free is to remain strong. We therefore support the efforts of President Reagan, Secretary Haig, and many others to regain our position of military preparedness — with a sincere hope that we will never need to use any of our weapons against any people anywhere.

8. We support equal rights for women.
We agree with President Reagan's commitment to help every governor and state legislator to move quickly to insure that during the 1980's every American woman will earn as much money and enjoy the same opportunities for advancement as her male counterpart of the same vocation.

Why do Norman Lear, George McGovern, the ACLU, and others continually attack the philosophies and programs of movements like Moral Majority Inc?

The answer is simple — Moral Majority Inc. is made up of millions of Americans, including 72,000 ministers, priests, and rabbis, who are deeply concerned about the moral decline of our nation, and who are sick and tired of the way many amoral and secular humanists and other liberals are destroying the traditional family and moral values on which our nation was built.

We are Catholics, Jews, Protestants, Mormons, Fundamentalists — blacks and whites — farmers, housewives, businessmen. We are Americans from all walks of life, united by one central concern — to serve as a special interest group providing a voice for a return to moral sanity in these United States of America.

9. We believe the E.R.A. is the wrong vehicle with which to obtain equal rights for women.
We feel that the ambiguous and simplistic language of the Amendment could lead to court interpretations which might put women in combat, sanction homosexual marriages, and financially penalize widows and deserted wives.

10. We encourage our Moral Majority state organizations to be autonomous and indigenous.
Moral Majority state organizations may, from time to time, hold positions not held by Moral Majority Inc.

WHAT MORAL MAJORITY INC. IS NOT:

1. We are not a political party.
We are committed to work within the two-party system in this nation.

2. We do not endorse political candidates.
Moral Majority Inc. informs American citizens regarding the vital moral issues facing our nation. We have no "hit lists." Some members of the media attempt to group Moral Majority Inc. with all so-called "new right" organizations. While we fully support the constitutional rights of any special interest group to target candidates with whom they disagree, Moral Majority Inc. has chosen not to take this course. We are committed to principles and issues, not candidates and parties.
Many organizations, called the "new right" by the media, are doing a noble work addressing political, domestic, and economic issues not addressed by Moral Majority Inc. We congratulate them on this contribution to America's renaissance. However, Moral Majority Inc. restricts its involvement to the moral issues defined above. For example, Moral Majority Inc. has no official position on the Panama Canal Treaty, Taiwan, or South Africa — as we are often falsely charged by our critics.

3. We are not attempting to elect "born again" candidates.
We are committed to pluralism. The membership of Moral Majority Inc. is so totally pluralistic that the acceptability of any candidate could never be based upon one's religious affiliation. Our support of candidates is based upon two criteria:
(a) The commitment of the candidate to the principles which we espouse, and
(b) The competency of that candidate to fill that office.
A careful polling of the several million Moral Majority Inc. members would prove that the religious affiliation of candiates had nothing to do with our individual voting habits last November.

4. Moral Majority Inc. is not a religious organization attempting to control the government.
Moral Majority Inc. is a special interest group of millions of Americans who share the same moral values. We simply desire to influence government — not control government. This, of course, is the right of every American, and Moral Majority Inc. would vigorously oppose any Ayatollah-type person rising to power in this country.

5. We are not a censorship organization.
We believe in freedom of speech, freedom of the press, and freedom of religion. Therefore, while we do not agree that the Equal Rights Amendment would ultimately benefit the cause of women in America, we do agree with their right to boycott those states that have not ratified the Amendment. Likewise, we feel that all Americans have the right to refuse to purchase products from manufacturers whose advertising dollars support publications and television programming which violate their own morality code.

6. Moral Majority Inc. is not an organization committed to depriving homosexuals of their civil rights as Americans.
While we believe that homosexuality is moral perversion, we are committed to guaranteeing the civil rights of homosexuals. We do oppose the efforts of homosexuals to obtain special privileges as a "bonafide minority," and we oppose any efforts by homosexuals to flaunt their perversion as an acceptable lifestyle and/or attempt to force their lifestyle upon our children. We view heterosexual promiscuity with the same distaste which we express toward homosexuality.

7. We do not believe that individuals or organizations which disagree with Moral Majority Inc. belong to an immoral minority.
However, we do feel that our position represents a consensus of the majority of Americans. This belief in no way reflects on the morality of those who disagree with us.

HERE IS HOW MORAL MAJORITY INC. IS CONTRIBUTING TO BRINGING AMERICA BACK TO MORAL SANITY:

1. By educating millions of Americans concerning the vital moral issues of our day.
This is accomplished through such avenues as our newspaper called the **Moral Majority Report**, a radio commentary by the same name, seminars, and other training programs conducted daily across the nation.

2. By mobilizing millions of previously "inactive" Americans.
We have registered millions of voters and reactivated more millions of frustrated citizens into a special interest group who are effectively making themselves heard in the halls of Congress, in the White House, and in every state legislature.

3. By lobbying intensively in Congress to defeat any legislation that would further erode our constitutionally guaranteed freedoms and by introducing and/or supporting legislation that promotes traditional family and moral values.
The passage of a Human Life Amendment is a top priority on the Moral Majority agenda. Moral Majority Inc. supports the return of **voluntary** prayer to public schools. We oppose mandated or written prayers.

4. By informing all Americans about the voting records of their representatives so that every American, with full information available, can vote intelligently.
We are non-partisan. We are not committed to politicians or political parties; we are committed to principles and issues that we feel are essential to America's survival at this crucial hour.

5. By organizing and training millions of Americans who can become moral activists.
This heretofore silent majority in America can then help develop a responsive government which is truly "of the people, by the people, and for the people" instead of "in spite of the people," which we have had for too many years.

6. By encouraging and promoting non-public schools in their attempt to excel in academics while simultaneously teaching traditional family and moral values.
There are thousands of non-public schools in America which accept no tax monies. Some of these schools are Catholic, Fundamentalist, Jewish, Adventist, etc. Some are not religious. But Moral Majority Inc. supports the right of these schools to teach young people not only "how to make a living," but "how to live."
Moral Majority Inc. does not advocate the abolition of public schools. Public schools will always be needed in our pluralistic society. We are committed to helping public schools regain excellence. That is why we support the return of voluntary prayer to public schools and strongly oppose the teaching of the religion of secular humanism in the public school classroom.

THE TIME FOR ACTION IS NOW:

Now is the time for all Americans to stand up for what is right in our nation and attempt to change that which is harmful and injurious.

Millions of Americans have already joined Moral Majority Inc. and have pledged their time, talent, and treasure to the rebuilding of this Republic.

The pornographers are angry. The amoral secular humanists are livid. The abortionists are furious. Full-page ads, employing McCarthy-like fear tactics, are appearing in major newspapers. The sponsors of these ads, of course, are attempting by these means to raise funds for themselves.

The opposition has every right to legally promote their goals and attack ours. But, certainly, we have that same right.

Therefore, we invite you to join our ranks. Moral Majority Inc. is a non-profit organization and does not give tax-deductible receipts for contributions. It is supported by Americans who are willing to invest in their country. We are spending millions of dollars at this time to return this nation to the values and principles on which it was built.

If you would like to receive a free copy of the *Moral Majority Report* newspaper, simply complete and mail the coupon below.

☐ **YES!** Please send me a free copy of the **Moral Majority Report**.

Name ______________________________

Address ______________________________

City ____________________ State ______ Zip ______

Mail to: **Moral Majority Inc.**
National Capitol Office
P. O. Box 190
Forest, VA 24551

WSJ

This ad is made possible by gifts from generous friends of the Moral Majority. If you wish to help, please send your check to the above address.

Exhibit 27

The Liberals...Do They *Really Care* About These Hungry Kids?

YOU'VE SEEN FULL PAGE ADS taken out by any number of Liberal organizations and "causes" that start with a picture like the one above. The ad copy is skillfully worded to touch the heart of any caring human being. As readers we are asked to send money to help poor homeless, starving people.

Do you have any idea what the sponsors of many of these ads are *really* doing with the donations they get?... how much of the money is going to the destitute, and how much may be *used to finance radical causes all over the world, to incite unrest, violence and civil war in unstable countries!*

What irony! They ask us to give money to "save the children"...from the very same wars that they have worked so hard to start!

You've no doubt heard of The World Council of Churches. Most Americans have been led to believe that this organization is dedicated to humanitarian causes. Did you know that this very same organization finances radical political groups all over the world—including bloodthirsty terrorists who torture their victims in ways that would turn your stomach? (Would you like to see proof? Write to The Church League of America and we'll send you the actual documentation, without charge.)

The TV screen probably has made you aware of the World Peace Council—the chief organizer of the recent mass demonstrations at the U.N. and in New York's Central Park, calling for a nuclear freeze and unilateral disarmament. Last year the World Peace Council's largest contributor sent them *forty-nine million dollars.* Who was that contributor? It was the Soviet Union.

And what of the Reverend Billy Graham? His record is a vivid example of how the political left has been systematically—and successfully—manipulating the evangelicals. During his recent trip to Moscow, Graham

used his world-wide reputation to present the Soviet Union as *hospitable* to religious freedom. Not only is this untrue, it does great harm to religious freedom all over the globe.

Graham's statements—and his socializing with agents of the KGB (Soviet secret police)—surprised many Americans, but not everyone. The Church League of America's files are *overflowing* with factual material that goes back 30 years, documenting Billy Graham's metamorphosis from a self-professed anti-Communist to a willing instrument of their propaganda.

Did you buy Jane Fonda's best-selling book on exercise? Or her record album? Or did you see one of her films? Do you know what *she* does with the millions in royalties that she collects? In a fully documented report on the subject, The Church League of America details the way that she is funding an attempt at the destruction of our free enterprise system—the very same system that made it possible for her to amass her enormous wealth.

What Is The Church League of America And Why Is This Ad Being Run?

The Church League of America is a non-denominational tax-free organization. It is composed both of clergy and laymen who are deeply concerned with the way the left wing and its radicals have managed to alter the religious values of many church leaders...successfully converting them into unwitting tools of political activism. The Church League deplores the techniques of slander, propaganda, deception and unprovable statements made by the radical left and so recklessly reproduced in the media. As a consequence the Church League has, over the years, compiled a massive library of *factual* records and documentation on the violence-

prone radicals of the political left. The Church League's library is routinely consulted by agencies of the U.S. government, local governments, and law enforcement agencies. The library is also available to any private company or individual who may have need to do research in this area.

Until recently, The Church League of America has, for the most part, limited its function to that of documentor of the facts about the left wing. But now we see religious groups of every kind—most of them well-intentioned but outrageously *deceived*—taking activist political positions on unilateral disarmament, El Salvador, events in South America, the Middle East and Africa. It has become a matter of sheer *survival* that Americans become fully aware of the way that the radical left is manipulating the churches and *USING* misinformed ministers, priests and laymen as potent weapons of an enterprise of violent social activism that can only *increase* poverty and hunger in the world, while it weakens societies of free men all over the planet.

So The Church League of America has taken on the tremendous job of spreading the word by running advertisements like this all over the country. But we can't handle it alone; we need YOUR help.

We are asking readers like yourself to join with us by making a tax-deductible contribution to this Church League campaign. Your contribution will be used *exclusively* to keep re-running announcements like the one you are reading now; not a penny will be used for any other purpose.

Help us to multiply these ads by sending as much as you can. If you can manage $10.00 or more the League will send, free, one or more of the publications described below. Before the subject leaves your mind... mail the coupon and join with us now!

Which Publications Will You Take FREE In Return For Your Help?

☐ **Billy Graham: Performer? Politician? Preacher? Prophet?** This brand new edition contains a complete documented description of Graham's recent trip to Moscow and his incredible pronouncements about "freedom of religion in the U.S.S.R." This absorbing book traces the record of the Billy Graham "crusades" back to 1951 and shows how his Moscow performance could easily have been predicted.

☐ **Betraying America: The Jane Fonda—Tom Hayden Axis.** The efforts of Jane Fonda and her radical left wing husband to stir up deliberately and to divide Americans against each other. What motivates this pair to work for America's destruction? Who are the persons and organizations behind them? The answers are *here;* you won't find them in the gossip columns.

☐ **How Liberals and Radicals Are Manipulating Evangelicals.** The struggle within the Christian Church between fundamentalist believers in the Bible's infallibility and the evangelicals who put current fashions in sociology, philosophy and anthropology on an equal basis with Holy Scriptures. How the liberals have swooped in to take control of the evangelical "troops" and turned them into supporters of Marxist causes.

☐ **How The Communists Use Religion.** This startling overview of the Russian Church reveals, fact by fact, that the "clerics" of the church actually are trained agents of the Soviet KGB. These self-same "religious leaders" are welcomed and fawned upon in the high church councils of the United States—and THAT is why they are immensely dangerous to the religions of the free world.

Church League of America
422 North Prospect Street, Wheaton, Ill. 60187

YES! I want to help spread the word about how the liberals and radicals are undermining American religious life, as well as our home and family life and our political system. I am making a tax-deductible contribution as follows:

☐ **$10** (Check any ONE book at left; we'll sent it free.)

☐ **$20** (Check any TWO books at left; we'll send them free.)

☐ **$35** (No need to check books; we'll send all four free.)

☐ My contribution is in another amount: $_____

Name_____

Address_____

City_____

State/Zip_____

Contributions to The Church League of America are tax-deductible under the authority of the U.S. Internal Revenue Code 501 (c)3.

Exhibit 28

A DIVERSITY OF OPINIONS REGARDING ABORTION EXISTS AMONG COMMITTED CATHOLICS.

A CATHOLIC STATEMENT ON PLURALISM AND ABORTION.

Continued confusion and polarization within the Catholic community on the subject of abortion prompt us to issue this statement.

Statements of recent Popes and of the Catholic hierarchy have condemned the direct termination of pre-natal life as morally wrong in all instances. There is the mistaken belief in American society that this is the only legitimate Catholic position. In fact, a diversity of opinions regarding abortion exists among committed Catholics:

- A large number of Catholic theologians hold that even direct abortion, though tragic, can sometimes be a moral choice.
- According to data compiled by the National Opinion Research Center, only 11% of Catholics surveyed disapprove of abortion in all circumstances.

These opinions have been formed by:

- Familiarity with the actual experiences that lead women to make a decision for abortion;
- A recognition that there is no common and constant teaching on ensoulment in Church doctrine, nor has abortion always been treated as murder in canonical history;
- An adherence to principles of moral theology, such as probabilism, religious liberty, and the centrality of informed conscience; and
- An awareness of the acceptance of abortion as a moral choice by official statements and respected theologians of other faith groups.

Therefore, it is necessary that the Catholic community encourage candid and respectful discussion on this diversity of opinion within the Church, and that Catholic youth and families be educated on the complexity of the issues of responsible sexuality and human reproduction.

Further, Catholics — especially priests, religious, theologians, and legislators — who publicly dissent from hierarchical statements and explore areas of moral and legal freedom on the abortion question should not be penalized by their religious superiors, church employers, or bishops.

Finally, while recognizing and supporting the legitimate role of the hierarchy in providing Catholics with moral guidance on political and social issues and in seeking legislative remedies to social injustices, we believe that Catholics should not seek the kind of legislation that curtails the legitimate exercise of the freedom of religion and conscience or discriminates against poor women.

In the belief that responsible moral decisions can only be made in an atmosphere of freedom from fear or coercion, we, the undersigned,* call upon all Catholics to affirm this statement.

To assist in our work please check one or more boxes below and send this coupon to:
The Catholic Committee c/o Catholics For A Free Choice, Inc. 2008 17th Street N.W. Washington, DC 20009

☐ I want to help you reach more people with this message. Here is my tax deductible contribution of $_____.
☐ Please send me additional literature.
☐ Please add my name to your Catholic Statement on Pluralism and Abortion.

NAME _____
ADDRESS _____
CITY/STATE/ZIP _____
PHONE _____

This ad is a project of the Catholic Committee. It has been paid for by Catholics For A Free Choice, Inc. Make your check payable to Catholics For A Free Choice, Inc.

CATHOLIC COMMITTEE ON PLURALISM AND ABORTION

Anthony Battaglia, Ph.D., Associate Professor, California State University • Roddy O'Neil Cleary, D. Min., Campus Ministries, University of Vermont • Joseph Fahey, Ph.D., Professor, Manhattan College • Elizabeth Schüssler Florenza, Ph.D., Professor, University of Notre Dame • Mary Gordon, M.A., author of *Final Payments* and *Company of Women* • Patricia Hennessy, J.D., New York City • Mary Hunt, Ph.D., Women's Alliance for Theology, Ethics and Ritual • Frances Kissling, Executive Director, Catholics for a Free Choice • Justus George Lawler, Executive Editor, Academic Bookline, Winston-Seabury Press • Daniel C. Maguire, S.T.D., Professor, Marquette University • Marjorie Reiley Maguire, Ph.D., Fellow in Ethics and Theology, Catholics for a Free Choice • J. Giles Milhaven, Ph.D., Professor, Brown University • Rosemary Radford Ruether, Ph.D., Professor, Garrett Evangelical Theological Seminary, IL • Thomas Shannon, Ph.D., Professor, Worcester Polytechnic Institute, MA • James F. Smurl, Ph.D., Professor, Indiana University

OTHER SIGNERS

Agnes P. Albany, M.A., Chestnut Hill College, PA • Everett Ballmann, Minot State College, ND • Michael H. Barnes, Ph.D., University of Dayton, OH • Barbara Bemache-Baker, Ph.D., Loomis Institute, CT • Kathryn Bissell, Wider Opportunities for Women, MD • Mary C.I. Buckley, S.T.D., St. John's University, NY • Ronald Burke, Ph.D., University of Nebraska at Omaha, NB • Mary J. Byles, Ph.D., Maryville College, MO • Ann Carr, Ph.D., University of Chicago Divinity School, IL • Rev. Joseph M. Connolly, S.T.L., pastor, Archdiocese of Maryland, MD • Margaret Cotroneo, Ph.D., University of Pennsylvania, PA • Patty Crowley, Chicago Catholic Women, IL • Barbara A. Cullom, Ph.D., Quixote Center, VA • Maryann Cunningham, S.L., Colorado • Mary Louise Denny, S.L., MO • Daniel DiDomizio, Marian College, WI • Maurice C. Duchaine, S.T.D., San Francisco, CA • Emmaus Community of Christian Hope, NJ • Margaret A. Farley, Yale Divinity School, CT • Darrell J. Fasching, Ph.D., University of South Florida, FL • Barbara Ferraro, Sisters of Notre Dame, WV • Maureen Fiedler, Ph.D., S.L., Catholics for the Common Good, MD • Silvio E. Fittipaldi, Ph.D., Pastoral Institute of Lehigh Valley, PA • George H. Frein, Ph.D., University of North Dakota, ND • Lorine M. Getz, Ph.D., Somerville, MA • Kevin Gordon, Director, Consultation on Homosexuality, Social Justice and Roman Catholic Theology, CA • Jeannine Gramick, School Sisters of Notre Dame, NY • Christine E. Gudorf, Ph.D., Xavier University, OH • Terry Hamilton, Woodstock/St. Paul Roman Catholic Community, NY • Jack Hanford, Th.D., Ferris State College, MI • Kathleen Hebbeler, Dominican Sister of the Sick Poor, OH • Patricia Hussey, Sisters of Notre Dame, WV • Caridad Inda, Council of Women Religious, MD • Dorothy Irvin, S.T.D., Dunbar, NC • Fr. Jerry Kaelin, O.F.M., Cincinnati, OH • Janet Kalven, Loveland, OH • Elizabeth Nelson Keating, Yale University, CT • Pat Kenoyer, S.L., Loretto Women's Network, MO • Joseph E. Kerns, S.T.D., Center for Christian Living, VA • Paul F. Knitter, Th.D., Xavier University, OH • Joseph A. LaBarge, Ph.D., Bucknell University, PA • Eleanor V. Lewis, Ph.D., Baltimore, MD • Wayne Lobue, Ph.D., Gilmour Academy, OH • Agnes Mary Mansour, Ph.D., Lansing, MI • Roseann Mazzeo, S.C., NJ • Bro. Ray McManaman, F.S.C., Lewis University, IL • Kathleen E. McVey, Ph.D., Princeton Theological Seminary, NJ • John A. Melloh, S.T.L., Milwaukee, WI • Joe Mellon, M.A., University of Notre Dame, IN • Diane Neu, M.Div., S.T.M., Co-director Women's Alliance for Theology, Ethics and Ritual, Washington, DC • Jeanne Noble, National Assembly of Religious Women, MD • Sr. Margaret Nulty, Sisters of Charity of New Jersey • Kathleen O'Connor, Ph.D., Maryknoll School of Theology, NY • Margaret A. O'Neill, Ed.D., Sisters of Charity of New Jersey, NJ • Ronald D. Pasquariello, Ph.D., Marist Brothers, Washington, DC • Richard Penaskovic, Ph.D., Auburn University, AL • Gerald A. Pire, M.A., Seton Hall University, NJ • Stanley M. Polan, S.T.L., Franklin Pierce College, NH • Dolly Pomerleau, Catholics for the Common Good, MD • John E. Price, S.T.L., Evanston, IL • Donna Quinn, National Coalition of American Nuns, IL • Jill Raitt, Ph.D., University of Missouri, MO • Maureen Reiff, Chicago Catholic Women, IL • John G. Rusnak, Ph.D., Phoenix, AZ • Mary Savage, Ph.D., Albertus Magnus College, CT • Jane Schaberg, Ph.D., University of Detroit, MI • Mary Jane Schutzius, Federation of Christian Ministries, Association of the Rights of Catholics in the Church, MO • Ellen Shanahan, Ph.D., Rosary College, IL • Emily Ann Staples, University of Minnesota, MN • Marilyn Thie, Sisters of Charity of New Jersey, Colgate University, NY • Sr. Rose Dominic Trapasso, Lima, Peru • Sr. Margaret Ellen Traxler, National Coalition of American Nuns, IL • Marjorie Tuite, Church Women United, NY • Alan F. Turner, Association for the Rights of Catholics in the Church, Valley Forge, PA • Judith Vaughan, National Assembly of Religious Women, CA • E. Jane Via, Ph.D., J.D., University of San Diego and Superior Court of San Diego, CA • Gerald S. Vigna, Ph.D., Pennsauken, NJ • Ann Patrick Ware, M.A., National Coalition of American Nuns, NY • Sallie Ann Watkins, National Coalition of American Nuns, CO • Mary Jo Weaver, Ph.D., Indiana University, IN • Virginia Williams, S.L., MO • Arthur E. Zannoni, Ph.D., University of Notre Dame Extension Program, IN

*Organizational affiliations are listed for purposes of identification only. Partial listing. This statement has been signed by many other Catholics. In addition, 75 priests, religious and theologians have written that they agree with the Statement but cannot sign because they fear losing their jobs.

Reprinted from the NEW YORK TIMES October 7, 1984

Exhibit 29

HEALTH CARE IN AMERICA

POVERTY OR HUMANITY?

"34½ MILLION AMERICANS STILL BELOW THE POVERTY LEVEL!"

Being poor is no sin. But, as Tevye says in *Fiddler on the Roof,* it's no great honor either. Particularly when you get sick and don't know where the money is going to come from to pay the hospital and doctor bills.

In the present public debate about medical costs, with its talk of "cost shifting" and "two-tiered health care," the poor and underprivileged seem almost to have been forgotten.

ADEQUATE HEALTH CARE

EACH OF US WILL HAVE TO CHOOSE

We in Catholic health care have been serving the health needs of the poor for nearly 2,000 years. Many of our health care facilities and sponsoring religious orders were founded for that purpose.

We believe that society has an obligation to make necessary health care available to all persons—whether rich or poor. In our efforts to find solutions to the current cost crisis in health care we must not ignore the special needs of the disadvantaged.

HEALTH CARE IN AMERICA. WHICH IS IT TO BE: POVERTY OR HUMANITY?

The more than 1,200 hospitals, nursing homes, systems, and sponsoring religious orders that make up The Catholic Health Association of the United States have made *their* choice.

The Catholic Health Association OF THE UNITED STATES **CHA.**

4455 Woodson Rd., St. Louis, MO 63134, (314) 427-2500

Exhibit 30

YOU'RE NEEDED AGAIN!

Around the world, U.S. armaments are *still* propping up dictators. And at home, the Pentagon squanders billions of our tax dollars on new weapons designed to fight a nuclear war. Military spending drains the economy and robs Americans of jobs.

Now, More Than Ever.

The Coalition for a New Foreign and Military Policy coordinates the grass roots lobbying efforts of dozens of religious, professional, peace and social justice organizations. We monitor key legislation and alert our nationwide activist network to the latest developments. And we help local activists tie their work into a coordinated national strategy.

We helped scuttle the B-1 Bomber. We worked with citizens all across the country to cut military aid to dictators in Chile, Uruguay, Argentina and the Philippines. *And now, we're going to have to do it all over again.* We have to challenge the sabre-rattling and militarism that puts the Pentagon ahead of our communities, our jobs, our environment and our schools.

We're working to end the arms race. We're working to make sure that U.S. aid supports human rights, not oppression. We're working to prevent U.S. intervention in El Salvador and Angola. And we're working for majority rule and authentic self-determination in South Africa.

Give Peace a Fighting Chance.

Ending the war in Indochina took the energy and commitment of millions of Americans. Building a new foreign policy will take the same commitment and more. That's where *you* fit in. If you're like us, you still want to put your energy and experience to work. Join us. You're needed again.

COALITION
For a New Foreign and Military Policy
120 Maryland Ave., N.E., Washington D.C., 20002

☐ **YES!** Sign me up for the Coalition's network and send me regular *Action Alerts* on key legislation, *Action Guides* on the issues and resources for local organizing work. Here's $20 for one year of Coalition materials.

☐ Tell me more about the Coalition and how I can get involved. Here's $2 for my information packet.

Name _____

Address _____City_____

State _____ Zip_____

The following organizations are members of the Coalition: American Baptist Churches USA, National Ministries ● American Friends Service Committee ● Americans for Democratic Action ● Business Executives Move for New National Priorities ● Center for International Policy ● Center of Concern ● Chile Legislative Center ● Church of the Brethren, Washington Office ● Christian Church (Disciples of Christ) Department of Church and Society ● Church Women United ● Clergy and Laity Concerned ● Council on Hemispheric Affairs ● Democratic Socialist Organizing Committee ● Episcopal Peace Fellowship ● Fellowship of Reconciliation ● Friends Committee on National Legislation ● Friends of the Earth ● Friends of the Filipino People ● Institute for Food and Development Policy ● Jubilee, Inc./The Other Side ● Mennonite Central Committee U.S. Peace Section ● Movement for a Free Philippines ● National Assembly of Women Religious ● National Association of Social Workers ● National Council of Churches ● National Federation of Priests' Councils, USA ● National Gray Panthers ● National Office of Jesuit Social Ministries ● NETWORK ● SANE ● Sisters of St. Joseph of Peace ● Union of American Hebrew Congregations ● Unitarian Universalist Association ● Unitarian Universalist Service Committee ● United Church of Christ, Board for Homeland Ministries ● United Church of Christ, Office for Church in Society ● United Methodist Church, Board of Church and Society ● United Methodist Church, Board of Global Ministries, Women's Division ● United Presbyterian Church, USA, Washington Office ● United States Student Association ● War Resisters League ● Washington Office of the Episcopal Church ● Washington Office on Africa ● Washington Office on Latin America ● Women's International League for Peace and Freedom ● Women Strike for Peace ● World Federalist Association ● World Peacemakers ● Young Women's Christian Association of the USA.

Cyn

Photo: Anthony Abuzeide

Exhibit 31

YOU CAN SAVE YOUR COUNTRY!

GET WASHINGTON TO STOP DEFICIT SPENDING... SEND IN YOUR 2¢ WORTH!

Right now the federal government is spending $4 for every $3 it takes in. This extra spending adds to the national debt. Interest on this debt costs the average American family over $2,500 a year. In 1984, 37% of every American's personal income tax went to pay the interest on the national debt.

Deficit spending is partly to blame for some of the problems with our economy—failing farms,

failing industries, the threat of fewer jobs and inflation.

Do something now to stop deficit spending. We can provide all Americans with affordable interest rates, a lower rate of inflation, and a strong economy.

If enough people speak up, we can assure a bright future for all Americans

Send Washington your 2¢ worth.

Clip this coupon now! Send it with your "2¢ worth" to the President, your Senators and Representative. If you like, toss in 2¢ change. It just might help get your point across.

Please do your best to help make a bright future for America by stopping deficit spending. Here's my 2¢ worth.

○ I support solutions that will reduce deficits substantially each of the next 3 years

○ I support a program that will lead steadily to a balanced Federal budget

○ I am willing to share in the sacrifices necessary to balance the budget

Name _____

Address _____

City/State _____ Zip _____

Published as a Public Service by:
The Dime Savings Bank of New York, FSB
First Federal Savings and Loan Association of Rochester
New York League of Savings Institutions
The Savings Banks Association of New York State
The Union Savings Bank

Exhibit 32

"*Every gun that is made, every warship launched, every rocket fired signifies, in the final sense, a theft from those who hunger and are not fed, those who are cold and are not clothed. This world in arms is not spending money alone. It is spending the sweat of its laborers, the genius of its scientists, the hopes of its children ...This is not a way of life at all in any true sense. Under the cloud of threatening war, it is humanity hanging from a cross of iron.*"

The Honorable Dwight D. Eisenhower, 1890-1969
34th President of the United States
Supreme Commander, Integrated European Defense Forces
From a speech before the American Society of Newspaper Editors, April 16, 1953

If you agree with President Eisenhower's statement,
please send this page with your personal comments
to your Congressman or Senator:

The Honorable (name)   The Honorable (name)
U.S. Senate   House Office Building
Washington, D.C. 20510   Washington, D.C. 20515

This message brought to you in the public interest by Joan B. Kroc
8939 Villa La Jolla Drive, San Diego, CA 92037

Exhibit 33

A DECLARATION OF WAR

The time has come to draw the line. Political Action Committees (PACs) have put Congress on the take. And *you're* being taken for a ride. Consider your health: PAC money from doctors helped convince Congress *not* to pass a bill that would help keep your hospital costs from skyrocketing. Consider your protection from fraud: PAC money from auto dealers helped convince Congress *not* to pass a bill that would require used car dealers to tell you what's wrong with the second-hand car you're buying. Consider your savings: PAC money from the dairy industry has helped to convince Congress, year after year, *not* to make needed cuts in dairy subsidies, which artificially inflate the price of the milk, butter and cheese you buy. Consider yourself *mute*. Your voice is being *drowned out* by the ringing of PAC cash registers in Congress.

Senator Robert Dole, Chairman of the Senate tax writing committee, says, "When these PACs give money, they expect something in return other than good government." These are contributions with a purpose—a legislative purpose. And **the PAC system works according to the golden rule, says former Congressman Henry Reuss: "Those who have the gold make the rules."**

We're not talking about illegal campaign contributions of the sort that ten years ago created a national scandal called Watergate. We're talking about $80 million in campaign contributions that are *perfectly legal,* creating a new national scandal corrupting our democracy. And *that* is a crime.

Unless we change our system for financing Congressional campaigns and change it soon, our representative system of government will be gone. We will be left with a government of, by and for the PACs.

We can't let that happen. We *won't* let that happen. Common Cause has declared war —— a war on PACs. Ours has always been a government of, by and for the *people*. We must keep it that way.   Common Cause.

But We Need Your Help!

Because even though there are Members of Congress who have spoken out against the PAC system, a majority have been unwilling to change it. It suits a special interest *they* have: getting re-elected. As Congressman Jim Leach says: "Clearly the collective judgment of Congress is that it's pro-incumbent to keep the current system, or they would have changed it by now."

Well, the only way they are going to change it is if enough citizens demand a change … fight for a change. And that's what we're doing. Because what's at stake is our democracy.

Join us. It's *People* against *PACs*. Plain and simple.

Please make your check payable to Common Cause and send to Common Cause, 2030 M Street, N.W., Washington, D.C. 20036. Thank you.

NAME

ADDRESS

CITY   STATE   ZIP

☐ I know that when citizens speak out together—like we did during Watergate—we *can* turn things around. Please sign me up on the "People" side of your war against PACs.

☐ To help this critical effort, I am enclosing a special contribution of:
☐ $20 (Annual Dues) ☐ $10 ☐ $35 ☐ $50 ☐ $100 ☐ $250 ☐ Other _____

☐ I am a member of Common Cause   QNY283
Residents of New York may obtain a copy of our last financial report from New York State Dept. of State Office of Charities Registration, Albany, NY 12231

A CONCEPTUAL FRAMEWORK FOR ADVOCACY ADVERTISING

Advocacy advertising can best be understood as a three-dimensional phenomenon: identification of sponsor's interest, intensity of advocacy, and specificity in identifying the adversary.

Identification of Sponsor's Interest

This dimension measures the extent to which the sponsor is willing to identify its own interests with the contents of, and programs advocated in, the advertising message. There are five states of this dimension:

Disinterested Sponsor. The sponsor is clearly identified. Its interests are connected with the message only in a very general way. The advocacy is of broad ideological or philosophical nature. The sponsor hopes that the reader will identify the message with the sponsor and view the sponsor as a public-spirited and forward-looking organization. Illustrative of this approach is an advertisement by Internorth Corporation urging people to vote [Exhibit 34]. A number of major corporate campaigns notably those of LTV, fall in this group. Other advertisements sponsored by a single company or a group of companies that are illustrative of this approach include: Drexel Burnham on tax reform and W. R. Grace on federal deficits [Exhibits 35–36]. An interesting ad in this group was recently sponsored by Computerland Corporation [Exhibit 37] and headlined "Why Computerland Decided Not to Send Money to Ethiopia." In this ad the company argued that we must seek long-term solutions to the problem of starvation in the Third World. The problem is not food shortage but, rather, inadequate distribution, low productivity, and government ineptitude. Thus it would be far more important for American business leadership to do what it does best, to help the economic growth of those countries.

Benevolent Sponsor. The sponsor's name is identified in the advertisement, but is presented only as indirectly related. The issue is presented as of broader public concern. Where solutions are suggested, the sponsor's role is minimized in a causal relationship with the problem, but emphasized in the solution. The advocacy appeal is of a general nature; the audience is exhorted to perform some voluntary action of self-help or self-sacrifice. A large number of industry-sponsored campaigns fall into this category. Examples can be found in the advocacy ads sponsored by the Chemical Manufacturers Association, the Canadian Petroleum Association, the Savings & Loan Foundation, the Edison Electric Institute, and the United Steel Workers. Other advertisements representative of this genre are those on the social and human costs of unfair trade and steel imports to a local community adversely affected by such imports, and those of the New York Medical Liability Reform Coalition on the high costs of medical malpractice insurance [Exhibits 38–39].

Exhibit 34

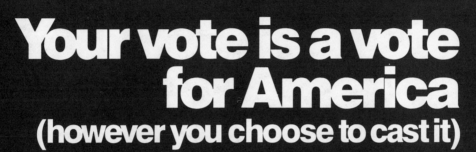

Your vote is a vote for America
(however you choose to cast it)

In a free society the very act of voting is important. For if too many of us fail to participate in determining who will govern, a minority can impose their will on the majority.

The freedom of choice we enjoy in America should not be taken for granted. It must constantly be protected by an intelligent, informed choice at the ballot box.

INTERNORTH

We work for America.

This ballot box dating to the early days of America's independence has been donated by InterNorth to Omaha's Western Heritage Museum.

InterNorth is an international energy-based corporation involved in exploration and production of oil and natural gas, natural gas transportation and distribution, liquid fuels and petrochemicals. International headquarters: Omaha, Nebraska

Exhibit 35

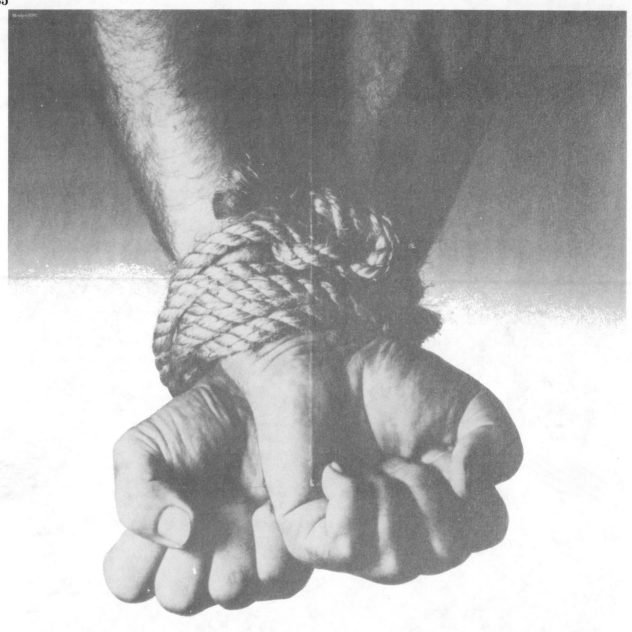

WHICH TAXES THE COUNTRY MORE, THE BILL OR THE WAITING?

Everyone's talking about tax reform. And that's the problem.

Because nobody's doing anything about it.

So while the controversy over the proposals rages, key sectors of the investment economy are coming to a screeching halt.

And no wonder.

Why make capital improvements if the very incentives for them are eliminated? Or even in doubt.

Why invest if the incentives for succeed-ing are reduced? Or even in doubt.

What are we saying about the fight against inflation, if indexing becomes a cornerstone of tax policy? No doubt there.

It may be years before real tax reform is legis-lated in this country.

But it's only a matter of time before the effect of that delay is felt.

Hopefully, the Administration will act responsibly and with speed.

Because the longer we wait for a tax bill, the less we may have to pay taxes on.

Drexel Burnham
Drexel Burnham Lambert Incorporated

Exhibit 36

IF THE DEFICIT GOES DOWN, HERE'S WHO TO THANK.
IF IT GOES UP, HERE'S WHO TO REPLACE.

UNITED STATES CONGRESS 1985

ALABAMA
Senate:
Jeremiah Denton (R)
Howell Heflin (D)
House of Representatives:
Sonny Callahan (R-1)
William L. Dickinson (R-2)
Bill Nichols (D-3)
Tom Bevill (D-4)
Ronnie G. Flippo (D-5)
Ben Erdreich (D-6)
Richard C. Shelby (D-7)

ALASKA
Senate:
Frank Murkowski (R)
Ted Stevens (R)
House of Representatives:
Don Young (R)

ARIZONA
Senate:
Barry M. Goldwater (R)
Dennis DeConcini (D)
House of Representatives:
John McCain (R-1)
Morris K. Udall (D-2)
Bob Stump (R-3)
Eldon Rudd (R-4)
Jim Kolbe (R-5)

ARKANSAS
Senate:
Dale Bumpers (D)
David Pryor (D)
House of Representatives:
Bill Alexander (D-1)
Tommy Robinson (D-2)
John Hammerschmidt (R-3)
Beryl Anthony, Jr. (D-4)

CALIFORNIA
Senate:
Alan Cranston (D)
Pete Wilson (R)
House of Representatives:
Douglas H. Bosco (D-1)
Gene Chappie (R-2)
Robert T. Matsui (D-3)
Vic Fazio (D-4)
Sala Burton (D-5)
Barbara Boxer (D-6)
George Miller (D-7)
Ronald V. Dellums (D-8)
Fortney H. (Pete) Stark (D-9)
Don Edwards (D-10)
Tom Lantos (D-11)
Ed Zschau (R-12)
Norman Y. Mineta (D-13)
Norm Shumway (R-14)
Tony Coelho (D-15)
Leon E. Panetta (D-16)
Charles Pashayan, Jr. (R-17)
Richard H. Lehman (D-18)
Robert J. Lagomarsino (R-19)
William M. Thomas (R-20)
Bobbi Fiedler (R-21)
Carlos J. Moorhead (R-22)
Anthony C. Beilenson (D-23)
Henry A. Waxman (D-24)
Edward R. Roybal (D-25)
Howard L. Berman (D-26)
Mel Levine (D-27)
Julian C. Dixon (D-28)
Augustus F. Hawkins (D-29)
Matthew G. Martinez (D-30)
Mervyn M. Dymally (D-31)
Glenn M. Anderson (D-32)
David Dreier (R-33)
Esteban E. Torres (D-34)
Jerry Lewis (R-35)
George E. Brown, Jr. (D-36)
Al McCandless (R-37)
Robert K. Dornan (R-38)
William Dannemeyer (R-39)
Robert E. Badham (R-40)
Bill Lowery (R-41)
Dan Lungren (R-42)
Ron Packard (R-43)
Jim Bates (D-44)
Duncan Hunter (R-45)

COLORADO
Senate:
Gary Hart (D)
William L. Armstrong (R)
House of Representatives:
Patricia Schroeder (D-1)
Timothy E. Wirth (D-2)
Mike Strang (R-3)
Hank Brown (R-4)
Ken Kramer (R-5)
Daniel Schaefer (R-6)

CONNECTICUT
Senate:
Christopher J. Dodd (D)
Lowell P. Weicker, Jr. (R)
House of Representatives:
Barbara B. Kennelly (D-1)
Samuel Gejdenson (D-2)
Bruce A. Morrison (D-3)
Stewart B. McKinney (R-4)
John G. Rowland (R-5)
Nancy L. Johnson (R-6)

DELAWARE
Senate:
William V. Roth, Jr. (R)
Joseph R. Biden, Jr. (D)
House of Representatives:
Thomas R. Carper (D)

FLORIDA
Senate:
Paula Hawkins (R)
Lawton Chiles (D)
House of Representatives:
Earl Hutto (D-1)
Don Fuqua (D-2)
Charles E. Bennett (D-3)
Bill Chappell (D-4)
Bill McCollum (R-5)
Buddy H. MacKay (D-6)
Sam Gibbons (D-7)
C.W. Bill Young (R-8)
Michael Bilirakis (R-9)
Andy Ireland (R-10)
Bill Nelson (D-11)
Tom Lewis (R-12)
Connie Mack (R-13)
Daniel A. Mica (D-14)
Clay Shaw, Jr. (R-15)
Larry Smith (D-16)
William Lehman (D-17)
Claude Pepper (D-18)
Dante B. Fascell (D-19)

GEORGIA
Senate:
Mack Mattingly (R)
Sam Nunn (D)
House of Representatives:
Robert Lindsay Thomas (D-1)
Charles Hatcher (D-2)
Richard Ray (D-3)
Patrick Swindall (R-4)
Wyche Fowler, Jr. (D-5)
Newt Gingrich (R-6)
George Darden (D-7)
J. Roy Rowland (D-8)
Ed Jenkins (D-9)
Doug Barnard, Jr. (D-10)

HAWAII
Senate:
Daniel K. Inouye (D)
Spark M. Matsunaga (D)
House of Representatives:
Cecil (Cec) Heftel (D-1)
Daniel K. Akaka (D-2)

IDAHO
Senate:
Steven D. Symms (R)
James A. McClure (R)
House of Representatives:
Larry E. Craig (R-1)
Richard Stallings (D-2)

ILLINOIS
Senate:
Alan J. Dixon (D)
Paul Simon (D)
House of Representatives:
Charles Hayes (D-1)
Gus Savage (D-2)
Marty Russo (D-3)
George M. O'Brien (R-4)
William O. Lipinski (D-5)
Henry J. Hyde (R-6)
Cardiss Collins (D-7)
Dan Rostenkowski (D-8)
Sidney R. Yates (D-9)
John E. Porter (R-10)
Frank Annunzio (D-11)
Philip M. Crane (R-12)
Harris Fawell (R-13)
John Grotberg (R-14)
Edward R. Madigan (R-15)
Lynn Martin (R-16)
Lane Evans (D-17)
Robert H. Michel (R-18)
Terry Bruce (D-19)
Richard J. Durbin (D-20)
Melvin Price (D-21)
Ken Gray (D-22)

INDIANA
Senate:
Dan Quayle (R)
Richard G. Lugar (R)
House of Representatives:
Peter Visclosky (D-1)
Philip R. Sharp (D-2)
John Hiler (R-3)
Dan R. Coats (R-4)
Elwood Hillis (R-5)
Dan Burton (R-6)
John T. Myers (R-7)
Lee H. Hamilton (D-9)
Andrew Jacobs, Jr. (D-10)

IOWA
Senate:
Charles E. Grassley (R)
Tom Harkin (D)
House of Representatives:
Jim Leach (R-1)
Thomas J. Tauke (R-2)
Cooper Evans (R-3)
Neal Smith (D-4)
James Lightfoot (R-5)
Berkley Bedell (D-6)

KANSAS
Senate:
Robert J. Dole (R)
Nancy L. Kassebaum (R)
House of Representatives:
Pat Roberts (R-1)
Jim Slattery (D-2)
Jan Meyers (R-3)
Dan Glickman (D-4)
Bob Whittaker (R-5)

KENTUCKY
Senate:
Wendell H. Ford (D)
Mitch McConnell (R)
House of Representatives:
Carroll Hubbard, Jr. (D-1)
William H. Natcher (D-2)
Romano L. Mazzoli (D-3)
Gene Snyder (R-4)
Harold Rogers (R-5)
Larry J. Hopkins (R-6)
Carl C. Perkins (D-7)

LOUISIANA
Senate:
Russell B. Long (D)
J. Bennett Johnston (D)
House of Representatives:
Bob Livingston (R-1)
Lindy Boggs (D-2)
W.J. "Billy" Tauzin (D-3)
Buddy Roemer (D-4)
Jerry Huckaby (D-5)
W. Henson Moore (R-6)
John B. Breaux (D-7)
Cathy Long (D-8)

MAINE
Senate:
George J. Mitchell (D)
William S. Cohen (R)
House of Representatives:
John R. McKernan, Jr. (R-1)
Olympia J. Snowe (R-2)

MARYLAND
Senate:
Charles McC. Mathias, Jr. (R)
Paul S. Sarbanes (D)
House of Representatives:
Roy Dyson (D-1)
Helen D. Bentley (R-2)
Barbara A. Mikulski (D-3)
Marjorie S. Holt (R-4)
Steny H. Hoyer (D-5)
Beverly B. Byron (D-6)
Parren J. Mitchell (D-7)
Michael D. Barnes (D-8)

MASSACHUSETTS
Senate:
Edward M. Kennedy (D)
John Kerry (D)
House of Representatives:
Silvio O. Conte (R-1)
Edward P. Boland (D-2)
Joseph D. Early (D-3)
Barney Frank (D-4)
Chester Atkins (D-5)
Nicholas Mavroules (D-6)
Edward J. Markey (D-7)
Thomas P. O'Neill, Jr. (D-8)
John Joseph Moakley (D-9)
Gerry E. Studds (D-10)
Brian J. Donnelly (D-11)

MICHIGAN
Senate:
Donald W. Riegle, Jr. (D)
Carl Levin (D)
House of Representatives:
John Conyers, Jr. (D-1)
Carl D. Pursell (R-2)
Howard Wolpe (D-3)
Mark D. Siljander (R-4)
Paul Henry (R-5)
Bob Carr (D-6)
Dale E. Kildee (D-7)
Bob Traxler (D-8)
Guy Vander Jagt (R-9)
Bill Schuette (R-10)
Robert W. Davis (R-11)
David E. Bonior (D-12)
George W. Crockett, Jr. (D-13)
Dennis M. Hertel (D-14)
William D. Ford (D-15)
John D. Dingell (D-16)
Sander Levin (D-17)
William S. Broomfield (R-18)

MINNESOTA
Senate:
David Durenberger (R)
Rudolph E. Boschwitz (R)
House of Representatives:
Timothy J. Penny (D-1)
Vin Weber (R-2)
Bill Frenzel (R-3)
Bruce F. Vento (D-4)
Martin Olav Sabo (D-5)
Gerry Sikorski (D-6)
Arlan Stangeland (R-7)
James L. Oberstar (D-8)

MISSISSIPPI
Senate:
John C. Stennis (D)
Thad Cochran (R)
House of Representatives:
Jamie L. Whitten (D-1)
Webb Franklin (R-2)
G.V. Montgomery (D-3)
Wayne Dowdy (D-4)
Trent Lott (R-5)

MISSOURI
Senate:
Thomas F. Eagleton (D)
John C. Danforth (R)
House of Representatives:
William (Bill) Clay (D-1)
Robert A. Young (D-2)
Richard A. Gephardt (D-3)
Ike Skelton (D-4)
Alan Wheat (D-5)
E. Thomas Coleman (R-6)
Gene Taylor (R-7)
Bill Emerson (R-8)
Harold L. Volkmer (D-9)

MONTANA
Senate:
John Melcher (D)
Max Baucus (D)
House of Representatives:
Pat Williams (D-1)
Ron Marlenee (R-2)

NEBRASKA
Senate:
Edward Zorinsky (D)
J. James Exon (D)
House of Representatives:
Douglas K. Bereuter (R-1)
Hal Daub (R-2)
Virginia Smith (R-3)

NEVADA
Senate:
Paul Laxalt (R)
Chic Hecht (R)
House of Representatives:
Harry Reid (D-1)
Barbara Vucanovich (R-2)

NEW HAMPSHIRE
Senate:
Warren Rudman (R)
Gordon J. Humphrey (R)
House of Representatives:
Robert C. Smith (R-1)
Judd Gregg (R-2)

NEW JERSEY
Senate:
Frank R. Lautenburg (D)
Bill Bradley (D)
House of Representatives:
James J. Florio (D-1)
William J. Hughes (D-2)
James J. Howard (D-3)
Christopher H. Smith (R-4)
Marge Roukema (R-5)
Bernard J. Dwyer (D-6)
Matthew J. Rinaldo (R-7)
Robert A. Roe (D-8)
Robert G. Torricelli (D-9)
Peter W. Rodino, Jr. (D-10)
Dean Gallo (R-11)
Jim Courter (R-12)
Jim Saxton (R-13)
Frank J. Guarini (D-14)

NEW MEXICO
Senate:
Jeff Bingaman (D)
Pete V. Domenici (R)
House of Representatives:
Manuel Lujan, Jr. (R-1)
Joe Skeen (R-2)
Bill Richardson (D-3)

NEW YORK
Senate:
Alfonse M. D'Amato (R)
Daniel Patrick Moynihan (D)
House of Representatives:
William Carney (R-1)
Thomas J. Downey (D-2)
Robert J. Mrazek (D-3)
Norman F. Lent (R-4)
Raymond J. McGrath (R-5)
Joseph P. Addabbo (D-6)
Gary Ackerman (D-7)
James H. Scheuer (D-8)
Thomas Manton (D-9)
Charles E. Schumer (D-10)
Edolphus Towns (D-11)
Major R. Owens (D-12)
Stephen J. Solarz (D-13)
Guy V. Molinari (R-14)
Bill Green (R-15)
Charles B. Rangel (D-16)
Ted Weiss (D-17)
Robert Garcia (D-18)
Mario Biaggi (D-19)
Joe DioGuardi (R-20)
Hamilton Fish, Jr. (R-21)
Benjamin A. Gilman (R-22)
Samuel S. Stratton (D-23)
Gerald B.H. Solomon (R-24)
Sherwood L. Boehlert (R-25)
David O'B. Martin (R-26)
George C. Wortley (R-27)
Matthew F. McHugh (D-28)
Frank Horton (R-29)
Fred Eckert (R-30)
Jack F. Kemp (R-31)
John J. LaFalce (D-32)
Henry J. Nowak (D-33)
Stanley N. Lundine (D-34)

NORTH CAROLINA
Senate:
John P. East (R)
Jesse Helms (R)
House of Representatives:
Walter B. Jones (D-1)
I.T. "Tim" Valentine, Jr. (D-2)
Charles O. Whitley (D-3)
William Cobey, Jr. (R-4)
Stephen L. Neal (D-5)
J. Howard Coble (R-6)
Charles Rose (D-7)
W.G. (Bill) Hefner (D-8)
J. Alex McMillan (R-9)
James T. Broyhill (R-10)
William M. Hendon (R-11)

NORTH DAKOTA
Senate:
Mark Andrews (R)
Quentin N. Burdick (D)
House of Representatives:
Byron L. Dorgan (D)

OHIO
Senate:
John Glenn (D)
Howard Metzenbaum (D)
House of Representatives:
Thomas A. Luken (D-1)
Willis D. Gradison Jr. (R-2)
Tony P. Hall (D-3)
Michael Oxley (R-4)
Delbert L. Latta (R-5)
Bob McEwen (R-6)
Michael DeWine (R-7)
Thomas N. Kindness (R-8)
Marcy Kaptur (D-9)
Clarence E. Miller (R-10)
Dennis E. Eckart (D-11)
John R. Kasich (R-12)
Donald J. Pease (D-13)
John F. Seiberling (D-14)
Chalmers P. Wylie (R-15)
Ralph Regula (R-16)
James Traficant (D-17)
Douglas Applegate (D-18)
Edward F. Feighan (D-19)
Mary Rose Oakar (D-20)
Louis Stokes (D-21)

OKLAHOMA
Senate:
Don Nickles (R)
David Boren (D)
House of Representatives:
James R. Jones (D-1)
Mike Synar (D-2)
Wes Watkins (D-3)
Dave McCurdy (D-4)
Mickey Edwards (R-5)
Glenn English (D-6)

OREGON
Senate:
Bob Packwood (R)
Mark O. Hatfield (R)
House of Representatives:
Les AuCoin (D-1)
Robert Smith (R-2)
Ron Wyden (D-3)
James Weaver (D-4)
Denny Smith (R-5)

PENNSYLVANIA
Senate:
Arlen Specter (R)
John Heinz (R)
House of Representatives:
Thomas M. Foglietta (D-1)
William H. Gray III (D-2)
Robert A. Borski (D-3)
Joseph P. Kolter (D-4)
Richard T. Schulze (R-5)
Gus Yatron (D-6)
Robert W. Edgar (D-7)
Peter H. Kostmayer (D-8)
Bud Shuster (R-9)
Joseph M. McDade (R-10)
Paul Kanjorski (D-11)
John P. Murtha (D-12)
Lawrence Coughlin (R-13)
William J. Coyne (D-14)
Don Ritter (R-15)
Robert S. Walker (R-16)
George W. Gekas (R-17)
Doug Walgren (D-18)
William F. Goodling (R-19)
Joseph M. Gaydos (D-20)
Thomas J. Ridge (R-21)
Austin J. Murphy (D-22)
William F. Clinger, Jr. (R-23)

RHODE ISLAND
Senate:
John H. Chafee (R)
Claiborne deB. Pell (D)
House of Representatives:
Fernand J. St Germain (D-1)
Claudine Schneider (R-2)

SOUTH CAROLINA
Senate:
Ernest Fritz Hollings (D)
Strom Thurmond (R)
House of Representatives:
Thomas F. Hartnett (R-1)
Floyd Spence (R-2)
Butler Derrick (D-3)
Carroll A. Campbell, Jr. (R-4)
John Spratt (D-5)
Robin Tallon, Jr. (D-6)

SOUTH DAKOTA
Senate:
James Abdnor (R)
Larry Pressler (R)
House of Representatives:
Thomas A. Daschle (D)

TENNESSEE
Senate:
James R. Sasser (D)
Albert Gore, Jr. (D)
House of Representatives:
James H. Quillen (R-1)
John J. Duncan (R-2)
Marilyn Lloyd (D-3)
Jim Cooper (D-4)
William H. Boner (D-5)
Bart Gordon (D-6)
Don Sundquist (R-7)
Ed Jones (D-8)
Harold E. Ford (D-9)

TEXAS
Senate:
Lloyd Bentsen (D)
Phil Gramm (R)
House of Representatives:
Sam B. Hall, Jr. (D-1)
Charles Wilson (D-2)
Steve Bartlett (R-3)
Ralph M. Hall (D-4)
John Bryant (D-5)
Joe Barton (R-6)
Bill Archer (R-7)
Jack Fields (R-8)
Jack Brooks (D-9)
J.J. "Jake" Pickle (D-10)
Marvin Leath (D-11)
Jim Wright (D-12)
Beau Boulter (R-13)
Mac Sweeney (R-14)
E. de la Garza (D-15)
Ronald Coleman (D-16)
Charles W. Stenholm (D-17)
Mickey Leland (D-18)
Larry Combest (R-19)
Henry B. Gonzalez (D-20)
Tom Loeffler (R-21)
Tom DeLay (R-22)
Albert Bustamante (D-23)
Martin Frost (D-24)
Mike Andrews (D-25)
Dick Armey (R-26)
Solomon P. Ortiz (D-27)

UTAH
Senate:
Jake Garn (R)
Orrin G. Hatch (R)
House of Representatives:
James V. Hansen (R-1)
Dave Monson (R-2)
Howard C. Nielson (R-3)

VERMONT
Senate:
Patrick J. Leahy (D)
Robert T. Stafford (R)
House of Representatives:
James M. Jeffords (R)

VIRGINIA
Senate:
Paul S. Trible, Jr. (R)
John William Warner (R)
House of Representatives:
Herbert Bateman (R-1)
G. William Whitehurst (R-2)
Thomas J. Bliley, Jr. (R-3)
Norman Sisisky (D-4)
Dan Daniel (D-5)
James Olin (D-6)
French Slaughter (R-7)
Stan Parris (R-8)
Frederick Boucher (D-9)
Frank R. Wolf (R-10)

WASHINGTON
Senate:
Slade Gorton (R)
Daniel J. Evans (R)
House of Representatives:
John Miller (R-1)
Al Swift (D-2)
Don Bonker (D-3)
Sid Morrison (R-4)
Thomas S. Foley (D-5)
Norman D. Dicks (D-6)
Mike Lowry (D-7)
Rodney Chandler (R-8)

WEST VIRGINIA
Senate:
Robert C. Byrd (D)
John D. Rockefeller IV (D)
House of Representatives:
Alan B. Mollohan (D-1)
Harley O. Staggers, Jr. (D-2)
Bob Wise (D-3)
Nick J. Rahall II (D-4)

WISCONSIN
Senate:
Robert W. Kasten, Jr. (R)
William Proxmire (D)
House of Representatives:
Les Aspin (D-1)
Robert Kastenmeier (D-2)
Steven Gunderson (R-3)
Gerald D. Kleczka (D-4)
Jim Moody (D-5)
Thomas E. Petri (R-6)
David R. Obey (D-7)
Toby Roth (R-8)
F. J. Sensenbrenner, Jr. (R-9)

WYOMING
Senate:
Malcolm Wallop (R)
Alan K. Simpson (R)
House of Representatives:
Richard B. Cheney (R)

Obviously, not everyone named here is personally responsible for creating America's outrageous deficits. But clearly, it is their responsibility to lower them. To end the insanity of $200 billion annual deficits.

Congress and the President share that responsibility with one whose name does not appear here. You.

Right now, the most important economic decisions of your lifetime are being made. In Washington. Without you.

Let your senators and congressional representative know exactly where you stand.

Write to them c/o U.S. Senate, Washington, D.C. 20510 or c/o House of Representatives, Washington, D.C. 20515.

This coupon is a good example of what you might say. Above all, keep your message simple.

If they work to bring down the deficit, they'll have earned your thanks. If they don't, they'll have lost your vote.

Dear ____________________

Please bring down the deficit now. If you don't, I'll vote for someone who will.

Name ____________________

Address ____________________

City __________ State _____ Zip _____

GRACE
One step ahead of a changing world.

Exhibit 37

WHY COMPUTERLAND DECIDED NOT TO SEND MONEY TO ETHIOPIA.

Today, many Americans, from school children to rock stars, are contributing money to provide short-term relief for the people of Ethiopia. Yet this effort will not supply the long-term solutions to the causes of hunger, which continue to devastate Sub-Saharan Africa and many other regions of the globe. We at ComputerLand believe it is time for the brightest, most powerful minds in Corporate America to develop the long-range programs that can eliminate World Hunger permanently, before the end of this century.

It isn't easy to ignore the emotions that television coverage of the tragedy in Ethiopia evokes. Scenes of starvation and death have haunted us constantly in recent months.

But put aside for a few moments, if you can, these terrifying images of the effects of hunger, and consider its causes.

For it is only when the causes of World Hunger are identified and attacked that any real progress will be made. And that the related problems of disease and overpopulation, so inextricably tied to hunger, will cease to torment the underdeveloped areas of our planet.

It is for these reasons that the ComputerLand Corporation decided to ask the most efficient problem-solving body in the world, American business leadership, to do what it does best.

SURPRISINGLY, FOOD IS NOT THE PROBLEM.

At this moment, while Ethiopia starves, there exists enough food for every man, woman and child on Earth.

Independent studies by The Presidential Commission on World Hunger, the Brandt Commission and the National Academy of Science all confirm there is ample cropland, agricultural technology and financial resources to grow, harvest and distribute the food necessary to end hunger everywhere, by the year 2000.

So the problem is not one of food, but of distribution.

Not a question of resources, but of logistics.

First, it is a matter of marshalling the expertise required to transfer the food, technical skills, agricultural equipment and medical supplies to the places on Earth they are needed.

In the longer term, ending hunger is a matter of helping these suffering countries develop strong, self-sufficient economies that can support their people, instead of depending on an endless chain of food shipments from abroad.

At ComputerLand, we believe there is no group in the world more capable of solving exactly these sorts of problems than the men and women who comprise Corporate America.

Their problem-solving abilities, management skills, business systems and their goal-oriented philosophy can get the job done with the utmost efficiency.

All that is needed to put this remarkable machinery to work is a fundamental decision that World Hunger is worth ending.

Not some day.

But now.

WHATEVER YOU ARE GOOD AT, THERE'S A NEED FOR IT.

Obviously, no one corporation, agency or government can shoulder the responsibility for developing a master plan to end World Hunger.

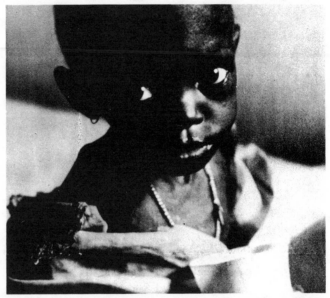

But be assured, there is an enormous need, somewhere in the world, for exactly the talents and experience your company possesses.

Whether you turn your attention to short-term relief or long-term solutions, your company's expertise, personnel and resources are what you can contribute.

Put simply, you should do what you do best.

Even if your business doesn't operate internationally or isn't directly related to food, farming, medicine or distribution, with a little thought you will find the connections that will complement the efforts of others.

In fact, a tool as simple as your telephone may be the best way to find other business people who need your skills to make a contribution of their own.

But most of all, you must make the decision that working to end hunger is a worthwhile priority. That hunger is a problem that your company can and will do something about.

Once you make that commitment, you will find many ways your organization can help.

And the benefits of such a commitment will serve your company well for years to come.

A TOUGH JOB WITH TERRIFIC FRINGE BENEFITS.

Obviously, helping to feed starving people is not bad for a company's image.

It is a clear demonstration of good corporate citizenship to many publics, including customers, stockholders and employees.

And there are more specific benefits to

ABOUT OUR COMMITMENT: ComputerLand Corporation, the world's largest and most experienced computer retailer, is a global network of over 800 retail stores operating in 24 countries. Our 10,000 employees are dedicated to providing computers and related products and services to businesses and individuals.

As part of our commitment to ending World Hunger, we have created a special department to provide you with complete information about ongoing programs, private relief agencies and government organizations to contact.

Ending World Hunger is a critical goal that requires a long-term commitment from corporate leadership. I urge you to make this an immediate priority.

Please write to me, Bill Millard, at:
OFFICE OF THE CHAIRMAN/WORLD HUNGER,
c/o ComputerLand Corporation,
30985 Santana Street, Hayward, CA 94544

be gained.

For instance, corporate educational programs not only improve worker skills in underdeveloped areas. They are also tax deductible costs of doing business.

Hard economic facts will also bear out that the end of World Hunger will create immense new markets for a wide spectrum of goods and services currently unsalable in these devastated areas.

Agricultural and industrial production for export in these countries will rise. Which will lead to profitable two-way international trade.

Large, vigorous and low-cost work forces will emerge virtually everywhere.

And the currently weak global financial system will be stabilized and strengthened, as long-term debts are repaid.

But besides these business benefits, we ask you to consider the other, more personal benefits you will reap.

For when your actions as a business executive help improve the lives of others, you have successfully integrated your professional skills with your values as a human being.

And you are practicing the finest form of business anyone can practice.

In fact, that is precisely why we at ComputerLand decided to run this ad.

As a communications organization, we decided not to contribute money directly to Ethiopia. But to use our time and resources to bring you this ongoing public forum, in the belief that the results will be more enduring and of greater effect.

In future weeks, we will speak to the business community about other aspects of the problem of World Hunger and what specifically can be done.

And we will continue our efforts until the goal is achieved.

Because when you consider the wealth of abilities and resources we possess here in America, while millions elsewhere starve, it would be unthinkable for us not to help.

ComputerLand

HUNGER WILL END WHEN WE MAKE ENDING HUNGER OUR BUSINESS.

© 1985 ComputerLand Corporation. ComputerLand is a registered service mark of ComputerLand Corporation.

Exhibit 38

The Aliquippa tragedy

What unfair trade has done to an American community

Aliquippa, Pennsylvania. The latest victim of unfairly traded steel imports.

Foreign steel, unfairly subsidized and unfairly dumped, is the principal culprit behind what's happened at the once-mighty Aliquippa Steel Works of LTV Steel. But there are other imports, threatening other industries just as vital to America. Textiles. Chemicals. Energy. Silicon Valley. The list goes on and on. How many more Aliquippas before this country moves to enforce fair trade?

One of the most disheartening tasks for a company is to announce the idling of a plant. It's not a question of bricks and mortar—we are talking about people's lives.

On May 17, LTV Steel Company gave notice to 1300 employees that most operations at the Aliquippa Works will be idled indefinitely.

This was a plant where in 1981 almost 10,000 people worked, forming the economic backbone of an entire community. This was a plant where photographers came to capture America's industrial might, and where the most productive steelmakers in the world made high-quality products to meet the world's demand.

Most important of all, this was a plant where $600 million was spent, most of it in the last 10 years, to modernize facilities and remain competitive.

LTV Steel has done everything possible to keep this plant going. But our losses in the first quarter of this year alone are estimated at $25 million. Over the last several years, product after product has been dropped; unit after unit shut down; employee after employee laid off. The community of Aliquippa has been crippled in the process.

Why did this grim change come about? Will there be more plant idlings in the steel industry like this one? The answer is yes—*unless America acts*.

We cannot say that every management move at LTV was correct. We cannot ignore the increase in steel-substitute products. And we cannot deny that costs—including employment costs—reached high levels.

Still, the truest answer to Aliquippa's trauma lies not in Pennsylvania, but overseas.

Unfair foreign competition, in the form of subsidized and "dumped" steel, intruded on product lines of steel bars, oilfield pipe and casing, continuous weld pipe, rod and wire, light structural steel, fence wire, and even nails—until we could no longer compete. What was finally left—pipe—now has an import penetration level of more than 60%.

LTV Steel, as well as the entire steel industry, has been pleading for fair treatment under our existing trade laws. Not protectionism, but fair trade. We can compete with anyone in the world in quality and price—*if* we all play by the same rules.

Last September, the Administration announced a plan to curb steel imports to the 18.5% level. Although this is a commitment to give away 18.5% of the U.S. market right off the top, we supported it in the best interests of all Americans and our trading partners.

But despite the considerable efforts of U.S. trade negotiators, little has happened. In fact, steel imports soared to the 30% level in January.

Unless these imports are curbed now, there will be more Aliquippas. Soon.

LTV Steel will continue to press for fair trade. All we want, and all our employees want, is a fair fight.

The LTV Corporation

AEROSPACE/DEFENSE · ENERGY · STEEL

63

Exhibit 39

Thank You, New York Times.

The New York Times *FRIDAY, APRIL 26, 1985*

What's the Cure for Bad Medicine?

In the opinion of New York actuaries, the medical malpractice insurance business is hurtling toward a disaster that could impair the medical-care system. Governor Cuomo is sympathetic, but offers a bill that would provide only symbolic relief. He and the Legislature need to think harder about the problem.

The costs of malpractice suits are rising nationally as medicine grows more sophisticated. Nowhere is the problem more severe than in New York City and its suburbs. In the 70's, the cost of malpractice claims increased 20 percent annually. In the 80's, the rate is curving alarmingly toward 30 percent. What especially worries the actuaries is the time it takes to settle a suit: now more than eight years. Claims being paid for past malpractice average about $150,000 today. Inflation will push the figure to $450,000 for malpractice occurring now.

•

Such figures spell deep trouble for the Medical Liability Mutual Insurance Company, the doctor-owned concern that insures 16,000 of New York's 22,500 private physicians. Its reserves total $1.15 billion but its potential liabilities may be $750 million more. The state insurance department recently authorized a premium increase of 55 percent, pushing the average cost to more than $20,000 a year in the metropolitan area and as much as $80,000 for some specialists on Long Island. Yet even such enormous increases may not be enough to keep the malpractice insurer afloat.

The prospect that doctors may thus not be able to find insurance at any price prompts state officials to consider "tort reform" — legislated limits on attorneys' fees and awards. The Governor's bill includes some curbs on fees and awards, but it avoids the tougher measure probably needed to contain the explosion in costs: a ceiling on damages for pain and suffering.

Such a ceiling would present difficult moral and practical issues. Would a limit wrongly squeeze the most severely injured victims the most? Should doctors be singled out for special protection? Nevertheless, a ceiling is not unprecedented. Courts in Indiana and California have upheld caps on liability, and the principle is recognized in worker's compensation and insurance of nuclear power plants.

The state trial lawyers' association, already campaigning passionately against even Mr. Cuomo's modest bill, insists no such stringent action is necessary. Why are doctors so upset, the lawyers ask, when most still pay only small percentages of their incomes for insurance? And how can the medical insurer be in trouble when it is making all of its payments with investment income?

The questions are disingenuous. Low malpractice premiums apply mainly upstate. Except for some successful specialists they are a genuine problem in New York City. They discourage doctors from some specialties. They drive up costs for middle-income patients. And they make it even harder to provide medical care in poor neighborhoods. As for paying claims out of investment income, the malpractice insurer is only 10 years old and hasn't yet had to pay out much; most of its cases are nowhere near settlement or verdict. Further, the high interest rates it has been earning are headed down, while inflation of payments heads ever higher.

The courts can't provide much justice for malpractice victims unless the malpractice insurance system works. That system is teetering. The crisis is real, and putting a ceiling on awards may be a sound remedy.

Copyright © 1985 THE NEW YORK TIMES

We Could Not Have Said It Better.

New York Medical Liability Reform Coalition
96 South Swan Street, Albany, New York 12210

Alliance of American Insurers
American Association
of Neurological Surgeons
American College of Obstetricians
and Gynecologists, District II
Business Council of New York State
Hospital Association of New York
State

Hospital Underwriters Mutual
Insurance Company

Medical Liability Mutual
Insurance Company

Medical Society of
the State of New York

Nationwide Insurance Company

New York Chamber
of Commerce and Industry
New York Conference
of Blue Cross/Blue Shield Plans
New York State Society
of Anesthesiologists, Inc.
New York State Society
of Surgeons

Acknowledged Self-Interest Sponsor. The sponsor is directly identified and openly associates its interest with those of the programs advocated in the message, such as ads by utility companies about air pollution standards promulgated by the Environmental Protection Agency. The reader is asked to take action that would be of immediate help to the sponsor, but would ultimately benefit the reader. Advocacy advertisements sponsored by Todd Shipyards, the League of Voluntary Hospitals and Homes of New York, and the Grumman Corporation are illustrative of this approach [Exhibits 40–42]. This approach has also been used by Lone Star Industries and Mobil Oil Corporation, among others. A variation of this strategy can be found in advertisements where incumbent corporate managements beseech their stockholders to vote for their plans in situations involving unfriendly or hostile takeover attempts.

Two recent advertisements by TWA and Gannett Corporation [Exhibits 43–44] present an interesting variation on this theme. TWA, which was confronted by an unfriendly acquisition offer from I. Cahn, the well-known corporate raider, sought to discredit Mr. Cahn by questioning his integrity and fitness to run an airline because it would not be in the best interest of the country. The ad states, among other things, that "TWA is a vital part of this nation's wellbeing. And because we [TWA management] view that role seriously, we are going to take whatever steps are necessary to protect the constituencies and communities we serve." And yet TWA's management was quite reluctant to entertain any proposals for employee stock ownership, or employee representation on the corporate board and in top management decision-making. TWA eventually agreed to a merger with Continental Airlines, which had earlier unilaterally abrogated its labor contracts by taking refuge under the Chapter 11 bankruptcy law. Gannett Corporation in its advertisement asked the company's stockholders to vote affirmatively on two management-supported amendments to the corporate charter. One amendment would require that anyone seeking to acquire the company must make a similar offer to *all* the shareholders, avowedly to ensure a "fair price" for all the company's stockholders. The second amendment would create staggered terms for board directors. Both provisions are considered helpful to the incumbent management in fighting off unfriendly takeover attempts.

Participative Sponsor. The sponsor's identity is apparent, but its interests are carefully disguised. Issues are presented as problems common to industry and also in the public interest. Advocacy campaigns by voluntary organizations and public interest groups fall in this category, along with many industry and trade group campaigns. Ingersoll-Rand Corporation's advertisement on coal as an element in a "balanced energy mix" is an illustration of this approach [Exhibit 45].

Exhibit 40

Six compelling reasons why the Arleigh Burke destroyer must be built on the West Coast.

The United States Navy will soon begin rebuilding its aging destroyer fleet with up to 61 ARLEIGH BURKE (DDG 51) class guided missile destroyers. These ships, equipped with the highly successful AEGIS combat system, will incorporate the most advanced technology available in antiair, antisubmarine, antisurface, amphibious and strike warfare capabilities. In conjunction with 28 AEGIS-equipped CG 47 class guided missile cruisers, 13 of which are already under contract at two Eastern yards, they will provide an impenetrable shield against surface, missile and aircraft attack as elements of the aircraft carrier battle groups so vital to our national defense.

There are six compelling reasons why the DDG 51 class lead ship must be built on the West Coast:

1 Maintain a geographically-dispersed AEGIS shipbuilding base. The two classes of AEGIS ships are too important to the Navy's forward defense strategy, and that strategy is too important to our national security, to concentrate all building resources in one geographic area. Selection of a West Coast shipyard for construction of the DDG 51 to supplement current CG 47 class cruiser construction facilities on the East and Gulf Coasts will avoid the financial and strategic risks of AEGIS program disruption or delay and ensure mobilization "surge" capacity.

2 Reduce "choke point" risk. All newly constructed aircraft carriers, submarines and AEGIS cruisers assigned to Pacific Fleet duty must be deployed by way of the Panama Canal since all of these ships are currently built only in Eastern yards. In addition to the long distance deployment bottleneck and logistics problems this situation can create, what is the alternative if access to the canal is threatened or denied in the future? Establishment of a West Coast source for AEGIS ship construction now will reduce rather than expand reliance on this potentially dangerous "choke point."

3 Establish AEGIS know-how on the West Coast to support the Pacific Fleet. Many AEGIS-equipped destroyers and cruisers will be stationed in the Pacific and will need convenient, capable facilities to provide service and repairs in minimum out-of-service time. Because the shipyards that build these sophisticated ships will be the best qualified—in fact, the only ones able—to service them effectively, this capability must be developed as quickly as possible on the West Coast to be available when the first AEGIS combatants go into Pacific Fleet service in 1985.

4 Keep defense programs competitive. The Navy's policy of maintaining competition among private shipyards on combatant ship construction programs has resulted in lower cost, improved quality and faster delivery, as exemplified by the FFG 7 class guided missile frigate program in which two West Coast yards and one East Coast yard shared in the construction program. Millions of dollars have been saved on this program and fleet readiness has been significantly improved through a procurement policy that mandated two-coast competition and building yard capability to directly support this class on both coasts.

5 Minimize total program cost. Support services (overhaul, repair, modernization, maintenance, etc.) over a ship's 30-year expected life cycle far exceed initial construction costs. Over the full term, cost-effective maintenance of Pacific-based DDG 51 class destroyers by the West Coast building yard will more than offset possibly higher acquisition cost caused by differences in regional wage scales, in addition to minimizing out-of-service downtime.

6 Capitalize on an available, qualified private sector resource. Todd's modern Los Angeles Division, which has an outstanding schedule and cost performance record on the FFG 7 class guided missile frigate program now winding down, backed by 25 years of experience in surface combatant construction, is fully qualified for the lead ship DDG 51 contract. Since 1976, Todd Shipyards Corporation has spent $120,000,000 of its own funds to create this technologically-advanced facility and its highly productive work force, an investment that will fully benefit the DDG 51 program.

The Navy needs AEGIS-equipped surface combatants, the Pacific Fleet needs experienced AEGIS support capabilities and our national defense urgently requires maintenance of a strong, knowledgeable West Coast AEGIS shipbuilding mobilization base.

The solution is obvious.

Todd Shipyards Corporation
One State Street Plaza, New York, NY 10004

DELIVERING THE SHIPS THE U.S. NEEDS—WHEN IT NEEDS THEM.

This advertisement appeared in THE WALL STREET JOURNAL, THE WASHINGTON POST and THE WASHINGTON TIMES.

Exhibit 41

HOSPITAL STRIKE

WHO'S TRYING TO BREAK WHOM?

In order to settle the hospital strike now entering its fourth week, the League of Voluntary Hospitals offered District 1199 two four percent wage increases during a two year contract. The Union responded with allegations of "union busting" and violence on the picket lines. Other unions, whose own negotiations with the City of New York are about to begin, have pledged support.

THE HOSPITALS OFFER IS FAIR BY ANY STANDARD

Compare the Hospitals' 4% annual offer with these facts:

- The cost of living for New York City workers rose only 2.5% in the last 12 months and is expected to remain below the 4% level.*

- So far this year major private industry settlements covering over 800,000 workers have averaged 2.6% the first year and 2.8% over contract life.**

- 1199 has settled in Rochester, New York and Baltimore for 4% each year. In Baltimore the Union gave up its welfare plan.

THE OFFER IS FAIR TO THE WORKERS

In their contract which just expired, all 1199 workers received wage increases of 15.6% while during that same period the cost of living rose only 6%. 1199 started these negotiations almost 10% ahead.

The lowest paid 1199 worker (aide, porter, maid, dishwasher, clerk, laundry worker) currently receives:

- A starting wage of over $15,000.
- 12 paid holidays
- 12 paid sick leave days
- two to four weeks paid vacation
- a generous pension plan with no worker payments

*Source: U.S. Bureau of Labor Statistics; percent rise over the most recent 12 month reported period for Urban Wage Earners and Clerical Workers—New York City.

**Source: U.S. Department of Labor Statistics News Friday, July 27, 1984.

- free released time training with stipends
- tuition refund
- a plan of hospital, surgical, physician, major medical, dental, optical and prescription drug benefits fully paid for by the hospitals.

THE OFFER IS FAIR TO THE HOSPITALS AND THE BILL-PAYING PUBLIC

In New York, the State Health Department controls and limits the prices hospitals can charge and the income they can receive. Within this system of health care cost containment, the hospitals have stretched the available dollars to the limit in trying to settle this strike. They have offered guaranteed wage increases but have neither asked for nor received guarantees from the State to pay for these increases. Based on current economic estimates the hospitals will not receive the income necessary to meet these increases. Insufficient funds mean reductions in medical care services and layoff of workers no matter when the strike ends.

DOES THIS SOUND LIKE "UNION BUSTING"?

Are the hospitals out to break the Union or is the Union out to destroy the hospitals?

The hospitals have no intention of trying to break the Union. They've lived with them for twenty five years and will live with them when this strike finally ends. They need their workers and want them to return to their jobs. The hospitals seek only a quick and fair settlement of this strike consistent with economic realities.

Despite the threats of increasing violence by the Union leadership and their disregard for the patients, the hospitals must, and will, continue to provide quality medical care to all who need it. They owe the communities they serve no less!

THIS STRIKE SHOULD END— NOW!

League of Voluntary Hospitals and Homes of New York

60 East 42nd Street, New York, N.Y. 10165 • (212) 687-3347

Exhibit 42

IN 1984
WE SAID MULTI-YEAR PROCUREMENT
COULD LOWER THE COST OF GRUMMAN'S
C-2A CARGO PLANES BY $89 MILLION.

WRONG.
IT'S $102 MILLION.

WE'RE ROLLING OUT THE FIRST THIS WEEK. BY THE TIME WE ROLL OUT THE LAST,
THE SAVINGS COULD BE EVEN BIGGER. THAT'S GOOD BUSINESS FOR AMERICA.

Only GRUMMAN.

Exhibit 43

What's fair is fair

Gannett Co., Inc. is proposing two amendments to its charter intended to help insure that all shareholders benefit fairly and equally from future stock price increases and that the company's successful policies are not abruptly changed.

The amendments cover:
- A "fair price" for all stock.
- Staggered terms for directors.

The fair price amendment helps insure that all shareholders must be paid substantially the same price as any other shareholder in any tender offer.

The board amendment helps to insure continuity and stability of policies and operations which have resulted in Gannett's record of 70 consecutive quarters (over 17 years) of uninterrupted earnings gains.

✓ Make sure you benefit fairly from any future increases in the market value of Gannett stock.
✓ Make sure your company doesn't risk an abrupt 180-degree change from its successful philosophy, policy and style.
✓ Vote for the proposed amendments in connection with the annual Gannett shareholders meeting May 21.*

*For more information see Gannett's April 1, 1985 proxy statement.
If you have questions or have misplaced your proxy card and need a new one, call Thomas L. Chapple or Jane L. Donnovan at (716) 546-8600.

GANNETT
THE NATION'S NEWSPAPER
USA TODAY
VIA SATELLITE

Exhibit 44

TWA

An Open Letter to Carl Icahn:

If you thought we'd just stand by and do nothing while you try to take over our company...

——— THINK AGAIN! ———

You secretly accumulated our stock for several weeks. Finally, you disclosed that you have bought one-fourth of our shares.

You have also been, as usual, vague about what your real intentions are—and, characteristic of your past actions, you have threatened to take over our company.

Well, Mr. Icahn, we have no intention of standing by and doing nothing while you play your Wall Street games with us.

TWA is a vital part of this nation's economic well-being. And because we view that role seriously, we are going to take whatever steps are necessary to protect the constituencies and communities we serve.

In case you're unaware who relies on us, let us elaborate:

- the other owners of nearly 24 million TWA shares of common stock, as well as the holders of our preferred and preference stock;

- the more than 27,000 TWA employees worldwide;

- the more than 60 U.S. cities we provide with dependable air service;

- the numerous cities and countries abroad which benefit from our acclaimed international flag service;

- the literally hundreds of vendors—from the aircraft manufacturers to the smallest stationery suppliers—who count on us for providing them with jobs; and

- finally—and of paramount importance—the more than 18 million passengers who fly 28 billion miles each year on TWA.

You see, Mr. Icahn, running a major airline is a big job, one that we don't take lightly. It's not like speculating with paper on Wall Street. You have to be proven "fit" to operate an airline—"fit" to manage; "fit" to raise the vast sums of money needed to maintain equipment safely and invest in new, modern aircraft; "fit" to comply with the many important rules and regulations that the various federal, state, municipal and international agencies demand of an air carrier.

In fact, we think you are so unfit we are asking our government's Department of Transportation to rule on your fitness to control an air carrier and we are suing you in state and federal courts.

So, Mr. Icahn, if you thought we'd just stand aside and do nothing while you try to take over our company—think again!

Running one of the world's most respected airlines is a heavy responsibility. We think it's a commitment you just can't handle.

Ed Meyer
President and CEO

Dick Pearson
Executive V.P and Chief Operating Officer

Exhibit 45

Ingersoll-Rand speaks out for the Coal Industry.

The advertisement on these pages is one of a series prepared by Ingersoll-Rand's Mining Machinery Group that deals with vital energy issues confronting our country today—and the steps that must be taken to insure an ample supply of energy for centuries to come.

Appearing over the next few months in The Wall Street Journal, these ads address a number of key issues in order to show how coal can contribute significantly to our country's balanced energy mix.

Ingersoll-Rand's Mining Machinery Group is pleased to stand up for the coal industry by bringing these critical issues to the attention of America's financial and industrial thought leaders. Add your voice to this cause; send today for the brochure and information packet offered in the advertisement.

Blackout 1994.

Coal can keep the lights on.

America must start preparing now for the growing energy demands of the next 20 years or the outlook could be rather dark, indeed. The Department of Energy has pointed out: Even though conservation of gasoline consumption is taking place, with a corresponding decline in dependence on foreign oil, the increasing growth in demand for electricity (approaching an annual rate of 3%) is creating a gloomy forecast. If this significant growth rate continues or increases, by the mid-to-late 1990's *it will be too late to fulfill it*. To meet even our nation's minimum additional requirements, the necessary power plants ought to be on drawing boards *today*.

The Department of Energy further estimates that by the year 2000 we will have to replace 25 to 30 percent of our total generating capacity—the equivalent of 150 new nuclear plants or 250 to 300 coal-fired plants.

What's our energy picture today?

The goal of our country's National Energy Policy Plan is to provide *an adequate supply of energy at a reasonable cost*; enough to meet our present and future needs. Our resources include energy reserves stockpiled or in the ground, such as oil, natural gas or coal; or proved sources, including nuclear and hydro-electric power; along with developing technologies that make use of solar power, wind, geothermal sources and biofuels.

This variety of resources represents the second objective of our energy policy: "to promote a balanced and mixed energy system."

Which energy source can we rely on?

The Secretary of Energy of the United States cautions, "The single most critical energy issue confronting this nation is our continued dependence on foreign oil. If I were a businessman making decisions regarding my future energy supply, I would not be willing to gamble on low-cost oil."

For generating baseload electricity, coal and nuclear energy are more economical over the long term than either oil or natural gas. However, the immediate future of nuclear power seems uncertain. What's more, reserves of oil and natural gas are decreasing while the costs of finding new reserves continue to rise.

Solar energy, wind energy, hydropower and geothermal systems essentially are technologies of the future and can, collectively, provide only about 11 percent of all the electricity generated by the year 2000.

Coal—a vital resource in the "balanced energy mix".

The U.S. possesses the world's largest recoverable reserves of coal, enough to provide the energy we need for centuries, at current and projected rates of demand.

According to the National Energy Policy Plan, coal production should increase more than any other fuel between now and the year 2000. But coal consumption has not grown in the last 5 years, and the future is unclear. In fact today, despite low oil prices, almost half (about $60 billion) of our trade imbalance of $130 billion per year is paid to import 5.4 million barrels per day of foreign oil. Think of the serious impact on our energy availability and our

economy when there is another oil shortage or prices again rise.

Coal's share of electric generating capacity is expected to grow from about 50% at present to 59% by the year 2000. But if we don't start plans now, we'll still have to depend on imported oil to meet our energy needs even then. It is also estimated that before 2000, oil and gas will be priced out of most utility markets. Thus, our nation *must* turn to coal for a continuing supply of energy.

If we expect to be prepared to respond to energy emergencies of the future—and the future starts today—we must recognize how essential coal is to the balanced energy mix. In order to help you understand the role of coal in our energy mix, we've prepared a booklet entitled, *Coal, America's Best-Kept Secret*. After receiving it, you may want to join your voice with others in taking a more firm stance on coal. Just return the attached coupon for your copy.

Ingersoll-Rand has pledged its resources to help propel American concern about our energy future into concrete action. Among other products, we manufacture machinery used to mine coal. But, that's not the only reason we're involved: mining companies will require equipment even if our energy

policies go unchanged. We're involved for the same reason you should get involved: because America must address its energy future, and act now.

Ingersoll-Rand
Mining Machinery Group
4201 Lee Highway
Bristol, VA 24201
Please send a copy of *Coal, America's Best-Kept Secret* and related materials to:

Name _____
Company _____
Address _____
City _____ State _____ Zip _____

INGERSOLL-RAND®
MINING MACHINERY

Elusive Sponsor. The sponsor's interests and even identity are carefully disguised to convey an aura of conscious disinterest. Group names are selected to indicate a broader public constituency than the group purports to represent. Issues are tailored to reflect public benefit without any mention of the sponsor's interest. Many single-interest groups, social activists, ideologically oriented organizations, and industry groups suffering from low public credibility or fighting adverse public opinion on an issue are likely to resort to this approach.

Intensity of Advocacy

This dimension measures the intensity with which an appeal is being made and ranges from emotional to reasoned persuasion and information. Emotional appeals are often identified with ads that fall into the categories of acknowledged vested interest and elusive sponsors. Emotional appeals often involve intangible or esthetic concerns and contain few specifics about what might be done or who should do it. Their emphasis is on building the reader's sympathy for the sponsor's action or position on an issue.

Most advocacy campaigns have one or more ads with primarily emotional appeals, or individual ads containing emotional appeals along with reasoned persuasion. Ad campaigns with environment and ecology as their primary theme are generally loaded with emotional appeals. Reasoned persuasion has been used in campaigns where sponsors attempt to identify their interests with those of their readers. The theme is "We are all in this together" or "We're doing our share, but we can't accomplish much unless everybody else does his share." Some information or data to appeal to one's reason is always provided so that a decision can be rationalized, although the actual reasons for making a given decision may be less than totally objective from the reader's perspective. Advocacy advertisements by public interest groups invariably contain a high level of emotional intensity, with an attempt to engage the reader's sense of morality and indignation against the adversaries identified in the ads.

When used by the general business community, these campaigns are generally associated with benevolent and elusive sponsors. Rational and informational appeals attempt to provide information to enable the reader to decide whether or not he/she should agree with the position taken by the sponsor. This appeal seems to have been more prevalent with disinterested sponsors, acknowledged vested interest, and elusive sponsors.

Specificity in Identifying the Adversary

The adversary can be classified into one or more of four categories: the general public, governmental agencies, competitors, and public interest or social activist groups. When the sponsor is a public interest group, the reverse would be the case. In many instances, the ultimate adversary may be someone or something other than that identified in the ad. The objective of the advertisement is to change attitudes in groups of people who may be in a position, either directly or indirectly, to influence the actions of the sponsor's adversaries in directions preferred by the sponsor.

Table 5 **Types of Advocacy Advertising**

Recognition of Sponsor Interest	Themes of Advertising Copy	Nature of Adversary
1. *Disinterested sponsor:* Sponsor's interest is carefully disguised.	General issues of public interest or with an ideological or philosophical content: support of free enterprise system, association of profits with growth, reduction in budget deficits, rational federal government regulation of business.	Government agencies and legislative bodies, news media, opinion leaders, academic institutions, public apathy and ignorance.
2. *Benevolent sponsor:* Sponsor's interests are presented as indirectly related.	Issues of interest to sponsor presented within the framework of overall social problems and suggestions for their solution. Public is exhorted to make sacrifices voluntarily.	Government agencies and legislative bodies, news media, opinion leaders, academic institutions, public apathy and ignorance.
3. *Acknowledged vested-interest sponsor:* Sponsor's identity and interests are directly associated with the advocated programs.	Open defense of self-interest, downgrading of opponents and their arguments.	Government agencies and legislative bodies, environmental and other public interest groups, other companies and industries opposed to the sponsor's interests, news media, and in the case of voluntary nonprofit groups, the business community and the power establishment.
4. *Participative sponsor:* Sponsor's interest is carefully disguised.	Issues presented as problems common to industry and in the public interest; e.g., regulation of our industry.	Governmental agencies and legislative bodies, public interest groups, competing industries, or firms that stand to gain from such regulation.
5. *Elusive sponsor:* Sponsor's identity and interest are carefully disguised to convey an image of conscious disinterest. Group names are selected to indicate a broader public constituency.	Issues are tailored to identify them with public benefit and general social concern, without any mention of sponsor's interests.	Sponsors of legislative programs or advocates of changes in current policies and political programs, be they governmental agencies or private groups, or business and industry groups.

Table 5 provides one attempt at classifying advertising campaigns within this framework. It should be helpful in understanding the broad range of activities that fall under the rubric of advocacy advertising.

IMPLEMENTATION STRATEGIES FOR ADVOCACY ADVERTISING

An effective advocacy campaign must have a clear focus in terms of its long-term objective and the intended target audience. The next set of issues has to do with the best means to accomplish this objective.

The strength of advocacy advertising for its sponsor lies in two elements: (1) The content of the message is controlled and defined in a manner most favorable for the sponsor; and (2) the environment of the message is carefully defined, so that the message is disseminated in a more hospitable environment. Even the most potent ideas may go awry if they are not communicated properly. An analysis of various advocacy campaigns, both in the United States and abroad, suggests that successful implementation involves several steps, discussed below.

Setting Campaign Objectives

A careful delineation of the sponsor's objectives is critical to the development of an effective campaign strategy. Two important issues must be borne in mind in establishing campaign objectives. (1) An advocacy campaign, more than most other types of advertising campaigns, not only influences existing public opinion, but also affects public expectations of the type of information about the sponsoring organization and its level of performance—both of which may turn out to be different than the sponsor was willing to provide. Moreover, once aroused, people may become cognizant of nonadvertised facets of a sponsor's activities and may evaluate them within the framework of pleadings made by the sponsor in an advocacy campaign. A sponsor, and especially a business sponsor, must therefore anticipate all significant aspects of the organization's operations that might become subject to unwanted public scrutiny. Another facet of this issue has to do with the changes in public policy being advocated in an advocacy campaign. Robert L. Dilenschneider of Hill & Knowlton observes:

> How high does one raise the public's level of expectation through advocacy advertising, and then, what programs are in place to fulfill that level? If a change in a law or regulation is being advocated, is that really possible, and what is the effect on overall public good? If a modification is being suggested in a company or in society, is that feasible, and how will that be effective over the long range? If expectations are raised to a level that cannot be realized, then the advocacy advertising itself is doomed to failure.[32]

The second issue has to do with the proper role for advocacy advertising in a total communications effort that also includes other forms of communication, notably unpaid communications incorporating news media relations that generate favorable publicity for the sponsor's policies and programs. A number of respectable public relations practitioners, and even corporate executives, have expressed misgivings about overreliance on advocacy campaigns to carry a sponsor's message on controversial issues of public policy (see the case study of Edison Electric Institute campaign). Observers like David Finn of Ruder Finn and Rotman; William P. Mullane, Jr. of AT&T; Kalman Druck, public relations counselor; and Robert Dilenschneider of Hill & Knowlton acknowledge the importance of advocacy advertising as a part of an integrated public communications campaign. However, they maintain that its impact and value are overblown, and that a sole or even primary reliance on it may be counterproductive in the long run.

Long-range unpaid communications—public relations and public affairs—can be much more effective in an advocacy situation. Look, for instance, at what congressmen and their staffs and regulators read. By and large they ignore ads and read constituent mail, newsclippings, watch television, and the like. These are generally programs or efforts generated through public relations or public affairs activities and not through advocacy advertising.[33]

The objective of a campaign must be defined in two dimensions:

- What public policy issues are to be communicated, and how well are they understood by the public or the target audience groups?
- What does the sponsor expect to achieve from the advocacy campaign?

For example, a sponsor who merely wishes to create public awareness of a public policy issue will opt for a long-term educational campaign; choose opinion leaders as the target audience; and develop messages using single or multiple authenticating sources as spokespersons. This approach has been successfully used by companies like Dresser Industries, LTV, and SmithKline Beckman. On the other hand, a company might wish to promote a variety of ideas, thereby identifying the sponsor as a public-spirited organization—for example, United Technologies and the LTV Corporation.

Another campaign objective may be to change public opinion on a specific issue within a short time. This campaign strategy will be quite different, depending on whether the sponsor stands to benefit from the advocated position or is acting primarily as a concerned public citizen. The advocacy campaigns by W. R. Grace, the Saving and Loan Foundation, and British Rail exemplify this approach.

An important aspect of an advocacy campaign is whether a company has articulated a program that provides a unifying standard for corporate policies and actions. This is the program with which the company must identify itself. It follows that advocacy campaigns by individual corporations that plead for business as a whole are likely to be less successful because a company cannot control the activities of other members of the business community. Advocacy advertising is generally more effective when it attacks an isolated issue on which the sponsor has been misunderstood or its position inaccurately reported. This is one of the reasons advocacy campaigns sponsored by industry groups tend to lack focus and are generally not as effective.

Sponsor's Public Credibility

An important element in the success of an advocacy campaign is the public perception of the credibility of the sponsor. Although a sponsor may effectively control the content of a message and carefully define the communication environment, the adversary nature of advocacy advertising makes it imperative that sponsors strive to make their messages credible to an otherwise skeptical and even hostile audience.

A stance of pure opposition—opposition as an end in itself, rather than some larger positive social commitment—is self-defeating and likely to be short-lived. Herbert Schmertz, vice-president for Public Affairs of Mobil Oil and the architect of that company's advocacy campaign, appreciates this concern when he says that his company has made a fundamental decision to make a significant intellectual commitment to the subject matter in its ad campaign, rather than giving it superficial treatment: "We probably lose readers. But in the long haul, unless you are prepared to put yourself on the line both intellectually and philosophically, you will never gain long-term leadership and recognition of substance."

We receive our communication cues from a variety of sources, most of which are not, and cannot be, controlled by the sponsor. Similarly, we interpret a particular message based on our prior attitude toward the sponsor and opinion on the subject being discussed. It is therefore not surprising that the oil industry's defense of its activities during the oil shortages of 1972–73 had little effect in changing the public's opinion of the oil companies or the believability of their public statements.

A new campaign by R. J. Reynolds follows somewhat similar logic. Designed to counter the public's growing hostility toward smoking and smokers, the ads use a reasoned approach to provide scientific information to correct the public's attitudes about the "second-hand smoker." It will be interesting to see whether such a campaign has any influence in changing public opinion about smoking hazards and public attitudes toward tobacco and cigarette smokers [Exhibit 46]. Another advertisement sponsored by Philip Morris Incorporated [Exhibit 47] protests the raw deal smokers are getting because many antismoking campaigns create discrimination against smokers by denying them use of public places in which to enjoy smoking and by fostering a general bias against and hostility toward smokers.

In an environment of low public credibility, a posture of self-righteousness on the part of the sponsor or defense of its position is highly suspect and is considered self-serving. This is especially true when the sponsor of such a message has long ignored public opinion and has been viewed as arrogant and uncaring. The most recent advocacy campaigns by organized labor are examples, and they are likely to suffer the same fate of those of the oil industry in the mid-seventies. Under these circumstances, the best strategy would be damage containment, with a message of partial repentance and a commitment to substantive change in those areas that are currently viewed by people as contrary to the public interest.

Voluntary nonprofit groups and social activists sometimes use this approach in a reverse manner, projecting their adversaries, in this case business and industry groups, as arrogant and uncaring. The objective is to project the sponsor as engaged in an uphill fight against a powerful adversary, with the aim of garnering public sympathy and support not only for the advocated position, but most important, for the group itself.

In the long run, the sponsoring institution must develop a political position, a position that is not merely self-serving, but that clearly embodies the public interest. The campaign by AIMS of Industry in the United Kingdom exemplifies the approach.

To overcome this problem, some corporations and industry groups

Exhibit 46

Second-Hand Smoke: The Myth and The Reality.

Many non-smokers are annoyed by cigarette smoke. This is a reality that's been with us for a long time.

Lately, however, many non-smokers have come to believe that cigarette smoke in the air can actually cause disease.

But, in fact, there is little evidence—and certainly nothing which proves scientifically—that cigarette smoke causes disease in non-smokers.

We know this statement may seem biased. But it is supported by findings and views of independent scientists—including some of the tobacco industry's biggest critics.

Lawrence Garfinkel of the American Cancer Society, for example. Mr. Garfinkel, who is the Society's chief statistician, published a study in 1981 covering over 175,000 people, and reported that "passive smoking" had "very little, if any" effect on lung cancer rates among non-smokers.

You may have seen reports stating that in the course of an evening, a non-smoker could breathe in an amount of smoke equivalent to several cigarettes or more.

But a scientific study by the Harvard School of Public Health, conducted in various public places, found that non-smokers might inhale anywhere *from 1/1000th to 1/100th of one filter cigarette per hour.* At that rate, it would take you at least 4 days to inhale the equivalent of a single cigarette.

Often our own concerns about our health can take an unproven claim and magnify it out of all proportion; so, what begins as a misconception turns into a frightening myth.

Is "second-hand smoke" one of these myths? We hope the information we've offered will help you sort out some of the realities.

© 1984 R. J. REYNOLDS TOBACCO CO.

R.J. Reynolds Tobacco Company

Exhibit 47

"...discrimination is discrimination, no matter what it is based on."

Smokers Get a Raw Deal

By Stanley S. Scott

The civil rights act, the voting rights act and a host of antidiscrimination laws notwithstanding, millions of Americans are still forced to sit in the back of planes, trains and buses. Many more are subject to segregation in public places. Some are even denied housing and employment: victims of an alarming — yet socially acceptable — public hostility.

This new form of discrimination is based on smoking behavior.

If you happen to enjoy a cigarette, you are the potential target of violent antismokers and overzealous public enforcers determined to force their beliefs on the rest of society.

Ever since people began smoking, smokers and nonsmokers have been able to live with one another using common courtesy and common sense. Not anymore. Today, smokers must put up with virtually unenforceable laws regulating when and where they can smoke — laws intended as much to discourage smoking itself as to protect the rights of nonsmokers. Much worse, supposedly responsible organizations devoted to the "public interest" are encouraging the har-

Stanley S. Scott is vice president and director of corporate affairs of Philip Morris Inc.

assment of those who smoke.

This year, for example, the American Cancer Society is promoting programs that encourage people to attack smokers with cannisters of gas, to blast them with horns, to squirt them with oversized water guns and burn them in effigy.

Zealots, stop maltreating cigarette users

Harmless fun? Not quite. Consider the incidents that are appearing on police blotters across America:

• In a New York restaurant, a young man celebrating with friends was zapped in the face by a man with an aerosol spray can. His offense: lighting a cigarette. The aggressor was the head of a militant antismoker organization whose goal is to mobilize an army of two million zealots to spray smokers in the face.

• In a suburban Seattle drug store,

a man puffing on a cigarette while he waited for a prescription to be filled was ordered to stop by an elderly customer who pulled a gun on him.

• A 23-year-old lit up a cigarette on a Los Angeles bus. A passenger objected. When the smoker objected to the objection, he was fatally stabbed.

• A transit policeman, using his reserve gun, shot and fatally wounded a man on a subway train in the Bronx in a shootout over smoking a cigarette.

The basic freedoms of more than 50 million American smokers are at risk today. Tomorrow, who knows what personal behavior will become socially unacceptable, subject to restrictive laws and public ridicule? Could travel by private car make the social engineers' hit list because it is less safe than public transit? Could ice cream, cake and cookies become socially unacceptable because their consumption causes obesity? What about sky diving, mountain climbing, skiing and contact sports? How far will we allow this to spread?

The question all Americans must ask themselves is: can a nation that has struggled so valiantly to eliminate bias based on race, religion and sex afford to allow a fresh set of categories to encourage new forms of hostility between large groups of citizens?

After all, discrimination is discrimination, no matter what it is based on. ☐

Copyright© 1985 by The New York Times Company. Reprinted by permission from the December 29, 1984 issue of The New York Times.

**Presented in the public interest by
Philip Morris Incorporated**

conceal their identities by creating public-spirited-sounding organizations such as Citizens for a Better Economic Environment, Californians for Common Sense, or Calorie Control Council. However, such concealment is seldom effective, and in the long run is quite likely to be counterproductive. One element of credibility would be a clear identification of the message with the sponsoring corporation and the willingness of the sponsor to state openly the nature and purpose of such advertising.

Public interest groups, on the other hand, have a distinct advantage in idea-issue campaigns because their names identify them with "good groups" or as on the "right" side of the issues. In the initial stages of a campaign on a public policy controversy, their messages may have a large measure of inherent believability that the opposition may try to dispel only at a risk of eroding its already low credibility. But if the advocating group has any long-term intentions, its staying power and public credibility will be subjected to greater media examination. Its messages are liable to lose their advantage if the group's representational character is questionable and its messages lack substance, or are not in accord with the notion of the public interest as perceived by most people. Thus advertisements sponsored by public interest groups may be quite successful as a one-shot phenomenon, only to go into oblivion, along with the group advocating it, once the issue has been resolved or intense public attention has subsided.

Advocacy campaigns must also reflect the long-term nature of the educational and attitudinal change in a sponsor's communication program. Campaigns developed on an ad hoc basis, under crisis conditions, invariably suffer from low public credibility because they project a self-serving image in a hostile external environment. On the other hand, if a sponsor continues to speak objectively on issues of social importance in which it has a vital stake, it builds a reservoir of credibility that can stand in good stead when it attacks inaccuracy or bias in the public statements of its critics.

An example of the difficulty in swimming against the rising tide of public opinion can be seen in the experience of AT&T with its advocacy efforts during the period when it was fighting the federal government's efforts at breaking up the company. As Mr. William P. Mullane, Jr., corporate vice-president of Information Services, AT&T states:

> As a business subject to the whims of public opinion and government fiat we have used advocacy advertising (or institutional advertising as we used to call it) since early in this century. We used it heavily in the turbulent years leading up to divestiture—with, some would say, less than total success. While we did enjoy certain isolated victories (mostly on pieces of legislation), obviously we did not win the war. As our chairman, Charles Brown, says, "Divestiture wasn't our idea." And yet it happened.[34]

Developing a Campaign Strategy

Advocacy advertising should be an integral part of a sponsor's total communication program, which in turn must bear a close relationship to the activities of the sponsor, the role it projects for itself in society, and the expectations of society for its performance. Too often, advocacy advertising is confined to what the sponsor wants the world to hear, rather than what the world wants the corporation to talk about. It should be a continuous program built around the long-range objectives of the sponsor.

Many institutional advocacy campaigns place a heavy burden on the mass media component of the campaign. All other elements of the communication mix are designed to promote "the advocacy tactics," rather than the total objective of the campaign. This is unfortunate, because such an approach tends to skew the reach of the message toward one segment of the targeted audience and may also distort the perception of the message. Instead, an advocacy campaign should be viewed as an integrated project in which different elements of the communications mix—press relations, direct mail, lecture circuit, and mass media—are carefully evaluated for their relative contributions to the overall campaign. The campaigns by W. R. Grace and the Edison Electric Institute demonstrate the success of such an integrated approach.

Selection of Target Audiences

Many advocacy campaigns—especially those oriented toward raising the threshold of public awareness and understanding of public policy issues—aim generally at the educated populace, without any attempt at the careful targeting common to product and service advertising. This approach is quite typical of many long-running advocacy campaigns, such as those of Mobil, United Technologies, and LTV.

There are, however, two exceptions:

- A sponsor may target its messages to those segments of the potential audience considered undecided and therefore "persuadables" on a particular issue. Bethlehem Steel, for example, developed an interesting approach to segmenting its audience in this manner. This approach also influenced that company's choice of media.
- A sponsor may want to reach influentials, such as political leaders, indirectly through their constituents or the general public, who will be encouraged to write to their elected representatives. This approach is generally used by sponsors who seek immediate action on a legislative issue and use the mass media to put pressure on decision-makers.

A novel form of this approach was used by the Edison Electric Institute. Confronted with growing public resistance to rising electric rates because of electric utilities' needs to raise large amounts of new investment funds, the EEI and its agency, Ruder Finn & Rotman, devised an integrated public relations program to create positive public opinion about the necessity of maintaining a financially healthy electric utility industry. EEI realized that state utility regulators were well aware of its member companies' needs for reasonable increases in their rates and felt that more supportive public opinion would make it possible for them to grant such rate increases when justified by costs and other relevant factors.

Selling an Idea Versus Selling a Product

Superficial similarities notwithstanding, product and issue advertising are very different in concept and must be dealt with differently in execution. Advocacy advertising, which is often short on information and dispassionate reasoning, tends to use emotional appeals. It is often distinguished by its graphics and artwork, an approach that does not do well in conveying abstract thought.

One may find this approach being increasingly used in advocacy commercials on television. However, unless used as a reminder or a reinforcing mechanism, these ads do little to create lasting changes in public opinion or to contribute to the quality and variety of information available to the public. In the long run, this tactic ends up by merely raising the noise level and debasing the rationale of advocacy advertising.

Stephen B. Elliott, director of corporate advertising, W. R. Grace & Co., takes a sharply different view. In a letter to the author, he states:

> I suspect you are biased against the use of television to convert people to a point of view, primarily because television gives you so little time to deliver any information and that constraint is so antithetical to your scholarly instincts. Still, I think you might be quite surprised to see how we have used television to generate publicity on television and in print around the country.
>
> We wanted to create greater public awareness and interest in the findings of the Grace Commission on government waste and also on budget deficits. There was no way we could have found a better medium than network television to create the kind of impact we wanted in the shortest possible time and at the most effective cost. Consequently, we prepared a network television commercial [Exhibit 48].
>
> I doubt if you have seen a network commercial quite like this one. In fact, it took us four months of bargaining to convince two of the three networks to show it. The very first night it aired on network news, we had 31,000 calls asking for our brochure on deficits. . . . We will run the commercial all this year, but the bulk of the budget will be spent in the first six months during the budget debate.[35]

Notwithstanding Mr. Elliot's enthusiasm for the heavy response to the commercial, the long-term effectiveness of this approach in changing public opinion in directions advocated by the Grace Commission remains to be seen. The favorable response to the commercial may be more a factor of the context of the message and the attention-getting qualities of the visuals. Public concern with federal deficits had already been heightened by the tremendous attention paid to it in the news media. And by alluding to the role of government spending and waste in contributing to this deficit, the commercial may make the viewers more comfortable with their prejudices, but will not necessarily enlighten them. The commercial can legitimately claim success in persuading people to ask for more details about the Grace Commission brochure. However, in the long run any changes in people's attitudes will have more to do with their perception of the equity and fairness with which budget cuts are

Exhibit 48

W.R. GRACE & CO.

"BABY" GXCP 4602

60 SECONDS

SFX: FOOTSTEPS.

MAN: Morning. Shall we get down to business?

Now that you've joined us, you'll enjoy numerous rights and privileges. But you will share certain problems, as well.

Specifically, you owe the United States government, in round numbers, $50,000.

BABY: Waaaaahhhhhh.
ANNCR VO: If federal deficits continue at their current rate,

it's as if every baby born in 1985 will have a $50,000 debt strapped to its back.

MAN: Let us review these figures for you.
ANNCR VO: At W.R. Grace & Co., we're not looking for someone to blame. We're too busy crying out for help.

Write to Congress. If you don't think that'll do it, run for Congress.

MAN: Now if you'll just sign here.

ANNCR VO: The last thing we want now is our kids

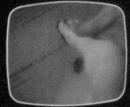

following in our

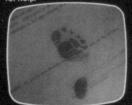

footsteps.

For a free booklet on the deficit and what you can do about it,

call 1-800-USA-DEBT.

At W.R. Grace, we want all of us to stay one step ahead of a changing world.

GRACE
One step ahead
of a changing world.

W.R. Grace & Co.

applied to different groups, and how the Grace Commission Report is reviewed and analyzed by commentators, scholars, and influential opinion leaders.

One reason for the failure of many advocacy campaigns may lie in the confusion that exists between the process of education, the procedures of advertising, and the purposes of propaganda. The purposes of education are to foster growth in comprehension of abstract ideas and concepts; to raise questions about prevailing beliefs; and to encourage intellectual inquiry. The purpose of propaganda is to inculcate a belief through all kinds of information—and even false information, if necessary. Advertising, on the other hand, is intended to provide answers that are definite and specific; to persuade people to do things; and in general to minimize inquiry and uncertainty in a society whose expectations have changed.[36]

Development of Message Content

Advocacy campaigns dealing with specific ideas, whether of a short- or long-run nature, are unique, one-of-a-kind phenomena. They are more like editorial messages or pleadings that must reflect the magnitude and scope of the public issue under discussion; the tone of the time, the nature of the place; and the character of the sponsor and the intensity of its commitment and of those opposing the sponsor's viewpoint and position.

Creativity, therefore, is very important in such campaigns. Moreover, since greater emphasis has to be placed on message substance than manner of delivery, development of message or ad copy requires significantly large resources for researching the issue. This is in sharp contrast to product advertising, especially consumer product advertising, where research emphasis is focused on the audience end and messages are designed based on that research. There is also relatively more weight given to graphics and visuals—the manner of delivery rather than the message itself.

A serious question therefore arises as to whether an advocacy campaign should be developed in-house or by an outside full-service advertising agency. This is not just a philosophical issue, but could be critical to the success of a campaign.

Strong arguments can be made for developing advocacy campaigns in-house.

- A sponsor has great technical expertise and knowledge of the issue that can provide the basic material for the ad copy. It can also more adequately anticipate and oppose critics' arguments. The best campaigns reflect not only the commitment, but the belief of the sponsor in the rightness of the idea, and its willingness to persuade, not exhort, people to see things its way.
- In-house campaigns use staff resources that are experts in their own areas and are also involved with corporate culture. They tend to develop messages that talk to the audiences as equals. Moreover, these messages also reflect the nonprofessional nature of the spokesperson as a communicator, lending more sincerity to the claims about the sponsor's commitment to a particular position on a public policy issue.

- In-house campaigns also tend to be more cost-effective. A large part of the cost is borne by a staff already employed by the sponsor. Direct cash outlays are minimized. Moreover, unlike an ad agency, whose income is directly related to the size of its media billing, the in-house staff has no incentive to increase the size of an ad budget for media buying. An ad agency executive, however, argues that the converse may also be true: "In-house resources may be utilized, but efficiencies in media against the stated objectives and target audiences may not be affected as well. Agency expertise, experience and media buying power account for a lot."[37]
- In-house campaigns create greater involvement by management—which in turn increases its understanding of the policy issues and makes it more sensitive to the corporation's external environment.
- Most in-house campaigns often use outside agencies in limited roles—for graphics, actual development of ads, in the selection of appropriate media, and in buying print space and air time.

Advocacy campaigns in which advertising agencies have played a larger creative role have been generally long on graphics and color, have low-key messages, and have greater visceral than cerebral appeal. They also tend to use electronic media much more than campaigns developed in-house. Thus it is quite easy to distinguish advocacy campaigns where ad agencies have played a major creative role. Campaigns by the Chemical Manufacturers Association, the Canadian Petroleum Association, Lone Star Industries, and the Association of American Railroads are illustrative of this genre of advertising. It should also not be surprising to see that most industry or trade association campaigns fall in this category. As was previously noted, the diverse nature of an industry group's membership makes it difficult for the group to take a sharply focused advocacy stance except in areas where the industry is fighting for its life in a highly hostile climate of public opinion, or is seeking a one-time legislative action. The committee approach and low-key advocacy make them suitable vehicles for advertising agencies.

Some agencies are making a concerted effort to develop expertise in creating and executing idea-issue campaigns. Two successful examples, both involving a single corporate sponsor rather than an industry association, are the cases of LTV (Ogilvy & Mather), and SmithKline Beckman (VanSant Dugdale).

Use of Authoritative Spokespersons

In addition to the credibility of the sponsor, the believability of an advocacy message is influenced by the character and authority of the spokesperson. Advocacy ads generally use one or more of the following sources to attribute the content of the message and/or to deliver the message.

1. Message stated in neutral, third-person terms.
2. A member of the sponsor's group speaks as authority for the message content and delivers it on the sponsor's behalf.
3. Person on the street as spokesperson.
4. Recognized outside authority—single or multiple—as message source.

Noncontroversial educational messages can generally use any or all of these. Choice of spokesperson or authority source becomes critical when the nature of the message is highly controversial, the sponsor's public credibility is low, and the external environment is hostile.

Research shows that a sponsor can improve the effectiveness of a message through the use of authoritative spokespersons when its credibility is low; when the subject matter is highly controversial, and when the external environment is hostile to the sponsor's interest.[38]

- An authoritative source who agrees with the sponsor's position and is so identified by the public has been found to be more believable than a representative of the sponsor's group or an ordinary person.
- When the single authoritative source used in the message is considered impartial or representing views with which the reader of the message is in agreement, credibility is high.
- A message is likely to have greater credibility when the source is a recognized authority, even though the reader may not agree with the views expressed in the advertisement.
- Advertisements using multiple authoritative sources representing all sides of a controversy tend to have greater credibility, even for viewpoints that represent the interests of the sponsor.
- A sponsor's spokesperson and his/her credibility is increased when the sponsor's views are presented along with those of other authoritative spokespersons on the subject.

Some of the best advocacy campaigns have been using single or multiple authority sources. Advocacy campaigns by LTV Corporation, SmithKline Beckman, Dresser Industries, and the Edison Electric Institute fall into this category. An advocacy advertisement sponsored by Dresser Industries used Nobel Laureate Edward Teller to argue in favor of nuclear energy. Although the ad appeared within days after the Three Mile Island accident, it received the largest unsolicited response by the company of any ad in the history of the *Wall Street Journal*.

Unfortunately there are also some troubling trends indicating that some business sponsors, particularly industry and trade groups, are resorting to tactics that border on disinformation.

- For example, some corporations are using well-known television figures to develop programs that bear strong resemblance to standard television news program formats. These programs do not present a balanced discussion of a given issue, but tout the corporate or industry position, thinly disguised as news. The journalists supposedly lend greater credibility to the program content.
- Corporations and trade groups are producing canned "backgrounders" and "live" interviews with executives on current issues. These programs are supplied free to radio and television stations. Independent stations, lacking adequate financial resources, appear only too willing to accept these materials and often use them on the air without identifying the sources. Mobil Oil, which is one of the leaders in using the advocacy approach in its ad campaigns, has also been one of the most significant suppliers of these simulated news and discussion programs.

Comparative Advocacy Advertising

A more recent development in advocacy advertising has been comparative advertising, in which different groups exchange charges or use advocacy ads to respond to claims made by the other group in its advocacy ads. Of course, this is the rule rather than exception in the case of political advertising in the United States, where candidates for political offices heap direct abuse and innuendos upon their opponents during an election campaign, with little concern for accuracy or even common civility.

Comparative advertising by nonpolitical groups and individuals has been used in three circumstances:

1. A sponsor takes an advocacy ad to denounce the position of another group. The most common examples are to be found in labor disputes or contract negotiations where corporate sponsors or unions denounce each other's position in public [Exhibit 7]. A variation of this approach was used by the United Steel Workers when it denounced the plans of U.S. Steel to import semifinished steel from the United Kingdom [Exhibits 8–9].

2. Another use of competitive advocacy advertising is used in hostile takeover or merger situations: Opposing groups address the stockholders of the acquiring corporation with claims and counterclaims as to which group has their best interests in mind.

3. A third variation has been used by two industry groups, the American Association of Railroads and American Trucking Association, which have attempted to refute each other's claims about public subsidies received by their respective industries, and to defend policies advocated by each of them.

This is a healthy development and should be of great benefit to the public. The approach serves as self-regulation because the sponsor realizes that opponents will not hesitate to dispute the accuracy of the sponsor's assertions in public, thereby putting extra pressure on the advertiser to be accurate. Public opinion studies following two of these campaigns showed greater awareness and understanding on the part of the public of the issues discussed and the relative positions of the groups on specific issues.

MEASURING THE EFFECTIVENESS OF ADVOCACY CAMPAIGNS

One of the most difficult problems with advocacy campaigns is to determine their effectiveness. Many advertising executives, both within and outside corporations, have argued against advocacy advertising on a number of grounds, but especially that it is not cost justified. Those using advocacy advertising profess to be satisfied with the outcomes of their campaigns. Naturally, most of the criticism comes from those who have not engaged in advocacy advertising. Critics also suggest that advocacy advertising, like other types of institutional advertising, is a "good time" phenomenon. Businesses do this to claim that they are responsible corporate citizens when profits are rising and companies are prospering, only to discontinue it when they face hard times. There is some truth to this allegation, as can be seen from the cases of Bethlehem Steel and SmithKline Beckman, both of which have reverted to conventional corporate image advertising after having been in the forefront of developing novel approaches to the use of advocacy advertising. More recently, the Association of American Railroads has changed its comparative approach to advocacy advertising and has opted for more conventional institutional advertising confined to extolling the good things about American railroads.

Evaluating the effectiveness of advocacy advertising entails some of the same problems confronted by all advertising; its effect is invariably combined with all other communication activities undertaken by a sponsor and therefore cannot be easily isolated. Furthermore, unlike product advertising, advocacy campaigns are designed for very different purposes that make conventional effectiveness measures of limited relevance.

Long-Term Editorial or Omnibus Campaigns

Advocacy campaigns that are primarily of an educational nature and designed to increase public understanding of a particular issue have to take a long-term perspective. Their success cannot be measured in traditional bottom-line terms. For example, how do we know the impact of an informed public on the federal government's expenditures for defense and national security or regulation of business?

A cynic might ask why one individual corporation, or a nonbusiness group for that matter, should concern itself with such issues, and even if it does, will it really make any difference?

The proper question, however, should be whether private institutions in a democratic society, corporations included, can afford to be passive about fundamental values that underlie the foundations of society. To put it differently, should we be concerned whether individuals vote or understand the values of a free society? Ray D'Argenio of United Technologies makes this point quite cogently:

> Every company has the responsibility to engage in an intellectual dialogue with the public. And it must be done consistently and over a long period of time. You have an obligation to yourself and to the nation to do that. There are times when business is under attack for keeping its mouth closed, and by not expressing its point of view.

Another corporate executive whose company is one of the most ardent users of advocacy advertising even argues against any notion of measurement:

> We are not following public opinion but leading it. It does not matter if people do not agree with us in the short run—just so they are willing to listen. By taking positions that are contrary to conventional wisdom we might actually be antagonizing some of our readers—but that is the price we are willing to pay.

Changing public opinion and attitude is a slow process and may have no direct or discernible relationship with traditional measures of awareness or recall of an ad immediately following its appearance. And yet, by more enlightened criteria, many of these campaigns have been successful not only in terms of improving public understanding of the issues involved, but also in gaining for the sponsoring corporation important public goodwill.

The LTV Corporation and United Technologies are illustrative of the phenomenon. They were conglomerates and not well known to the public. LTV also suffered from a negative public image because of the business record of James Ling, the master entrepreneur who founded the company.

The LTV campaign, which presented opposing viewpoints on specific issues in its ads (including findings of public opinion surveys) was very successful. It generated more than 35,000 requests for additional materials on issues discussed in the ads. The advertisements in the *Wall Street Journal* alone generated more than 6,000 unsolicited letters in a single year.

The Edward Teller ad on nuclear power sponsored by Dresser Industries generated more than 5,000 requests for copies. Various groups and corporations reprinted the ad in local newspapers and other in-house publications at their own expense. Dresser Industries' estimates it reached over 9 million readers.

Similarly, United Technologies' now-classic "The Girl" ad was a phenomenal success. It generated great response from women's organizations all around the country and has been the subject of numerous newspaper and television stories, in addition to thousands of copies being distributed all over the world. SmithKline Beckman's two-year advocacy campaign generated more than 82,000 requests for additional information.

Most companies engaging in educational or informational advocacy campaigns put a high value on letters from their readers, especially when these letters express individual viewpoints and seek additional information about the issue.

Specific Issue-Related Campaigns

Advocacy campaigns in this category include, among others, those of Kaiser Aluminum, Rodale Press, Bethlehem Steel, AFSCME, and Edison Electric Institute. When companies are launching campaigns that focus on specific issues linked with a company's activities, benchmark studies are sometimes carried out to determine the target audience's knowledge and understanding of those issues and their opinions of the company. The success of a campaign is then measured in terms of shifts in people's opinions on certain dimensions from the benchmark. Some of the major advocacy campaigns have used this approach: Bethlehem Steel, Commercial Union, Canadian Petroleum Association, Chemical Manufacturers Association, American Association of Railroads, SmithKline Beckman, British Railways Board, LTV Corporation, and Kaiser Aluminum. They offer excellent approaches to the use of benchmark studies prior to a campaign launch. Canadian Petroleum Association, for example, went so far as to establish specific targets for shifting people's opinions on various issues following different phases of its advertising campaign. Each phase of the campaign was tied into the previous phase accomplishing its objective. It is also interesting to note that a majority of advocacy campaigns in which field studies are used are also the ones where outside ad agencies have played a relatively larger role in creating and implementing the campaign.

While benchmark and other follow-up studies are important, placing too much emphasis on them in determining campaign strategy may have serious drawbacks.

- The measurement is viewed only in terms of positive movement from the benchmark data. However, in a hostile external environment, the mere arrest of a decline in people's opinion on a given issue may be an important and worthwhile result.
- Public opinion studies measure current opinion and how it might have been influenced by an ad campaign. However, this measure is unstable, especially when no other measure exists that would link a change in opinion to a specific action. Attitude changes on public policy issues evolve slowly, and one cannot predict at what point a person's attitude will have been influenced by the message of an ad. A person may claim not to have been influenced by an ad at one time, but may evaluate the same information differently at a future time in view of other information that later came to his/her attention. Campaign decisions made on the basis of pre- and post-studies may actually suggest incorrect conclusions.

Short-Run Single-Issue Campaigns

These campaigns involve persuading the target audience to take certain actions, such as to write to their elected representative to vote for or against a particular bill or proposed law. The success of these campaigns is easily measured in terms of whether a particular law was enacted. The examples of the Savings & Loan Foundation in the case of the "All Savers Certificate" and the W. R. Grace campaign to lower capital gains taxes are illustrative of the great success that can be achieved through this strategy. There are, however, certain caveats:

- Both campaigns used a multiplicity of communication channels, print advertising in the mass media being only one of them.
- There was strong public support, although there was official antipathy to the issue. Thus it was a question of mobilizing public opinion to bear on a reluctant political leadership.
- Even the best campaigns will not succeed where there is strong public hostility toward the sponsor or against the policy position advocated by the sponsor. All the efforts of the oil companies were unsuccessful in preventing the passage of the windfall profits tax during the Carter administration.

Studies also show that while both the tobacco and bottling industries have had occasional successes in referendum fights against legal restrictions on smoking in public places and for bottle-return deposit laws, it has been largely a losing battle as more and more communities have been enacting some form of legislation affecting these industries.

Research in Ad Readership

Some sponsors have gone so far as to mimic the procedures of developing an ad campaign typical of product advertising. Both the issue and the manner of its treatment are carefully developed through focused group interviews; ad copy and storyboards are pretested for audience reaction; and the success of individual ads is measured through readership surveys. One of the most elaborately planned, researched, and executed campaigns of this type has been that of the Canadian Petroleum Association.

While these campaigns have hallmarks of scientific research and professional execution, their results have been disappointing. I have found such campaigns to be generally bland, nonprovocative, and with little to commend them in terms of raising readers' intellectual curiosity and inducing them to think. Like placebos, they have the appearance of a remedy but leave no mark on the user.

Conventional market research, although desirable, has limited usefulness for advocacy campaigns. The educational character of the ideas discussed and the long-term time horizon make short-run, immediacy-oriented measures inappropriate for evaluating these campaigns. A sponsor must believe that, like the value of education, what it is doing needs to be done and then determine how far it wants to go to pursue that objective, given its institutional character and value system. There are no short-cut approaches to the problem and there are no short-term measures to the evaluation of the success of the approaches.

In summary, in the last ten years there has been a significant increase in the quality and sophistication of the advocacy campaigns undertaken by corporations. This is especially true of the print media, where advocacy ads seem mostly to have discarded emotional messages. Instead, they concentrate on discussing issues in terms of expert opinion, corporate viewpoint, or even both-sides viewpoints from responsible and highly credible spokespersons. Most of this effort is sincere, honest, and open, and its growth has enriched the public debate.

At the same time, there has been a great increase in the number and diversity of nonbusiness groups using advocacy advertising. And some of the business and nonbusiness groups have been resorting to advocacy advertising not to raise the level of public debate, but to demean it, not to improve the quality of public decision-making, but to deteriorate it by manipulating public opinion through the use of disinformation and emotional rhetoric.

Increased access to the marketplace of ideas carries with it an obligation to use such access in a responsible manner. The business community has the most to lose from public misinformation and so should take every step to improve the quality of public information and debate. Large budgets and air time are unlikely to buy happiness and credibility for corporations unless this opportunity is used intelligently and in a manner that will earn the business community public respect and trust.

When properly employed, advocacy advertising contributes to greater understanding by the public of the sponsor's position in meeting society's expectations. None of this, however, will come to pass if restraint is not exercised in the use of advocacy advertising. If we are content primarily to pursue partisan propaganda in our communications, the consequences could affect every aspect of our society. It will not reduce the scope of conflict, but enlarge it. It will not contribute to the quality and diversity of public information, but worsen it. In the final analysis, greater freedom to talk would be a pyrrhic victory indeed if in the process public trust in the sponsor's credibility is lost. There would be greater noise, but not necessarily more intelligent discussion. Critics of the business community, who also engage in advocacy campaigns, deserve no more respect if they continue to label all business claims as self-serving and contrary to public interest while they refuse to recognize any other viewpoint as representative of the larger public interest except their own, or to be interested in hearing viewpoints that are not variations of their own. We would thus create an environment where mutual distrust is fostered and the public interest is poorly served. As Robert L. Dilenschneider comments:

> If this nation continues to receive an ever increasing glut of advocacy advertising, we are putting the readers of such ads in a position where, (1) they tune them out; or (2) they are interested and then have to choose sides. In choosing sides we set up a controversy that, if propelled to the extreme, could be quite unhealthy. Specifically, right now America appears to be at peace with itself. The populace, based on all of the polls, appears to be saying, "we are happy with our country, we are happy with the direction in which it is headed, we are happy with our leadership." I certainly don't want to comment on our leadership on a pro or con nature. But advocacy advertising that continues to suggest "things are wrong" will upset the mood of the nation after a prolonged period of time. I don't think the United States can afford right now to slip back into a period like the 1960s.[39]

NOTES

1. S. Prakash Sethi, *Advocacy Advertising and Large Corporations* (Lexington, MA: D. C. Heath, 1977).
2. Ibid., pp. 7–8.
3. Ibid., *Valentine* v. *Christensen*, 316 U.S. 52 (19420; Thomas Emerson, "Toward a General Theory of the First Amendment," *Yale Law Journal,* 72 (1963), p. 877; and Martin H. Redish, "The First Amendment in the Market Place: Commercial Speech and the Value of Free Expression," *George Washington Law Review,* 39 (1970), p. 29.
4. Sethi, note 1; Charles E. Ludlum, "Abatement of Corporate Image Environmental Advertising," *Ecology Law Quarterly,* 4 (1974), pp. 247–278; "Notes: Freedom of Expression in a Commercial Context," *Harvard Law Review,* 78 (1965), p. 1191; "Developments in the Law, Deceptive Advertising," *Harvard Law Review,* 80 (1967), p. 1004; *Banzhaf* v. *FCC,* 405 F.

2d 1082, 1101–02 (D. C. Cir. 1968) cert. den.; and Steven J. Simmons, "Commercial Advertising and the Fairness Doctrine: The New FCC Policy in Perspective," *Columbia Law Review,* 75 (1975), pp. 1083–1087.

5. *First National Bank of Boston, et. al* v. *Bellotti, et. al,* 98 S. Ct. 1470 (1978); *Anderson* v. *The City of Boston,* 439 U.S. 1060, 99 S. Ct. 822 (1979).

6. *First National Bank of Boston* v. *Bellotti, et. al,* supra note 3, pp. 348, 1419, citing *Virginia State Board of Pharmacy* v. *Virginia Citizens Council,* 425 U.S. 748, 764, 96 S. Ct. 1817, 1827 (1976).

7. S. Prakash Sethi, Testimony in "IRS Administration of Tax Laws Relating to Lobbying (Part 1)," *Hearings Before a Subcommittee of the Committee on Government Operations, House of Representatives,* 95th Congress, 2nd Session, July 18, 1978, pp. 381–455.

8. For some examples of general criticism of the news media from both liberal and conservative perspectives, see Michael Botein and David M. Rice, *Network Television and the Public Interest* (Lexington, MA: D. C. Heath, 1980); Francis W. Watson, Jr., *The Alternative Media: Dismantling Two Centuries of Progress* (Rockford, IL: The Rockford College Institute, 1979); Ben H. Bagdikian, *The Effete Conspiracy: And Other Crimes of the Press* (New York: Harper, 1974); Fred W. Friendly, *The Good Guys, The Bad Guys and the First Amendment* (New York: Random House, 1975); and Nelson Smith and Leonard J. Theberge (eds.), *Energy Coverage—Media Panic* (New York: Longman, 1983). This is a publication of The Media Institute, a public interest group based in Washington, DC, that is generally critical of the news media and their coverage of news and issues involving the business community. Some other publications of The Media Institute include *TV Coverage of the Oil Crises: How Well Was the Public Served* (1981); *Crooks, Conmen and Clowns: Businessmen in TV Entertainment* (1981); *Television Evening News Covers Nuclear Energy: A Ten-Year Perspective* (1979); and Robert L. DuPont, *Nuclear Phobia—Phobic Thinking about Nuclear Power* (1980). In addition, there are a host of other case histories alleging media mistreatment. The most notable of these are Illinois Power Company, Dow Chemical, Exxon Corporation, and the National Council of Churches. Copies of pertinent material and videotapes are available from the respective institutions.

9. S. Prakash Sethi, *W. R. Grace & Co., New York: A Short-Burst, High-Intensity, Saturation Campaign in Advocacy Advertising* (1985), and *Kaiser Aluminum, Oakland, California: Use of Advocacy Advertising to Counteract Alleged Inaccuracies and Bias in News Reporting, and to Seek Access to Broadcast Media* (1985).

10. Sethi, *Advocacy Advertising and Large Corporations,* pp. 73–104; and Sethi, "Advocacy Advertising," in Duncan McDowell (ed.), *Advocacy Advertising: Propaganda or Democratic Right?* (Ottawa: The Conference Board, 1982), pp. 25–36.

11. Sethi, *Advocacy Advertising and Large Corporations,* pp. 73–104, 289–318.

12. Sethi, note 7.

13. W. R. Grace, note 9; S. Prakash Sethi, *The LTV Corporation: An Issue Advertising Campaign Emphasizing Discussion of Alternative and Opposing Viewpoints to Elucidate Ideas and Encourage Public Discussion; United Technologies: An Unusual Two-Pronged "Soft" Issue and "Hard" Advocacy Advertising Program; SmithKline Beckman Corporation: An Issue-Information Advertising Campaign to Stimulate Public Discussion of Important Public Policy Issues through Dissemination of Authoritative Views of Well-known and Nationally Recognized Experts;* and *AIMS of Industry: Issue Advertising Campaign by a Nonprofit Group, Aggressively Advocating the Virtues of the Free Enterprise System,* 1985.

14. *ORC Opinion Index,* May 1981, Opinion Research Corporation, Princeton, NJ.
15. *The Roper Reports* #82-10 and #84-10, The Roper Organization, New York.
16. S. Prakash Sethi and Nobuaki Namiki, *Public Perception of and Attitude toward Political Action Committee,* Research Program in Business and Public Policy, Center for the Study of Business and Government, Baruch College, The City University of New York, New York, 1984.
17. S. Prakash Sethi, *Association of American Railroads, Advocacy Advertising Case Study,* 1984.
18. Testimony of S. Prakash Sethi before the Commerce, Consumer, and Monetary Affairs Subcommittee of the House Government Operations Committee, July 18, 1978, pp. 14–18; Testimony of Victor L. Lowe before the Subcommittee on Commerce, Consumer, and Monetary Affairs, House Government Operations Committee on Tax Deductions for Grassroots Lobbying, May 23, 1970; Auditing of Political Advertising by Electric Utilities and Gas and Oil Companies, July 16, 1976.
19. Peggy Dardenne, "Cost of Corporate Advertising," *Public Relations Journal,* 1980–1984, yearly survey published in November of each year.
20. *Current Company Practices in the Use of Corporate Advertising, 1981: ANA Survey Report* (New York: Association of National Advertisers, 1982).
21. Data provided by ANA.
22. See various issues of *Initiatives and Referendum Report,* published monthly by Free Congress Foundation, Washington, DC; David B. Magleby, *Direct Legislation: Voting on Ballot Propositions in the United States* (Baltimore: Johns Hopkins Press, 1984).
23. Common Cause, "The Power Persuaders: A Common Cause Study of What the Federal Lobby Law Does Not Reveal about the Special Interest Lobbying in the Carter Energy Package," Washington, DC, 1978.
24. See note 18.
25. S. Prakash Sethi, "Advocacy Advertising. Text of Remarks at the Public Affairs Conference on Advocacy Advertising," sponsored by the Conference Board of Canada, Toronto, Canada, November 25, 1981. See also Mark G. Yudof, *When Government Speaks: Politics, Law and Government Expression in America* (Berkeley: University of California Press, 1984); and David G. Tuerck, *The Political Economy of Advertising* (Washington, DC: American Enterprise Institute, 1978).
26. *Hearings Before a Subcommittee of the Committee on Government Operations, House of Representatives,* 95th Congress, 2nd Session, "Problems in the Relationship Between the Commerce Department's Maritime Administration and National Maritime Council, a Private Organization; Tax Treatment of National Maritime Council Expenditures for the 'Don't Give Up the Ships' Advertising and Public Relations Campaigns," Washington, DC, July 20–21, 1978; *Report on Problems in the Relationship Between the Commerce Department's Maritime Administration and the National Maritime Council, a Private Trade Organization,* House Committee on Government Operations, 95th Congress, 2nd Session, October 2, 1978.
27. McDowell, *Advocacy Advertising,* p. 6.
28. O. J. Firestone, *The Public Persuader: Government Advertising* (Toronto: Methuen, 1970), p. 83.
29. Statement by Jean-Jaques Blais, federal minister of supply services, May 1981, quoted in McDowell, *Advocacy Advertising,* p. 7. Similar statements have been made by other government ministers under the prime ministership of Pierre Trudeau when the Liberal party was in power in Canada.
30. S. Prakash Sethi, *British Railways Board, Advertising Campaign,* 1984.
31. Ibid.

32. Robert L. Dilenschneider, president and chief operating officer, national operations, Hill & Knowlton, Inc. Letter to the author dated December 31, 1984.

33. Ibid.

34. William P. Mullane, Jr., corporate vice-president, information services, AT&T. Letter to the author dated January 14, 1985.

35. Stephen B. Elliott, director of corporate advertising, W. R. Grace & Co. Letter to the author dated January 4, 1985.

36. Irving Kristol, "On Economic Education," *Wall Street Journal,* February 18, 1976, p. 20.

37. Letter to the author dated January 30, 1985, by Linda Cheeseman, account supervisor, Ogilvy & Mather Advertising. Ms. Cheeseman has been managing the LTV account for her agency.

38. James Jaccard, "Toward Theories of Persuasion and Belief Change," *Journal of Personality and Social Psychology,* 40 (1981), pp. 260–269; Shelly Chaikkn, "Heuristic versus Systematic Information Processing and the Use of Source versus Message Cues in Persuasion," *Journal of Personality and Social Psychology,* 39 (1980), pp. 752–766; Michael H. Birnbaum and Steven E. Stegner, "Source Credibility in Social Judgment: Bias, Expertise, and the Judge's Point of View," *Journal of Personality and Social Psychology,* 37 (1979), pp. 48–74; William B. Lashbrook, William B. Snavely, and Daniel L. Sullivan, "The Effects of Source Credibility and Message Information Quantity on the Attitude Change of Apathetics," *Communication Monographs,* 44 (August 1977), pp. 252–262; Ruby Roy Dholakia and Brian Sternthal, "Highly Credible Sources: Persuasive Facilitators or Persuasive Liabilities?" *Journal of Consumer Research,* 3 (March 1977), pp. 223–232; Paul M. Kohn and Suzi Snook, "Expectancy-Violation, Similarity, and Unexpected Similarity as Sources of Credibility and Persuasiveness," *Journal of Psychology,* 94 (1976), pp. 185–193; Stuart J. Kaplan and Harry W. Sharp, Jr., "The Effect of Responsibility Attributions on Message Source Evaluation," *Speech Monographs,* 41 (November 1974), pp. 364–370; Raymond G. Smith, "Source Credibility Context Effects," *Speech Monographs,* 40 (November 1973), pp. 303–309; R. Glen Hass and Darwyn E. Linder, "Counterargument Availability and the Effects of Message Structure on Persuasion," *Journal of Personality and Social Psychology,* 23 (1972), pp. 219–233; Erwin Bettinghaus, Gerald Miller, and Thomas Steinfatt, "Source Evaluation, Syllogistic Content, and Judgments of Logical Validity by High- and Low-Dogmatic Persons, *Journal of Personality and Social Psychology,* 16 (1970), pp. 238–244; and Kim Giffin, "The Contribution of Studies of Source Credibility to a Theory of Interpersonal Trust in the Communication Process," *Psychological Bulletin,* 68 (1967), pp. 104–120.

39. Dilenschneider, note 32.

Part II CAMPAIGNS TO ENCOURAGE PUBLIC DEBATE AND DIALOGUE

Section A   *PRESENTATION*
OF AUTHORITATIVE
VIEWPOINTS ON MAJOR
SOCIAL ISSUES

Chapter 2   DRESSER INDUSTRIES, INC.,
DALLAS:
ADVOCACY ADVERTISING USING EXPERTS
TO SUPPORT CORPORATE VIEWPOINTS
ON PUBLIC POLICY ISSUES

On July 31, 1979, a two-page advertisement with a very catchy headline, "I was the only victim of Three-Mile Island," appeared in the *Wall Street Journal* [Exhibit 1]. The quote was from Dr. Edward Teller, the renowned nuclear scientist. The ad was a response to the intense antinuclear publicity generated in the media by various activist groups opposed to nuclear power following the accident at the Three-Mile Island (TMI) on May 7, 1981.

The ad was sponsored by Dresser Industries, Inc., a Dallas-based corporation with interests in various facets of energy and high technology. From all accounts it was a very bold response, presented in a hostile sociopolitical environment, when everyone and everything seemed to be against the nuclear power industry.

In the advertisement, Dr. Teller strongly defended the use of nuclear power on grounds of cost, safety, energy independence, and national security. Teller stated, among other things, that safe measures for disposing of nuclear wastes were indeed available but could not be adopted for want of a decision by the federal government. Summing up the case for nuclear power, even in the light of the TMI accident, he stated that two lessons had been learned:

Research assistant: Josette Quiniou.

Exhibit 1

"I was the only victim of Three-Mile Island."

"On May 7, a few weeks after the accident at Three-Mile Island, I was in Washington. I was there to refute some of the propaganda that Ralph Nader, Jane Fonda and their kind are spewing to the news media in their attempt to frighten people away from nuclear power. I am 71 years old, and I was working 20 hours a day. The strain was too much. The next day, I suffered a heart attack. You might say that I was the only one whose health was affected by that reactor near Harrisburg. No, that would be wrong. It was not the reactor. It was Jane Fonda. Reactors are not dangerous.

Now that I am recovering, I feel compelled to use whatever time and strength are left to me to speak out on the energy problem. Nuclear power is part of the answer to that problem, only a part, but a very important part.

I have worked on the hydrogen bomb and on the safety of nuclear reactors. I did both for the same reasons. Both are needed for the survival of a free society. If we are to avoid war, we must be strong and we must help to generate the progress that makes it possible for all nations to grow and prosper.

And what is the greatest present-day threat to the prosperity and even the survival of nations? A lack of energy. Both developed and developing nations are threatened.

The citizens of the United States have just begun to recognize the impact of the world's growing energy shortage. Gasoline lines, electrical brownouts and higher prices are minor irritants. They are nothing compared to what may lie ahead. In a struggle for survival, politics, law, religion and even humanity may be forgotten. When the objective is to stay alive, the end may seem to justify the means. In that event, the world may indeed return to the 'simpler' life of the past, but millions of us will not be alive to discover its disadvantages. When our existence is at stake, we cannot afford to turn our backs on any source of energy. We need them all.

When it comes to generating electricity, we especially need nuclear power. Contrary to what Nader and Fonda and their friends such as Sternglass, Wald and Kendall, would have you believe, nuclear power is the safest, cleanest way to generate large amounts of electrical power. This is not merely my opinion – it is a fact. Due to the lessons learned at Three-Mile Island, the nuclear way of generating electricity will be made even safer.

I have attempted to respond briefly to some of the questions which people ask about nuclear power. The problems that these questions raise are problems because of political indecision or public fear. Technically, they are non-problems, because the dangers they imply either do not exist or else we have the know-how to solve them. I am absolutely convinced of it, after a lifetime of work as a nuclear scientist.

I was once asked how I would like for my grandson, Eric, to think of me and my life's work after I am gone. Eric is nine years old. He is a terrible guy – he beats me at the game of "GO." I am enormously fond of him, but I have not given much thought to what he will someday think of my life's work. I have given a great deal of thought to whether he will be alive in the next century, and whether he will be living in freedom or in slavery. If he is living under communism, he will know I was a failure.

I believe that we have reached a turning point in history. The anti-nuclear propaganda we are hearing puts democracy to a severe test. Unless the political trend toward energy development in this country changes rapidly, there may not be a United States in the twenty-first century.

The President has recognized the danger of the energy shortage. As yet, he has given only some of the answers. I think – I hope – that democracy has enough vitality to evaluate the risks and to recognize the great benefits of nuclear power to human health and well-being, and to the survival of our free society."

Q. How dangerous is the release of low-level radiation from a nuclear power plant?

A. If you sat next to a nuclear power plant for a whole year, you would be exposed to less radiation than you would receive during a round-trip flight in a 747 from New York to Los Angeles.

Let me put it another way: The allowable radiation from a nuclear plant is five mrems* per year. In Dallas, people get about 80 mrems per year from the natural background of buildings, rocks, etc. In Colorado, people get as much as 130 mrems per year from the natural background. Therefore, just by moving from Dallas to Boulder you would receive ten times more radiation per year than the person gets who lives next to a nuclear power plant.

mrems is as appropriate as mil to make comparisons

Q. How much radiation were the people around Three-Mile Island exposed to during the accident?

A. Let me put it this way. Your blood contains potassium 40, from which you get an internal dose of some 25 mrems of radiation in one year. Among the people not working on the reactor, a handful may have gotten as much radiation as 25 mrems.

Q. Should "spent" nuclear wastes be reprocessed to save the plutonium and other by-products?

A. Yes. Plutonium, for example, is as valuable as the original uranium fuel, because of its potential use to produce still more energy. In the end, reprocessing is needed to make nuclear energy abundant and lasting.

Q. Is there a danger that the plutonium produced by nuclear reactors might be stolen by terrorists and used to construct homemade nuclear explosives?

A. I believe that reactor products can be properly safeguarded from terrorists. This can be much more easily done than the guarding of airplanes. Also, any terrorist who puts his mind to it can come up with ways to terrorize a population that are less dangerous to himself than handling plutonium. The answer is not to get rid of the reactors — let's get rid of the terrorists.

Q. Will the expansion of nuclear power by other countries enable them to produce nuclear weapons?

A. Unfortunately, yes. This is already happening. Two-thirds of the reactors in operation in the free world today are outside the United States. Since we can't stop other nations from building nuclear plants or weapons, what we must do is find better solutions to international problems. An energy-starved nation is much more likely to make and use nuclear weapons as a last resort to survival. The only way to prevent that is to see to it that there is enough energy to go around, and to strengthen cooperation and confidence among the nations.

Q. What have we learned from the accident at Three-Mile Island?

A. Two things. First, that nuclear reactors are even safer than we thought. Despite many human errors and a few mechanical failures at Three-Mile Island, the damage was contained. No one was killed, or even injured. We have also learned that a lot can be done by better educated, better paid and more responsible reactor operators, and by a more efficient display of the state of the reactor by modern instrument panels.

Three-Mile Island has cost $500-million, but not a single life. We must pay for safety and, even after we have paid for it, nuclear energy is the cheapest source of electrical power. It is most remarkable that in the case of nuclear energy we are paying for our lessons in dollars, not in lives.

Q. Can a nuclear reactor explode like an atomic bomb?

A. No. Energy cannot increase fast enough in the reactor. Therefore, it is absolutely impossible for a nuclear power plant to explode like a bomb. For this to happen, the laws of nature would have to be repealed.

Q. What is the risk of nuclear power compared to other forms of producing electricity?

A. It is far safer than coal or hydroelectric power, but all three are necessary to meet our need for energy. It may sound strange to say it, because coal has been around so long, but we know more about controlling radiation than we do about controlling the pollutive effects of burning coal. And, of course, a dam has no backup system to protect those who live below it. Indeed many of these people have lost their lives and more their homes.

Q. I live within 50 miles of a nuclear power plant. What are my chances of being injured by a nuclear accident?

A. About the same as being hit by a falling meteor.

Q. What about the effect of an earthquake on a nuclear plant?

A. At the first sign of a tremor, the reactor would shut down automatically. Also, reactors are built to withstand enormous structural damage. The only man-made structures I can think of that are more stable are the pyramids of Egypt.

Q. Is it true that we still have no satisfactory way to dispose of nuclear wastes?

A. No. Ways do exist. What we have *not* had is a decision by our government on which way to go. Waste disposal is a political problem, not a technical problem.

Q. How much radioactive waste materials are produced by nuclear plants?

A. At the moment, about 12½ % of our electricity is generated by nuclear power. If all of it were produced this way, the wastes from these plants over the next 20 years would cover a football field to a depth of about 30 feet. To dispose of this waste a mile underground would add less than one percent to the cost of electricity.

Dr. Edward Teller was born in Hungary and educated in Germany. He came to the United States in 1935 and worked extensively on nuclear developments during and after World War II. He led the earliest efforts to ensure the safety of nuclear power reactors and to achieve clean power generation. In recent years he has concentrated increasingly on the varied aspects of the coming energy shortage, and has argued for utilization of every feasible form of energy. Active in national programs to explore peaceful uses of nuclear power, Dr. Teller is a Senior Research Fellow at the Hoover Institution, Stanford, California, and Professor Emeritus at the University of California.

Dr. Teller's newest book, *Energy from Heaven and Earth* (W. H. Freeman & Co.), traces the origin and development of energy, from 15-billion years ago to the present day and in the future. Authoritative, amusing and easily understood, it is highly recommended to all who seek a balanced perspective on the energy situation.

Limited copies of this message from Dr. Teller are available on request to Dresser Industries, Inc., Dresser Building, Dallas, Texas 75201.

DRESSER INDUSTRIES

Dresser Industries is one of the world's leading and most diversified suppliers of technology, products, and services to industries involved in the development of energy and natural resources, including oil, gas, coal and hard minerals.

For the fiscal year ended October 31, 1978, consolidated net sales and service revenues amounted to $3.05 billion, and net earnings were $203.9 million.

To learn more about Dresser, please write for our Annual Report.

> First, that nuclear reactors are even safer than we thought. Despite many human errors and a few mechanical failures at Three-Mile Island, the damage was contained. No one was killed, or even injured.
>
> Three-Mile Island has cost $500-million, but not a single life. We must pay for safety and, even after we have paid for it, nuclear energy is the cheapest source of electrical power. It is most remarkable that in the case of nuclear energy we are paying for our lessons in dollars, not in lives.

The response to the ad was phenomenal. It was the most successful ad ever run in the *Wall Street Journal*. The *Journal* did an advertising flyer on it that was used in its marketing effort. The ad suddenly thrust Dresser Industries into the forefront of U.S. corporations that had begun to speak out on public issues.

The rationale for the ad is provided by Ed R. Luter, Dresser's senior vice-president for finance, and the executive primarily responsible for its advocacy ad campaign:

> On the problem of nuclear power, all of the no-nukes like Jane Fonda, or Ralph Nader, were getting a tremendous amount of publicity. They were staging big rallies in Washington, D.C., and opposing nuclear power in any form. It was an emotional issue that they were exploiting. They had lost their Vietnam issue as something to get attention, so they shifted to nuclear power. Once again the news media was simply not adequately presenting both sides of the story.
>
> We had little selfish interest in this case. There are a few products that we sell for nuclear power plants, but it is no major part of our business. But we thought that nuclear power is important to this country and its future development. It is one source of energy that we have that will last for a long, long time. Therefore, we decided that the other side of that story should be told. Dr. Teller was the obvious choice to interview because he is very vocal on the subject and also one of the greatest experts in this country on nuclear power.[1]

COMPANY BACKGROUND

Dresser Industries, Inc., is among the world's leading suppliers of technology, products, and services to energy industries dealing with oil, gas, coal, and nuclear power. Headquartered in Dallas, Texas, the company operates in more than 150 countries and employs 57,000 people, of whom 43,700 work in domestic facilities. Its total revenues reached $4.6 billion in 1981. Through a strategy of internal growth and extensive acquisition, the company now operates in five major product groupings: petroleum, energy processing, refractories and minerals, mining and construction, and industrial specialty products.

John V. (Jack) James is chairman, president, and chief executive officer of Dresser Industries, Inc. He is a very outspoken individual. As a result, he is involved in many outside groups, such as the Conference Board, The Business Roundtable, The Chamber of Commerce of the United States, and The Business Council. In addition, he is a member of the president's Export Council.

STRATEGY FOR DEVELOPING AN ADVOCACY CAMPAIGN

Initial Decision

In 1971, John J. McKetta, professor of chemical engineering at the University of Texas, and chairman of the advisory committee on energy to the secretary of interior in 1970–71, published an article in which he predicted a severe energy shortage. Dresser published that article in the company's 1971 annual report. As the 1973 embargo made his predictions come true, he updated his article for the 1977 report, again forecasting drastic energy shortages. According to a company spokesperson: "We got such a response to that article from our own shareholders that we decided it would be a good subject for nationwide publication. We received letters by the hundreds from shareholders congratulating us for publishing the article. That really was what gave us the idea of starting to speak out on matters of importance to the country and to Dresser." An interview with McKetta, presented in a question-and-answer format, became the first ad [Exhibit 2].

Other circumstances also contributed to Dresser's decision to engage in advocacy advertising. The oil embargo and the energy crisis required Dresser to furnish comprehensive information to its constituencies. As the crisis impinged on the American economy and welfare, it gradually evolved into a greater public issue, making communications from a large stakeholder such as Dresser almost obligatory.

The Objective

The primary objective of such a program is to provide a counterpoint to all the publicity generated by antibusiness activists and environmental groups. A more specific reason for launching a public information campaign is offered by Dresser's CEO:

> One of the problems we have is getting people to understand the economic effects of regulations issued from Washington. This concerns us because it affects our business and our employees. We think that there has been a great deal of legislation that's been put into the mill without a lot of careful consideration.[2]

Decision-Making Process

Ed Luter has the prime responsibility for picking the issues. It is not a regular ad campaign in the traditional sense of the word. Management waits for an issue to arise that someone should speak out on.

Ideas are first presented to Jack James, the CEO, and if he agrees that they are sufficiently important, a go-ahead is given. There is a lot of dialogue and exchange among corporate executives. It is a very cooperative but quite short decision process. The board of directors, or the outside members of the board, do not play any direct role in the selection process. However, they are informed about what is going to be published. Thus they are not surprised when questions come from acquaintances.

The Energy Crisis: Why the country's over a barrel, and what you can do about it.

Every citizen should be informed.

Reading this report will alarm you. It will make you concerned. It will also make you informed on an energy situation made confusing by short-term expediency and self-serving rhetoric.

Unfortunately, for all of us, the gasoline shortage of 1973 and the natural gas shortage of 1977 were not just temporary malfunctions of the U.S. energy supply system. In this question and answer interview, prepared originally for Dresser shareholders, Dr. John J. McKetta, a leading energy authority, cites evidence to show these problems were only the tip of the growing U.S. energy crisis iceberg.

We are not going to escape all the consequences of our energy neglect over the past years. But, as informed and concerned citizens, we can minimize our problems down the road . . . by conserving energy and by encouraging our Congressmen to take corrective action now, before it is too late.

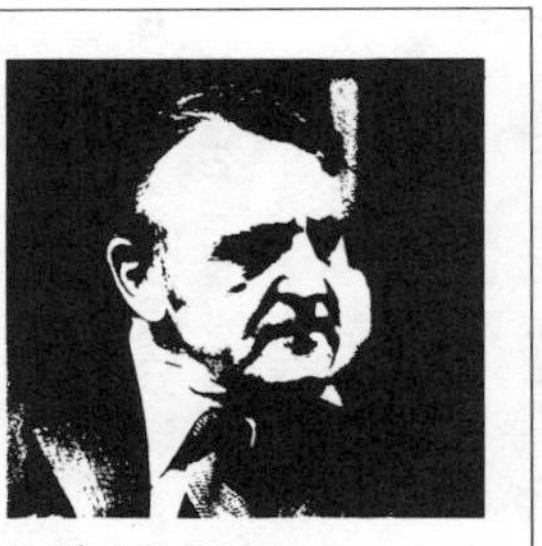

Dr. John J. McKetta is Professor of Chemical Engineering at the University of Texas and among the country's most qualified spokesmen on the subjects of energy and environment. In 1970-1971, he served as Chairman of the Advisory Committee on Energy to the Secretary of the Interior and, during that period, was among the first authorities to call attention to the serious energy problem facing a then unaware United States. His predictions have been chillingly accurate.

Dr. McKetta is a charter member and a director of the National Council for Environmental Balance. He was Chairman of the Committee on National Air Quality Management for the National Academy of Science and Engineering, 1970-75. In 1976, Dr. McKetta received the coveted Lamme Award from the American Society of Engineering Education, the Joe J. King Professional Engineering Achievement Award and the Triple E Award from the National Environmental Development Association for outstanding contributions to the national issues of energy, environment and economics. He is widely published internationally on these subjects as well as chemical technology, processing and design.

Dr. McKetta's wide scope of interests and accomplishments make him exceptionally well qualified to present a balanced, expert opinion and timely warning about the threatening nature of our country's energy situation today.

Q. Dr. McKetta, for more than a decade you have consistently stated that the United States energy situation was growing progressively worse. Is that still your view?

A. In 1971, I termed the circumstances serious. But we have since passed that point. We are now facing disastrous consequences from our inability to meet our energy needs.

Q. What are our chances of rectifying our energy predicament?

A. Unfortunately, since the gravity of our problem was spotlighted by the Arab oil embargo in 1973, almost everything we have done has tended to worsen the situation. Time is running out on us. Even if we could move tomorrow to develop a workable energy policy and were able to implement it at once, we would still experience at least a deterioration in our standard of living in this country by 1985. If we do not move quickly, the situation will become dire.

Q. Would you please elaborate on what you mean by dire?

A. I mean that we will experience deep and painful disruptions in our whole economy. We will have a severe recession by 1985, brought about by shortages of domestic energy. In fact, unless we move immediately, there will be an energy shortage in the United States that we simply cannot imagine at this time. Most of this is, and will be, caused by the vote consciousness and shortsightedness of our government in energy matters.

If we allow our energy programs to drag on as they are today, I predict the government, by 1985, will have on its payrolls a large number of "regulators" who will appear at our homes to make certain that we maintain low temperatures in the winter and high temperatures in the summer, and that our clothes dryers are permanently disconnected. Air conditioners in automobiles will be banned and we will drive on Saturday and Sunday for emergency purposes only.

I further predict that escalator use will be prohibited, elevator use severely limited, that unemployment will be as high as 14 percent, prime interest rates as high as 15 percent and that we will have the worst recession in the history of the country.

Q. Since the oil embargo, the prices of crude oil have gone up substantially; drilling activity has been increasing steadily and the Federal Power Commission recently set a new price ceiling of $1.42 per thousand cubic feet on new interstate natural gas. Haven't these factors brightened the domestic energy outlook?

A. The $1.42 price level has not been fully resolved. If it were, it would improve to a small degree the economics of gas production. Still, all the factors you cite can do little, if anything, to prevent the disasters we face. The increase in drilling activity has been insignificant when weighed against the problem.

In 1974, the U.S. produced 9 million barrels of oil per day. The figure declined to 8.5 million in 1975, and declined again in 1976, even while demand was rising at higher than expected rates. We aren't gaining in production — we are continuing to lose ground. We aren't moving toward energy self-sufficiency; we are moving farther away from it.

Just a few years ago, we were importing about 25 percent of the oil used in this country. In 1976, we imported approximately 45 percent, and the figure is still growing. Our increasing dependence on imported oil brings greater risks of another embargo, and more intimidation in the conduct of our foreign policy. This endangers and jeopardizes our nation.

Since 1956, out total energy demand growth rate has outstripped our total energy production growth rate, causing a disturbingly high growth rate in energy imports.

Q. What about energy sources other than oil and gas? Can we count on them to close the gap between our production and demand?

A. Our projection regarding other U.S. energy sources has declined substantially between 1970 and 1975. In 1970, we estimated that all of our energy sources could provide 95 quadrillion British Thermal Units by 1985. Our 1975 estimates show that we were overly optimistic and now we expect only 62 Q's from all energy sources by 1985. (1 Q equals one quadrillion British Thermal Units. This is the energy in 1 trillion cu. ft. of gas or 46 million tons of coal or 180 million bbls. of oil or 243 million megawatt hours.)

While our predictions of oil and gas production by 1985 have been revised downward by 3 Q's, predictions of supplies of other energy sources, such as coal, nuclear, geothermal, solar and synthetics, have been revised downward by almost 30 Q's. The outlook now is that coal will be the only energy source other than oil and gas that can make a significant contribution to our energy supplies over the next ten years. Nuclear energy, for example, will provide only about 9 Q's by 1985, if all planned nuclear plants are actually built.

At the same time, 1975 predictions of 1985 energy demand have been revised upward from the 1970 estimates. The chart shows the supply and demand estimate made in 1970 and the 1975 revisions through 1985. As may be noted, the gap between the supply and demand estimates widens perilously. What's more, in 1976, it appears that we will not be able to produce even at the low level of the 1975 estimates.

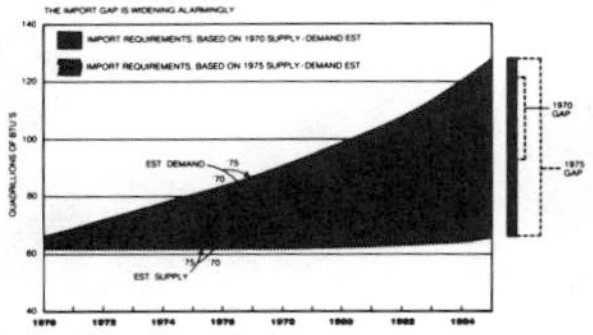

Obviously, we must make every effort to develop all energy sources, but oil, gas and coal are the only ones that can make a significant contribution to our needs in the immediate future, or, at least, the next two decades. We have no choice but to concentrate our efforts on hydrocarbons, especially oil and gas, until other sources of energy are able to share the load — probably around the year 2000.

Q. What are the consequences of our rising energy imports?

A. First, we must conclude that our increasing dependence upon imported oil could result in a profound and dangerous weakness in the U.S. position abroad. Today, for example, we face the dilemma of supporting Israel, with whom we have religious and friendly ties, or supporting the Arab states, whose oil supply is vital to our nation.

Second, there is the specter of economic disaster. In 1976, the U.S. cost of imported energy liquids will be $37 billion. It was only $6 billion in 1973. If we project import trends based on our 1970 production and demand projections, we would need to import 8 billion barrels of oil during the year 2000. The cost of that amount of fuel could be over $200 billion. This is equivalent to 20 million new jobs at $10,000 per person per year. If we use 1975 projections for production and demand, the situation becomes even more disastrous.

We should also keep in mind that our rising bill for energy imports has the same effect as if our tax bill were increasing . . . the result is that industry has less funds to provide new jobs and consumers have less funds available to spend to support employment.

Q. Is our growing dependence on imported oil proof that the United States is running out of oil and gas?

A. No, the tragedy of our problem is that the crisis is developing even though expert scientific studies indicate there are sufficient domestic resources of crude oil and natural gas to last for the foreseeable future, and certainly until other energy sources, such as nuclear power, develop to the point of supplying the greater part of our needs. As of 1975, the U.S. had proved recoverable reserves of about 228 trillion cubic feet of gas and 34 billion barrels of oil. Estimates of undiscovered U.S. recoverable potentials go as high as 750 trillion cubic feet for gas and 104 billion barrels for oil.

Q. You mentioned earlier that in addition to oil and gas, coal must be used more extensively. Why is its use limited now?

A. In 1970 the Mine Safety Act and EPA regulations caused declines in the production and usage of coal. Twenty-two percent of the total mines were closed during 1970-71. Since that time, restrictions on the use of high sulfur coal have decreased usage. Production and usage have risen since 1971, but 1975 levels will have to triple by 1985 if we are to approach self-sufficiency.

Q. What must be done to reverse the energy situation in this country?

A. Simply stated, we must close the gap between supply and demand. More precisely, we must adopt an energy policy that establishes specific objectives and provides the incentives and controls required to achieve them.

Our strategy should be to increase domestic production and reserves of oil and gas over the short term, say to 1990, to gain time for development of our alternate energy resources.

Q. Specifically, what steps should be taken to accomplish this?

A. One of the first steps should be to return to a free market for energy. If we decontrol the price of oil and gas, we will have higher prices. Although basically unpopular, higher prices would help correct our energy situation in two ways: first, they would slow demand; second, they would spur domestic exploratory drilling, which would eventually increase both our production and reserves. We know from the experiences of other countries that when gasoline costs more than a dollar a gallon, consumption drops substantially.

Higher prices for oil and gas would also encourage greater recovery of oil and gas from existing wells. Only about 35 percent of known oil deposits is recoverable using present technology. Higher prices would allow technological advances which, in turn, would contribute to improvement in recovery rates of existing oil reserves. Also, there are known natural gas deposits that are not now commercial; higher prices would change the economics, encourage drilling in those fields and help increase our gas production.

In addition, we need to triple the use of coal, because it represents our most abundant and easily accessible source of domestic energy.

Q. Do you have other thoughts about making the problem less severe?

A. In addition to accelerating our production, we need to conserve energy through more efficient use. One area subject to significant improvement is power generation. For example, the conversion of natural gas to electricity results in an energy loss of over 30 percent. Also, we should convert immediately to coal for electrical power generation, especially in states that do not produce large quantities of natural gas.

We should declare a moratorium on automotive catalytic converters and exhaust gas recirculation devices, except in the few cities with special environmental problems, and put lead back into gasoline so that we could return to the more efficient engines for automobiles.

We must become reasonable about environmental demands and establish trade offs between energy development and environmental constraints. We need to review many of the obstructive governmental regulations. We have to take a more rational approach to the prudent use of nuclear energy. Finally, research must be increased to develop every practical energy source as rapidly as possible.

Q. Is it too late to head off our energy shortage?

A. Yes, it is too late to completely eliminate the gap between supply and demand over the next 15 years. Some of the actions we just discussed, however, would decrease oil demand by about 2 million barrels per day and increase the oil supply by some 3 to 4 million barrels per day by 1985.

As I said at the outset, time is running out. No matter what we do, we are going to feel the adverse effect of the energy crisis on our living standards.

America has the resources to solve our energy problem. Our only hope is that the U.S. Congress will put national interests above politics and adopt a comprehensive energy policy that will reduce our energy problem to manageable proportions.

Every citizen can help.

The threat of growing energy shortages and rapidly-rising costs bring new urgency to the need for a comprehensive U.S. energy policy.

In the development of an energy policy, your Representatives and Senators need the views and support of all citizens.

Let your elected representatives in Congress know how you feel. In most communities, a listing of these officials is contained in the telephone directory under "United States Government — Congressional offices." Or, you may write to your legislators c/o House of Representatives, Washington, D.C. 20515 or c/o United States Senate, Washington, D.C. 20510.

Additionally, every citizen should do all that he or she can about energy conservation. Many helpful booklets on how to save energy are available free or at nominal cost from the Federal Government or local utilities.

Time is very important . . . act now.

Limited copies of the interview with Dr. McKetta in booklet form are available upon request to Dresser Industries, Inc., Dresser Building, Dallas, Texas 75201.

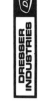

Dresser Industries, Inc., together with its subsidiaries, is a leading supplier of engineered products and technical services to energy and natural resource industries around the world.

For the fiscal year ended October 31, 1976, consolidated net sales and service revenues amounted to $2.23 billion, and net earnings were $156.8 million.

A majority of these revenues was derived from the sale of products and services to energy-oriented industries, including oil and gas exploration, oil and gas drilling and production, gas transmission and distribution, petroleum and chemical processing, production of electricity, marketing of petroleum products, and coal mining, preparation and handling.

Industrial markets accounted for the remaining revenues and included a broad range of basic industries.

Since 1971, sales, net earnings and earnings per share have increased at annual compounded rates of 23%, 37% and 30%, respectively.

To learn more about Dresser, please write for our Annual Report.

DRESSER INDUSTRIES

Dresser . . . a world leader in serving energy and natural resource industries with highly engineered products and sophisticated technology.

The company does not have a structured approach to environmental scanning in terms of what major issues are emerging, tracking them systematically in terms of their importance to the company, and then getting a public position on these issues. Instead, it relies on management's expertise in the areas relevant to the company, and the feeling of senior executives as to what is current and important to political leaders, the general public, and the news media. Dresser also does not undertake public opinion surveys to measure public interest or feelings about a particular issue. Luter observed: "We have some feel for public opinion although we have not done any surveys. We are not very great on hiring people to do public opinion surveys for us. We are not too sure how thorough and accurate they are. We depend mainly on our own reactions we get from our audience. We can tell from the responses that we get that it has had quite a bit of effect. For example, we have tracked the responses as to the number of people that wrote in for our annual reports as a result of reading the ads."

In selecting issues, Dresser follows three general principles:

1. Avoid discussion of issues that are the subject of U.S. foreign policy or national security.
2. Address only those issues where the company has some expertise and knowledge and can speak with authority.
3. Do not mix Dresser's own problems or interests with the general discussion of an issue in terms of its implications for the national agenda.

Thus although the company has a very strong interest in exporting oil exploration and production technology to the USSR, it has chosen not to speak on the issue in its advocacy advertisements because Dresser's views "might conflict with national policy of the administration, whoever is in office." Similarly, in discussing the South Africa issue, the company did not refer specifically to its own efforts in South Africa or its position on the Sullivan principles. They were fully stated in Dresser's proxy material and in correspondence with people who wrote about it.

In 1977, Dresser ran four advertisements. Of these, one dealt with the issue of energy shortage, and one with nuclear power. Dresser also ran two advertisements dealing with the constraints imposed by the U.S. government on overseas trade by American corporations. During 1977, there were two pieces of legislation before Congress on the boycott. One was the Ribicoff amendment to the tax bill, and the other was a bill making it illegal to comply with the Arab boycott. Dresser was opposed to both bills. The corporation also did not think that the news media were giving equal treatment to both sides of the story. Therefore, it decided that someone should present the other side of the case on this important issue [Exhibit 3].

There were no advertisements in 1978. During 1979, the company ran two ads, one with Teller's statement on TMI and nuclear energy, and the other one an update of McKetta's 1977 ad. There was an ad in 1980, and it attempted to dispel the myth that there was any "real" energy shortage in the United States [Exhibit 4]. During 1981, Dresser addressed two issues in its advocacy ads, the first one dealing with U.S. investments in South Africa [Exhibit 5] and the other with the adequacy of energy resources in the United States [Exhibit 6].

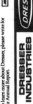

500,000 American jobs hang in balance as Congress considers more boycott legislation.

Every citizen should be informed.

There are times when the best solution to a sticky problem is not the passing of more laws. This is one of those times.

Action by Congress is threatening:
- **500,000 U.S. jobs**
- **Billions of dollars of national income**
- **U.S. influence in Middle East peace negotiations**
- **One of our important energy sources**

In this question and answer interview, Dr. Richard D. Robinson, one of the nation's leading authorities on international business, comments on the far-reaching effects of current legislative countermeasures to the Arab boycott.

It's a problem with which all Americans should be concerned. As informed and concerned citizens, we can stem this tide and correct some of the harmful action already taken by encouraging our Congressmen and the Administration to take corrective action now before it is too late.

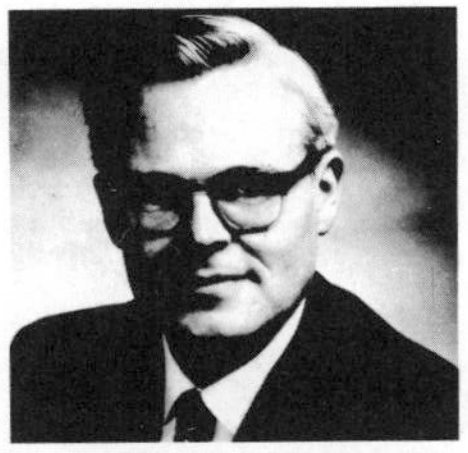

Dr. Richard D. Robinson is Professor of International Management at the Alfred P. Sloan School of Management, Massachusetts Institute of Technology. He is one of the earliest educators in the United States to do research in the field of international business. As early as 1958, Dr. Robinson was writing about the impending conflicts between the multinationals and the poorer countries and urging Western corporate management to rethink traditional notions of ownership and control. He was first to suggest the idea of the "fade-out" of foreign ownership in the case of mature enterprises. In 1963 he wrote a pioneer book, International Business Policy, the thesis of which was that Western business was likely to imperil its operations in the lesser developed countries unless it became more sensitive to the economic interests and political aspirations of the host countries. In the absence of such sensitivity and responsive corporate policies, he predicted increased expropriation of foreign assets and the forced spin-off of foreign ownership. Over the years, he has gained a reputation as a friendly and honest critic of international business.

He is the author of one of the leading textbooks in the field, International Business Management: A Guide to Decision-Making, which is widely used in graduate schools of business and management. He is a founder and past president of the Academy of International Business, a Fellow in L'Academie Internationale de l'Organization Scientifique, lecturer for the U.S. Department of State's Foreign Service Institute, consultant on innumerable international projects, former Turkish Area Specialist for the American Universities Field Staff, and former foreign correspondent for the Chicago Daily News Foreign Service in the Middle East. His most recent book is National Control of Foreign Business Entry—A Fifteen Country Study.

Q. **Dr. Robinson, other than the energy crisis, what do you consider to be the greatest challenge to the U.S. economy?**

A. There are two. First, the U.S. economy is becoming integrated with the world economy, which means massive internal adjustments. In the long run, these should serve the welfare of all. Second, the U.S. economy is shrinking relative to the rest of the world. Therefore, our perspective and policies must shift accordingly. Let's face it, our share of world trade is growing smaller. So is our gross national product, as a percent of global product. The percentage of the world's largest corporations based in the U.S. is declining. And, to the extent we can measure it, even our share of the world's technological innovations—inventions and patents—is doing the same. We have virtually *no* unique technology to offer the world market, and few unique skills.

Q. **That's a bleak picture.**

A. No, it's not bleak—we're merely joining the world as a co-equal partner. *But*, it *could* become *very* bleak if we persist in passing costly—and unnecessary—laws.

Q. **What laws are you referring to?**

A. Uppermost in my mind at the moment is the Ribicoff Amendment to the 1976 Tax Reform Act, which is already in effect, and the anti-boycott legislation now being written in both houses of Congress.

Q. **How do they affect the economy?**

A. They make it difficult—perhaps impossible—for U.S. firms to compete with the Europeans and Japanese in one of the richest markets of the world—the Middle East.

Q. **What do we have to lose?**

A. Income and jobs. The U.S. stands to lose $16-billion in outstanding service and construction contracts in Saudi Arabia alone, plus another $4-billion a year in sales of direct civilian exports, and $9-billion in military goods and services. A good estimate of the annual total for U.S. sales of goods and services to Saudi Arabia is approximately $15-billion a year. Let's translate that into jobs in the U.S.: If 20% of the $15-billion represents labor, that amounts to $3-billion a year. At $15,000 per job per year, that equals 200,000 direct jobs in the U.S. That's a *very* conservative estimate. It reflects only sales to Saudi Arabia. If sales to all 18 Arab nations are included, the total probably is closer to 500,000 jobs, *at least*. That's 500,000 jobs we will *not* have in the U.S. if the Ribicoff Amendment is allowed to stand and similar restrictive laws are passed. The loss of 500,000 jobs is likely to mean at least another $5-billion added to welfare expenditures in the U.S.

Q. **And you think that legislation to prevent compliance with the Arab boycott will have this effect? Don't the Arabs need American products and technology too much for that to happen?**

A. The answer is, simply, "no". As I said before, we have lost the technological lead we once enjoyed after World War II. The fact is, we are even now supplying less than 15% of the Arab's imports. Even this share has required the greatest effort on the part of U.S. businesses in the face of intense competition from Europe and Japan. With very few exceptions, in the areas of certain sophisticated technology, the Arabs can buy anything they need from other countries.

Q. **And bills now being written in Congress will complicate this still further?**

A. Yes, by adding criminal sanctions and loss of export permits to the loss of tax incentives and other financial supports already included in the Ribicoff Amendment.

Q. **Isn't there justification for these laws on moral grounds?**

A. Let's reverse the situation. Say the U.S. is at war with Japan. Naturally, we would not buy Japanese goods or permit U.S. firms to sell to Japan. And we could develop a good argument for not doing business with any foreign firm that was selling to Japan if we thought it had the effect of sustaining the war effort. Likely, we would develop a list of such firms—a blacklist, if you will. Such firms would be denied trading rights in the U.S., and no U.S. firm could do business with them under the threat of criminal sanctions. And, if the principal officers of foreign firms *not* on the list became loud proponents of the Japanese war effort, if they raised money to support it or otherwise aided Japan's military effort, any good, loyal American would say that they, too, should be blacklisted. In fact, that's what we did in World War II. There was no moral issue involved.

Q. **But the argument in this instance is not one of military aid so much as racial and religious discrimination.**

A. That argument would have some validity, if true. But it isn't. I know personally of U.S. firms doing substantial business in Saudi Arabia, and elsewhere in the Arab Middle East, which employ many people of Jewish origin. Those firms have been under *no* pressure from the Arabs.

It's also worth noting that, of the 50,000 requests for boycott compliance recently made public by the Commerce Department, apparently only 26 were found to be discriminatory on racial or religious grounds. These seem to have been corrected subsequently by diplomacy. It is easy for Americans to believe that religious equality is the reason for opposing the Arab boycott, because we *want* to be a people who are not afraid to stand up for human rights. And, also, because we are committed to the continuation of Israel as a viable state. But neither Israel nor religious equality is the issue here. We must understand that or suffer the consequences. Israel and the Arab countries are countries at war.

Q. **What is the motivation behind the laws in the U.S. then?**

A. In some cases, it is a misguided effort to prevent discrimination in world trade as well as in U.S. employment. In other cases it is an attempt to weaken the Arab position in the Middle Eastern conflict—to bring the Arabs to heel.

Q. **And it won't work?**

A. Definitely not. There is no way an American company or its affiliates or employees can bring such pressure to bear on a sovereign state, whether acting singly or together. Our backing out of the Arab market will have no appreciable effect on the Arabs, except possibly to increase the prices they pay for imports by perhaps 1 or 2 percent. But it *will* seriously reduce the leverage, the communications, and the influence we have to work with them toward peace in the Middle East. Also, I very much doubt that it is in the interest of pro-Israel groups in this country to allow this situation to develop. Surely, even the most ardent Israeli supporters do not want their activities to be identified with the loss of half a million American jobs. The anti-Israel backlash from such an event—yes, it could easily become an anti-Semitic backlash—could be tragic. The price is simply too high to pay, especially when we realize that it would deny the Arabs very little. In short, such countermeasures are counterproductive, because the penalties do not flow through to the Arab states—they stay right here at home.

Status—anti-boycott legislation

The appropriate U.S. House of Representatives and Senate Committees have completed work on differing versions of anti-boycott legislation. It is impossible, therefore, to state the specific provisions which will be included in the final version of this legislation. As early as next week, the full House and Senate might consider and vote on the two different versions. The number of the Senate Bill is S. 69 and the House Bill is H.R. 5840.

Both Bills contain broad prohibitions which would, in effect, make it virtually impossible for U.S. firms to do any substantial business with Arab countries without violating both U.S. criminal and civil laws. Each of these Bills as currently drafted provides some specific exceptions from the prohibitions to permit U.S. firms to conduct certain limited transactions with or in Arab countries.

The exceptions are so qualified that even at best U.S. firms currently doing business in the Middle-East will find it more difficult, if not impossible, in most instances to continue their operations, and firms trying to do business in that area for the first time may find it impossible to do any business without violating U.S. law.

While the Senate version presently appears to be more realistic in allowing some business to continue, it is anticipated that there will be efforts on the Senate floor to so qualify the exceptions that they either are eliminated or become so narrow that, for all practical purposes, the exceptions would be useless and little or no business could be conducted between U.S. companies and Arab countries.

Q. **Why are the Japanese and Europeans not in the same boat?**

A. They are, in the sense that their firms are subject to the same boycott rules. But the Japanese and Europeans are accustomed to abiding by the laws of other countries when doing business with them. The boycott, therefore, is not even a controversial issue for them. Exports are basic to their national economies. They do everything they can to support and encourage exports, including government-guaranteed financing and tax incentives, boycott or no boycott. I would imagine that they are thoroughly amused by our dilemma. Their sales will grow as ours decline. Talk about exporting jobs from the U.S.—this is the most effective way I know.

Q. **And you think anti-boycott legislation will boomerang on the Middle East peace talks?**

A. More knowledgeable people than I have said it, people who have, themselves, been involved in the Middle Eastern political negotiations. By interrupting trade between the U.S. and Arab states, we can only harden the attitudes of both sides in the peace negotiations. The Saudis are going to blame Israel for the result, and it is going to make the markets in which the Saudis buy even more competitive. They'll have to pay slightly more. I can't help but believe this will affect military sales as well. Anti-boycott legislation is extremely dangerous to our economy, to peace in the Middle East, and to the Israeli cause. Congress can pass any laws it wants to, but it must understand the trade-off and the consequences of what it does. If there are any political gains to be realized by anti-boycott legislation—and I don't think there are—the American people will pay dearly for them. And no one outside the U.S. will care.

Q. **According to recent newspaper articles, the committees in both the House and the Senate have completed their work on anti-boycott legislation and most of the objectional provisions to U.S. business have been either removed or significantly modified. Do you agree?**

A. Some press accounts describe the anti-boycott bills as being much more harmless than they, in fact, are. Both the Senate and House bills in their present form are highly restrictive. They will, in my judgment, cause enormous losses of business for U.S. firms. Under them, for example, it is a criminal action (punishable by fines and/or imprisonment of executives) if a company, on its own initiative, knowingly substitutes a non-blacklisted source of goods for a blacklisted source to fulfill a shipment to Arab customers. Under the House version, a company would be subject to criminal penalty if it provides goods from a non-blacklisted source unilaterally selected by an Arab customer, if it knew that such selection was boycott-related. This restriction doesn't recognize the rights of sovereign countries to decide what and whose products they will buy.

Q. **What is the solution, then? What has to be done?**

A. The first thing, in my judgment, is to repeal the Ribicoff Amendment. Then Congress should *not* pass any of the current anti-boycott proposals. Second, we should follow the advice of a friend of mine, Richard Nolte, who was United States Ambassador to Egypt at the time of the 1967 Arab-Israeli war, and who is now executive director of the Institute of Current World Affairs. Here's what he has to say:

"If the *real* interest is to modify the Arab boycott and its application, the effective way to do so is by quiet diplomatic effort, where successes have already been achieved. The key to removing it altogether is a peaceful settlement of the Arab-Israeli dispute. If, instead, new anti-boycott legislation is passed, especially an extreme version, it will be not only a self-inflicted wound for us but a 'red flag' for the Saudis. They will take it as a destructive act of hostility and discrimination. They will take it as evidence that United States Middle East policy is still in thrall to Israel.

There has to be a better way. Must we persist in casting the Saudis in an adversary role? They have gone to great lengths to emphasize their desire to cooperate with the United States, not least in seeking peace in the Middle East with justice and security for all. In view of the very great importance to us of that objective and the Saudi connection in general, the proposed legislation deserves a very careful second look."*

*New York Times, February 18, 1977, p. A-27

Every citizen can help.

Due to the importance of this proposed legislation to employment and national income, your Representatives and Senators need the views and support of all citizens.

Let your elected representatives in Congress know how you feel. In most communities, a listing of these officials is contained in the telephone directory under "United States Government—Congressional offices." Or, you may write to your legislators c/o House of Representatives, Washington, D.C. 20515 or c/o United States Senate, Washington, D.C. 20510.

Time is very important . . . act now.

Limited copies of the interview with Dr. Robinson are available upon request by mail to Dresser Industries, Inc., Dresser Building, Dallas, Texas 75201 or by calling 214/745-8982

Dresser Industries, Inc. is a leading supplier of engineered products and technical services to energy and natural resource industries around the world.

For the fiscal year ended October 31, 1976, consolidated net sales and service revenues amounted to $2.23 billion, and net earnings were $156.8 million.

To learn more about Dresser, please write for our Annual Report.

DRESSER INDUSTRIES

Exhibit 4

When your head's in the sand, there's a lot still exposed.

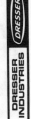

Q. Dr. Hill, what is your assessment of our energy situation today?

A. We are living in a dream world. There is plenty of gasoline. There were no electrical brownouts this summer. There appears to be no shortage of heating oil for this winter. The natural gas companies are promoting sales again. The problem is that all dreams end. Ours will end, too, sooner or later.

Q. What will end it?

A. I'm not sure. The OPEC nations could stop production or raise prices beyond anyone's ability to pay, or several oil-dependent nations could start a war over Middle Eastern oil supplies. Or something could happen to close the Straits of Hormuz through which flows a third of the world's oil supplies — anything of this order.

Q. And if one of those things happens, then what?

A. Then it's a toss up whether we survive or not.

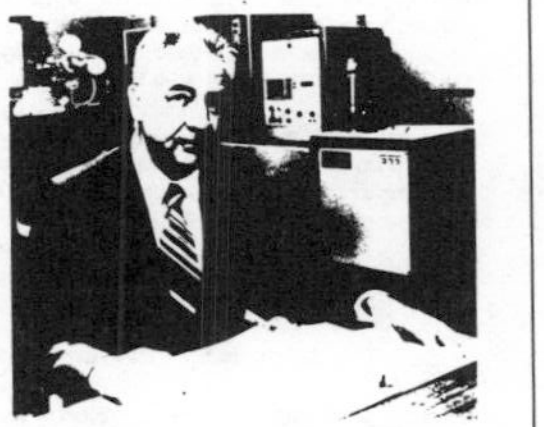

Dr. George R. Hill is the Envirotech Professor in the Department of Chemical Engineering at the University of Utah.

He was Director of the Fossil Fuel Power Plants Department and Assistant Director for the Fossil Fuel and Advanced Systems Division of the Electric Power Research Institute (EPRI), Palo Alto, California.

Prior to joining EPRI, Dr. Hill was Director of the Office of Coal Research at the U.S. Department of the Interior. He joined the Department of the Interior in 1972, after serving as Dean of the College of Mines and Mineral Industries at the University of Utah for six years.

Earlier, Dr. Hill served as professor and department chairman in the Department of Fuels Engineering at the University of Utah.

The author of over 90 scientific and technical publications, Dr. Hill was the recipient of the American Chemical Society's Storch Award in 1971 for contributions to fundamental research on the chemistry and utilization of coal and related materials.

Dr. Hill serves on the Board on Mineral and Energy Resources of the National Academy of Science and National Academy of Engineering, where he is serving as the Chairman of the Editorial Board for *Chemistry of Coal Utilization* for the 1980 updated version. He is also a member of the Fossil Energy Advisory Committee of the Department of Energy, and he serves as a member of the State of Utah Energy Conservation and Development Council.

Q. Couldn't we just make do with less?

A. We would *have* to make do with less. A great deal less, when you consider that we depend on OPEC for almost half the oil we use in this country, and we have nothing to take its place. Reduce our oil supply by 40% and you would see factories shutting down, ships sitting at their docks, driving limited to official and emergency purposes. There would be massive shortages of food and other goods, and unemployment would be beyond anything we can imagine.

We would be easy pickings by any dictator who promised "to lead us out of this mess". Militarily, we would be a sitting duck.

Q. You think something like this will happen?

A. We have done nothing to prevent it.

Q. Can we prevent it?

A. Not in the short term. We might have, had we started seven years ago after the first oil embargo. Now we are facing a catch-up time of five, maybe ten years before we can turn the situation around.

Q. Ten years? It didn't take us that long to gear up for World War II!

A. That's true. But energy wasn't a problem in 1940. Also, we weren't hamstrung by a federal bureaucracy as we are today. And we had Pearl Harbor to shock us into action.

Q. Are you saying it will take a Pearl Harbor to bring us around to solving our energy problem?

A. I hope that something less will do it. But the OPEC embargo didn't convince anyone. Or gasoline lines. Or Iran. Or the Russian invasion of Afghanistan. And today we are listening to — sleeping through — the news of war between Iraq and Iran. I am wondering what it *will* take to wake this country up to the need to develop its own energy resources.

Q. Is energy self-sufficiency another dream, or do we have the resources to be self-reliant?

A. We have the resources.

Q. What are they?

A. Petroleum, coal, oil shale, natural gas, nuclear power, hydroelectric, plus the potential of greatly increased use of geothermal, solar and other supplementary power sources. You name it, we've got it. We are better off in some areas than others, but we are not developing any of these sources as well or as fast as we might.

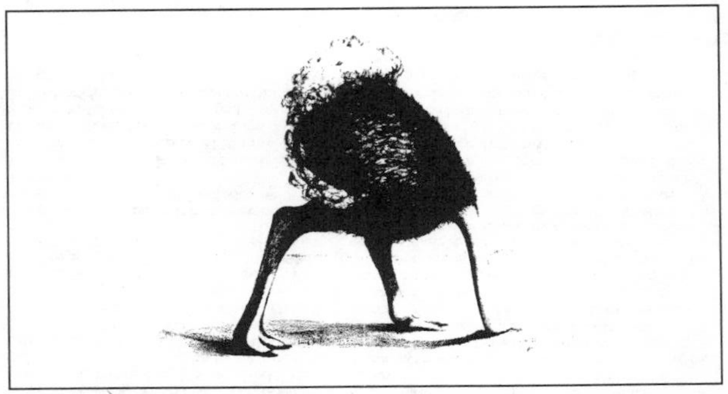

Q. Why not?

A. It's popular right now to blame Congress and, of course, some Congressmen can be blamed for shortsightedness and for lacking the courage to stand up to highly vocal anti-growth pressure groups. But the real hangup is not with Congress. It is with the regulatory agencies. Here you have layer upon layer of bureaucrats, some unable or unwilling to make a decision, and others who seem to be deliberately sabotaging the energy program.

Q. Sabotaging? How?

A. By leaving proposals in the "in" box for months. By encouraging — and even financing — activist groups to drag out the process in public hearings or by bringing spurious lawsuits. Or by silently backing demonstrators — even training them at taxpayer's expense. Or by confusing the public with oversimplified statements about the promise of solar power or alarming them with statements against nuclear power plants. It all has the same result — to freeze us in our tracks.

Q. Why are they doing this?

A. They are not together on that. As Tom Hayden, one of the Chicago Seven said, "First we make the revolution, then we decide what for." But, in general, they advocate more government control over the sources of production, and greater distribution of wealth. They also want a no-growth society free of all risks, even if this means turning back the calendar on progress. Such a society, of course, denies opportunity to those at the bottom of the economic ladder and takes away individual freedoms. It also ignores the threat to our national security and to that of other nations friendly to us.

Q. Are they succeeding in that?

A. I think they are. That is why, in my opinion, we are seeing virtually no progress in developing our water and mineral resources. That's why nuclear power is in such turmoil. That's why there have been no significant increases in coal production, even though we have enough coal in the United States to last for hundreds of years, and even though we can make everything from coal that we can from petroleum.

Q. Dr. Hill, since coal is your special area of expertise, let me ask you — of all our energy resources, isn't burning coal the most dangerous to the environment?

A. It would be if we went back to burning it the way it was done during the industrial revolution. But we don't have to do it that way today. We now have the technology to mine coal, to burn it, or to process it or convert it into other usable energy forms — and to do all these things in ways that are safe to the environment and to human life.

Q. What about such things as "acid rain"?

A. Coal is taking a bum rap for acid rain. It's true that rain is more acidic in some parts of the world than in others, but it is just possible that this is largely due to the burning of high sulphur oil, not to coal, alone.

Fortune magazine, not long ago, made a case for the build-up of acid rain in the northeastern U.S. by saying that the sulfates from the west were being carried east by the prevailing winds, and that this was the reason for high concentration of sulfates over the eastern U.S. But, then, you would expect to see a gradual buildup of sulfate concentrations all across the United States rather than just in the east. But you don't.

Q. When coal is burned, it does produce more carbon dioxide than oil or natural gas. There are those who fear that, if enough carbon dioxide reaches the atmosphere, it will cause world temperatures to increase — which is the so-called "greenhouse effect" — and melt the polar ice caps, causing tidal flooding and the like. What do you say to this?

A. Well, for one thing, there seems to be a cooling of world temperatures right now, which goes contrary to that theory. But let's assume that the amount of carbon dioxide in the atmosphere *does* continue to build. At the rate of less than ½ of 1% a year, which is the rate of increase determined by the World Climate Conference in 1979, it would be sometime in the middle of the next century before the buildup would become significant.

In their view, and mine, that is plenty of time to conduct the research we need to find ways of controlling the effects of carbon dioxide from fossil fuel combustion on climate. It is also time enough, if necessary, to redirect many aspects of the world economy and energy production.

The plain fact is that what we know about carbon dioxide does *not* justify delaying the expansion of coal use. That's not just my opinion. It was the conclusion reached by more than 80 scientists from 16 countries who participated in the World Coal Study in January of this year.

I do not want to belittle the genuine concerns people have about developing any of our energy resources, coal included, but the truth is we are faced with a much more immediate threat to life than a buildup of carbon dioxide or acid rain.

For the next ten years, we must see to our *survival.*

That means we must develop every energy and fuel resource that we can. We will continue to work to ensure that our survival occurs in a world that is pleasant and safe to live in. In the meantime, we cannot afford to stand around with our heads in the sand.

This energy problem is not going to solve itself.

What Is Your Shock-Resistance Factor?

Beginning with the electrical blackout of New York City in 1965, Americans have received a number of "shocks" about the energy situation. Looking back, any one of them might have been enough to galvanize the country into action. And, yet, 15 years later, here we are, more dependent than ever on foreign oil imports. Is it true that action by Congress lags the will of the people? Or are we, the people, still not convinced there is a problem? How many shocks did it take to convince *you?*

After each of the "shocks" listed below, put a check in the box opposite *if that shock did not convince you that America has an energy problem. Stop* checking when you feel you were convinced there *is* a problem. To compute your Shock-Resistance Factor, see below:

	NOT CONVINCED:
1. **Electrical blackout of New York City**	☐
2. **The OPEC embargo**	☐
3. **Lines at the gasoline pumps**	☐
4. **Carter's "Moral Equivalent of War" speech**	☐
5. **Gasoline price increases**	☐
6. **Electricity price increases**	☐
7. **Natural gas availability/price increases**	☐
8. **The trouble in Iran**	☐
9. **Russian invasion of Afghanistan**	☐
10. **Iran-Iraq conflict**	☐

Total boxes checked ______

Add the number of boxes you checked. The result is your Shock-Resistance Factor. The higher the number, the more resistant you are to energy shock. The lower the number, the more likely you are to support an all-out energy development program for America. If your S-R Factor is 5 or below, what are you doing about it?

MAIL YOUR RESULT TO US
Use this coupon to send us your Shock Resistance Factor. If we get enough replies, we will publish the National Shock Resistance Factor.

DRESSER INDUSTRIES
BOX 718
DALLAS, TEXAS 75221

My Shock-Resistance Factor is ______

NAME ______

ADDRESS ______

CITY ______ STATE ______ ZIP ______

Limited copies of this message are available on request to Dresser Industries, Inc., Dresser Building, Dallas, Texas 75201

Dresser Industries is one of the world's leading and most diversified suppliers of technology, products, and services to industries involved in the development of energy and natural resources, including oil, gas, coal and power.

To learn more about Dresser, please write for our Annual Report.

DRESSER INDUSTRIES

Exhibit 5

A message to American investors in South Africa

"Your withdrawal from South Africa will be seen as a lack of faith in your own democratic system."

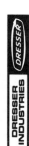

Q. Mrs. Mvubelo, do you think apartheid is beginning to change in South Africa?

A. The apartheid laws have failed dismally. A healthy and growing economy saw to that. The emergence of the Afrikaner businessman has ensured apartheid's permanent demise. Black workers are valued assets, educated and trained black workers even more so. Laborers are no longer in demand for things machines can do. We are not faced with the practical considerations which led to the French Revolution or those which brought the Communists to power in Russia. We are not in the static status situation of peasants or serfs.

Q. As you see it, what is the most important question facing South Africa at the present time?

A. The most urgent and pressing problem in South Africa at this time is the political accommodation of the urban blacks.

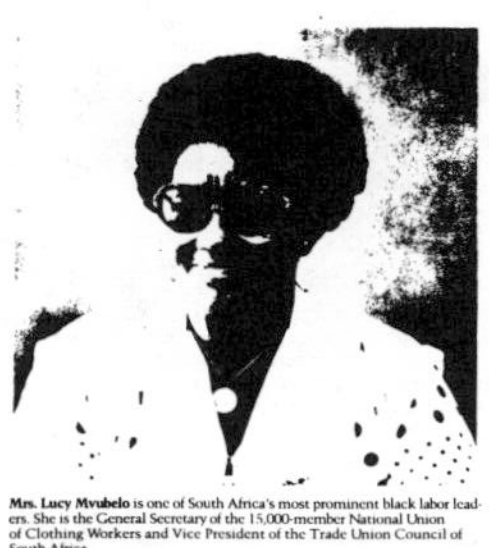

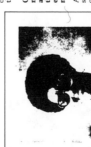

Mrs. Lucy Mvubelo is one of South Africa's most prominent black labor leaders. She is the General Secretary of the 15,000-member National Union of Clothing Workers and Vice President of the Trade Union Council of South Africa.

Born in Johannesburg in 1920, she has been active in the labor movement all of her adult life. Since 1953, she has held prominent positions in the National Union of Clothing Workers, during which time the membership has increased more than ten-fold, a significant achievement during a period of great difficulty for organized black labor. Her union is now the largest black trade union in South Africa.

Until recent changes in the law, the National Union of Clothing Workers was unregistered and, therefore, not officially recognized. Despite this fact, Mrs. Mvubelo succeeded in gaining de facto recognition for the union within the garment industry.

From 1959 to 1964, Mrs. Mvubelo was appointed to the Women's Section of the International Labor Organization to represent black women workers. She was elected to a second five year term, but was prevented from continuing in office when South African participation in the I.L.O. was terminated in 1964. She also serves on the Executive Committee of the multi-racial Women for Peace Movement. In April, Mrs. Mvubelo will receive the honorary degree of Doctor of Social Science, *honoris causa*, from Rhodes University of Grahamstown.

Lucy Mvubelo is convinced that foreign investment offers the best hope of economic progress for South African blacks, both because it increases the demand for workers and because of the influence of foreign-based companies.

After meeting with Mrs. Mvubelo, syndicated columnist William Raspberry wrote that, "Although many internationally respected black South Africans differ with her on the question of disinvestment, Lucy Mvubelo is no government stooge. Indeed, she has spent a good many years fighting her government on one front or another." Mr. Raspberry noted that, "Mrs. Mvubelo said she has risked her freedom to argue with the Minister of Planning that some of the government's policies are creating artificial unemployment among blacks in South Africa. She is willing to risk personal embarrassment to tell Americans that disinvestment would do the same thing."

The following interview was adapted, with Mrs.Mvubelo's permission, from an earlier interview that appeared in the Winter, 1980 issue of *Lincoln Review*, a publication of The Lincoln Institute for Research and Education.

Q. What about the South African "homelands" policy which has created allegedly independent new black states such as Transkei and Bophuthatswana?

A. For better or worse, the South African Government policy of creating independent black republics is or will be an accomplished fact. Nine such republics are planned, and three are already independent—Transkei, Bophuthatswana and Venda. These will soon be followed by Ciskei. Once political independence has been granted, it cannot be taken away. Can you imagine what the world's press would have to say about, for example, the invasion by South African forces of the unrecognized Republic of Transkei? Therefore, as much as we dislike and disapprove of this carving up of South Africa, we have to accept that it is an accomplished fact and cannot be changed. Thus, we are left to consider the key question of the urban blacks, those who are so closely integrated with the whites, coloreds and Asians in South Africa that they cannot be separated out and have absolutely no desire to be anything else but South African citizens.

Q. Do urban blacks consider themselves primarily to be members of particular tribes, such as the Zulu or the Tswana, or do they view themselves as South Africans who desire the equal rights of citizenship with those of other races?

A. This is an important distinction. To consider the position of the urban blacks is really to consider the situation of Soweto, the apartheid-created black city on the outskirts of Johannesburg, a city with a population of over a million black persons from every black ethnic group in South Africa as well as its neighboring countries. The inhabitants of Soweto are thus anything but a homogeneous society, yet they have much in common. Soweto is urbanized, industrialized, Christianized and totally dependent on the economic structure controlled by the white man.

Q. Are you saying that urban blacks, such as those in Soweto, have formed a new community which has replaced the previous tribal identity and loyalties which Soweto residents had when they first came to the area?

A. Yes, this is certainly now the case. The divergent groups of Soweto have been molded into a society that gives prominence not only to its politicians, but also to a variety of other people. The inhabitants of Soweto have much in common, but theirs is a dependent society. It is dependent for political rights on the white Afrikaner government and for its economic well-being on English-speaking whites.

Q. What, then, do the urban blacks of South Africa think about their future?

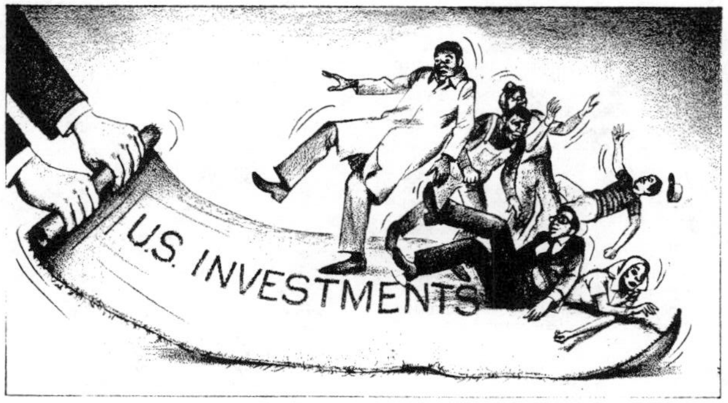

A. The urban black, whose responsibility it is to decide the future political and economic advancement of blacks in South Africa, is faced with the question of whether equality is to be achieved by evolution or revolution, or by the mythical process of the outside world boycotting South African trade and the disinvestment of foreign capital.

Q. What is your own opinion concerning these alternative courses of action?

A. In my view, revolution is totally unacceptable. It is only the far left wing or communist elements which still see revolution as an answer. For any revolution to be successful, it must have the popular support of the people—or at least the majority of the people—and it must have the support of the intellectuals of the society. The concept of communism is alien to Africa and even more so to the well-informed blacks in South Africa.

Q. Are there any circumstances under which you think that revolution would be an appropriate means for achieving black equality in South Africa?

A. Revolution as a means of gaining political power can only become a popular concept in a situation which is static and devoid of the future hope of change and the solution of problems. It requires a state of affairs in which a man can have no hopes for himself or for his children. But today's situation in South Africa is neither static nor sterile.

Q. Many opponents of apartheid in the United States, including many black Americans, have urged a boycott of South African goods as a way to improve race relations in South Africa and push that country to racial equality. What do you think of this approach?

A. Those in __our__ country who urge a boycott of South African goods and the disinvestment of Western capital are simply a small fringe of desperate revolutionaries. They realize that the basic condition from which revolution can arise does not exist, thus the world must create it. Who will suffer? Clearly the greatest hardships would fall on my people, the black people. They will be the first to lose their jobs. They will be left to die of starvation. They will be the first to be killed in a revolution.

Q. What do you see as the way to bring black South Africans into a position of equality with whites?

A. Clearly, there is only one solution, and that is by way of evolution, by negotiation, and utilization of all opportunities which arise, by cooperation when necessary and resistance when necessary.

Q. Has evolution accomplished much so far?

A. It has accomplished a great deal. Remember, in 1948, with the election of the present South African Nationalist Government, there was the beginning of a concerted effort to keep the black man in his place. His very slight voting power was destroyed. Wherever possible, he was reduced to the status of laborer. Job reservation measures excluded blacks from most trades and professions. A never-ending list of laws was passed to keep the black man down. But all of these efforts are crumbling, or have already crumbled. South Africa has a new Prime Minister and a definite new direction is being taken. Full trade union rights have been granted to blacks. Training facilities are now available. Job reservation is dead. The Group Areas Act is regarded as applying only to residential areas and neutral business areas will be created in which any businessman can operate.

Q. But aren't some of these things simply surface changes which keep the underlying inequality of the races basically unchanged?

A. To say that the changes are "cosmetic" is to misunderstand. It is not plastic surgery any more, but is much nearer to a heart transplant, for a change of heart has taken place. We have really entered a new phase: rights and privileges are being extended to blacks, to coloreds, to Asians. I am convinced that this process will continue provided that South Africa remains economically sound.

Q. You believe that a boycott or a policy of disinvestment would slow down the pace of change?

A. There is no doubt about it. Large scale unemployment, although affecting mainly the blacks, can also affect the whites, and the old story of jobs for whites will once again become a major issue. Repressive laws will again be demanded.

Q. How would South African blacks view a withdrawal by American business?

A. American culture has had a tremendous influence in South Africa, not only on whites but even more so on blacks. The black man sees in the situation of the American Negroes a comparable situation. We feel a common sympathy for Americans. It is still good business in South Africa for a label to say, "Made In U.S.A." Your withdrawal from the South African scene can only be to your own disadvantage. It will be seen as a surrender to the revolutionary philosophies of the East and a lack of faith in the very democratic capitalistic system which you represent. Remaining in South Africa and increasing your stake will be a boost to the evolutionary process which is now taking place. It will be encouragement that the freedom which is so cherished by the Americans can also be ours.

Q. Not long ago, Jesse Jackson visited South Africa and called for an end to U.S. investment in the country. Did you meet with Mr. Jackson?

A. I had an appointment with Jesse Jackson and waited for three hours but he never appeared. He didn't meet the black in the street while he was there. He met only the affluent, and the radicalized intellectuals. I called his hotel many times but was never able to get through to him. We are angry about his call for disinvestment. Before he made such a statement he should have met with black workers—those who would be affected. He called for disinvestment, then he left—he went home. Many blacks said, "Who called on him to speak for us?" Imagine him telling business to withdraw. What will happen to the people who lose their jobs? His only alternative is a war and revolution he will not have to fight.

Q. Do you think the South African government was mistaken to invite Jesse Jackson to the country?

A. No, it was good for him to come and for the government to let him. If he really looked at things he would have seen that we blacks in South Africa are often better off than those in so-called "free" black states. Letting Jackson in shows a certain liberalization on the part of the government. They now seem to be taking the view that critics in the U.S. and elsewhere should be invited in to see things for themselves. We are angry, however, when outsiders tell us that violence is the only way to achieve change. It will be my children's blood which will be shed. We don't want to destroy what we have built.

Q. Do you believe that outside observers understand the problems which South Africa faces in all of their complexity?

A. The answer is no. Too many critics are simplistic. They must consider the vastness of our problem: The blacks are divided into nine groups, with thousands more having come in from other states; our whites divided into English- and Afrikaans-speaking, and originating from every conceivable European nation; we also have in our midst considerable numbers of Indians, Pakistanis, Chinese and Malays from the Far East, and Turks, Syrians and Lebanese from the Middle East. Just as diverse as our people are, so diverse are their religious beliefs. "How to solve our racial problems?" is the foremost question of every thinking South African, and to all of us one answer has been dismissed: Violence. There are still advocates of violence. As you well know, violence has become a lucrative world-wide phenomenon. So, regrettably, we will have our own I.R.A., Bader-Meinhof or Black Panther movement. Whatever it may be, it will remain a minority, even in South Africa.

Limited copies of this message are available on request to Dresser Industries, Inc., Dresser Building, Dallas, Texas 75201

About Dresser

We offer more products and services for the petroleum, natural gas, coal and synfuel markets than any other company. Anywhere.

Our headquarters are in Dallas, Texas. We employ 53,000 people and operate in over 100 different countries around the world. In 1980 we reached our 100th birthday and $4.0 billion in sales.

To learn more about Dresser, please write for our Annual Report.

DRESSER INDUSTRIES DRESSER

Exhibit 6

Can everyone be wrong who says we are running out of oil and gas to produce in this country?

A. "YES."

Q. Mr. Halbouty, whatever happened to the energy crisis?

A. If by "crisis" you mean "shortage," I will say again—as I have said many times, *the United States has no energy shortage!* What we have had is a shortage of wisdom and environmental policies were drafted, adopted and enforced. That's why we are dependent on our energy resources, and that's why we have not developed our energy resources. Now what we have done to OPEC for about half of our petroleum energy needs. *That's* the crisis. And *that* hasn't changed.

Q. Well, can it be changed?

A. Yes, it can be changed and I'm sure it will be changed. As a start, the Executive Action taken by President Reagan in the first few days of this Administration to deregulate crude oil, gasoline and propane has shown the country and the world that the time has come to stop the over-regulation of the free market by the government. I am of the opinion that the entire energy industry will see the dawn of a new era in operations and productivity resulting from the unshackling of unnecessary regulations and controls. Changes of this kind will create the incentives to explore and find more domestic oil and gas and to develop and produce some of our other sources of energy.

Q. A lot of important people say we are running out of oil and gas to produce in this country.

A. I reject such pessimism, absolutely. The premise that we are running out of oil and gas is without merit. The pessimistic doomsayers form their opinions without regard to established geoscientific principles. We are discovering new fields every day, and will continue to do so as long as we have potentially rich areas which have not been explored or adequately explored. As an earth scientist I am extremely familiar with the geology of this country. I know it from coast to coast and from border to border, and I declare *unequivocally* that *significant* oil and gas reserves remain to be found and will be found in this land of ours.

Q. What makes you so sure?

A. Knowledge. Knowledge makes me sure. I *know* how oil and gas are formed and under what conditions, and I *know* that we have not even *begun* to explore all the places oil and gas might exist. Why, today only about 20% of the total land area of the United States is either producing oil and gas or is under lease for exploration. And less than 4% of the 528 million acres of our Continental Shelves have ever been leased for exploration. How can people say there is nothing to be found either onshore or offshore? Also, until recently, explorers have been content to go after the easy finds—the geological anomalies that are easily located and mapped by geophysical instruments. On the other hand, it has been by *accident* only that many of the *subtle* trap fields—those rich, unpredictable reservoirs such as the 7-billion-barrel East Texas field—were discovered. The subtle traps are more numerous and equally This makes further exploration all the more challenging. But they are there—waiting to be found. Also, geoscience is providing exploration-ists with views and ideas of finding oil and gas that were unthought of previously.

Q. How do you account for reports that the industry is drilling more wells and producing less?

A. The industry is not producing less gas. Look around you! We have a surplus of gas—it's running out of our ears—and the 1978 Gas Policy Act, which restricts how to use it, is plain asinine. Also, the 1978 Gas Policy Act should be abolished and gas should be deregulated.

Q. What about declining oil production? That is pretty well documented.

A. The reason we are not seeing more oil production is because too much drilling is going on in the wrong places! Most of it is in-fill drilling in proven and producing fields. Spacing patterns in existing fields have been reduced, enabling more wells to be drilled in known areas. All this will draw down our known reserves faster. What we need to have is

---

more wildcatters drilling out in the boondocks, where there is a possibility of finding *new* reserves. In the past, too many wildcatters were turned off by price controls and bureaucratic red tape, and had no incentive to explore and drill costly wildcat wells. Since President Reagan decontrolled oil last January, exploration in the so-called boondock areas has gradually increased and will continue to do so.

Q. Where is this undiscovered oil and gas likely to be?

A. Tell me where it *isn't* likely to be! Amazing progress is being made in geology, geophysics and petroleum engineering. People in these fields are employing new ideas and utilizing new concepts and equipment which permit exploration, development and production in areas and under conditions that were once considered impractical. Geoscientists are not so inclined to dismiss an area as unsuitable for petroleum production as they once were.

Q. Such as?

A. The *Western Overthrust Belt* is a good example of the changes in exploration thinking. Eight years ago, if a geologist or geophysicist had recommended that his company drill a well in that area, he would have been considered insane. Now it is one of our most prolific producing areas. Looking into the future and as another example of changes in geological thinking, the *Appalachian Overthrust Belt* was completely disregarded for years. Now it appears that sedimentary rocks necessary for oil accumulation may extend more than 100 miles farther east in the Belt than was thought originally. This *doubles* the potentially promising area for oil and gas exploration *from New York to Alabama!* Or take those areas in western New Mexico, western Colorado, western Utah, Arizona, Nevada, northern California, Idaho, Oregon and Washington. None of this vast western frontier has been explored adequately. Neither have the Outer Continental Shelves. Nor have the present producing basins been explored to their full dimensions.

Q. How about the Gulf Coastal area of the United States? Some say it has peaked out.

A. This province is one of the most densely drilled petroleum basins in the world. More than 820,000 wells have been drilled in only two of the states, Texas and Louisiana — an average of one well per square kilometer. And yet, exploration activity in this basin is greater today than it's ever been and is increasing.

Q. Are there other basins like this?

A. Yes, and it is doubtful that *any* basin or province in this country can be classified as thoroughly evaluated. Finds are

---

still being made in mature producing areas, and there are scores of untested possibilities that could yield large new quantities of petroleum in most all of them.

Q. Are you just as bullish on the amount of natural gas yet to be found in the United States?

A. The gas potential in the United States is almost beyond comprehension. It is completely safe to say we have enough undiscovered natural gas, if it is sought, to take care of our needs for at least the next century. The consensus is so that there are between 500 and 1000 *trillion* cubic feet of natural gas yet to be discovered in the United States. That is *in addition* to our proven reserves of 195 trillion cubic feet. So there is in this country enough gas, discovered or discoverable, to support economic growth for the next 35-50 years, at least, and probably longer.

Q. When you add to this the large amounts of coal we have in this country, it makes one wonder how we got into this situation of being energy dependent.

A. That's right. If you're talking about *known* energy reserves, we have 60 times more coal than oil and 40 times more coal than gas. Much of it is located on federal lands. Its the same with oil and gas. And, also, development and production of synthetics are being held back particularly because of the extremely strict controls of the Clean Air Act.

Q. How much land does the government own?

A. 775 million acres—one-third of the nation's total land area. Most of this is in states with the highest oil and gas potential. For example, the federal government owns more than 48% of Wyoming, 47% of California, 37% of Colorado, 33% of New Mexico—and 98.5% of Alaska!

Q. How much of that is open to oil and gas leasing?

A. Only about one acre out of seven. And yet that small amount provided 7% of the crude oil and 6.1% of the natural gas produced in this country last year. Imagine the increase in production if those lands were explored. Out of off-shore lands, which may contain one-fourth of the undiscovered recoverable oil and gas in the entire country, need to be leased and explored as soon as possible. Our total public lands offer an enormous oil, gas and mineral potential, but access to these resources has been denied us by excessive environmentalism and controls. *This is a major factor which increased our dependence on imports. We must* return to the common sense policy of multiple-use of federal lands. We must stop keeping public lands as instant wilderness areas without a thorough evaluation of the natural

---

resources they contain so that those resources could be developed and produced if they are needed in the future.

Q. And if we don't?

A. Then we become further dependent on foreign oil. It's not for nothing that the Russians are extremely desirous to control the Middle East. And, let me tell you something else. We are dangerously dependent on imports for minerals, such metals as chrome, cobalt, manganese, antimony, titanium, molybdenum and platinum. These minerals are *absolutely essential* to a modern industrial economy and are *indispensable* to our national security. *We have no alternative but to develop our own resources without delay.*

Q. What's the answer, then? Do we have to choose between wrecking the environment or having enough energy and minerals?

A. No, it needn't be an either-or situation. Years of experience in the United States and abroad have demonstrated industry's capability and willingness to respect and protect the environment. It is possible for us to recover fuels and minerals with out altering the environment significantly.

Q. Significantly?

A. Yes! Our devotion should be to prevent *permanent* unsettling effects on the environment. And that we can do! It is becoming standard practice not only to restore the surrounding where exploration, development and production took place, but also to enhance the environment by improving the chances for survival of existing and future animal and plant life. Industry today is more involved with protecting the environment than most of the so-called environmentalists.

Q. How would you classify the Union Oil blowout off Santa Barbara in 1972?

A. It was small and not permanently destructive. It was not even particularly damaging. The beach off Santa Barbara has returned to normal and I find normal for that area means some continuous seepage of *oil*—no, not from wells, but from the oil sands which exist in and above the ocean floor in that area. Why do you think they call this permanent point on the coast "Coal Oil Point"? Oil has been seeping from the ocean floor off Santa Barbara since time immemorial. It is characteristic of the geology of the area, and it hasn't destroyed the environment off Santa Barbara. The Union Oil blowout reason was replaced by mass hysteria inflamed by the media and over-zealous environmentalists.

Q. What about some of our other energy sources and synthetics?

A. I feel that we must continue to research and develop energy from nuclear, solar and geothermal power. Synthetic fuels also hold great promise for the future energy self-sufficiency of the country. But I strongly feel that private enterprise should be responsible for the development of these sources, *NOT* the government. Those who raise the cry for government subsidies and "handouts" should realize that whenever the government "gives" us something, it "takes" much more away.

Q. Mr. Halbouty, what do you consider the most important steps that should be taken to increase our domestic production of oil and gas?

A. I think now is the time for reappraisal and readjustment. It is time for the new Administration to regulate the regulations. We must have a common sense, realistic approach to cooperation between government and business. We must bury forever the useless and counterproductive knee-jerk antagonism between the two.

First, all punitive controls and regulations should be eliminated.

Second, we should open more offshore areas and also more of the restricted onshore areas for energy and mineral exploration.

Third, conservation should be practiced, but it should be done on a voluntary basis. Legislative mandates should be kept to a minimum.

Fourth, the free market—the free enterprise system—should be permitted to operate without federal interference, and

Fifth, and this above all, the government should get off and stay off our backs.

If these things are done, I am convinced that within five years a positive trend will be established that, if continued for another decade, will provide the nation with a most respectable energy self-sufficiency.

Q. Are you encouraged by the new attitude in Washington?

A. President Reagan's announced objectives have convinced me that America is about to enter a new era of growth and productivity. It will not be limited to energy alone, but will extend to all areas of our economy. Americans are desirous—indeed, they are *hungry*—to have this country returned to the ideals and principles upon which it was founded—freedom to trade, freedom to build, and freedom to live as happily as possible. To preserve these rights we must return to the healthy processes of a free market system.

I have observed that there is a strong positive attitude throughout the country that the new Administration will formulate a viable energy policy which will serve our country well, economically and strategically. I am personally convinced that under President Reagan's leadership, this nation can have such a policy.

DRESSER INDUSTRIES

Limited copies of this message are available on request to Dresser Industries, Inc., Dresser Building, Dallas, Texas 75201.

Dresser Industries is one of the world's leading and most diversified suppliers of technology, products, and services to industries involved in the development of energy and natural resources, including oil, gas, coal and power.

To learn more about Dresser, please write for our Annual Report.

Michel T. Halbouty is an earth scientist and engineer whose career and accomplishments in the fields of geology and petroleum engineering have earned him recognition as one of the world's outstanding geoscientists.

A graduate of Texas A&M University, he holds Bachelors and Masters degrees in both geology and petroleum engineering, a Professional Geological Engineering degree, and a Doctor of Engineering degree (HC) from Montana College of Mineral Science and Technology. Currently, he is Chairman of the Board and Chief Executive Officer of the Michel T. Halbouty Energy Co.

Over the years, he has continued to explore new techniques and new concepts of advanced oil and gas exploration, production and development. The newest of these, which he strongly supports and advocates, is the use of remote sensing from spacecraft to enhance the overall global petroleum and mineral exploration effort.

Mr. Halbouty has contributed several books and 230 scientific articles to the literature of petroleum geology and petroleum engineering. He has lectured throughout the world to scientists on the philosophy of petroleum exploration, new techniques and concepts. He is an outspoken proponent on the future of the energy economy and puts into action what he believes by offering solutions, applying his knowledge to existing problems, and offering solutions.

As Chairman of President Reagan's Energy Policy Advisory Task Force and as a Leader of his Transition Team on Energy, he has spent much of his time and expertise to help ensure the economic energy stability of our country.

(illustration caption) EVERYONE KNOWS WE ARE RUNNING OUT OF OIL AND GAS TO FIND ANYWAY!

(labels on illustration) ENVIRONMENTALISTS · OVER-REGULATION · BUREAUCRACY · DISINCENTIVES · SHORT-SIGHTED POLICIES · GAS PRICE CONTROLS · FEDERAL LAND LOCKUP · U.S. WILDCATTER

Dresser, along with many other large U.S. corporations, has been attacked by various church groups, notably the Interfaith Center on Corporate Responsibility (ICCR) of the National Council of Churches, for its investments in South Africa. ICCR also urged Dresser to agree to abide by the Sullivan Principles, advocated by Rev. Leon Sullivan, a black leader and a member of the General Motors board of directors, setting down certain requirements for U.S. companies operating in South Africa. According to Luter:

> We decided to tackle this issue because we were being harrassed. We do business in South Africa. We have not signed the Sullivan Principles. We have adopted principles of our own that are identical, but we would not sign Sullivan's because we would not commit to his requirements for semi-annual reporting and on-site inspection. We think that is a door that we should not open up as a practical matter, and also as a matter of principle, because we report, I guess, to something like 100 governmental agencies in this country alone. We report to governmental agencies in about 80 to 90 other countries that we do business in and those are mandatory requirements.
>
> If Sullivan can come along and say: "Sign up with me, and let me inspect your plants and submit these voluminous reports to me," that is unacceptable to us. Anybody can do that on any issue. We offered to become a signatory to the principle. But we said we won't agree to your inspection and reporting requirements, and we told him why. I talked personally to a member of his staff and he said: "Well, we understand your position, and we would rather you not sign the principles with those reservations. There are 130 other companies who have already signed them. They would also want to be released from those requirements, and that wouldn't be good for our movement." So we parted on a friendly basis.
>
> Subsequently, we became the subject of attention of the ICCR. At its direction, the Episcopal Church filed a shareholders' resolution and we published it in our annual report two years ago and they got a lot of publicity on it. They tried to come back this year [1981], but they were late in filing their resolution, and so we are not publishing it this year.

There was one ad in 1982 on the subject of developing U.S. mineral resources. Luter observed:

> Senator Barry Goldwater has been very vocal on that subject. He feels very strongly that we are shackling ourselves and endangering our own safety by not developing our mineral resources in areas where we depend 90 to 100% on other countries like South Africa and Russia for some of our critical mineral needs. And yet, we have these hundreds of millions of acres in "the lower 48" and Alaska that we cannot develop. We think there needs to be some change in that situation.

Targeted Audience and Media Selection

Dresser ads are addressed to the general public, which "as voters should let Washington know what they think and how they feel about important social and economic issues," says Luter. The publication is limited to the *Wall Street Journal* because of budgetary constraints. However, a consortium of companies has asked to help sponsor some of the ads in major U.S. newspapers at their own expense. Thus, in the case of the Teller ad in 1979, the reprint ran in the *Washington Post, St. Louis Dispatch, Houston Post, Chicago Tribune, Los Angeles Times, Atlanta Constitution, New York Times,* and *San Francisco Chronicle.* None of these companies identified themselves publicly—they just reprinted the ad. The Dresser logo was deleted, but not the reference to the availability of reprints, which enabled them to give Dresser credit.

Despite the large audience TV can reach, Dresser does not consider it a potential medium for future campaigns. As Luter comments: "I don't think television is as cost effective as the print medium. Television time is very expensive. If you use a 30-second spot with a message like ours, I doubt that many people would remember. When people see something like this in print, they may clip it, or it may stay with them for a longer time, and it is a lot less expensive."

The company has also used some of the ads in its in-house organs. The reprints are supplied to all of Dresser's operating units for communicating with employees and local communities.

Copy Format and Execution

Once an issue is selected, the company identifies an outstanding expert on that subject, and seeks his/her cooperation in eliciting his/her views through an interview. The material is reduced to a question-answer format that becomes the basis of the ad copy. The experts are not paid any fee for the interview; instead, the company donates a sum of money to the interviewee's favorite charity in return for allowing it to publish the interview.

The company does not use any outside advertising agency and does all the work in-house "because we think we can do a better job in our own public relations department. We have never felt the need for an ad agency, because we know what we want better than they know. We also do our own annual reports. We use an agency to do the art work for the annual report, but all the text, the format and everything else we develop ourselves."

Costs and Budgets

Dresser has no set budget for its advocacy campaign, since the cost depends on the number of issues and insertions per year. So far, expenditures have ranged between $150,000 and $250,000 per year. This amount, however, understates actual costs, because a major part of the work is done by employees of the company.

Mini-ad Campaign

In addition to the two-page spread in the *Wall Street Journal*, Dresser also runs a series of ads on a regular basis called the "Think About Series." Starting in 1980, they appear on the first Monday of every month in the *Wall Street Journal,* and are very different from the two-page spreads.

The rationale for these advertisements, according to Luter, is as follows:

> We have had a long list of subjects that we would like to make at least some comment on, but we could not afford to spend the money to run them as two-page spreads in the *Journal.* They are much easier to do. We find a quote from somebody, and all we have to do is make a phone call and get permission to use it. It is a standard format. There is no additional art work. It is a very inexpensive way to get a lot of issues before the public.

These advertisements cover a wide variety of subjects, but most of them fall within the general categories of energy resources, nuclear power, excessive regulation, and the news media. Copies of a selected number of ads from this series are presented in Exhibits 7 through 10.

EFFECTIVENESS OF THE PROGRAM

Dresser does not undertake any readership surveys on its ads. Instead, it relies primarily on unsolicited responses from readers, and requests for reprints. Based on these criteria, the campaign has been highly successful. The most successful ad was undoubtedly the Teller ad [Exhibit 1]. As of March 1980, more than 5,000 responses were recorded. Including secondary distribution via reprint rights, about 9 million people were exposed to the message of this ad. Nevertheless, it is difficult to estimate the total number of people who read the ad. As Judi Murrell, manager of shareholder communications, said:

> The actual distribution of reprints is approximately 72,000, but companies would ask for reprint rights for the ad which they would include in their billing to customers, or other kinds of controlled mailing, and they would tell us about the size of their circulation. It appeared in several newspapers. Of course, we can find out the circulation of the newspaper, but how many people read one copy? We did not even attempt to estimate that number.

The first McKetta ad [Exhibit 2] generated over 1,400 responses and 42,000 requests for reprints. Accounting for secondary distribution through reprint rights, this ad reached over 216,300 people. Another important ad in terms of public response was the ad on nuclear power [Exhibit 3, 1977], which reached over 265,000 people. The remaining ads generated more modest responses.

Exhibit 7

Is This Really Necessary?

Steel companies are already spending more than $600 million annually to meet environmental regulations. Steel is subject to about 6,000 Federal regulations of all types (affecting actual steelmaking operations) and has at least 27 Federal agencies looking over its shoulder at all times, often with overlapping regulatory domains. The paperwork burden of one steel firm in 1978 was 92,000 pages of reporting to 112 agencies of the Federal, state, and local levels.

The Regulatory Action Network: Washington Watch. Chamber of Commerce of the United States

Exhibit 8

Lord, Deliver Us

"The Lord's Prayer contains 56 words, Lincoln's Gettysburg Address 268, and the Declaration of Independence 1,322 words," notes an Arthur Andersen & Co. study of regulatory impact, commissioned in 1978 by the Business Roundtable. "But a government regulation on the sale of cabbage requires 26,911 words!" Examining the impact of just six Federal agencies, the Andersen study found they cost just 48 Roundtable companies a total of $2.6 billion in 1977—43% of what those firms spent on research and development that year and 16% of their combined net income.

– Industry Week
September 29, 1980

Exhibit 9

TV: Here's Mud In Your Eye

Make no mistake—business *does* get a bad rap on television entertainment shows. When actors appear as business men and women in TV situation comedies or adventure stories, two out of three times it is as crooks, con-artists or clowns. At least half the time, corporate executives are depicted as being involved in illegal activities. This treatment is not limited to individuals— business in general is almost never portrayed as a socially useful or economically productive activity.*

Dramatic license has its place, but at a time when we're concerned with revitalizing the economy, providing jobs and meeting foreign competition, does Hollywood's message (supported by advertising paid for by large corporations) serve the public interest?

*Based on a Media Institute study of 200 TV programs telecast during the 1979-80 season.

Leonard J. Theberge, President
The Media Institute
Washington, D.C.

Think About It.

DRESSER INDUSTRIES *DRESSER*

Exhibit 10

Look, But Don't Touch

The federal government owns 34 percent of all the on-shore land in the United States. These federal lands include many of the most promising areas for energy resource development, yet they account for only 8½ percent of U.S. energy production today from oil, gas, coal and uranium. More than 500 million acres of publicly owned land—i.e., two-thirds of on-shore federal lands (or more than one-fifth of the entire on-shore United States)— are closed to mineral exploration altogether. And the amount being withdrawn or severely regulated is still growing. Why?

P. W. J. Wood
Executive Vice President
Cities Service Company

NOTES

1. Statement of Ed R. Luter, senior vice-president for finance, Dresser Industries, Inc. Unless otherwise specifically stated, all direct quotes are from Dresser executives in personal interviews with the author.
2. Quoted in Grover Heiman, "Jack James Directs Dresser's Destiny, Texas Style," *Nation's Business,* November 1979.

Section B   *PRESENTATION OF MULTISIDED MESSAGES THROUGH AUTHORITATIVE SPOKESPERSONS IN SINGLE ADVERTISEMENTS*

Chapter 3   THE LTV CORPORATION, DALLAS:

AN ISSUE ADVERTISING CAMPAIGN EMPHASIZING DISCUSSION OF ALTERNATIVE AND OPPOSING VIEWPOINTS TO ELUCIDATE IDEAS AND ENCOURAGE PUBLIC DISCUSSION

Among the many corporations and industry groups engaged in advocacy advertising, LTV holds a unique place in that it is the only company that has dared to provide a paid communication format which presents alternative viewpoints and expert opinions—some opposed by the company, and even contrary to its immediate interests—on issues the company considers important to itself and to the national public policy. There are other companies, like Dresser Industries, Inc., of Dallas, and SmithKline Beckman of Philadelphia, that have provided paid advertising space to publicize the views of well-known and highly credible experts on major public policy issues. However, their views were generally in agreement with those of the sponsoring companies. Corporate critics and cynics have argued that LTV's choice of experts, even those opposing LTV's views, is tempered in terms of "moderate" critics who

---

Research assistant: Mohamed Allam.

are "acceptable" to LTV, and who would not argue the opposing viewpoint forcefully. However, an analysis of various advertisements shows that while the opposing viewpoint is not represented by the extreme fringe, the spokespersons are certainly well informed, and have exceptionally good credentials for their authoritative views on the subjects under discussion.

But the fact remains that this is the first campaign of its kind, in which a "multiple-viewpoint" approach has been used to discuss controversial issues of social importance. Even if one were to accept the notion of a slight bias in favor of "moderate" opponents, their stature would preclude any notion of their being spokespersons for the company.

Another important characteristic of the LTV campaign has been its policy of avoiding those issues that are being debated or voted in Congress at a given time. The company has wanted to avoid the accusation of engaging in lobbying. Instead, it has attempted to keep its campaign essentially apolitical and focused on discussing major issues of public policy.

Despite its novel approach, LTV has achieved tremendous success in establishing an identity for itself among the investing public, opinion leaders, and large segments of the public as a responsible and forward-looking company. This is particularly remarkable considering the extremely low point from which it had to come, given its problems in the conglomerate era of the late 1960s and early 1970s. The LTV campaign thus offers an excellent example of the use of idea-advocacy advertising to create a favorable corporate institutional identity.

LTV—HISTORICAL BACKGROUND

A company's communication philosophy is invariably a product of its history, traditions, and corporate ethos; of its people, and primarily its management and chief executive officer; its product mix and lines of business; and the external environment within which it must conduct its business. Nowhere do these factors appear more forcefully than in the case of LTV in shaping its current corporate philosophy and attitude toward political involvement and commitment to speaking out on public issues.

If the 1960s was the era of "go-go" conglomerates, then LTV and its founder and architect, James J. Ling, were its superstars. In 1965, the company that then bore Jim Ling's name ranked 204th on the *Fortune* list. In just four years, it had catapulted to number 14. *Fortune* referred to LTV in a major article as "Jimmy Ling's wonderful growth machine," terming it the fastest growing company in America. Under his banner, LTV simply exploded across the business horizon. The company was the subject of front-page stories in the *Wall Street Journal*, and Ling was interviewed by *Playboy* and was on a multitude of talk shows.[1]

LTV was in the thick of the merger mania of the sixties, and one of its most adroit players. For example, in 1968 alone, there were about 4,500 mergers in the United States, and 26 of the companies on *Fortune*'s 500 had disappeared from the scene. In its rise to the 14th largest manufacturing company from 204, LTV had acquired a large number of companies during the four-year period between 1965 and 1969. In the process, the company became the darling of Wall Street, and by the late summer of 1967 its stock had catapulted to $203 per share on a presplit basis.

LTV's high profile was immeasurably influenced by Ling's personality. There was just enough of an anti-Establishment aura about Mr. Ling to give him special appeal for the young people of that era. And just enough of it, also, to disturb business leaders around the country, who saw in the conglomerate movement a threat to themselves and their own enterprises.

Fall from Glory

Unfortunately, the fall from the towering heights of fame and prosperity was just as steep and precipitous as the rise. Like a house of cards, it did not take long for adverse winds to bring Ling's entire edifice tumbling down. In the latter half of the 1960s, political opposition had started to rise against the conglomerates. For LTV, the mortal blow came in 1968 when Ling directed his attention toward that most traditional of American businesses, the steel industry. In his most ambitious venture to date, he reached out and acquired Jones & Laughlin (J&L), a venerable and respected member of the steel community.

The Nixon administration came to office at this time, and pledged to "go after the conglomerates." It went after the one with the highest profile, LTV. An antitrust suit was filed, and was bitterly contested by all sides. It was ultimately settled with a consent decree under which LTV was permitted to keep J&L, but the acquisition was marred by the ensuing protracted, bitter, and costly fight. Combined with the collapse of the economy and of the stock market in 1970, the whole thing proved to be the undoing of both LTV and James Ling. By December 1970, he was forced out of the company he had created, and the stock had plummeted from a post-split $169 a share to $7\frac{1}{8}$.

The New LTV—The Consolidation Phase

The early 1970s were quite painful for LTV and were devoted primarily to a program of consolidation and rebuilding. Paul Thayer, who had headed the company's aerospace operations, was installed as chief executive. The consolidation and redirection effort continued through much of the 1970s. The old name, Ling-Temco-Vought, was dropped, but the familiar LTV symbol was retained, and the company adopted the name it has today, The LTV Corporation.

The lineup of industries in which LTV was involved was reduced from about ten to five. Eventually, the whole enterprise was combined into four components, steel, energy, aerospace, and ocean shipping. With a simplified structure, the company gradually moved away from its holding company mode and in 1978 became an operating company. Major changes were also made in management, including the arrival of Raymond A. Hay to serve as president.

At this point, LTV moved to acquire the Lykes Corporation in what was then the biggest merger in U.S. business history. Best known for its steamship business, Lykes also owned Youngstown Sheet & Tube, a steel company that, blended with Jones & Laughlin, overnight made LTV the nation's third largest steel company. Tucked away into the Lykes group was a real crown jewel named Continental Emsco, a leading supplier of products and services to the oil and gas industry, and a company with exceptional growth prospects.

The year 1978, which culminated in the merger in December, was a pivotal one for LTV. It was also a year when the stock had dropped to an all time low of $5\frac{1}{8}$. LTV entered 1979 as a basically new company, but one with many communications problems.

CEO—Paul Thayer

Paul Thayer, chairman and chief executive officer of LTV, was elected to his present position in July 1970. An ace combat pilot during World War II, he joined Chance Vought Corporation in 1948 as a test pilot, leaving it in 1950 to join Northrop Aircraft as chief of its Experimental Flight Test Program. He returned to Chance Vought in 1951, and by 1955 had become a vice-president for sales and service, and was elected to its board of directors. In 1961, Chance Vought merged into Ling-Temco-Vought, and he became a director of LTV. Four years later, when the company was reorganized, Thayer was named president of LTV Aerospace Corporation, the successor of Chance Vought.

BRIDGING THE CREDIBILITY GAP

The communication problem facing LTV was twofold: (1) LTV was still scarred by the wounds of its conglomerate days. "Conglomerate" was a bad word on Wall Street, and the professional investment community did not quite trust LTV. (2) The reconstituted LTV was regarded as the old conglomerate in new clothing, and because it was engaged in four widely different industrial activities, investment analysts found it difficult to follow.

Consequently, while LTV had entered an era of stable and predictable earnings and growth, it was not so recognized by the investment community. The company's stock prices reflected that indifference and ignorance. According to John Johnson, LTV's vice-president of advertising: "LTV was much like the woman who, after undergoing an extended period of therapy, said she felt like she was all dressed up, but had no place to go."

PRECOMMUNICATION PHASE—MARKET SURVEY

By the end of 1979, the company began looking into the ways to bridge its credibility gap. According to John Johnson:

We had not only a low profile, which meant that we were not really recognized by Wall Street, but it showed, perhaps even more dangerously, that we had a shadow residual image of the late 1960s, which meant that in those areas where we were recognized, we had a negative public image.

Our price earnings ratio was extremely low and the stock was, in our opinion, very much undervalued. We saw, looking into the future, where there would be a need to raise investment capital. At some point in time, we would also become interested again with mergers and acquisitions. So with all things considered and knowing that you cannot tell your story through the press, certainly not alone, we felt that the time had come for us to develop a well thought out, well conceived corporate advertising program.

Benchmark Individual/Institutional Survey, November–December 1979

As a first step, the company undertook an opinion survey to measure the public image of and attitude toward LTV. The survey was conducted in November–December 1979, and involved interviews with 401 individuals and institutional investors. This survey was a follow-up to a similar survey conducted in February 1979 which had led to a $500,000 traditional corporate institutional advertising campaign aimed at generating name recognition and awareness of financial strength and profit performance among the investment community. The major findings of this survey were not very encouraging and are summarized below.

Attitudes. There had been no change as yet on the key criterion of advertising effectiveness in LTV's overall reputation. In the February 1979 survey, not *one* of the 400 respondents rated LTV "the best company overall." In December, after six months of advertising, only three respondents (1 percent of the total sample) rated it "best." Among the nine competitive conglomerates evaluated, TRW was rated highest in both waves, with 30 percent in the preadvertising benchmark wave and 28 percent in the first postadvertising wave considering it the best overall.[2]

In both the February and December waves, LTV was rated poorest among nine competitive conglomerates on most of the nine image characteristics asked about.[3] The most common view of LTV was that it was a conglomerate. Eighty-five percent in the February preadvertising wave and 82 percent in the December postadvertising wave put it in that category. However, a large proportion of respondents, 63 percent in December, also thought of LTV as an aerospace company; while 55 percent called it a steel company. Relatively few saw it as a transportation company (31 percent) or food company (20 percent).

The December postadvertising wave showed no significant change on respondent's attitudes toward the issue of mergers. On a scale of 1 to 10, where 10 meant "strongly agree" and 1 meant "strongly disagree," 22 percent of the respondents were willing to agree (scale positions 8, 9, or 10) that the merger created production efficiencies. The statement that the merger produced a stronger corporation was agreed upon by 29 percent of all respondents. In the December postadvertising wave, only 16 percent agreed that the merger would create an investment opportunity.

Awareness (Selected Findings). *Conglomerates:* Recognition of selected conglomerate names was high in both the February and December advertising studies. Ninety-one percent of the respondents in the preadvertising wave and 83 percent in the postadvertising wave knew of LTV. However, the name was not one that apparently came to mind very frequently when investors thought about conglomerates. Only 8 percent in February and 7 percent in December mentioned LTV without being prompted. *Merger:* Awareness of the LTV-Lykes merger declined between February and December among both institutional and private investors (from 67 percent in February to 52 percent in December). *Advertising awareness and recall:* Twenty-three percent of the Benchmark sample said they had seen LTV advertising. The postadvertising wave in December indicated that there was a significant decline in the number of respondents (from 23 to 17 percent) who said they had seen LTV advertising. Generally, most respondents were vague about what had been in the advertising.

Commenting on the findings, Ogilvy & Mather, Inc., the advertising agency responsible for both the conventional institutional advertising campaign and the benchmark surveys, concluded:

> The first campaign had not changed the investors'—both private and institutional—view of LTV. The campaign had not had much time—six months—to make its impact felt. Further, it came at a particularly difficult time. Prior to the LTV-Lykes merger, the business press had given LTV and its future a lot of attention. Much of this coverage was negative, focused on the merger as a way to revitalize ailing companies, and on questions about whether this merger would meet its objectives.[4]

Ogilvy & Mather, however, felt that there was still good reason to believe that the current campaign should be stronger not only in terms of the spending pressure behind it, but in terms of copy as well.

DEVELOPING A NEW CAMPAIGN STRATEGY—ISSUE ADVERTISING

The survey and the subsequent soul searching made LTV's senior executives realize that they had "rather severe communications problems," and that they had to "develop a unique approach that would be different from what everyone else was doing." Johnson states:

> We had some very long and heated debates about what our approach should be. The agency initially felt that we ought to tell a very hard financial story. That is to say a very specific, rifleshot type story to the financial community about our financial progress. But we felt that we were not ready for that kind of an approach. Financial magazines and newspapers were full of institutional advertising that was loaded with bars and

charts and barrels of chest thumping. But it is the dullest kind of advertising.

Moreover, it was an absolute trap in another important sense as well. I think that once you commit yourself to bragging about financial performance, you had better be sure that you can deliver on it. However, as far as LTV was concerned, there were too many variables. I felt that we had not yet reached a point where we could predictably sustain that kind of a campaign. We were going to have our ups and downs. LTV is in some very cyclical businesses—steel, defense, even the energy business has proven to be cyclical. It has gone to hell in a handbasket in 1981–82.

We know that given all the corporate clutter with which we were competing, we'd have to do it in a highly distinctive way to avoid being simply part of the crowd. We also decided that if we were going to advertise, we would respect the intelligence of our readers.

Target Audience

The first step in the process was to decide who would be the target audience for the company's communications. Knowing it is difficult to be all things to all people, LTV decided to focus its message at the investment community, and within that context its first order of priority was to reach individual investors. This was the semi-pro who had a fair amount of discretionary income, who was interested in the company's stock, and the group to which LTV felt it had the best access.

The company was also interested in the institutional investment community, but not quite to the same degree. It wanted to tell its story to the business community; it wanted to reach opinion leaders and the managerial level of its employees. All of them were the LTV target audience.

Another important target group was the lawmakers and regulators in Washington. The company had concluded long ago that not only its fortunes, but those of the entire business community were vitally affected by laws and regulations made in Washington.

Campaign Objectives

The main objectives of the company's corporate advertising were to establish a favorable climate for merger and acquisition, to build pride among its employees, and to touch the opinion leaders. LTV, however, thought it had a particular problem to deal with, not the least of which was credibility. Because LTV had an extreme high growth record in the late 1960s which then declined sharply in the 1970s, it wanted to approach this in a very thoughtful way. Accordingly, the objective was to position the company vis-à-vis the various industries in which LTV operated—steel, energy, aerospace, defense, and ocean shipping. This was to be done through the eyes of outside experts who were looking into the decade of the 1980s.

The Decision-Making Process

The process of decision-making both as to the launch of the campaign and the choice of issues was highly informal, and confined primarily to two people, John Johnson, vice-president of advertising, and Julian Scheer, senior vice-president of public affairs, who is located in Washington, D.C.

It is also interesting to note that unlike most corporations with strong advocacy advertising campaigns, LTV's CEO, Paul Thayer, had not involved himself directly in the campaign except at the formal approval level. He is, however, kept fully informed and sometimes makes suggestions as to the choice of spokespersons to be used in the copy. However, this should not be taken as an expression of lack of interest. On the contrary, it may be a reflection of the corporate culture with which the entire senior management is involved. The corporation, by its own statements, is "committed to the political process." Paul Thayer has a strong record of involvement in national affairs and is known for his outspoken views, even when they run counter to prevailing opinion among important segments of the business community.

John Johnson describes the sequence of events that led to the 1980 campaign in this way:

> As we entered the 1980s, LTV was an $8 billion company, coming on the scene as an important factor in the business community. Once again, we were going to be active in the merger and acquisition business, but not this time as a high flyer. All of our acquisitions would have to be in related fields and make good business sense. Our image in the business community and Washington would be just as important as the image on Wall Street. We needed to achieve a relatively high profile again, but as a responsible, thoughtful company that was one of the leaders in its various industries.
>
> Julian Scheer and I started by discussing the various ways by which we can reach our target audiences efficiently, consistently, and effectively. We felt that we really needed to tell our story through the eyes of outsiders who could look at the industries in which we were in from an objective viewpoint. And then we could tell our stories against the background of what they had to say about those industries.
>
> Julian is extremely knowledgeable about the Washington scene. He had been working on the Hill for LTV for a number of years. He had a strong interest in the political process, and had been trying to establish a higher level of visibility and recognition with the Congress and regulatory agencies. Remember, that in the final analysis, in many ways LTV was seriously damaged from Washington, when the acquisition of Jones & Laughlin took place. We had become a target company, and a lot of the problems that hit our company in the 1970s evolved out of what transpired in Washington. We recognized that the political audience and political constituency were very important to us. Therefore, we needed to come forward in a non-threatening way, and as a company that was a good corporate citizen.

Johnson felt that one of the ways by which the company could project a forward image would be to somehow tie it with the major issues of the 1980s. Julian immediately bought the idea, out of which was born the campaign in which the issues were tied to the political arena through a discussion of the views of all major presidential candidates.

THE 1980 CAMPAIGN—FIRST WAVE

Working with Ogilvy & Mather Houston, LTV's ad agency, the company developed a two-segment program for 1980 aimed at probing the future of the industries in which it operates. LTV's strategy was to position itself in terms of the outlook for its industries in the new decade, and to position itself vis-à-vis those industries. Both campaigns would be united through one strategic focus: LTV would be the corporation that is "Looking Ahead." This eventually became the slogan and the new banner for the LTV issue advertising program.

As a first step, LTV decided to take advantage of the enormous public interest in the 1980 presidential primaries. Using the exceptionally high news value of the primaries, and the need for an airing of issues vital to business as a distinctive jumping off point, it provided a forum for the leading presidential candidates. This forum constituted wave 1 of LTV's 1980 corporate advertising program.

The campaign was organized around six major issues: increased productivity, inflation, energy, environmental protection, national defense, and foreign policy [Exhibits 1–4 are illustrative].

Each ad was captioned at the top with "LTV Looking Ahead." Below it was the subject of the ad, for example, "America's Foreign Policy," followed by a subheading, "The Leading Presidential Candidates Discuss the Direction It Should Take." The opening paragraphs of each ad read:

> LTV is looking at the future of U.S. business. A key to the future is who will lead this country into the next decade and how that person feels about business issues. The American Enterprise Institute for Public Policy Research polled the leading presidential candidates on issues the Institute considered vital to America. This ad presents the candidates' point of view on foreign policy [or whatever issue is presented in the ad].
>
> In this series, the LTV Corporation endorses no candidate or political position. We are providing this forum to the candidates for the benefit of LTV's employees, shareholders, and the business community.

Ten candidates were represented in the first two ads. However, as the campaign progressed, some candidates dropped out of the running, with the result that there were only seven candidates in the fifth and sixth ads of the series. The campaign at once accomplished a number of things:

1. It established LTV as a forward-looking company, interested in public issues.
2. American Enterprise Institute (AEI) was invited to sponsor the series because federal election laws prevented the company from direct

LTV. Looking Ahead

The leading presidential candidates tell what steps they would take to stimulate capital formation and increase productivity.

LTV is looking at the future of U.S. business. A key to the future is who will lead this country into the next decade and how that person feels about business issues. The American Enterprise Institute for Public Policy Research polled the leading presidential candidates on issues the Institute considered vital to America. This ad presents the candidates' views on capital formation.

In this series, the LTV Corporation endorses no candidate or political position. We're providing this forum to the candidates for the benefit of LTV's employees, shareholders and the business community.

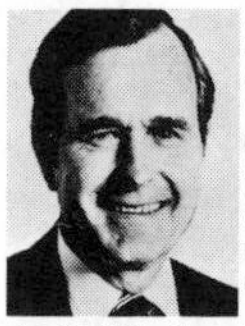

George Bush, Republican, Texas. Economists now confess that many of the old rules of their profession no longer seem to work in today's world, but there is one rule that is still irrefutable: rising productivity is the key to a rising standard of living.

In the quarter century after World War II, productivity in the U.S. rose at about 3 percent a year and Americans enjoyed the greatest surge of prosperity in our history. In the 1970's, productivity was cut in half and then in half again—and incomes went into a stall. Then in 1979, productivity actually dipped into negative figures—and income fell.

As U.S. productivity during the 70's dropped to the lowest level of all the major industrialized democracies, many of our most important industries—autos, steel, textiles, etc.—also came under enormous competitive pressure.

Clearly, one of our overriding tasks in the 80's is to restore the vigor and vitality of our economy:

- We must pursue disciplined fiscal and monetary policies to halt the inflation that is so severely inhibiting capital formation.
- We must overhaul the tax laws that now penalize savings and investment. Rules governing depreciation, expensing of research and development, and credit for job training—all must be reformed.
- And we must lift the regulation burden that is now retarding innovation and causing great waste and inefficiency.

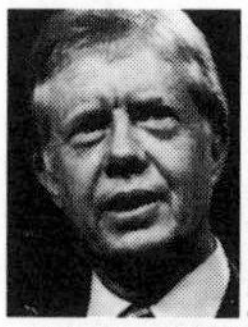

President Jimmy Carter, Democrat, Georgia. In 1978, I established the National Productivity Council. Three months ago, I announced the Administration's Industrial Innovation Initiatives, which will help boost our nation's productivity. The steps include establishment of a special center within the National Technical Information Service to improve the flow of knowledge from Federal laboratories and research and development centers, so industries can be better informed of technological opportunities.

Other steps are the strengthening of the Federal government's capacity to provide domestic industries with information on foreign research and development activities.

The Administration's program includes strengthening our patent system, clarification of anti-trust policy, and placing special emphasis on encouraging the development of small innovative firms.

My program includes strengthening our patent system, clarification of antitrust policy, and placing special emphasis on encouraging the development of small, innovative firms.

Improvements in productivity also require increased investment. The Revenue Act of 1978, approved by me, allocated a larger than normal share of the tax reductions to corporate tax reduction—including a change in the capital gains tax. My anti-inflation program helps; economic stability has a positive effect on investment. And when the economic situation allows for a tax cut in the 1980's, this Administration will look to cuts that increase productivity without stimulating inflation.

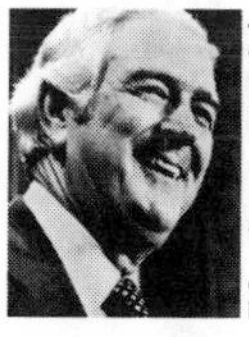

John B. Connally, Republican, Texas. For too long now, our economy has been frustrated and stagnated by Federal tax policies which encourage consumption while penalizing savings and investment.

As a result, our American productive plant has become the oldest in the industrial world. Our productivity growth lags far behind that of Japan, Germany, France, Canada and even the United Kingdom.

We're going to have to change this trend if we are to maintain a growth economy. Nothing is more critical in the change than encouragement of capital formation. And that requires a new tax philosophy.

I have advocated the stimulation of individual savings—the creation of a "taxpayer's nest egg account," of up to $10,000 with its earnings secure from Federal taxation so long as it remains invested in a bank, savings and loan or common stock. Such a plan would encourage the building of a small estate for the average wage earner and create enormous new capital for investment.

I would combine that with revision of current depreciation policies to encourage investment in new plants to achieve greater productivity. We should provide for the recovery of the cost of any building within ten years, any equipment within five years, and any rolling stock within three years.

I am convinced that these two actions would produce enormous new growth and prosperity.

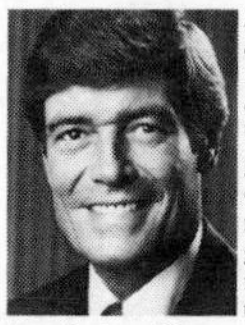

Philip M. Crane, Republican Congressman, Illinois. High taxes are crippling our economy. By taking a big slice of any economic gain, the government is reducing the incentive and resources for continual growth. We desperately need a permanent, across-the-board bracket reduction of at least 30 percent to restore the reward for working, saving, producing, investing, and growing, as my good friend and colleague, Jack Kemp, has proposed.

This is, however, only a beginning. Savings in this nation are the lowest in any major industrial nation: only 3.3 percent of disposable income in 1979. With the government borrowing to cover its deficits and discouraging private savings with inflation and taxes, the lending institutions have a limited supply of money on hand. Its price has to be high. Eliminating all taxation on savings would help to restore the encouragement to save.

To raise a paltry $6 billion (less than 1 percent of what it spends), the government also imposes inheritance taxes. This is, by definition, a tax on widows and orphans. Although designed to break up concentrations of wealth, these taxes only seem to break up small businesses and farms which may be about to prosper despite enormous tax burdens when their owner commits his last dignified taxable act: he dies. Estate and gift taxes should be entirely eliminated.

In addition, we must increase the investment tax credit to 15 percent, accelerate depreciation allowances on capital investments, abolish double taxation of dividends, and index the tax code. Until we restore the reward for capital formation, businesses will not have the resources to expand and hire new employees. With the tax changes I have suggested, America can become again the world's most productive nation.

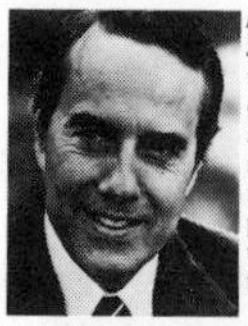

Robert Dole, Republican Senator, Kansas. A country with a tax system that encourages consumption and discourages investment, savings, and capital formation is engaged in a policy that will eventually threaten the essence of its freedom.

Unfortunately, the United States has for too long been on such a course. Among major industrialized nations, our country ranks last in savings as a percent of income, last in fixed investment as a percent of GNP and last in productivity growth. Is it any wonder that we have uncovered the secret of prolonged high levels of inflation even during times of low economic growth?

The only solution to this problem is also no secret. We must radically restructure our tax system. Some small but important steps have been taken in recent months. Congress reduced the capital gains tax rates last year and this past December the Senate added a savings interest and dividend exclusion amendment to the energy tax bill.

Much more remains to be done. We must reduce the regular rates on all sources of individual and corporate income as well as further reduce the capital gains rate. Outdated historical cost depreciation methods must be replaced with a simpler, more accelerated method. The double taxation of corporate profits and dividends must be reduced. And special tax credits for research and development must be enacted.

Our current dilemma cannot be reversed overnight, but the prescription is clear and the first major steps are long overdue.

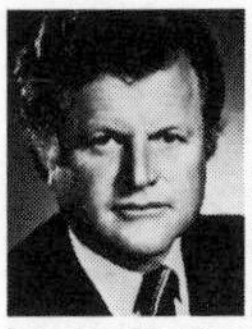

Edward M. Kennedy, Democratic Senator, Massachusetts. A top priority on our economic agenda must be a major new national commitment to the twin goals of productivity and innovation. That means new incentives for savings and investment, for entrepreneurs and business firms. I see five major initiatives that can be used to reach these goals.

- First, we must provide additional incentives to encourage capital formation and to enable industries to bring their plants and equipment into the modern world. It is time to revise the tax treatment of depreciation to insure that it is better designed to meet the four important goals of capital formation, efficiency, equity and simplicity.
- Second, we must devise targeted incentives to stimulate ventures that hold the promise of substantial innovation.
- Third, we must revamp the antiquated patent system, so that competitive forces can play a greater role in generating innovation in the economy.
- Fourth, we must provide small business firms with new incentives to stimulate innovation. In recent decades, small business has accounted for nearly half of all major U.S. innovation.
- Fifth, we must revitalize the foundation for new technology by strengthening the nation's basic and applied research and by bolstering education and career development for scientists and engineers.

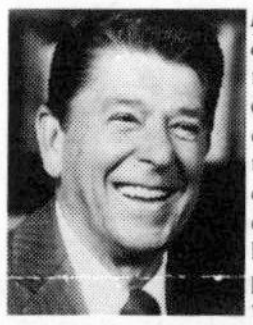

Ronald Reagan, Republican, California. We're right in worrying about declining American productivity. Higher productivity means we can produce more with the same effort. It takes people who have better ideas. It takes people with savings to invest in those ideas. And it takes motivated workers to implement them.

You can't increase productivity by making people at every level work harder for less pay. They need better tools and rewards equal to their effort.

By blaming Americans themselves for being less productive, the government is again ignoring the effect of its own policies. The Federal income tax is a tax on all individual productivity—on labor, on savings and investment, on enterprise. These tax rates climp steeply with income. But what's worse, they are not adjusted for inflation. Every time inflation raises your income, but not your buying power, you are still pushed into a higher tax bracket. Over the past decade, this combination of inflation and steep tax rates has reduced the rewards for higher productivity, and individual productivity has suffered.

When government takes more of one person's income the larger it is, and gives it to someone else for having a smaller income, each person suddenly has more to lose by earning more. The government has effectively raised the tax on the effort of both.

Americans have not become too lazy to work, or complacent with their accomplishments. We are being punished for working, for saving, for investing, for growing, by a thoughtless government which is quickly becoming the major partner in their families' income.

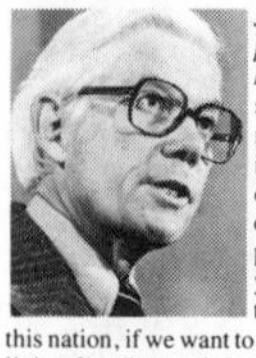

John B. Anderson, Republican Congressman, Illinois. Properly understood, capital formation is not a "business" concern, it is a very "human" concern. If we want an economy that is capable of producing 3 million jobs a year, if we want to reduce the incidence of poverty in this nation, if we want to provide a rising standard of living for all Americans, then we will have to promote greater capital formation. The capital formation issue must be treated in a broad, comprehensive fashion. First, we must boost the availability of capital by encouraging Americans at all levels to boost their savings and investment. I have suggested, for instance, that we ought to move gradually towards a $750 ($1500 for married couples filing jointly) savings and dividend income exclusion. We must also take another look at the taxation of capital gains; the recent surge in inflation has largely neutralized the capital investment incentives contained in the 1978 law. Second, we must liberalize and simplify the existing tax depreciation allowances for capital assets. I favor the adoption of the 10-5-3 approach contained in the proposed Capital Cost Recovery Act. Finally, we must recognize the role that technology and R&D play in promoting capital expansion by boosting our R&D effort through tax incentives and the removal of regulatory impediments.

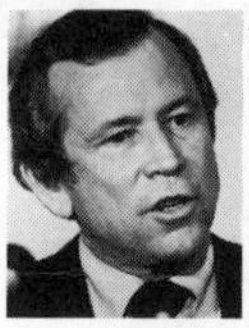

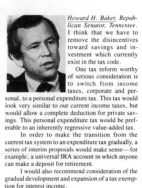

Howard H. Baker, Republican Senator, Tennessee. I think that we have to remove the disincentives toward savings and investment which currently exist in the tax code.

One tax reform worthy of serious consideration is to switch from income taxes, corporate and personal, to a personal expenditure tax. This tax would look very similar to our current income taxes, but would allow a complete deduction for private savings. This personal expenditure tax would be preferable to an inherently regressive value-added tax.

In order to make the transition from the current tax system to an expenditure tax gradually, a series of interim proposals would make sense—for example, a universal IRA account in which anyone can make a deposit for retirement.

I would also recommend consideration of the gradual development and expansion of a tax exemption for interest income.

We must eliminate the false notion that because a market may not work perfectly in some situations, that automatically means the government will do better. A less than perfect free market may well be better than a less than perfect government regulatory system.

An increased rate of government investment, and research and development expenditures, is long overdue. The share of government spending in these areas has fallen markedly in the last 15 years. We need to expand both government and private investment, and government and private R&D expenditures in order to expand technology and increase and modernize our capital stock. If we do not do so, we will not be able to compete effectively on world markets.

In my view, these changes and others would provide an enormous stimulation to capital formation and promote the long-term growth and increased productivity which is the core of our national strength.

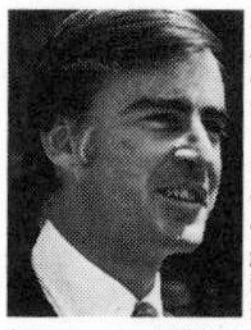

Edmund G. Brown Jr., Democratic Governor, California. We cannot continue to perpetuate the myths of the 50's and 60's by inflating our economy with deficit spending. Instead of more government programs, we must encourage investment — through tax incentives and selective assistance—to rebuild this nation's industrial base and stimulate new technology. We must shift the ethic, the attitude of this country from borrowing and consuming to saving and investing. In my campaign I have called for a reindustrialization of our society, a move away from planned obsolescence and waste to greater efficiency, conservation and stewardship. Our country has both the people and the resources. We must mobilize them by retooling, rebuilding and reequipping this nation so that we can compete during the 1980's. I am confident that our leadership in agriculture, in electronics, in aerospace and a host of other industries can be enhanced and can form the basis for a renewed long-term productivity. But we have to wake up this country. We have to wake up to the fact that we are facing the turn in the road. The complacency, the smug games that are being played in Washington are not going to make it in the 1980's.

More from the candidates

The candidates were asked to speak out on other subjects including the environment, government regulation, inflation, and energy. We will present their statements on the issue of the environment in the next ad in this series.

If you would like a copy of the candidates' views on all subjects, send for our free booklet, "The Candidates 1980." Requests on your letterhead should be mailed to: Candidates, The LTV Corporation, P.O. Box 225003, Dallas, Texas 75265, or call (214) 746-7734.

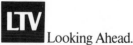

LTV Looking Ahead.

The LTV Corporation, Dallas, Texas

Steel: Jones & Laughlin Steel, Youngstown Sheet and Tube • Energy Products and Services: Continental Emsco Company • Aerospace/Defense: Vought Corporation, Kentron International • Food: Wilson Foods Corporation • Transportation: Lykes Bros. Steamship

The American Enterprise Institute for Public Policy Research is a nonpartisan, nonprofit, research and educational organization. This material is part of ongoing AEI research, partially funded by an LTV grant.

The leading presidential candidates discuss America's number one domestic problem: inflation.

LTV is looking at the future of U.S. business. A key to the future is who will lead this country into the next decade and how that person fee!s about business issues. The American Enterprise Institute for Public Policy Research polled the leading presidential candidates on issues the Institute considered vital to America. This ad presents the candidates' views on inflation.

In this series, the LTV Corporation endorses no candidate or political position. We're providing this forum to the candidates for the benefit of LTV's employees, shareholders and the business community.

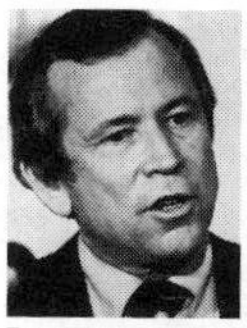

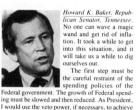

Howard K. Baker, Republican Senator, Tennessee. No one can wave a magic wand and get rid of inflation. It took a while to get into this situation, and it will take us a while to dig ourselves out.

The first step must be the careful restraint of the spending policies of the Federal government. The growth of Federal spending must be slowed and then reduced. As President, I would use the veto power, if necessary, to achieve this goal.

We must provide real incentives for savings and investment, thereby making resources available for the improvement of economic productivity. A greater rate of investment in energy research and technology will also assist in solving the energy crisis which is playing havoc with our economic system.

A Baker Administration would devise a comprehensive plan to dismantle regulations that impede competition and drive up costs and prices.

We must eliminate the counter-productive impact of the threat of wage and price controls. The prospect of such action invites people to hedge against it, either in setting prices, or negotiating long-term contracts for material, equipment or labor. Controls and the threat thereof only exacerbate the market distortion which is at the core of our economic problems.

We must restrict the growth of the monetary supply until the inflation rate has been substantially reduced. The inadequate fiscal policies of the Carter Administration have caused the Federal Reserve to monetize the debt with record high interest.

It is imperative that we formulate a schedule of tax cuts for various segments of the economy over the next four years. We must announce that schedule in advance and stick to it, thereby allowing the American wage-earner and business executive to make spending, savings and investment decisions with a degree of certainty.

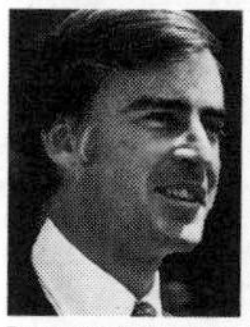

Edmund G. Brown Jr., Democratic Governor, California. I am convinced that the direction of the country must change. Productivity rates are declining, the dollar is weaker, inflation is almost beyond control and the situation abroad is becoming increasingly unstable. But instead of seeking to rebuild our strength, the leadership in Washington continues to offer more government programs, more budget deficits, more basic weakness. Simply by continuing to print more money, the Carter Administration and Congress can, in effect, kid the American people that hard choices don't have to be made. Therefore, I would support the balanced budget amendment that is now pending before the Senate Judiciary Committee. I would place a freeze on Federal employment and would allow no new programs to be added to the budget until other programs are trimmed. In the long run, I want to control inflation by shifting this country from an era of excess consumption, fueled by public and private debt, to an era of investment in our environmental, technological and human assets.

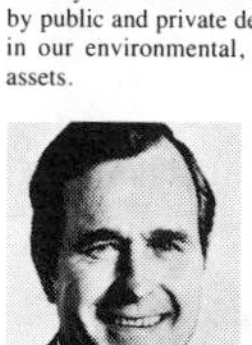

George Bush, Republican, Texas. Three years of Carternomics have been devastating for America. Inflation last year was three times what it was when this Administration was elected—and, in fact, hit the highest level in more than 30 years. Purchasing power last year declined by 5.3%; interest rates and home prices hit record highs, and savings rates hit record lows.

Tragically, this Administration seems paralyzed in the face of adversity. Its new economic forecast calls for yet another year of double-digit inflation, and its new budget calls for yet another massive increase in taxes.

The Carter Administration falsely proclaims that all of our problems are rooted in OPEC price increases; they are *not*. Weak leadership, in Washington, is at the heart of our problem.

It is time to abandon the counsel of despair that we hear from the White House and to find a new counsel of hope. If we act wisely—on energy and on inflation—we have it within our power to conquer both problems together and emerge as a great and resilient people once again.

We can and we will bring inflation under control if we adopt a coordinated program to:

—Balance the Federal budget by controlling spending and limiting the growth of goverment;

—Revitalize the economy through supply-side tax cuts to generate jobs, encourage savings, investment, and energy efficiency;

—Reduce the crushing tax burden for American taxpayers, and

—Prune the thicket of conflicting and redundant regulations and laws that stifle creativity, economic growth and productive investment.

The fundamental economic facts are simple. It is time for the government to face up to them. I am committed to ensuring that we do so.

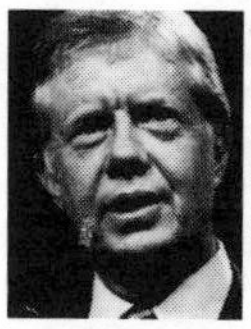

President Jimmy Carter, Democrat, Georgia. This inflation took 15 years to build up; it cannot be eliminated overnight. The Administration's anti-inflation program was designed to cope with the very special inflation factors confronting our nation. So far, double-digit price increases have been heavily concentrated in the areas of energy and housing. In the short-term, the goal of anti-inflation policy must be to "quarantine" these increases and prevent them from spilling over into the basic wage-price structure of our economy. This calls for public restraint — in the form of a tight budget and restrained monetary policy—and private restraint.

This program has been successful in the face of very difficult circumstances. Increases in 1979 compensation did not increase any faster than in 1978—despite very high energy inflation. I have submitted a tight budget for Fiscal Year 1981. Continued cooperation with wage and price guidelines is essential.

Over the longer term I believe this nation must address the structural problems that create and drive inflation. This means increasing productivity and freeing resources for private use—which I have begun by submitting a tight budget for Fiscal 1981; this means reducing the burden of excess regulation — which I have done with my regulatory reform program. It also means reducing our vulnerability to outside shocks. The Administration's grain reserve program protects the U.S. economy from sudden price increases caused by a worldwide crop failure. And, most importantly, my energy program is designed to loosen the hold OPEC has on our economy.

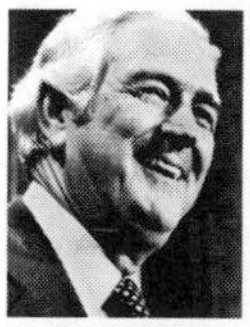

John B. Connally, Republican, Texas. There is no great mystery about inflation. When you print more money without producing more goods and services, you're going to have it.

One of the greatest contributors to inflation is excessive Federal government spending. Another is the cost of imported energy. During the past decade, deficit spending has totalled a staggering $325 billion. In 1979 alone, the Federal goverment spent $30 billion more than it took in.

My first act as President would be an all-out effort to restrain Federal spending and balance the budget. I believe this could be done within two years without reducing any essential programs. At the same time, I would begin a crash program to achieve energy self-sufficiency.

I would also take aggressive steps to reduce or eliminate our foreign trade deficit, another major contributor to inflation and our eroding dollar.

Finally, I would place far more emphasis on incentives for savings and investment to modernize our nation's aging industrial base. Only if we have such modernization of our plants and equipment can we hope to compete with our more efficient competitors in world markets and achieve the increased productivity that is the ultimate answer to inflation.

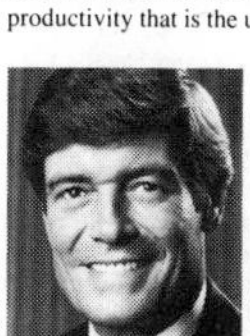

Philip M. Crane, Republican Congressman, Illinois. Before discussing inflation remedies, it is essential to define our terms. Inflation is an expansion of the money supply in excess of productivity increases. Neither business nor labor causes inflation, though they are often blamed by those who advocate restricting their wages and prices. The Federal government causes inflation. The Federal Reserve System resorts to money expansion to finance the monstrous deficits created by Congress. This practice is called "monetization" of debt in Washington. In the rest of the country it is called counterfeiting, and it has the same effect. It makes the money worth less; that results in higher prices; that causes labor to seek higher wages; and that compounds the price spiral problem. Business and labor, however, are not causing the problem; they are only responding to the goverment-created problem.

To solve the problem, we must amend the Constitution to restrain Federal spending. My proposal, introduced in Congress long before the concept took root nationwide, would forbid any Federal spending in excess of thirty-three and one-third percent of the average national income. The Federal budget has grown 400% over the last 15 years. Unless we place a constitutional check on the growth of government spending, it will continue to inflate the currency and injure pensioners, wage-earners and savers.

Studies indicate that such an amendment linking growth in Federal spending to growth in personal and national income would produce budget surpluses in two years. Any surpluses should be rebated in tax cuts and used to retire the national debt.

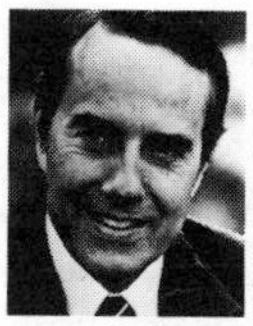

Robert Dole, Republican Senator, Kansas. There is no simple solution to the serious inflation problem that this country is facing. Years of reckless spending, an often incorrect monetary policy, increasing unproductive expenditures on Federal regulation and a lack of a responsible energy policy have created this economic problem.

There are, however, several specific steps that will both slow inflation to tolerable levels and that will prevent its recurrence in our society.

First, fiscal policy—the government's taxing and spending policy — must be basically altered. Excessive government spending contributes fundamentally to inflation by pumping more money into the economy without correspondingly increasing production. We must cut spending now and pass a constitutional amendment that limits spending and taxing and requires a balanced Federal budget.

Secondly, tax policy in this country has tended more and more in recent years to discourage needed capital formation and to encourage consumption. A healthy private sector requires a large capital stock to increase its productivity and its international competitiveness. Tax policy must be radically restructured to this end.

The nation's monetary policy—essentially the control of the economy's supply of money and credit —is also an important element in fighting inflation. By cutting budget deficits, the Congress can decrease the pressure on the Federal Reserve Board to expand the money supply. Further, through their oversight functions, the President and the Congress can encourage sound monetary policy.

Thirdly, the Congress should act to eliminate much of the current, unnecessary Federal regulations. The country must be made aware of the huge costs which the economy pays for this activity and every Federal regulation should be reviewed to determine if it is worth its cost. Those which do not measure up, must be eliminated.

Numerous other important steps must also be taken. For example, this country must develop a rational energy policy. We cannot continue to ship billions of dollars overseas to purchase oil while discouraging domestic energy production.

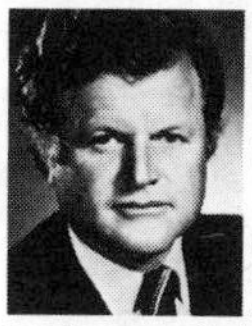

Edward M. Kennedy, Democratic Senator, Massachusetts. The Carter Administration has failed utterly to control inflation, with last year's rate of 13.2% the worst since 1946. Its short-run anti-inflationary efforts have been inadequate and unfair, and its long-run answers have been non-existent. The underlying structural economic problems must be addressed, beginning immediately.

First, I would urge carefully targeted tax incentives and patent reform to encourage innovation and retooling of our industries in order to promote greater productivity.

Second, I would encourage competition by removing burdensome regulation where competition would thereby be enhanced and by focusing anti-trust enforcement on the largest concentrated sectors of the economy.

Third, I would make American firms more competitive abroad by unifying America's governmental policies and offices relating to trade and by improving the financial and technical assistance terms American firms can offer when they seek to sell abroad.

Finally, I would undertake a comprehensive energy policy aimed at reducing our dependence on foreign oil through direct conservation investments in industry, business and residences, supporting coal production and utility conversion to coal, and developing appropriate other alternative forms.

The above steps are aimed at the long-term underlying problems. In the short-term, to break the back of the inflation psychology, I have proposed a 6-month freeze of wages, prices, interests, rent and profit followed by fair mandatory controls for a limited additional period. Similarly, to reduce our dependence on OPEC I have proposed short-term gasoline rationing to reduce imports over three years in an amount equal to the 1.7 million barrels per day we now import from the Persian Gulf. These latter actions are the unpleasant last resorts forced on us by the mismanagement of economic and energy policies by the Carter Administration, which has now become irretrievable.

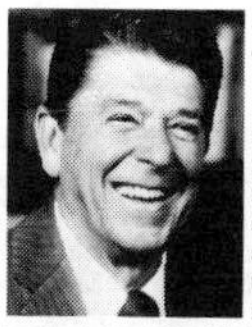

Ronald Reagan, Republican, California. I'll attack inflation sensibly.

First, I will tell our monetary authorities that they have only one job—to restore and maintain a sound dollar at home and abroad. Deficits may tempt the government to print new dollars, instead of paying back its debt with honest money. We must remove that temptation by balancing the budget, but we do not have to succumb to it in the meantime.

Second, I will ask Congress to act immediately in beginning the necessary reform of our tax system. In 1979, personal income increased 12 percent but taxes rose at a faster rate, up 15.8 percent. Mr. Carter's new budget projects total tax receipts to be 21.6 percent of GNP in 1981 and 24.2 percent of GNP in 1985, an all-time historic high for peacetime or wartime.

We need to restore the rewards for working and saving by cutting income tax rates and adjusting them automatically for inflation. My goal will be to cut the tax rates of all Americans by approximately 30 percent during my first term in office.

Third, I will attack excessive Federal spending. The U.S. General Accounting Office says that up to $50 billion, or one-tenth, of the Federal budget is simply wasted, every year.

Finally, I believe we need to accept the fact that Federal over-regulation of the economy has exceeded the bounds of sensibility. Where costs exceed benefits, the regulators must desist.

Inflation is not caused by people or businesses. And you don't cure inflation by removing the nation's incentive to grow strong once again.

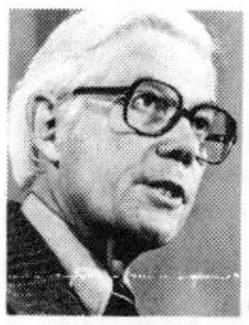

John B. Anderson, Republican Congressman, Illinois. Any program to deal with inflation necessarily involves an element of sacrifice. The unwillingness of the public and their elected representatives to make those sacrifices explains, no doubt, the failure of our recent endeavors. Sacrifice, in the form of fiscal restraint, must be the focal point of any anti-inflationary strategy. Continued reliance upon a monetary tourniquet to stem the hemorrhage of deficit spending invites recession and unduly penalizes small businessmen and other segments of our society. It must be understood, however, that fiscal restraint involves public sacrifice. Achieving a balanced budget will require us to forswear major new spending initiatives like national health insurance or the questionable MX missile system. It will require us to trim our more wasteful spending programs, particularly some of the categorical grant-in-aid programs like the Law Enforcement Assistance Administration. More importantly, it will require us to defer a general tax cut. A balanced budget, however, is not a cure-all. We must also boost our productivity by increasing savings and investment through selective tax cuts and boosting our R&D effort. Finally, we must come to grips with our ever more costly dependence on foreign oil. Here too, an element of sacrifice is required. In the short-term we must rely upon our most cost-effective energy option: conservation, or in more appropriate terms, enhancing our energy productivity.

More from the candidates

The candidates were asked to speak out on other subjects, including energy, capital formation, and the environment. We will present their statements on the issue of energy in the next ad in this series.

If you would like a copy of the candidates' views on all subjects, send for our free booklet, "The Candidates 1980." Requests on your letterhead should be mailed to: Candidates, The LTV Corporation, P.O. Box 225003, Dallas, Texas 75265. For details, please call (214) 746-7734.

LTV Looking Ahead.

The LTV Corporation, Dallas, Texas.

Jones & Laughlin Steel • Youngstown Sheet and Tube • Kentron International • Lykes Bros. Steamship • Continental Emsco Company • Vought Corporation • Wilson Foods Corporation.

The American Enterprise Institute for Public Policy Research is a nonpartisan, nonprofit, research and educational organization. This material is part of ongoing AEI research, partially funded by an LTV grant. Printed by permission.

Exhibit 3

LTV. Looking Ahead

America's foreign policy: the leading presidential candidates discuss the direction it should take

LTV is looking at the future of U.S. business. A key to the future is who will lead this country into the next decade and how that person feels about business issues. The American Enterprise Institute for Public Policy Research polled the leading presidential candidates on issues the Institute considered vital to America. This ad presents the candidates' views on foreign policy.

In this series, The LTV Corporation endorses no candidate or political position. We're providing this forum to the candidates for the benefit of LTV's employees, shareholders and the business community.

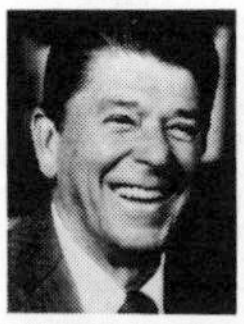

Ronald Reagan, Republican, California. In my view, the United States must first decide upon its priorities for the 1980's and then move swiftly to formulate and implement realistic policies to achieve those priorities. Central to this task must be a long-range strategy designed to protect American interests and create conditions of stability in our economy and in the world in which global economic order can expand.

If a single word could be used to describe the 1970's, "disappointment" might be an appropriate one. Not only did we fall short of achieving a durable peace based on solid accomplishments, but we actually retreated from the world, often as though we should be ashamed of ourselves for past misdeeds.

I do not think that we can enter the decade of the 1980's with an outlook of gloom or despair; rather, the "image" we present to the world must faithfully reflect the reality of America, its values and its goals.

Because so many in the world look up to our country as a living example of freedom in action, and while I believe we must live up to those expectations whenever possible, the challenge of the 1980's demands that we once again pursue our national interest with the resources at our disposal. Without behaving in a narrow, nationalistic way, we must put American interests first.

This means rebuilding our dissipated strength, and the best and only way to do this is by releasing the vitality of our great country from the artificial restraints of massive governmental regulation. Remove those restraints, restore individual initiative and provide the conditions for rapid, dynamic growth in all sectors of our lives: those are the essential preconditions for pursuing an active role in the world and for defending our vital interests.

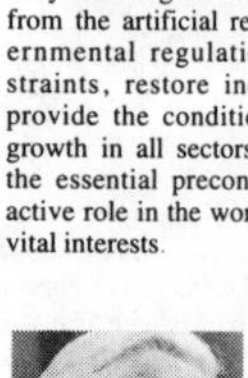

John B. Anderson, Republican Congressman, Illinois. The United States should stand for peace, improvement in the standard of living for all people, and the pursuit of human rights for all peoples. While we should not shrink from military competition with the Soviet Union, our primary instruments to achieve our goals should be diplomatic, economic, political, and technological. We should rekindle the creative and innovative minds of our scientists and engineers who can tap the resources of space, earth, our oceans, and the human mind to provide services, technologies and products to improve the quality of life for all. We should use the international airwaves to proclaim the benefits of our free enterprise system. We should use our capacity to feed the hungry and the poor to cement relations with the developing nations of the world. And if necessary, we should demonstrate our will to use force to defend critical American interests abroad.

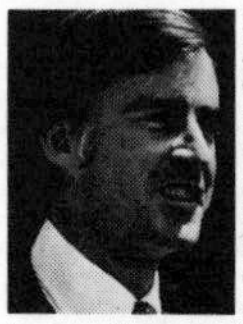

Edmund G. Brown Jr., Democratic Governor, California. The world has changed profoundly during the last 25 years as 100 new countries have come into the family of nations. Many of them have become strong and productive. As a result, we should no longer try to maintain the role of policeman of the free world. We need as part of our foreign policy a recognition that the time has come to demand of our allies and of other nations that they assume greater responsibility for their own defense and vital interests. A President has to understand this new role and explain it to the American people. We should look on this new approach as a constructive development and encourage regional groupings of nations to act for their common defense, allowing America to provide its greater strength and technology and military capacity in a partnership fashion. Whatever actions we take, they should be guided by our fundamental commitment to freedom and self-determination.

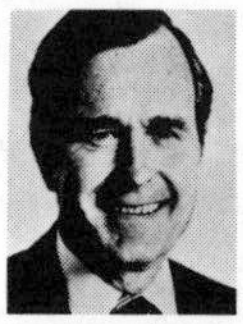

George Bush, Republican, Texas. When I worked in China as U.S. representative there, one of the first things I learned was that, in writing the word "crisis," the Chinese join together two other symbols — one standing for "danger," the other for "opportunity."

That is very much the way I see the world today. We are now on the threshold of a dangerous decade for America. Our strategic forces are more vulnerable than at any time in our history, our nation is extraordinarily dependent on OPEC oil, our alliances are frayed, and the Soviets are on the march.

Clearly, this is a time of peril. But with courage and creativity, it can also be a time of opportunity for America:

- We can seize this opportunity to finally repair our military forces by reversing the do-nothing policies that have characterized the Carter Administration for so long.
- We can seize this opportunity to free ourselves from foreign oil by removing governmental controls over our own producers and stepping up our conservation efforts.
- And we can seize this opportunity to rebuild our relationships with others by forging a new set of partnerships based upon shared interests in defense, energy and economic matters. Instead of beating old friends over the head because we disagree with their internal policies, we should work with them to advance mutual goals — and in the process, we will serve the cause of human freedom everywhere.

Carterism has failed because it has neither had a coherent sense of what it wants nor the discipline to stick to what it says.

By adopting a new course — a course that we follow steadily and consistently — I am convinced that we can ease the Russian bear back in his cage and create once again a more peaceful world.

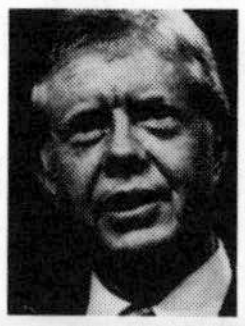

President Jimmy Carter, Democrat, Georgia. This Administration is determined that the United States remain the strongest of all nations — economically, morally, ethically and militarily. This continued strength is necessary if the United States is to be a beacon for other nations to follow.

In my State of the Union address, I outlined several steps the United States will take so that American ideals and interests prevail. I said: "We can thrive in a world of change if we remain true to our values and actively engaged in promoting world peace."

The paths taken by the United States in the next decade will include continuing to work for peace in the Middle East and Southern Africa, working with our allies to protect our vital interests in the Persian Gulf, continuing to build our ties with developing nations and respecting and helping to strengthen their national independence, and continuing our commitment to support the growth of democracy and the protection of human rights.

I have pointed out that "We must face the world as it is," and this includes the continued competition with the Soviet Union. The Soviet invasion of Afghanistan, for example, is a key example of the need to maintain our readiness.

Regarding what I expect will be a decade of rapid change, I said: "But America need have no fear. We can thrive in a world of change if we remain true to our values and actively engaged in promoting world peace."

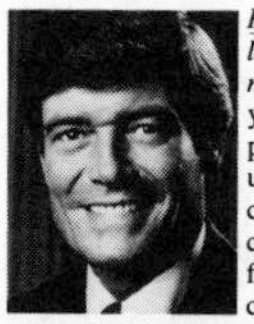

Philip M. Crane, Republican Congressman, Illinois. For the past four years American foreign policy has been a failure, a disgrace. American prestige, American credibility, American influence have declined continuously and precipitously. Since President Carter assumed office we have failed to offer strong and effective response to the Soviet-armed Cuban Afrika Korps adventures in Angola and Ethiopia. We abandoned longtime friends and allies in Iran and Nicaragua while allowing admittedly destabilizing forces to prevail. We were irresolute in the face of the introduction of Soviet combat troops, advanced nuclear-capable fighter-bombers and improved submarine servicing facilities in Cuba. Is it any wonder that our friends perceive us as weak, that they doubt our willingness to confront a Soviet challenge, whether direct or through surrogates, wherever it may occur? We cannot expect other pro-Western, free nations to support our ideals and consider them precious if we are unwilling to stand up for them. We cannot foster and champion the spread of basic human freedoms and counter Soviet aggression if we sit idly by and watch Americans taken hostage and sovereign nations overrun by Soviet tanks.

The time has come for us to act. We must develop a cohesive, comprehensive foreign policy and pursue it actively. We must spend whatever is necessary to regain military superiority. We must assure our friends and allies that we are willing to stand firmly behind our principles.

We must reestablish a reputation for standing behind our commitments and friends. Our idealistic support for human rights is the foundation of our foreign policy, but that commitment must be tempered with the realistic awareness that the world is as it is, not as it ought to be, and that we cannot make it over in our own image. We should be mindful of Ben Franklin's admonition — "A good example is the best sermon."

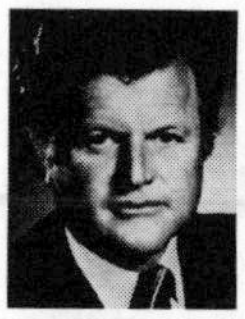

Edward M. Kennedy, Democratic Senator, Massachusetts. America's situation internationally has lurched from crisis to crisis under the Carter Administration. U.S. prestige has dropped around the world. Our allies have lost confidence in us and our adversaries have lost respect.

I believe the primary obligation of the President is to reassert our strength in a credible fashion, reassure our allies, and reclaim our standard as the defenders of freedom.

A strong defense is the cornerstone of foreign policy, and I support military spending and strengthened intelligence capabilities necessary to assure the national security of the United States. I am in favor of both effective, verifiable arms control agreements and critically important weapons systems.

With regard to the Soviet Union, I prefer predictable, firm, and credible policies that insure unacceptable costs for aggression. But, let us not foreclose every opening to the Soviet Union. Afghanistan is not the first abuse of Soviet power, nor will it be the last, and it must not become the end of the world. Ten months after the Cuban Missile Crisis—a far greater threat to American security than Afghanistan—the U.S. Senate ratified the nuclear test ban treaty by an overwhelming vote.

The task of statesmanship is to convince the Russians that there is a reason for fear, but also reason for hope, in their relations with the United States.

More from the candidates

The candidates were asked to speak out on other subjects including government regulation, inflation, capital formation, increased productivity, defense, energy, and the environment.

If you would like a copy of the candidates' views on all subjects, send for our free booklet, "The Candidates 1980." Requests on your letterhead should be mailed to: Candidates, The LTV Corporation, P.O. Box 225003, Dallas, Texas 75265, or call (214) 746-7734.

For another look at the vital issues facing the country, watch a new ten-part series, "Ben Wattenburg's 1980," on Public Television beginning May 18. Check local listings for program date and time.

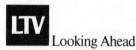

LTV Looking Ahead

The LTV Corporation, Dallas, Texas

Steel: Jones & Laughlin Steel, Youngstown Sheet and Tube • Energy Products and Services: Continental Emsco Company • Aerospace/Defense: Vought Corporation, Kentron International • Food: Wilson Foods Corporation • Transportation: Lykes Bros. Steamship

LTV. Looking Ahead

Exhibit 4

America's national defense: the leading presidential candidates discuss their ideas for strengthening this country's position.

LTV is looking at the future of U.S. business. A key to the future is who will lead this country into the next decade and how that person feels about business issues. The American Enterprise Institute for Public Policy Research polled the leading presidential candidates on issues the Institute considered vital to America. This ad presents the candidates' views on defense policy.

In this series, The LTV Corporation endorses no candidate or political position. We're providing this forum to the candidates for the benefit of LTV's employees, shareholders and the business community.

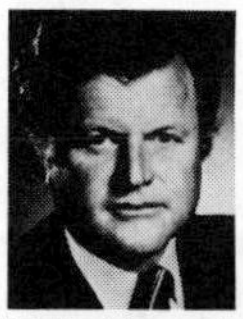

Edward M. Kennedy, Democratic Senator, Massachusetts. As we look ahead at the decade before us, our emphasis should be not only on strategic deterrence but developing and strengthening a general-purpose force that is fighting-trim, equipped with workable and working weapons, and relevant and ready for the conduct of various regional missions.

The military balance between the United States and the Soviet Union is central in discussing national defense. Soviet military forces are now the equal of our own; approximate military parity is a fact of life. I have no doubts that in this decade the Soviet Union will steadily work to improve its military forces—upgrading the accuracy of its strategic forces, deploying a new generation of aircraft and armed vehicles, and strengthening its ability to reach foreign lands beyond Afghanistan and other nearby places.

Similarly, the U.S. must modernize and expand its military force in concert with its Atlantic and Pacific allies, in response to increased turbulence in such vital regions as the Middle East, the Persian Gulf, and southwest Asia, and in relation to the capabilities of the U.S.S.R. The crucial question is how do we accomplish the important task of strengthening our forces and making them usable, so that they are a credible deterrent and capable of defending Western interests.

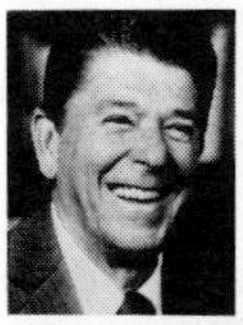

Ronald Reagan, Republican, California. My first priority would be to embark on a program of rebuilding American military strength. Selectively and prudently, we must commit our resources to achieving this goal.

We have permitted ourselves the luxury of believing that our principal adversary, the Soviet Union, shares our hopes for peace and our trust in mutual restraint through good example. That this leads to policies endangering our national security is now abundantly clear.

At a minimum, we must move quickly to restore the principal elements of the last Republican defense budget and just as swiftly establish strategic goals.

Finding the resources to do this job will definitely not be easy, but I believe we can take an initial step by redirecting the misspent resources presently being consumed by a huge governmental bureaucracy. This cannot be done effectively, or at all, without the assistance of the Congress.

Specifically, restoring the credibility of our deterrent power must come before anything can be accomplished.

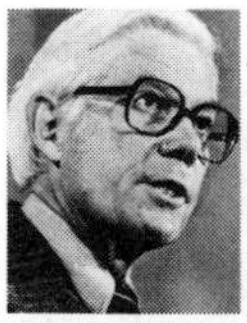

John B. Anderson, Republican Congressman, Illinois. Several key elements, in addition to a strong, mobile military establishment, are necessary to preserve and enhance the security of our nation. First, we need a strong, innovative research and development community within and outside the government. Second, we need an intelligence community better able to identify threats and opportunities. Third, we need improved cooperation among our allies on defense, energy, economic, and other political areas of common interest. Fourth, we need to better insulate our economy from foreign interference with our energy and raw material supplies. Finally, we need to demonstrate both our willingness to cooperate with other nations in such diverse fields as arms control, science and technology, and cultural affairs and our willingness to compete in military forces, political propaganda, and economic matters. By demonstrating both our competitive and cooperative spirit through deed as well as word, I believe our nation will encourage international cooperation and be more secure in the long term.

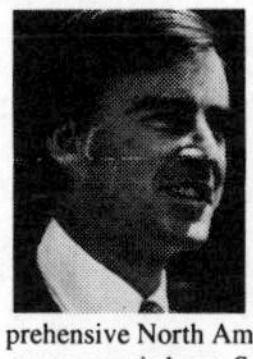

Edmund G. Brown Jr., Democratic Governor, California. The first element of a sound defense policy is a robust domestic economy. We need to reindustrialize in the 1980's, encouraging productivity and investment as part of a comprehensive North American strategy to rebuild our economic base. Secondly, we need to enter into mutual defense *partnerships* with our major allies, in Europe, Japan and the Middle East. The United States can no longer afford to guarantee the world's security as a sort of global policeman. Thirdly, we need to pursue realistic arms control and a mutuality of interest among superpowers, resisting jingoistic pressures to mindlessly step up the cold war. Such a defense policy will make us strong enough to promote a vision of global cooperation where possible and political nonmilitary competition where necessary.

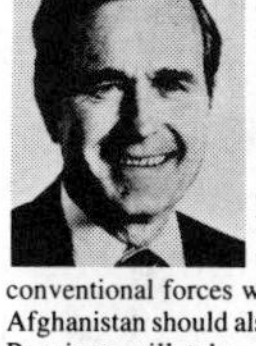

George Bush, Republican, Texas. Fortunately, the country has finally woken up to the fact that we are entering a decade of great danger. For the first time in our history, our strategic forces will be seriously vulnerable to Soviet attack and our conventional forces will be inferior. Events in Afghanistan should also leave no doubt that the Russians will take advantage of weakness wherever they find it.

It is thus obvious that we must press forward with a sustained buildup of our forces. Among our highest priorities should be development and deployment of a new manned bomber, a long-range cruise missile, a greatly strengthened, three-ocean navy, and expanded airborne and seaborne tactical forces.

I also support draft registration for both men and women, and I would like to see an immediate investigation of the readiness of our military troops. If the facts demand it, we should not hesitate to increase financial incentives for those in uniform or even to return to the draft. I am confident that our young people will rally as the need is there.

These changes may cost money—more than is called for in the Administration's new budget. But we can no longer afford policies built more on bluff than true brawn.

In my view, Mr. Carter has proven himself unfit to continue as Commander in Chief. Over the past three years, in the face of a massive Soviet buildup, he cut nearly $40 billion from the projected defense budgets of President Ford. One weapons system after another has been delayed or cancelled.

Even his recent conversion to higher spending was wrung from him only as a concession in order to win approval of the SALT Treaty. We should not be taken in by a sheep in wolf's clothing.

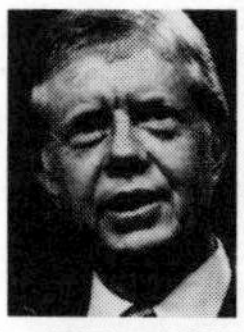

President Jimmy Carter, Democrat, Georgia. Since taking office, this Administration has sustained annual real growth in defense spending, necessary to overcome the many years of declining real defense budgets in the late 1960's and 1970's.

The Administration's defense program emphasizes these areas: 1) ensuring that our strategic nuclear forces will be equivalent to those of the Soviet Union and capable of deterring any nuclear aggression; 2) upgrading our forces so the military balance between NATO and the Warsaw Pact will continue to deter the outbreak of war; 3) providing forces to give us the ability to come quickly to the aid of friends and allies around the globe, and 4) ensuring that our Navy continues to be the world's most powerful. This program includes the cruise missile production to modernize our strategic air deterrent, B-52 modernization and upgrading the strategic submarine missile force.

The new MX missile will enhance the survivability of our land-based intercontinental ballistic missile force. In addition, the program calls for accelerating our ability to reinforce Western Europe with massive ground and air forces.

Also, recognizing that our national interests are critically dependent on a strong and effective intelligence capability, I am recommending we provide America's intelligence community with charters which can permit it to operate more effectively and without excessively cumbersome or self-defeating administrative requirements.

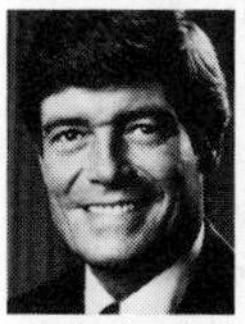

Philip M. Crane, Republican Congressman, Illinois. The United States must be militarily superior. The nature of geopolitical competition with the Soviet Union demands it.

True peace is only attainable through strength. America is currently perceived as being in a weakened state. The President has created this perception by remaining excessively preoccupied with obtaining peace through unilateral concessions.

If we are to avoid that trap, we need to take steps now to restore our strategic and conventional force structures to meet the Soviet challenges in the 1980's and 1990's.

President Carter has eroded our position vis-à-vis the Soviets with drastic cuts in defense spending. He cut $5 billion from the last Ford defense budget. He slashed $57 billion from Ford's five-year defense program proposal. He cancelled the B-1 bomber. He vetoed funding for the nuclear aircraft carrier. He shelved development and deployment of the neutron weapon. He delayed the cruise missile, Trident missile and submarine, and MX ICBM programs. He closed the Minuteman III ICBM production line. These cuts have fed the global perception that the United States is but a shadow of its former self.

To regain superiority we must revitalize our defense and intelligence programs. That means increased funding. We must allocate more defense funding for Research and Development, an area we have traditionally excelled in but have allowed to slip considerably. We must craft our defense posture to deal with Soviet capabilities, not speculation as to their intentions. We must regain superiority in strategic weapons. Unless we build a strong mix of strategic defenses, we will never be able to survive a nuclear attack.

We must strengthen our military capabilities. We need to insure that our active forces are up to combat levels of manning, equipment, weapons, and ammunition of the qualities necessary to meet the needs of the 1980's. The same approach must be applied to the reserves and National Guard. All this will require an increased defense budget.

The United States must also undertake a military strategy which positions our forces in or near areas of instability and provides the capability for rapid reinforcement.

Finally, any military presence and capabilities we develop must be coupled with an active, coherent foreign policy aimed at discouraging and denying Soviet adventurism in the region involved.

More from the candidates

The candidates were asked to speak out on other subjects including government regulation, inflation, capital formation, increased productivity, energy, and the environment. We will present the candidates' views on American foreign policy in the next ad in the series.

If you would like a copy of the candidates' views on all subjects, send for our free booklet, "The Candidates 1980." Requests on your letterhead should be mailed to: Candidates, The LTV Corporation, P.O. Box 225003, Dallas, Texas 75265, or call (214) 746-7734.

For another look at the vital issues facing the country, watch a new ten-part series, "Ben Wattenburg's 1980," on Public Television beginning May 18 at 10 P.M., E.D.T.

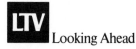

LTV Looking Ahead

The LTV Corporation, Dallas, Texas

Steel: Jones & Laughlin Steel, Youngstown Sheet and Tube • Energy Products and Services: Continental Emsco Company • Aerospace/Defense: Vought Corporation, Kentron International • Food: Wilson Foods Corporation • Transportation: Lykes Bros. Steamship

sponsorship, as it would constitute a form of political campaign contribution that was proscribed by law. However, an important side effect of AEI sponsorship, as the intermediary to solicit the views of the candidates, was that it conveyed to the candidates the seriousness with which the project was being handled, and that their views would be carefully scrutinized by leading scholars, opinion leaders, news media, and the general public.

3. LTV served a very important public service function by providing all candidates a forum to speak on issues at the same time, and to address one issue at a time, in a limited space. It forced them to articulate their views so that the readers could compare and evaluate them; and by making the candidates put their views in writing, succinctly and briefly, it made them commit themselves in a manner that would be difficult for them to disavow at a later date.

4. The campaign brought LTV to the attention of the candidates and their multitudes of staffs, and other important segments of the political and intellectual leadership of the two major parties. This helped lay the groundwork for future contacts for the company.

The Free Booklets

Clearly, the ads could present the views of the candidates only in a capsule form. Therefore, LTV put together the complete statements of the candidates in a booklet entitled "The Candidates 1980," and invited the readers of each ad to write to LTV for a free copy.

Media Schedule

Starting with February 19, the ads ran every Tuesday for eight weeks, to coincide with the spring primaries. They were full-page ads and were carried in the national editions of the *Wall Street Journal*.

Development of Copy Format

LTV subscribes to the notion that an intelligent reader requires and expects substantive information and therefore is willing to read through long copy. As evidence, it points out that *Fortune* did an adverbation study on this issue with LTV's high-technology ad. It was the second most noted ad in the book, and the first most read. The authors produce their own original material, which is edited by the ad agency people to conform to style and space constraints. The material attributed to LTV management is produced in-house by the company, with the assistance of the research staff.

THE 1980 CAMPAIGN—SECOND WAVE

The success of the campaign with presidential candidates encouraged the company to forge ahead with further involvement in political issues.

The candidates debate campaign had allowed the company to enhance its image with the financial community, and also deal with all the things it wanted in the political arena.

Using essentially a similar format, LTV decided to focus on those areas where its various subsidiaries were involved. On each topic, the views of from five to six experts would be sought and presented, together with the views of a senior management representative of LTV. The company's subsidiary engaged in the activity would also be given top billing in the advertisement. This would serve the dual purpose of increasing public awareness of the issues, and also create greater investor visibility for various segments of LTV's business.

LTV went to extreme lengths to ensure that the experts chosen would represent diverse—although mutually supportive—perspectives. The success of the company in achieving this objective could be seen from the list of notables who accepted LTV's invitation to express their views in the company's ad forum. The series was presented under the rubric of "LTV Looking Ahead," which became the main theme of the company's entire issue advertising program.

The program included four advertisements:

1. "The Peacemakers: The Ultimate Irony. To Make Weapons for War and Pray for Peace" [Exhibit 5]. The ad provided views on the necessity of adequate defense preparedness to ensure long-term peace. Those expressing views on the subject included The Right Honorable Margaret Thatcher, prime minister of the United Kingdom; Senator Ernest Hollings, chairman of the budget committee; Dr. William J. Perry, U.S. under secretary of defense for research in engineering; Mr. Wolfgang H. Demish, senior analyst for the investment firm of Morgan, Stanley, & Company; Frank Borman, former astronaut, chairman and president of Eastern Airlines; and Mr. Paul Thayer, chairman of the board and CEO of the LTV Corporation. The ad also identified LTV's subsidiaries, Vought Corporation and Kentron International, which are engaged in aerospace and defense work.

2. "America's Merchant Fleet: Adrift In the Doldrums. Can It Find a Course Back To World Prominence?" This ad dealt with the issue of national support for a merchant fleet for the United States. It argued for the need for greater federal subsidies to maintain America's merchant fleet.

3. "The Energy Finders: They Have Searched Around the World, Under Land, Sand and Sea. Where Next?" In this ad, five energy experts discuss future prospects for attaining energy independence for the United States, and the costs and challenges associated with harnessing different types of energy resources. LTV's Continental Emsco subsidiary is identified as engaged in energy-related activities.

4. "The Steelmakers: Yesterday's Symbol of Strength & Stability. In Trouble Today. What about Tomorrow?" [Exhibit 6]. This ad discusses the problems of America's steel industry in terms of investments, productivity, and the need for a more realistic regulatory, environmental, and tax environment.

Exhibit 5

The Peacemakers: The ultimate irony. To make weapons for war and pray for peace

LTV's Vought Corporation & Kentron International are in Aerospace/Defense; We asked world leaders and industry experts to look ahead.

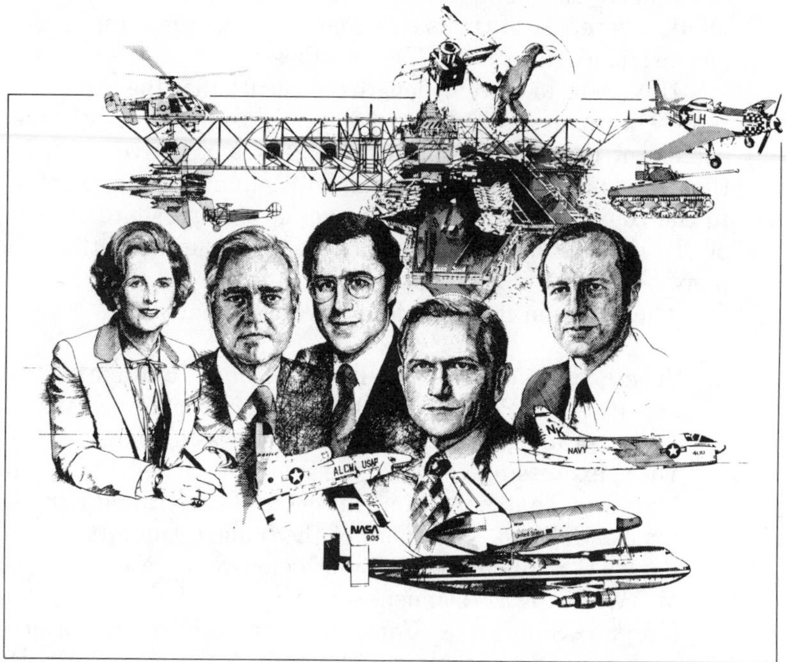

LTV acknowledges the distinguished contributors to the second edition of LOOKING AHEAD. The illustration, we think, is befitting the knowledge and historical perspective they bring to the subject matter. From left to right: Prime Minister Margaret Thatcher, Senator Ernest F. Hollings, Mr. Wolfgang H. Demisch, Mr. Frank Borman and Dr. William J. Perry.

LTV is a multinational, multi-billion-dollar American-based corporation. It is involved primarily in five industries. Aerospace/Defense is one of the five. We asked the British Prime Minister, a leading U.S. Senator and three other experts to share their thoughts with us regarding the future of this important industry.

MARGARET THATCHER: The dangerous decade

The Right Honorable Margaret Thatcher, M.P., is Prime Minister of the United Kingdom.

The last 10 years haven't been a happy period for the Western democracies, domestically or internationally. We face a new decade. I've called it "the dangerous decade" — dangerous because the challenges to our security and to our way of life may, if anything, be even more acute than in the 1970's.

We can argue about Soviet *motives*. Meanwhile they expand their armed forces on land, sea and air. They continually improve the quality of their armaments. They and their allies outnumber us in Europe. Their men, their ships, and their aircraft appear ever more regularly in parts of the world where they have never been seen before. Their Cuban and East German proxies do likewise.

Modern weapons are totally destructive and immensely expensive. And it's in no one's interest that they should be piled up indefinitely. It makes good sense for both sides to seek agreements on arms control which preserve the essential security of each. And we in Britain have therefore supported the talks on Strategic Arms Limitation and on Mutual and Balance Force Reductions.

But the *fact* is: the Russians have the weapons and are getting more of them. And it is simple prudence for the West to respond. We in Britain intend to do that to the best of our ability and at every level.

These thoughts were also expressed before the Foreign Policy Association meeting during the Prime Minister's most recent visit in the United States.

ERNEST F. HOLLINGS: Either rebuild or accept permanent inferiority

Mr. Hollings is the United States Senator from South Carolina and Chairman of the Budget Committee.

America is in a defense depression. An Army supposedly mobile is shy 60,000 vehicles. A Navy to cover three oceans can only cover an ocean and a half. In the Air Force, the planes are older than the pilots. We have three Marine landing divisions but the equipment for only one. Mid-level technicians leave the services in droves because of inadequate pay. We are short 27,000 technicians in the Navy, 46,000 Army noncoms and 2,500 Air Force pilots. Lulled into complacency by SALT Agreements and the ridiculous notion that to compete is destabilizing and provocative, we concede the field to the Soviets. During the past decade, they have outspent us in defense by $240 billion. They have a larger navy, an overwhelming army, a stronger air force and now they are surpassing us in strategic weaponry. With the perception of superiority, they throw their weight around on every continent.

Our need is commitment. Commitment in dollars, commitment in determination to defend freedom. We either rebuild or accept permanent inferiority. If there is to be credibility in our commitments, such as the Carter Doctrine, we cannot draw the line by cutting the defense budget. We must provide higher military pay; adequate training, operations and maintenance; more planes and ships; and stepped-up research and development. Expensive? Yes, $10 billion more a year. But as John C. Calhoun said, "Those who would enjoy the blessings of liberty must undergo the hardships of sustaining it."

WILLIAM J. PERRY: Modernization needed to counter aggressive actions

Dr. Perry is United States Under Secretary of Defense, Research and Engineering.

For years we have acknowledged that the Soviet Union held a quantitative lead in military equipment, but believed that our qualitative lead would more than compensate for this. It is time to reexamine that belief and to reject the complacency that went with it. During the decade of the 1970's, the Soviet Union made a major advance in the development and production of defense material, and as a consequence will enter the 1980's in a dramatically different defense posture than they had as they entered the 1970's.

We are behind quantitatively in deployed equipment and are falling further behind because of disparities in equipment production rates. While we are still ahead in defense technology, we are in danger of losing that advantage because of massive Soviet spending in defense R&D.

But we also have some distinctive advantages: a superior technological base, a competitive industry with greater productivity, and allies with a substantial industrial capability.

The 1980's threaten to be a period of growing international tension and danger for the U.S. if the Soviet Union continues its military buildup and its aggressive attempts to expand political influence. A primary objective of our force modernization is to provide a military capability with strength sufficient to deter or counter those aggressive actions. In that regard, five specific areas of emphasis should be noted: (1) We must maintain unambiguous nuclear deterrence; (2) We must greatly improve our anti-armor capability; (3) We must improve our ability to deploy forces rapidly; (4) We must maintain our tactical air superiority; (5) We must maintain our naval superiority.

The FY 1980 Department of Defense Program for Research, Development, and Acquisition, prepared for the 96th Congress, Second Session, is included in the book Looking Ahead.

WOLFGANG H. DEMISCH: Aerospace must be weaned from government dependence

Mr. Demisch is a senior analyst with the investment banking firm of Morgan Stanley & Co. Incorporated.

We believe a doubling of defense procurement over the next five years is a strong probability.

Such a surge will help the industry's equity market performance, even though it may also exacerbate existing supply shortages to the point where allocation and profit controls again become necessary. Tight supply will, however, hasten the operational maturity of the new electronics-based military technologies, as production of these systems can be stepped up much faster than production of complex vehicles such as warships or tanks.

Unfortunately, experience shows that military demand provides only short-term prosperity. To achieve long-term growth, aerospace must be weaned from its government dependence. This requires a technology-intensive, prospectively very large commercial market. The commercial exploitation of space, now being made possible by the reusable Space Shuttle, may represent the needed opportunity.

By the mid decade, routine Shuttle operations will open the new habitat for industry.

The communications suppliers, already the principal commercial users of space vehicles, will then experience another quantum jump in capability and flexibility, based on the large structures the Shuttle makes possible. Manufacturing companies have thus far been less active, but the unique zero g, high-vacuum space environment is particularly appropriate for producing ultrapure drugs and specialized electronic materials.

By the end of the decade, therefore, these space applications promise to link aerospace to three of the fastest growing industries in the world. Moreover, the work will provide the basis for a much broader commercial space development program. Space will be the foundation of the long-term prosperity of the industry.

FRANK BORMAN: In the airline industry, a decade of profound change

Mr. Borman is the Chairman and President, Eastern Airlines.

In the aerospace and defense fields, as well as in the airline industry, I believe we must see a consolidation of our technological advances of the past and a successful integration of current technology into a vital, resilient and effective national posture. Inevitably that will mean greater concentration on the organizational and personal side of the equation rather than on the technical or scientific side. Let me use the airline industry as an example.

Few products or services available to Americans on a daily basis offer more value in real terms than an airline ticket. In spite of the ravages of inflation, until recently air transportation was one of the more price-stable products in the marketplace. The credit goes in large measure to the advancement of aviation technology.

Under cover of the enormous productivity increases afforded by the rapid introduction of new technology, many airlines grew lethargic. Airline employees of every category along with the passengers became prime recipients of the material rewards of modern, advanced equipment. The end to the halcyon days should have been predictable in the late 60's. A plateauing of the technological advances coupled with unprecedented increases in the price of fuel and burgeoning labor costs began to affect the price of a ticket in the middle to late 70's.

Increasing ticket prices brought a cry of concern from consumers and political forces. The agreed solution signed into law by President Carter in 1978 was to deregulate the domestic industry, effectively introducing competition on a far broader scale in an attempt to restore price stability to our product. Deregulation has, in my opinion, been effective in doing just that. However, continuing inflation exaggerated by the enormous increase in fuel prices has compounded even the most competitive marketplace.

The challenge for the industry in the 80's then will be to couple the modest technological improvements of the new generation of airplanes with increased labor productivity thus helping to restabilize ticket prices. I believe that this trend will necessarily filter throughout the aerospace industry and the armed forces of the country.

LTV: In the forefront of technology

A message from Paul Thayer, Chairman of the Board and Chief Executive Officer, The LTV Corporation.

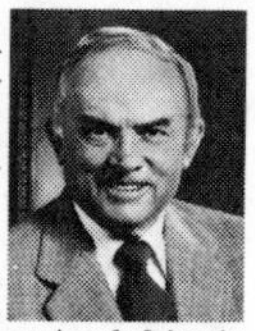

LTV, through its aerospace subsidiary Vought Corporation, has a long and proud history as an important contributor to the nation's defense strength. Vought, in fact, is this country's second oldest continuous producer of military aircraft. It has developed and produced a distinguished line of aircraft that includes such names as Corsair, Kingfisher and Crusader. Vought's A-7, still in production, currently forms the backbone of the Navy's carrier-based strike force.

As the nation's defense needs have changed, so has our strategy for meeting those needs. In the past three years we significantly increased our capabilities in the growing field of tactical missiles, considerably broadening and diversifying our technological base in the process. A major challenge to this strategy was met with the recent selection of Vought by the U.S. Army to produce its Multiple Launch Rocket System (MLRS). The MLRS also will assist our allies and is expected to be co-produced in Europe for NATO. A multibillion dollar program, MLRS will not only improve Vought's outlook, but will contribute significantly to the free world's defense capability.

This is not to say that LTV's aerospace group, which also includes Kentron International, supplier of high-technology support services, will focus its future solely on tactical missiles. While broadening our missiles and space capabilities, we also intend to stay in the military aircraft business, to expand our subcontracting strengths in both the commercial and military aviation sectors, particularly in high-technology areas, and expand the market for Kentron's services.

The aerospace/defense business will not be without problems in the 1980's, but the overall outlook is positive. We are positioning ourselves to play a vital part in the growth we see ahead for this new decade.

More information available

As a corporation, LTV is committed to careful planning. To plan intelligently, it is vital to constantly and pragmatically look ahead. As part of this program, we asked twenty-five experts from different fields to give us their perspective on the future of the industries in which LTV is active. We're now publishing their viewpoints in a book titled *Looking Ahead*. For a free copy write: Looking Ahead, P.O. Box 225003-J, Dallas, TX 75265, U.S.A.

The LTV Companies

The LTV Corporation is involved in five different industries. STEEL: Jones & Laughlin Steel, Youngstown Sheet and Tube; ENERGY PRODUCTS AND SERVICE: Continental Emsco Company; AEROSPACE/DEFENSE: Vought Corporation, Kentron International; FOOD: Wilson Foods Corporation; OCEAN SHIPPING: Lykes Bros. Steamship.

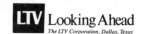

LTV Looking Ahead
The LTV Corporation, Dallas, Texas

The Steelmakers: Yesterday's symbol of strength & stability. In trouble today. What about tomorrow?

LTV's Jones & Laughlin is in steel; We asked 5 experts with different vantage points to look ahead.

It was said of the men who pioneered this industry, "They came to a country of wooden towns and left a nation of steel." You can't put past glory in the bank.

Today, you don't have to look further than the headlines in this very publication to see that the domestic steel industry has problems. We feel it is a good time to take a realistic look at the future of steel. Our five experts did just that. Here are highlights from their reports.

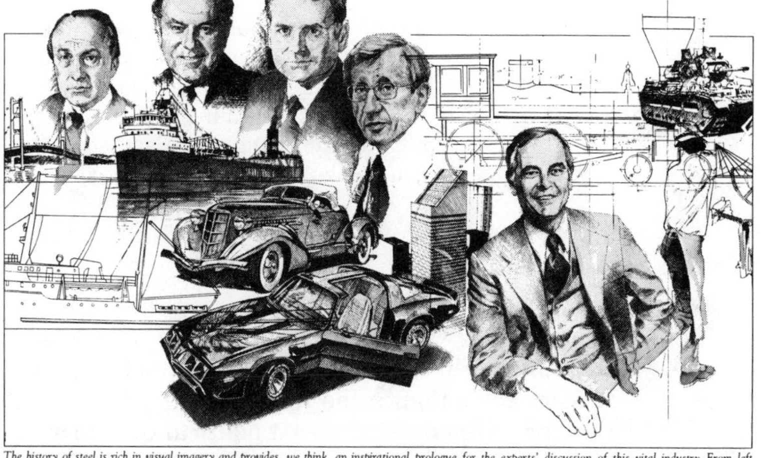

The history of steel is rich in visual imagery and provides, we think, an inspirational prologue for the experts' discussion of this vital industry. From left to right: Eugene Frank, Lloyd McBride, Harold A. Poling, Dr. Richard M. Cyert and Thomas J. Whitaker.

Lloyd McBride: On productivity, innovation, capital & "write-offs"

Mr. McBride is President, United Steelworkers of America.

The immediate and pressing need for the American steel industry is a rapid increase in productivity. Ordinarily we think of productivity improvement as the percentage change in the ratio of output divided by input. We should think of productivity in terms of all its factors, including the cost of money, energy, waste, poor planning, and demoralized employees.

The first requirement of ever-improving productivity is vigorous and persistent technological improvement. Productivity is 75 percent innovation.

> Today our steel industry needs billions of dollars to bring its mills up to competitive technology with that of the companies in Japan and Western Europe. The money must come from one or more of four sources: profits, loans, wages or taxes. The industry is now operating at or near zero profit level because of reduced utilization of facilities and obsolescence. Thousands of good jobs are at stake.

Steelworkers will share any sacrifices that must be made by all Americans to restore a vigorous, inflation-free economy. However, the huge capital requirements cannot be deducted from wages.

Compared to steel companies in Europe and Japan, American steel companies have glacially slow write-off periods of capital investments. The companies need fast write-off periods of capital investments. The companies need fast write-offs to generate the funds needed to make technological improvements. Productivity, then, is partly a function of national tax policy. Politics are involved. *What does the U.S. Congress want to do to help the steel industry?*

And what about the effect of imports on the steel industry? We have given up enough of our domestic markets to foreign producers. Our markets are wide open; theirs are closely controlled. We put profits first; they put market share first and profits follow. We practice free trade; they practice national interest.

We must trade with our allies. But we must work out orderly, disciplined trading arrangements. We have to do this government to government. And we must do it soon.

Richard M. Cyert: The vicious circle must be broken

Dr. Cyert is President, Carnegie-Mellon University, Pittsburgh, Pennsylvania.

Inadequate profit leads to inadequate investment. Inadequate investment leads to obsolete plants. Obsolete plants lead to poor productivity. And poor productivity leads to...

That is the vicious circle that must be broken or the industry will proceed to extinction. It can be broken.

The key is to produce the conditions whereby the industry can be made profitable, and, thereby, attract new investment. A major step is for government to pledge a nonintervention policy on prices. The level of inflation experienced in the country gives evidence that the control of steel prices does not effectively control inflation.

Of equal importance is the control of dumping. Such control may fly in the face of hard-core free traders. The argument is made that America should take advantage of getting another country's resources at bargain prices; however, we cannot allow short-run gains to eliminate a domestic industry.

Dumping can be controlled only by quotas or by a pricing mechanism such as trigger pricing. The latter has difficulties for enforcement but can be modified to be more effective than in the past. Trigger pricing is to be preferred over quotas. As a mechanism to prevent dumping it is more likely to encourage competition.

By eliminating price controls, and by controlling dumping, government will establish the basic conditions that will enable the industry to survive without handouts from society.

In order to get the industry moving forward *more rapidly,* five additional changes would be effective:

> 1. Regulatory agencies, in particular the EPA, should recognize that eliminating an industry is a cost to society.
> 2. The depreciation period for new investment should be significantly shortened.
> 3. The uncertainty of the environmental standards should be eliminated.
> 4. The Justice Department should approve company consortia for research and development projects.
> 5. Labor and management should work together to improve productivity.

If we allow the industry to be demolished, we must resign ourselves to being in the hands of foreign producers. OPEC has given us empirical evidence of how effectively an international cartel can function.

Eugene Frank: Survivors of current crisis should prosper

Mr. Frank is a steel economist with the investment banking firm of M. Waddell & Towne Inc.

Regardless of what skeptics may say, the world is now—and will be for some time to come—in the "Steel Age." Currently, the world is in a period of oversupply of steel. The energy crisis has sent economies into a tailspin, prompting many steel-producing nations to use their steel industries' exports as a cushion against unemployment and to obtain currency to pay for their oil. Because the U.S. marketplace is the most open in the world, it has served as the dumping ground for excess foreign production and as a result has become the burial ground for a number of American steel plants.

Approximately 20 plants have been closed and currently eighty thousand steelworkers are unemployed—a crisis of epidemic proportions.

Dumping has hurt both the competitive American industry and the government-owned or government-subsidized foreign steel industry, which has resulted in a rationalization of the world steel industry. As a result, when world demand picks up—as it will—the supply will not be there.

Sometime during the decade of the 80's steel will be in short supply in the world markets. If the liquidation of our domestic industry continues, the United States alone would become dependent, like we are for oil, upon unreliable foreign sources of supply for 50-70 million tons of steel by 1990.

> For two decades the United States has been without a sound domestic economic plan, the absence of which has started a slide of the U.S. toward being a second-rate industrial power.

In the very near future our government must decide if it wants a viable domestic steel industry and a strong industrial base for this nation. A sound sectional plan for steel, because of its unique status, could serve as a format for other industries under siege.

To solve the steel crisis, the U.S. must enforce its trade laws by eliminating trade abuses, balance its pollution goals with its economic goals, provide adequate capital retention by shortening depreciation, install favorable investment tax credits through reform of our tax laws and reduce the number of oppressive regulations now suffocating all of industry.

For those companies, plants and communities that survive the current crisis, the steel needs of our economy alone are so great—that if the domestic industry is allowed to serve those needs—a bright future for the industry and the nation would be assured.

Harold A. Poling: The need for Auto/Steel Reliance has never been more urgent

Mr. Poling is Executive Vice President, Ford Motor Company, North American Automotive Operations.

To meet foreign competition, as well as to satisfy government requirements and customer demands for more fuel-efficient vehicles, U.S. auto manufacturers are engaged in a massive restructuring of their product lines that will entail an almost total retooling of the industry at an estimated cost of between $70 and $80 billion during the 1980-84 period.

> The auto companies are developing more fuel-efficient engines and power trains at an accelerating pace. But the complementary approach of reducing vehicle weight—a critical factor in fuel economy — is equally necessary in order to design and produce cars of sufficient size to preserve the interior comfort and safety Americans want and need for family and long-distance travel. For this, the car makers look to the steel industry to develop lighter but equivalent strength steels for chassis, bodies and other components.

Further expansion in the use of automotive high-strength steel is being held back by a need for improved heat-to-heat, and even coil-to-coil, consistency in order to achieve greater predictability in forming and welding. Development of new steels with added and/or different properties could replace certain present steel commodity applications, resulting in lighter or less expensive materials. Other automotive needs that might be met by innovative solutions from the steel industry are lighter weight, yet equivalent strength tubing to replace bars; hot-rolled bars with closer tolerances and improved surface conditioning in place of more costly cold-finished bars; and modified alloy bar chemistries that would eliminate certain alloying elements presently in low supply or only available from foreign countries.

The steel industry is making significant progress in meeting our needs. Nevertheless, we are hopeful that a greater investment of capital and technological resources may be even more productive of the cost-effective innovations that will ensure continuation of the steel industry's position as the leading supplier of materials to American auto manufacturers.

These are difficult and demanding times for both the auto and steel industries. Their reliance on each other has never been more urgent or subject to greater market pressures. I am confident, however, that by working as closely together throughout the 1980's as we have done in the past, the traditional partership of America's two most vital industries will succeed in providing the American people with the most dependable, fuel-efficient and desirable automobiles available anywhere in the world.

Thomas J. Whitaker: A bright future for metal service centers

Mr. Whitaker is President, Edgcomb Metals Company, a wholly owned subsidiary of The Williams Companies, Tulsa, Oklahoma.

The industrial might of the United States is dependent upon a viable domestic steel industry. While other materials can be substituted for steel in certain applications, the fact remains that steel will continue to be the backbone of industry for the foreseeable future.

> Given this country's reliance on steel, a viable steel industry is imperative to the well-being and defense of the nation; therefore, the rebuilding of the decaying domestic steel industry must be addressed.

A good starting point would be passage of the Jones-Conable Capital Cost Recovery Act. Had the provisions of this Act been in effect during the 1974 through 1978 time frame, the domestic steel industry would have generated an additional $4 billion of capital funds with which to modernize its facilities. This would have represented a capital recovery rate of roughly 60 percent versus the actually experienced rate of 30 percent.

As the vital link between the standard output of the producing mills and the fluctuating requirements of the nation's metal-consuming industries, metal service centers are expected to thrive in the uncertain environment of the 1980's. Metal service centers, which process and distribute roughly 20 percent of the steel produced in the United States through approximately 1,600 companies, provide a means for metal users to move costs out of their system through efficient processing capabilities and common inventories.

In my opinion, the uncertain environment of the 1980's will create an ever-increasing reliance on metal service centers as the vital link in the steel producer-to-consumer chain. I feel as though metal service centers will be handling as much as 25 percent of domestic steel production by 1985, solidifying their position as the domestic steel producers' largest customer.

LTV: Positioning ourselves for the future

A message from Raymond A. Hay, President, Chief Operating Officer, The LTV Corporation.

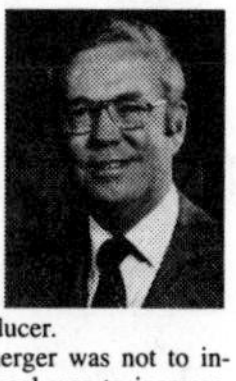

Following our merger with Lykes Corporation in December 1978, which combined the operations of Jones & Laughlin Steel and Youngstown Sheet and Tube under one management, we became the nation's third largest steel producer.

The goal of the merger was not to increase our size: the goal was to increase our strength. To create a stronger, more competitive force within the industry. The realization of that goal — because of the merger and the modernization program undertaken at our Pittsburgh and Aliquippa works — was apparent in our 1979 operating results.

But the real test for our company and industry lies in the future. We are now in difficult times. Almost all of the major steel markets are weak. It is pure conjecture as to when they will recover. (The major exception is the tubular market—to which we are a leading supplier.)

> Importantly, the postmerger LTV steel group entered these difficult times in a much better position than it has enjoyed in the past. For example, we are now one of the few companies producing *all* of its steel with modern and efficient basic oxygen and electric furnaces.

Our goal is to continue this progress—lowering our costs, improving productivity and achieving greater profitability — and thus position ourselves for the future.

Many experts predict that in the 1980's world demand for steel will overtake supply. We are not counting on a worldwide shortage. We do, however, look for a gradual improvement in the supply/demand relationship and are reducing production costs to competitive levels so that we can capitalize on the return to reasonable profit levels such an environment will provide.

Our ability to participate in any coming period of prosperity will be determined in part by a number of factors beyond our control.

Clearly, changes are in order and must be made quickly. LTV believes America's future as a world power lies in part in the recognition that a revitalization of one of our most important and basic industries must become a high priority.

To Be Continued

In future editions, other industry leaders and specialists will look ahead at the other industries in which LTV is involved. A collection of all of the reports will be made available in book form at the conclusion of the series. To reserve a free copy write: LTV — Looking Ahead, P.O. Box 225003-C, Dallas, Texas 75265.

The LTV Companies

The LTV Corporation is involved in five different industries. STEEL: Jones & Laughlin Steel, Youngstown Sheet and Tube; ENERGY PRODUCTS AND SERVICE: Continental Emsco Company; AEROSPACE / DEFENSE: Vought Corporation, Kentron International; FOOD: Wilson Foods Corporation; OCEAN SHIPPING: Lykes Bros. Steamship.

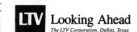

LTV Looking Ahead
The LTV Corporation, Dallas, Texas

Media Schedule and Target Audience

The 1980 media schedule consisted of 16 full-page ads in the *Wall Street Journal,* followed by *Barron's* with 10 two-page spreads, and *Forbes* and *Financial World* with one insertion each. LTV's allocation of a substantial part of its budget to the *Journal* was deliberate. According to Johnson:

> We use the *Journal* because we think that, more than any other single publication, it reaches the audience that we want to reach. It reaches the investment community par excellence, it reaches the business community, it reaches our managers, it reaches many of the thought leaders, so it really is the umbrella publication that we use for our program.

Supportive Activities

In addition to widespread distribution of "The Candidates 1980" and "LTV Looking Ahead" booklets, LTV undertook a series of other activities to support and enhance the impact of its advertising campaign.

The company produced a political directory and calendar that were sent to opinion leaders across the country. LTV also started holding an annual Washington seminar, which continues to date. Its purpose was to expose the corporate management to key issues, to bring them face to face with provocative thinkers and innovators on a broad range of subjects. The seminars have included an outstanding array of speakers—Abba Eban, the novelist Anthony Burgess, Tom Wolfe, Dean Rusk, to name just a few. After each seminar, the company published a book incorporating the views and comments of the speakers. These books were distributed throughout Washington and to opinion leaders across the country.

Hand in hand with all this, LTV also has a program called "Blitz the Cities." In this program, every year corporate executives visit anywhere from four to eight cities, where they cover a broad spectrum of the audiences the company is trying to appeal to with its advertising—financial analysts and brokers, government officials, customers, employees, shareholders, and the press.

LTV also supports a PBS program, "The Lawmakers," a WETA-TV show, which gives it a good visibility with Congress and has helped make LTV better known in Washington.

Campaign Effectiveness

LTV took great pains to measure the effect of its 1980 campaigns. Two waves of tracking studies were conducted in 1981 through phone interviews. Among their major findings were these:

1. *Awareness* of LTV had shown a marked increase. As a conglomerate, 89 percent of the respondents were aware of LTV. Of the respondents, 76 percent were cognizant (aided or unaided) of LTV as a steel

company. Investors' awareness (aided or unaided) of those companies involved in the merger—Lykes, Jones & Laughlin, and Youngstown Sheet & Tube—had declined since the benchmark study.

2. *Advertising awareness* of LTV also indicated a notable gain. Investors' unaided awareness level for LTV advertising was at 6 percent—a significant increase from the previous waves. Thirty-five percent of the institutional and individual investors had seen or heard LTV advertising (on an aided or unaided basis).

3. The *image of LTV* had shown some modest gains. The proportion of investors stating LTV as "best" displayed significant gains on the following attributes: speaking out on key political issues facing business; being a spokesman for the future of businesses they were in; and involved in several very different industries.

4. The *overall image of LTV* as "having the best overall reputation" was still relatively low. According to Ogilvy & Mather: "This is an extremely difficult measure to improve upon through advertising, especially for skeptical investors, who require more concrete evidence of success. Nonetheless, over the last four waves there were indications of gradual improvement in the overall image of LTV."

There were other positive signs, although the company is reluctant to take credit for them. Johnson states:

> We have had good news on the stock prices front, although it is impossible to establish direct causality with our advertising or any other single factor. This is an area in which my skepticism level is very high, i.e., the affect of advertising on stock prices and stock activity for the short term. A study was conducted by our ad agency from June 24 to September 29 to measure stock activity on the day the ads appeared versus the days when there was no advertising. It showed net stock changes. There were advances related to the Dow Jones Industrial averages, advances, and declines. In addition, during 1980 the stock price went up from 7-3/4 to 20-3/4. And new buy recommendations were forthcoming from a number of advisory services. During this period, LTV was on the most active list almost daily.

In summary, the 1980 program accomplished a more favorable awareness of the corporation. It appeared to have had a positive impact from an investment standpoint. It generated a solid advertising response. It provided a focus for LTV at a time when it didn't want to talk about a track record which it didn't have, but which it was expecting to establish in the future. It promoted employee morale and built a stronger corporate spirit within the company. And it began building a new image of LTV.

THE 1981 CAMPAIGN—DEVELOPMENT OF A NEW STRATEGY

The success of the 1980 campaign, and LTV's own desire to enhance its public image as a company with strong interest in the propagation of new ideas and stimulation of public discussion, led it to evolve a highly innovative, and in many ways quite risky, strategy of issue advertising. The underlying assumptions and essential elements of this strategy say as much about the corporate ethos as they do about the creative talents of its developers.

1. An issue must be discussed intelligently and cogently in order to sustain a reader's interest and help him/her formulate an opinion.
2. Most arguments have more than two sides; therefore, to the extent possible, multiple viewpoints should be presented.
3. An issue is best presented by the person who is an expert on that subject, and who advocates a particular policy position. Therefore, the spokespersons for various viewpoints should be not only experts in their respective areas, but have credibility, high visibility, and national and international stature.
4. Public opinion is extremely important in the ultimate resolution of any public policy issue. To this extent, the company commissioned the Opinion Research Corporation of Princeton, NJ, a prestigious survey research firm, to undertake a national poll of public opinion on the particular issues under discussion.
5. On each issue, LTV would provide its own views, expressed by Paul Thayer, CEO, or another member of senior management.
6. Utmost care was taken to select the speakers from the widest possible spectrum of opinion on an issue. Here again, the company was extremely successful in attracting spokespersons who were recognized experts with high credibility and public visibility.

Development of Ad Copy

The ad copy called for the presentation of four opinions—one representing the case for the issue, one against, the third representing a summary of public opinion as discovered by ORC surveys, and the fourth representing the views of LTV.

The outside spokespersons were asked to prepare a 1,500 word statement expressing their views. These statements were boiled down to 150 words for inclusion in the ads. The edited versions were reviewed and approved by the authors of the statements before they were included in the ads.

In most cases, the speakers did not accept any fee for the right to publish their views. However, in a number of cases, the authors were paid a modest fee (seldom exceeding $5,000) to prepare an article on their views.

The larger versions of the papers were collated and published in a booklet series under the rubric of "Looking Ahead." These booklets were widely distributed among Washington leaders, news media, and the many people who wrote LTV for copies of the ads and for additional information about the issues.

Copy Themes

The 1981 campaign focused on six major issues: (1) America's technological lead [Exhibit 7]; (2) federal support of the U.S. maritime industry

[Exhibit 8]; (3) greater access to federal lands and national wilderness areas for mining, and oil and gas exploration; (4) energy self-sufficiency; (5) trade protectionism [Exhibit 9]; (6) America's defense responsibility for the rest of the world [Exhibit 10]. An analysis of the 1981 campaign showed certain important trends:

1. The choice of issues was limited to energy, transportation, defense, and international trade, areas where LTV had vital business interests. Some of the issues in the new debate format were similar to the ones used in the 1980 campaign, when the company was attempting to raise investor consciousness with particular issues, and at the same time create greater recognition for its subsidiaries.
2. The many diverse and opposing viewpoints were presented intelligently. The stature of the spokespersons was such that it would be preposterous to presume that their views could be anything but strictly their own. Moreover, the format lent itself to articulate and vigorous debate.
3. The choice of issues was, in some ways, rather narrow. The company avoided a discussion of some of the other major economic issues of the day, where a great deal of confusion existed and public debate might be desirable and highly pertinent—for example, supply-side economics, federal budget deficits, high unemployment.
4. The company had not chosen to discuss other important issues of public policy, which although not strictly economic in nature, nevertheless had strong implications for the private sector, such as the role of private enterprise in curbing social ills, entitlement programs, transfer payments, and private enterprise zones. This is especially unusual in view of the fact that LTV has chosen to undertake a highly visible political profile, and its CEO, Paul Thayer, is active in national economic issues, being the current chairman of the U.S. Chamber of Commerce.

LTV management recognizes these attributes of its advertising program, and offers the following explanation:

1. LTV is not Mobil Oil, either in resources or corporate philosophy. It does not wish to cover the waterfront and speak out on every conceivable issue.
2. LTV's advertising is not adversarial, but informational. The company does not wish to confront its opponents, or to castigate them as ignorant or ill-informed.
3. LTV's primary emphasis is to encourage national dialogue on major issues of public importance, but on issues that are also important to its activities and its market performance. For this reason, the choice of issues has to be somewhat narrow and related to LTV's primary interests. Comments Johnson:

> We come at this advertising from our own unique position. There may be nobody else in the United States that has the same set of problems that we had. I think it's important to understand that. We did not come into this with the idea that we're going to change the world overnight or influence the political process. But we did want an acceptance and understanding for this com-

Exhibit 7

LTV. Looking Ahead

Has America's technology lead slipped?
Industrialist and educator agree, yes.
Disagree as to why

INFLATION MAIN CULPRIT

Dr. Simon Ramo
Director and Co-Founder,
TRW Inc.

How do we regain technological superiority? Hosts of negative factors, not involving science and technology, have become bottlenecks...

If broad technological inferiority should come to characterize America, living standards certainly would drop, our security would be threatened, and our economic competitiveness in world markets would collapse.

Unfortunately, America's technology position has deteriorated. It is not that we have lost the innovative touch. Instead, hosts of negative factors, not involving science and technology per se, have become dominant bottlenecks to progress.

Poor "real" earnings

The main problem is inflation, which has led to poor real earnings by technological corporations and low cash flows.

Since taxes are paid on stated (and inflated) profit figures, not real ones, many corporations have been taxed nearer to 80 percent of true earnings than the reported 40 percent, the useful cash flows often being less than dividends paid.

Not surprisingly, the limited funds now available for investment typically are put into "safe" technology changes, those representing only small increments. *Bold technology advances too often call for more risk investment than is to be expected in our inflationary economy.*

If we could halt inflation and create tax incentives for investment, most of America's technology lag would soon evaporate. New products would blossom to create more job opportunities. Improved methods would be developed to enhance productivity and lower costs—providing the base for further growth.

Another handicap to the nation's realization of the full benefits of technology advance has been the growing adversary relationship between government and business. Ours is not (and never was) a totally capitalistic, free-market society. We are a hybrid—partially a free-enterprise economy and a government-controlled one. *The secret to success is to arrange the best functions for the private sector and the government.*

One simple formula won't establish these optimum missions. The government-private split of roles and responsibilities for energy activities, for instance, needs to be different from that for the sponsoring of basic research, or for military weapon system development, or for protecting the environment, or for stimulating the computer-communications revolution.

One simple answer? No!

Most importantly, we cannot hope to arrive at the most sensible relationships by espousing either of two exaggerated views: 1) Since profit-seeking enterprise cannot act objectively in the national interest, government control is the answer. 2) Since government is a wasteful, incompetent bureaucracy, we should leave everything to the free market.

LACK OF INITIATIVE BLAMED

Robert C. Seamans, Jr.
Dean, School of Engineering,
Massachusetts Institute of Technology

Years after the energy embargo, the U.S. is still debating the advantages of various technologies rather than mounting concerted programs...

I must assert that the U.S. is falling behind its true potential in many technical areas. Note that Japanese radios, TV's, hi-fi's, automobiles and steel, to mention a few products, are not only lower priced, but usually of higher quality.

Our annual growth in productivity has dropped from over 3 percent in the 60's to less than 1 percent in recent years.

The U.S. can still mount technical effort of the highest quality, as evidenced by the recent Voyager pictures of Saturn and its moons. But years after the energy embargo of 1973-74, the U.S. is still debating the advantages of various technologies rather than mounting concentrated programs to conserve energy and to make alternate fuels available.

Clearly, the U.S. must become less dependent on imported oil, just as the U.S. must protect its environment, improve worker safety, and provide more efficient transportation, food delivery and health care. *These objectives cannot be accomplished without the innovative use of advanced technology.*

Many factors adversely influence the U.S. capability to innovate. Investment in new technology can have long-term, favorable consequences, but corporations are judged quarterly by their short-term profits.

Capital for new plants and facilities is difficult to form at present high interest rates, but the U.S. must invest today to supply needed, high-quality and low-cost products and services tomorrow.

Most commitments must be made privately, but the risk in some cases may be so great and the scale of operations so large, that government financing is required—as in the development of fusion reactors.

A "trained brain" shortage?

Advancement, whether privately or publicly funded, depends heavily on a steady flow of scientifically and technically qualified individuals.

The number of engineers graduating at the bachelor's level has increased in the past ten years. But the number is not sufficient to satisfy today's demand.

During the past decade the number of engineering students graduating at the doctoral level has fallen by over 25 percent, thereby jeopardizing the U.S. capability for future education and innovation. The U.S. educational system from secondary school to postgraduate study cannot satisfy U.S. technical needs without stronger support from both government and industry.

Self-proclaimed experts and sincere, but uninformed, individuals advocate a return to a simpler world.

This causes many to doubt the need for advanced technology. Certainly, technology hasn't always been used thoughtfully—for the benefit of mankind. But...the U.S. cannot provide for the future without it.

WHAT THE PUBLIC THINKS.

Reported by Kenneth Schwartz
Vice President, Opinion Research Corporation

To simplify the issue, call it "The technology race." Americans see their country winning in space; losing on the highway.

"With respect to technology in general, is the United States now the world leader, or have some other countries overtaken us?" That was the leading question on this issue.

U.S. overall leader

Of the 1,008 people contacted in a nationwide telephone survey conducted for LTV by Opinion Research Corporation, the majority (52 percent) believe that we are the world leader in technology.

However, 36 percent think we are losing out to other countries. "No opinion" accounted for the remaining 12 percent.

Space exploraton

What about specific technology? In the area of space exploration, a resounding 68 percent felt America was first. The Soviets trailed with 22 percent. Interestingly, the poll was taken in March, one month *before* the successful space shuttle flight.

After space, we asked for an opinion on which country is the technological leader in different major industries.

Steel production

A majority of Americans believe their country is the technological leader in steel production: 54 percent versus second place Japan with 19 percent. West Germany was a distant third with 3 percent.

Electronic products

It was a different story when it came to electronic products. Here, it was virtually a tie between the U.S. and Japan: 43 percent and 39 percent, respectively. But the higher the level of education, the more likely people were to believe that Japan has a technological edge. For example, 52 percent of the respondents with "some college or more" named Japan the electronics leader—against 41 percent "voting for" the U.S.

Automobiles

As for automobiles...Japan was the clear winner. A majority of 56 percent of Americans polled named Japan as the technological leader. The U.S. was second with 26 percent, West Germany third with 6 percent.

The "educated guess"

Again, the higher the education, the more likely they were to name Japan as the automobile leader. In fact, among those with "some college or more" the margin was 65 percent for Japan—versus 20 percent for the U.S. Among the "less than high school" group, the tally was 44 percent favoring Japan versus 35 percent for the U.S..

WHAT LTV BELIEVES

Speaking for LTV, Paul Thayer
Chairman of the Board and Chief Executive Officer

If the huge lead America built in technology has eroded—let us hear the news as reveille, a call to action. Not as taps...

LTV believes that an ongoing exchange of ideas between industry, educators and government is a sign of good health. We also believe the future belongs to those who seize the initiative.

We're calling special attention to the technology issue because it is a fundamental question in our society; and because we at LTV are a technology focused company. Our Vought Corporation is on the leading edge of space and defense technology, and we are applying advanced technology in all of our other industries—energy, steel and ocean shipping.

LTV cheered the recent success of the space shuttle because Vought technology played an important role in Columbia's safe return. We also cheered because we are Americans.

LTV shares the concerns expressed by Dr. Ramo and Dean Seamans. On a positive note, the space shuttle is a dramatic example of what can happen when America makes its commitment to excellence.

Report on Vought

LTV has made progressive moves at Vought. Not many years ago, Vought was considered to be an airplane company. Airplanes are still part of our business. But only part. Today Vought is a high-technology contractor, a company that must be categorized by its capability, not by its end product.

The point is best made with examples. The U.S. Army's Multiple Launch Rocket System is the cornerstone of a growing rocket and missile business. The U.S. Air Force Space Division's Air-Launched Anti-Satellite Weapon is another major ongoing project. Vought is involved with the U.S. Navy's Supersonic Tactical Missile Project. Work on new Boeing 757 and 767 programs are progressing. It is a long list.

Overall, Vought's sales in 1980 were up nearly $100 million to $652 million. The future is bright with a backlog of over $1.5 billion.

Other issues will be discussed

This is one of a series discussing issues critical to the LTV companies. Responsible spokespeople with distinct views—usually opposite-are heard from in each. Current public opinion is also reported.

What are your views? Let them be known. Write your elected officials. If you own stock in a technology company, write the chairman. To be put on the LTV Issues mailing list write me, Paul Thayer, P.O. Box 225003-2A, Dallas, TX 75265.

The LTV Companies

Jones & Laughlin Steel, Continental Emsco Company, Vought Corporation, Kentron International, Lykes Bros. Steamship Co., Inc.

The inspiration for this series was the question, "What are the most critical issues facing the industries in which LTV is active?"

The LTV Corporation
Dallas, TX 75265

Should America continue to subsidize its merchant fleet? Two top economists disagree

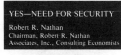

YES—NEED FOR SECURITY

Robert R. Nathan
Chairman, Robert R. Nathan Associates, Inc., Consulting Economists

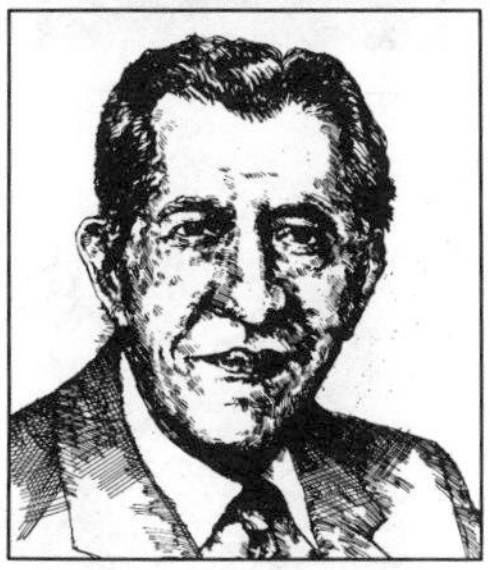

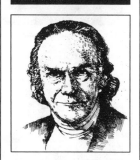

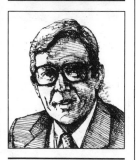

There are serious security considerations . . . it is appropriate that stern economic criteria be applied . . .

Given the huge and continuing subsidies and other costly provisions that are needed for international liner operations, it is impossible to justify the continuation of America's merchant marine on purely economic grounds. The costs of constructing vessels in the United States and their operating costs are so high relative to costs of foreign shipyards and operators as to preclude—at least for the present and foreseeable future—the prospects for a successful United States merchant marine without subsidies.

Therefore, economists could conclude that this country would be better off by letting our merchant marine either compete or disappear. However, there are serious security considerations which, in my judgment, warrant a program to assure at least that minimum available level of ocean shipping facilities to provide some degree of contribution to our national security.

Air transport of military manpower and equipment has improved, but there are still substantial military needs for ocean shipping facilities.

If we do conclude that a subsidized American merchant marine is justified on security grounds, as I believe, then it is entirely appropriate that the sternest economic criteria ought to be applied in deciding how best to achieve that security objective at the lowest possible cost.

Many experts in the marine field currently have doubts whether the present practices and procedures are compatible with the objective of carefully scrutinizing the costs essential for fulfilling the minimal ongoing security needs of the United States.

Recurring reviews

Most obvious, there should be recurring reviews—perhaps once every three to five years—of the methodology and the data sources which serve as the bases for determining levels of construction and operating differential subsidies. With dramatic changes occurring in productivity, inflation and other international competitive conditions, the government should try to assure reasonable balance between essential incentives and minimal subsidies. Government subsidies should not underwrite excessive profits; rather the costs of capital in setting subsidies should take into account realistic risk factors.

There are private United States carriers who transport on their own account or who are engaged in domestic coastal or international tramp operations, who are not directly subsidized. However, they do benefit from certain cargoes that are reserved for U.S.-flag companies and they move at higher than international tariffs. For that preferential cargo they are protected from foreign competitors and presumably from U.S.-subsidized carriers.

In summary, incentives of a non-direct subsidy nature should be sought, multiple operating incentives should be avoided and strict monitoring of financial results should be a firm requirement.

NO—IT DOESN'T WORK

Allen R. Ferguson
President, Public Interest Economics Center

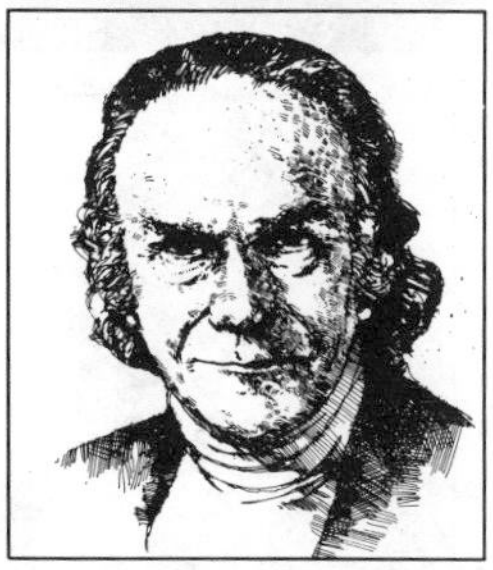

We cannot make the American-flag fleet competitive by continuing to subsidize its inefficiencies . . .

Why can't the American merchant marine swim; why can't it compete—at least without Federal support? In fact, much of it can and does compete. Hundreds of ships owned by American corporations operate under Liberian, Panamanian and other "flags of convenience."

The more visible part of the American-owned fleet, subsidized American-flag ships in scheduled liner service, however, cannot compete *under present* law. Two major restrictions hobble them:

(1) They may sail only American-built ships manned only with "citizen" crews. Failure to do either precludes them from receiving subsidies or from serving the domestic trade.

(2) U.S. shipyards are far less efficient—less productive—than are foreign yards and American crews are more expensive—that is, are less productive per wage dollar—than foreign crews.

As the capital intensity of ocean transport increases, with containerization and greater ship size and speed, the burden of the crew requirement will decline, but the burden of sailing American-built ships will increase.

We *cannot* make the American-flag fleet competitive by continuing to spend some three-fourths of a billion dollars per year to subsidize its inefficiencies, and billions more, indirectly, to protect it from competition in the domestic trades.

We *can* make it competitive by removing the legal requirement that U.S.-flag carriers operate American-built ships. Eventually, removing the mandate to use American-citizen crews or so changing it as to reduce its incentives to inefficiency would also be sound, but less important and politically harder.

It is sometimes argued that defense needs dictate that U.S.-built ships be used and subsidized in ocean commerce. In fact, essential shipbuilding capacity is sustained under naval contracts. Most of the subsidized ships are of little use to the military, as naval authorities have testified; the advocates of construction subsidies dare not put them into the Defense budget because they fear (rightly) that military planners would find other expenditures more important. Real military needs could be better met by buying cargo ships in the open market and holding them in the reserve fleet. That fleet has proven to be extremely valuable in military crises. The reserve fleet is obsolete, but could be renewed at bargain-basement prices.

Thus, an administration devoted to free enterprise could make the American merchant marine competitive by "stroke-of-the-pen-technology" and could save taxpayers and consumers hundreds of millions of dollars. With such a simple change the domestic trade could also be opened to free competition, reducing the price of oil and lumber in the Northeast and of nearly everything in Alaska and Hawaii.

WHAT THE PUBLIC THINKS

Reported by Kenneth Schwartz
Vice President, Opinion Research Corporation

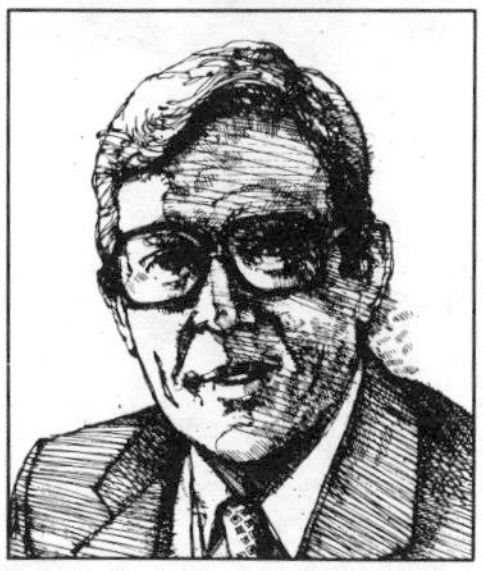

The reality is, this is not a "hot issue" with the public. But among those who know "something" . . . 62 percent favor subsidy.

It is important that we put this information into the proper perspective. On LTV's behalf, ORC polled 1003 people between May 14-17, 1981. However, before we reached the specific question on subsidy, we first asked, *"How much have you heard or read about the size and condition of the United States merchant shipping fleet?"* A great deal? A fair amount? A little? Nothing at all?

Results: great deal, 3 percent; fair amount, 13 percent; little, 45 percent; nothing at all, 38 percent; don't know, 1 percent.

We then asked the 61 percent of the original respondents who answered *"great deal, fair amount or little"* some subsequent questions. So, please keep in mind that the next section of this column deals only with answers given by that 61 percent who professed at least a little knowledge of the subject.

How did they respond to the topic addressed here by the two distinguished economists, Nathan and Ferguson? *"Would favor or oppose the Federal Government providing financial subsidies for a merchant shipping fleet?"*
In favor: 62 percent. Opposed: 25 percent.
No opinion: 13 percent

Three other questions relative to views on the merchant fleet were asked. (The responses are in parenthesis.)

(1) From what you have heard or read, how would you describe the size and condition of the U.S. merchant shipping fleet? Would you say it is adequate for our country's needs (19 percent)? Somewhat inadequate (48 percent)? Or very inadequate (22 percent)? No opinion accounted for the remaining 11 percent.

(2) As far as you know, can our merchant shipping fleet compete satisfactorily with foreign fleets (yes, 19 percent)? Or has our fleet fallen behind competitively (fallen behind, 64 percent)? No opinion, 17 percent.

(3) Is the defense of our country in any way dependent on the strength of our merchant shipping fleet (yes, 72 percent)? Or doesn't the merchant shipping fleet play any role in our defense (no role, 12 percent)? No opinion, 16 percent.

Consistent with earlier poll

Interestingly, we conducted a similiar poll for LTV in March 1981, but we had not asked the question on subsidies. The May findings are consistent with the March poll. The major exception being that the number of people who claimed to know "a little" rose from 36 percent in March to the 45 percent in May. This meant that a larger number (61 percent vs. 52 percent) were eligible to answer the second tier of questions. The greatest shift in opinion between the two polls came on the question regarding the U.S. fleet's competitiveness with foreign fleets. In March, 32 percent felt we could compete. In May, only 19 percent felt so.

WHAT LTV BELIEVES

Speaking for LTV, Paul Thayer
Chairman of the Board and Chief Executive Officer

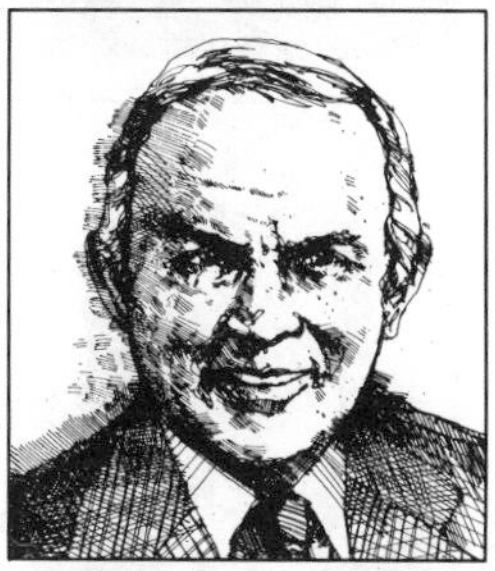

LTV is focusing attention on this issue because we believe it is an important one—and one that is widely misunderstood.

A strong American merchant marine is essential to our country's well-being and security. The U.S. needs a healthy maritime industry. Given the realities of international shipping today, that requires subsidies.

The U.S. merchant marine is made up of privately owned companies such as our own Lykes Bros. Steamship Co. These companies are efficient, innovative and progressive. Their seagoing and shoreside personnel are U.S. citizens. Their ships are built in U.S. yards to the world's highest standards, helping to support the shipbuilding base our Navy depends upon. An example is the unique SEABEE barge-carrying ships developed by Lykes. These 875-foot vessels carry thirty-eight 1,000-ton capacity barges across the ocean, reducing shipping time and costs. Our three SEABEE vessels are regarded as ideal for defense transportation needs and they stand available—as do the 43 other vessels of our Lykes fleet—if required. If the Navy had to build and operate its own cargo-carrying fleet, the cost to taxpayers would be enormous, and the time delay dangerous.

Advantages of foreign competitors

The efficiency and innovation of the U.S. merchant marine cannot offset the cost advantages enjoyed by foreign competitors, who may enter our commerce and ports without duty or restriction. A growing number of foreign lines are government-controlled and do not operate for profit.

These ships are built and manned by workers whose wages are far below American levels. Subsidies are designed to make up the difference between our on-board wage levels and the composite cost of our competition. They do not guarantee a profit to U.S. companies. They do not cover shoreside costs. They do not place the U.S. operator at parity with foreign competitors.

Defense needs alone justify support for a merchant marine. But there are other reasons. The private U.S.-flag merchant fleet serves our country's commercial needs. These companies are alert to the needs of our exporting and importing firms and help to maintain fair ocean freight charges. The U.S. fleet contributes to our balance of payments and protects the public from dependence on foreign carriers for essential materials and goods.

The industry has served us well. Maritime subsidy programs, averaging about $400 million per year, are a small price to pay for such a vital national asset.

Our own Lykes Bros. Steamship Co., Inc. operates a fleet of 46 modern ships on trade routes covering five continents and U.S. ports on the Gulf, West and South Atlantic coasts and the Great Lakes.

What are your views? Write your elected officials. To be put on the LTV Issues mailing list write me, Paul Thayer, P.O. Box 225003-3A, Dallas, TX 75265.

The LTV Companies: Jones & Laughlin Steel, Continental Emsco Company, Vought Corporation, Kentron International, Lykes Bros. Steamship Co., Inc.

The inspiration for this series was the question, "What are the most critical issues facing the industries in which LTV is active?"

LTV

The LTV Corporation
Dallas, TX 75265

Exhibit 9   LTV. Looking Ahead

Does U.S. industry need trade protection?
"Realistically, yes..." says Kirkland.
"Counterproductive," argues Crandall.

U.S. NEEDS PROTECTION	LOOK BEYOND POLITICS	WHAT THE PEOPLE THINK	WHAT LTV BELIEVES
Lane Kirkland President, AFL-CIO	Robert W. Crandall Senior Fellow The Brookings Institution	Reported by Kenneth Schwartz Vice President, Opinion Research Corporation	Speaking for LTV, Paul Thayer Chairman of the Board and Chief Executive Officer

"...the cry of protectionism is never raised against protectionist governments; only against U.S. exporters who complain."

"...the arguments for trade protection ignore some rather fundamental political and economic forces which severely limit their validity."

"...people believe that American companies are falling behind..."

"...for the future of American industry to be successful, America must be able to compete equitably."

U.S. NEEDS PROTECTION

As American-flag ships vanished from the seas after World War II, seamen were told this was, after all, a manufacturing nation, not a service nation. Export, not transport, was where the jobs were.

After 30 years of export deficits, it is said the U.S. should emphasize service in its trade policy. The loss of steel plants in Pennsylvania, auto plants in New Jersey, railroad parts in California, shoes and machinery plants in Missouri and electronics, glass, rubber and aluminum nationwide are acceptable because this is a service economy.

Economic diversification only answer

In the eyes of the AFL-CIO, neither of these simple arguments holds water. The United States must be a diversified manufacturing, agricultural and service economy, with a complete range of basic industrial and technological products. Anything less fails to develop the resources and industries this nation needs to provide full employment and rising living standards. That is the goal. Trade policy is one means of pursuing that goal, not an end in itself.

Those who speak of "free trade" as if such a thing still existed talk as if the United States has many barriers to trade and other countries very few. The reverse is true. Other nations have planned economies, import restrictions, export requirements and export subsidies.

No U.S. exporter has free access to the markets in Japan or Brazil, let alone such countries as Romania or the Soviet Union. And yet, the cry of "protectionism" is never raised against protectionist governments; only against U.S. exporters who complain.

These are increasingly in short supply. It is easier to close U.S. plants, open new ones abroad, enjoy protection within these markets and export freely to the United States and third markets. Industry gets every encouragement to do so from U.S. policymakers, who deny help to American producers in the U.S. while deploying an array of subsidies for overseas investments.

Changing the balance

U.S. tax and trade policies have led to a world in which the principal traders are now multinational banks, corporations and governments, often working in partnership, destroying the industrial fabric of the United States while charging the U.S. with "protectionism." As long as this imbalance remains, the losses from foreign trade will be much higher than the gains for most Americans.

What America needs is a fair trade policy that takes account of the real world, in which free trade does not exist.

No country need apologize for giving weight to its own national interest; for the United States to ignore its people's needs is suicidal in the long run.

LOOK BEYOND POLITICS

Any period of economic adversity creates political pressures for "temporary" protection of domestic industries from import competition. Both labor and management argue that trade restrictions will allow industry to modernize, to reduce unemployment, and to be relieved from "unfair" foreign competition and its effect upon prices. The political appeal of these arguments is obvious. One needs only to look at the protection the U.S. government has given producers of textiles, shoes, clothing, meat, sugar, television sets, steel, and even automobiles.

Unfortunately, arguments for trade protection ignore fundamental political and economic forces which severely limit their validity. First, protection is usually counterproductive. Relieved of foreign competitive pressures, domestic producers are likely to adjust more slowly to economic circumstances. The steel industry has benefited from protection for all but four of the past twelve years. No one can seriously argue that this "temporary" respite has induced the industry to accelerate its modernization program.

Altering collective bargaining

Secondly, it weakens the resolve of management at the collective bargaining table. The most noticeable effect in the steel industry has been the sharp acceleration in its wage rate which began precisely when the first restrictions on steel imports were being negotiated. Now the industry pays $20 per hour for its labor and finds it difficult to compete with the Japanese and Koreans (or even the Canadians).

Perhaps the most disquieting result of trade protection is its permanency. Government cannot know whether it is easing an industry's temporary problems or creating a permanent ward of the state.

Removing all import restrictions on textiles or apparel is now unthinkable. We should not succumb to pressures for creating similar government wards out of our automobile or steel industries, even if other countries choose to subsidize their failing industries. American workers and consumers are not helped by a policy of sheltering businesses which are no longer competitive.

Finally, we must consider the effect of retaliation by foreign governments on our exporters. Trade protection for our dying and weak industries will reduce the demand for exports from our high-technology and farming sectors as foreign governments are forced to retaliate. We only need to look back on the 1930's to see how such trade policies can convert a recession into a depression. Surely, no one is well served by a trade war.

This is Mr. Crandall's opinion and not that of other staff members or trustees of The Brookings Institution.

WHAT THE PEOPLE THINK

How the American public feels about the very sensitive issue of foreign competition is an issue which is not only crucial to the nation's economy, and the LTV Corporation, it is a concern in almost every household.

To gain a better understanding of the depth of these feelings, Opinion Research Corporation conducted a nationwide telephone survey in March of 1,008 people. They were asked, "To begin with—from all that you have heard or read, would you say that American companies are holding their own or falling behind in competition with foreign companies?"

Six in ten Americans believe that U.S. companies *are* falling behind, while 29% think they are holding their own. The other 11% had no opinion.

More importantly, the proportion of people believing American industries are falling behind rises significantly as income rises.

Believe American companies are falling behind in competition with foreign companies

Under $10,000 family income	50%
$10,000–$14,999	57%
$15,000–$24,000	65%
$25,000–$49,000	68%
$50,000 or more	73%

We next asked if they would favor restrictions on imports. Four in ten of those who see American companies falling behind our foreign competition believe we should have restrictions on some imports. One in five would favor restrictions on all imports.

Percentage of Americans favoring restrictions on imported goods

Restrictions on all imports	23%
Restrictions on some imports	40%
No restrictions	32%
No opinion	5%

Of those favoring restrictions, the overwhelming majority favor restrictions on automobiles—75%. Other restrictions on goods and services were not so widely mentioned.

In sum, Americans are keenly aware of foreign competition and concerned about its impact on the U.S. economy. They also know that U.S. trade policies will have to change.

WHAT LTV BELIEVES

Open competition is an American legacy. Our nation's industrial success has been built upon that legacy. But, when the world's producer nations each play by a different set of rules, competition alone isn't enough.

American tax and consumer dollars helped make foreign competition as formidable as it is today. We accept that as a fact of business life. What we cannot accept are practices such as the dumping of government-subsidized, foreign-made steel into the U.S. market—steel sold at below the cost of the most efficient producer. In other words, when unfair trade practices are pursued, we believe our government must exercise a restraining hand. In the long run, carefully measured intercession will bolster rather than deter competition.

American business, on its own, must continue to produce more efficiently if it is to succeed in the world marketplace. LTV has recently embarked upon a $400 million capital expenditure program to modernize many of the steelmaking facilities of its steel subsidiary, Jones & Laughlin, the nation's third largest steel producer. This should strongly enhance J&L's ability to compete. Additionally, J&L has benefited significantly from a remarkably effective productivity improvement program.

1981 will be an important year for LTV's Jones & Laughlin steel group and our Continental Emsco energy products and services group. Strong demand for products—drilling equipment/supplies and tubular products—will have a positive impact on our revenues.

J&L is the nation's largest supplier of pipe to the oil and gas industry. Concurrently, new orders for Continental Emsco's drilling equipment are running far ahead of last year. In both cases, as the number of active drilling rigs and pipelines under construction continues to reach record levels, our activities in both areas will also increase.

LTV is dedicated to becoming increasingly competitive in the areas in which it operates—and to the principle of open competition. But for the future of American industry to be successful, America must be able to compete *equitably*. This will require more than hard work and capital investment. It will require U.S. and international trade policies that truly recognize the world marketplace as it exists today, and provide protection and fair play for *all* the participants. The end result will be a more balanced industrial environment. And that will benefit the *consumer* as well as industry.

The LTV Companies: Jones & Laughlin Steel, Continental Emsco Company, Vought Corporation, Kentron International, Lykes Bros. Steamship Co., Inc. To receive the LTV Issues series through the mail, write LTV Issues, P.O. Box 225003-6A, Dallas, TX 75265

The inspiration for this series was the question, "What are the most critical issues facing the industries in which LTV is active?"

The LTV Corporation
Dallas, TX 75265

Exhibit 10

What is America's defense responsibility for the rest of the world? Sadat vs. one of America's brilliant educators

ACCEPT RESPONSIBILITY

Anwar Sadat
President
Arab Republic of Egypt

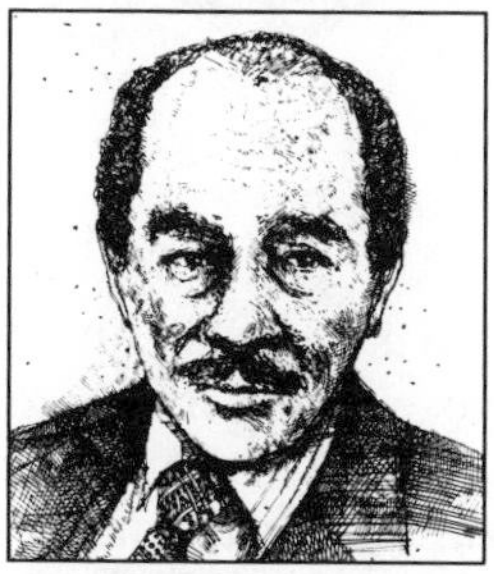

Democracy is essentially a matter of ethics, and in a democracy we must stand ready for a daily test of ethics.

Throughout the 70's you Americans suffered from your Vietnam complex. This gave the Soviets their freedom of action.

In Africa and the Middle East, the Soviets have built three belts of security for themselves. The first belt stretches from Angola to Mozambique. The second belt runs from Afghanistan through the anarchy of Iran, then South Yemen, Ethiopia, and finally Libya. The third belt is now under construction. Libya and Syria are starting a union together. The Soviet Union has already signed a treaty with Syria. This would be automatic in the case of Libya.

Look at the map. These three belts are clearly seen. They threaten us. We are a small country. But if the Soviets try to consolidate these belts, I shall fight.

If you in America do not again take up your responsibilities, as the first superpower of the world and the one which supports peace, all of us are doomed. We shall see the Soviet Union in the Persian Gulf as well as in the Mediterranean. We shall see them putting their puppets everywhere. And we know what it means to be a puppet of the Soviet Union. They foreclose people's dreams. They cancel out all logic. For they themselves are robots. It is only the head of the party who can act.

The forces of peace can win. I have dealt with the Soviet Union for a long time. If you check them, they will pull back.

For three years I have told the Americans this. I have said to the United States and the Western European nations that I will give them facilities to defend their position in the Persian Gulf. The collapse of the oil facilities there could mean the collapse of Western civilization. Without this oil the factories will stop. Look at all your tanks in NATO. Without oil they are scarecrows.

Of course to share our facilities with you and to cooperate in other economic matters is not only in your interest. It is in our interest. To whom will we send our oil, if not the West? Who will give us the know-how to rebuild our countries? Who will in the end share with us the nuclear energy to replace oil, if Western civilization collapses?

The Soviet Union will not give us these things. They have new technology in the military field only.

In the 80's there must be a new peaceful order in the world. I believe that we in Egypt can participate. To protect this order, the U.S. must accept its responsibilities.

You Americans did not ask me for facilities to reach the hostages in Iran. But one day I came and said that I was ready to give the United States such facilities.

I remain ready to offer any facilities that will help you reach the Gulf states. The face of the United States has changed for us. From that of the policeman—who represented imperialism and colonialism—to that of the peacemaker.

NO RESPONSIBILITY

Noam Chomsky
Massachusetts Institute of Technology
Professor of Linguistics

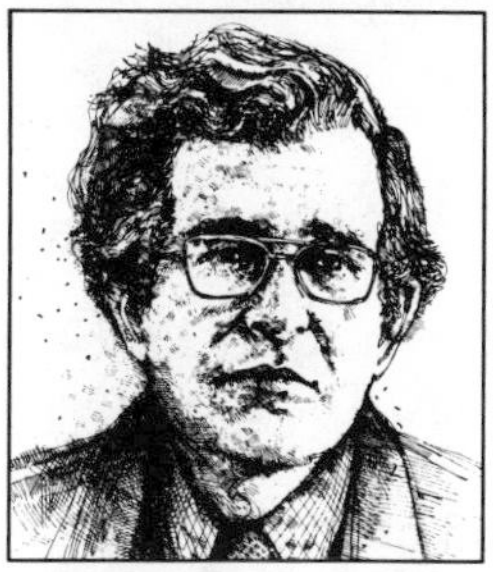

States use their power to defend the "National Interest," a mystification devised to conceal the special interest of those with domestic power.

Typically, the "defense of the national interest" policy is disguised in high-sounding rhetoric, which we dismiss with contempt when the official enemy "defends freedom and socialism" by sending tanks to Berlin, Budapest, Prague or Kabul, while solemnly reciting it when our own state acts in a similar way.

When the U.S. Air Force began the systematic bombardment of rural South Vietnam in 1962, it was defending those who were concerned over the "domino effect" of a successful nationalist-communist revolution that might be emulated elsewhere. The aggression was masked as defense against "internal aggression" by Vietnamese—indeed, South Vietnamese.

In support of "free" people?

In 1947, Truman announced that the U.S. would "support free people who are resisting attempted subjugation by armed minorities or by outside pressures," specifically, the Greek royalist elites and Nazi collaborators restored to power by the British Army, by then unable to repress the rebellion caused largely by British-backed terrorism.

The U.S. proceeded to defend the Greeks from "internal aggression" by supervising a program of massive repression, tens of thousands of political prisoners and exiles, political executions, reeducation camps, forced population removal, etc., exactly as any rational person reading the Truman doctrine would have predicted. In this case too, what was feared was the domino effect.

When the U.S. backed an invasion force in Guatemala in 1954, overthrowing a mildly reformist democratic government and installing a regime whose descendants still administer a huge reign of terror, it was defending the "national interest" but nothing else. The same is true of the destruction of the peasant society of northern Laos, the arming of mass murderers in Indonesia and El Salvador, and on and on.

Cold war victories

In each case, the propaganda system invokes the threat of the superpower enemy, exactly as the USSR does. The cold war has been highly functional for the superpowers, providing each with a framework for carrying out its designs within the reach of its power. Hence its persistence, despite the threat of mutual annihilation.

The world, however, is not what it once was. The relative decline of Soviet and American power brings forth new and increasingly assertive rivals. The EEC is moving slowly toward a more independent role, which may engage it in conflict with the U.S. in the Middle East and elsewhere. Similarly, Japan.

Before long, pursuit of the "national interest" may require new programs, new forms of violence and terror, and new rhetoric.

WHAT THE PUBLIC THINKS

Reported by Kenneth Schwartz
Vice President, Opinion Research Corporation

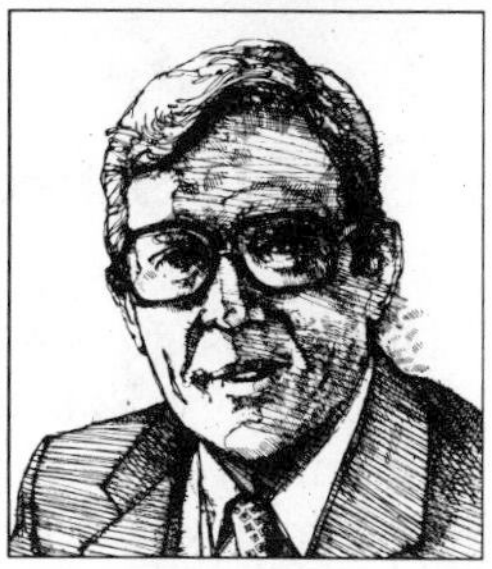

It all depended upon the kind of military help we mentioned. Advisors? Yes. Troops? No.

"How much responsibility, if any, do you think the United States has to protect other countries from takeovers or military action taken against them?" That was the question we asked the American public.

Of the 1,008 people contacted in a nation-wide telephone survey for LTV by Opinion Research Corporation, seven in ten believe that the U.S. has at least a fair amount of responsibility to undertake such protection, while 25 percent believe the U.S. has little or no obligation to do so. The remaining 5 percent have no opinion on the subject.

However, Americans are quite selective when it comes to the kind of military help they believe the U.S. should give a foreign country threatened by aggression.

Advisors vs. troops

"If a foreign country that is being threatened by aggression asks for protection, would you favor or oppose the United States sending military advisors?" Sixty percent said they would be in favor of such a move; 27 percent were opposed. Another 4 percent said "it depends"... while 9 percent had no opinion.

What does the public think about other key issues?

What do people think about subsidizing the U.S. merchant fleet? How do they rate America's technological capability against the rest of the world's? What are their attitudes toward opening up the American wilderness for oil, gas and mineral exploration?

LTV's Issues mailings report on the public's attitudes toward those and other subjects of importance to American business in general—and to The LTV Corporation in particular.

The issues are also discussed by responsible spokespeople with conflicting points of view. If you would like to be on our mailing list, write LTV-ISSUES, P.O. Box 225003-4A, Dallas TX 75265.

The question of sending troops provoked an entirely different response. Only 26 percent favored sending troops into a foreign country threatened by aggression that asked for protection. Fifty-seven percent registered their opposition to such a move. Six percent said "it depends"...and 11 percent had no opinion.

Sending and selling weapons

We also asked a question regarding *whether you would favor or oppose supplying weapons to a threatened country.* In favor: 42 percent. Opposed: 40 percent. It depends: 5 percent. No opinion: 13 percent. This was the only question where there wasn't a majority for one side of the issue or the other.

The majority of people would favor *selling* arms to a friendly or neutral foreign country. In favor of selling arms: 53 percent. Opposed: 31 percent. It depends: 12 percent. No opinion: 4 percent.

WHAT LTV BELIEVES

Speaking for LTV, Paul Thayer
Chairman of the Board and
Chief Executive Officer

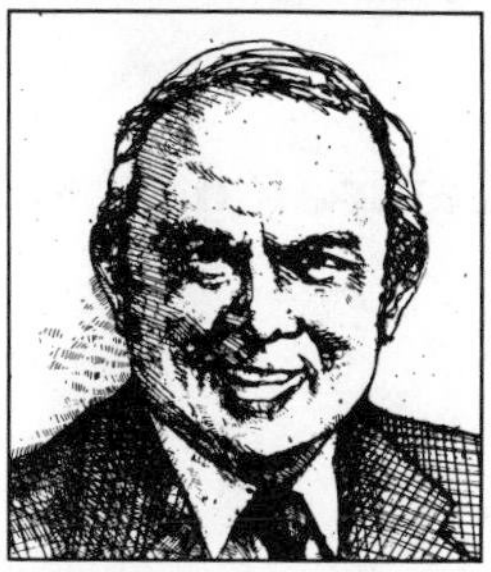

LTV supports President Reagan's proposal that America restore its own military capability.

We want to focus attention on this issue—but also present a balanced view. We're grateful to the Egyptian Embassy for helping us arrange for President Sadat to appear in our Forum. We also wish to thank Dr. Chomsky.

In a report to Congress last year, the Defense Department estimated that the Soviets had spent a total of *350 billion dollars more* on defense during the 1970's than we did. Last year, the Soviets devoted 12 percent of their GNP to defense—compared to our allocation of 5 percent. The Soviets have 3.5 million people in uniform compared to our 2 million. They enjoy a 2-to-1 advantage in tactical combat aircraft: a 3-to-1 advantage in tanks and armored vehicles; and a 4-to-1 superiority in attack submarines. *How should we assess this?*

Secretary of Defense Caspar Weinberger said, "It is neither reasonable nor prudent to view the Soviet military buildup as defensive in nature. It would be dangerously naïve to expect the Soviet Union—if it once achieves clear military superiority—not to try to exploit their military capability even more fully than they are now doing."

LTV believes we must honor our defense commitments. But to do so we must operate from a position of strength. In terms of real dollars, we are spending on defense today roughly what we were spending after the Korean War. As a percent of Gross National Product our defense outlay today is substantially less than it was in the early 1960's. President Reagan is redressing this dangerous trend. We support him in this needed effort. An effort aimed at improving our defenses, while still seeking to avoid an uncontrollable and unaffordable arms race.

In the final analysis increased defense spending will not make us more secure. Defense dollars must be spent wisely. We cannot afford a huge arsenal of weapons at the cost of a sick economy. Again, we feel the President is on the right track. His program to revive our economic strength, and the spirit of America, is every bit as vital to world security as the effort to strengthen our military posture.

LTV—through its subsidiary, Vought Corporation—has contributed to serving the free world's defense needs since World War I. We are dedicated to providing superior aircraft, missiles and technology at the lowest possible cost. The defense business is not always a popular one. When the issues are clearly defined, however, we think most people see it to be a necessary one.

Defense technology is one part of LTV's business, but one we take pride in as an instrument through which we help the nation meet its commitments in the continuing struggle for freedom.

The LTV Companies: Jones & Laughlin Steel, Continental Emsco Company, Vought Corporation, Kentron International, Lykes Bros. Steamship Co., Inc.

The inspiration for this series was the question, "What are the most critical issues facing the industries in which LTV is active?"

LTV
The LTV Corporation
Dallas, TX 75265

pany. We didn't want people to think—well, here comes this big conglomerate again. Running around, gobbling up companies.

4. This same philosophy explains the choice of media by LTV for its campaign. While a large number of other corporations include such opinion leader magazines as *Atlantic Monthly* and *Harper's,* and communication magazines like *Washington Journalism Review* and *Columbia Journalism Review,* LTV has confined itself to business and financial community magazines, with the sole exception of *Smithsonian.*

Campaign Costs and Media Schedule

The campaign ran between April 1981 and February 1982, and cost approximately $2.5 million. The media coverage was far more extensive than in previous years. Nevertheless, it was heavily concentrated in financial newspapers and magazines. The relevant publications and number of inserts were: *Wall Street Journal* (14), *Barron's* (10), *Fortune* (6), *Forbes* (7), *Business Week* (7), *Institutional Investor* (6), *Registered Representative* (3), *Newsweek* (Executive) (3), *Smithsonian* (6), and *Time* (2).

Effectiveness of the Campaign

LTV is very satisfied with the results of its two campaigns and plans to continue them in the future. The company believes that issue advertising is like a learning program which must be continuously sustained over a long period to be reliable and effective.

In addition to the tracking studies discussed earlier, LTV is particularly proud of the thousands of unsolicited letters it received from the readers of its various ads. The company received over 25,000 requests for the booklets from its candidates' views and industries campaigns. These requests were totally unsolicited. The volume of reader mail differed for different ads. However, the *Wall Street Journal* ad series (1980) generated a total of almost 6,000 letters, followed by *Forbes* (2,700), and *Barron's* (750). According to Johnson:

> It was very gratifying—the thoughtful content of the letters, praising LTV for its statesmanship role in providing this provocative and informative forum—and we were pleased with the large number of respondents who asked to be put on our mailing list and who asked for the annual report.

THE 1982 CAMPAIGN

The 1982 campaign essentially followed the 1981 format, but with two significant modifications: (1) The issues selected were much broader in scope and addressed public policy concerns that transcended the narrow and immediate interests of the company. The campaign moved LTV one step closer to stimulating public discussion of issues that are still in the formulative stages. (2) Rather than surveying general public opinion, ORC surveyed and reported the views of opinion leaders. It was felt that since the dimensions and scope of these issues had not yet been fully delineated, a dissemination of informed views of the nation's opinion leaders would be more relevant to the discussion of the issues.

Copy Themes

Four issues were addressed in the 1982 campaign:

1. The Role of Individual Investors in America's Stock Markets [Exhibit 11]. It is common knowledge that equity capital in large American corporations is increasingly owned by institutional investors such as trust funds and insurance companies, and managed by professional managers. These managers, with their fiduciary responsibilities, are primarily interested in increasing short-run returns on their investments, and move in and out of corporations at the first sign of problems, rather than staying in and helping correct those problems. The advertisement examines the problem from different perspectives, and examines what, if anything, might be done to encourage greater individual participation in the stock market.

2. The second advertisement, "Can Labor and Management Form a More Successful Partnership?" [Exhibit 13], looks at the traditional adversarial relationship between America's management and organized labor, and raises the question whether, in view of declining American productivity and increasing foreign competition, this relationship should be re-examined in order to develop more participatory and cooperative forms of labor-management relations.

3. The third advertisement examined the question of increasing foreign investment in the United States. Traditionally, the United States has been the largest investor in foreign countries. While these investments, in most cases, have been a positive factor in the economic growth of the countries involved, there have also been some real and imagined adverse consequences. American multinational corporations have been accused of exercising control over the economies of these countries, transferring obsolete technology, and making exorbitant profits. In many cases, the U.S. government has used American multinational corporations as instruments of its foreign policy—for example, imposing restrictions on the French and British subsidiaries of American companies in exporting equipment to the USSR for the construction of the Trans-Siberian gas pipeline.

4. The fourth ad in the series was titled "Corporate Social Responsibility: Where Does It Begin? Where Does It End?" [Exhibit 12]. While American corporations have come a long way from the notion that the only social responsibility of the corporation is to make money for its stockholders, the debate is by no means over. No one disagrees that a corporation must be profitable, survive, and grow, in order to fulfill its primary economic function. The debate is, however, not on

Exhibit 11   LTV Looking Ahead

Is there a future for individual investors in America's stock market?

William Freund and Jude Wanniski voice their opinions

Recently, more individuals have been investing in the stock market, but they've been investing less. What will the future hold? That is the topic of the following Looking Ahead report — another in a series focusing on issues critical to business.

An Optimistic View

**Dr. William C. Freund
Senior Vice President
and Chief Economist,
New York Stock Exchange**

Is there a future for individual investors in America's stock market? A resounding *yes.*

But success depends in large part on the individual's perception of his relationship to the market. Too often an individual sees the market as an overwhelming or mysterious force run by huge institutions.

This attitude of 'market as adversary' overshadows the very real financial and psychological benefits offered by individual involvement.

Why is individual shareownership desirable? It gives each of us our own direct stake in our economic system. It works to diffuse economic power to help keep our competitive system responsive to the majority of the population. It helps unify 'owners' and 'workers' in the common goal of intensifying productivity growth for the economic good of all.

Boosting productivity

The last point is particularly significant. Currently, this country is in a productivity slump which impairs our ability to compete domestically and in world markets. Recent New York Stock Exchange studies indicate the importance of boosting productivity growth. And one way of accomplishing this is to eliminate the wall which now seems to exist between management and labor. A key to destroying the barrier is individual involvement in the market, for employees can then assume a direct equity interest in the companies they work for as well as American enterprise in general. They, in short, join management through their association in the market. The economy as a whole, as well as the individual investor, will be well served by such a move. The U.S. needs unprecedented amounts of new equity capital to help finance the renewal and modernization of its businesses. Through increased equity investments, individual investors can help launch a new era of capital formation, rising productivity, and real economic growth. If that happens, millions of individuals should reap the rewards of investment in stock.

Individual involvement in the stock market is a key to productivity growth — indeed to protecting our current economic system.

Toward this end, the New York Stock Exchange does everything in its power to assure that the rights of individual investors are at all times protected. For example, on the Exchange, an individual's order to buy or sell at a specific price has the right to participate in even the largest transactions by institutional investors. Through close regulation and surveillance of the marketplace, we do our best to see to it that nobody — individual or institution — trades on the basis of inside information.

Clearly, there is a need for the individual investor in the stock market. And more people are investing in stocks, especially at younger ages. That is a strong vote in favor of the proposition that there *is* a future for individual investors in America's stock market.

Strengthen Dollar First

**Jude Wanniski
President, Polyconomics**

Over the past decade, the stock market was a downright dangerous place for people to put their savings. A hundred dollars invested in stocks was worth, on average, only $54 nine years later after correcting for inflation. In the decade ahead, the stock market may become a delightful place to be, but only if our government changes its

policy toward our American dollar.

The stock market, after all, is by far the best gauge of the health of the national economy. And the entire dollar economy, worldwide, got off the track a little more than ten years ago because of a drastic change in the government's policy toward our currency.

With reduction in tax rates and a sound dollar restored, the stock market will again be a desirable place for investors.

Specifically, President Nixon on August 15, 1971, ended the government guarantee that the dollar would be worth a specific amount of gold. The change was based on the notion that by devaluing our currency, we could buy fewer goods abroad and sell more American goods in the export market, thereby increasing the number of American jobs.

The real effect was to damage the dollar as a standard of value. Its price, in real goods, has fluctuated dramatically, first with the worst inflation in our history, now with one of the most serious deflations. Since 1973, real national output *per employee* has risen by only 1.9 percent. There has been an illusion of expansion, but it has been achieved only by forcing wives out of the home to work and by pulling students away from their books.

A dramatic turnabout

Only when our government restores the dollar's guarantee will we see real economic expansion and a rising standard of living. But when it happens, it will happen dramatically. With faith in the dollar restored, interest rates will fall to low levels and the economy will blossom with the return of long-term credit. The housing and automobile industries, which rely on the availability of credit, would lead the way in a buoyant economy and a buoyant stock market.

And yes, we need to get the *individual* investor back into the market, especially those willing to take the risks in developing new enterprises.

Buying stock is buying a piece of the future. And with the benefit of our hindsight, the future looks potentially bright. There has already been a major shift of attitude against tinkering with the dollar's value. And the government has now seen that the tax system cannot be used to punish productive effort and investment.

Much remains to be done. But when the reduction in tax rates is finally in place, and a sound dollar restored, the stock market will be a much more comfortable place for the American investor to be.

What Opinion Leaders Think

**Reported by
Kenneth Schwartz
Vice President,
Opinion Research Corporation**

In the eyes of the nation's opinion leaders, the individual investor's participation in stock market trading will decline or stay the same rather than increase.

The Opinion Research Corporation surveyed 500 opinion leaders in the worlds of business, media, academics, labor, government, and public interest groups to learn their views of the future of individual investors in the stock market. Interviews were conducted on behalf of The LTV Corporation in February 1982.

The general outlook for participation by the individual investor is pessimistic — prediction

For a number of reasons, leaders feel that individual participation in the stock market will not increase in the near future.

of decreased participation is especially high among labor leaders (51%), public interest group leaders (46%), and academics (44%). Only business executives seem somewhat optimistic — 39% feel participation will increase, though as many as one in three feel it will do no better than stay the same.

Leaders who think individual trading will decrease were asked why. The prime reason was that other financial vehicles, such as pension, money market, and mutual funds are more attractive than the market to today's more sophisticated investors. Another important reason is general concern over economic conditions, inflation and stock market instability. High interest rates and the lack of available cash also are cited.

Institutional involvement thought positive

Opinion leaders as a group do not seem overly concerned about the growing dominance of stock market trading by institutional investors. Overall, in fact, 37% of those surveyed felt this institutional activity was "good" as opposed to 27% who termed it "bad". The main exception was the group of public interest group leaders: 43% of that group felt institution involvement was a bad trend.

Leaders were asked their views on the effectiveness of recent tax law changes:

Will tax changes be effective in increasing individual investment or should there be more incentives?			
	Changes will be effective	More changes needed	No opinion
Total Opinion Leaders	42%	49%	11%
Business Executives	61%	39%	5%
Media Representatives	31%	66%	3%
Elected Government Officials	45%	41%	14%
Labor Union Leaders	29%	60%	11%

Those who think further changes in tax laws are needed think the two most significant incentives would be (1) eliminate or revise the capital gains tax and (2) eliminate double taxation of dividends.

How LTV Is Involved

**Speaking for LTV,
Paul Thayer
Chairman of the Board
and Chief Executive Officer**

The Stock Market. Is there a future in it for the individual investor? Apparently a great many individual investors think so. Today, one in every seven Americans is a stockholder. And almost half of those shareowners are in families with incomes below $25,000 a year.

Millions of individuals in this country own stock in the companies for which they work. Through various employee stock purchase plans, they develop a direct financial involvement in the future of their companies and in the growth of our enterprise economy in general.

The strength of the market system and the nation behind it promises a bright future for the individual investor.

Individual involvement in the market is the very cornerstone of our democratic enterprise system. But is there a future in it for people who want to buy a stake in that system? There is if that system and the nation behind it are as strong as I believe them to be.

The stock market is an important economic barometer. A recovery in the market usually is the forerunner of recovery from a recession. Of equal importance, the stock market is a barometer of the national mood, reflecting the level of confidence people feel in the country.

Long-term optimism

At the moment, the nation is in evident economic turmoil. The stock market is reflecting this and participation by individual investors has correspondingly waned. In the short term, this is an understandable adjustment to present realities. For the long term, I believe that we can solve our problems — and emerge from the present turmoil stronger than ever.

This country has enormous resilience, a strong collective will and a demonstrated history of overcoming adversity. I believe we will become increasingly competitive internationally, more productive, and able to meet the difficult challenges that face us. I also believe that government, labor, and business will have to work in closer harmony than in the past to make this possible.

Given this latter development, we can look forward to a vibrant economy and to a stock market that will offer a promising future for the prudent, informed individual investor.

About LTV

The LTV Corporation is a diversified operating company involved in four different industries: ENERGY: Continental Emsco Company; STEEL: Jones & Laughlin Steel; AEROSPACE/DEFENSE: Vought Corporation; OCEAN SHIPPING: Lykes Bros. Steamship Co., Inc.

If you'd like a free booklet with expanded statements by *Looking Ahead* participants, to be published at the conclusion of this series of reports, write Paul Thayer, Chairman, The LTV Corporation, P.O. Box 225003-12A, Dallas, TX 75265.

LTV

The LTV Corporation
Dallas, TX 75265

Exhibit 12

Corporate social responsibility: Where does it begin? Where does it end?

Lewis Lehr and Paul MacAvoy speak out

Social, community, and cultural groups are turning increasingly to corporations for support. To what extent should corporations respond? This is the subject of the following Looking Ahead report — another in a series of discussions focusing on issues critical to the business community.

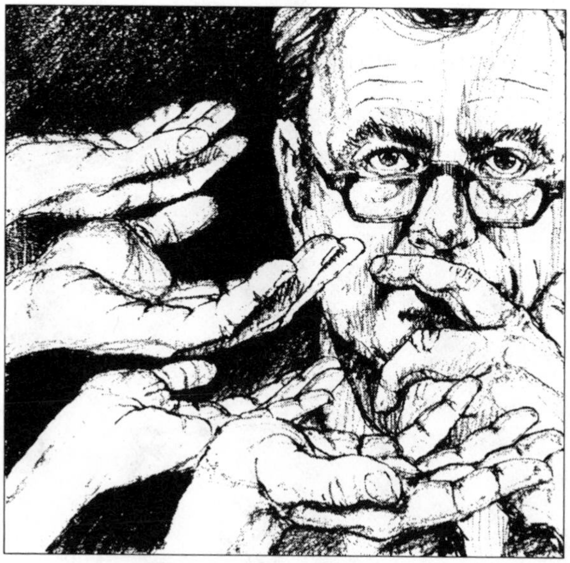

Enlightened Self-Interest

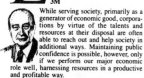

Lewis W. Lehr
Chairman and CEO,
3M

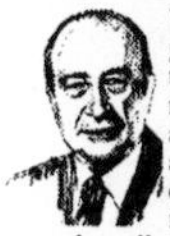

While serving society, primarily as a generator of economic good, corporations by virtue of the talents and resources at their disposal are often able to reach out and help society in additional ways. Maintaining public confidence is possible, however, only if we perform our major economic role well, harnessing resources in a productive and profitable way.

More corporate philanthropy is certainly desirable at a time when private sector leadership is being sought to fill gaps in support for existing social programs. But the broad base of corporate responsibility must remain a pervasive social consciousness in all of our dealings, respecting the legitimate interests of customers, suppliers, employees, stockholders and neighbors. Only when the bills are paid, the payroll met, the customer served and our owners fairly rewarded can we add in any responsible way the "frosting on the cake."

My view is that the needs and interests of society are *not* in opposition to those of business. Public interest and private profit are compatible. Our challenge is to find innovative ways in which self-interest *and* the common good can be served.

For a company to be responsible to its community is more than altruism — it is good business.

For a company to be especially conscious of its responsibility to the communities in which it operates is more than altruism. It is good business, and good for business.

A fleet of vans for more than a thousand commuting employees may strike some as an expensive fringe benefit and others as a worthy conservation initiative. In fact, the program is largely a self-funded one which saves our company what it would otherwise have spent on parking lots and ramps.

Pollution prevention is more than an obligation which business owes to society. It is rather an obligation we owe to ourselves and our communities. And pollution prevention can pay off in our bottom line.

Carefully focused and well-leveraged corporate philanthropy can likewise serve as a channel for enlightened self-interest. My own company's interest is clear in the millions given each year to education. We expect to benefit from a well-educated citizenry.

Whether the giving is in time or money, expertise or judgment, it can surely be in the stockholders' interest . . . if the result is a society more conducive to the long-range survival and success of corporate endeavor. Anything less than an innovative response by corporations to the current challenge may well put future profits at risk.

Economic Efficiency the Priority

Dr. Paul MacAvoy
Professor of Economics,
Yale University

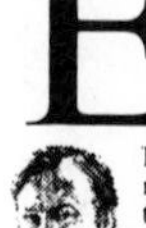

In recent years, there have been mounting pressures on the corporation to serve social interests as well as private investors. These pressures intensify as the Reagan Administration cuts back on government social programs and calls on corporations to fill the void. But at the same time, increased domestic and international competitiveness makes it more necessary than ever for the corporation to accelerate investment so as to provide better and cheaper goods and services which consumers are willing to buy, rather than those of competitors. The corporation cannot use the same cash flow to benefit social interest groups and make investments.

How can such social and efficiency objectives be reconciled? Certainly not by the example of how well the government has traded one off against the other. The difficult choices of "how much more" that confounded government social programs have been passed on to the corporation without any indication of how to make them.

There are even more basic problems than just finding the limits of conflicting responsibility. The corporation as now constituted cannot, given its legal obligations, pursue charitable enterprises. It is set up so that if management deviates substantially from the pursuit of investor returns to pursue social policy objectives, it becomes a takeover target by other companies and even dissatisfied stockholders. Furthermore, antitrust and regulatory policies in this country are designed to achieve maximum investment, and deviations such as price fixing are not condoned on grounds that they are in the public service, as defined by charitable groups. What the company can do as a matter of business strategy is to make investments and conduct operations so as to produce the highest possible returns to stockholders. In a competitive economy, such as we now have, this enhances investment, which increases productivity, innovation and the total volume of goods and services for all consumers.

The primary public policy concern of the large corporation is to generate the highest possible returns to investors.

When the corporation invites various social or political constituencies to share in the basic returns from investment, this system breaks down. Sooner or later, these socially responsible constituencies require obsolete plants to be kept in operation, or employment to be maintained in a recession. Doing these things resolves social conflicts, but destroys the corporation as an investment institution.

Furthermore, to practice social policy consistently, the corporation would have to be "democratized" to make it responsive to these other constituencies. This would require that community and labor leaders, and church members be added to the board of directors to represent such interests. After all, present board members have no expertise in representing such interests. But a board elected by such constituencies would undermine the pursuit of economic objectives which the corporation does better than any other institution.

What Opinion Leaders Think

Reported by
Kenneth Schwartz
Vice President,
Opinion Research Corporation

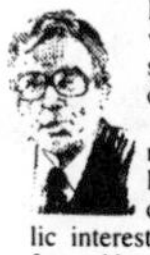

In today's society, the corporation is viewed as more than an economic institution; it must also meet certain social responsibilities.

This is the principal finding of a nationwide survey of 500 opinion leaders in business, media, academics, labor, government, and public interest groups. The interviews were performed by the Opinion Research Corporation on behalf of The LTV Corporation.

Leaders feel corporations must be socially responsible, but those outside business are skeptical as to whether business will accept the financial burdens of responsibility.

The vast majority of those in every subgroup polled believed that the corporation *does* have certain social responsibilities. Labor union leaders were nearly unanimous (97%) in this belief, and most other groups concurred. The one exception is academic leaders — almost a quarter of this group, 23%, felt that a corporation is solely an economic institution.

To what degree should business be responsible for the social, cultural and educational programs formerly provided by the Federal government? Overall, 57% feel that business has at least a fair amount of responsibility. Public interest group leaders are most firm in this belief — 88% consider business responsible for such programs, while less than half of the academic leaders (41%) feel this way. Business executives are divided on this issue: 47% believe they have a great deal or fair amount of responsibility, 45% think they have little or no responsibility.

Areas of responsibility

Opinion leaders who say business should assume some responsibility were given a chance to react to the importance of business support in a number of areas. Ninety percent of this group overall consider providing more employment opportunities and job training programs for the unemployed and minorities as very or somewhat important. Other areas evaluated as important were expanded services/benefits for employees, such as day care, van pooling, or health services; support of educational institutions; additional support of established community services and charities; support of scientific research outside the company; increased support for cultural activities and development of new social service programs for the community.

Whether business actually will assume financial responsibility in these areas is another matter. A majority of opinion leaders overall think business will do so in supporting educational institutions (61%), employee benefits (59%), funding community services and charities (56%) and providing jobs for unemployed (54%). But leaders are divided on how business will support science and the arts — and almost two-thirds (64%) think business will *not* assume the financial responsibility of developing new social service programs for communities.

Consistently, business executives seem more confident than other opinion leaders that corporations actually will assume financial responsibility in areas considered most important.

How LTV Is Involved

Speaking for LTV,
Paul Thayer
Chairman of the Board and
Chief Executive Officer

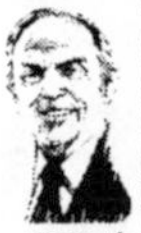

The relationship between the American public and American business has had, like any other long-term relationship, its definite ups and downs. Sometimes, business has been viewed as the darkest villain, interested only in profits; at other times, business has been applauded as the engine which moves the nation to marvelous economic and technological feats.

America's businesses have risen quite effectively to meet the challenges of social responsibility.

And out of these ups and downs, our relationship is changing to one in which the public acknowledges a business's need for efficiency and profitability, while corporations understand social needs and their role in them.

Clearly, the corporation cannot be a dispassionate bystander. The evolutionary process which has made business such a force in American society also heaps a great deal of social responsibility on business. By and large, I believe America's businesses have risen quite effectively to meet those challenges.

Interrelated responsibilities

The first and foremost responsibility of business remains its function as employer, supplier of goods, and profit maker. This must be uppermost in the minds of business decision-makers as they set policies and make strategic decisions.

But the corporation's economic responsibilities are so closely related to overall social responsibility that they cannot be ignored. It takes people to work factories, it takes natural resources to produce goods — and people and resources and communities must remain healthy for business to be healthy. They must be enriched in order for business to be enriched.

The argument that contributions to worthy social programs and causes deprive stockholders of the profits they deserve is no longer really a valid one. Those who invest in our corporations also enjoy the fruits of a better society. I feel that our willingness to share some of our profits to serve our communities is a move that stockholders understand, expect, and endorse.

I am confident that in the ever-evolving relationship of corporation and public, the many aspects of our society can and will benefit.

About LTV

The LTV Corporation is a diversified operating company involved in four different industries: ENERGY: Continental Emsco Company; STEEL: Jones & Laughlin Steel; AEROSPACE/DEFENSE: Vought Corporation; OCEAN SHIPPING: Lykes Bros. Steamship Co., Inc.

If you'd like a free booklet with expanded statements by *Looking Ahead* participants, to be published at the conclusion of this series of reports, write Paul Thayer, Chairman, The LTV Corporation, P.O. Box 225003-14A, Dallas, TX 75265.

LTV

The LTV Corporation
Dallas, TX 75265

Exhibit 13

LTV: Looking Ahead

Can labor and management form a more successful partnership?

Douglas Fraser and A.H. Raskin share their views

Union leaders, business executives, and long-time labor observers are aware of the need for change in the labor-management relationship. This is the topic of the following Looking Ahead report — another in a series of discussions focusing on issues critical to the business community.

Six Important Changes

Douglas A. Fraser
President, United
Automobile Workers

The labor movement should concentrate its energies in six basic areas in the years ahead.

First, labor must seek to extend the principle of democracy to the workplace itself. Rather than challenging unsound corporate decisions only after those decisions have been made, labor should have a voice — a meaningful voice — in corporate decision making from the start.

We should expand the input, participation and power of the working people who build our products and provide our services. And corporate America should embrace that participation as a resource of great value.

Second, unions must seek mechanisms that provide workers with greater job security.

We are currently experiencing the worst economic downturn since the Great Depression. Workers with 15 and 20 and 25 years' seniority suddenly have found themselves indefinitely or even permanently out of work.

Labor must work toward the day when contractions in the work force will be managed by attrition, rather than by the cruel, inhumane and wasteful practice of throwing able-bodied and willing workers on the economic scrap heap.

In a number of arenas: corporate, political, social, international, labor must take on a new role.

Third, in this age of multinational corporations, unions must redouble their efforts to develop a vigorous and coordinated worldwide labor movement.

The corporations that bargain across the table with U.S. unions are often multinationals functioning in many countries with widely varying working conditions. Labor's goal must be to harmonize the variables of labor cost so that companies compete on the basis of product innovation, efficiency, quality and other factors — rather than by driving wages to the lowest common denominator.

New efforts in productivity

Fourth, labor must support efforts to improve quality and productivity. That is in the best interest of workers. The U.A.W., for example, has pressed the auto companies on the quality issue, because our members' jobs are at stake.

Fifth, unions must do a better job of communicating, both with the public and their own members.

Opinion polls rank unionists right down at the bottom of the list. Despite all labor has done on behalf of social, political and economic justice for so many, including millions who never belonged to a union, the public regards us too often as a negative force.

We must redefine more vigorously the role of

labor as a positive, progressive institution that seeks not just gain for a few, but for all — and particularly for those in our society without the power to represent themselves.

And, in addition to organizing the unorganized, labor must spend more time unionizing the organized. Our strength rests in an informed, active and committed membership. The old trade union shibboleths won't be enough on which our younger union members can base their relationship with their union.

Sixth, labor will have to redouble its efforts in the political area.

In the years ahead, the gains which labor will seek won't be won at the negotiating table — but in the statehouses and in Congress.

Labor must update its use of the political technologies so effectively employed by Big Business. And we must press for reforms to prevent elections from being sold to the highest corporate bidder.

By working toward change in these six areas, the union can start to redefine its role as one which will benefit not only labor, but *all* Americans.

Seeds of Trust Planted

**Abe H. Raskin
Associate Director
The National News Council**

Powerful labor unions, traditionally geared to the pursuit of "more," are currently accommodating to the unpleasant necessity of settling for less. Awareness that the United States is in a fight for economic survival has prompted one union after another to agree to freeze wages and sacrifice prized work rules as a contribution to saving jobs and keeping sick industries alive.

Are unions finally recognizing that adversarial attitudes carried over from the turbulent 1930's are poor armor for confronting the infinitely more complex industrial challenges of the 1980's? Or will this accommodating spirit, born of mass unemployment and fierce global trade competition, disappear when the economy gets stronger?

My own conviction is that both the need and the opportunity have never been greater for chipping away the antagonisms of the past and establishing a fruitful new relationship built on cooperation by management and labor. The key lies in restructuring the lines of command in the workplace to make workers full-fledged partners in shaping the decisions that directly affect their jobs.

Treating workers as adults with worthwhile ideas about how to improve the business, rather than as children in constant need of direction, pays dividends in productivity, quality, and job satisfaction. There is nothing visionary about this approach; it is the essence of the teamwork system on which Japanese efficiency and good workmanship are built.

Workers must become full-fledged partners in shaping the decisions that directly affect their jobs.

America is ripe for speedy progress in the same direction as evidenced by the agreements being made right now by giant companies and unions which provide for increased employee involvement and shared authority. Management is surrendering some of its sacrosanct prerogatives in favor of imaginative new arrangements for more shop-floor democracy. Profit-sharing funds and employee stock ownership plans are symptoms of the change that is making the worker's voice heard at every level, up to the executive suite and the boardroom.

It would be ridiculous to suggest that acceptance of the partnership idea is universal at this stage. Too many unionists still cling to the "hate the boss" philosophy which they acquired in bloody battles on the picket lines; too many employers see the present as a period for cracking down on unions and for making their own rule more ironclad.

My hope is that no clumsy misstep on either side will push us back into the sterility of conflict. That would be suicidal for both.

What Opinion Leaders Think

**Reported by
Kenneth Schwartz
Vice President, Opinion
Research Corporation**

Opinion leaders in groups as diverse as business executives, media representatives, labor union leaders, public interest groups, academics and government officials strongly favor a more cooperative relationship between management and labor. That was the response of 500 opinion leaders questioned in February 1982 by Opinion Research Corporation on behalf of LTV. Overall, 7 out of 10 polled responded they strongly favor a positive change in the relationship of labor and management. Labor union leaders (86%) and business executives (76%) are most enthusiastic in this regard.

Leaders believe a new era of labor-management relations is dawning — but how long it will take to come is in dispute.

There is also consensus on the reasons *why* most opinion leaders think that a new era of labor-management relations is dawning. "Need for increased productivity" is seen as very or fairly important by 93%. Opinion leaders are also nearly unanimous (92%) in viewing "international competition" as a factor which will lead to an improved labor-management relationship. Other reasons cited include "need for job security" (80%), "slower economic growth in many basic industries" (77%), and "trend to automation" (75%). Significantly, all subgroups, with few exceptions, tend to agree on the relative importance of the reasons evaluated.

Disagreement on time frame

This unanimity of opinion breaks down, however, when opinion leaders were asked how long they think it will take for a change in labor-management relations to occur. The response of the overall opinion leaders and of selected subgroups is as follows:

When opinion leaders expect a significant positive change in labor-management relations.			
	Within two to three years	Within four to five years	Longer than five years	Not at all
Total Opinion Leaders	50%	13%	14%	19%
Business Executives	60%	13%	11%	11%
Labor Union Leaders	43%	6%	25%	26%
Elected Government Officials	50%	17%	14%	14%
Academics	29%	8%	23%	31%
Public Interest Groups	28%	9%	20%	37%

The final issue was worker participation in

decision making affecting jobs. While 63% of labor leaders strongly favor this, only 25% of business executives do. Overall, opinion leaders feel it will take some time for any change in participation to occur. Four leaders in ten think it will take longer than five years; about one in eight feel a change won't occur at all.

How LTV Is Involved

**Speaking for LTV,
Paul Thayer,
Chief Executive Officer
and Chairman of the Board**

Americans from every walk of life are now recognizing the devastating effect that uncooperative feelings between unions and management have on national productivity. Some are calling for "new" partnerships to be forged to overcome the difficulties many U.S. companies are facing.

No meaningful partnership between management and unions will be achieved, however, until we deal with several basic issues that unions tend to overlook.

Primary among these is the need to recognize that each company is unique. Each has its own peculiar problems and its own set of opportunities. Each has differing resources to bring into action for the long-term good of the company and its employees. Union leaders — particularly at the international level — need to be more sensitive to individual company situations and to long-term solutions to problems. Where this is not the case, the results can stifle growth and even bring about unnecessary job losses and business failures.

Both management and workers have a mutual interest: the success of the companies for which we work.

Much is being said today about shared decision making, but this an obligation that rests solely with those who have responsibility for the consequences of those decisions. That is true whether you are a business manager or a union leader. Management cannot abdicate this most important of its responsibilities, vested in it by the shareholders.

Seeking information needed for sound decisions is another matter. Much work is needed in this area in every company whether the employee is a manager or is represented by a union.

The sharing of ideas, criticisms, suggestions and knowledge of the task at hand is the key to intelligent, effective decisions that will benefit everyone. Management must have this input from all employees, union represented or not, and labor leaders equally must seek information if their advocacy is to be informed and appropriate to the local situation.

In the final analysis, management and workers have a mutual interest. Each of us is an employee and each of us has a stake in the success of a common venture: the company for which we work.

About LTV

The LTV Corporation is a diversified operating company involved in four different industries: ENERGY: Continental Emsco Company; STEEL: Jones & Laughlin Steel; AEROSPACE/DEFENSE: Vought Corporation; OCEAN SHIPPING: Lykes Bros. Steamship Co., Inc.

If you'd like a free booklet with expanded statements by *Looking Ahead* participants, to be published at the conclusion of this series of reports, write Paul Thayer, Chairman, The LTV Corporation, P.O. Box 225003-13O, Dallas, TX 75265.

profits per se, but on how they are earned—on how such externalities as environmental costs are borne by the society, how corporations might involve themselves in helping those groups who are adversely affected in the process of producing goods and services, and what responsibilities corporations should have to the larger community.

Media Schedule

The primary media for the campaign again was the *Wall Street Journal*, with ten insertions between July and November 1982, followed by *Fortune* and *Smithsonian*, with one insertion each.

NOTES

1. James C. Tanner, "Mergers Play Key Role as James Ling Builds Electronics Empire," *Wall Street Journal*, May 16, 1960, p. 1; "The 500: A Decade of Growth," *Fortune*, July 15, 1966, p. 213; Stanley H. Brown, "Jimmy Ling's Wonderful Growth Machine," *Fortune*, January 19, 1967, pp. 137–138; "Ling: The Merger King," cover story, *Newsweek*, October 9, 1967, pp. 71–81; "Jim Ling's Instant Conglomerate," *Forbes*, November 1, 1967, p. 42. LTV was receiving extensive coverage in the news media during the late 1960s. For example, in *Wall Street Journal* alone, there were 42 stories on LTV in 1965, 66 in 1966, 109 in 1967, 140 in 1968, and 158 in 1969.
2. The other companies included in the survey were TRW, Bethlehem Steel, Northwest Industries, Gulf-Western, Cooper Industries, Armco Steel, National Steel, and IC Industries.
3. The image characteristics measured were: being innovative, being growth-oriented, being competitive, meeting planning objectives, being financially sound, having strong management, responsive to needs of marketplace, self-sufficient in raw materials, having profitability, being honest and trustworthy, speaking out on key political issues facing businesses, and being a spokesman for the future of businesses they are in.
4. James Robins, "Merger of Lykes into LTV Given Holder Approval: Union Valued $188 Million Creates Third or Fourth Largest U.S. Steelmaker," *Wall Street Journal*, December 6, 1978, p. 6. For a discussion of the rise and fall of conglomerates and their economic implications, see John Brooks, "Annals of Finance—The Go-Go Years," *New Yorker*, Part 1, June 23, 1973, p. 40; Part II, July 2, 1973, p. 35; Part III, August 13, 1973, p. 58. Part II contains a discussion of Jim Ling's activities. See also George J. Benston, *Conglomerates Mergers: Causes, Consequences, and Remedies* (Washington, D.C.: American Enterprise Institute, 1980); Harry H. Lynch, *Financial Performance of Conglomerates*, (Boston: Division of Research, Graduate School of Business, Harvard University, 1971); and David Stone, *An Economic Approach to Planning the Conglomerate of the 70's* (Princeton, NJ: Auerbach Publishers, 1970).

Chapter 4

SMITHKLINE BECKMAN CORPORATION, PHILADELPHIA:

AN ISSUE-INFORMATION ADVERTISING CAMPAIGN TO STIMULATE PUBLIC DISCUSSION OF IMPORTANT PUBLIC POLICY ISSUES THROUGH DISSEMINATION OF AUTHORITATIVE VIEWS BY WELL-KNOWN AND NATIONALLY RECOGNIZED EXPERTS

Between March 1979 and February 1982, SmithKline Beckman Corporation undertook a major advocacy campaign in the *Wall Street Journal, Newsweek,* and *Time.* The avowed purpose of the campaign was to create greater public awareness of and generate more discussion on certain issues of public policy that the company felt were not being adequately addressed among important segments of the nation's opinion leadership.

An equally important added purpose was to create a recognition among the company's major constituencies—stockholders, suppliers, the financial and investment communities—that SmithKline was a respon-

---

Research assistant: Mohamed Allam.

sible corporate citizen whose concerns were not limited to the immediate matters of products and services, but extended into those areas of public policy and public opinion that ultimately affect all corporations and the future of private enterprise in the United States.

SmithKline thereby became part of a small group of U.S. corporations that have elevated issue-advocacy advertising from the low road of rather brazen advocacy of particularly self-serving solutions of public policy issues to the high road of enlightened discussion of important public policy issues, albeit those in which corporate and business interests have a significant stake.

The campaign was suspended in February 1982, immediately prior to SmithKline's acquisition of California-based Beckman Instruments Corporation. A company spokesman stated that the two events were not related. The campaign was suspended because of a change in corporate strategy, when it was decided that "our limited resources should be devoted to more traditional institutional advertising aimed at increasing name recognition for the corporation."

SMITHKLINE BECKMAN CORPORATION— HISTORICAL BACKGROUND

SmithKline is primarily a health care company engaged in the manufacture and marketing of ethical drugs, proprietary medicines, animal health products, and both ethical and proprietary products for eye and skin care. Through its network of clinical laboratories in the United States and Canada, it provides medical laboratory services. SmithKline also participates in industrial fields through its line of ultrasonic and electronic instruments. In 1982, SmithKline Beckman, the merged total entity, achieved $3.0 billion in sales from its worldwide operations.

Beckman Instruments, Inc., acquired in March 1982, is a broadly based international manufacturer of diagnostic and laboratory analytical instruments and related chemical products, industrial instruments, control systems, and precision electronic components. Beckman's products are used widely in medicine and science, and in a broad range of industrial applications.

Robert F. Dee is chairman of the board of SmithKline Beckman Corporation. He joined the company in 1948 and, after holding a variety of positions, became a group vice-president in 1967. He was elected to the board of directors in 1969, became SmithKline's president in 1972, chairman of the board in 1976, and served as chief executive officer from 1972 to 1982. He has had a long-standing concern about the lack of understanding and appreciation of the business role in society on the part of important segments of public opinion. In a recent article, he commented:

> Some communicators appear not to think enough. If they did, they would have a better understanding of our economic system, capitalism, and would be less hostile to it than some of us perceive them to be. The irony of such hostility is that the entire structure of our communications, especially its tech-

nology, rests on our ability to innovate. And we can only advance in technology by amassing capital to finance innovation. The choice is between state capitalism, communist or socialist, or our democratic capitalism. This choice should not be obscured by opaque logic in our communications.

Business people are thinkers of a different breed. The world of academe may not see them as thinkers of great importance. And no doubt very few business people would view themselves as distinguished thinkers in the academic sense. Riskers of capital, certainly. Quantifiers, admittedly. But philosophers, hardly. Yet those in business spend a great deal of time thinking, although they often have little to say. They have consequently earned a reputation for the kind of torpor usually associated with semi-submerged hippos basking in the sun.

Business people in the democracies do, after all, plan and make the products and supply the services that keep most of the world's living beings fed, housed, clothed, medicated, and even amused. It's true that our industries also at intervals produce the instruments of human destruction. Yet without our disasters, we might also be deprived of such things as nuclear energy, rocket shuttles, Nobel prizes, and a wide range of beneficial technologies. The use of science is never without risk.

In a world confronted by increasing miniaturization and the growing role of microchip technology, the content and function of communications will change. Communications are shrinking the globe. And the pace is mounting. If all the technological advances of world history were graphed on a one-year calendar, most of the action would appear a few minutes before New Year's Eve.

Thought and technology move in tandem. There may be a short lag between the two, but ultimately they match up. Human perceptions grow to embrace entirely new generalizations, new assumptions. Technology and the new findings of science have already altered our perceptions of time and space.[1]

Antecedents to the Issue-Information Advertising Campaign

In 1978, SmithKline introduced its first corporate image advertising program since the early 1960s. Designed to draw the attention of the investment community and enhance the corporate identity, the campaign emphasized SmithKline's research-oriented activities. The campaign ran in the print media in Chicago, San Francisco, and Philadelphia through the Business Network[2] magazine group and in the West and East Coast editions of the *Wall Street Journal*.

With the introduction of Tagamet and its immediate success, public awareness of SmithKline's presence was assured, as was the attention of all professional money managers. The success of the ongoing corporate advertising was therefore clouded. The ads themselves failed to produce any direct feedback. According to one corporate spokesperson:

With continuing good prospects for our corporate business performance, the specific goal of further acquainting potential buyers of our shares with the company as an investment opportunity seems less urgent. As a consequence, we have been able to turn our attention to more general corporate goals in thinking about advertising prospects for the future.

It's almost certainly true that we still have a long way to go in making the corporation widely known to the many audiences whose good opinion we'd like to earn. So in thinking about the next campaign, we've made our objectives more general than those on which we based the last campaign.

The seeds for the company's issue-advertising campaign were planted in early 1975, when Irving Kristol, the distinguished neo-conservative scholar, gave a talk to the SmithKline managers. In his speech, he urged company executives to begin forming a "constituency" that was aware of and receptive to the ideas supported by the corporate community of America. Robert Dee, chairman of the board, recalled:

> It seemed like a good idea in an age when constituencies of all kinds have great political impact. We began with a modest effort of communication, through a program called "Issues for Action," with our employees, shareholders, suppliers, customers, and friends. The format was an unpretentious six-page leaflet. Its main claims to distinction were that it was written in plain English and the topics were those people were deeply concerned about: inflation, the national debt, government overspending, taxation, declining American productivity, reduced research output, a falling dollar, foreign trade deficits, savings.

The intent of the "Issues for Action" program was to share ideas about "urgent public issues and to encourage citizens to engage in the political process by voting, by direct political action, and by communicating with their elected political representatives." The mailing list eventually grew to over 90,000 names and represented people from all segments of the population. "Many seemed fascinated by the curious phenomenon of a businessman who was not speaking of 'free enterprise,' but rather of the growth potential of 'capitalism'—and of the errors of a federal government that had been hemorrhaging the assets of its taxpayers for years."

The Decision-Making Process

In late 1978, the company decided to build on the success of its "Issues for Action" program by broadening its reach through an issue-advocacy program. Research data had showed that there were about 12 million young, upwardly mobile, reasonably affluent, college-educated, community-involved, investing, property-owning readers of news publications who could be encouraged through advertising to support sound government. SmithKline's management felt that these people could be a potent force for putting pressure for action on a seemingly indifferent Congress and a sluggish administration.

The idea for the new type of campaign was initiated by the board chairman, Robert Dee, and was enthusiastically supported by the executives in the corporate and public affairs departments. The rationale behind the campaign was best articulated by Mr. Dee:

> In communications, we're rapidly approaching the point at which the contents of one human mind will be almost instantaneously transferable to others, worldwide. This is sure to have an impact on all of our values: social, cultural, political, ethical, and economic.
>
> It's a fascinating time; it's a disquieting time. But above all, it's a time for integration.
>
> We have reached a juncture when all elements of American society must merge, not fractionate; when business, science, academe, religion, and government must share insights as humankind pushes toward a way of living that we can only begin to imagine.
>
> The business person as communicator has a part to play in this process. Doing so is socially desirable and politically valid.

Once the decision to launch the new type of ad campaign was made, a task force was established to develop a strategy for implementing the decision.

SmithKline's decision-making process differed in a number of important ways from that of some of the other companies, such as W. R. Grace and United Technologies, with highly innovative and successful issue-advertising programs.

- The process was quite formal and structured.
- It had a more extensive and close involvement of the advertising agency both in the design and implementation stages. This was unusual when compared with many other corporate advocacy campaigns, where ad agencies played only a minor role.
- The monitoring and evaluation functions were performed on a continuous basis, also with the close involvement of agency people.

SmithKline's CEO, once the basic policy was established, delegated implementation of the program to his staff and the advertising agency. Throughout, however, he played an active role in guiding its strategy. According to Andrew Gillinson, a former agency officer who has joined the corporate affairs staff:

> Mr. Dee's vision—of the modern corporation's responsibility to communicate on issues critical to society's well-being—inspired the campaign. His vision guided us in its development. Understandably, then, he paid close attention to the work of staff and agency, especially in the selection of issues for commentary.
>
> The chairman scrupulously reviewed each finished draft and frequently made editorial suggestions, mainly for clarity and brevity. He was particularly concerned, too, that the commentaries point not only to problems but also to remedies. Mr. Dee invariably gave the final say whether a particular commentary would be published.

In general, by the time copy was submitted for review by Mr. Dee, we felt that the issue it addressed was one of considerable interest to him and to the board. As a result, it was rare that an ad had to be delayed or canceled at that late stage.

Objectives of the Campaign

The objectives of the campaign as established by the corporation were these:

1. To increase public visibility of SmithKline Corporation so that its name is widely known, and people have positive feelings about the company.
2. To demonstrate that SmithKline Corporation is alert to human needs and shares the public concern about the social, political, and economic problems that confront all Americans.
3. To show that SmithKline Corporation is mature and thoughtful, to communicate a sense of security about the company's good judgment and social awareness, and to convey its concern for the betterment of the health of people around the world.
4. To convince readers that the public sector's performance should be judged by the same criteria as the private sector's—productivity, effectiveness in achieving goals, efficiency, and cost effectiveness.

Having decided on the main objectives, the company invited a number of advertising agencies to make presentations. Agencies were not given very specific instructions except for overall financial-budgetary targets and the company's expectations of what it wanted to accomplish. A number of agencies made presentations, and SmithKline selected the Baltimore-based VanSant Dugdale agency to handle the campaign. This agency had considerable prior experience in managing political and electoral campaigns and had the reputation for being sophisticated in handling public policy issues.

A small committee was set up to develop and implement the campaign strategy. It was comprised of three SmithKline executives: William E. Learnard, executive vice-president of corporate affairs; William L. Grala, vice-president, public affairs; and Gustav Gumpert, director of creative services. The agency representatives were Daniel J. Loden, then chairman of the board of VanSant Dugdale; Raymond Sachs, executive vice-president; and Andrew Gillinson, vice-president (currently with SmithKline, but at that time working with VanSant Dugdale). In addition, on occasion media and research people were also brought in to sit on the committee. One notable outside member was Robert Hessen, a noted historian and resident scholar at the Hoover Institution, a conservative think tank based in Palo Alto, California.

The committee concluded:

Corporate advertising as it's now practiced, with a few exceptions—like Mobil—has no message that appeals broadly to what people are concerned about—money, jobs, inflation, a declining dollar, the frustrations stemming very largely from economic, social, and political mismanagement by government. We want to talk about what people are thinking about.

The advertising strategy was therefore going to be a variant of the "Issues for Action." However, instead of featuring corporate spokespersons or the man on the street, it was going to use authoritative independent spokespersons. Thus was born the campaign theme "Forum for a Healthier American Society."

It was an advocacy campaign, but with a different twist in that SmithKline was not advocating anything specific—except realistic solutions to pressing social, economic, and political problems. The main intent was to make it possible for people to share their ideas with the public. According to a corporate spokesperson:

> We decided that we can't tell what America's thinking by ourselves. We need help. We need the help of an Omaha housewife, for example, who knows what's wrong with our economic system because her grocery bill went up 12% in a month. Or Irving Kristol, who knows what's wrong with our government because he's been studying it for two decades. Or the office manager who knows what government does to people because her job is to handle the OSHA paperwork—all 60 filing cabinets of it—for one of the nation's largest firms.
>
> We need Martin Feldstein [Harvard economist and currently chairman of President Reagan's Council of Economic Advisors] to say what's wrong with Social Security—not us. We need somebody to say why the dollar is failing; why our balance of trade is sinking; why the welfare system is spending half its tax money on administration; why we're encouraging high prices for food through government agricultural price support.
>
> These are things Americans are thinking about. These are the things they want authentic answers to. But not from us. They want to hear it from the horse's mouth, the horse in this case being the frontline people who have the answers that make sense.
>
> It seemed to us that the advertiser who buys space to put what America's thinking before the public will be doing a great service—a public service in the public interest.

With these goals in mind, the company conceived of a new philosophy that mingled "the fascination of the personal testimonial, the freshness of the man-in-the-street interview, and the flair of the professional Big Thinker." The rationale for the campaign was based on three premises:

1. Americans are people-oriented. They want to know what people are thinking about. They want confirmation for their own intuitions, and they want reassurance that what they think is shared by others.
2. America is changing. The interests of the public are more and more lining up with the interests of business. People now see that in our struggle against inflation, spendthrift government, and the foggy thinking of bureaucrats, we're all in the same lifeboat.
3. Americans are fed up with phoniness in advertising. They don't want

to be massaged with facts about the glories of business institutions. They want to know what business is doing to help them. They want to be sure that business is on their side.

Use of Advertising Agency

Another interesting aspect of the SmithKline campaign was its heavy reliance on an advertising agency to develop and implement a campaign strategy. Most other corporations with strong and successful advocacy campaigns emphasize the availability and use of in-house expertise, and generally downplay the role of the agency except in buying media time or developing layouts, art work, graphics, and so on.

A company spokesman suggested that it helped to take some of the burden off the corporate staff that would otherwise have to pay close attention to the day-to-day detail of running a campaign. He went on to say that SmithKline's agency, VanSant Dugdale, "is a unique resource in that a number of its principals have long been concerned with political and public policy issues." Being close to Washington, the agency people were also involved with trade associations and lobby groups, and were in touch with other special interest groups.

EXECUTION OF THE CAMPAIGN

Target Audience

As stated earlier, the target audience for SmithKline's advertising program was comprised of adults who had attended college, and who came from upper-income households. The emphasis was to seek out and reach "thinking Americans"—people who had an interest in current events, an inclination to be reflective, and the capacity for self-determination and self-expression. In addition, the company analyzed the media coverage of about 8 million people who were classified as activists—persons who had engaged in three or more public or civic activities during the preceding twelve months. These activities included such things as writing to a newspaper editor or a public official, addressing a public meeting, running for a political office, or helping in a political campaign.

There was also an attempt, as in the case of Bethlehem Steel's advocacy advertising campaign, to match various targeted audiences with the four campaign objectives. It was felt that objective 1 probably applied to investors and consumers; objective 2 to consumers and politicians; objective 3 to politicians and investors; and objective 4 to businesspeople generally and to consumers. It was recognized, of course, that there would be audience overlap for each of these objectives. However, as first approximations, these target audiences appeared to be a good start.

Criteria for Issue and Author Selection

The committee devoted a great deal of attention to the selection of issues and choice of authors. This was not based on a formal environmental or issue scanning system. Overall, the issues must present a challenge, and there must be an agenda for the future. Leading issues of the day were tested against a set of criteria. These were:

1. Was the issue of current major importance?
2. Was it a subject that would require presidential or congressional action?
3. Was it a subject that affected in a major way the revitalization of America?
4. Was it a subject where it was possible to present an intelligent point of view that would help establish a direction and a constituency?

The prime responsibility for selecting potential spokespeople rested with the advertising agency. The spokespeople had to have high public credibility for their views and, if possible, high name recognition. In all, the views of 24 spokespeople were presented in the campaign. An overwhelming majority of these were scholars, academicians, authors, or public statesmen [Table 1]. Authors wrote their own commentaries and were paid an honorarium averaging about $3,000.

Table 1 **Authors Used in the SmithKline Campaign**

- William E. Simon, a senior advisor to Booz, Allen & Hamilton, Inc., and a senior consultant of Blyth, Eastman, Dillon & Co., Inc.
- Ben J. Wattenberg, a senior fellow at the American Enterprise Institute, co-editor of AEI's magazine *Public Opinion,* and chairman of the Coalition for a Democratic Majority.
- René Dubos, professor emeritus at the Rockefeller University, New York City; eminent scientist and Pulitzer Prize-winning author; chairman of the Committee of International Experts that provided the United Nations Environment Programme guidelines.
- Martin Feldstein, professor of economics at Harvard University, and president of the National Bureau of Economic Research.
- George Roche, president of Hillsdale College, Michigan, since 1971; director of seminars at the Foundation for Economic Education.
- Dr. Walter E. Williams, associate professor of economics at Temple University, and a distinguished scholar of the Heritage Foundation.
- Dr. Herbert Stein, A. Willis Robertson Professor of Economics at the University of Virginia; chairman of the President's Council of Economic Advisors until 1974.
- Eric P. Schellin, chairman of the board of trustees of the National Small Business Association.
- Michael Novak, resident scholar in religion and public policy at the American Enterprise Institute; the author of ten philosophical works and two novels.
- James Dale Davidson, writer, lecturer, and scholar; chairman of the National Taxpayers Union in Washington, DC.
- Marva Collins, who after fourteen years of frustrated teaching in public schools, in 1976 founded Westside Preparatory School and put into practice beliefs despised by officialdom.

Table 1   **(Continued)**

- John F. Lehman, president of Abington Corporation; served as special counsel and senior staff member to the National Security Council.
- Amitai Etzioni, professor at George Washington University and founder and director of the Center for Policy Research; served as a senior advisor in the White House, 1979–80.
- Allan H. Meltzer, John M. Olin Professor of Political Economy and Public Policy at Carnegie-Mellon University and co-chairman of the Shadow Open Market Committee.
- Walter Laqueur, chairman of the International Research Council of Georgetown University; professor at Georgetown University.
- David Kelley, assistant professor of philosophy at Vassar College.
- William C. Mott, executive director of the Council on Economics and National Security; has been president of both the Capital Legal Foundation and the National Legal Center for the Public Interest.
- Theodore L. Eliot, dean of the Fletcher School of Law and Diplomacy at Tufts University; was special assistant to the secretary of state and executive secretary of the State Department.
- Thomas Sowell, professor of economics at UCLA; a senior fellow at the Hoover Institution.
- Margaret N. Maxey, assistant director of the South Carolina Energy Research Institute; member of the Medical Radiation Advisory Committee.
- Michael J. Malbin, resident fellow at the American Enterprise Institute for Public Policy Research in Washington; an adjunct associate professor of politics at the Catholic University of America.
- Frank Vogl, United States economics correspondent for the *Times* of London; author of the book *German Business After the Economic Miracle*.
- George Gilder, director of the International Center for Economic Policy Studies, and chairman of the Economic Roundtable at the Lehrman Institute.
- Allen Weinstein, professor at Georgetown University; executive editor of the *Washington Quarterly*.

Issues

As can be seen from the various advertisements, SmithKline's choice of topics centered mainly on broad issues of public policy, and specifically as they pertained to hazards of big government. While an admirable course of action in itself, the selection process raises certain important questions. For example:

1. Why shouldn't the company stick to those subjects where it has expertise, such as the pharmaceutical industry? There are issues here that would be of great interest to the public. There is the controversy about brand name and generically equivalent, albeit lower-cost, alternatives. Another issue might be the exploding costs of health care and how they might be best contained. A third topic might be the real or alleged loss of innovativeness on the part of the American pharmaceutical industry.
2. Even where broad issues of public policy are chosen, they deal with topics that have been prominent in the news media, such as inflation and overregulation. The choice of well-known authorities, while

highly desirable for public visibility and credibility, also runs the risk of espousing only those views that have been expressed before, in a variety of forums, and have almost become part of the conventional wisdom. Thus, one might reason that these messages might provide comfort to "true believers," but they do not add significantly either to the setting of the public agenda by bringing before the public heretofore undiscussed but important issues, or by enriching the quality of public debate by bringing new ideas and approaches to bear on already established but difficult issues.

Andrew S. Gillinson of SmithKline acknowledged the validity of these concerns and offered the following rationale for the company's strategy:

> On the opposite side of the expertise coin is the public feeling that a company speaking out may have a vested interest and, therefore, might be biased. We felt, for example, that if we spoke out publicly about patent law and certain flaws in it that are detrimental to public health, our arguments might be heavily discounted.
>
> More important, perhaps, is that the company's management, and more specifically its chairman and CEO, felt that there were issues beyond those mainly affecting our industry that were of great public concern. Certainly tax and fiscal policy have a great impact on any corporate or individual citizen. The management felt that there were broad, urgent national issues that deserved to be considered more widely and more thoroughly than was the case, and therefore they took priority.

Ad Copy Format

Another unusual feature of this campaign was the enormous attention paid to the visual impact of the advertisement—a trait more often associated with product or corporate image advertising than issue-advocacy advertising. An analysis of other corporate advocacy campaigns shows that highly artistic visuals are invariably an indication of a strong ad agency influence on the campaign.

VanSant Dugdale created a four-color, four-page advertising format [Exhibit 1], a "Commentary Unit" that consisted of:

- First page with a challenging title
- Expert commentary on the second and third pages
- Comment by Robert F. Dee, chairman and CEO of SmithKline Corporation, on the fourth page, along with an offer of additional material

Under the heading "The Concern" (both heading and copy were slightly changed from one advertisement to another), Dee states that SmithKline Corporation is among the world's most research-intensive pharmaceutical and health-related products company. Because people generally agree that this work is socially useful, even vital, the company could be content to go quietly about its business—providing needed products, good jobs, and respectable return on investments. He goes on to say:

But in good conscience we cannot pay attention to problems of health and ignore threats to personal freedoms and to the economic security of Americans. That is why we sponsor the SmithKline Forum.

We believe in the economic realism upon which the United States is founded. We hold that human rights and prosperity flourish in a climate of individual responsibility and suffocate in an atmosphere of authoritarianism and paternalism.

About America's business, he contends that business not only must provide things that enhance the quality of life, but ". . . also to help preserve and improve the economic, political, and social systems essential to the well-being of all Americans."

Individuals also have a responsibility to go beyond their everyday life and to involve themselves in issues of public concern.

In our society, public policy is often the key to solving problems. If public policy is to be sound, it must result from government by the people. But only you as a private citizen can make good government a vigorous reality—by voting and communicating regularly with your elected representatives, beginning at the community level.

We hope that ideas expressed in the SmithKline Forum will help you form your own opinions. We hope you'll make it your business to know the views of representatives and candidates, impress your views upon them, and support those in government who faithfully represent your basic convictions.

We Americans dare not take our rights and our prosperity for granted. We must guard them constantly and jealously, or awake one day to find them gone.

At SmithKline we believe that now is the time for all of us to act—in America's behalf and in our own behalf.

It would appear that this was the first and only advocacy campaign with such an expensive look and feel about it. The campaign had an aura of opulence, an extremely beautiful package, perhaps conveying the impression of an important product.

The four-color, four-page format was used only in *Newsweek* and *Time*. The *Wall Street Journal* format consisted of a full-page black-and-white advertisement, with the guest editorial and photo appearing first, followed by the SmithKline message. The insertions in both publications occurred roughly every six weeks during 1979 and 1980, and every eight weeks during 1981.

SmithKline's issue advertisements also used very long copy and thus were quite different in style and content from some of the other campaigns dealing with similar issues, such as those of Lone Star Industries, Commonwealth Edison, and Mobil Oil. Andrew Gillinson of SmithKline observes:

Our company, by its very nature, prefers to deal with issues substantively. We do not wish to make appeals for public support on the basis of emotion, but on the basis of fact.

Exhibit 1

The SmithKline Forum for a Healthier American Society   Vol. III   No. 6   September 1981

Human Rights. No More Small Men.

It is wrong to say "first bread, then [...] Novak. Democratic capitalism delivers f[...]

"A state which dwarfs its men, in order that they may be more docile instruments in its hands…will find that with small men no great thing can really be accomplished."
—JOHN STUART MILL, 1859

In 1948, most of the world lay gripped in poverty and much of it lay under the rubble of the most devastating war in human history. That year, when the United Nations ratified the Universal Declaration of Human Rights, there were only 49 independent nations in the world. The triumph of Allied armies in Asia, North Africa and Europe had carried Western civilization, particularly the United States, to its highest point of historical prestige.

It was quite natural, in those days, that the formulations of the Universal Declaration of Human Rights should have been modelled on the Bill of Rights of the United States, and on the concepts, institutional experiments, and ideals about which Abraham Lincoln spoke at Gettysburg. He observed that the Civil War was, "testing whether that nation, or any nation, so conceived and so dedicated, can long endure."

Can Nations Based on Human Rights Endure?

The foundation of human rights is the limited state.

Neither the Thousand Year Reich contemplated by Hitler nor Stalin's state was conceived to be limited. At Auschwitz alone, Hitler killed four million persons of almost every European nationality and, in all the death camps, he killed at least twelve million. According to Aleksandr Solzhenitsyn, Lenin and Stalin between them killed 65 million of their fellow citizens in a terror that began in 1923 and continued during and after the war in a vast, dark and sprawling Gulag.

That is why Pope John Paul II as one of his first acts visited Auschwitz and later, at the United Nations, recalled that the Declaration of Human Rights owes its origin to so much bloodshed, so much anguish, already endured in our century of unlimited states.

Imagine what the Universal Declaration of Human Rights would have been had Hitler won the war or if Stalinism had everywhere prevailed. Words about human rights would have had no more substance than the paper on which they were inscribed.

What Is a Limited State?

In the first place, a limited state is one which does not impose a philosophy, does not hack humans to the mold of the "new man," does not forbid liberty of conscience. A limited state is a state "under God"— in operational terms, a state separated from, and under the judgment of, the transcendent claims of the free individual conscience.

Second, a limited state is prevented, as if by a moat, from intruding into the homes of its citizens. They have rights against the state. Law itself is conceived to be not solely an expression of the will of the state, but a set of limitations *upon* the will of the state. The law regards individuals as the source of inalienable rights.

This is a magnificent conception. It stands as a defense against all forms of collectivism. No matter how sweeping or how total the claims of states may be, these claims crash into impenetrable walls at the boundary of individual conscience.

Yet of all forms of political economy, none so thoroughly limits the state, and none so thoroughly respects the right of individuals, as democratic capitalism—that is, those two dozen or so nations which are democratic in polity, at least partly capitalist in economy, and liberal and pluralistic in ethos.

The Greatest Social Power in the World

Democratic capitalism is not the Kingdom of God. It is not without sin. It is a system much in need of improvement, and subject

Exhibit 1

berty," concludes theologian Michael
edom with economic development.

at all times to continuous lawful revolution.

Still, by limiting the state, democratic capitalism liberates the energies of individuals and whole communities. By respecting the unpredictable potential of the individual, it unleashes the greatest social power in the world, a power which in 200 short years has transformed the world.

For when the system of democratic capitalism first appeared in history, about 1800, the population of the world was not quite 900 million. Today, through creative inventions, advances in medicine, and economic development pioneered by democratic capitalistic societies, living human beings number 4.4 billion.

For Even the Poorest Nations

Still, the task of feeding, clothing, and housing these new millions demands immense new productive skills. Vast new wealth must be created. Great mountains of goods are needed for schools, clinics, homes. Simple things, like clean running water, are in many places still not available. Refrigeration and electric lights, basic sanitation and reliable sources of food, are inexcusably absent.

Thus, the economic development first imagined by Adam Smith in his *Inquiry into the Nature and the Causes of the Wealth of Nations* (1776) is a still unfinished task. Perhaps in one more century, by the year 2076, all the poorest nations will have experienced decisive economic growth. But that hasn't happened yet.

Lincoln said this nation could not endure, half-slave and half-free. Neither can the world long endure, half-slave and half-free—or half-starved and half-fed.

Human Rights and Economic Development

For the future, two points are crucial. Adam Smith did not write about the wealth of *Individuals,* or even the wealth of *Scotland,* but about the wealth of *Nations.* The fundamental intention of democratic capitalism is to raise the material base of all nations, of every part of humankind.

Second, human rights and liberty are not merely the goal for which

wealth is to be created. They are the means of creating it.

The world needs to know that human rights work, that liberty is effective, that the practical choice is not "first bread, then liberty." Systems which deny liberty in the name of bread usually produce neither bread nor liberty.

The experiment with human rights which is conceived in liberty, and dedicated to the proposition that all men are created equal, is also an experiment in economic development. If all humans are equal, each must be free to make significant economic decisions—and if they are so free, the greatest social energy within the universe will be released.

It is wrong to pit human rights against economic development, to deny the former in the

(continued)

Michael Novak is a former Ledden-Watson Distinguished Professor of Religion at Syracuse University and is the author of ten philosophical works and two novels.

His books and articles have appeared in many languages, and his new book, The Spirit of Democratic Capitalism, *will be published in February, 1982, by Simon & Schuster.*

Novak is a Resident Scholar in Religion and Public Policy at the American Enterprise Institute.

© 1981 SmithKline Corporation

Exhibit 1

name of the latter. It is not only morally wrong, or politically wrong. It is also economically wrong. Free persons dream. Free persons invent. Free persons create. Freedom enriches, for wealth is not fixed but created.

The dream of democratic capitalism, which gave rise to the Bill of Rights, is not solely a moral dream or a political dream; it is also an economic dream.

With Due Respect

Respect for human rights inspires moral dynamism. Respect for human rights generates political vitality. Respect for human rights releases economic energies. It does all three of these at once.

Economic development is fundamentally an achievement of the human spirit. The imprisonment of that spirit in so many places, in so many ways, not only denies inalienable rights, but causes starvation and misery. Without respect for human rights, technical assistance is hollow, outside aid merely hides decay, and proven technologies fail. At the heart of hope lies the wit of individuals choosing for themselves.

The experiment of human rights works.

—Michael Novak

Views expressed by participants in the SmithKline Forum are their own.
© 1981 SmithKline Corporation

SmithKline Corporation
H21/NW914, P.O. Box 7929
Philadelphia, PA 19101

For more of Michael Novak's thoughts on democratic capitalism, send for your free copy of his book, *Toward a Theology of the Corporation*. We will also include other Commentaries published in this Forum and several of SmithKline's *Issues for Action* pamphlets.

_____
name

_____
street address or box number

_____
city/town   state   zip code

Growth

For you and for SmithKline, a healthier future depends on ideas.

The United States and SmithKline Corporation have grown up together. In 1830, when America was still in its infancy, SmithKline also set out from Philadelphia on a journey of human adventure.

Today, SmithKline is a world leader in science and technology. We are principally a health care company—researching, developing, manufacturing and marketing prescription medicines, over-the-counter medicines, animal health products and eye care products.

We also supply medical laboratory services and, with advanced ultrasonic and electronic technologies, we take part in the medical and industrial instruments field.

In 1978, SmithKline sales first topped the $1 billion mark. This year our sales will exceed $2 billion—with price increases accounting for just a small fraction of that growth. In 1980 alone, we created 1,500 new jobs.

SmithKline and its 21,000 people worldwide continue to make substantial investments in themselves. We offer you this SmithKline Forum series of ideas as a further investment in the health of this country—and of our world.

Ideas move the world. We hope they move you.

Robert F. Dee

Robert F. Dee
Chairman of the Board and
Chief Executive Officer
SmithKline Corporation

SmithKline
CORPORATION

There are also some serious qualifications to be made to the conventional wisdom that advertising copy must always be short. It really depends upon the audience's potential involvement with the subject matter. You may see short copy for soap and long copy for automobiles. The decision about which automobile to buy, as opposed to which bar of soap to buy, is one that the consumer gives a good deal more consideration. Similarly, we found that we would engage the attention of readers on a subject like inflation much more thoroughly than we would, let's say, on an issue of narrower concern, or less urgency, e.g., education vouchers. We did not run an advertisement on that issue. That issue was not selected because it would have enjoyed a comparatively low level of intrinsic interest and, therefore, could not have sustained an audience's attention over the course of a thousand, or twelve hundred words.

The advertisements also urged readers to send in a coupon, provided in the ad, should they wish to receive copies of *Issues for Action* or, in later ads, additional material by the guest commentator.

Media Strategy and Advertising Budget

The ad agency conducted studies to match target audience characteristics with readership profiles of various magazines and newspapers that were considered potentially appropriate vehicles for the ad messages because they provided a suitable news and editorial environment.

The target audience was defined as individuals who were literate, empathetic, and responsive. These characteristics were then put into certain demographic variables:

- Literacy: Those having attended college.
- Empathy: Upper-income adults exhibiting "conservative" qualities, who were likely to favor SmithKline's position. This objective was broadened to include educated people who exhibited ambivalence in terms of their political philosophy.
- Responsiveness: Individuals engaged in multiple public activities and receptive to "issue-oriented" campaigns.

An analysis of syndicated marketing data, primarily Simmons and Target Group Index, indicated that the primary target of the type desired by SmithKline approximated 3 million people. An intermedia analysis compared magazines, television, and radio as suitable vehicles to carry the SmithKline message. Four-color pages in magazines, 30-second television commercials, and two-thirds page black-and-white newspaper advertisements were compared at budget levels of $1.3 and $3 million. Based on this research, it was concluded that at the lower level of $1.3 million, coverage in magazines afforded the best opportunity for reaching the intended target audience of 3 million people. Studies showed that the *Wall Street Journal* and *Business Week* would best meet the target audience criterion.

Exhibit 2

The Malignant Growth of Federal Spending

The SmithKline Forum for a Healthier American Society Vol. I. No. 1 March 1979

Commentary:

William E. Simon examines the true cause of the inflation that can put an end to our way of life.

"The best way to destroy the capitalist system is to debase the currency."
—Nikolai Lenin

"By a process of inflation, governments can confiscate, secretly and unobserved, an important part of the wealth of their citizens. By this method they not only confiscate, but they confiscate arbitrarily; and while the process impoverishes many, it actually enriches some...There is no subtler, no surer means of overturning the existing basis of society than to debauch the currency. The process engages all the hidden forces of economic law on the side of destruction and does it in a manner that not one man in a million is able to diagnose."
—John Maynard Keynes

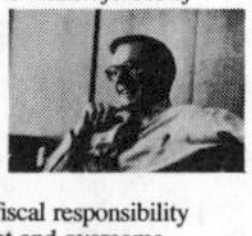

The fight to restore fiscal responsibility to our national government and overcome inflation is, above all, a fight for the freedom, dignity and prosperity of all Americans—a fight that compels the utmost support of anyone who cherishes those values.

Americans are a practical and compassionate people. It is vital, therefore, to broaden understanding of the misguided policies that hobble American productivity, and to demonstrate that the poor, the elderly, the sick and the disadvantaged have everything to gain from an orderly move away from big spending and big government. For this aspect of the fight, we must arm ourselves with the facts.

If the poor did not exist, the collectivists would have to invent them.

Despite a quintupling of the Federal budget (from under $100 billion to over $500 billion) in just eighteen years, rationalized as the cure for a host of social ills, the record of accomplishment is dismal.

A little math clearly illustrates the inefficiency and actual effect of government programs. By dividing the number of America's officially defined poor in 1975 (25 million) into the *increase* in annual Federal expenditures for social welfare between 1965 and 1975 ($209 billion), we discover that had we simply given the money to the poor, each would have received some $8,000 a year. $32,000 for a family of four! Instead, the bulk of this enormous wealth has been absorbed in the process of bureaucratic redistribution. In effect, government has forced the privately employed middle class to finance the growth of a publicly employed (and far less productive) middle class—at the cost of rampant inflation, due primarily to government's ceaseless spending beyond its means and its excessive printing of money.

Since 1930, government spending at all levels has risen from ten percent to forty percent of total national income. The Federal government has already become the dominant force in our society. It is the biggest single employer, the biggest consumer and the biggest borrower.

If government spending and taxing trends of the last two decades persist for the next two, government will so dominate the economy that the State will control many of the most important personal decisions of its citizens. And if our economic freedom disappears, history warns us, our personal and political freedoms also will disappear.

The fleecing of America.

Consider the staggering Federal debt that has resulted from a string of seventeen deficits in the past eighteen years. Consider the deceptively low figure of nearly a trillion dollars, quite apart from the additional seven-trillion-dollar mortgage on the future represented by Social Security and other vast obligations.

Interest payments on the debt amount to some fifty billion dollars a year, making them the third largest item in the Federal budget after transfer payments (redistribution of wealth programs) and defense. That is an average of a thousand dollars a year from every American household. And, of course, the debt is not being paid off. It is being continuously refinanced at increasing cost. And still the deficit spending continues.

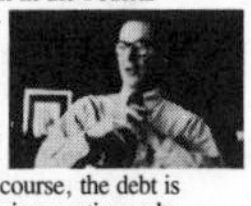

The average American must now work until mid-May of each year to pay Federal, state and local taxes. But burdensome taxation and debt are only two of the Federal government's three ways of sustaining its pointless spending spree. The third is printing money.

Greenbacks, greenbacks everywhere.

Between 1967 and 1978, the government caused the money supply to grow nearly three times as fast as the economy's true output, fueling inflation and allowing the government to make payments on its debt with dollars worth far less than those originally borrowed from the citizenry. This debasement of the currency is not only unconscionable trickery, it is the route to financial and economic collapse. Not only does it steal the fruits of past and present labors from Americans, it also courts disaster.

Inflation must be identified for what it is: not grease for the economic machine, but the most vicious hoax ever perpetrated for the expedient purposes of a few at the cost of many; a clear and present danger to the progress of our economy and the standard of living of all Americans.

Let us clarify the way the insidious cycle of spending, taxing, borrowing and inflation cripples the private sector.

- Excessive taxation for the alleged purpose of social welfare confiscates resources from the most productive sector of the economy and transfers them to the least productive.
- Government's borrowing to finance spending beyond its tax revenues usurps the majority of funds in the private financial markets, leaving private enterprise little with which to modernize, increase productivity and create lasting jobs.
- Government's excessive printing of money to pay its debts dilutes the value of the dollar and generates inflation.
- Inflation encourages individuals to spend and borrow for present consumption at the expense of saving and investing for the future. America devours her seed corn as citizens follow government's example, living beyond their means.

Tyrants without jackboots.

We can identify other ways in which big government is trampling the free enterprise system (such as the overregulation of business at an annual cost of over $125 billion), but let us now see *why* our government continues the destruction of an economic system that has brought us the greatest prosperity, the highest standard of living, and most important, the greatest individual freedom in the history of mankind. Why have politicians been so eager to increase spending year after year?

The answer lies in human nature—in the same immense forces of self-interest that the free enterprise system benignly channels into the creation of wealth. It lies, specifically, in insatiable appetites for power and position—the appetites of politicians who hold that nobody was ever reelected by promising less, and who have discovered that popular spending need not be financed with unpopular new taxes as long as there is deficit spending, money creation, and the resultant cruel and hidden tax of inflation.

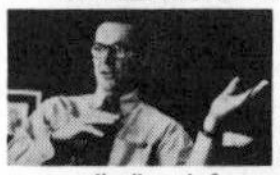

How can we rid ourselves of the small group of professional officeholders who continuously take wealth from everyone and redistribute it for purposes they alone deem important? As a beginning, I recommend limiting the terms of Congress to twelve years, and a single six-year term for the presidency. These changes would give us citizen lawmakers who would return home and live under the laws they had enacted; lawmakers who would be less concerned with reelection than with America's long-range interests.

It's later than we think.

The irrational, unrealistic fiscal, monetary, tax and regulatory policies of nearly half a century have so damaged our economy that financial collapse is probable within this century unless the trend is quickly reversed.

If collapse does occur, the United States will, in my judgment, simultaneously turn into an economic dictatorship. So many citizens have been trained to see the government as economically omniscient and omnipotent, and to blame all economic ills on "business," that disaster could easily bring popular demand for a takeover of the major means of production by the State. Legal precedent and ideological justification exist. It would take little to accomplish the transition.

Political courage and public wisdom are our only hope for preserving the premier economy of the world, as well as our individual freedoms.

We must make all Americans aware of the fact that the fundamental guiding principles of American life have been reversed, and that we are careening with frightening speed toward socialism and away from individual sovereignty, toward centralized coercion and away from free choice.

We must generate broad-based support for a plan to reduce the growth of Federal spending, match the growth of the money supply to the true growth of the economy, reduce taxes and eliminate unnecessary regulation. We must save our votes for politicians committed to such a plan.

The ultimate choice.

The longer we delay the hard decisions, the less likely we are to succeed. The American people must now decide whether they will sell the liberty that is the envy of the world for the empty promise of the Welfare State, or whether they will restrict government to its proper functions: defense of the nation, protection of the helpless from the avaricious, and creation of an environment for sustained economic growth through sensible fiscal, monetary, tax and regulatory policies.

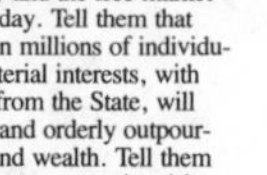

Personal and political freedoms are inseparable from economic freedom. Tell those who characterize the fight for liberty as "reactionary" that in the context of history coercion is clearly reactionary and liberty progressive. Tell them that the twin ideas of human liberty and the free market were born only yesterday. Tell them that allowing millions upon millions of individuals to pursue their material interests, with minimal interference from the State, will unleash an incredible and orderly outpouring of inventiveness and wealth. Tell them that lack of vision threatens to extinguish the brightest light ever to appear in the long night of tyranny and privation that is the history of the human race.

Tell them about America.

—W.E. Simon

William E. Simon was Secretary of the Treasury from 1974 to 1977. He also served as Deputy Secretary of the Treasury, 1973 to 1974, and as Chairman of the Economic Policy Board, the Federal Energy Office, and the East-West Foreign Trade Board. Mr. Simon is now a Senior Advisor to Booz, Allen & Hamilton, Inc., and a Senior Consultant to Blyth Eastman Dillon & Co., Inc.

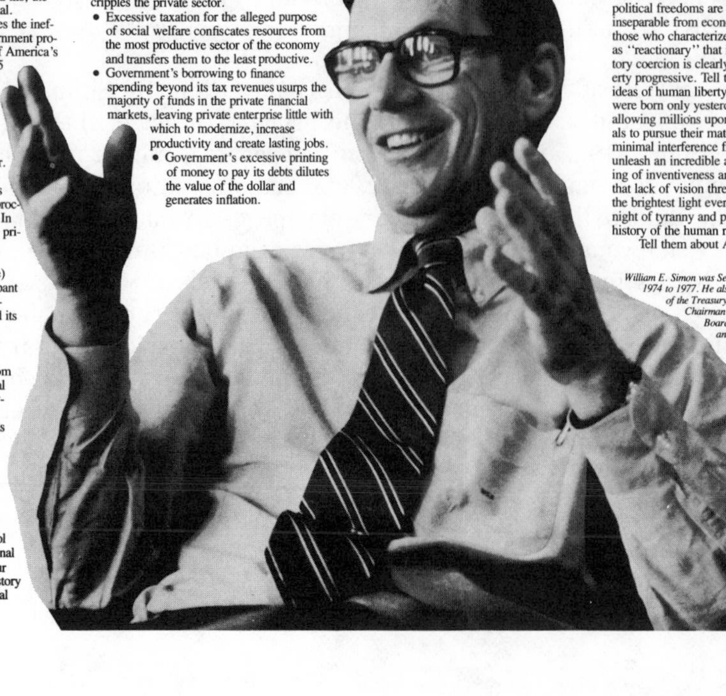

The Concern.

SmithKline Corporation's two-level approach to health.

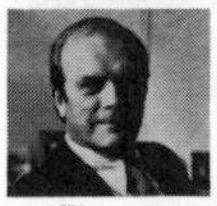

SmithKline is providing this forum on social, political and economic issues because the health of Americans and the health of American society are of concern to us.

We are among the world's most research-intensive companies. We are engaged primarily in the research, development, manufacture and marketing of medicines and other products used in health care. Consequently, we are deeply concerned about the health of individuals.

But we also feel a concern about the social, political and economic health of society as a whole—because we think the body politic requires as much attention and care as the human body.

We are convinced that a healthy America is a socially conscious America. And we are convinced that social consciousness requires individual initiative and individual action. This forum is our way of taking action. It is our contribution to the social well-being of America. Its purpose is to put before you positive ideas about social, political and economic issues that all Americans are now confronting.

In the months to come, we will extend this forum to others whose thoughts we believe contribute to a healthier American society.

It would be impossible to present a complete spectrum of thought on any one issue. Our object is to advance ideas that are rooted in the economic realism upon which the United States is founded: the proposition that human rights and material well-being flourish in a climate of freedom and individual responsibility—and suffocate in an atmosphere of authoritarianism and paternalism.

We believe this program is a meaningful way for a major corporation in American society to communicate. Our commitment of resources for the purpose is a matter of social conscience, and we believe it is in the interest of our shareholders, employees, customers and suppliers, all of whom are profoundly affected by the health of our nation and its economy.

A course of action.

Ideas are sterile unless acted upon. But what action should you as a private citizen take?

We suggest that, to the extent you find truth in ideas of social, political and economic significance, your responsibility is to share them and work to see them reflected in public policy.

The disturbing estimate is that barely a third of Americans eligible to vote did so in the latest congressional elections. Moreover, the sole act of voting every few years does not assure that elected officials understand your wishes.

We suggest, then, that you write regularly to your representatives at every level of government. Begin today. Make your views known, know the views of representatives and candidates, and support those in government who faithfully represent your basic convictions. Experience has shown this to be an effective way of making your personal opinion work for the good of all Americans.

At SmithKline we believe it is time for all of us to act—in America's behalf, and in our own behalf.

Robert F. Dee

Robert F. Dee
Chairman of the Board and
Chief Executive Officer

SmithKline
CORPORATION
H20/W322, P.O. Box 7929, Philadelphia, Pa. 19101

If you would like to receive SmithKline's *Issues for Action*, a series of informative pamphlets on subjects of social, political and economic significance, please complete this coupon and mail it to the address above.

name

title and company (if any)

street address or box number

city state zip code

Views expressed by participants in the SmithKline Forum are their own and are not necessarily those of the management of SmithKline Corporation.

© 1979 SmithKline Corporation.

Exhibit 3

The Creed of the Class B Optimist

The SmithKline Forum for a Healthier American Society Vol. I, No. 2 April 1979

Commentary:

Ben J. Wattenberg, eminent analyst of national trends, makes his argument for confidence in America's future.

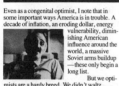

Even as a congenital optimist, I note that in some important ways America is in trouble. A decade of inflation, an eroding dollar, energy vulnerability, diminishing American influence around the world, a massive Soviet arms buildup—these only begin a long list.

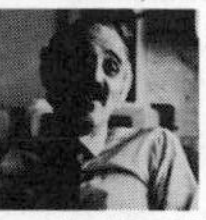

But we optimists are a hardy breed. We didn't waltz through the flames of the Sixties only to be blown away by the icy draughts of the Seventies—or, for that matter, to stand paralyzed in fear of the oncoming Eighties.

How do we manage these days? There are still Class A optimists around. They say, "We have no big problems. It will all work out all right." And there are Class B optimists, like me, who say, "We do have big threatening problems. But we are a very strong country, and now (at last!) we are recognizing our problems. If we now have the will to apply our strengths to our newly recognized problems, why, it will all work out all right."

Consider our current situation.

How Strong We Are

We have heard a lot recently about our economic dilemma. Declining productivity, governmental overregulation, innovation lag, foreign buy-out, and so on—real problems, to one degree or another. But the case has been made that America is falling victim to "the English Disease"—a not-so-slow unraveling of the economic system caused by inflation and promiscuous government spending, leading to a decline of national potency. The value of the pound sterling eroded, we're told, and England's primacy disappeared. The American dollar has eroded, we're told, and the American Century is ending.

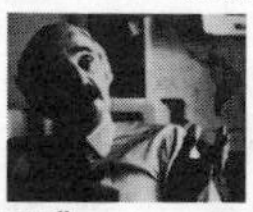

Harrumph! America is not a small island with an anomalous empire—an empire that would have dissolved under the pressure of events even if the pound sterling had remained undebauched.

Without pooh-poohing our real economic problems, which deserve not even a single pooh, it might be useful to list a few of America's often unthought-about economic strengths.

England is a little nation that has to buy food to feed its people. America is the world's largest supplier of food to others. England is perhaps the major nation most dependent on others. America, by contrast, is perhaps the most autarkic—a continental nation of incredible resources, including the largest coal reserve in the world. Furthermore, the U.S. today produces as much oil as Saudi Arabia! These sorts of natural resources remain in place come hell, high water, inflation, recessions, depressions or almost any other prospective economic horror scenario.

Human Factors, Too

All that's in the ground, of course. But we do all right above the ground. It's said we're falling behind in the technology race. Maybe so—but maybe not. Of the last 19 Nobel prizes awarded in scientific fields, 14 went to Americans! Hardly a sign of a nation running out of curiosity.

The fact that we are the superpower of technology has helped lead to another situation that is not likely to change soon: we are an international political superpower. The cliché has it that we are "the leader of the free world"—and that is an accurate cliché. One can engage in any manner of yen worship, Deutschemark homage or Swiss franc idolatry, and still not come up with a plausible scenario that passes the torch of Western leadership to any other nation or combination of nations.

There's another cliché that deserves mention: "America is the arms merchant of the world." Sometimes that's said as if it is something bad, something to be tut-tutted about. Wrong. Not worth even a single tut. In a volatile world where power so often determines policy, it is better that we have such a lever than not.

Our strength goes beyond the tangible as well. There has been, for example, a great deal of dire breast-beating that can be summed up as, "Help! America is Being Raped by Foreign Investors!" But America has been unique in its handling of foreign investment. Other countries have sometimes nationalized it. We've been smarter. We've naturalized it! Foreign capitalists send their venture capital here, send their sons to keep an eye on it, they marry American girls, the grandsons are American, so too are their posterity, and the original venture capital. One is tempted to ask whether we're talking about rape or seduction.

Indeed, we ought to think more about why that foreign capital is coming to America. True, foreign investors cite the cheap dollar. But what they stress is that America is the most politically stable nation in the world. Hardly the hallmark of a tottering society, inflation or not.

We also ought to think about the fact that the U.S. is a target not only for investment but for people. Public opinion polls taken all over the world show that the U.S.—for all its well-publicized ills—is the place to which most earthlings would emigrate if they had a chance.

Recognizing Our Problems

So America remains a very strong country.

Even strong countries can have big problems. In recent years, America's biggest problem has been that we were unwilling to recognize what our big problems were. Indeed, history tells us that is one of the pitfalls of democratic forms of government: a sometime somnambulism in times of growing danger. The English listened to Chamberlain, not Churchill. But rather suddenly, much of that has changed. A remarkable confluence of dire events and conditions has brought our problems front and center. In one sense, that's more good than bad; grounds for optimism, not pessimism. You have to see the boil in order to lance it.

A growing domestic inflation hit a flash point in California last year with the passage of Proposition 13 and the so-called "tax revolt." One may disagree about the merits of Proposition 13 and about what sort of tax-and-spending changes ought to be made, but one clear thought is now permeating the entire political spectrum: government spending, one cause of inflation, must be subject to a more disciplined scrutiny.

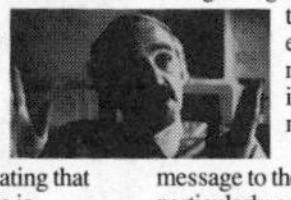

The voters sent that message to their elected leaders in a particularly eye-opening way—via the ballot box. And that message at this time is creating the condition precedent to getting our economy back in order.

That eye-opener was delivered to us—by us. But another fact of life was dropped upon us from the outside. The tumult in Iran underscored what should have been apparent five years earlier: the Western democracies cannot afford to leave themselves energy-vulnerable to a Middle East political circumstance that is perhaps best seen as a cauldron sitting on a tinderbox resting on a volcano.

As this is written, the person with the most direct control over the American energy situation, the strength of the dollar and our balance of payments is not President Carter. It's not Secretary Schlesinger. It's not the president of Exxon. It is a 78-year-old man with a beard and a turban in Iran.

And finally, there is the issue that is probably the most important of our era. That issue can perhaps be best capsulized as two questions: (a) are we prepared to have our children grow up in a world where the Soviet Union is the most powerful military force? And (b) what is to be America's role in the world during the last fifth of this century? For a half dozen years now, these questions have loomed like a dark but often unrecognized rain cloud over the American condition. Suddenly it seems as if one external event may serve to convene a massive consciousness-raising session—before the thunderstorm. It now seems likely that the SALT II treaty will be debated by the U.S. Senate for several months. That debate should force us to look not only at missile equivalencies, but at overall Soviet armed strength, at Soviet geopolitical expansion—and force us, too, to ask those two haunting questions.

One Last Ingredient

The question before the house can now be framed simply enough. Do we have the national will to apply our strength to our newly-recognized problems?

Americans, I believe, respond to identifiable problems. Especially so when, once recognized, they aren't anywhere near insurmountable. Unlike the English situation thirty years ago, our problems are quite within the range of our ability to deal with them.

If the Soviets are making mischief because they believe that their growing military power now lets them call the shots, then the first step toward telling them that they will never—never—win an arms race is to increase American defense expenditures. That is not much of a problem. American arms spending absorbed 9% of our gross national product in 1960. Today that figure is 5%.

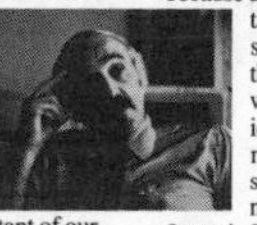

Maybe we now have to go back up to, say, about 6%. To justify that, we must understand only one very sad but very true idea: the level of our defense spending is set in Moscow. Unfortunately, the Soviets are lending credence to that idea every day.

Similarly, if the rise in nondefense spending must be held down for awhile to deal with inflation, that too is manageable without Uncle Sam becoming Uncle Scrooge. In 1960, the percentage of the GNP going for social welfare expenditures was 11%. Today it is 21%. And it is becoming apparent that poor people are not helped by letting inflation rage.

Solving our energy problems, of course, is not simply a matter of moving dollars from Column A to Column B. But the transfer of our energy independence to the old man with the turban is in large part a self-inflicted wound. America, not the Middle East, made it difficult to mine coal and next-to-impossible to produce nuclear power; decisions made in America led to long delays in drilling for American oil; American policy, not the Ayatollah's, ranked the snail darter more important than hydroelectric power. What America did, America can undo, or more properly, can do more moderately.

The Future

So that's why I remain a Class B optimist. We have problems. We are strong. We have been forced to recognize our problems. And I believe that we will apply our strength to our problems.

If we do, the American Century will not end just yet. And in the year 2000, no one will be writing articles about the American Disease.

—B.J. Wattenberg

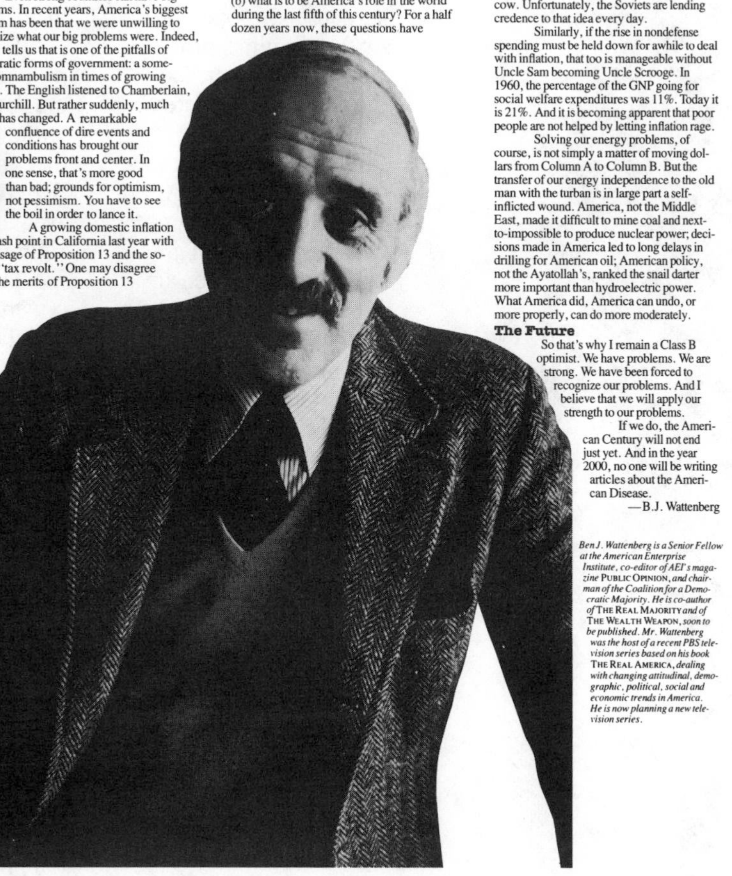

Ben J. Wattenberg is a Senior Fellow at the American Enterprise Institute, co-editor of AEI's magazine PUBLIC OPINION, *and chairman of the Coalition for a Democratic Majority. He is co-author of* THE REAL MAJORITY *and of* THE WEALTH WEAPON, *soon to be published. Mr. Wattenberg was the host of a recent PBS television series based on his book* THE REAL AMERICA, *dealing with changing attitudinal, demographic, political, social and economic trends in America. He is now planning a new television series.*

The Concern.

SmithKline Corporation's two-level approach to health.

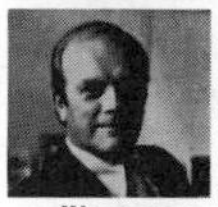

SmithKline is providing this forum on social, political and economic issues because the health of Americans and the health of American society are of concern to us.

We are among the world's most research-intensive companies. We are engaged primarily in the research, development, manufacture and marketing of medicines and other products used in health care. Consequently, we are deeply concerned about the health of individuals.

But we also feel a concern about the social, political and economic health of society as a whole–because we think the body politic requires as much attention and care as the human body.

We are convinced that a healthy America is a socially conscious America. And we are convinced that social consciousness requires individual initiative and individual action. This forum is our way of taking action. It is our contribution to the social well-being of America. Its purpose is to put before you positive ideas about social, political and economic issues that all Americans are now confronting.

In the months to come, we will extend this forum to others whose thoughts we believe contribute to a healthier American society.

It would be impossible to present a complete spectrum of thought on any one issue. Our object is to advance ideas that are rooted in the economic realism upon which the United States is founded: the proposition that human rights and material well-being flourish in a climate of freedom and individual responsibility–and suffocate in an atmosphere of authoritarianism and paternalism.

We believe this program is a meaningful way for a major corporation in American society to communicate. Our commitment of resources for the purpose is a matter of social conscience, and we believe it is in the interest of our shareholders, employees, customers and suppliers, all of whom are profoundly affected by the health of our nation and its economy.

A course of action.

Ideas are sterile unless acted upon. But what action should you as a private citizen take?

We suggest that, to the extent you find truth in ideas of social, political and economic significance, your responsibility is to share them and work to see them reflected in public policy.

The disturbing estimate is that barely a third of Americans eligible to vote did so in the latest congressional elections. Moreover, the sole act of voting every few years does not assure that elected officials understand your wishes.

We suggest, then, that you write regularly to your representatives at every level of government. Begin today. Make your views known, know the views of representatives and candidates, and support those in government who faithfully represent your basic convictions. Experience has shown this to be an effective way of making your personal opinion work for the good of all Americans.

At SmithKline we believe it is time for all of us to act–in America's behalf, and in our own behalf.

Robert F. Dee

Robert F. Dee
Chairman of the Board and
Chief Executive Officer

SmithKline
CORPORATION
H20/W419, P.O. Box 7929, Philadelphia, Pa. 19101

If you would like to receive SmithKline's *Issues for Action*, a series of informative pamphlets on subjects of social, political and economic significance, please complete this coupon and mail it to the address above.

name ______________________

title and company (if any) ______________________

street address or box number ______________________

city ______ state ______ zip code ______

Views expressed by participants in the SmithKline Forum are their own and are not necessarily those of the management of SmithKline Corporation.

© 1979 SmithKline Corporation.

Commentary:

Presented by The SmithKline Corporation

Dr. René Dubos, renowned scientist order and rejects world government.

Let ecological consciousness begin at home.

On many occasions, I have lectured in colleges where students are deeply concerned about the quality of the environment, but everywhere I have had two kinds of experience that account for the title of this essay. The students are eager to discuss the global aspects of environmental problems, but they do not seem disturbed by the messiness of their cafeterias and other public rooms. My message to them is that thinking in a global way is a useful intellectual exercise, but no substitute for the care of the place in which one lives. If we really want to do something for the health of our planet, the best place to start is in the streets, fields, roads, rivers, marshes, and coastlines of our communities. This essay is an elaboration of my message to the students.

Toward global consciousness.

During the 1970's, huge international conferences were organized by the United Nations to discuss the contemporary problems of humankind. These megaconferences began with resounding statements of global concern and with clarion calls for international cooperation. As the meetings progressed, however, the discussions of concrete topics were usually diluted in a flood of ideological verbiage. At the end of a conference, efforts to set down a statement of consensus resulted in resolutions so broad in meaning that only few of them could be converted into action programs. Yet, I believe that these conferences had a beneficial influence which was not apparent to me while I was involved in them.

They helped to generate a global awareness of certain dangers that are now threatening all nations. This is not a small achievement because thinking globally is not natural to human beings. Our intellectual and emotional processes are not adapted to a global view. It is only when people from all parts of the world listen to one another's problems that they realize how crowded we are on our small planet, how limited are its resources, and how multifarious are the dangers to which we are all exposed.

The economics of environmentalism.

Another contribution of the international conferences was to dramatize the diversity of conditions on our planet. While there was much posturing and propagandizing through the conferences, the delegates learned from their contact with representatives of other countries that global problems appear in a different light depending upon the local situation. At the 1972 Conference on the Human Environment in Stockholm, the environmental purists discovered that abject poverty is the worst form of pollution and that poor countries have legitimate reasons to be more interested in economic development than in the ecological gospel. At the 1976 Habitat Conference in Vancouver, the delegates of poor countries complained of exploitation by industrialized countries, but nevertheless wanted to learn from them how problems of water supply, low-cost housing or sustainable rural development could be solved by advanced technologies.

Energy and other global problems best solved locally.

The most practical achievement of the international conferences may have been, however, to reveal that the best and often the only way to deal with global problems is, paradoxically, to look for solutions peculiar to each locality.

Exhibit 4

and author, embraces pluralistic world

Our planet is so diverse, both physically and socially, that its problems can be tackled with precision only by dealing with them at the national or, even better, at the regional level, in their unique natural and cultural contexts. Three examples will suffice to illustrate the necessity of the local approach to global problems.

- The low cost of petroleum and natural gas, and the ease with which these fuels can be shipped and used anywhere in the world, were responsible until recently for the illusion that fairly uniform technological policies could be formulated for the planet as a whole. Fossil fuels, however, are becoming much more costly and soon will be in short supply. Different kinds of renewable sources of energy are being considered to deal with this situation. For example, nuclear fission, solar radiation, the biomass, the wind, the tides, the waves, etc. Each one of these sources of energy has advantages and objections peculiar to it and, unlike petroleum and gas, each one is much better suited to one natural or social condition than to others. Solar radiation has a better chance to be developed on a large scale in highly insolated areas—the biomass in densely wooded areas—the wind where it

---

Dr. René Dubos, Professor Emeritus at the Rockefeller University, New York City, eminent scientist and Pulitzer Prize winning author, was Chairman of the committee of international experts that provided the United Nations Environment Programme guidelines. Supported by the National Endowment for the Humanities, he founded the René Dubos Forum, which focuses on humanistic and social aspects of environmental problems, managed by Total Education in the Total Environment, Inc. (TETE), a non-profit organization in Bronxville, New York.

© 1979 SmithKline Corporation

blows in a fairly dependable manner—coal where the pollution it inevitably causes will be least objectionable—nuclear fission in industrialized countries that are most deficient in other energy resources and where the public is therefore more likely to accept the risk of massive unpredictable accidents. Just as the shift from hydroelectric power to coal, then to petroleum and gas made certain heavy industries move from New England to the Appalachians and then to Texas, so we can anticipate that there will be many different local solutions to the global energy problem.

- Desertification (referring not to natural deserts, but to areas which are rendered desertic by human activities) is a problem of increasing gravity in many parts of the world. In an attempt to control the spread of desertification, the United Nations Environment Programme (UNEP) first formulated programs which were transnational, in the sense that they dealt with vast continuous areas of deserts stretching across several countries. However, this plan has been abandoned because the human practices leading to desertification differ from country to country. The desert unit of UNEP has recently decided that before receiving international help the individual countries should create their own projects fitted to their particular social conditions.

- The recommendations of the Habitat Conference were fairly explicit with regard to supplies of clean water or of decent shelter because these biological necessities can be defined in scientific terms. In contrast, the recommendations were quite vague with regard to cultural matters or quality of life because these values have intense local and individual characteristics that transcend scientific determinism.

Hazards of globalization.

In my opinion, it is fortunate that practical necessities will compel a local approach to global problems. Globalization would mean more standardization and therefore less diversity, which in turn would slow down the rate of social innovation and of qualitative growth. Another danger of globalization is that excessive interdependence of systems increases the likelihood of collective disasters if any one of the subsystems fails to function properly as a result of accident or sabotage.

Finally, we may soon reach a state, if we have not reached it already, at which the technological, economic and social systems become so huge and so complex that the human mind cannot cope with their comprehension, let alone their management. There is a better chance for creativity, safety, and manageability in multiple, fairly small systems, aware and tolerant of each other, but jealous of their autonomy.

E pluribus unum.

Skepticism concerning the value of globalization does not imply isolationism. There are good reasons to believe that we can create a World Order, not a World Government, in which natural and social units maintain or recapture their identity, yet interplay with each other through a rich system of communications. This is beginning to happen through the 16 specialized agencies of the United Nations such as the World Health Organization, the World Meteorological Organization, the Food and Agricultural Organization, and the UNEP, which I mentioned earlier. My hope is that we shall learn to create for humankind a new kind of unity out of ever-increasing diversity.

—René Dubos

Commentary:

presented by SmithKline Corporation

James Davidson describes how a the USA on a perilous course.

...at the beginning of the dynasty, taxation yields a large revenue from small assessments. At the end of the dynasty, taxation yields a small revenue from large assessments...

—14TH CENTURY SCHOLAR*

The United States now faces challenges as serious as any in its history. Though present dangers are less clear than those of the 1860s and the 1940s, they threaten our society no less gravely.

In the past, when massive internal conflict or external force might have destroyed the nation, our unquestioned economic strength saved us. Today our economic strength is in question—and with it, the rights and

the prosperity that characterize America. This time, you and I will determine the outcome.

Stumbling Toward Disaster.
The US economy has begun to fail—largely as a result of unsound government policies. Overtaxation of work, saving and investment—as well as other types of government mismanagement—have virtually halted the growth of America's economic output. This means less real income for the ordinary citizen. It has already brought the decline of America's once dominant influence in global markets and in international affairs.

We must reject, then, any argument that America can not afford economic growth; that we have reached environmental or other "limits." Our quality of life stands threatened by foreign disorders and by the twin specters of inflation and unemployment at home.
We cannot afford to forego growth. We are no longer rich enough.

Automatic Confiscation.
A typical working couple who earned $23,000 in 1979

handed over to government more than $7,500 in taxes of all kinds. Americans now pay, on the average, 38 cents in taxes out of each dollar they earn.

Though Congress hasn't boosted income tax rates since the early 1950s, inflation has. Workers who gain income to make up for inflation are boosted into higher-rate tax brackets. Every time you get a 10% raise, your taxes go up by 16%. This process can quickly make you poor. In fact, if your family is like seven of every ten in America, you have less buying power than you had in 1969.

Under these conditions, you probably can't save money. Even if you could you probably wouldn't. Inflation would wipe out any interest, even if it weren't taxed.

All of this is bad for you and terrible for the country, because two-thirds of the money available for economic growth—for new jobs, more productive technologies, increased tax revenues—comes from individual savings.

The Leisure Society.
Whether you're making a living or living on public assistance, taxes leave you little incentive to work longer or harder. Over the entire range of incomes, about half of all households would now pay about fifty cents in taxes on any extra dollar they might earn.

Does it disturb you that the traditional American values of hard work and thrift have been turned upside down? Does it disturb our elected representatives? If it did, they could easily do something about it.

Introduction to History, translated by Franz Rosenthal, Bollingen Series XLVIII. Reprinted by permission of Princeton University Press

Exhibit 5

olicy of excessive taxes has set

They could make substantial cuts in spending and balance the budget. They could reduce income tax rates. They could make it possible and sensible for people to save.

Sorry—Too Risky.
If you have a stake in a corporation (as one of 30–40 million shareholders or as one of 80–100 million pension plan participants) you are subject to multiple taxation— taxation that shows up as higher prices for everyone.

First, tax law recognizes that depreciation (wearout of tools, buildings, etc.) is a cost, and so it's deductible from total income. But the law computes depreciation on the original *purchase* price of an

asset—not on the price of replacing it when it wears out, when inflation has raised its cost considerably. So, what appear to be profits may in fact be losses.

Second, the company's stated earnings are taxed (at high rates) before any part of them can be distributed to shareholders.

Third, when shareholders receive earnings in the form of dividends, they are taxed again—as personal income.

Fourth, if a shareholder sells stock at a profit (often an artificial "inflation profit") the gain is taxed, even if it is not used for consumption but is immediately reinvested.

This enervating drag on business and industry discourages people from investing. The average after-tax rate of return on investment— even in major corporations—has been reduced to a pitiful 4% a year.

Labor and Capital— The Starving Partners.
Unable to attract sufficient investment, US industries cannot modernize to compete with more efficient production facilities abroad. The average plant in the USA is twenty years old. In Japan it's only ten years old.

Trillions of dollars of new capital will be needed to rebuild and expand our industries in the 1980s, to create jobs for people entering the labor market. But the money will be forthcoming only if present tax and regulatory policies are changed.

New capital strengthens America's production base and raises national income—without adding to inflation. And since 1947, about three-fourths of such additional income has gone not to "capitalists" but to workers. If people fully understood this fact, labor unions and individual workers would be lobbying furiously for reform of corporate, dividend and capital gains taxation.

Feasting at Public Expense.
Where can cuts in federal spending be made so that both tax reduction and budget balancing can be achieved? There is no department or agency in government that could not spend money more wisely. Budget cuts, in many cases, would stimulate better service for the public. The most significant cuts, however, must be made in income "transfer" programs—programs that take money from Peter and give it to Paul— because they represent such a major portion of federal spending. In addition, government must get out of its habit of bailing out, subsidizing,

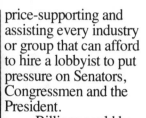

price-supporting and assisting every industry or group that can afford to hire a lobbyist to put pressure on Senators, Congressmen and the President.

Billions could be saved by eliminating programs that reward special interests while providing little or no benefit to the public.

Regaining Our Balance.
Lowering tax *rates*—for individuals and for businesses—would not mean lowering tax *revenues* permanently. On the contrary. Lower tax rates, accompanied by new restraint in government spending, would free funds to finance rapid growth of new and existing businesses. It is highly likely that lower tax rates would, within two or three years, lead to major growth of the total private earnings base from which public revenues flow. 20% of $1.50 is more than 25% of $1.00.

We are told that the 1981 federal budget does reflect "restraint" because its 14% increase over the 1980 budget is not much in "real"

(continued)

James Dale Davidson, writer, lecturer, scholar, is Chairman of the National Taxpayers Union in Washington, D.C. He was educated at the University of Maryland and at Pembroke College, Oxford. His book The Squeeze, *about the economic decline of the middle class, will be published in April by the Summit Books division of Simon and Schuster. N.T.U. is headquartered at 325 Pennsylvania Ave., S.E., Washington, D.C. 20003*

© 1980 SmithKline Corporation

ADVERTISING CAMPAIGN—1979

The major focus of the 1979 campaign was big government and its influence on energy (oil) prices, inflation, and individual freedom. The message was best exemplified in an advertisement entitled "The Malignant Growth of Federal Spending," expounding the views of William Simon [Exhibit 2]. In this ad, Simon argues that the fight to restore fiscal responsibility is, above all, a fight to control inflation, and to preserve our dignity, freedom, and prosperity. He compares big government to a tyrant, and suggests that the poor, the sick, and the socially disadvantaged have a great deal to gain from an orderly move away from big federal deficits. Other advertisements in this broad category were: Martin Feldstein, "Three Threats to Our Standard of Living"; George Roche, "The Federal Assault on Independent Education"; Walter Williams, "Minimum Wage, Maximum Folly"; Herbert Stein, "Freedom, the Reliable Energy Source"; and Eric Schellin, "Small Business, Shackled Giant of Innovation."

The campaign also covered two related but peripheral topics addressing the issues of optimism in America's future, and support for a pluralistic world. In "The Creed of the Class B Optimist," Ben J. Wattenberg makes a strong case about America's future and decries critics who find America nothing more than a basketful of problems [Exhibit 3]. René Dubos, "Think Globally, Act Locally," preaches against the tendency toward globalism and world government in the form of various UN agencies as a mechanism to solve world's environmental, energy, and other problems. While it is highly desirable to think globally in terms of the scope of the problem, Dubos says the best approach to solve them is through local action, taking into account diverse local conditions [Exhibit 4].

ADVERTISING CAMPAIGN—1980

The 1980 campaign continued its emphasis on the dangers of big government. However, another major topic was added dealing with America's defense and the dangers of international communism. Two peripherally related issues addressed in the 1981 campaign were those of America's values, and the antibusiness bias in the news media. There was a total of eight advertisements in 1980. The specific headings were: Michael Novak, "Irony, Tragedy, Courage"; James Davidson, "The Exhausting of America"; John Lehman, "As Criminal as War Itself"; Amitai Etzioni, "America's Most Critical Choice"; Allan Meltzer, "Big Government: Democracy's Deadly Creation"; Walter Laqueur, "The Crisis of Leadership"; David Kelly, "Bad News, America."

Typical of the genre of the dangers of big government advertisements were those by James Davidson and Marva Collins. In his commentary, James Davidson, chairman of the National Taxpayers' Union, argues that through a policy of excessive taxation, the federal government is leading the nation on a potentially disastrous economic course [Exhibit 5].

Exhibit 6

Irony, Tragedy, Courage.

The SmithKline Forum for a Healthier American Society   Vol. II   No. 1   February 1980

Commentary:

Through the eyes of theologian Michael Novak, free people may gaze steadily on the boiling passions of the Eighties.

Freedom is a system based on courage.
—Charles Péguy

Irony dominates our era. A socialist system which is a dismal economic and political failure stirs tremendous ideological fervor around the world, while democratic capitalism, based firmly on a record of unparalleled liberty, equality, and prosperity, is rejected as morally unworthy. At the end of 1979, flames rose from U.S. embassies in Iran, India, Turkey, Libya, and Pakistan.

Libyan leader Muammar Kadafi, no paragon of liberty, says sharply: "An explosion of hatred toward America is taking place. Everybody hates America, everybody, not only the Moslem countries. Because everybody is or has been oppressed by America and sooner or later will revolt against America..."

The Crime of Success.

In 1952, the great Protestant theologian Reinhold Niebuhr wrote that the substantial human successes of the United States would supply the reason for other nations to condemn it: "We are ironically held responsible for disparities in wealth and well-being which are chiefly due to differences in standards of productivity. But they lend themselves...to the Marxist indictment, which attributes all such differences to exploitation. Thus every effort we make to prove the virtue of our 'way of life' by calling attention to our prosperity is used by our enemies and detractors as proof of our guilt."

Under the rumble and clatter of the first Soviet tanks in Afghanistan, the Iranian "students" did not turn their bitterness from the "covert imperialism" of the U.S.A. to the flaunted imperialism of the U.S.S.R.

Thou Shalt Covet.

For seventy years, Marxism was a theory only. A majority of the world's nations have now put it into practice. Its economic failures drag the planet down. Since the Soviet Revolution there have been sixty-two years of "bad weather"; socialist nations cannot feed themselves. Yet the more Marxism fails, the stronger it seems. For Marxism is, as expatriate Marxist historian Leszek Kolakowski has shown, a matrix for expressing any form of resentment. It institutionalizes envy (one of the most persistent and universal of human vices, prohibited twice in the Ten Commandments). It makes tyrants feel secure. It legitimizes every abuse of liberty they undertake.

"The power of the non-Communist world...is held responsible for every ill inhering in the whole historic situation," Niebuhr wrote. "The Marxist theory has the advantage of satisfying a deep instinct in the human heart. It places the blame for an unfortunate situation entirely upon others."

Unreason Amplified.

Socialism works better in theory than in practice. Democratic capitalism works better in practice than in theory. Inarticulate common sense has led to greater justice than ideology has. Yet in our era facts do not seem to count. Mobs everywhere—and rulers—are moved by symbols, images, passions, and ideologies.

Mass communications, ironically, have speeded up this irrational process—ironically because nearly every technology of mass communication was invented or enhanced in the hated United States. We are told that the "students" holding U.S. hostages in Iran spent their free time attending propaganda movies and listening to tape recorders.

Too Early a Dawn?

Our forefathers were borne along by an uncommon cultural dynamism. Did they oppress Libya, an advanced culture in the eighth century A.D.? The U.S. did not exist before 1776. It remained an underdeveloped nation until the time of our grandparents.

Was it a fault that modernity began early in our culture? One modern Islamic leader told his people: "For 13 centuries, in each of which [this] country ought to have taken a great leap forward, it has remained motionless and backward. We are now faced with the consequences of this neglect, and must make amends for the torpor of the past." He went on: "If the Great Lawgiver of Islam were alive today to see the progress of the world, he would confirm the complete harmony of his true teachings with the basis and the institutions of the civilization of today."

The Familiar Stench.

Tragedy also dominates our era. Yet the great Mexican novelist Carlos Fuentes thinks that in the West the notion of progress replaced the notion of tragedy: "...once you believe that you are ordered to progress, failure becomes not tragedy but a crime. Those who oppose you are no longer your equals but figures of evil." In truth, many in the West retain a vivid sense of tragedy and of their own past. Many still struggle to reconcile modernity with the Judaism, Christianity or other great religion of their hearts.

A tragic sense is no more than common sense. Over 100 million Europeans have lost their lives through violence in this century, 4 million in the crematoria of Auschwitz alone. It is a calumny on the West to hold that only the Third World knows tragedy.

Even now we live in fateful times. Democratic capitalism, burning as a fitful flame in perhaps two dozen beleaguered nations in the world, may not long survive. The destiny of civilization may once again be decided, not by reason or morality, but by force of arms. If starved of oil, democratic capitalism in Italy, in France, in Germany and in Japan may flicker out before the end of this century.

As 1979 in so many ways echoed 1939, the 1980s already have about them the smell of the 1940s.

Wisdom and Pessimism.

To comprehend the spiritual depths of democratic capitalism it is not necessary, then, to hold a sunny secular optimism. Quite the opposite; the great founding documents both of democracy and of capitalism recognize full well the evil in the human heart. For this reason, they labor upon pragmatic checks-and-balances, empowering persons and institutions to resist the omnivorous state apparatus which has dominated human history.

Perhaps the course of democratic capitalism will be all too like that of a meteor flashing briefly across the centuries. (Adam Smith's first—and rather primitive—"manifesto" of democratic capitalism first appeared in 1776.) Perhaps the tyrannical central state will once again swallow the sectors of liberty, and history will relapse into its traditional torpor and backwardness.

If democratic capitalism does perish, it will not be because its economic system produced a lesser prosperity. It will not be because its political system permitted a lesser range of liberties and civilities. It will be because its cultural leaders never perceived, never expressed, and too poorly defended its moral ideals—and, therefore, on the field of battle it fell.

Loneliness and Courage.

The people of the United States need to be armed against the dangers to liberty in the 1980s—armed both militarily and in spirit. We very much need a better theory about our system, a vision of its goals and disciplines. Since we cannot expect to be loved, we shall undertake the lessons of an ironic sense of life. And in a sense of the tragedy of life we shall find reasons enough for noble words and acts.

In this world, there are no excuses. There is no place to hide. Not even liberty comes free.

—Michael Novak

When Michael Novak taught at Stanford University he was twice in three years voted one of the two "most influential professors" by the senior class.
Novak is the author of ten philosophical works and two novels. His books and articles have appeared in many languages, and his twice-weekly column "Illusions and Realities" is syndicated by the Universal Press Syndicate.
Novak is a Resident Scholar in Religion and Public Policy at the American Enterprise Institute.

The Purpose.

Why SmithKline is sponsoring these ideas for a healthier American society.

People write to us at SmithKline in response to these articles. Many say how much they like them and encourage us to continue. And some say they are puzzled why we are sponsoring the series. They ask how it helps our business.

We answer every letter by saying that SmithKline is mainly in the health business—prescription and over-the-counter medicines as well as equipment and services that improve American health care.

To improve people's health we have to stay healthy as a company. And we firmly believe that SmithKline's business health—like your well-being—depends on a healthy American society.

At the moment America has many problems. We have global crises, energy shortages, an unstable dollar, a lag in scientific discovery, low productivity, a huge government debt, a balance of trade that works against us—and a crushing burden of inflation that is eroding every citizen's buying power every day.

America has many highly intelligent people who believe they have reasonable solutions for some of these problems. And the purpose of this Forum is to share their ideas with you.

Individual Action— An Absolute Necessity

These crucial issues of public policy can be discussed forever. What we really must do is take action on them.

We believe it is essential, therefore, that *you as a private citizen* reach a conclusion about what you believe. Then you must vote your opinion at every election by choosing candidates in whom you have confidence. And you must regularly share your views with your elected representatives by writing to them.

At SmithKline we are convinced that the time for all of us to act—in America's interest and in our own—is *now.*

Robert F. Dee

Robert F. Dee
Chairman of the Board and
Chief Executive Officer
SmithKline Corporation

SmithKline
CORPORATION
One Hundred Fiftieth Anniversary 1830–1980

SmithKline Corporation
H20/W229, P.O. Box 7929
Philadelphia, PA 19101

If you would like to receive SmithKline's Issues for Action, a series of informative pamphlets on subjects of social, political and economic significance, please complete this coupon and mail it to the address above.

name

title and company (if any)

street address or box number

city   state   zip code

Views expressed by participants in the SmithKline Forum are their own.

© 1980 SmithKline Corporation

Commentary:

presented by SmithKline Corporation

Pay the price of peace while peace urges defense analyst John Lehman.

Until war is eliminated from international relations, unpreparedness for it is well nigh as criminal as war itself.
—DWIGHT D. EISENHOWER

Against spreading Soviet adventurism and our ailing economy, the guns-or-butter debate today stands out starker than ever. But the old political game, treating defense as just another social service competing for funds, will dangerously confuse present efforts for sound defense policy.

To evaluate sums as vast as this year's $140 billion for defense, the mind grasps for a steady reference. Politicians perennially refer to last year. The Republic did not fall, so we must have spent enough; and surely there was "fat" enough for politically attractive cuts this year. This tradition, and our Constitution's prohibition of long-term military funding, blinds us to the result of accumulated yearly compromises: we are in very deep trouble.

Self-reliance and Self-defense.

Do not be intimidated by the protective jargon of the priesthood of defense experts. The important issues involve only common sense applied to facts and simple axioms.

Axiom I: *It is a harsh world.* To assure peace we need to be invincible in war.

Orderly international commerce, secure (not exploitative) access to energy and mineral resources especially, is vital to the democracies. Complete denial of foreign oil would bring economic collapse—and war. Less publicized are bauxite, cobalt, titanium, nickel, tin, zinc, chromium, platinum, and manganese. We import more than

60% of our requirements of each, and we are steadily losing access to them through political-military actions directed against the West. The lead time to purchase titanium sponge, for example, has gone from 12 weeks in 1976 to 90 weeks, and prices have more than tripled.

Scarcities, our adversaries know, worsen our debilitating inflation.

Axiom II: *The purpose of defense is deterrence*—persuading another that action against us will bring him more harm than gain.

Since possible actions against us range from kidnapping to thermonuclear attack, our capability to dissuade must be commensurately broad and assure successful action if an adversary is not deterred. Bluffs will fail over time.

Our defense policy is failing to deter, as demonstrated by recent events: the Soviet brigade in Cuba, Cuban forces in Africa, the spectacle in Iran, the invasion of Afghanistan. Adversaries are not dissuaded from seizing Americans, threatening our friends, or constricting our vital resources. The world sees our adversaries benefit more than suffer.

Chamberlain lamented after Munich, "Our past experience has shown us only too clearly that weakness in armed strength means weakness in diplomacy."

From Strength to Weakness.

A decline and a disparity of effort sustained for fifteen years explains our massive defense failure. Since 1970, the Soviets have outspent us in defense by more than $240 billion, and in strategic weapons by 270%. Our effort has shrunk

from 8.2% of GNP in 1964 to 5% today—the lowest since 1938. The Soviets are spending 13% to 15% of GNP on their military.

We are now unlikely to prevail in violent conflict if deterrence fails.

Exhibit 7

nd security can still be bought,

The Soviets could, by full-scale effort, shut the Persian Gulf and cut the jugular of the West. Our Navy, outnumbered three to one in surface ships and in attack submarines, barely equal in Naval aircraft, can no

longer simultaneously protect the vital sea-lanes in the North Atlantic, the Mediterranean and Southwest Asia—even by abandoning the western Pacific as planned. In Central Europe we could not prevail with conventional weapons. In addition, the growing imbalance in *strategic* systems may lead the Soviets to believe they can attack the U.S. itself and survive retaliation.

The Generous and the Brave.

The expression "behind the power curve" describes an aircraft's inability to overcome accumulated drag and avoid crashing, even with maximum engine power. Our defense posture is nearing a similar peril. In such critical areas as personnel retention, shipbuilding and weapons procurement, recovery is possible only by drastic action now.

It takes eight years to replace a skilled tech sergeant and a decade to revive a closed shipyard. An aircraft cut from the budget costs nearly twice the price two years later.

Experienced military people are leaving in droves. They have lost up to 25% of their purchasing power since 1972. A typical Virginia-based Petty Officer maintaining F-14 fighters, working sixteen hours a day during his annual six or eight months at sea, makes less per hour than a cashier at MacDonald's. His family qualifies for public assistance. Small wonder that the services are short some 70,000 noncommissioned officers.

The F-14 pilot, trained at a cost of $1 million to fly a $25-million machine, has a 23% chance of dying in peacetime if he stays twenty years. We pay him $24 thousand a

year and a dollar for each day away from home. The Air Force expects to be short 3,500 pilots next year.

Even the most dedicated are near the breaking point.

The Cost of Neglect.

Operations and Maintenance funding also has eroded. Fuel cuts have reduced pilot flying hours significantly, hurting readiness, safety, and retention. We scrimp at a terrible cost: last year, 74 Navy men died in 127 crashes due mainly to aircrew or maintenance errors.

The Army's plight from repeatedly delayed modernizations is described in chilling terms by its senior R&D officials. Unless large numbers of new fighting vehicles, attack helicopters and battlefield air-defense systems appear in the mid-80s, said one, "I don't see how we can win any war that might be fought."

For the Navy, this year's budget request is the seventh in seven years that procures fewer combat aircraft (72) than needed to stay even with peacetime attrition (180).

To catch up with these deferrals, taxpayers will pay billions

(continued)

John F. Lehman, Jr. has served as Special Counsel and Senior Staff Member to the National Security Council, as a Delegate to the Mutual and Balanced Force Reductions Talks, and as Deputy Director of the Arms Control and Disarmament Agency.

Since 1977 Dr. Lehman has been President of Abington Corporation. He holds degrees in International Law and Diplomacy from Cambridge University, a B.A. from St. Joseph's College, and a doctorate in International Relations from the University of Pennsylvania.

Lehman's best known work is The Executive, Congress and Foreign Policy. *He is an officer flying A-6s and Skyhawks in the U.S. Naval Reserve.*

© 1980 SmithKline Corporation

Commentary:

presented by SmithKline Corporation

Why do American TV viewers
industry and commerce? Philosopher

*The spirit of truth and the spirit of freedom—
they are the pillars of society.*
—Henrik Ibsen

It's seven o'clock. Do you know what's happening?

If you are watching the network news, you may or may not. If you are watching a network story on business, probably not. That fact both angers and worries a growing number of people.

Last year, for example, on the day Mobil reported third-quarter profits, CBS correspondent Ray Brady did a "standupper" in front of a Mobil station, explaining how oil companies could be avoiding taxes by disguising domestic earnings as foreign. When Mobil objected that it did no such thing, it transpired that Brady had no evidence. The misdeeds were hypothetical. CBS defended the segment on the ground that Mobil was never mentioned by name, but the company was smeared nonetheless.

And That's the Way It Is?

Mobil's was an extreme case, but business anger runs deepest over less obvious patterns of misrepresentation. Business seems to appear in the news only when some problem can be laid at its door: acid rain falling, products being recalled, the greasing of palms in tropical lands. Profits are reported in a manner that seems calculated to inflate the public's conception of them. Corporate explanations have been twisted or cut so often that many executives no longer speak to journalists. Some companies, in self-defense, make their own videotapes of interviews.

The pressures of the medium are partly to blame for shoddy reporting. Journalists must decide what is news, then investigate and package it, in an unrelenting race against the clock. To make matters worse, most of them feel at sea in the complexities of finance and technology that underlie business stories. But there is an antibusiness bias as well, in the form of attitudes that shape and color the news.

Through a Glass Darkly

Journalists tend to share attitudes common among those who work with ideas. Most seem to feel, for example, that manufacturing and commerce are mundane activities, devoid of idealism, drama, heroes. Hence the inner life of business, with all its excitement and achievements, is passed over in silence. The television audience sees almost nothing of the tumult of innovation, the unceasing generation of jobs and wealth, the sometimes heroic efforts required to keep the flow of goods moving, the countless ways in which corporate products have made life safer and richer. Business becomes newsworthy only in those marginal cases when it can be made to seem dangerous.

During a recent two-week period, for example, the networks used the occasion of a rate increase for Metropolitan Edison to recall the accident at its Three Mile Island nuclear plant. They also ran stories on the dumping of toxic wastes, faulty tires, an allegedly unsafe tractor, and pilots' complaints about airline safety procedures.

During the same period, the networks ignored every business achievement of note: Mobil's announcement that it would invest another $1.35 billion in its North Sea fields; reports of oil and gas finds in Montana, Canada, Colombia, and Indonesia, and exploration elsewhere; IBM's introduction of a line of cheaper and more powerful computers; Sharp Manufacturing's plan to introduce the first pocket-size minicomputer; the success of two entrepreneurs in putting together capital for a Coca-Cola bottle plant in the South Bronx, raising hope for that economic desert—the list goes on.

When business can't be portrayed as dangerous, it is usually presented as exploitative. For that is another prevalent attitude. Most journalists tend to be suspicious of the profit motive. Despite the harmony of interests that a free market promotes, they assume profits are won at the expense of workers, consumers, the environment. In their search for victims of corporate avarice, journalists have often doctored the facts to fit the assumption. Conversely, government measures to control business are routinely described as victories for workers or consumers, even if the measures eliminate jobs or raise prices.

Exhibit 8

see a dangerously distorted picture of
David Kelley looks at media bias.

This bias may also explain Tom Bethell's finding, in a study* for the Media Institute, that the media tend to blame business for inflation. In 1978 and 1979 one network ran 200 stories on inflation. Specific price increases were mentioned 123 times, with the implication that they were the causes of inflation, not the effects. Federal deficits and expansion of the money supply, now held by economists as the chief cause of inflation, were mentioned in only 17 stories. In frequency of reference, these government activities ranked just ahead of bad weather as forces blamed for inflation.

The Horns and the Hounds

The aversion to profit goes still deeper—deeper than any worry about exploitation could explain. For many in the media, profit seems to have the moral flavor that pleasure had for the Puritans. Like Cotton Mather, they are haunted by the suspicion that someone, somewhere, is getting too much. The result is not merely a tendency to exaggerate profits, but a standing presumption of corporate guilt in general.

Thus the wildest rumors are taken seriously on the air—like the mythical oil tankers waiting off New Jersey for the price to rise, mentioned by ABC and NBC during the first energy crisis of 1973–74. Lavish and uncritical attention is paid the conspiracy theories of the antibusiness left. Alleged infractions of government regulations are reported in an atmosphere of perfidy exposed, and three-time felons often receive fairer coverage than companies that stand accused. As the victim of this witch hunt, business is left with the burden of proving its innocence.

But not on media time. NBC covered a Federal Trade Commission report criticizing the life insurance industry, but ignored the industry's rebuttal in Senate hearings. All three

networks, which have aired suspicions that the major oil companies favor their own service stations over independents, were silent last May when an Energy Department report found no evidence of the practice.

All this bias and inaccuracy helps paint a picture, and the picture has power. That is what has business not only angry but worried. Two-thirds of the populace rely primarily on television for their news. Is it any wonder that public confidence in business has dropped sharply in the last decade, or that a majority of Americans believe, for example, the energy crisis was contrived by the oil companies? Is it any wonder the political climate encourages oppressive controls on business, eroding economic freedom and washing it down the Potomac? Business leaders feel they are drowning in a sea of misinformation.

Congress Shall Make No Law...

Journalists often hide from allegations of bias under the mantle of the First Amendment, claiming to hear in such charges the Censor's distant tread. They complain of the chilling effect.

That is the sound of one knee jerking.

The First Amendment means that no one, including those in the media, is immune from critics. If the media claim that business, government and other institutions are responsible for their actions, for turning out, in effect, a good product, the media must recognize the implication that they are

equally responsible for the objectivity of their reporting.

But criticism does not imply any design on press liberties. Those who value economic freedom know the effects of government controls too well to wish them on journalists. Informed people in business are concerned, for example, about the recent spate of court decisions that leave reporters more susceptible to government investigation and less capable of investigating government.

As for the antibusiness attitudes that filter the news, they are the residue of anticapitalist ideas that have reigned among intellectuals for a century, and ideas can be countered only by better ideas. All parties to this argument need the freedom to speak their minds.

Real liberty of speech and thought, however, is impossible without economic freedom. That freedom

(continued)

David Kelley received a Ph.D. in philosophy from Princeton University in 1975, and is now Assistant Professor of Philosophy at Vassar College. Among his other activities, he has addressed the Mont Pelerin Society on the morality of capitalism, commented on affirmative action for WNEW-TV, and written extensively for Barrons Business and Financial Weekly on the media and the role of ideas in the marketplace.

At present Kelley is completing a book The Evidence of the Senses.

*Tom Bethell, "TV, Inflation and Government Handouts"—*The Wall Street Journal,* July 8, 1980.

© 1980 SmithKline Corporation

A cutoff of vital foreign min... William Mott, would cripple America

...and the seven empty ears blasted with the east wind shall be seven years of famine.
—JOSEPH, IN GENESIS 41:27

Across mineral-rich southern Africa a chill wind now blows from the East, threatening to freeze key American industries in their tracks and to hurl millions of us out of work. This wind threatens every American pocketbook. It threatens our nation's economic survival. But few can see a wind in the distance.

U.S. Senator Jack Schmitt sees. This professional geologist, whom NASA so respected that it sent him to the moon, has warned his Senate colleagues:

Not far in the future awaits sudden recognition of a "materials crisis" with the possibility of more devastating effects than our current "energy crisis".

Who has listened to him, or to Senator McClure? Has the House of Representatives listened to Congressman Jim Santini, sounding alarms for several years? Said Santini to the press:

The U.S. is dangerously reliant—as it was and remains in energy—on foreign sources for key minerals...This poses, of course, serious risks and adverse consequences to both our economy and defense.

We import over 50 percent of more than 20 of the minerals *essential* to our country. In some critical minerals, such as manganese, cobalt, chromium and platinum, we import nearly all of our annual needs.

The Stuff of Nightmares

Joseph, interpreting the Pharaoh's dreams in ancient times, warned Egypt to stockpile grain to avoid *natural* disaster. Our seers,

relying on studied facts and reasoned projections, today warn us we risk disaster of political and military making. And they too urgently advise stockpiling—to lessen the danger of America's dependence on unstable foreign sources of essential minerals.

How vulnerable are we? Consider that 98 per cent of the world's known reserves of manganese ore are in southern Africa and in the U.S.S.R. Without manganese it is difficult if not impossible to make iron and steel. For chrome ore the figure is 96 per cent. Without chromium we cannot produce high-temperature and high-pressure alloys essential for electricity-generating turbines, for nuclear reactors, for advanced aircraft and for the petrochemical industry.

Cobalt, too, is necessary for electric turbines, for jet engines and for high-speed machine tools. Southern Africa holds only 25 per cent of the world's cobalt reserves, but we import 97 per cent of our needs —more than half from Zaire and Zambia.

As for platinum-group metals—essential for automobile catalytic converters, for no-lead gasoline and for aspirin (we'll need it)—southern Africa accounts for 86 per cent of world reserves, and the U.S.S.R. 13 per cent.

Domestic sources of these minerals either do not exist or their mining is severely restricted by our own environmental policies.

Honey for the Bear

As surely as our economy runs on oil, it is built of metal. And as surely as the Soviets are encircling the Persian Gulf—by invading Afghanistan, by supporting Iraq and by placing their Cuban and East German surrogates in Ethiopia and in South Yemen—they are trying to gain control of southern Africa, the Saudi Arabia of minerals.

The Soviet motive for depriving the U.S.A. and its allies of vital minerals is nothing less than the historical Communist aim. Economic chaos could well collapse the capitalistic system. The Soviets seek, meanwhile, to secure the resources of southern Africa for themselves. Experts believe the Soviet Union has not sufficiently developed its own minerals-production capacity to meet its future industrial and defense needs. The U.S.S.R., moreover, badly needs our technologies and

Exhibit 9

als, warns national-security analyst
industry, economy, and defense.

goods. For these it must have Western currencies. By obtaining minerals at low cost from the nations of southern Africa and reselling them at high prices to the West, the Soviets could, to paraphrase Lenin's purported saying, buy more than enough of our "rope" to hang us.

Smash and Grab

Today there are Cuban troops in 15 African countries, including some 25,000 in Angola, right next door to Zambia, Zaire, Namibia and Zimbabwe—all treasure troves of minerals critical to our economy.

25,000 troops may seem few, but Soviet arms, logistic aid and air support are at hand. And, as history shows, even a small band of well-equipped military or political agents can shatter a fragile chain of mines, railways, processing plants and ports.

Are the Cubans present, as some observers wishfully have suggested, as a stabilizing force? Galina Orionova, a recent defector from Moscow's "Institute of U.S. Studies," knows better. Says this plain-spoken woman, who cannot understand why the West is so surprised at Soviet incursions into the Third World:

The Soviet government behaves like any ordinary Soviet consumer. He grabs anything which happens to be on the counter, even if he doesn't need it, knowing that tomorrow it may no longer be available.

It is vain to hope that the Soviet Union—miserably inept at producing items of value for world trade—will forsake force and subversion as means to economic and political ends.

Ready or not, we are in a

Resource War, cold or hot, with the U.S.S.R.

Military preparedness is only part of a proper U.S. strategy in the Resource War—in southern Africa and in the Persian Gulf region. But we must recognize the umbilical cord between supplies of critical minerals and our national defense. Without them we cannot build a ship, a plane or a tank. This is why today we have

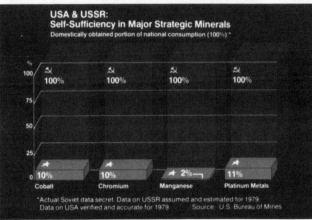

USA & USSR:
Self-Sufficiency in Major Strategic Minerals
Domestically obtained portion of national consumption (100%)*

100%	100%	100%	100%
10% Cobalt	10% Chromium	2% Manganese	11% Platinum Metals

*Actual Soviet data secret. Data on USSR assumed and estimated for 1979
Data on USA verified and accurate for 1979   Source: U.S. Bureau of Mines

stockpiles—woefully small as they are. This is one reason we need to rebuild America's merchant marine and to provide for more adequate armed forces—fully able to protect the sealanes that carry materials vital to our economy and to our defense.

A Plan of Action

We Americans are suffering, and may yet agonize, because of our shortsightedness about energy. A similar lack of vision about minerals could destroy us. We have our Josephs, but no omnipotent Pharaoh who can decree immediate measures to preserve the realm. We have only ourselves and, within our system, we need desperately to take the following steps before a minerals crisis strikes us with at least the force and effect of an oil crisis:

■ *Establish a Council on Minerals and Materials to develop and implement a national minerals policy, including—*
(**A**) a sweeping review of our stockpile laws, policies and programs.
(**B**) an audit of existing stockpiles. They must be brought up to presently authorized levels without delay.
(**C**) a reshaping of policy so as to open government stockpiles to industry (via a trigger mechanism) if certain events occur, or to encourage private stockpiling by user industries through special tax incentives. Stockpiles now are restricted to defense needs.
■ *Re-evaluate our foreign policy in view of our materials dependency.*

In particular, we must stop treating South Africa as a moral leper and look on her as a necessary ally. With respect to our sea routes for supply of Mideast oil and southern African minerals, she is one of the most strategically located nations in that part of the world. We must, through the efforts of American business, labor

(continued)

RAdm. Wiliiam C. Mott, USN (ret), is Executive Director of the Council on Economics and National Security, a project of the National Strategy Information Center, an independent foundation.

Mott served recently as a member of the task force appointed by Governor Reagan to recommend executive and legislative action on the problem of critical minerals. President Reagan now has the report of that task force.

Mott served in the White House under President Roosevelt and in the Pacific during World War II. He subsequently worked for Presidents Truman and Eisenhower.

Mott, an attorney, has been president of both the Capital Legal Foundation and the National Legal Center for the Public Interest.

© 1981 SmithKline Corporation

Commentary:

presented by SmithKline Corporation

Salute the capitalist entrepreneur
They dream, then act, and enrich ou

"In spite of their natural selfishness and rapacity, though they mean only their own conveniency, though the sole end which they propose from the labors of all the thousands they employ be the gratification of their own vain and insatiable desires…they are led by an invisible hand…without intending it, without knowing it, to advance the interest of society."

ADAM SMITH, 1776

With these famous words about businessmen, Adam Smith, the world's leading apologist for free enterprise, created a catastrophic schism in the soul of modern capitalism. If he is right, Western society suffers from a deep conflict between its economic system and its religious values.

With friends like Adam Smith, it is fair to say, businessmen hardly need enemies. Yet, in my belief, businessmen are the heroes of the market economy. While Smith and other pro-capitalist economists offer many more sophisticated arguments *for* the system, their essential view of the nature and motivation of capitalists is insidiously false. They fail to explain in any convincing way the sources of economic growth and progress. Why do free enterprise economies succeed when self-interest, after all, is just as common in any torpid bureaucracy or stagnant socialist regime?

Capitalism: The Giving of Gifts

The fact is that capitalism is good and successful not because it miraculously transmutes personal avarice and ambition into collective prosperity but because it calls forth, propagates, and relies upon the best and most generous of human qualities.

The process of capitalist investment, for all the obvious differences, bears a close relationship to the ritual gift-giving that anthropologists have discovered to be universal in primitive life. These gifts are not offered without the expectation of a return; the outcome depends on the voluntary responses of others. In order to make a successful gift, the giver must first suppress his own appetites (save) while at the same time figuring out the desires of the recipient. To the extent the recipients value the gifts more than the givers, the profits of the system—in this case, the circles of human sympathy—will expand.

The giving impulse in modern capitalism is no less prevalent and important, no less central to all creative and productive activity, than in a primitive tribe. Look at the unending offerings of entrepreneurs: investing capital, creating products, building businesses, inventing jobs, accumulating inventories. These contributions—all long before any return is received, all without any assurance that the enterprise will not fail—constitute a pattern of giving that dwarfs in extent and in practical generosity any primitive rite of exchange. Giving is the vital impulse and moral center of capitalism; give and you will be given unto is its fundamental law.

Money as a Means, Not an End

Capitalists are motivated not chiefly by the desire to consume wealth or indulge their appetites, b by the freedom and power to consummate their entrepreneurial idea Whether piling up coconuts or designing new computers, they are movers and shakers, doers and givers, obsessed with positive visio of change and opportunity.

Are they greedier than doctor or writers or professors of sociolog or assistant secretaries of energy or commissars of wheat? Their goals

seem more mercenary, but this is only because money is their very means of production. Just as the s ologist requires books and free tim and the bureaucrat needs arbitrary power and the scientist must have laboratory, the capitalist needs cap to fulfill his role in launching and financing enterprise. Are capitalis self-interested? Presumably. But t crucial fact about them is their dee interest and engagement in the wo beyond themselves, impelled by th imagination, optimism and faith.

Exhibit 10

says social philosopher George Gilder.
ives.

The Traveling Bazaar

The rewards of capitalists, however, do not simply constitute a tribute to virtue or an accommodation or a particular style of professional fe. Entrepreneurs must be allowed retain wealth for the practical reason that only they, collectively, can ossibly know where it should go, to whom it should be given. Successful apitalism confronts the potential nvestor, public or private, with millions of small companies (nearly 16 million in the U.S.), scores of thousands of them lurching forth every ear with growth rates of between 20 nd 40 percent and more, and suffering from crises of expansion and cash low. It offers a vast Babel of business plans and projects presented vith every imaginable combination f managerial, marketing, engineering and huckstering skills, all inscrutbly mixed in a teeming marketplace f corporations, limited partnerships, roprietorships, franchises, concessions, spreads and deals of every escription.

The investor must appraise vast traveling bazaar of new products, the overflow of a million garages and laboratories, hobby shops and machinery "skunkworks," companies all claiming "new breakthroughs," takeoff trajectories, unique product niches, firms offering fame and fortune and tax shelter, providing low cost fuel, high margin fast food, automatic profits in mail order marketing, forty-seven magazines the world needs now, the people's airline, fourteen plausible cures for asthma, the perfect coffee cup, all demanding huge infusions of instant capital, all continually bursting beyond the ken even of banks and experts, let alone government planners, regulators, and subsidizers.

The flood of protean growth can be comprehended and sustained only by investors who have money of their own and who can share in and pass on the profits as they gain new knowledge and investment skills.

Who Loves the Entrepreneur?

The fatal problem of a system without accumulations of personal income and without the possibility of large profits is not the lack of incentives but the lack of dynamism and flexibility. It is capitalism that best combines the desire and ability to do good and create value, with the resources to accomplish these goals.

Yet the contribution of these businessmen is easy to misunderstand. These capitalists provide a continuing challenge both to men who refuse a practical engagement in the world—on the grounds that it is too dangerous or corrupt—and then to men who demand power over others in the name of ideology or expertise, without first giving and risking their wealth. It is not surprising, therefore, that the chief source of

the incomprehension of capitalism is the intelligentsia, one of the many aristocracies which preen themselves on a contempt for bourgeois or "middle class" values and which refuse to acknowledge the paramount role of individual enterprise in the progress of the race.

Mind Over Manner

Adam Smith himself misunderstood. His error was to found his theory on the mechanism of market exchanges themselves rather than on the business activity that makes them possible and impels their growth. In effect, he subordinated a higher and more complex level of activity—the creation of value—to a lower level, its measurement and exchange.

In *The Wealth of Nations,* Smith implies that in some possible mystical way the market process precedes and subsumes the process of production. However, man, not mechanism, is at the heart of capitalist growth. Although a marketplace may work

(continued)

George Gilder is Program Director of the International Center for Economic Policy Studies and Chairman of the Economic Roundtable at the Lehrman Institute. His latest book, Wealth and Poverty, *is exerting a major influence on public policy in the United States. Gilder's previous works include* Sexual Suicide *and* Visible Man, *among others. He contributes to* The Wall Street Journal, Harper's Magazine *and many other publications.*

© 1981 SmithKline Corporation

Commentary:

presented by SmithKline Corporation

Press freedoms and economic
The defenders of each must now unite.

At the UN the Third World Countries usually vote with the totalitarian states, thereby almost paralyzing that organization. But the UN is one of the few forces on which our common hopes for a better world are based.
—SOVIET DISSIDENT ANDREI SAKHAROV, MOSCOW, 1975

The United Nations has become what Daniel Patrick Moynihan, former American Ambassador to the UN, once called it. It has become "a dangerous place." The world organization now poses two related threats to the dream of a planet filled with free societies.

- Governments that oppose international *press* freedoms intend to establish through the UN a "New World Information Order". They hope to achieve that allegedly benign goal by 1983, one year ahead of George Orwell's fictional timetable for tyranny's triumph.

- Enemies of international *economic* freedoms, mostly the same countries, seek to implement through the UN a "New International Economic Order". They have left its schedule less definite.

The "new order" in information would, as a main aim, grant governments and UN agencies insidious new authority: to "regulate" both the gathering and the international transmission of news.

The economic "new order" envisions, among other things, mandatory transfer of unspecified billions in Western technology and financial resources to underdeveloped —and largely unfree—societies. Its sponsors rarely acknowledge that since World War II, the United States has funded more humanitarian activities than all other nations combined.

Those battling the new order in information, however, and those struggling against the new order in world economic affairs have cooperated hardly at all. Business and the media throughout the developed world harbor deep mutual suspicions.

High purpose perverted.

The UN was planned originally as a practical, collective postwar forum from which to mobilize against future aggression. Today a UN majority comprised mainly of unfree and partially free societies has transformed that body into one which

United Nations Headquarters, New York City

periodically assaults the values and resources of free societies.

Imagine Franklin Roosevelt and Harry Truman, the UN's true godfathers, discovering a UNESCO*-sponsored coalition of tyrannies and their accomplices hatching elaborate plots to muzzle free world news media, all in the name of correcting alleged "omissions" and "imbalances" in coverage. "Positivity is news," declared Zimbabwe's Director of Information revealingly. "Negativity is not news."

Imagine, also, the reaction of Americans who sponsored efforts like UNRRA (UN Relief and Rehabilitation Agency), the Marshall Plan, Point Four, and other global postwar assistance programs when confronted with the UN's *economic* new worlders. These "reformers" are determined to swell and control, through a pack of violently anti-

*UNESCO stands for United Nations Educational, Scientific and Cultural Organization and is not to be confused with the more admirable UNICEF—United Nations Children's Emergency Fund.

American UN agencies, the major stream of aid and investment coming from the West into Less Developed Countries (LDCs).

The free press counterattacks.

Recognizing that the New World Information Order imperils freedom, 63 leaders of independent news organizations from 21 countries met last May in Talloires, France.

The Talloires delegates accurately described the goal of their adversaries as, essentially, a *New World Propaganda Order*. Their declaration endorsed values long cherished by free people: "We support the universal human right to be fully informed, which right requires the free circulation of news and opinion. We vigorously oppose any interference with this fundamental right."

The Talloires meeting marks a historic turning point for world press liberties.

Carrots and sticks.

Since Talloires, the defenders of global press freedom have adopted a shrewd carrot-and-stick strategy. Whenever the subject has arisen at the UN, Western and moderate Third World representatives have answered new order advocates with efforts to implement information measures outside of UNESCO's control. These include training programs and communications technology-sharing schemes designed to strengthen resistance to government pressures by independent journalists in LDCs.

As the free media began fighting back, it became apparent that on these issues no unified "Third World" exists. Rather, treatment of the media has varied widely. Researchers at Freedom House, a leading human rights organization, found that two dozen LDCs permit most or all essential press freedoms while three dozen permit some. Only in a hard core—about four dozen

Exhibit 11

reedoms are under attack in the U.N. rgues historian Allen Weinstein.

Third World tyrannies—has an independent press been destroyed as completely as in the Communist bloc.

The lessons seem obvious. With Western technical aid, we should concentrate on strengthening the media in societies that show some resolve to resist state domination of communications. We should deal differently with countries where government controls the press completely and where foreign journalists suffer harrassment, arrest and even physical injury. We should demand from them a complete accounting in UN forums after each brutal violation of press liberties.

Forestalling worldwide state control of news gathering and distribution will require other steps.

Western diplomats should continue to insist that the UN's professional staff observe scrupulous neutrality in the struggle over press freedoms. In the past, UN staff have often served as new order cheerleaders.

We should allow no further covert UN efforts like the subsidizing of propaganda supplements in 16 major world publications. How appalling that puff pieces for both new orders— economic and information— should have appeared last year (without the credit line, "PAID FOR BY ENEMIES OF THE FREE WORLD") in such journals as Japan's *Asahi Shimbun*, Germany's *Frankfurter Rundschau*, Austria's *Die Presse*, Pakistan's *Dawn*, Italy's *La Stampa*, Mexico's *Excelsior*, India's *Indian Express*, Yugoslavia's *Politika*, Senegal's *Le Soleil*, and France's flagship paper, *Le Monde*!

Plums and persuasion.

The defenders of economic freedom, led by President Reagan at Cancun, also have begun to fight back. They have rejected LDC extortion as a method for negotiating over resources with developed societies.

The LDCs, to be sure, possess valuable raw materials and important markets. But the developed countries hold coveted technologies and vital capital, as well as their own natural resources and *indispensable* markets.

By selectively offering and withholding our markets, skills and capital, we can convince the often unstable regimes of poor countries that neither stability nor prosperity can be obtained through bureaucratic coercion.

With or without clear policies by the governments of their developed home countries, however, private companies ultimately will do business *only* with countries where they are treated fairly. They will go and stay only where their stakeholders are assured security for their investments and opportunity for earnings.

The United States should miss no chance, at the UN and elsewhere, to make those facts of life plain.

Not-so-strange bedfellows.

The free world press has paid scant attention to the parallels between UNESCO's regulatory plans for journalists and efforts by other UN agencies to sponsor both the New International Economic Order and a host of additional restrictions upon private investment and trade in developing countries.

Yet both press and business should recognize the clear convergence of their interests in halting two comparably dangerous schemes. Unfortunately, all too many journalists
(continued)

Allen Weinstein is University Professor at Georgetown University. At Georgetown's Center for Strategic and International Studies, he is Executive Editor of The Washington Quarterly, *whose readership includes government decision makers, business leaders, diplomats, and scholars, as well as subscribers in 65 other countries.*

Formerly a member of the Editorial Board of The Washington Post *and a Professor of History at Smith College, he also created and moderated the public affairs television series,* "Inside Washington." *His latest books include the award-winning* Perjury: The Hiss-Chambers Case *(Knopf) and the third edition of* Freedom and Crisis: An American History *(Random House).*

© 1982 SmithKline Corporation

The issue of national defense and the dangers of communism is the theme of John Lehman's commentary, "As Criminal as War Itself" [Exhibit 7]. In his commentary, entitled "Irony, Tragedy, Courage," Michael Novak talks about the values of liberty, individual, and freedom [Exhibit 6]. And finally, the issue of media bias against business is covered by David Kelley in "Bad News America" [Exhibit 8]. It argues that since the media claim that business and other institutions are responsible for turning out a good product, the media must also recognize their own responsibility toward objectivity and fairness in reporting about business.

THE 1981–82 CAMPAIGN

The 1981–82 campaign focused on four issues, inflation, energy, defense, and basic American values. The issues were covered through nine advertisements. The defense issue was addressed by Rear Admiral William C. Mott in "Resource War" [Exhibit 9] and by Theodore Elliott in "Dangers from the Dismal Empire." The value issues were addressed by Michael Novak in "Human Rights. No More Small Men" and by George Gilder in "The Heroes of Growth" [Exhibit 10].

Finally, in a commentary by Allen Weinstein, "Danger at the U.N." [Exhibit 11], the issue of press freedom at the global level is addressed. Weinstein comments on the recent efforts by some Third World and Communist bloc countries to curb press freedoms. He argues forcefully against such measures, warning that freedom of the press and economic freedoms are not separable and that we should defend both to protect individual freedoms everywhere in the world.

Media Schedule and Budget

The campaign ran from March 1979 through February 1982, at a total cost of $6.3 million. In 1979 and 1980, the entire campaign was conducted in the national editions of *Newsweek* and the *Wall Street Journal*. During 1981, the number of insertions in the *Wall Street Journal* was greatly reduced and *Time* magazine was added to fill the gap. The single advertisement in 1982 was run in *Newsweek* and *Time*. The media schedule was an average of one insertion every six weeks, or approximately nine insertions per year for three years (March 1979–February 1982). This estimate was calculated as follows:

$$52 \text{ weeks} \times 3 \text{ years (length of campaign)} = \frac{156 \text{ weeks}}{25 \text{ ad units}}$$

$$= 6.2 \text{ average insertion frequency}$$

MEASURING CAMPAIGN EFFECTIVENESS

Reader Responses

Each SmithKline advertisement contained a coupon which the reader was urged to fill in and return to receive more information. Beginning with the advertisement featuring Michael Novak in September 1981, SmithKline offered, free of charge, additional material by the author of the commentary so that the reader could learn even more about the author's views. The packet also contained specific instructions as to how the reader could make his or her views known to elected representatives. The company received about 82,000 written responses from readers requesting additional information [Table 2]. Although the company did not undertake any systematic analysis of these responses, the letters were almost totally supportive of the company's advertising campaign and its treatment of the issues.

Tracking Studies

SmithKline undertook two studies to measure the effectiveness of its ad campaign. These studies were conducted by Yankelovich, Skelly, and White.

The first study was conducted in February 1980. The sample consisted of 6 preliminary focus groups in five cities, followed by 612 interviews conducted in 11 major markets from coast to coast. This sample was drawn from the target audience—the 12 million upscale, educated adults in the United States. There was also an additional study of a sampling of 71 readers who had responded to a SmithKline advertisement and asked for literature. The total interview base was thus 683.

The results were extremely reassuring. The reach of the program (the percent of the universe who read *Newsweek* and/or the *Wall Street Journal*) was 60 percent, which is the reach estimated in the original media plan. Translated into numbers of readers, this indicates that about 7.2 million of the targeted audience read *Newsweek* and/or the *Wall Street Journal*, and 1.3 million recalled SmithKline advertisements, extending the original target of the "Issues for Action" pamphlets dramatically.

SmithKline had effectively reached its target audience, and also effectively communicated with them. For example:

• Those recalling the campaign had an awareness of SmithKline that was 82 percent higher than the nonreaders, and their "very favorable impressions" of the company was 2.5 times greater.
• Those recalling the campaign were 40 percent more likely to take a position on the issues in the advertisements than nonreaders, and 57 percent more likely to write their congressman or other government official.
• Recallers of the campaign were 58 percent more likely to take time to read the company's annual report than nonreaders, and 71 percent more likely to take a position in favor of the company, if it were in

Table 2   **Written Responses to Issue-Advocacy Advertisements Placed by SmithKline in *Newsweek* and the *Wall Street Journal***

1979	Title	Subject	Response
Simon	"The Malignant Growth of Federal Spending"	Federal spending	4,200
Wattenberg	"The Creed of the Class B Optimist"	Perspective on American future	1,200
Dubos	"Think Globally, Act Locally"	Global pluralism	1,500
Feldstein	"Three Threats to Our Standard of Living"	Savings incentives	2,800
Roche	"The Federal Assault on Independent Education"	Independent education	3,400
Williams	"Minimum Wage, Maximum Folly"	Minimum wage	4,000
Stein	"Freedom, the Reliable Energy Source"	Energy	2,400
Schellin	"Small Business, Shackled Giant of Innovation"	Small business	2,900
1980			
Novak	"Irony, Tragedy, Courage"	Democratic capitalism	7,500
Davidson	"The Exhausting of America"	Taxation	5,000
Collins	"Free the Children"	Quality education	3,500
Lehman	"As Criminal as War Itself"	Defense spending	3,600
Etzioni	"America's Most Critical Choice"	Reindustrialization	2,600
Meltzer	"Big Government, Democracy's Deadly Creation"	Big government	2,900
Laqueur	"The Crisis of Leadership"	National leadership	2,400
Kelley	"Bad News, America"	Media bias	5,000
1981			
Mott	"Resource War"	Scarce minerals	2,400
Eliot	"Danger from the Dismal Enterprise"	Soviet-American relations	1,300
Sowell	"Inflation: The Bill for Our Illusions"	Inflation	2,700
Maxey	"Fear of Fission"	Nuclear energy	1,600
Malbin	"Who Rules, America?"	Congress	900
Novak	"Human Rights. No More Small Men"	Human rights	9,300
Vogl	"Faith, Hope and Prosperity"	Faith, hope, and prosperity	1,800
Gilder	"The Heroes of Growth"	Entrepreneurship	3,200
1982			
Weinstein	"Danger at the U.N."		3,800
Total			81,900

a dispute with the government, and 67 percent more likely to write their congressman in favor of the company in such a dispute.

- Eighty-three percent of those who had seen the campaign wanted to see more such ads in the future.

The sample of the 78,000 readers who responded to the campaign was even more positive in their response to all of the points.

The study also pointed out two minor weaknesses of the campaign: (1) SmithKline's corporate identity was not well established and could be stronger. (2) The reasons for SmithKline's running the campaign were unclear to many readers.

The 1981 Evaluation Research: Second Survey

In June and July 1981, Yankelovich conducted 143 personal in-depth interviews with key individuals in government and academia. In government, interviews were conducted with senators and representatives plus senior congressional, White House, cabinet, and other executive branch aides. In academia, the survey covered top administrators of small liberal arts colleges and deans, professors, and department heads of large universities.

Forty percent of those interviewed in government and 32 percent of the academics recalled the SmithKline campaign. These government and academic opinion leaders recalled corporations speaking out in advertising in three groups. Mobil, Exxon, and General Motors were most often mentioned. The next group was SmithKline, Shell, and United Technologies. The third group included a widely scattered number of companies including Gulf, U.S. Steel, and W. R. Grace.

A number of legislators reported that the issues discussed in the ads were being brought to their attention by constituents, and in some cases SmithKline ads were being cited. College administrators also stated that the ads had been called to their attention, and some professors reported that they had used the ads in class.

Reaction to the SmithKline campaign was favorable. Opinion leaders felt that it was appropriate for SmithKline to speak out on issues because it was seen as "their right." Speaking out was also seen as an obligation to present the "corporate point of view." A majority of those interviewed in government stated that campaigns like SmithKline's stimulated public action. The academic community was a little less likely to believe that a campaign like this stimulated such public action. Their reservation was based on the premise that they felt the campaign would not appeal to the general public, because it would be "over their heads."

There was no evidence that the campaign was creating a backlash. Because SmithKline's competence was seen in health-related areas, the motivation for the corporation venturing beyond health in these ads was not clear and in some cases was therefore suspect. Criticisms of the campaign were minimal; they focused on the perceived wordiness and one-sidedness of the advertising.

The campaign had increased awareness and knowledge of issues; it had stimulated action. However, it had not rapidly increased familiarity with SmithKline or added significantly to knowledge of the company. It was probable that the campaign functioned best in increasing familiarity with SmithKline among those people who responded to the advertisements and received additional corporate information. This was true in the 1979 research among upscale readers of the *Wall Street Journal* and *Newsweek*.

Because this was qualitative research with in-depth personal interviews with a small number of people, statistics were less meaningful than the tone of the interviews.

Reflecting on the campaign, Andrew Gillinson observed:

> I believe that among certain key potential constituencies, the prestige of the company was raised, and it came to be thought of as a socially concerned and activist organization. That was true in government and even in academe, where we encountered some hostility to corporate advocacy advertising. We created awareness of another facet of the corporation.
>
> At the same time that the campaign was going on, Mr. Dee was fairly active in public speaking, and he continued the "Issues for Action" pamphlet series. After the campaign was initiated, by the way, the pamphlets were graphically redesigned to project the same identity—i.e., the red and blue stripes were borrowed from the advertising layout and lent back to the very series that inspired the advertising campaign.
>
> The press coverage in the trade and general interest media, although not overwhelming, was largely complimentary. The negative comments from readers of the campaign were few and far between. One self-criticism of the campaign was that the name SmithKline Corporation was not widely enough known at the outset of the campaign and, therefore, the money that was dedicated to this campaign might have been better spent in raising the level of public awareness of the corporation. Rather than reaching the largest possible audience to achieve that goal, however, we concentrated on a narrower constituency and made strong gains there.
>
> I would like to emphasize our impression that the campaign succeeded in attracting to the corporation a thoughtful constituency. We feel that should we have a need for support from the public generally, this constituency could be turned to. This point was borne out by in our research. People surveyed indicated that they would be more likely to take the corporation's part should it come into a dispute with a government agency.

Epilogue

Soon after SmithKline acquired Beckman Instruments, Robert Dee relinquished his position as CEO to Henry Wendt, who was at that time president and chief operating officer. At about the same time, the issue advertising campaign was terminated because the new CEO felt the communication priority should be awareness of the new company among the financial and scientific communities, better achieved for the time being through more conventional corporate institutional advertising campaigns (the "Issues for Action" series continues to be published).

NOTES

1. Robert F. Dee, "The Hippos Are Astir," *Public Communication Review,* Boston University, School of Public Communications, Fall 1981, pp. 10–12.
2. The Business Network is comprised of the following magazines: *Business Week, Dun's Business Month, Money, Nation's Business, Newsweek, Sports Illustrated, Time, U.S. News & World Report.*

Section C OMNIBUS CAMPAIGNS DISCUSSING ISSUES OF PUBLIC POLICY

Chapter 5 UNITED TECHNOLOGIES CORPORATION, HARTFORD, CT:

AN UNUSUAL TWO-PRONGED "SOFT" ISSUE AND "HARD" ADVOCACY ADVERTISING PROGRAM

The headline in a full-page advertisement in the *Wall Street Journal* of May 23, 1979, simply read: "Let's get rid of the girl. . . . Like you, she has a name. Use it." The ad was not signed. One could not even see a logo. There was only a brief note in small type at the bottom stating that reprints of the ad could be obtained by writing to Harry J. Gray, chairman, United Technologies [Exhibit 1]. The ad chided businessmen for being insensitive and for conscious neglect by referring to women employees as "the girl." It suggested that men take a giant step forward and begin calling women by their first names. It read in part, " 'The girl' is certainly a woman when she is out of her teens," and urged readers to treat her with the respect she deserves.

The advertisement was an instant success and has since become a classic. It generated a tumultuously emotional response from readers, and the company was overwhelmed. Within hours of publication, numerous supportive calls from women across the country reached United Technologies headquarters. Organizations such as the National Secre-

---

Research assistant: Josette Quiniou.

Exhibit 1

Let's Get Rid Of "The Girl"

Wouldn't 1979 be
a great year
to take one giant
step forward
for womankind
and get rid of
"the girl"?
Your attorney says,
"If I'm not here
just leave it with
the girl."
The purchasing agent
says, "Drop off your
bid with the girl."
A manager says,
"My girl will get
back to your girl."
What girl?
Do they mean
Miss Rose?
Do they mean
Ms. Torres?
Do they mean
Mrs. McCullough?
Do they mean
Joy Jackson?
"The girl"
is certainly
a woman when she's
out of her teens.
Like you,
she has a name.
Use it.

taries Association, the International Ladies Garment Workers Union, the Center for Working Women, *Ms. Magazine,* and a host of others called or wrote to express their support of the message. The ad also became the subject of news stories in a large number of newspapers, magazines, and even television shows.[1]

Eight secretaries at Endowment Research Corporation in Boston sent Harry Gray a huge bouquet of flowers. A woman stockbroker promised that she would push UTC stock all day if she was sent a reprint. The corporation also earned a seven-minute ovation at the National Secretaries Association's annual meeting.

If there ever was a single piece of communication or message that would elevate a company from a virtual nonentity with the general public and provide it with a highly visible and positive entity, this ad would certainly rank as a creative message that touched a responsive chord with large segments of the general public.

UNITED TECHNOLOGIES CORPORATION

The sponsor of the ad, United Technologies Corporation, is a large, diversified manufacturer, based in Hartford, Connecticut, with 1981 revenues of $13.7 billion. In 1982 UTC ranked 20th on the Fortune 500 list. It is the seventh largest manufacturing company in the United States and employs about 190,000 people, of which 46,000 work outside the country. In most cases, the company's various operating divisions are far better known than the parent.

Back in 1971, when Harry Gray was recruited from Litton Industries, Inc., UTC's outlook was bleak. The company, then known as the United Aircraft Corporation, was a stagnating $2 billion manufacturer of jet engines, helicopters, and other aerospace products, and was almost exclusively dependent on the volatile aerospace market, with half of its sales to government. Sales and earnings were declining steadily, with a reported deficit of $43.9 million in 1971–72 stemming from a $137 million writeoff to cover customer warranty expenses on the Pratt & Whitney JT9D engine built for Boeing's new 747 Jetliner. Therefore, the board decided to rejuvenate United Aircraft through diversification and by hiring an outsider who would be experienced in the acquisition game.

Harry Gray's acquisition program concentrated on companies in the $500 million to $1.5 billion sales range, with product technology compatible with that of UTC.[2] He wanted companies with large, possibly dominant, market shares to get the greatest profits from product improvements and made use of UTC's technological strengths. Among the major acquisitions were Essex International (1974), Otis Elevator (1975), Ambac Industries and Dynell Electronics (1978), and Carrier and Mostek (1979).

UTC's operating units are divided into three major types of activities. (1) *The power sector.* This includes Pratt & Whitney, the world's leading producer of aircraft jet engines. (2) *The building systems sector.* This includes Carrier Corporation, the largest manufacturer of air conditioning equipment and operating worldwide; and Otis Elevator Company, the world's leading manufacturer of elevators and escalators. (3) *The electronics sector.* This includes Mostek Corporation, the designer and manufacturer of integrated circuits and other semi-conductor products; the Essex Group, producing wires and cables for residential and commerical uses; Hamilton Standard, building control devices for commercial and military aircraft and spacecraft; Norden Systems, making control displays and minicomputers for space and military uses; and the Microelectronics Center, which supplies circuits for the electronic products of UTC divisional subsidiaries.

Finally, three separate entities must be added. Inmont, the world's largest producer of printing ink and a leading manufacturer of paints for cars; Sikorsky Aircraft, an international leader in design and production of helicopters; and the United Technologies Research Center, carrying out basic and applied research with more than 1,000 scientists, engineers, and technicians.

Top Management

UTC's board of directors consists of 18 directors, only 5 of whom are inside directors. Most of the outside directors have conventional business backgrounds and hold senior positions in other major corporations or investment-finance related institutions. There are, however, two academics on the board, one of whom is a woman.

The corporate management structure is a lean one, with the headquarters staff consisting of no more than 450 people, including secretaries and mailroom boys. This provides for easy access to senior management and a close-knit, informal management style.

The CEO

Harry J. Gray, chairman, president, and chief executive officer, joined United Technologies in 1971. His educational background is in journalism and marketing. Before joining UTC, he held executive positions with Greyhound Corporation and Litton Industries. His detractors describe him as tough and aggressive, one who swallows up companies. However, his associates contend that is only one aspect of his personality. He has a great deal of patriotism and deep feeling for his country.

He also has a flair for attracting attention. "He flies practically everywhere in a Sikorsky helicopter, to the point that choppers have become symbolic of Gray—just as Gray himself has become a symbol of the high-stake takeover game. His angular features and mischievous grin fit his swashbuckling image."[3]

Gray is quite involved in top business councils dealing in issues of public policy. Among others, he is a member of the Business Council, the Economic Club of New York, and the Conference Board.

ANTECEDENTS OF THE AD PROGRAM

The reasons for originating the ad program were twofold. The first set of reasons pertained to problems of corporate identity that were peculiar to United Technologies. According to Raymond D'Argenio, UTC's senior vice-president, communications:

> Our problem at United Technologies can be simply put. Few people know who we are, and what we do—despite the fact that we are now 20th on the *Fortune* list, and grow faster every year.
>
> Yet, ironically, almost everyone knows our divisions and their products—Otis elevators, Sikorsky helicopters, Pratt & Whitney aircraft engines, Carrier air conditioners, to name just a few.
>
> United Technologies needs to become better known in order to attract investors, to attract engineers and scientists, and to get that modicum of respect and understanding that all companies need to grow profitably in the years ahead.[4]

The rapid growth of the company and the acquisition program were not without their problems. Some of the acquisitions were strongly resisted by the acquired companies—for example, Otis Elevator and Carrier Corporation. At the same time, the diversification program caused many Wall Street analysts to lose interest in UTC stock because of its ambiguous and complex product mix. Aerospace analysts found the company too complicated to study, and specialists in multi-industry companies had to familiarize themselves with its operations. The confusion, or rather the lack of awareness among financial analysts and the investing public, and between its subsidiaries and the parent company, led UTC's management to undertake a corporate advertising program.

The second objective, although quite compatible with the first one, was more rooted in a philosophy about the role of the corporation in society, and reflected, as it must, the philosophies, ideological bent, and personal beliefs of its chief executive, Harry J. Gray, which in turn permeated the entire corporate culture. The company was concerned with an "all-pervasive anti-technology sentiment in this country, which has been growing and gaining momentum for years." UTC wanted to impart a favorable feeling about technology and at the same time to project United Technology as a leader in advancing and applying technology as a positive force for solving problems and improving the quality of life.

The company felt very strongly that it should take part in the formulation of public policy and national agenda. According to D'Argenio:

> Every company has the responsibility to engage in an intellectual dialogue with the public. And it must be done consistently and over a long period of time. You have an obligation to yourself and to the nation to do that. There are times when business is under attack for keeping its mouth closed, and by not expressing its point of view.
>
> Just consider for a moment the atmosphere we face in the 1980s. Our country's dependence on the rest of the world is increasing—in economic, political, and other spheres. The growth of special interest groups continues to fragment American society. People become more belligerent as their discontent and cynicism grow—as the "American dream" becomes less and less attainable. And we all know that corporations are highly visible targets for people's frustrations and complaints.
>
> For too long, we have ceded the arena of public opinion to antibusiness activists, expressing our viewpoint only as a defensive reaction. By taking part in the public policy process with verve and effectiveness, UTC's objective was to demonstrate that

it was run by intelligent people and that the company was willing to speak out on things that mattered in the American society. It was also felt necessary to express sensitivity to the changing social trends, and not merely to assert the business viewpoint in a defensive reaction to the ground ceded to antibusiness activists.

If these public attitudes toward business continue to grow, and if the current ideas of antigrowth and antitechnology continue to spread, then all of us are in for some rough times, indeed. Today, we are being called upon to perform more specific tasks—to win converts to a specific course of action our company wants to follow, or to a specific political or economic position our company supports.

CAMPAIGN STRATEGY—THE DECISION-MAKING PROCESS

The initiation of the campaign came about through informal discussions among two or three top people, and primarily between Raymond D'Argenio and UTC's chairman, Harry Gray. There were no formal detailed studies or position papers as to the rationale for the two campaigns, the selection of issues, identification of targeted constituencies, or opinion surveys to measure the effectiveness of those campaigns.

The choice of issues is made on an ad hoc basis among a very small and informal group of corporate executives. These executives are tuned to each other's thinking, share common opinions on public issues, and agree on UTC's needs and objectives. They feel that they know rather well what types of issues they are going to confront.

The idea of the campaign was the brainchild of Ray D'Argenio, UTC's senior vice-president, communications. When he joined the company in 1977, he decided that something needed to be done in the area of corporate communications in response to the growing public backlash against technology. He found Harry Gray and other senior executives highly responsive, and got the go-ahead.

The ad copy for most of the advertisements is developed in-house. Management thinks that very few people in advertising agencies can handle issue analysis and understanding on a consistent basis. No one on the corporate staff considers himself an expert in advertising, but advertising is treated like anything else, based on the executives' own reactions and those of friends and associates whose opinions and experience they respect. In addition, UTC's management felt that no agency could project the image of the corporation as it would like. Within the UTC senior management staff there was a wealth of experience and knowledge about the issues the company wanted to address, and a deeply felt instinct as to how the company should be projected to the larger public.

UTC's CEO is very actively involved in the decision-making process for both the "soft" issue and "hard" advocacy campaigns. He suggests items. He reviews every ad, and he rewrites a lot of them. As one corporate spokesperson observed: "People don't realize it that he [Gray] is one of the few CEO's in the country with a M.A. in Journalism for starters. He has a keen appreciation of the power of communications, and he recognizes good things when they happen as quickly as he recognizes bad things."

In substance, two men at UTC, Chairman Harry Gray and Senior Vice-President, Communications Ray D'Argenio, are the prime force behind UTC's ad campaign. The UTC board of directors, however, is apprised of the campaign and informed about its progress. UTC's board has a Public Policy Committee which consists of seven members, all of whom are outside directors. This committee receives regular reports on UTC's external affairs activities, including corporate contributions and communications programs.

THE "SOFT" ISSUE CAMPAIGN

The "soft" issue campaign, most identified with UTC, consists of a once-a-month ad in the *Wall Street Journal* appearing every second or third Thursday of the month. The decision to launch the campaign was quite informal, eclectic, and quick, and in many ways reflects UTC's management style.

The series was started in February 1979. The company was looking for an innovative approach that would raise its message above the overwhelming mass of dull corporate advertising that was inundating the media, and wanted to stress its mastery of high technology and innovation. The best way to communicate these characteristics to the public was to demonstrate the creativity developed within UTC.

The idea for the campaign was suggested by Richard Kerr, a free-lance writer. Kerr, a former New York advertising agency owner, suggested an approach that would give people something to think about, rather than telling them what to think. Kerr is the creative mind behind the series. The copy addresses itself to individuals, with a message relevant to their concerns. The success of the series is based primarily on the fact that everybody can identify with these situations and share these concerns. The conversational tone, expressed through short sentences and simple words, was certainly helpful in getting the reader's attention. The messages are kept deliberately brief; they are unrelated to UTC's business; and they are not directed at readers as businesspeople or investors, but as human beings. Most unconventional of all, there is not even a bold or prominent display of UTC's name or logo, except for a small print notation at the bottom indicating that reprints may be requested by writing to Harry Gray, chairman of United Technologies Corporation.

Classification of Themes

The ads cover a variety of human issues, like the prejudices, foibles, weaknesses, and strengths for which there may be latent recognition, but which people are often too embarrassed to admit. They gently twit people's conscience and urge them to think and do something about those issues without specifically telling them what to do.

An analysis of the ads shows that they can be broadly classified into five categories: human prejudices, our need to communicate with others, creativity, achievement, and patriotism.

The most famous example of the messages dealing with human prejudices is, of course, "The Girl" ad, asking for recognition of women who work in offices and chiding businessmen for referring to female employees as "the girl." In a similar vein, the valuable role of women in America's history and today's society is emphasized through the example of Eliza McCardle, President Andrew Johnson's wife [Exhibit 2]. Other ads pay tribute to women for their skills as homemakers [Exhibit 3] and focus on handicapped persons in the same positive light.

The role of individualism and creativity is emphasized through messages that stress how people with ideas and perseverance are able to create useful things that contribute to human happiness and social welfare [Exhibit 4]. The rewards of personal achievement are also highlighted. The potential of an individual using his or her creative and intellectual ability is emphasized. The messages urge active and positive behavior toward achievement in education and work, arguing that the main component for success is willingness and constant verve [Exhibit 5].

The last theme deals with patriotism and emphasizes American pride and the achievement of the country as a nation [Exhibit 6]. Whereas all the other themes focus on individual behavior, this series of ads advocates the well-being of the nation.

THE OP-ED CAMPAIGN

Since their inception in March 1977, UTC Op-Ed messages have appeared weekly in the three major local newspapers in Connecticut—the state with the largest concentration of UTC employees. These ads deal not only with public policy issues, but also with topics of regional interest. During the first two years of the program, selected ads with broader appeal were occasionally published in the *Wall Street Journal, Washington Post,* and *Washington Star.*

From the very start, the idea behind the program was to make it national as soon as possible, and to run it on a more regular schedule. Even though the campaign was successful in Connecticut in the very first year, the type of audience did not necessarily represent opinion leaders in the United States. Therefore, in the second stage a more influential audience was sought. In 1980, UTC messages appeared each month in *Harper's,* the *Atlantic,* and every other week in the *Washington Report* published and distributed by the U.S. Chamber of Commerce. In 1981, other national journals were added: *The New Republic, National Review, Commentary, Foreign Affairs, New York Review of Books, Technology Review,* and in 1982, *The Economist.*

Exhibit 2

Do You Owe Something To An Eliza McCardle?

She met a
tailor
when he was twenty.
He had never been
to school.
She married him.
Taught him
to
read,
write,
spell.
He learned fast.
Became President.
Inherited
post-Civil War
reconstruction problems.
Beat an
impeachment rap
by just one vote
after trying to
fire his Secretary of War
for justifiable reasons.
Bought Alaska
from the Russians
for $7 million.
Lost his try at a
second term.
Ran for
U.S. Senate instead,
and won.
His name?
Andrew Johnson.
America will reach
its full maturity
when
an Andrew
does the
same
for an Eliza.

© United Technologies Corporation 1981

Exhibit 3

The Most Creative Job In The World

It involves
taste,
fashion,
decorating,
recreation,
education,
transportation,
psychology,
romance,
cuisine,
designing,
literature,
medicine,
handicraft,
art,
horticulture,
economics,
government,
community relations,
pediatrics,
geriatrics,
entertainment,
maintenance,
purchasing,
direct mail,
law,
accounting,
religion,
energy
and management.
Anyone who can
handle all those
has to be somebody
special.
She is.
She's a homemaker.

Exhibit 4

Get Out Of That Rut

Oscar Wilde said,
"Consistency is
the last refuge of
the unimaginative."
So stop getting up
at 6:05.
Get up at 5:06.
Walk a mile at dawn.
Find a new way
to drive to work.
Switch chores with
your spouse
next Saturday.
Buy a wok.
Study wildflowers.
Stay up alone all night.
Read to the blind.
Start counting
brown-eyed blondes
or blonds.
Subscribe to an
out-of-town paper.
Canoe at midnight.
Don't write to your
congressman,
take a whole scout
troop to see him.
Learn to speak
Italian.
Teach some kid
the thing you do best.
Listen to two hours of
uninterrupted Mozart.
Take up aerobic dancing.
Leap out of that rut.
Savor life.
Remember, we only
pass this way once.

Exhibit 5

In The Next 45 Seconds Your Resume May Not Look So Hot

You may be
proud of how
far you've come.
But here's a
tough old bird
whose score you
might have trouble
matching.
He not only
reached for
the stars.
He grabbed
a handful.
He was a lawyer.
A congressman.
A governor.
An Indian brave.
An ambassador *to*
the United States.
Commander in chief
of an army.
President of a republic.
A United States senator.
And the
only
American
to have one of
our ten largest
cities named
after him.
That's an achiever!
Take your carefully
worded resume out of
your drawer
and set it beside
Sam Houston's record.
Time's running
out.
You better get
moving.

Exhibit 6

You're The Finest

In just 200
years,
your country,
through freedom
and hard work,
has changed the world.
In agriculture,
industry,
education,
medicine,
law,
transportation,
and on and on.
No country can
match America's
record
in religious freedom,
civil freedom,
human rights,
the importance
and dignity of the
individual.
We do have our differences.
But when we join together
in times of crisis,
our strength is
awesome.
Among all the
world's nations,
America still
stands out front.
You're an American.
You're the finest ever—
and don't you ever,
ever
forget it.

The Copy Format

All these ads are developed in-house, where Frank Giusti, director of editorial and news service, is responsible for writing the ad copy. The messages are cleared through the communications and legal departments, as well as by other executives whose expertise may be relevant to the message in the ad copy. They are ultimately approved or rejected by Gray, who personally reviews each and every advertisement.

The format of UTC's Op-Ed ads is quite different from other companies' ads, except those by Mobil. They are presented as little editorials with two columns, a headline, and UTC's logo. The rule is not to go beyond 50 typewritten lines in small characters. Since the Op-Ed program started, the company has used the same format to raise the recognition level among readers and build a corporate image.

Advertising Budget

The advertising budget for the two campaigns is quite modest compared to other major corporations. The total amount allocated for the communication program in 1981 was $6 million, of which $2 million was spent for UTC's half sponsorship of "Meet the Press" every Sunday. The Op-Ed program costs $350,000 annually, whereas a corporation like Mobil spends millions of dollars for the same type of program. Within this budget, the monthly campaign in the *Wall Street Journal* costs over $1 million for the entire year. This amount also includes the printing and making of reprints. Presently none of the ads have been published in the *New York Times*, despite a strong interest in it. Cost considerations led to choosing the *Wall Street Journal* only instead of both publications for the monthly campaign. The actual partition between the *Wall Street Journal* campaign and the weekly Op-Ed ads is not a matter of controversy. The tradeoff between the two appears unlikely, despite the budget constraint. The monthly *Journal* ads have generated a momentum the company wants to sustain.

Analysis of the Op-Ed Campaign

The annual Op-Ed program is broadly divided into two parts: one-third dealing with corporate image, and two-thirds with more general issues. The advertisements tend to reflect UTC management's philosophy and present its viewpoint.

The issues covered run the whole gamut of public policy issues, ranging from defense of private enterprise to national defense, overregulation of business, news media bias, big government, U.S. exports, high technology, and international treaties. For ease of understanding, the ads have been classified into various categories [Table 1; also see Exhibits 7–16].

Table 1   **Classification of UTC's Op-Ed Advertisements**

I. Corporate Image Advertising

Interest Identification	Type of Issue Addressed	Illustrative Advertisements
Benevolent sponsor: Sponsor's interests presented as indirectly related.	Corporate philanthropy; impact of corporate activities on the community	
Self-serving sponsor: Sponsor's interests are the main focus of the message.	Corporate financial performance; new products; recognition of superior employees; support of United Way	

II. Advocacy Advertising

Disinterested sponsor: No direct immediate benefits for the sponsor are envisaged.	Support of free enterprise system Role of profits International treaties Crime on the streets	"Let's Hear It for Profits" [Exhibit 7]
Benevolent sponsor: Sponsor's interests are presented as indirectly related.	Support for Reagan's economic program Increases in defense spending Reduction in federal spending Support for higher education Antibusiness bias in the news media Clean air, toxic waste disposal	"Soviet Military Power" [Exhibit 8] "A Brake on Spending" [Exhibit 9] "Campus and the Corporation" [Exhibit 10] "Crooks and Clowns on TV" [Exhibit 11]
Acknowledged vested-interest sponsor: Sponsor's interests are directly identified and aggressively defended.	Corrective ads challenging inaccuracies in news stories Defense of Op-Ed advertising program Defense of corporate merger	"America's Finest Fighter Engine" [Exhibit 12] "What Are We Doing on the Op-Ed Page?" [Exhibit 13]
Participative sponsor: Sponsor's interests are identified with those of the industry and business in general. Issues are presented as common to industry and also in the public interest.	Export promotion—Eximbank Government red tape; overregulation Repeal of laws requiring union wage rates on federal construction jobs International production sharing by multinational corporations	"Unshackle the Yankee Trader" [Exhibit 14] "Red Tape and Abalone" [Exhibit 15] "Bulldoze Davis-Bacon" [Exhibit 16]

Exhibit 7

Let's Hear It for Profits

Bah, profits! Big, *bad* profits; rarely are they referred to as *good*. They're scorned as "excessive," "windfall," "obscene" and worse by those who find it expedient, for political or other reasons, to flog business profits.

Too many people are swallowing that kind of balderdash . . . whether it's about oil company profits or any company profits. There's widespread misunderstanding about profits, what they are and what they do.

What they are is the fuel — the lifeblood — of America's entire economic system. What they do is work for all of us, supporting and advancing the quality, standards, and institutions of our society.

Profits are what's left over to a company after the cost of doing business. In a way, they are to a company what personal savings are to an individual. When a wage-earner gets his paycheck, he allocates it to meet family expenses and pay bills. If there's anything left over, perhaps he sets some aside for future needs.

Profits, in a sense, are corporate savings. But they're not stashed away. They're put to work for people.

First of all, close to half of a company's profits go to the government. One of every seven dollars collected in federal taxes comes out of corporate earnings. Corporate income taxes, totaling tens of billions of dollars a year, help support all the services, functions, and programs that people expect from government, ranging from protection of the environment to aid to education.

Companies reinvest profits in their business to build for the future. The money is used to construct factories, expand capacity, modernize equipment, innovate, create new products — all productive activities that provide more and better jobs. More jobs mean more wages, generating more tax revenue for government.

Profits are distributed, in part, as dividends to the people who invest their money in the business. When they're paid out this way, profits are taxed a second time, as income to the recipients.

Dividends are paid to such investors as pension funds, churches, and colleges. Thus, a lot of business profit goes directly into social benefits.

Business gives huge sums to hospitals, colleges, the United Way, the arts, and assorted community and charitable causes. Corporate philanthropy depends on profits.

One misconception about profits centers on their size. National surveys show the prevailing public belief to be that business profits come to about 30 cents on each dollar of sales. Actually, profits are closer to a nickel on the sales dollar. When people are asked to specify what they consider a fair and reasonable profit, most give a figure two or three times the actual level.

Profits make our system work. They feed both the private and public sectors. Without healthy profits, there can't be a healthy country. Improved living standards, economic and social progress, expanded opportunities for people — they all grow out of profits.

UNITED TECHNOLOGIES

Pratt & Whitney Aircraft Group • Carrier Corporation • Otis Group • Essex Group • Hamilton Standard
Sikorsky Aircraft • Power Systems • Chemical Systems • Norden Systems • United Technologies Research Center

Exhibit 8

A Brake on Spending

The mood of the citizenry seems clear, both from the results of the 1980 elections and public opinion polls taken since then. Rein in big government, people are saying. Get control of federal spending.

At last, it's sinking into the national consciousness that flinging public money at every conceivable social and economic need hasn't really worked to bring about the kind of society that most people want. What it *has* done is helped plunge America into the doldrums of economic sluggishness, unchecked inflation, unemployment, and budget deficits.

The cost of government has been barreling out of control since the mid-1960s. It took us as a nation some 185 years to reach $100 billion in federal spending in 1962. It took only nine years to raise outlays by the second $100 billion; only four years to add another $100 billion; and only two years to pile up still another $100 billion.

During the last two decades, while the nation's population rose 23%, the federal budget soared by more than 500%.

We're living beyond our means — and paying for it with the cruel, concealed tax of inflation. Long gone is the time when we demanded that government keep its spending in line with its income. Even as tax revenues have risen year after year, spending has gone up even faster. The result: deficit stacked upon deficit, fueling inflation.

In good times and bad, the government has been supplementing its tax revenues by borrowing money. It thus competes with its own citizens for, and drives up the cost of, available money. It siphons off funds that could be used for private investment in productive activities to create jobs.

Meanwhile, all the borrowing has sent the public debt ballooning upward. Right now it's closing in on *one-trillion dollars*.

Among the new folks in power in Washington, there's a heartening resolve to put our fiscal house in order. President Reagan is determined to work toward a balanced budget as part of his efforts to get the economy moving. And there is a sense of receptivity on the people's part. In a major national poll earlier this year, 70% of the public said they'd prefer a balanced budget to a tax cut if it came to a choice.

Matching federal outgo to income will take time. The profligacy of decades can't be undone in a year or two. It will demand steadfastness, political courage, and a toning down by all of our tendency to turn to the government to fund solutions to almost every problem. Nor should budgetary restraint be achieved at the expense of people genuinely in need. They must be protected.

Still, no program or department of the federal government should be immune from scrutiny to determine where money can be saved, projects deferred, payrolls tightened, activities reduced, efficiency improved.

The belt-tightening will pinch. Coming to grips with the size, cost, and complexity of the federal government will require sacrifices by virtually everyone — business included.

UNITED TECHNOLOGIES

Pratt & Whitney Aircraft • Carrier • Otis • Essex • Inmont • Sikorsky
Hamilton Standard • Mostek • Elliott • Jenn-Air • Norden • Research Center

Exhibit 9

Soviet Military Power

Some scraggly bands are given to pooh-poohing the Soviet threat. They seem to view the Kremlin's denizens as little more than a bunch of burly teddy bears of mildly mischievous bent. Well, those folks can draw little comfort from a new report issued by the U.S. Department of Defense.

Entitled *Soviet Military Power,* the report is a distillation of briefings given to the defense ministers of NATO countries. In 100 pages of facts, figures, charts, maps, and pictures, it details the relentless buildup of military might being pursued by the Soviet Union. It tells of an unstanched flow from Soviet production plants of new weapons systems, tanks, missiles, artillery, ships and aircraft.

Even as Russia's domestic economy sputters and stumbles and the Russian people struggle against denial and deprivation, the Kremlin pumps vast sums into its military machine. This money is funding a massive buildup of forces, the projection of Soviet power far from Soviet boundaries, and the use of proxy forces to support revolutionary factions and conflicts. It all adds up to a mounting threat to international stability.

The Pentagon report notes that the Soviet armed forces now number more than 4.8 million men. A total of 180 divisions —motorized rifle, tank, airborne—are stationed in Eastern Europe, the U.S.S.R., and Mongolia, and are in combat in Afghanistan. The Soviets have 50,000 tanks and 20,000 artillery pieces in the field.

In Eastern Europe alone, there are more than 3,500 Soviet and Warsaw Pact tactical bombers and fighters. In each of the last eight years, the Soviets have built more than 1,000 fighters—many times the U.S. output.

They have eight classes of submarines and eight classes of major surface warships currently under construction. And they are constantly adding to their nuclear warheads deliverable against Western Europe, China, and Japan.

Soviet military production capacity is awesome. It consists of 135 major military industrial plants totaling some 10,000 acres of floor space—a 34% increase over the last decade. In 1980 these plants produced more than 150 different types of weapons systems.

What's especially troubling is the rapidity with which the Soviet Union is forging ahead in technology—the foundation of know-how that spawns military capability. Technologically, the U.S. is still out front. But the Soviets are narrowing the gap. During the 1970s, they dramatically reduced America's lead "in virtually every important basic technology," the Pentagon says. They are now believed to be ahead in some advanced spheres, such as high-power lasers.

In the report's preface, Secretary of Defense Casper W. Weinberger points out that a clear understanding of Soviet armed forces, their doctrine, capabilities, strengths, and weaknesses "is essential to the shaping and maintenance of effective U.S. and allied armed forces."

With clarity and force, *Soviet Military Power* contributes to that understanding. Copies of the report are obtainable, at $6.50 each, from the Superintendent of Documents, U.S. Government Printing Office, Washington, D.C. 20402.

UNITED TECHNOLOGIES

Exhibit 10

Campus and the Corporation

There are growing grounds for concern about the health and vitality of higher education in America. Public and private universities face troubled futures rooted in fiscal uncertainties that strike at the heart of the educational mission.

Budgets and endowments are being ravaged by inflation. Faculty salary scales are under pressure; pay dropped by 20% in constant dollars during the last decade. Enrollments are on the decline, particularly in graduate studies. Bright young people are turning away from academic careers. With their budgets squeezed, universities are deferring needed maintenance. They are stinting on books for their libraries and instruments for their labs.

All this threatens the continued quality of on-campus teaching, scholarship, inquiry, innovation, and research: functions vital to the underpinnings of knowledge in our democratic society.

Take basic research, or the search for knowledge that enables us to do more things in better ways. At least 60% of all the basic research in the U.S. is done by universities. On-campus research and development in 1979 exceeded $5 billion in value, and more than $3.5 billion of the total represented basic research, as distinct from applied research and engineering development.

The U.S. government has been the principal sponsor of basic research at universities. However, government support has been weakening in recent years. One measure of hope is the increasing involvement of the business community in supporting university research and in contributing in other ways to the strengthening of higher education.

Still, there's large room for growth in corporate help for education. "Business has gained a clearer understanding of the role of the universities and the value of free inquiry," notes the Committee for Corporate Support of Private Universities. "One result is a substantial increase in business support of higher education — measured in inflated dollars. But in constant dollars, it has risen only marginally." What's especially disturbing is that many corporations give little or nothing to higher education.

Inducing more companies to support higher education is the task taken on by the Boston-based committee. It is not a fund-raising agency. Rather, it is an advocate, an exhorter, working to foster closer relationships between campus and the corporation.

Corporations turn to the campus for the talented, trained people they need. They draw on the ideas and innovations that flow from university scholarship and research. So business has a direct self-interest in getting closer to the higher education community, finding out what the needs are, and helping to fill them. There are many ways to help: direct research grants, capital contributions, matching employees' gifts to universities, fellowships for young teacher-scholars, cooperative projects in teaching and research.

Increasing ties of understanding and support are being formed between business and education. Such links are mutually valuable. They serve both institutions, along with the broad public interest. They should be multiplied and strengthened.

UNITED TECHNOLOGIES

Exhibit 11

Crooks and Clowns on TV

See the dastard. Hiss at him. See the dolt. Hoot at him. They're both businessmen, TV variety.

In the skimpy fare served up as network entertainment night after night, the business world is peopled mostly by ne'er-do-wells and nincompoops. Likely as not, businessmen and women are portrayed on the tube as schemers and lawbreakers, a la J.R. Ewing, or else they're bubble-heads bumbling about and mouthing off for laughs, in the manner of Archie Bunker.

Such are the key gleanings of a study, first of its kind ever done, looking into the way television depicts people in business. The study found that two out of every three businessmen on television come across as foolish, greedy, or evil. In the prime-time view, over half of all corporate chiefs commit illegal acts, ranging from fraud to murder. Some 45% of all business activities are shown as illicit. Only 3% of TV business people behave in ways that are socially and economically productive.

The study, titled *Crooks, Conmen and Clowns: Businessmen in TV Entertainment,* was done by The Media Institute, a Washington-based research organization that seeks to improve the level and quality of media coverage of business and economic affairs. If the institute's researchers wound up their work bug-eyed and babbling, that's understandable. They peered at 200 episodes of the top 50 series on ABC, CBS, and NBC: sitcoms, shoot-'em-ups, dramas, and the like. The sample excluded all specials, sporting events, and news programs.

Analyzing the shows' content and characters, the institute confirmed what some of us in business have long been squirming about: As pictured by the floppy-necked quiche nibblers who dream up network series, most businessmen are either blackguards or buffoons. "Businessmen on prime-time television are consistently shown in an unflattering light," The Media Institute said. "Sixty-seven percent are portrayed in a negative manner—as criminals, fools, or greedy or malevolent egotists—while only 25% are shown in a positive light."

The bigger the business, the more unfavorably its practitioners are painted. The leaders of large companies tend to be cast as out-and-out crooks, lesser executives as mere miscreants, and small businessmen as dimwits. In TV's vision of business, ethics are about as rare as rowboats in the Sahara.

Why the perverse portrayals? Leonard J. Theberge, president of The Media Institute, points out that TV entertainment adheres to a simplistic format of good versus bad. In years past, "bad" was personified by such societal stereotypes as minorities, ethnic groups, and women. Happily, such stereotypes have all but been eliminated. Still, the bad-guy slot remains to be filled. Business folks, it seems, make suitably handy villains and knuckleheads.

Theberge notes, too, the existence of "cultural reasons which might explain a bias by TV writers against businessmen. For example, it is not a new phenomenon for creative artists to look down on the commercial sector."

Two ironies obtrude. One is that the networks whose shows project businessmen as scoundrels and jesters are themselves commercial enterprises run by, yes, businessmen. The other is that the programs denigrating business are supported by advertising dollars from—you guessed it—business.

UNITED TECHNOLOGIES

Exhibit 12

America's Finest Fighter Engine

Pratt & Whitney Aircraft's F100 jet engine is the most advanced military aircraft engine operating in the world today.

The F100 weighs about 3,000 pounds and produces roughly eight pounds of thrust for every pound of its weight. No other engine in the world's inventory can match the F100's thrust-to-weight ratio.

This is why the U.S. Air Force selected the F100 to power two of America's front-line fighter aircraft: the twin-engine McDonnell Douglas F-15 and the single-engine General Dynamics F-16. Thanks to the F100, both of these fighters can outperform any other aircraft they are likely to face in air-to-air combat. And that's why the F-15 holds every world time-to-climb record from sea-level to 60,000 feet.

More Push Per Pound

Engine thrust-to-weight ratio is crucial to aircraft performance. High push-per-pound means faster acceleration and offers greater maneuverability. And these are factors that help decide who flies home after a fight.

Outstanding Readiness Record

The F100 has been on active duty with the U.S. Air Force since 1974. Although it is still a maturing engine, it has built an outstanding record of reliability and safety. The F100 engine, operating in the U.S. Air Force wing deployed at Bitburg, Germany, has achieved a readiness record greater than 92%, which is comparable to military engines that have been in service 20 years or longer. In a surprise inspection a few months after receiving its F-15s, the Bitburg wing passed the stringent operational readiness test with flying colors. This was a real tribute to the F100's reliability and performance.

Allies Build F100

Four of America's NATO allies—Belgium, Denmark, the Netherlands, and Norway—are co-producing F100 engines for their own fleets of F-16 fighters. In fact, the performance of the F100 was one of the important factors in the selection of the F-16 by these countries.

Fortune Distorts Facts

We at United Technologies are extremely proud of the F100. We are disturbed that a recent issue of *Fortune* magazine carried a highly misleading, distorted and outdated article about the F100. The one-sided article paints a false picture of the F100's capabilities and accomplishments. We want to set the record straight. That's why we are giving you these facts.

A Superb Safety Record

America's fleets of F-15 and F-16 fighters have more than 110,000 hours of flight time, with an unexcelled safety record for modern jet fighters.

Fewer "Teething Troubles"

All military fighter engines have experienced problems during their development and introduction into operational service. To provide combat superiority, they must constantly push forward the frontier of engine technology. Unforeseen problems are expected...and inevitable. But the F100 has experienced fewer difficulties than any other engine at the same stage of maturity.

Unparalleled Qualification Tests

The F100 successfully completed the toughest development test program ever undertaken. The final qualification test required 150 hours of operation simulating the most severe in-flight service. This test included 30 hours of continuous operation at simulated flight speeds of 2.3 times the speed of sound. A combat aircraft may only spend an hour or two at this speed during its entire lifetime.

Costs Under Target

An F100 engine costs less today than it did in 1973. In fact, we're delivering engines to the Air Force at lower costs than the target levels set in 1975. Our aggressive cost-reduction program will save American taxpayers more than $250 million during the production of the first 1,900 engines.

Stall/Stagnation Understood

Fortune said the causes of this curious phenomenon are still not completely understood, even by some leading engine specialists. But Pratt & Whitney Aircraft and the U.S. Air Force *do* understand why it has occurred and what changes are needed to avoid it. All changes have been approved by the Air Force except one, which is in the works. The approved changes are now being implemented.

Ready to Defend America

Our nation can rely on the excellent performance and reliability of the F100 engine. It stands ready to fulfill its mission of powering our front-line fighter force for more than a decade to come.

America has a winner in the F100 jet engine.

UNITED TECHNOLOGIES

Pratt & Whitney Aircraft Group • Otis Group • Essex Group • Sikorsky Aircraft
Hamilton Standard • Power Systems Division • Norden Systems • Chemical
Systems Division • United Technologies Research Center
United Technologies Corporation, Hartford, CT 06101

Exhibit 13

What Are We Doing On the Op-Ed Page?

Four years ago this week, we ran the first of these editorial advertisements. Its heading was the same as the one atop today's message. Ever since then they've been appearing every week, 52 weeks a year.

Selections from the series are published regularly in two of America's premier thought magazines, *Harper's* and *The Atlantic*, and in a national newspaper published by the U.S. Chamber of Commerce. This year they're running in additional national journals, among them *The New Republic, National Review, Commentary, Foreign Affairs,* and *Columbia Journalism Review.*

It's been invigorating and rewarding for us to participate in the arena of ideas through this series and to get readers' reactions to our views. Plenty of people have been vocal in taking issue with what we have to say. We've been pilloried as often as praised in letters to the newspapers where our ads appear.

Some readers have expressed outrage that newspapers sell advertising space for a company to voice a viewpoint instead of pitch a product. Their notion seems to be that corporations should be exempt from constitutional guarantees of free expression; that newspaper opinion pages are somehow sullied when they present a business opinion.

We'd guess that a goodly number of people turn to this space each week, if only to find out what we're spouting off about. In one ad published only in four Connecticut newspapers, we offered free paperback versions of William Simon's book, "A Time for Truth." We expected perhaps 300 requests at most. We got almost 1,500.

Reaction to any given ad can run from pole to pole. After we voiced concern about the growth of single-issue politics, one reader replied angrily that whoever wrote the message had "a mind of monstrous stew." On the other hand, a midwestern U.S. Senator of ultra-liberal persuasion wrote in to say it was "one of the most thoughtful and well-written advertisements I have ever read."

Some of our weekly editorials have been inserted in the Congressional Record. Others have been widely reprinted. A piece on teacher burnout brought us a letter of praise from the president of the National Education Association. Warming to the same ad, another reader sent us a 17-page letter, a pile of newspaper clippings, and a list of suggested reading.

In our kickoff message of four years ago, we told readers what we'd be talking about in this space. We said at the time:

> We'll speak out on some of the concerns we have — and perhaps you have: things like jobs, energy, national defense, transportation, pollution, inflation, taxes, bureaucracy, social problems. We'll express our views on public issues .... We'll tell some of the things we're doing and thinking and planning as a corporation.

> We'll be talking about business, sometimes not necessarily our business, but areas of concern to thoughtful citizens. And we'll be talking about technology. That's a subject of paramount interest to us as a technology company, designing and building products created through the application of scientific and engineering disciplines.

In the months ahead, we'll continue to speak up on these and other matters. We hope you'll give us a hearing.

UNITED TECHNOLOGIES

Pratt & Whitney Aircraft • Carrier • Otis • Essex • Inmont • Sikorsky
Hamilton Standard • Mostek • Elliott • Jenn-Air • Norden • Research Center

Exhibit 14

Unshackle the Yankee Trader

When products built in the U.S. are sold abroad, good things happen economically here at home. Most important of all, jobs are sustained and created. Every $1 billion in exports represents an estimated 40,000 jobs in America.

Overseas sales of U.S. goods generate tax revenue for our government. Each $1 billion in exports means $400 million in federal tax revenue.

Exports soften the impact of inflation. They help shore up the dollar. They provide the wherewithal, in the form of foreign exchange credits, to pay for the things we buy from abroad. That's especially critical in the light of America's dependence on foreign producers for much of our oil.

When the U.S. performs poorly in world trade, the effects cut right across our entire economy. Jobs are lost. Inflation is fueled. Living standards decline.

America has become laggard as an international trader. For 1977, 1978, and 1979, our international trade accounts were in the red by more than $75 billion. That's the total by which U.S. imports exceeded exports. Just as worrisome, our *share* of world trade is declining.

A sound way to offset the costs of oil imports is to raise exports of manufactured goods. Yet, in the manufactured-goods sector of exports, the U.S. is losing ground to competitors. This country exports less than 20% of its manufactured goods. That compares with about 40% for Japan, 45% for France, 55% for West Germany, and 70% for Great Britain.

During the decade of the '70s, U.S. manufactured exports rose threefold, while West Germany's increased over four times and Japan's climbed better than five times. Look at the three countries' trade surpluses in manufactured goods in 1979: U.S. — $4.5 billion; West Germany — $59 billion; Japan — $72 billion.

To promote exports, other industrialized nations spend up to six times what the U.S. does as a percentage of the national budget. Abroad, government and industry often pull together with well-meshed export policies and programs to achieve national economic goals. All too often the U.S. government, in contrast, places impediments in the paths of its exporting companies.

Perhaps that's about to change. The pro-trade climate seems to be brightening. In Washington and elsewhere, there's growing awareness that exports are a vital underpinning to a strong national economy. Increased attention is being trained on the need to stimulate exports through such measures as replacing export disincentives with incentives, slashing away the restrictive red tape that fetters exporters, and strengthening the Export-Import Bank in its job of helping to arrange financing for foreign buyers of American-made products.

Let's now convert this rising export consciousness to action. Let's cut loose the Yankee Trader in world markets.

UNITED TECHNOLOGIES

Pratt & Whitney Aircraft • Carrier • Otis • Essex • Inmont • Sikorsky
Hamilton Standard • Mostek • Elliott • Jenn-Air • Norden • Research Center

Exhibit 15

Red Tape and Abalone

Abalone is a Pacific mollusk prized at table. With demand growing and supplies declining, a California entrepreneur named George S. Lockwood had the idea of going into the business of producing the snail-like creatures under controlled conditions. He was quickly enmeshed in a web of red tape spun by government regulators. He raised money, devised an innovative way of spawning and raising abalone, and remodeled an old sardine cannery. As *Reader's Digest* tells the tale, it took him months to get the necessary permits from his local planning, building, and finance departments, along with licenses from five different offices of the state Department of Fish and Game.

Enter the feds. Lockwood needed a supply of denatured alcohol to check abalone tissue for disease. This meant getting a permit from the U.S. Bureau of Alcohol, Tobacco, and Firearms. With the permit came federal inspectors. He needed chloral hydrate for his work. This meant getting a permit from the Drug Enforcement Administration. And more inspections, these by the Food and Drug Administration.

One day two state safety inspectors turned up. They'd heard there was a "serious ozone hazard in the abalone breathing room." Actually, there was no such room. There *was* a small ozone generator, purchased at the suggestion of another government agency. In any case, the inspectors conceded they were not equipped to measure ozone. So they'd conduct a safety inspection. At day's end, they cited Lockwood for 14 violations.

One was for an "ungrounded" electric typewriter. Lockwood found that the brand-new typewriter was double-insulated and labeled as such by the manufacturer. The district safety director later admitted the citation never should have been issued. Yet he refused to lift it, insisting that Lockwood would have to appeal. He did appeal ten of the citations, at considerable cost. Seven were reversed. When the inspectors finally brought in ozone-measuring gear, they found the ozone level was lower than it is in Los Angeles.

Lockwood was fended off by bureaucrats for nearly a year when he tried to find out about U.S.-funded research in abalone raising. Getting the data eventually through the Freedom of Information Act, he learned that federal funds were being used to duplicate his technology, which was then made available to potential competitors. He flew to Washington and persuaded a key congressional chairman to have the funding stopped.

Since his facility was discharging water containing abalone's organic waste into the ocean, Lockwood was directed to obtain the same permit required for a large sewage treatment plant. No matter that abalone have been giving off waste for hundreds of thousands of years without government regulation. Or that the water his company discharged was actually cleaner than the water it took in.

He wanted to attach several small plastic pipes to an existing steel pipeline stretching from his building into the bay. This required a permit from the Army Corps of Engineers. He hired an architect to make drawings of the pipes. But his application was denied—it had the wrong kind of arrows and lettering. Fuming, he called his Congressman and two Senators. An hour later he learned his permit would be approved.

To expand, Lockwood bought the building next door, planning to move his scientific laboratories to the third floor. The local planning department turned thumbs down — it had no record of a third floor at the address. The planners were unmoved by Lockwood's protests that the third floor was built with the rest of the building 35 years ago. He'd need a new permit from the city and formal approval from the Coastal Zone Administration. Rather than go through more hassle, he decided to keep his lab where it was. By then, he had dealt with a total of 45 bureaucracies.

The wonder of it all is that his business is flourishing. Many a small business isn't so successful in bucking government regulators.

UNITED TECHNOLOGIES

Pratt & Whitney Aircraft • Carrier • Otis • Essex • Inmont • Sikorsky
Hamilton Standard • Mostek • Elliot • Jenn-Air • Norden • Research Center

Exhibit 16

Bulldoze Davis-Bacon

Back in 1931, amid the great depression, Congress passed a law known as the Davis-Bacon Act. At the time, it made sense. The government was undertaking large-scale public works in an effort to put people back to work and arrest the economy's tumble. The purpose of the law was to prevent itinerant, unscrupulous contractors from taking advantage of the country's hard times by low-bidding for construction work through the use of cheap, non-local labor.

A full half-century after its enactment, Davis-Bacon is still on the books, a legislative leftover from the depression. Nowadays, in effect, it's a super-minimum wage law that forces private employers to pay more to workers on federally supported construction projects than they pay to employees in privately financed projects.

Specifically, the law requires contractors on federal or federally assisted construction projects, over $2,000 in value, to pay their workers the wage "prevailing" for each trade in similar projects in the local area where the construction is being done.

In many cases, the "prevailing" wage is interpreted as the union scale —even in localities where the majority of comparable private construction is done by non-union contractors. Davis-Bacon has evolved into a taxpayer-subsidized prop for wages, in turn pushing up costs, in an already high-wage industry in which employees are paid an average of $13 an hour.

The law drives up construction costs to the federal government. It gouges states, cities, towns, and counties receiving federal matching funds to build such public projects as highways, airports, sewage treatment plants, parks, hospitals, and the like. As Davis-Bacon inflates the total cost of such projects, the local government's share rises.

In 1979 Congress' watchdog agency, the General Accounting Office, took a hard look at Davis-Bacon and recommended its repeal on grounds that it drives up government costs, fuels inflation, and disturbs local wage patterns. The Carter Administration, in a study, found that through administrative changes alone in the law, the government could save over one billion dollars yearly and reduce inflation appreciably.

That Davis-Bacon inflates construction wages artificially is acknowledged by economists both liberal and conservative. Repeal of the law has been advocated by organizations as divergent in their viewpoints on most issues as Common Cause and the U.S. Chamber of Commerce, along with newspapers such as the New York Times, Washington Post, and Wall Street Journal.

Eliminating Davis-Bacon would save the federal government billions of dollars a year; stimulate competitive bidding for federal construction work; enable local governments to get more construction for their money; open up opportunities for construction employment among minorities and youths, many of whom are now unable to get into tightly controlled union apprenticeship programs; and wipe out costly and burdensome red tape in government and industry.

Whatever its merits were 50 years ago, Davis-Bacon is totally without warrant today. It's an archaic statute — unjust, inimical to the public interest, inflationary, and a waste of taxpayers' dollars. It should be wiped off the books.

UNITED TECHNOLOGIES

An advocacy campaign of such long duration and intensity is quite likely to develop a set of patterns that express an underlying corporate philosophy, and UTC is no exception. An analysis of advertisements in the Op-Ed series leads one to the following observations:

- The ads cover a broader spectrum of public policy issues which are in line with concerns expressed by large businesses in America.
- The issues also reflect the concerns of a major corporation like United Technologies, with strong interests in aerospace, defense, and international business.
- The issues are discussed in a sharp, precise style. Complex explanation and elaboration of nuances in various viewpoints are avoided; the emphasis is on making a point positively, directly, and forcefully.
- To increase the credibility of the message, the copy refers to anonymous experts, and the message is presented in a third-person style. In some cases, specific authoritative sources are also cited.
- In a program of this size, sometimes there appear inconsistencies; policies advocated in one ad may run counter to recommendations made in another ad.

Spectrum of Issues Covered

Harry Gray strongly feels that American business should participate actively in the formulation of public policy in the United States. Ray D'Argenio states:

> I believe people *do* want to hear from business. After all, labor unions have a point of view. Individuals have a point of view. Activists have a point of view. Corporations have a point of view. It's just that not enough have spoken up to let people know what that point of view is.
>
> No one can come to this company now after five years, and say how do you stand on such and such an issue. God knows we have taken a stand on practically everything from crime in the streets, to deregulations, and everything else in between. No one can say that we are not engaging in a dialogue with people in the marketplace of ideas, and working with people to come up with public policy positions that are going to guide this country. I am not saying that our ads are going to have tremendous influence. They are only a drop in the bucket. It would be better if there were 10 drops or 50 drops like it. Business then would be really filling its intellectual responsibility to the public.

One-Sided versus Two-Sided Messages

UTC executives concede that developing a two-sided or a multisided message would be more interesting and would give the message more credibility. However, they feel they could not use this approach because:

- Such advertisements are more difficult to write and edit. It is hard to present the other side's viewpoint.
- UTC is buying space to present its point of view. The company is *editorializing* a position, *its* position, and not debating an issue in a neutral manner.
- It is not the company's obligation to give expression to its critics. "The Naders, Jane Fondas, and other activists of this world would have no problem reaching their audiences. They are much better at public relations than we will ever be. They know how to get the media, how to move the media, and contrive stories in a way that give the news media what it wants."
- If UTC presented other viewpoints as well, it would just double its budget and reduce by one-half its ability to state what it feels should be said.

Inconsistencies in Corporate Positions

In some of the Op-Ed ads, the positions taken seem to conflict with those taken in other ads. For example, some Op-Ed pieces advocated support for President Reagan's economic programs and urged brakes on federal spending and cuts in entitlement programs; other pieces advocated increases in defense spending and enlargement of Eximbank's lending authority. Moreover, while the earlier ads advocated reduction in federal budget deficits, as part of President Reagan's economic program, UTC was silent when President Reagan's budget later came up with deficits exceeding $120 billion. As a major defense contractor and builder of airplane engines, UTC stood to gain significantly from increased defense spending and Eximbank lending authority.

A UTC spokesperson agreed that at first glance these would appear to be contradictions. The company has also received a number of letters, and there have been letters to the newspapers which ran these ads, to the effect that the company was not consistent in its advocacy of cuts in federal spending and a balanced budget. Frank Giusti, director of editorial and news services, and the author of most of the Op-Ed pieces, acknowledged that he had agonized the most over his company's position concerning the Eximbank. However, the company feels that there is indeed justification for such an approach:

> We believe in strong national defense. And in terms of priorities, if there is a choice to be made, we would advocate increased defense spending even at the cost of larger budget deficits.
>
> Export subsidies through Eximbank are important to UTC to compete in the world markets for the sale of jet engines, where other governments subsidize their domestic industries. We would prefer that no government should subsidize its domestic industries. However, we did not choose "no subsidy" as our Op-Ed position, because the senior management felt that support of Eximbank loan authority was a more realistic and viable alternative.

Use of Authoritive Sources

Many of the Op-Ed pieces start out by saying, "There are those who say . . . .," or use anecdotal information about misuse of entitlement programs ("Growth of the Wrong Kind,") and senseless regulation ("Red Tape Regulation"). The third-person narrative implies that there is an authoritative source for this information, while in fact it might be a subjective opinion. The second approach may create an impression that these are not isolated incidents, but are symptomatic of what is wrong with our entitlement programs and government regulation in general. The news media and social activists have been severely criticized for taking isolated incidents of business malfeasance and, through innuendo and guilt by association, implicating the entire business community. And yet some of UTC's ads could also be criticized for following a similar strategy.

When asked to elaborate, a UTC spokesperson suggested that the use of the "straw man approach" was based on stylistic considerations, and was not intended to misguide readers, who were quite intelligent and sophisticated. As to the use of anecdotal information, Ray D'Argenio observed:

> Suppose we were to say that 90% of the people working for the government are doing a good job and that regulation is working, and that 10% are bad, and here is an example of the 10%. The point may have been made more accurately, but not necessarily more effectively. When you do the "Abalone" thing [Exhibit 15] it stays in your mind and you remember it. Our stories are factual and accurate. We couldn't even begin to match the exaggerations and untruths thrown at us by antibusiness social critics.

In advocating increased expenditures on national defense ["Soviet Military Power," Exhibit 9], UTC used as its authoritative source a Pentagon study which described in elaborate charts and photographs the growing military power of the Soviet Union. This report was widely criticized in the media, and by some well-known experts in the United States and Europe on Soviet military power. They characterized the study as highly exaggerated and aimed at persuading Congress to approve an enlarged defense budget.

When asked whether UTC should have pointed out the reservations of many respected experts about the accuracy of the report which was cited in the advertisement as the basis for advocating greater defense spending, a UTC spokesman responded:

> We were aware of the criticism of the Report. However, we did not agree with these criticisms. Furthermore, to acknowledge these criticisms in our ad would be to lend credence to them, and would also be tantamount to using a two-sided approach in our advertising, which we had chosen not to do.
>
> This report was not the only reason for our advocating a greater national defense effort. There have been numerous other studies, and our own experts tell us that we are lagging behind

the Soviet Union in our military preparedness, and we must make a determined effort to catch up.

EFFECTIVENESS OF UTC'S ADVERTISING PROGRAM

The response to UTC's campaigns has been overwhelmingly positive. By the end of 1981, 2.5 years after the beginning of the *Wall Street Journal* series, the company had received over 350,000 letters requesting more than 1.5 million reprints. The "Girl" ad alone had generated requests for over 52,000 reprints within a year of its publication, and requests are still coming in although the ad ran in May 1979.

The company has not undertaken a systematic analysis of the letters to develop a reader profile. However, since the letters have come from all over the United States, they are considered to be a good indicator of widespread awareness of the company's program. Most of the letters are long and thoughtful, giving comments on readers' experiences on the particular topic. Since people had manifested interest, answering such letters was an opportunity to have them learn something about UTC. Each letter writer received a reprint of the requested ad with a note, and a booklet describing UTC's activities and products. In addition, a copy of the latest color spread reprint (corporate image advertising) from the *New Yorker* magazine, and the latest quarterly report, were also sent in case readers were interested in investing in the company. Observes Ray D'Argenio: "In a subtle way we might be building a nice little constituency. So if there is a time when we get into trouble we can call upon them. We have done the same thing with our shareholders."

Christine Rothenberg, director of advertising, also views the impact of these ads in terms of emotional responses they evoke and their human interest value.

> Many of the letters that come in response to the *Wall Street Journal* campaign are from shareholders. The vast majority of them say, "it makes me particularly proud to be a shareholder in this company when I see what you are doing in your ads."
>
> Our ads have given us a unique identity which would be very hard for anyone to imitate. The average reader of even the *Wall Street Journal* considers business as cold, uncaring, and impersonal.

It is not clear whether letters from individuals can translate into investor loyalty. A very large part of UTC stock is held by institutional investors "who are not going to give two-bits whether they are impressed with your advertising."

UTC also believes that these ads have created tremendous employee loyalty and pride, even among lower-level employees. "When you go into some of our plants, you will see an ad that we ran—'I Take Pride in My Work'—posted at different locations."

Op-Ed Program

UTC has not yet undertaken any tracking studies, although it feels they would be relevant for the Op-Ed program. But the company gets some idea about the effectiveness of the campaign through research done by the *Wall Street Journal,* or gets the results from other companies that also publish in the *Journal.*

Public response in terms of letters to the Op-Ed Program has not been as large and has not been systematically solicited. Nevertheless, when one ad, published only in four Connecticut newspapers, offered a free paperback version of William Simon's book, *A Time For Truth,* 1,500 requests were received, whereas UTC expected no more than 300. Another notable for its impact was the one where UTC urged people to support the automotive industry. All the automobile makers ran it in their house organs. A local radio station ran it on the air, and local TV stations mentioned it on their news programs. The governor of Michigan sent Harry Gray a personal thank you note for running it.

NOTES

1. See, for example: *Boston Herald American;* May 28, 1979, *Chicago Tribune;* September 2, 1979, *Vogue,* September 1979, *Sun-Sentinel,* September 11, 1979; *New York Times,* May 27, 1979, *The Charlotte News,* October 29, 1979; *The Kansas City Star,* August 28, 1979; *Minneapolis Tribune,* June 17, 1979; *Los Angeles Times,* June 10, 1979, *Los Angeles Herald Examiner,* April 22, 1979; *The Detroit News,* April 16, 1979; and *Advertising Age,* June 25, 1979.
2. "What Makes Harry Gray Run," *Business Week,* December 10, 1979, pp. 74–79.
3. A. H. Ehrbar, "United Technologies' Master Plan," *Fortune,* September 22, 1980.
4. Interview with the author. Unless otherwise expressly stated, all direct quotes with UTC executives are from personal interviews or written communications with the author.

Part III CAMPAIGNS IN SUPPORT OF PARTICULAR IDEOLOGIES

Chapter 6   **AIMS OF INDUSTRY, UNITED KINGDOM:**

A POLITICALLY ORIENTED ADVOCACY CAMPAIGN AGAINST NATIONALIZATION OF BRITISH INDUSTRY AND OTHER POLICIES OF THE LABOUR PARTY

Between March and May 1983, Aims of Industry launched an intensive advocacy advertising campaign to inform the public against the dangers of nationalization of industry in Britain and the dire consequences that would follow if Britons were to return the Labour party to power in the national elections that were to take place on June 9, 1983.

The campaign was astutely timed, professionally designed, and expertly executed. It combined both the political and the ideological goals of Aims—defeat of the Labour and Socialist parties in the elections, which it feared would lead the country toward nationalization and subvention of free enterprise. This campaign was the latest in a string of notable campaigns that Aims had launched in previous years against nationalization of various British industries and other programs and policies of the Labour government and the Labour party that were di-

_____

Research Assistant: Mohamed Nabil Allam.

rected toward broadening the scope of the government in the management of the nation's economy in general, and certain targeted industries in particular.

The seeds of the campaign, however, were planted in September 1982. At the time there was considerable speculation that new elections would be called within the next 18 months. Shortly before the Labour party was due to be convened, Michael Ivens, director of Aims, found out that "nationalization" was going to be a major element in the Labour party's election platform. He foresaw a golden opportunity to one-up the Labour party by preempting the press coverage; to force the Labour party to "own up" to the issue; and to make voters aware of the issue.

Thus on Sunday, September 21, 1982, he personally typed up a press release titled "Nationalization Bombshell for Labour" and hand-carried it to all the newspapers on Fleet Street. The result was tremendous press coverage, with banner headlines. The press release quoted Ivens as challenging the Labour party by saying that if "the Labour Party have any sense, they will drop their nationalization plans. If they don't do this at the Labour Party Conference next week, we have a massive advertising and poster campaign up our sleeve" [Exhibit 1]. This aggressiveness, and a willingness to challenge and to take risks, coupled with a superb finesse in capturing favorable media attention, distinguishes Aims from other groups, and has given it a great deal more success that would have been otherwise possible. Aims does not claim total credit for the landslide victory of the Conservative party under Mrs. Thatcher's tutelage. It would, however, appear that the Aims advertising campaign played a very effective and supportive role.

Aims of Industry has certain characteristics that are quite similar to some political and ideologically based organizations in the United States. For example, its support of politically conservative candidates makes it an ideological twin of the National Conservative Political Action Committee (NCPAC), which has spent millions of dollars in paid political commercials in the last two general elections with the objective of defeating liberal Democratic candidates for the U.S. Congress and Senate. However, there are certain important differences between Aims and similar groups either in the United States or in Great Britain. For example:

1. The product that Aims of Industry promotes is intangible—the idea of free enterprise. Unlike the political parties, it is not primarily concerned with electoral activities. Unlike the steel companies, it is not concerned with manufacturing, except for the manufacture of propaganda. By contrast with the British Iron and Steel Federation, Aims of Industry is not an industrial trade association regularly negotiating with government departments on behalf of a particular industry. Its terms of reference are broader and more vague than those of many other institutions in Britain. In the words of a spokesman, it is "an ideological pressure group," supporting the ideology of free enterprise and opposing the "errors" of socialism.

2. Aims of Industry is concerned with party politics. As its director, Michael Ivens, has explained: "Obviously we're political, but politics is not the prerogative of parties." The organization is free to engage in controversies of a partisan nature, because "Aims of Industry does

Exhibit 1

FOR RELEASE: MORNING PAPERS, TUESDAY, SEPTEMBER 21, 1982
NATIONALIZATION BOMBSHELL FOR LABOUR

A bombshell for Labour's nationalization policies is provided by a new survey* carried out by National Opinion Polls on behalf of Aims of Industry, the free enterprise organisation. Nearly two-thirds (63%) said "No" to more companies being nationalized. 62% said that nationalized industries were less efficient than free enterprise.

Only 16% of those polled felt that more companies should be nationalized, whereas 63% were opposed. Only 15% thought that more nationalization would make living standards go up whereas 41% thought they would go down. Only 12% felt that nationalized industries are more efficient than free enterprise industries, whereas 62% thought they were less efficient.

Labour's "Programms 1982" calls for nationalization or re-nationalization of companies in the construction, building materials, cement, glass, telecommunications, road haulage, electronics, ports, forestry and timber, pharmaceuticals and health equipment, North Sea oil, electrical engineering, bricks and tiles, mineral rights and production facilities, banking and private health industries.

The NOP survey of Labour Party supporters will provide even more headaches for Mr. Foot. Labour supporters were seriously divided on the question of more nationalization with only 38% in favour, 35% against, 19% don't knows, and 7% saying it depends which companies. Only one in four Labour supporters (26%) felt that more nationalization would make living standards go up and only one in four (25%) felt that nationalized industries were more efficient. Half as many again (38%) felt that nationalized industries were less efficient.

Conservative voters reject nationalization. 85% think that no more companies should be nationalized, 63% think that more nationalization would make living standards go down, 82% think nationalized industries are less efficient than free enterprise industries.

68% of Alliance supporters reject more nationalization (12% are in favour); 38% felt that more nationalization would make living standards go down (12% think living standards would go up); 66% thought that nationalized industries are less efficient than free enterprise industries (10% said more efficient).

"If the Labour Party have any sense, they will drop their nationalization plans," said Michael Ivens, Director of Aims of Industry, which is supported by thousands of companies and federations. "If they don't do this at the Labour Party conference next week, we have a massive advertising and poster campaign up our sleeves," he said.

*"Public Attitudes to Labour's Policies on Nationalization"; Aims of Industry, 40 Dougty Street, London WC1N 2LF.

not have to negotiate with the government or avoid treading on people's toes, unlike other employers' organizations."

3. Aims is supported by major corporations and industry groups and its governing council is composed of leading corporate executives. In many ways it has elements of both the Business Roundtable and the National Association of Manufacturers (NAM) in the United States.

4. Unlike NCPAC in the United States, Aims' advocacy campaigns are not directed against the election of individual political candidates. Instead, they focus on issues that are part of a political party's agenda. This strategy is largely due to the nature of British politics, where political parties are ideologically oriented, national in character, and party platforms play a greater role in elections and subsequent governance than in the United States.

5. Aims is also a research organization, similar to the American Enterprise Institute (AEI) and the Heritage Foundation, in that it initiates and sponsors studies on various aspects of the workings of the economic system. Aims' reports, based on these studies, are widely disseminated to promote public education.

Aims represents a conservative—or libertarian—viewpoint. Still, it is an independent organization and does not profess to be aligned with any party. According to Mr. John Lyle, former chairman of the governing council of Aims:

> That approach continues today. Aims has opposed extremists, whether Communist, Trotskyist or National Socialist. Aims was, in fact, the first national organization to attack the National Front in its booklet "Blackshirts Under the Bed." A difficult problem for Aims of Industry is what problems to take up and what problems to leave to others. Sometimes Aims has recognized that it is the only organization in the field at that time; this applied, for example, to its defence of press freedom and its attack on internal censorship by the print unions. The resource war and the relationship between industry and defence is something that Aims would have preferred to leave to others. But as no others were forthcoming we took up the subject and then we were followed by our friends in the United States, France and West Germany.[1]

This case raises a number of issues of both a strategic and a tactical nature that deserve careful analysis for their possible application in similar campaigns in the United States and other countries.

1. How effective is the strategy of combining advocacy-issue advertising with electoral campaigns? What are the risks associated with such a strategy?
2. Given the fact that Aims is financed by the business community, how does its sponsorship affect the credibility of its messages, especially with intellectual elites, opinion leaders, and those segments of the public who hold opinions different to those advocated by Aims?
3. Among the most successful advocacy campaigns in the United States have been the ones that carried long messages, often using third-party authoritative sources, to make detailed presentations of com-

plex issues. Aims' messages, on the other hand, are short, rhetorical, and based more on emotional than rational appeals. How effective is such an approach likely to be, given that advocacy-issue advertising's target audience is primarily opinion leaders, the messages are carried in the elite media, and the issues covered are quite complex and serious?

4. A related issue is the use of humorous cartoons to convey the ad message. Does the humorous approach symbolize frivolity, and might it detract from the serious nature of the subject matter?

5. Close association and active participation of business corporations in politics carries with it the risk of polarization of public opinion and may cause greater division between business and labor groups. Might not such an approach lead to adverse reaction and retaliatory response from the unions and the Labour party in terms of industrial conflicts and greater regulation of industry, once the Labour party comes to power?

AIMS OF INDUSTRY—BACKGROUND

Aims of Industry was organized in 1942 by a group of businessmen worried about the growth of economic controls in wartime and fearful of their continuance and extension after the war. The election of a Labour government in 1945 made the fear a reality. It also increased the importance of Aims, since the measures it opposed were immediately affecting the operations of business.

By the end of 1946, Aims was being briefed by industrial bodies to act on their behalf in negotiations of all kinds where publicity was needed. When the Liverpool Cotton Association, for example, was threatened with extinction and its own protests were being ignored by the Board of Trade, it asked Aims of Industry to take up its case. The Smithfield Meat Importers, in danger of nationalization, put themselves in the hands of Aims of Industry. The Railway Companies Association and the Road Haulage Association, with their whole membership facing obliteration by the transport bill, briefed Aims of Industry to put their case for survival. In each case, and on behalf of industry as a whole, Aims of Industry went to work by presenting the facts. By 1947, it had a record of solid achievement as the only public relations organization for industry.

During the life of that Labour government, the organization grew quickly. One of its major campaigns during this (1947–1951) period was conducted on behalf of Tate and Lyle, the largest sugar processor in Great Britain. To get a mandate from its shareholders, the board of Tate & Lyle called an extraordinary meeting of its shareholders, who voted over 80 percent in support of the campaign. The company also received strong support from its employees. The company called in Aims of Industry to assist in the direction of the campaign. The campaign that followed has become a classic of its kind, one that is still used as a case history for students of public relations.

The campaign used a cartoon character in the shape of a sugar cube. It was created by the doodling of artist Bobby St. John Cooper. It was an impudent animated sugar cube, christened "Mr. Cube." The advantage of having Mr. Cube was that he could say the most outrageous things and get away with it [Exhibit 2]. By a stroke of genius, the organizers realized that they had a truly mass medium at their disposal in the form of sugar packets that reached millions of housewives and provided a "literally free" medium of mass communications.

The campaign was directed at the mass electorate through a great variety of media techniques, including the printing of antinationalization cartoons and slogans on the firm's sugar packets. At this time the extension of nationalization was a major political issue of concern to both parties, and as sugar was rationed, supplies of this basic consumer commodity could not be taken for granted. After the 1951 election, the Labour party abandoned its pledge to nationalize the sugar industry.[2]

The success of the Mr. Cube campaign had a tremendous effect on Aims and greatly influenced its programs and strategies. In the process, Aims became a nationally recognized institution and an important voice for free enterprise. Many political cartoonists in leading newspapers started using Aims as a spokesperson for presenting conservative views on the working of the economy [Exhibit 3]. Moreover:

1. Aims became more aggressive in publicly opposing government policies. In the 1960s and 1970s, Aims undertook major advertising campaigns to warn the public of the consequences of Labour's nationalization policies.
2. It has taken strong positions against such issues as the expanding scope of local governments, compulsory or closed shop unionism, press censorship through the press unions' refusal to print messages they disapprove, and extremism.
3. Aims has opposed the growth of bureaucracy in the EEC and was the first British organization to oppose compulsory trade union membership on company boards. The present threats of the Fifth Directive make that campaign still essential.
4. Aims has published and widely distributed fact-filled reports and pamphlets in support of its advocated positions.
5. Aims set up July 1 as Free Enterprise Day, accompanied by the presentation of Free Enterprise Awards, and this has led many in the United States to follow suit. President Carter proclaimed July 1 as International Free Enterprise Day.
6. Aims of Industry has given help and advice in setting up free enterprise organizations in Latin America, Scandinavia, and Australia. Aims and its sister organization in Norway, Libertas (which sprang from a wartime resistance movement), joined to create cooperation in Europe by free enterprise organizations. This has now led to cooperation on an international scale.
7. Aims' objectives are not merely negative in character; it also advocates that industry should be responsible as well as enterprising.

Organizational Goals and Objectives

Aims describes its objectives, among others, as:

• To defend free enterprise and freedom

Exhibit 2

Mr. Cube at work.

Exhibit 3

Press cartoons from the
Nationalization Campaign.

Exhibit 3

Milestones

AIMS AND HUMOUR

Aims' message is usually a serious one, but satire and humour are sometimes appropriate. Aims' activities have also been the subject of cartoons in the press: here are a few amusing examples.

The man who dreamt...
...of 5 years' more Socialism.

Issued by Aims in the interest of a return to Freedom and Enterprise.

The man who dreamt...
...the Government had nationalized construction and building. And woke to find that Labour is planning to do just that.

Issued by Aims in the interest of a return to Freedom and Enterprise

Dickens' sharp comment on the vast number of people who do not pay rates for 'Londoners and the Rates'.

(with acknowledgements to Marc and The Times).

Exhibit 3

'But, darling — everybody's got a red under the bed!' (with acknowledgements to Jak and the Evening Standard). This appeared at the time that Aims was running its reds under (and in) the bed campaign to warn the public that extremists in the trade union movement were planning to overthrow Ted Heath's government.

Humorous cover — but hard-hitting contents on the new bureaucrats.

'It's either something to do with Free Enterprise Week or things are worse than we thought' (with acknowledgements to Mac and the Daily Mail).

Stanley says...

"There must be a quicker way to bankrupt them!"

Issued by Aims of Industry in the cause of free enterprise.

'Of course I'm non party and non political — down with Wilson' (with acknowledgements to Vicky and the Evening Standard).

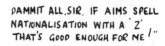

DAMMIT ALL, SIR. IF AIMS SPELL NATIONALISATION WITH A 'Z' THAT'S GOOD ENOUGH FOR ME!"

(with acknowledgements to Punch).

Exhibit 3

Industry is being held back and you're paying!

Let FREE ENTERPRISE get things moving again

Issued by Aims of Industry, the non-party organisation – in the interest of Free Enterprise.

A lot of people would benefit from British Industry coming under State control...

The French.
The Germans.
The Dutch.
The Italians.
The Swiss.
The Austrians.
The Americans.
The Japanese.

and a lot more wouldn't.
British industry.
British workers.
British shareholders.
British consumers.

AiMS

Jetter Lane, London EC4A1AX
dustry in defence of free enterprise.

All this is going to cost you a lot of money.

You may have a bill soon for thousands of millions of pounds. It is going to cost vast sums of money for a Labour Government to take over and buy into many industries and companies. And the bill will be met by the taxpayer.

You will also meet the bill because nationalized industries tend to make a loss. And they are subsidised by the public. All this means you will pay more and your money will buy less. So what can we do about it? We must make our voices heard.

Say 'NO' to the Elephants

NATIONAL-IZATION   STATE CONTROL.

Issued by Aims of Industry against Labour's plans to take over British industry.

IF THE STATE TAKES OVER...

IT'S YOU WHO STAND TO LOSE ■ State control of free enterprise firms will cost millions ■ New State companies will cost millions more ■ Make no mistake—it's _you_ who'll have to pay if they take over ■ Free enterprise is fairer ■ It puts the customer first ■ It keeps prices keen ■ It encourages competition ■ It gives you plenty of choice at home—and does a more efficient job than the State could ever do when it comes to selling British goods abroad ■ So it's up to you.

SAY NO TO NATIONALIZATION
ISSUED BY AIMS OF INDUSTRY
the non-Party organisation for Free Enterprise

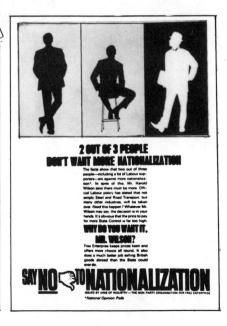

2 OUT OF 3 PEOPLE DON'T WANT MORE NATIONALIZATION

The facts show that two out of three people—including a lot of Labour supporters—are against more nationalization*. In spite of this, Mr. Harold Wilson says there must be more Official Labour policy has stated that not simply Steel and Road Transport, but many other industries, will be taken over. _Need this happen?_ Whatever Mr. Wilson may say the decision is in your hands. It's obvious that the price to pay for more State Control is far too high. **WHY DO YOU WANT IT, MR. WILSON?**

Free Enterprise keeps prices keen and offers more choice all round. It also does a much better job selling British goods abroad than the State could ever do.

SAY NO TO NATIONALIZATION
ISSUED BY AIMS OF INDUSTRY — THE NON-PARTY ORGANISATION FOR FREE ENTERPRISE
*National Opinion Polls

- To create a public belief in free enterprise so that the government can make the right decisions and companies can achieve their objectives
- To oppose, and wherever possible reduce, unnecessary government intervention by state ownership, control, or excessive bureaucracy
- To expose the problems industry faces from excessive state or local government spending
- To emphasize that freedom for the individual is inseparable from freedom of enterprise, and that the purpose of government is to preserve and protect individual and economic freedom—not to restrict it
- To identify and make widely known attempts from whatever source to undermine the authority of a freely elected government or to attack freedom and free enterprise
- To advise and assist companies, federations, and trade associations in their relationship and dealings with government, the political parties, the trade unions, the press, radio, and television
- To encourage the realization that the interests of all engaged in an enterprise—employees, managers, shareholders—are indivisible, and that all should therefore work together for its prosperity
- To encourage an understanding that our economic prosperity must, in the end, depend on adequate national defense
- To work with similar organizations abroad that are engaged in the fight for free enterprise

Structure and Decision-Making Process

Aims of Industry is governed by a twenty-three-member council, including a chairman. The current officers of Aims are: Mr. Nigel Mobbs, chairman; Sir John Reiss, BEM, president; Lord Taylor of Hadfield, vice-president; and Mr. Michael Ivens, director. "President" is an honorific title and is usually given a chairman upon his retirement. The chairman is the head of the council and chairs the council meetings. In addition, there is a Scottish committee of ten members, with its own chairman.

Aims' organization structure offers it tremendous flexibility in moving quickly when circumstances demand immediate and timely action. According to Michael Ivens:

> I meet with my council chairman once a fortnight and we discuss issues that are currently at hand. We would also get one or two members of the Council involved who would be interested in specific issues. However, when an occasion arises, and I want to attack somebody through our advertisements or press releases, I go ahead and do it, and seek my Council's approval afterwards. I have this relationship with my Council. If they want to get rid of me they can. That's fine. Most times with an advertising campaign, I would tell them first. We have a very free run here. My Council has always backed me. We have tremendous mutual trust and respect.
>
> Because of this and because we are very often agonized by seeing too many opportunities, we tend to overwork. We are regarded by the press as overkillers. We can't stand not to get into the act.

Michael Ivens came to Aims in 1972 with over fifteen years of experience in industry, and with a number of years in communications and journalism. Author of numerous books and articles, he is also a published poet. He is an active participant in initiating policy decisions in consultation with the council, and is in charge of executing strategy and also, with his staff, of implementing Aims programs and activities.

Aims is financially supported by a corporate membership of over 1,200 companies, and 10 federations and associations representing more than 35,000 companies. Aims is a company limited by guarantee, which is uniquely British in its conception. Such a corporation must be a nonprofit company. In the event such a company fails, the law limits the liability of the shareholders to a maximum of £1, whereas in an ordinary company the directors' liability would extend to a great deal more money.

Aims receives strong support from business and industry. In many cases, corporations and federations are unwilling to get directly involved in political and electoral issues. They do not want to upset the government or unions and prefer to keep a low profile. Instead, they provide financial and other resource support to Aims to undertake these campaigns. Says Michael Ivens: "Our advantage is that we don't provide our victims with any targets to shoot at. We do not reveal the names of our corporate supporters. Moreover, not all companies in an industry will be supporting us on a given issue. Therefore, the unions do not have a specific company or industry to target for undue pressure.

Aims' fundraising is also quite unusual, both because of what Aims is and also because of the peculiarities of British tax law. Under British law, corporations are allowed to make political contributions, provided they are disclosed to the shareholders in the annual report. Labour unions also make political contributions through funds raised from their members as political dues. A union member signs a pledge card to the "Levy Fund," which is called "opting in."

When the Labour party came to power in 1975, the law was changed. Instead of "opting in" to the Labour party, all workers who belonged to trade unions would automatically be assumed to pay the Labour party levy unless they were to "opt out." The immediate effect was dramatic. Where previously something like 47 percent of union members were paying the political levy, the number jumped to over 75 percent.

In the 1960s, when the Labour party was in power, it wanted to reduce industry's financial support to the Conservative party. The Labour government amended the Companies Act and required that all companies disclose their political contributions or donations. Companies were also to disclose contributions or donations to any group whose activities affected support or nonsupport for a political party. This was done specifically with Aims in mind. As a consequence, a number of companies could have been afraid to make contributions to Aims. To get around the problem, Aims came upon a very creative solution. Instead of accepting contributions, it now accepts only payments for services rendered. To make it even more legitimate, Aims started paying value added tax (VAT) on its receipts. The companies making such payments did not have to make any disclosure and be subjected to pressure by Labour or any other political group.

Aims' normal operating budget ranges between £350,000 and £400,000 a year. However, during election years, or to run special advertising campaigns, it may raise additional funds that could fluctuate from £200,000 to £500,000, depending on the particular campaign.

THE 1983 CAMPAIGN—THE FIGHT FOR FREE ENTERPRISE

The plans for the 1983 campaign were formulated within the background of the Labour party's platform which, among other things, called for:

- A massive state ownership and control of the British economy. Industries and companies affected would include banks, insurance, electronics, pharmaceuticals, health equipment, construction and building materials, road haulage, shipping, ports, forestry, timber, and oil.
- All industries and companies denationalized by the current Conservative government would be renationalized.
- Privatization would be stopped. There would be an attack on private medicine and private health insurance programs.
- Pension funds would be liable for use for political investment, and trade unions would be given greater power over the management of these funds.
- The land of tenant farmers would be nationalized. This represents 34 percent of agricultural land.
- Banks would be controlled. It would be a case of "cooperate or be nationalized."

The Labour party platform also made certain other proposals which Aims considered to be against the best interests of Great Britain as well as its industry and commerce. The Labour party's National Executive Committee had prepared a statement on the financial institutions which was approved by the party's 1982 annual conference. This statement was based on the report of the Labour party's Financial Institutions Study Group, "The City—A Socialist Approach."

According to Aims, the report made sweeping proposals on pension funds. Among other things:

- Institutions would be expected to fund a new National Investment Bank (NIB) and take up agreed volumes of NIB bonds. The government would guarantee a return on this investment "to allay fears that the funds would be directed into unprofitable activities," but no mention was made of how any such shortfall would be made good. Pension funds would be required to hold a minimum of their assets in government debt.
- A new Securities Act would be passed to set up a Securities Commission with which pension funds would have to register.
- Exchange controls would be reintroduced, and there would be restrictions on overseas portfolio investment.
- The report also suggested the formation of Agreed Development Plans (ADPs), which would discuss investment strategies for large pension funds.
- The report asserted that the main obstacle to a shift from investment

in secondary markets to direct pension fund investment in individual companies is "the funds' lack of expertise." The statement stated that the public sector borrowing requirement (PSBR) would increase as public sector spending was used to boost the economy, but that "we do not accept that high public borrowing means high interest rates."

Political Environment of the Campaign

To counteract the threat of the Labour party's plans, Aims decided to undertake an advocacy campaign to inform the British public about the dangers to the nation's economy and their own self-interest should the Labour party's program come to pass. In launching this campaign, it could not have found a more hospitable political environment.

A national public opinion survey was conducted in August 1982 to assess the implications of the Labour party's present policy on nationalization, and also to test the views of the public on the relative efficiency of nationalized industries and free enterprise.

Some of the major findings of the survey were these:

- 63 percent thought there should be no more companies nationalized. This included 85 percent Conservatives and 68 percent Alliance. Labour voters were seriously divided, with 35 percent opposed to more nationalization and 38 percent for (and a further 7 percent saying it depends on which companies).
- 16 percent of respondents thought that more companies should be nationalized. A further 4 percent said it depended on which companies.
- 41 percent of all respondents thought that more nationalization would make living standards go down, 15 percent thought that more nationalization would make living standards go up, 28 percent thought that it would make no difference, and 17 percent did not know.
- One Labour voter in four thought more nationalization would make living standards go up, 39 percent thought it would make no difference, and 17 percent thought living standards would go down.
- 12 percent of voters thought that nationalized industries were more efficient than free enterprise industries, 62 percent thought them less efficient, 6 percent thought it varied, 4 percent said it made no difference, and 16 percent were don't knows.
- One Labour voter in four (25 percent) felt that nationalized industries were more efficient, while nearly four Labour voters out of ten (38 percent) felt nationalized industries were less efficient.
- 82 percent of Conservative voters and 66 percent of Alliance voters thought free enterprise industries more efficient. Only 5 percent of Conservative voters and 10 percent of Alliance voters considered nationalized industries more efficient.

The findings of the survey reinforced national trends that had been emerging in the country for the last decade. For example:

- The majority of the public is opposed to more nationalization. Over the years, something like 90 percent of Conservatives, 80 percent of

Liberals (and now Social Democrats) and 50 percent of Labour voters have opposed more nationalization.

- Nationalization, as an issue, ranks number 4 or 5 in subjects that determine the way people vote.
- There has been a tremendous move away from socialism by the young in the last ten years. In the October 1974 election, for example, the Conservatives got 9 percent of the 18 to 23 vote. In the last election, this moved up to 45 percent, and that figure is holding.

Aims also undertook a survey of the business community concerning the Labour party's proposals on the use of pension funds. This questionnaire was sent to 250 companies and elicited over a 75 percent response. The respondents included trustees of pension funds, pension fund managers, insurance companies and brokers, and pension consultants. Some of the major findings of this survey were:

- Overall, there was total disapproval from the entire industry for the proposals.
- 100 percent of respondents disapproved of the Labour party's proposals for government direction of pension fund investment, and 100 percent felt that the proposals would not benefit members of pension funds.
- 99 percent of respondents were against investing in government debt on a compulsory basis.
- 90 percent believed that the proposed National Investment Bank would not provide a more efficient source of funds for industry than existing methods. There was no approval for this suggestion, with 10 percent saying "don't know."
- 80 percent of respondents felt that a restriction on overseas portfolio investment would reduce the growth potential of pension funds and therefore benefits for members.
- 90 percent of respondents rejected Labour's assertion that high public borrowing would not mean high interest rates.
- Most respondents (72 percent) thought that pension funds had benefitted by the abolition of exchange controls; only 7 percent disagreed.
- 79 percent disagreed with Labour's statement that pension funds "lacked the expertise" to invest directly in individual companies; only 13 percent agreed.

Moreover, the survey drew an unusual volume of supplementary comments, indicating the serious consideration given the survey by respondents. Many respondents stressed that workers should be able to feel confident pension funds were sacrosanct and run for their benefit and that there should be no scope for any organization, whether the company itself, the government, or a trade union, to raid the fund. Many made the point that, with experiences like De Lorean and massive losses in nationalized industries, government had a poor record in directing and monitoring investment monies and finding investment winners.

There was also concern that the proposals would entrust large sums to the whims of politicians, but it would be companies, their workers, pensioners who had already retired, and pension fund trustees who would have to foot the bill if those whims went wrong. It was felt by many trustees that their duty to maximize the yield of the funds entrusted to their care—and hence improve benefits to members—was incompatible with attempts to provide investment money for politically motivated social objectives. In such a situation, there could be a conflict with the trust law, resulting in trustees being placed in the position of disobeying the government's directives or being liable for action for breach of trust by pension fund members.

Development of a Campaign Strategy

The campaign strategy had six important elements:

1. Identify issues through public opinion surveys and political intelligence and experience, on which the Labour party was likely to be vulnerable to voter hostility.
2. Force these issues into the open by taking the initiative and going public long before either of the two parties was ready to confront them.
3. Use a constant barrage of press releases to maintain momentum, generate press interest, and create a heightened news environment.
4. Harness the energy thus created through a hard-hitting advertising campaign.
5. Confront the television networks with their past record of pro-labour bias in their election-related public affairs programming and ensure that Conservative party views received fair and equal coverage.
6. Involve the largest possible number of corporations, business associations, and industry leaders in becoming active on the electoral issues and speaking publicly about them.

James Knox, an experienced advertising executive with *The Spectator,* a conservative British political opinion magazine, observed:

> Aims started issuing press releases and advertising about three or four weeks before the election was even announced. To me, it was a softening up exercise. They [Aims] were really trying to weaken the case for nationalisation before the battle officially commenced.

Selection of Target Audience

Public opinion research indicated that distinct groups must be separately cultivated through specific appeals and then coalesced into a broader constituency. These were:

1. People who were not familiar with the Labour party's platform or understood its implications—the "don't knows" part of the voting public
2. Influentials and opinion leaders
3. Present and potential supporters

Aims realized that Labour's plans were not merely not understood by the public, but that their import was inadequately grasped by many Conservative leaders and by influential people in the news media as well. Therefore, the objective was both to inform and to educate the general public and the opinion leaders.

Campaign Theme

The primary theme of the 1983 campaign, as with most other Aims' campaigns, was that nationalization would be paid for out of people's savings and also by their pensions. A subsidiary theme focused on specific industries that were to be nationalized to emphasize the fact that Labour would virtually nationalize the banks and direct pensions in order to pay for nationalization.

Another subsidiary theme was to stress that the Labour party, if elected, was likely to move to the Left on the same lines as a moderate Labour administration that was swiftly overthrown by extremists in local elections in London's municipal governing body, The Greater London Council.

EXECUTING THE CAMPAIGN STRATEGY

Building Industry Coalitions

The first step was to encourage industries and companies to speak out during the election. The Aims director visited most major federations and associations. He was afraid the "low profile" was the fashionable stance, although most of them were delighted that Aims was going to fight. On the other hand, Aims did get some of them to break ground and speak out.

For example, at the suggestion of Aims, the Institute of Directors cooperated in persuading eighteen major industrialists to sign a letter to be sent to the news media dealing with election issues. It received a good deal of publicity on television, radio, and in the press.

Fundraising

Aims felt that it would need £500,000 to run an effective campaign. However, contacts with potential supporters made it appear that because of the poor economy, the most that could be expected would be £250,000. This was the amount for the budgeted campaign.

One of the approaches to raise funds, but equally important to let people know that Aims was going to launch a campaign against the Labour party's election platform, was to develop a brochure that was mailed to all potential contributors. This brochure presented the reasons for the campaign, the campaign strategy, and also included some sample advertisements. It contained a coupon that could be used to send contributions. The advertisement drew over £10,000 in individual contributions [Exhibit 4].

Exhibit 4

SUPPORT THE FIGHT FOR FREE ENTERPRISE CAMPAIGN

We wish to support the campaign with a payment of
£. . . . . . plus VAT at 15%

We enclose a cheque payable to Aims of Industry

Name. . . . .
Position held. . . . .
Organisation. . . . .
Address. . . . .
. . . .
. . . .
Telephone number. . . . .

Please complete and return this to David Yockney,
Deputy Director, Aims of Industry, 40 Doughty St, London
WC1N 2LF (01-405 5195).

ALL FINANCIAL SUPPORT IS TREATED CONFIDENTIALLY

Registered in England No: 457622   VAT Registered No: 244 6295 51

Ensuring Fair Television Coverage

Aims believed that television news coverage and public affairs programming during the 1979 election was highly biased toward expressing the Labour party viewpoint. Its research had shown that in the last election, three times as many trade union representatives appeared during election commentaries compared to representatives of the business community. The research also showed that sometimes even the Labour party's slogans were used as a backdrop for Labour spokespersons appearing on a given program. Aims conducted similar research during the big national steel strike in 1981, and found similar results: Roughly three times as many trade union representatives appeared on radio and television as business and industry members.

As a preamble to the 1983 election, and armed with its research findings, Aims made strong representations to both the BBC and commercial television and radio executives with a view to discouraging them from pursuing similar policies in these elections. The effort was quite successful. Ken Daly, deputy director of Aims, observed:

> We said to the broadcast media that unless we receive a fair treatment we will make protestations to the Home Secretary and the Prime Minister. We told them that we would send copies of our letters [letters that Aims had written to the radio and television executives] all around the place. We made it a bit uncomfortable for them to ensure that this [the unfair coverage] was not going to happen this time. What was very interesting about this election was they [the broadcast media] absolutely played down the trade unions, unions did not receive a free platform. BBC even took a trade union program off television. In fact, this was the most blatant pro-union program we had on television. We were quite happy about that. The broadcast media played the two sides much more fairly this time than they had done before.

Preelection Press Coverage

An integral part of the campaign strategy was to maintain a news momentum concerning the electoral issues, the dangers of the Labour party's program, and the activities of Aims. This was achieved through a continuous flow of press releases timed to anticipate major events of the campaign, the Labour party actions, or to coincide with Aims' own tactics.

As stated previously, the first shot was fired on September 21, 1982, with a press release entitled "Nationalisation Bombshell for Labour" [Appendix A]. This was immediately followed by another release on September 28, 1983, under the headline "Worst Dose of Nationalisation Ever." The press release asserted that "immediately after the war, it was a question of nationalising some inefficient industries. Now it's a matter of taking efficient companies from a wide variety of industries. Our foreign competitors must be delighted." It stated that "Aims of Industry will mount a £1 million campaign against these proposals. The first big cheque has already come in."

Aims issued five more press releases between January 6 and April 2, 1983. The January 6 release charged that proposals by the Greater London Council (GLC) "to bring the police under their thumb would move London to becoming not just a Trotskyist state but a police state." The release was commenting on a GLC report seeking to transfer control of the Metropolitan Police and Scotland Yard to politically appointed local police committees. In the fourth release, dated February 9, 1983, "Pension Funds Say 'No' to Labour's Plans," Aims provided some of the major findings of its survey of 250 pension funds managers, which showed an almost total opposition to the Labour party's proposal to impose government direction on pension fund investment.

The fifth release, March 18, 1983, "Enormous Demand for Destination Disaster Leaflet—Satirising Labour's Nationalization Plans," talked about an astonishing demand for the leaflet even before it was published. With a cover by Cummings indicating that the Labour party wanted Britain to join the "Nationalization Express" which had failed so grievously in the Soviet Union and Eastern Europe, it also included a scheduled journey that revealed Labour's plans should it win the election. The stops included Foot's Folly, Benn's Bridge, Perilous Shore, Militants' Maze, Kaufman's Kloister's Cave, and finished up at Marxist Junction, where there was a final stop for National Bankruptcy. The leaflet was not merely amusing; it showed Labour's plans to nationalize the pharmaceutical industry, direct pension funds, nationalize twenty-five top companies, introduce state ownership in many industries, particularly the banks, and nationalize everything the Conservative government had denationalized. Aims director Ivens declared that the demand for the leaflet would pass the 1 million mark.

The sixth release, dated March 23, 1983, again assaulted the Labour party's nationalization plans. Headlined "Labour's Plan Is Blatant Robbery to Support Nationalization," it claimed that "Labour's plan to grab £6 million of the public's savings for socialist projects and their attack on the banks was blatant robbery. To justify it and also the assault on the banks in the name of unemployment was sheer dishonesty." The release stated that much of the money would be used for Labour's nationalization policies, which would make people poorer, create unemployment, and destroy the value of their savings. In the release Aims also announced that its first advertisement attacking these plans would appear that week and that a national campaign was to start in April.

The last release was dated April 2, 1983, and announced the launch of a national advertising campaign to attack Labour's nationalization proposals. In the press release, Michael Ivens declared that he was receiving tremendous favorable response and financial support for the campaign. "They [the business community] realise the Labour's policies would wreck our economy and their business." The release went on to describe different advertisements that would attack Labour's plans to take over pension funds for state investment and the plans to nationalize the banks. Another advertisement with a striking hammer and sickle would deal with Labour's plans to nationalize all the land of tenant farmers, which amounted to 34 percent of all agricultural land. This, the advertisement would state, was a first step to implementing Labour's policies to nationalize all farmland. The campaign would use cartoons designed by the distinguished artist and cartoonist Cummings, and would be backed up by studies, booklets, research reports, and leaflet distribution to homes throughout the country.

Advertising Campaign

The campaign had four components:

1. Print ads in major national newspapers and provincial newspapers
2. Publication of special reports dealing with issues of concern to special constituencies—farmers, retirees and all wage earners who would be affected by state control of pension funds, the pharmaceutical industry
3. Leaflets to satirize Labour's policies
4. Two car stickers entitled "A Free Enterprise Needs Freedom," and "Freedom Needs Free Enterprise"

Implementation of the Print Advertising Strategy

Before the campaign launch, Aims' advertising agency, Allen, Bradley & Marsh, conducted focus group research where participants discussed Aims' previous advertisements. One conclusion was that the groups did not like political advertising that was aggressive, hard-hitting, and controversial. They tended to prefer softer versions. According to an Aims' spokesperson:

> This gave us very lively discussions with our agency. Our instincts and our previous experience was that despite any displeasure that hard political advertising might cause some members of the public, we just had to go ahead with it. After a good deal of discussion we instigated a hard-hitting campaign. We were helped by the fact that our agency, when they saw it was essential, gave us their enthusiastic support.
>
> We have found that this kind of fundamental discussion is essential in a political advertising campaign. The air has to be cleared so that the advertising agency's approach to conventional advertising is harmonised with our approach to political campaigning. And of course changes had to be made also on our side. It means that we tend to get involved rather more than conventional clients in selecting newspapers, writing the ad copy and suggesting graphics. But we are very dependent on the professional skills of the advertising agency—in this campaign skilled buying by the agency gave us an exceptionally high return on capital invested.

In developing their advertisements, Aims relied on techniques that had proved their worth in previous campaigns. These included sharp headlines, short messages, and biting humor—all designed to catch attention and get the message across while at the same time have supporters laugh and get opponents angry. Michael Ivens describes his rationale for the advertising as follows:

Our first priority was to reach the largest number of people holding opinions on different issues that stretched the entire spectrum from extremely positive to extremely negative.

The most important thing in influencing people is contrast. If you put a red dot on a black field, it will stand out. Over the years, we have found this also applies to cartoons. Because a cartoon is very different, people notice it. A good one-inch cartoon can be much more effective than a one-page advertisement. Second, there is a long history in communication research showing a positive relationship between communication and pleasure. And cartoons are associated with communication and pleasure. Third, when you're working on a limited budget, you're getting more observations per inch.

Michael Forsyth, a conservative MP elected to the Parliament for the first time in 1983, and a public relations and advertising expert, makes a similar observation:

The electorate is not very sophisticated about the issues. Nor are people that interested in learning about them. If you take an advertisement in a newspaper about pension funds, if they [the people] have read this headline and got half the message, you're lucky.

It's true that people who have a vested interest, one way or the other, are a more sophisticated section of the electorate. However, this group is a very tiny minority, which is both fully aware of the arguments on an issue, and has already made up its mind as to which side it stands on.

A number of other advertising executives in London interviewed by the author made similar observations. However, they did not have any empirical data to show whether an alternative approach had been tried, and if so, with what effect.

This approach, however, runs counter to another important need of advocacy advertising, to reach opinion leaders and educated readers who want to be persuaded on the merits of an argument, rather than slick graphics and emotional appeals. Research in the United States tends to prove this point, that copy with well-reasoned arguments attracts large readership in newspapers and magazines that draw educated and well-informed readers.

Michael Ivens, however, maintains that the British situation is quite different and not directly comparable with that of the United States:

Our first objective is not to reach the opinion leader with the message, but to show him that the advertisement is being used. Let's take one opinion leader who was clearly reached, and that's Mrs. Thatcher, the prime minister.

There are two kinds of opinion leaders. There's the opinion leader that we want to be on our side, and he knows that this is being done. The other opinion leader is our opponent. We want to enrage him into making statements that would put him to public ridicule and hurt his cause.

We've done it very successfully. Our advertisements have really angered Tony Benn, one of the leaders of the Labour Party.

He is quite an honest politician. He actually has a preference for saying what Labour policies are. This has worked to our advantage.

The campaign used a total of nine advertisements. The first ad, "Don't Let Labour Play Politics with Your Savings," stated that despite the failures of nationalization in Britain and abroad, the lesson still remains unlearned by the Labour party. The advertisement asserted that nationalization would lead to the use of personal savings for political ends rather than sound business objectives and would have grave implications for every individual in Britain. The ad ran a total of five times in three different newspapers [Exhibit 5].

The second advertisement, "What Will You Give to Help Us Defeat Labour's Plans for Nationalization," argued that not everyone understood that Labour planned to take many of Britain's most efficient industries and put them under state control. This is not fully understood by the British public, and that's why Aims needed financial support for its campaign to put those facts before the public. The ad ended with the question, "Will You Support Us Now—or Like the French, Choose Socialism and Regret It Later?" The ad ran only once in the *Daily Telegraph* [Exhibit 6].

The third ad, "Don't Let Labour Feed Off Our Money," dealt with the topic of the inefficiencies and losses of the nationalized industries. It suggested that nationalization had not worked in the past, was not likely to work in the future, would starve private industry of investment capital, and was a misguided response to Britain's needs. The ad ran a total of 14 times in 6 newspapers.

The fourth ad, "Don't Let Labour Make Our Farmers Take a Hammering," argued that if Labour won the next election, it would nationalize the lands of all tenant farmers, which was the biggest threat to British farming in centuries. The ad ran a total of 4 times in 3 different newspapers [Exhibit 7].

The fifth and the sixth advertisements had similar headlines, "Don't Let Labour Feed Off Our Money," and discussed the adverse effects of the Labour party's nationalization program. The sixth advertisement, however, brought in the SDP, the Social Democratic party or the Alliance, by asserting that the SDP and the Liberals had in the past cooperated with Labour, and a vote for SDP would in fact be supporting the Labour party's program. These two advertisements were by far the most intensively used messages in the campaign, with ad 5 running 28 times in 17 different newspapers and ad 6 running a total of 52 times in 26 newspapers.

The seventh ad, entitled "Don't Let Labour Carry Britain to Extremes," reminded voters of what happened when Labour won the election for the Greater London Metropolitan Council. In short order, the moderates were ousted and extremist elements took over. The advertisement suggested that a similar fate awaited Great Britain if Labour won the June 1983 general election. The ad ran a total of 8 times in 8 different newspapers.

Exhibit 5

DON'T LET LABOUR PLAY POLITICS WITH YOUR SAVINGS.

Labour's sweeping schemes to harness some £6 billion saved or deposited with the country's financial institutions, have, at last, been revealed.

<u>They will borrow</u> £6 billion out of personal savings–your savings, to finance state investment on terms yet to be explained.

<u>They promise legislation</u> to give union leaders half the seats on the boards that run pension schemes.

<u>They will virtually nationalize</u> the banks. And they will set up a State Investment Bank based on the public's money.

<u>They will take</u>, but what will they return? Money for pension funds has got to be invested with security. Where, under a future Labour government, will that security come from?

Using personal savings for political ends rather than sound business objectives has grave implications for every individual in Britain.

It underlines the tragedy that, despite the failures of nationalization here in Britain and abroad, the Labour party hammer on and on–the lesson still unlearned.

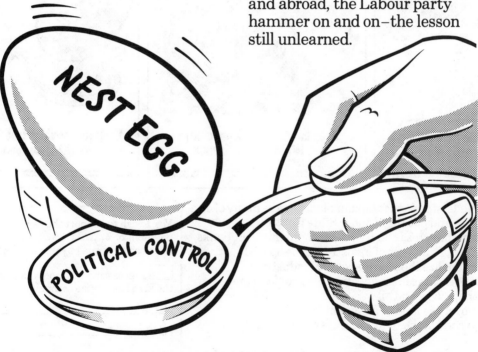

Keep your savings free from politics–say NO to nationalization.

This is one of a series of advertisements by Aims of Industry in support of free enterprise and a society free from unnecessary political control. Aims of Industry, 40 Doughty Street, London, WC1N 2LF. Tel: 01-405 5195

Exhibit 6

WHAT WILL YOU GIVE TO HELP US DEFEAT LABOUR'S PLANS FOR NATIONALIZATION?

DON'T LET LABOUR DICTATE WHAT THE BANK MANAGER DOES WITH YOUR MONEY.

Whatever sort of account you hold, your bank doesn't just put your money in a drawer until you want it back again.

That money is invested, with security. And it's managed by persons responsible to the account holders. In short, to you.

Now Labour plan virtually to nationalize the banks.

More often than not, nationalization produces enormous losses. How safe do you think your money will be under State Control?

And it's not just you who will be affected. Everybody will—because banks are a major source of investment in industry. If the banks are required to use their money politically by a Socialist government the prosperity of all Britain will suffer.

Nationalization has failed in the past. It will fail again. The Labour party cannot alter that fact.

Keep your money free from politics— say NO to nationalization.

This is one of a series of advertisements by Aims of Industry in support of free enterprise and a society free from unnecessary political control. Aims of Industry, 40 Doughty Street, London, WC1N 2LF. Tel: 01-405 5195

DON'T LET LABOUR FEED OFF OUR MONEY.

The losses of nationalized industries are costing the taxpayer billions of pounds.

Yet the Labour party have pledged a sweeping programme of nationalization if they win the next election.

Where will the money come from for this? The answer is from the taxpayer. And from people's savings. And from pension funds.

And private industry will be starved of investment capital.

Where, then, will be our hopes for economic recovery? Where, then, will be our dreams of national prosperity?

Twenty-six miles from Dover lies an answer. The French swept a Socialist government into power with policies of nationalization. They are paying for it dearly now.

Despite the repeated failures of nationalization here and abroad, Labour persists.

It's tragic, and a misguided response to the needs of Britain here and now.

Keep industry free from politics— say NO to nationalization.

This is one of a series of advertisements by Aims of Industry in support of free enterprise and a society free from unnecessary political control. Aims of Industry, 40 Doughty Street, London, WC1N 2LF. Tel: 01-405 5195

DON'T LET LABOUR PLAY POLITICS WITH YOUR SAVINGS.

Labour's sweeping schemes to harness some £6 billion saved or deposited with the country's financial institutions, have, at last, been revealed.

They will borrow £6 billion out of personal savings–your savings, to finance state investment on terms yet to be explained.

They promise legislation to give union leaders half the seats on the boards that run pension schemes.

They will virtually nationalize the banks. And they will set up a State Investment Bank based on the public's money.

They will take, but what will they return? Money for pension funds has got to be invested with security. Where, under a future Labour government, will that security come from?

Using personal savings for political ends rather than sound business objectives has grave implications for every individual in Britain.

It underlines the tragedy that, despite the failures of nationalization here in Britain and abroad, the Labour party hammer on and on–the lesson still unlearned.

Keep your savings free from politics— say NO to nationalization.

This is one of a series of advertisements by Aims of Industry in support of free enterprise and a society free from unnecessary political control. Aims of Industry, 40 Doughty Street, London, WC1N 2LF. Tel: 01-405 5195

Not everyone understands that Labour plans to take many of our most efficient industries and put them under State Control.

The assault is right across the board–on companies, on banks, on pension funds, on land. Few areas of industry will be spared.

Labour will nationalize the pharmaceutical industry.

They will take over firms in engineering, electronics, construction, shipping, road haulage and oil.

They will take over the land of all tenant farmers.

They intend to control the banks and use pension funds for political ends.

In short, they are planning a major attack on free enterprise. One which would see sound business principles shattered by political ideology, and put the savings and security of every individual at grave risk.

So far, this is not fully understood by the British public. That's why we need a great deal of money for a major advertising campaign to put these facts before the British public–before the next election.

We need financial support. Will you support us now–or like the French, choose Socialism and regret it later?

Support the free enterprise campaign

say NO to nationalization.

This is one of a series of advertisements by Aims of Industry in support of free enterprise and a society free from unnecessary political control.
Aims of Industry, 40 Doughty Street, London, WC1N 2LF. Tel: 01-405 5195

Yes, I wish to support the campaign with a payment of £...................plus VAT at 15%.
I enclose a cheque payable to Aims of Industry

☐ Please send me more information about the Free Enterprise campaign.

Name_____

Position held_____

Organisation_____

Address_____

_____

_____

Telephone number_____

Please complete and return this to David Yockney, Deputy Director, Aims of Industry, 40 Doughty St., London, WC1N 2LF. (01-405 5195).

Reg. No. England 457622 VAT Reg. No. 244 6295 51

All financial support is treated confidentially.

Exhibit 7

DON'T LET LABOUR MAKE OUR FARMERS TAKE A HAMMERING.

If Labour win the next election they will nationalize the land of all tenant farmers –34% of all agricultural land.

They will then attack the rest, in line with the policy stated in their Programme, 1982:

"The demands for the public ownership of agricultural land is, and always has been, an integral part of the Labour Party's philosophy."

This is the biggest threat to British farming for centuries.

It is a purely political attack on one of the most efficient farming industries in the world.

You have only to look at the Soviet Union to understand the gravity of the implications: productivity is so low, they must turn to the USA for food.

We cannot afford to let political ideology disrupt a stable and efficient industry.

Yet, tragically, the Labour Party hammer on and on–the lessons of repeated failure, here and abroad, still unlearned.

Keep Farming free from politics– say NO to nationalization.

This is one of a series of advertisements by Aims of Industry in support of free enterprise and a society free from unnecessary political control. Aims of Industry, 40 Doughty Street, London, WC1N 2LF. Tel: 01-405 5195

The eighth ad in the campaign, "Remember the Liberal/Labour Pact?" warns the voters against the new alliance, the Social Democratic party, by reminding them that it was the Liberals who kept the Labour party in power in 1977–78 and thereby supported Labour's initiatives for a closed union shop, nationalization, and other socialist anti-free enterprise measures. The ad ran a total of 7 times in 7 different newspapers [Exhibit 8].

The ninth ad in the campaign was exactly the same as the third, fifth, and sixth ads in the series; the issue itself was dropped while the headline and the picture were kept. The ad ran a total of 2 times in 2 different newspapers.

Media Schedule and Campaign Cost

After some early shots in the *Spectator* at the end of March and the beginning of April, the campaign started in earnest in the week beginning April 18, 1983, and continued right up to the eve of polling day. A total of 121 advertisements were placed in 53 newspapers. It is estimated that 25 million adults were covered by the schedule, and that they would have seen the campaign advertisements on about four occasions. It is also estimated that about 80 percent of A, B, C1, C2 readers had four opportunities to see the advertisements. A graphic representation of the total insertions for different advertisements is presented in Exhibit 9. The campaign was budgeted at £250,000, with approximately £50,000 allocated to the provincial newspapers.

Publication of Special Reports

Four booklets were published during the campaign. The first was "British Farming under Threat of State Land Monopoly," by Professor Donald Denman. This appeared during the first week of the campaign and received extensive coverage in the national, local and agricultural press. In addition, Professor Denman was interviewed on the BBC Scotland agricultural program "Landward" and on Independent Radio News and also on Southern Radio and local programs in Teeside and Belfast.

In the second week of the campaign, Aims published "If Labour Win," by Roger Rosewell, former industrial organizer of the Socialist Workers party. This pointed out that if the GLC *putsch,* which brought in Ken Livingstone after the GLC campaign had been led by a so-called moderate, were repeated in the general election, the electorate could end up with Tony Benn as prime minister. The booklet was advertised in selected newspapers in the national press with the heading, "Don't Let Labour Carry Britain to Extremes."

In the third week Aims published "The Labour Attack on Private Pensions—It's Your Money They're After," by Dryden Gilling-Smith, a leading author on pensions. In the final week, the organization published "Pharmaceutical Nationalization Will Damage Britain," which was an Aims study of the damage Labour's plans could do to this very successful industry. The facts used in this report were provided by the pharmaceutical industry.

Exhibit 8

REMEMBER THE LIBERAL/LABOUR PACT?

The Liberals kept the Socialist government in power from March 1977 to Autumn 1978.

The Liberals therefore helped maintain the closed shop and government by the trade unions. They also helped to keep in existence Socialist policies on industry, nationalization and the economy.

And, of course, SDP leaders have supported Socialism, nationalization and the closed shop over the years when they were leaders of the Labour party, and singing the Red Flag at Labour party conferences.

Are they really going to change now?

Keep industry free from politics- say NO to nationalization.

This is one of a series of advertisements by Aims of Industry in support of free enterprise and a society free from unnecessary political control. Aims of Industry, 40 Doughty Street, London, WC1N 2LF. Tel: 01-405 5195

Exhibit 9

**Aims of Industry Advertising Campaign:
Frequency of Advertisement Insertions**

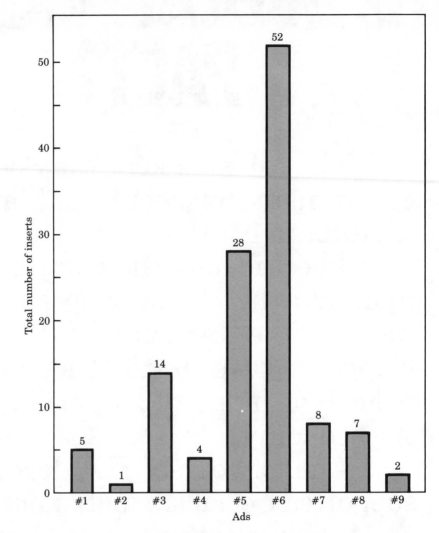

EVALUATION OF CAMPAIGN EFFECTIVENESS

Aims did not undertake any systematic research as to how many people were reached by the campaign and how many were affected by it so as to influence their voting choices. Such research would be very difficult to conduct during the short period in which the campaign was carried out and because of the existence of a host of other messages, both supportive and contradictory, that bombarded at the voters. The evaluation therefore has taken two other courses: (1) opinions of influential leaders who were directly affected by the campaign, and (2) news media coverage.

Leaders' Opinions

It would appear that Aims advertisements and other campaign materials received considerable attention from opinion leaders. The Conservative party expressed strong appreciation for Aims' contribution to the election. The prime minister based no less than three of her speeches on Aims advertisements. The themes were: nationalization had to be paid for from savings, pensions, and future inflation; if elected, a Labour government would move to the Left; and the SDP leadership and the Liberal leadership had helped Labour governments in their nationalization policies.

According to Lord Taylor of Hatfield, vice-president of Aims:

> I believe Aims played a very vital role in the Conservative victory during the 1983 elections. Because of the legal restrictions on the political parties during elections, Aims could start its campaign before CP and it could continue up to the day of voting in the elections. Moreover, we could say many things which the CP either would be reluctant to say or may be couldn't say. For example, we made a great play of the fact that the Socialists proposed to take the savings of people which would be squandered on their stupid schemes.
>
> We also have had information from a wide variety of people who were helping and canvassing in various constituencies.

Another observation was made by Graham Mather, who ran a hard campaign in a Labour constituency and lost by a very narrow margin:

> In my particular constituency, Aims would have an impact largely through the national press advertising, and to a more limited degree through an advertisement they placed in a local free weekly newspaper. The advertisements provided good material that conservative volunteers could use to canvass votes. It also gave me a high recognition factor because the advertisements were advocating the same issues as I was.
>
> In particular, the advertisement dealing with the threat to savings was very important. My constituency had a much higher than average proportion of older people. My ability to refer to a non-Conservative Party source about the threat to people's savings and pension funds posed by Labour's plans added to the credibility of my message.
>
> Surprisingly, Aims's agriculture advertisement also received tremendous attention in my constituency. Although it is primarily an industrial constituency, because of boundary changes, it now includes quite a number of small farms, and tenant farms. It was very helpful for me to use a non-party source and to show that industry-supported campaign organization had identified these threats at an early stage.
>
> Aims booklets were also quite helpful because they provided detailed and convincing arguments on issues that were of concern to my constituents and were identified in the advertisements. The booklets discussed issues in a way in which local candidates could use them to their advantage. Aims crystallized the issues and, in fact, pre-empted them. It was much

later in the campaign that ministers like Norman Fowler, and eventually the Prime Minister, began to refer to the issues identified by Aims as their key issues. I think Aims performed a very useful service by testing the water.

Another perspective is offered by Michael Forsyth, a first-time Conservative MP from Scotland:

> Aims was very effective in helping to brand the Labour party manifesto as being extremist. In particular the use of cartoons and language, direct as it was, was very effective in getting across the idea of the Labour Party's program being in conflict with individual freedom and, more importantly, privacy in such matters as bank accounts and pensions.
>
> As a campaign, Aims' was one amongst the very many inputs to which the electorate was exposed. People tend to switch-off and become very bored. I think Aims' campaign was much more effective than any of the other things that were done by business organizations.

Reaction from the News Media

Aims campaign generated tremendous media coverage. In large part it was due to the well-orchestrated effort of press releases, but equally important, it was the choice of issues, their timing, and the aggressive, and often abrasive, style and content that could not be ignored.

The coverage included major national newspapers, *The Times* and *Sunday Times, Daily Telegraph, Daily Express, Financial Times,* and *The Guardian,* and a host of provincial newspapers.

Aims' press campaign was mentioned on two successive nights in the BBC Newsnight program's election roundup, which included the presenter, John Tusa, holding up Aims' Lib/Lab advertisement and saying, "This appears on Friday and makes no bones about its targets." More than fifty articles appeared in various newspapers commenting on different issues raised by Aims and the potential impact of the Aims campaign on elections.

In an article on the occasion of the Aims 1982 presentation of the National Free Enterprise Awards, the *Times* stated that Aims, which at one time was considered on the right-wing "fringe of political thinking," has moved to "the centre of conventional government wisdom." Describing Aims policies and activities as it turned forty, the *Times* observed:

> Naturally, this has led Aims to become something of a hate figure among the left—a position it positively relishes and encourages. Mr. Ivens says most forcefully that the organization is not party political, even though its defence of the free enterprise system is more likely to find support within the Conservative Party than elsewhere.

The *Times* also gave good coverage to Aims press releases and issues covered in its advertising campaign. For example, in a long article, Lionel Barber (*Times,* May 29, 1982) commented on the joint letter of twenty industrialists, sponsored by the Institute of Directors and Aims of Industry, which attacked the SDP–Liberal Alliance. The *Times* asserted that this campaign would split business. The anti-Labour move, inspired by the right-wing business lobby groups, Aims of Industry, and the Institute of Directors, would undermine the CBI's (Confederation of British Industry) strenuous efforts to remain apolitical and avoid any public endorsement of Mrs. Thatcher and the Conservative party. It would also embarrass the Association of British Chambers of Commerce, which stresses that it too is apolitical. It quoted Michael Ivens as saying that in the election too little attention had been paid to the business policies of the main parties, particularly Labour's proposals to withdraw from the EEC: "Labour's plans for nationalisation are more dangerous than in 1945—they get at the whole base of the economy."

The *Financial Times* (May 13, 1983) carried a story on land nationalization using material from the research and special publications sponsored by Aims and also stated that this issue would be one of the major themes of Aims' advertising campaign.

Reporting on the Aims campaign, the *Daily Telegraph* (June 3, 1983) stated that the intervention was in contrast to the low profile adopted by other organizations, and in some quarters it was felt the tactic might backfire. There was also excellent coverage in *The Guardian* through such articles like "Right-wing Attack on Labour Farm Plan" (May 13, 1983), and (Tribune, December 31, 1982) " The Hard Men Behind the Iron Lady."

EPILOGUE

Although the elections are over, Aims is busy planning a number of activities to ensure that the Conservative party continues to reduce the role of government in all walks of life in England, and to keep people reminded of the potential dangers to their society and way of life if the Labour party were to return to power. Some of the issues under active study for action include these:

- Reduction in the bureaucracies of the London Educational Authority and National Health Authority
- The relationship between local governments and the central government
- Advocacy against amendments of the parent regulations at the UN level
- Reform of EEC's agricultural policy
- The European Parliament — opposing proposals for providing board seats to worker (union) representatives on all corporations incorporated in the EEC

NOTES

1. A personal history of AIMS of Industry, *40 Years Fighting for Free Enterprise, Freedom Needs Free Enterprise,* AIMS of Industry, London, 1982, p. 6.
2. See H. H. Wilson, "Techniques of Pressure—Anti-Nationalization Propaganda in Britain," *Public Opinion Quarterly,* 15: 2 (1951).

Part IV CAMPAIGNS CALLING FOR DIRECT ACTION ON THE PART OF THE PUBLIC

Chapter 7

W. R. GRACE AND COMPANY, NEW YORK:

A SHORT-BURST, HIGH-INTENSITY SATURATION CAMPAIGN IN ADVOCACY ADVERTISING

1978 was the year when President Carter and the U.S. Congress were aiming to revise the tax treatment of capital gains in order to reduce some of the alleged preferential treatment accorded capital gains. The Carter administration considered such a course not only good economic policy, but also defended it on the basis of equity in the treatment of different sources of income. The fact that it made good politics in an inflationary environment did not escape the administration's attention either.

In this essentially indifferent, if not hostile environment, W. R. Grace undertook a communications campaign to educate the public and opinion makers that good economic policy lay not in reducing the preferential treatment of capital gains taxes, but in liberalizing it. In a short four-month campaign of well-coordinated mass media advocacy advertising, press relations, and formal and informal contacts with members of Congress, the company was instrumental in elevating the level of public debate on capital gain taxes to the point where the business viewpoint was given a more intelligent and sympathetic hearing. What started out

---

Research Assistant: Ingrid Schwindt.

as a move to increase capital gains taxes from 49 to 52 percent ended up as a reduction in capital gains taxes from 49 to 28 percent. As a catalyst for such a change, the Grace campaign can take a large measure of credit for its role in the reduction of capital gains taxes.

THE ANTECEDENTS

Grace had undergone major changes in the past two decades. From a company that once earned 93 percent of its income from holdings in Latin America, it had developed into a diversified corporation with about 90 percent of its income from operations in the United States, Canada, and Europe. It had evolved from a trading and shipping company to an international corporation that produces chemicals, engages in coal and oil exploration, and serves the consumer directly in the retailing and restaurant industry. The firm's headquarters are located in New York. In 1977, Grace's sales amounted to over $4 billion, compared to $1.9 billion in 1968. By 1979, those sales had grown to $5.3 billion.

Until it launched its advocacy campaign on the tax issue, Grace's only advertising experience (except for promotion of its goods and services) involved corporate advertising. A major corporate advertising campaign had been launched in April 1976, when company officials realized that the public still perceived Grace as a shipping company, despite the firm's divestment of this line of business in the late 1960s. Grace had hoped to make potential investors aware of its new image with its corporate advertising campaign, the first one in the company's 125-year history. Although many company officials, including the president, had thought corporate advertising was a waste of money prior to this first attempt, the company had budgeted over $1 million directed primarily toward this purpose in 1978.

The Advocacy Campaign's Building Blocks

The following elements of the design and execution of Grace's advocacy campaign are noteworthy:

- Strong involvement of the top management, and especially the executive officer.
- Specificity of the issue. The campaign was built around one issue, capital gains taxes, and offered one solution, reduction in capital gains taxes, which would lead to increased capital formation and economic growth.
- Solid research on the issue preceding the campaign.
- A well-coordinated campaign in which mass media advertising was an integral part of a comprehensive communication effort and different communication instruments and channels were used for specifically targeted audiences.

Investor taxation is a subject that had long concerned J. Peter Grace, chief executive officer of W. R. Grace, who had been largely responsible for the company's change of direction and growth during the last two decades. According to Stephen B. Elliott, Grace's corporate advertising manager:

> As is so often the case, the advocacy campaign was the inspiration of the company's chief executive officer, J. Peter Grace. Early in January of 1978, Mr. Grace became convinced that the 49% federal capital gains tax rate was a "disincentive" to economic growth. And he began to speak out to those audiences he believed would best understand what was a fairly sophisticated argument.
>
> At the beginning of 1978, there was little public debate on the subject of capital gains taxes. In fact, at that time, it was President Carter's intention to *increase* the maximum capital gains tax rate to 52%. No one was yet speaking out against this point of view. They would soon enough.

The formal campaign evolved from Mr. Grace's speeches. It was a saturation campaign, well timed to reach specific audiences and to have the most impact on their opinions at critical decision-making points.

Involvement of the CEO

At Grace's direction, the company's economic department conducted an analysis of how, for instance, the U.S. capital gains structure compared with that of other countries. From this analysis evolved a 49-page study on the theme of capital gains. The covering letter to the 49-page analysis bore Grace's personal signature.

Focus on the Issues

The careful honing of the issue and its timely execution played an important part in the campaign. According to Antonio Navarro, Grace's vice-president of corporate communications, an issue campaign should be addressed in a manner that is specific, clearly conceived, and well documented. Tone must be delicately defined. He further noted:

> The company must have something to say for itself and the public. The issue must not be so self-serving that it repels the reader. And it must not be so slanted toward the public good that it is not believed. What you should have is a reasonable combination: an ad where a legitimate concern of the company can be recognized but, at the same time, where the concept to be sold and the action recommended go beyond the narrow company interests to benefit a broader sector of society . . . or, better yet, the majority of its citizens. . . . Such a combination is difficult, but not impossible to achieve.[1]

Taxation became a major issue in 1978. There was widespread discontent against big government, rising inflation, and concomitant high taxes. One of the manifestations of this discontent was the passage of

Proposition 13 in California, which put a limit on property taxes. It was passed by a landslide on June 16, 1978.[2] During the talks about taxes, the issue of lower capital gains taxes had also been raised in Washington, and for the most part the idea was either viewed negatively or not debated much at all. In proposing to increase capital gains tax rates, President Carter was continuing a trend that had resulted in a doubling of the maximum rate during the past decade. Furthermore, Carter threatened time and again to veto any tax bill that included a reduction in capital gains taxes. Congress also was essentially negative. Only a small group of fiscal conservatives, notably former Congressman William Steiger of Wisconsin, had any interest in the concept of lower capital gains taxes.[3] Even the business community was less than enthusiastic. Most major business organizations, including the Business Roundtable and the Business Council, had chosen *not* to make lower capital gains taxes a high priority in their 1978 lobbying efforts, in effect conceding the "impossibility" of the cause. The only private sector support came from the Securities Industry Association.[4] With the prevailing opinions at the time on capital gains, and with the issue before Congress, J. Peter Grace felt he had to speak out on this subject.

DEVELOPMENT OF A CAMPAIGN STRATEGY

Organization

The company went about its plan in a deliberate and methodical manner. Instead of simply letting an advertising agency plan and implement a campaign, a company task force was formed in the spring of 1978 to carry out the effort. This team included Robert M. Coquillette, executive vice-president, whose responsibilities then included corporate communications and advertising; Leonard Kamsky, vice-president, business economics; Francis D. Flanagan, Washington-based vice-president; and Antonio Navarro, vice-president, corporate communications. With the blessings of Grace, an extensive study of capital gains taxes was undertaken by the company's economic department. The result of the study was, according to the firm, a strong descriptive argument pointing to a high correlation between economic growth and capital gains.

Research

The company's research findings, compiled in its 49-page report, were entitled "The Disincentivization of America." The title highlighted the study's focal point—the impact of investor taxation on capital formation and economic growth. With this report, which contained 22 pages of charts and statistical analyses, Grace attempted to "deliver specific, convincing evidence to Congress in order to counter each of the major challenges then being raised against lower capital gains rates."

The task force was, however, concerned whether such a quantitatively oriented report would have any impact because of the potential difficulties in communicating its findings. According to Navarro:

When we actually started the campaign, we didn't know what to expect. We had a communications effort the likes of which had never been done before, at least to our knowledge. We were speaking quantitatively to audiences that some people said could not begin to understand the complex issues. . . . In fact, a deliberate strategy was to present information to the public and to Congress in a somewhat crude form. One thing I wanted to avoid was any kind of "Madison Avenue" slickness.[5]

The Campaign Theme

The campaign theme chosen was the "Disincentivization of America," which was also the title of the company's economic report on the adverse impact on the U.S. economy of capital gains taxes. The theme contained a three-point reform program:

1. Reduction in the maximum tax on capital gains to its pre-1969 level of 25 percent from the then current maximum of 49.1 percent.
2. An easing of the double taxation of dividends by raising the maximum deduction provided to investors on dividend income to at least $1,000 or $2,000 from the existing $100.
3. An end to the heavy government deficit spending of 1974–1978, which, Grace said, was a major source of inflation.

To maximize the campaign's impact, the task force decided to monitor its progress on a continuous basis so that changes in strategy could be made immediately. To keep currency and timeliness, only newspapers were to be used for print advertisements. According to one company spokesperson: "We did not use magazines, as we were writing ads while the legislative debate was proceeding. We needed a fast-breaking environment, for what we were doing here was developing arguments against those we were facing in legislative debate." Each ad was to be keyed to the specific issues debated at that time in Congress. Readers of the ads were asked to write to their representative on the capital gains tax issue.

The Targeted Audiences

An extensive in-house discussion, with inputs from Mr. Grace, led the task force to select four groups for attention in the campaign: U.S. representatives and senators, chief executives of Fortune's 1000 companies, editors of 665 U.S. newspapers, and the general public. The first three groups were to be reached through a direct mail campaign, while the last group was to be reached through an ad campaign. The mailing to members of Congress was designed to lobby on behalf of investor tax relief. The mailing campaign to chief executives of the Fortune 1000 companies was designed to gain needed support from other corporations. The mailing campaign to 665 major U.S. newspapers was aimed at publicizing the issue. For maximum impact, personal contacts by company representatives with media chiefs and members of Congress were to follow the mailing campaign. The advertising campaign to the general public would attempt to educate Americans on the capital gains tax issue. The company also communicated with 62,000 Grace employees and Grace stockholders, in each case asking them if they thought "our" point of view was worth commenting upon, to write to their representative.

Campaign Costs

The direct media costs of the ad campaign were a little over $300,000. These costs did not include the very substantive cost of time spent by Grace executives. The company did not take any tax deductions for this advertising, since the ads were asking the public to act and as such fell under the IRS guidelines covering indirect lobbying, and therefore were ineligible for deduction. The primary print media were the *Wall Street Journal, Washington Post,* and the *New York Times,* with occasional advertisements appearing in other leading regional newspapers.

NEWSPAPER ADS

Grace had planned initially to run four separate ads. However, as the campaign unfolded and the subject received some controversial publicity on whether a reduction of capital gains taxes would benefit the small investor, Grace ran three additional ads. The last two were based on the company's additional research and stressed that the middle-income investor would benefit most from lowering the capital gains tax rate.

By keying each ad to a specific set of issues that developed, Grace was able to counter President Carter's main arguments for raising capital gains taxes. For example, in early June, the president proclaimed that capital gains received "preferential" treatment, and that the small and middle-income investor would benefit least from a reduction in capital gains taxes. Grace, however, showed that the tax on capital gains was, in fact, higher than on ordinary income, and that the small investor would benefit most from a reduction.

An analysis of Treasury records by Grace researchers showed that the average holding period of a stock was 7.2 years. With that in mind, the researchers looked at what a 7 percent annual inflation rate would do to a wage earner with a capital gain equaling his/her annual salary and taken at the end of a seven-year holding period. It was shown that if in any given year an individual were to make $25,000 in earned income and also make $25,000 from the sale of an asset, the effective real tax rate would be 24.1 percent on the earned income and 57.7 percent on the capital gain, or 2.4 times higher—a clear case of "disincentivization." The same applied to wage earners at the $12,500 salary level, where the capital gains tax rate would be 1.9 times the rate on earned income.

The newspaper ads used in the campaign were developed by the Marschalk Company, the agency which had been producing the corporate advertising for Grace. Marschalk did not play any role in the preparation of the 49-page report or the covering letter. It was essentially the agency's job to take, at the company's bidding, four ideas that appeared in the lengthy memorandum and translate them for public consumption. "What the agency contributed was a way to communicate to the general public the kinds of ideas that obviously we were trying to communicate in a more sophisticated manner to a more sophisticated audience.[6]

Reflecting on the planning stage of the campaign, Stephen B. Elliott, Grace's corporate advertising director, stated: "The process was a team effort. We wanted to incite the reader but at the same time to be absolutely accurate. Our task was to create a deliberate tone which was also dramatic enough to keep the reader's interest. A ticklish balance to maintain."

Each ad was composed of a simple black-and-white layout with a large headline. The text, in smaller print, informed the reader of the company's point of view on the capital gains tax issue and presented a three-point program on the subject. In the lower righthand corner, Grace identified itself as being "One Step Ahead of a Changing World."

The ads were run in the following order:

1. Taxflation—"Let's Stop Taxflation" [Exhibit 1]
2. Underinvestment—"Let's Give Investment a Chance" [Exhibit 2]
3. Decapitalization—"Taxes Up. Productivity Down" [Exhibit 3]
4. Individual investor—"The Small Investor" [Exhibit 4]
5. Composite of the four previous ads—"Taxes Are Taking the Freedom Out of Free Enterprise"
6. Tax loss—"Paying Taxes on a Loss"
7. Long step needed—"The House Taxation Bill"

The goal was to cover the major population centers of the country at the lowest possible cost. Each ad was initially run in the *Wall Street Journal* and the *Washington Post* before it appeared in the other chosen publications.

The first ad appeared in the *Wall Street Journal* and the *Washington Post* on June 9, 1978. It was pegged directly to a previous news article that had quoted a congressional aide as saying some big companies opposed investor tax relief and didn't have their own shareholders' interests at heart. "Well, here's one corporate management that does have its shareholders' interests at heart, especially when taxation and inflation are striking at the very roots of our society and our economy," the ad declared. The ad went on to document how investors pay heavy tax rates on both dividend income and capital gains, and added: "An economy which depends on private capital for growth can't afford to bite the hand that feeds it."

Letters from the public soon began trickling in to Grace's offices supporting the company's stand, even though the company had not asked for a response, but had instead urged readers to write to representatives of Congress.

Exhibit 1

Let's stop taxflation before it brings our economy to a standstill.

A recent issue of a major business publication carried this statement:

"Stockholders be damned: Some big firms oppose tax relief for shareholders.

"Congress has practically ignored a proposal to end 'double taxation' on dividends: once as corporate income, again as dividend income to shareholders."

The article then quoted a congressional committee aide as saying:

"Corporate managements don't have shareholders' interests at heart."

Well, here's one corporate management that does have its shareholders' interests at heart, especially when taxation and inflation are striking at the very roots of our society and our economy.

We believe that shareholder tax relief is urgently needed.

And double taxation of dividends isn't the only problem. For certain tax brackets, capital gains are taxed *three* times.

They're taxed once through the computation of regular taxes. Then, because they're a tax preference item, they're taxed again—this time by reducing the amount of salary or wages eligible for treatment as earned income subject to the advantages of a 50% tax ceiling. Finally, they're taxed a third time through the so-called minimum tax.

To make matters worse, inflation erodes the real value of dividends or capital gains. As a result, much of what the shareholder receives is nothing more than illusion.

Taxflation—the combination of taxation and inflation—is destroying all we work for:

- If income stays the same, purchasing power declines. A dollar put away in 1965 buys only 50¢ today.
- If income keeps pace with inflation, the wage earner finds himself in increasingly higher tax brackets which more than offset gains in purchasing power.

What's our program for stopping taxflation? We suggest you write the Chairman of the House Ways and Means Committee, the Chairman of the Senate Finance Committee, or your elected Senators and Representatives, and tell them to:

1. *Stop the unprecedented government deficit spending which has become a major cause of inflation.*

2. *Stop double taxation of dividends by excluding dividend income from federal taxation—at least to some reasonable annual amount, like $1,000 or $2,000 per taxpayer.*

3. *Reduce short-term capital gains tax to a maximum of 25% and, on a sliding scale, lower that tax rate to zero for assets held over ten years.*

An economy which depends on private capital for growth can't afford to bite the hand that feeds it. And taxflation is doing just that.

Writing your Congressman to stop taxflation is one way to make sure our economy continues to make sense.

One step ahead of a changing world. GRACE

chemicals • natural resources • consumer products

W.R. Grace & Co., 1114 Avenue of the Americas, New York, N.Y. 10036

Exhibit 2

Let's give investment a chance while there's still something left to invest.

The combination of taxes and inflation has all but destroyed the incentive to invest in the American economy. And recent proposals to raise capital gains taxes would further reduce that incentive.

We call this process "disincentivization." And, as you can see from the table below, it's bringing business investment and economic growth to a standstill:

	CAPITAL GAINS TAX RATE		REAL U.S. INVESTMENT GROWTH RATE	REAL GNP GROWTH RATE
	Maximum	Based on $75,000 Gain	Average of 5 Years Ending on Year Shown	Average of 5 Years Ending on Year Shown
1968	25.0%	25.0%	8.0%	4.8%
1973	35.0	27.5	3.9	3.3
1977	49.1	30.6	1.7	2.7
1979	52.5*	36.5*	?	?

*Per the Administration's Tax Reform Proposal

As tax rates on capital gains increase, investment and economic growth rates decline.

At W.R. Grace & Co., we think the best way to trigger new investment is to *reduce* the tax on capital gains.

According to Chase Econometrics Associates, a reduction in the maximum tax rate on capital gains to 25% would free billions of dollars for investment in American business. Enough to create some 440,000 jobs. Enough, in fact, to produce $16 billion in *added* tax revenues by 1985.

What's more, we can further stimulate investment by reducing taxes on dividends.

The present law taxes dividends twice — once as corporate income, then as dividend income to investors. Reducing the taxes on dividend income would free more capital, increase productivity, and create even more jobs.

How can investors — both large and small — get the tax relief they need to keep our economy growing? We suggest you write the Chairman of the House Ways and Means Committee, the Chairman of the Senate Finance Committee, or your elected Senators and Representatives, and tell them to:

1. *Reduce the short-term capital gains tax to a maximum of 25% and, on a sliding scale, lower that tax rate to zero for assets held over ten years.*

2. *Stop double taxation of dividends by excluding dividend income from federal taxation — at least to some reasonable annual amount, like $1,000 or $2,000 per taxpayer.*

3. *Stop unprecedented government deficit spending which has become a major source of inflation.*

An economy which depends on private capital for growth can't afford to bite the hand that feeds it. And increasing taxes on investment dollars would do just that.

Writing your Congressman to lower investor taxes is one way to make sure our economy continues to make sense.

One step ahead of a changing world. **GRACE**

chemicals • natural resources • consumer products

W.R. Grace & Co., 1114 Avenue of the Americas, New York, N.Y. 10036

Exhibit 3

Taxes up. Productivity down. Could we be doing something wrong?

America can no longer afford to ignore the fact that its productivity has fallen behind.

And, as you can see from the table below, compared to other countries, taxes on investor capital have retarded U.S. growth in productivity and in GNP:

| | 1977 Maximum Capital Gains Tax | ECONOMIC PERFORMANCE – 1962-1977 | | |
		Investment as a % of GNP	Average Annual % Increase in Productivity	Average Annual % Increase in Real GNP
Japan	0%	32.0%	8.4%	8.3%
France	0	22.8	5.7	4.8
Netherlands	0	23.7	6.9	4.6
Belgium	0	21.8	6.9	4.0
Germany	0	24.8	5.5	4.0
U.S.	49.1	17.5	2.7	3.5

High productivity requires a high level of investment for plant and equipment. But investment as a percentage of GNP (17.5%) is lower in the U.S. than in any of the other countries shown above.

The reason is simple. An increasing capital gains tax rate has reduced the profitability of equity investment. With inflation compounding the problem, investors have fled the market. The result has been a marked drop in capital formation — especially for small companies:

CAPITAL RAISED BY COMPANIES HAVING A NET WORTH OF UNDER $5 MILLION		
Year	No. of Offerings	Funds Raised ($ in Millions)
1969	698	$1,367
1971	248	551
1973	69	160
1975	4	16
1977	30	118

Between 1969 and 1977, offerings dropped a staggering 95.7%. At W.R.Grace & Co., we think the best way to stimulate investment and productivity is to reduce the tax burden on investors. Yet, recent proposals to raise capital gains taxes would further *reduce* the incentive to invest.

Experts argue that a reduction in the maximum tax rate on capital gains to 25% would free billions of dollars for investment in American business. Enough to create some 440,000 jobs and to produce $16 billion in *added* tax revenues by 1985.

How can investors — both large and small — get the tax relief they need to keep our economy growing? We suggest you write the Chairman of the House Ways and Means Committee, the Chairman of the Senate Finance Committee, or your elected Senators and Representatives, and tell them to:

1. *Reduce the short-term capital gains tax to a maximum of 25% and, on a sliding scale, lower that tax rate to zero for assets held over ten years.*

2. *Stop double taxation of dividends by excluding dividend income from federal taxation — at least to some reasonable annual amount, like $1,000 or $2,000 per taxpayer.*

3. *Stop the unprecedented government deficit spending which has become a major source of inflation.*

An economy which depends on private capital for growth can't afford to bite the hand that feeds it.

Writing your Congressman to lower investor taxes is one way to make sure our economy continues to make sense.

One step ahead of a changing world. **GRACE**

chemicals • natural resources • consumer products

W.R.Grace & Co., 1114 Avenue of the Americas, New York, N.Y. 10036

Exhibit 4

The small investor:
An endangered species.

You don't have to be a millionaire to have a stake in the capital gains tax debate.

Small investors — indeed, all Americans — will be directly affected by this issue. And it's quickly coming to a head.

On the one hand, there are those who favor proposals to reduce the maximum tax rate on capital gains.

The Administration, on the other hand, rejects these proposals, claiming they would bring windfall profits to the rich, while leaving the average American in the lurch.

But the facts are that nearly two-thirds of total capital gains are realized by individuals with adjusted gross incomes of *under $50,000*. At W.R.Grace & Co., it is precisely the small investor we want to support. The individual whose right to property is being threatened by inflation and taxes. Each of these investors would benefit from the proposals, and *all* Americans would share in the other economic benefits which would result from reduced capital gains taxes.

Consider the following:

- Over the past ten years, the U.S. economy has steadily deteriorated, as shown in the table below:

THE DETERIORATING U.S. ECONOMY (5 Years Ending in Year Shown)				% Deterioration 1968-1977
	1968	1973	1977	
Real GNP (Average Annual % Change)	4.8%	3.3%	2.7%	(43.8)%
Unemployment Rate (Average %)	4.2	5.0	6.7	(59.5)
Real Business Investment (Average Annual % Change)	8.0	3.9	1.7	(78.8)
Inflation (Average Annual % Change)	2.6	5.0	7.7	(196.2)
Federal Deficit (Average, $ Billions)	$(4.7)	$(9.9)	$(38.2)	(712.8)
Maximum Capital Gains Tax (Single Year Rate)	25.0%	45.0%	49.1%	(96.4)

- Reversing these economic trends will require vigorous and productive investment in American business.

- Yet, the combination of 50% capital gains tax and 7% inflation has made it exactly 2.4 to 3.1 times tougher now to realize the same real profit from an investment than it was in the mid-sixties.

- This increased investment risk has all but crushed the incentive to invest. So much so that individual participation in equity markets declined 26% between 1968 and 1976. Like an endangered species, the choice for the small investor has been: flight or fight. So far, he has fled.

A deteriorating economy affects *every* American, regardless of income level or tax status.

Our point is simple and obvious. The best way to stimulate investment — and hence the economy as a whole — is to reduce the taxes that are forcing investors to turn away from equity markets.

Some experts say that reducing the maximum capital gains tax rate to 25% would free billions of dollars for productive investment. Enough to create some 440,000 jobs. Enough, in fact, to add $16 billion to federal revenues by 1985.

If you, too, think the small investor is an "endangered species," we urge you to write the Chairman of the House Ways and Means Committee, the Chairman of the Senate Finance Committee, or your elected Senators and Representatives, and tell them to:

1. *Reduce the short-term capital gains tax to a maximum of 25% and, on a sliding scale, lower that tax rate to zero for assets held over 10 years.*

2. *Stop double taxation of dividends by excluding dividend income from federal taxation — at least to some reasonable annual amount, like $1,000 or $2,000 per taxpayer.*

3. *Stop the unprecedented government deficit spending which has become a major source of inflation.*

An economy which depends on private capital for growth can't afford to bite the hand that feeds it. And heavy taxes on investment dollars are doing just that.

Writing your Congressman to lower investor taxes is one way to make sure our economy continues to make sense.

One step ahead of a changing world. **GRACE**
chemicals • natural resources • consumer products

W.R. Grace & Co., 1114 Avenue of the Americas, New York, N.Y. 10036

THE DIRECT MAIL CAMPAIGN

On June 16, 1978, seven days after the first advertisement of the campaign had appeared in the *Wall Street Journal* and the *Washington Post*, Grace mailed its 49-page report, "The Disincentivation of America," to members of Congress. Each report was sent with the covering letter bearing Mr. Grace's signature. Congressman Al Ullman, chairman of the House Ways and Means Committee, was sent a similar letter [Appendix].

The covering letter carried some statistical highlights from the report and explained "how the combination of taxes and inflation, i.e., taxflation, had all but destroyed the incentive for the individual to produce and to invest," and how a significant reduction in the capital gains tax rate would trigger billions of dollars of new investments and ease inflation pressures at minimum cost in federal revenues. In fact, some experts were arguing at the time that a rollback of capital gains taxes to 25 percent would produce $16 billion in added tax revenues by 1985.

A week after this broad mailing, the company ran its second ad. Unlike the first advertisement, the second contained a chart, added after company officials saw that the Grace economic report had been impressive largely because of its profusion of hard-hitting charts. Elliott noted that it was Mr. Grace's idea to include charts in the ads. He admitted that he, as an advertising director, had initially been skeptical as to whether "people would actually respond to charts."

The second ad was headlined: "Let's Give Investment a Chance While There's Still Something Left to Invest." The chart showed that during the previous decade, real growth rates in U.S. investment and in GNP were steadily on the decline, while capital gains tax rates were being increased. The second ad also touched on one of the central points of the campaign, that a reduction in capital gains rates might actually result in higher dollar tax revenues through an unlocking of investment dollars. Grace repeatedly cited a study produced by Chase Econometrics indicating that a rollback of capital gains taxes to 25 percent would produce $16 billion in additional tax revenues by 1985.

Grace was generating a great deal of attention, both for itself and for the tax issue it was raising. As the campaign intensified, so did the public debate over taxation. To gain greater support in Congress, the company began rallying its own executives and managers to the cause, asking them to write their senators and representatives if they agreed with the company's position.

The third ad appeared on June 23, 1978. It was entitled "Taxes Up. Productivity Down. Could We Be Doing Something Wrong?" This ad contained a chart showing that the number of small companies able to raise new investment dollars through the equity market had dramatically declined between 1969 and 1977. The trickle of letters to Grace headquarters was now turning into a small stream. A key breakthrough for the company came on June 26, when the *Wall Street Journal* reprinted Mr. Grace's original letter to Congressman Ullman as a guest article on its editorial page. That same day, President Carter held a press conference in which he said, "But neither they [the American people] nor I will tolerate a plan that provides huge tax windfalls for millionaires and two bits for the average American."[7]

Carter had good reason to be worried. The campaign for lower capital gains taxes was gaining momentum. On July 2, the *Los Angeles Times* reprinted Peter Grace's letter to Ullman as a guest article, and the following day the *New York Daily News* ran a lengthy editorial supporting Grace's position and opposing that of the president. On July 12, the company responded directly to the president's press conference claims with its fourth ad. Under the headline, "The Small Investor: An Endangered Species," Grace argued: "You don't have to be a millionaire to have a stake in the capital gains tax debate. Small investors—indeed, all Americans—will be directly affected by this issue. And it's quickly coming to a head." The ad went on to note Carter's assertion that lower capital gains taxes would bypass the needs of the average American. "But the facts are that nearly two-thirds of total capital gains are realized by individuals with adjusted gross incomes of under $50,000," the ad said. This ad drew by far the greatest public response. Letters of support were now pouring into W. R. Grace's offices at a rate of more than 100 a day. To keep the public interested, Grace ran a fifth ad on July 25—a composite of the four previous ads—under the headline: "Taxes Are Taking the Freedom Out of Free Enterprise."

Press coverage also increased dramatically, as capital gains taxation emerged as a significant public issue. The *Baltimore Sun* ran an article on the Grace campaign headlined "Capital Gains Tax Cut Would Help Little Investors, Too." The *Newark Star-Ledger* published an article under the title: "Grace Warns Nation Is Hurt by Taxflation." All told, at least 106 newspapers in 31 states carried news articles quoting from Mr. Grace's original letter to Congress, from the economic report, or from the company's ads.

THE FIGHT INTENSIFIES—RESULTS

Throughout July, it became increasingly evident that the House was likely to approve at least some reduction in capital gains taxes. By now the company had analyzed its additional research of the Treasury records, and was ready to put up a fight with newly found data which showed that capital gains did not receive "preferential treatment" and would not benefit only large investors, as the administration had been claiming. On August 4, 1978, Grace sent another letter to Congressman Ullman documenting the detrimental impact of high inflation and tax rates on the middle-income taxpayer. "As you know, Mr. Ullman, this is precisely the group which the President claimed would benefit least—about 'two-bits' worth—from a reduction in capital gains taxes," Grace stated.

The ads running subsequently included charts highlighting the company's additional findings. The sixth advertisement appeared on August 24, entitled "Paying Taxes on a Loss Just Doesn't Make Sense." The ad stressed the effect of a 7 percent annual inflation rate on the middle-income taxpayer, and suggested again that this person's capital gains tax rate was dramatically higher when compared with the tax rate for earned income than that of investors in other income brackets.

On August 10, 1978, Grace published a special issue of its company newsletter containing reprints of the first four ads, excerpts from press coverage and letters, as well as an update on the status of the campaign. The news letter was circulated to the company's 62,000 employees, and asked them to write to their representatives if they considered that the company's point of view had merit.

Action in Congress

Congressional mail kept flowing in. Finally, in late August the House approved tax legislation that included a reduction in the maximum capital gains tax rate to 35 percent—both a victory and a disappointment to Mr. Grace, who still sought a maximum 25 percent rate.

With the bill now moving to the Senate, the company made its first direct attempt to rally W. R. Grace shareholders through a dividend stuffer mailed on September 7. In addition, on September 12, Mr. Grace wrote to Senator Russell Long, chairman of the Senate Finance Committee. This letter contained essentially the same information and arguments that had been made to Congressman Ullman on August 4. The letter was followed by the seventh and final ad, the cleverest of the series. In an obvious pun on Long's name, the ad was headlined, "The House Taxation Bill: A Long Step Is Still Needed."

Senator Long was impressed by the economic arguments being put forth by Grace, and reportedly was amused by the headline. From the beginning, there was a widespread feeling that Senator Long would swing to the side of lower capital gains taxation if the supporting data were strong enough to justify such a stand. Indeed, he soon expressed himself in favor of a bigger tax cut than the House bill provided. He and his committee voted to reduce the maximum capital gains tax to 25 percent instead of the 35 percent voted by the House.

On October 15, Congress sent President Carter the Revenue Act of 1978, including a reduction in the maximum capital gains tax rate to 28 percent. The president, despite earlier protestations, signed the bill on November 6, 1978.

How Successful Was the Campaign?

In retrospect, it would appear that the company was successful in bringing about a change in public and congressional opinion in favor of lower capital gains taxes. The arguments were made in an intelligent and dispassionate manner and contained little appeal to emotion. Grace had a clear objective in mind when it launched its "communications" campaign—the reduction of capital gains taxes—and it was not afraid to take a position on the subject. Elliott observed: "We took a particular issue, we knew what we thought about that issue, and we carried through the arguments in every form of communications that we could."

Company officials seemed to be delighted with the results of the campaign. Mr. Grace himself says he learned two lessons from the effort. The first, that "one small voice can, in fact, be heard if you have the right information directed to the right people." The second, that "there seems to be a growing, widespread appreciation that government by itself is not going to provide prosperity. We must look to private capital to do this, and that must be encouraged."

The press coverage of the campaign and the arguments made therein was indeed extensive. Most major nationally known newspapers devoted additional space to endorsing Grace's arguments favoring a reduction in capital gains taxes. Congressional response was also quite good. Over 100 legislators wrote to Grace, some with their own plans for reduction in taxes. Senator Long considered Grace's documentation "fantastic," and said it was Mr. Grace more than any other person who catalyzed the grassroots movement for lower rates. Without this grassroots movement leading to the support of the public and influential officials on the capital gains tax issue, "we would most likely not have succeeded," noted Grace.

The company believes that not only has it been successful in regard to the capital gains tax issue, but also that, through the synergistic effect of corporate advocacy advertising, it has created a positive image for itself, even though this was not the specific objective of the advocacy campaign. Navarro feels that both campaigns "further the cumulative impact of Grace's communications effort [to the institutional and individual investor] in that they reveal the style and rationale behind Grace's management decision process."

The firm, however, is quite cognizant of the efforts made by other companies, groups, and individuals that created the overall environment which contributed to the success of Grace's campaign. States a company official:

> We were not alone in this effort. Had we been alone, we would likely *not* have succeeded. This was the period of Proposition 13. This was the time of Bill Steiger's tax reforms. This was a moment when the public, according to Senator Russell Long, had for the first time in a decade come to the conclusion that capital gains taxes should be taxed differently than they had been. In other words, a grassroots movement had been created.
>
> The fact that the campaign was successful is a tribute to Congress and to the common sense of the American people. They realized from the arguments that were presented that a capital gains tax reduction would spur investment growth and job generation, and perhaps even affect GNP growth.

EPILOGUE

News reports during the June–October 1978 period show a strong relationship between the campaign and the turn of political events in Washington that started with opposition to lower capital gains taxes and ended with the enactment of the tax cut.

Consider the following sequence of events:

On May 5, 1978, G. William Miller, chairman of the Federal Reserve Board, said that "cutting capital gains taxes was not currently the best way to encourage business investment."[8] Miller believed that liberalizing depreciation rules or increasing the investment tax credit would generate more new investment for each dollar of tax revenue lost to the Treasury.

On June 22, 1978, the White House claimed that at this time it was "unthinkable that a Congress controlled by Democrats would approve a cut in capital gains taxes.[9] The Carter administration, however, began to change its mind when Representative James Jones (D., Oklahoma), who had introduced a proposal to cut the maximum tax on capital gains to 35 percent from 49 percent, declared that he had the support of Republicans as well as the majority of Democrats serving on the House Ways and Means Committee for his plan. Thus, in the middle of June the Carter administration was "making a last-minute attempt to keep the House Ways and Means Committee from approving a cut in capital gains taxes.[10] To achieve this, the administration was prepared for a compromise on the tax package it had introduced in January 1978.

Congress, however, failed to act on President Carter's January tax package. Instead, it appeared that the Jones' proposal or the alternative plan submitted by Representative William Steiger, who favored a reduction in capital gains taxes to a maximum of 25 percent, might be passed by Congress. The president warned that he might veto these proposals. Despite these threats and President Carter's assertion on June 26 that a reduction in the capital gains tax rate would "provide huge tax windfalls for millionaires and two bits for the average American,"[11] the administration submitted a new tax package to Congress that included a reduction of the maximum rate on capital gains to 35 percent from 49 percent. The *Wall Street Journal* reported on July 19, 1978: "Jimmy Carter's tax package, limping since the President proposed it in January, was sidelined perhaps for good, and replaced by a measure Mr. Carter has threatened to veto. . . . Yesterday, it was pushed aside by a bill that contains few of Mr. Carter's proposed reforms and would cut the maximum rate on capital gains to 35 percent from 49 percent."[12]

This new plan on capital gains taxes was approved by the House in August and moved to the Senate. The vote in the Senate Finance Committee was 13 to 1 in favor of the Senate's more generous version of capital gains tax reduction. The *Wall Street Journal* stated:

> A substantial cut in capital gains taxes moved one step closer to reality as the Senate Finance Committee voted to exclude 70 percent of long-term gains from regular income tax instead of the current 50 percent . . . along with changes in the minimum and maximum taxes contemplated by the committee, the higher exclusion would reduce the top rate on capital gains to 25 percent, about half the 49 percent under existing law.[13]

President Carter was very upset by the Senate's largesse which, together with other tax reforms, would have reduced federal taxes by $29.3 billion, as compared with the House's overall reduction of $16.3 billion. However, the House bill would have benefitted mostly the relatively wealthy taxpayers, while the Senate's bill included a slightly better break for middle- and low-income families. Representative Al Ullman and Senator Russell Long were thus urged by Mr. Carter to work out a compromise between the Senate's version the House's plan. A compromise was reached on October 23, 1979. According to *Time,* the new law was enacted "to encourage risk-taking investment, [and] taxpayers can exclude completely from their taxable earnings 60 percent, instead of the current 50 percent, of the gains realized from the sale of capital assets; in no case will an investor have to pay more than 28 percent taxes on capital gains, a cut from the present maximum of 49.1 percent."[14]

NOTES

1. "W. R. Grace & Co. Corporate Communications Newly Spiced with a Commitment to Advocacy Advertising," *Madison Avenue,* February 1979, p. 94.
2. "A Backlash to the Tax Revolt," *Business Week,* July 31, 1978, p. 69.
3. Representative Steiger had co-sponsored a tax bill, the Steiger-Jenkins-Hanson Act in Congress. He subsequently defended his stand on capital gains taxes in a letter to the *New York Times,* June 14, 1978. Appendix A, Grace's letter to Ullman, includes an excerpt from Steiger's comments.
4. Ed Colloton, "How to Develop an Advocacy Program," *The Corporate Communications Report: A Bimonthly Newsletter on Current Trends in Investor Relations and Accounting* (New York: Corp. Co. Services, Inc., 112 East 31 St., New York 10016), 10, 3 (January 1979), p. 2.
5. Cited in *Madison Avenue,* p. 94.
6. Ibid., p. 94.
7. "Grace's Battle on Capital Gains—Gains Ground." *Grace News* (in-house publication), special edition, August 1978.
8. "Miller States Position on Capital Gains Taxes," *New York Times,* May 5, 1978, p. 33.
9. John Pierson, "Carter Tax Package May Be Cut in Effort to Stop Paring of Capital Gains Taxes," *Wall Street Journal,* June 22, 1978, p. 6.
10. Ibid.
11. As cited in "Grace's Battle on Capital Gains—Gains Ground," *Grace News.*
12. "Carter Tax Plan Sidelined as House Unit Will Look at Cutting Capital Gains Rate," *Wall Street Journal,* July 19, 1978, p. 3.
13. "Capital Gains Tax Cut Voted by Senate Panel," *Wall Street Journal,* September 22, 1978, p. 3.
14. "Congress Gets the Antitax Message," *Time,* October 23, 1978, pp. 30–31.

APPENDIX

W. R. GRACE & CO.
GRACE PLAZA, 1114 AVENUE OF THE AMERICAS
NEW YORK, N.Y. 10036

J. PETER GRACE
PRESIDENT

June 16, 1978

The Honorable Al Ullman
House of Representatives
Washington, D.C. 20515

Dear Mr. Ullman:

For some time now, I have been concerned about the inability of our economy to generate the investment needed for continued growth.

Most people don't realize it, but investors who bought stocks or bonds in 1968 — and paid taxes on the gains — were left at the end of 1977 with 33¢ to 76¢ of the purchasing power of the original dollar, depending on the type of investment. Those who put their money in savings banks did no better.

These negative returns to investors understandably reduced the incentive to invest. Underinvestment, in turn, results in a slower rate of growth and higher levels of unemployment. Listed below are the disturbing trends in these fundamental sectors of the economy:

Average of Five Years Ending In:	Real Business Investment	Real Gross National Product	Unemployment Rate
	(Annual % change)		(Annual %)
1968	8.0%	4.8%	4.2%
1973	3.9	3.3	5.0
1977	1.7	2.7	6.7

We cannot hope to maintain satisfactory levels of growth and employment without a healthy rate of investment. If our economy is to continue to provide jobs and an adequate income for future generations — if, in short, the structure of our society is to endure — the trend of decelerating investment must be reversed.

Instead, in 1969 the federal government brought about a significant deterioration in the investment climate by a sharp increase in the capital gains tax. This change in the ground rules of our economy was followed by the unfavorable trends in business investment and GNP shown above. At the same time, inflation and the federal deficit began to move to dramatically high levels:

	Maximum Capital Gains Tax Rate	Inflation Average of 5 Years Ending on Year Shown	Federal Deficit Average of 5 Years Ending on Year Shown
			(billions)
1968	25.0%	2.6%	$ (4.7)
1973	45.0	5.0	(9.9)
1977	49.1	7.7	(38.2)
1979	52.5*	?	?

*Per the Administration's Tax Reform Proposal

The doubling of the maximum tax rate on capital gains since 1968 has unquestionably affected the growth of new investment and has thus reduced the country's productivity. Increased productivity and reduced federal spending are two critical factors in the country's desperate fight against inflation. And yet, just this week, we learned from the Bureau of Labor Statistics that, for 1977, productivity declined in 25 of the 66 industries monitored by the Bureau, compared with only 10 declining in 1976.

This unsettling situation was updated with commendable brevity by Representative Steiger in a recent letter to the editors of *The New York Times* defending his bill to reduce taxes on capital gains:

". . . I am also upset about a few other percentages: 6.1 percent unemployment, 10 percent inflation, an 11 percent increase in Federal spending, a 17 percent decline in individual stock market participation since 1969, and a negligible percentage of equity issues for new high-technology firms in recent years."

In the analysis attached to this letter, I try to show in more detail how the combination of taxes and inflation, i.e., taxflation, has all but destroyed the incentive for the individual to produce and to invest. The most productive members of our society—those who strive to get ahead and, in the process, better both themselves and the nation—are pushed by inflation into ever-higher tax brackets, thereby offsetting any real increase in income. To compound the felony, capital gains are taxed at rates which, when the effect of inflation over the years is recognized, border on confiscation.

This, in my view, strikes a body blow to the motivation on which this country was founded and has prospered. It is what I call the "disincentivization" of America.

Chief among these disincentives, as I have already indicated, is the counterproductive taxation of capital gains. A significant reduction in the tax rate on capital gains would trigger billions of dollars of new investment and ease inflationary pressures at a minimum cost in federal revenues. In fact, some experts argue that a rollback of capital gains taxes to 25% would produce $16 billion in *added* tax revenues by 1985. Whether or not one believes such forecasts, the following comparative table for 1962–1977 should make an impression on even the most ardent skeptic:

	Business Investment as a % of GNP	Average Annual % Increase in Productivity	Average Annual % Increase in Real GNP	Maximum Capital Gains Tax
Japan	32.0%	8.4%	8.3%	0
France	22.8	5.7	4.8	0
Netherlands	23.7	6.9	4.6	0
Belgium	21.8	6.9	4.0	0
Germany	24.8	5.5	4.0	0
United States	17.5	2.7	3.5	49.1%

I believe it would be difficult to ascribe fully to coincidence the fact that some of the fastest growing economies in the world are also those where the investor is not penalized for his courage and success.

To provide the tax relief that the productive elements of our country need to keep our economy growing, we suggest that legislation and administrative measures be adopted to bring about the following:

1. Reduce the short-term capital gains tax to a maximum of 25% and, on a sliding scale, lower that tax rate to zero for assets held over ten years. An alternative to reach substantially the same results would be the indexing of the tax structure to adjust for inflation, as done successfully by other countries such as Canada. When considering changes in the taxation of capital gains, it would be well to bear in mind that capital gains represent only about 3% of total federal tax revenues.
2. Stop double taxation of dividends by excluding dividend income from federal taxation—at least to some reasonable annual amount, like $1,000 or $2,000 per taxpayer.
3. Stop unprecedented government deficit spending, which has become a major source of inflation.

I urge that Congress recognize and correct the disincentives to savings and investments implicit in our tax system. The opponents of capitalism call for increased government participation in the economy. What is really needed is the restoration of incentive. And *that,* in my opinion, is the proper prerogative of government.

Sincerely,

J Peter Grace

Attachment

Chapter 8   # KAISER ALUMINUM AND CHEMICAL CORPORATION, OAKLAND, CA:

USE OF ADVOCACY ADVERTISING TO COUNTERACT ALLEGED INACCURACIES AND BIAS IN NEWS REPORTING AND TO SEEK ACCESS TO BROADCAST MEDIA

On July 24, 1981, ABC premiered a new late-night news and public affairs program called "Viewpoint." The concept behind "Viewpoint" was to give critics of television news a forum for rebuttal. Among the three stories included in the first program, one concerned Kaiser Aluminum and dealt with an episode aired on April 3, 1980, in ABC's primetime news magazine, "20/20." Kaiser Aluminum had been waging an intense battle in the courts, the federal regulatory agencies, and in the news media, charging "20/20" coverage to be inaccurate and biased, and seeking adequate response and rebuttal time in a suitable forum.

The "Viewpoint" program did provide a format and response time, which Kaiser Aluminum considered both appropriate and satisfactory, thus bringing to a close at least one battle between the television net-

Research Assistant: Mohamed Nabil Allam.

works and large corporations. Kaiser Aluminum had also sought paid access on television and radio to air its views or encourage discussion of issues deemed important in terms of public policy. Many companies, notably Mobil, have sought similar access, with only limited success. Some other companies, such as Illinois Power, have tried other means. They have produced and distributed a response tape to achieve similar ends. The Kaiser Aluminum case provides a broad perspective on the nature of the problems, views of opposing parties to the conflict, and most important, how differently the public interest is defined by various groups that call for methods which are diametrically opposed.

KAISER ALUMINUM—THE CORPORATION

Kaiser Aluminum and Chemical Corporation is headquartered in Oakland, California. In 1982, Kaiser Aluminum ranked 136th on the *Fortune* list of 500 largest industrial corporations, with annual sales of $3.2 billion and 26,250 employees worldwide. It is a diversified international company with major operations in aluminum, industrial and agricultural chemicals, fertilizers, refractories, real estate, and international trading. Kaiser Aluminum operates throughout the world, and has especially large mining operations in Australia and manufacturing facilities in Western Europe.

Cornell C. Maier, Kaiser Aluminum's chairman of the board and chief executive officer, is a man of strong convictions and eclectic personality. He joined the company in 1946, immediately after graduating in electrical engineering from the University of California. In 1971 he was named general manager of the corporation, with direct responsibility for the day-to-day operations of the company's diversified and multinational activities. He was elevated to the position of CEO in July 1978, and was elected chairman of the board in 1978.

Because of Maier, Kaiser Aluminum is heavily involved in community-related projects both at the local and national level. He attributes his crusading interest in social responsibility and free enterprise to his upbringing. Born of poor parents 57 years ago in Herried, South Dakota, a village of 500, he was reared by his mother, who scratched out a living for Cornell and his sister by working as a grocery and department store clerk. He served in the Army Air Corps during World War II.

Maier spends a considerable amount of time speaking out on public issues. For example, he came out forcefully against Proposition 13 (even while encouraging a group of employees who wished to take an opposite stand to voice their views.) His rationale for his position: The amendment was the wrong way to achieve necessary lower taxation because it would hurt young people and the poor.

KAISER ALUMINUM'S FORAY INTO ISSUE ADVERTISING

Prior to 1979, Kaiser Aluminum's corporate advertising used the traditional approach of building corporate image. The company does not engage in direct consumer advertising, since it sells its products solely to industrial users. However, in 1979 it decided to devote its advertising resources to a public discussion of issues. According to Ronald Rhody, corporate vice-president for public relations and advertising:

> We started in our plant city communities. Our objective was to draw people's attention to those issues we felt to be of specific concern to those communities. The issues ranged from the need for adequate power to the more general discussion as to why profits are necessary, or to the sort of social and economic contributions we make to the community. We used only newspapers in 1979. [Exhibits 1–2]

The following year the company added radio, using local employees to deliver the corporate message [Exhibit 3]. This proved to be quite successful. At this time, the company also decided on a broader regional approach and began to experiment with television. Pre- and post-market tests in five cities showed that television would be a powerful medium to raise public awareness on those issues, and would also cause some positive change in terms of attitudes toward those issues.

Advocacy Commercials for TV

Kaiser Aluminum developed three commercials, and following network procedures submitted them to the three networks for their approval. The proposed commercials dealt with three issues:

1. Need for a national energy plan
2. The burden of unnecessary government red tape
3. The threat to the free enterprise system

The action line in all these commercials was: "Whatever your views, let your elected representative know now."

All the three networks (CBS, NBC, ABC) immediately rejected the commercials on the basis of network policies, which precluded airing of controversial issues through paid commercials. CBS asserted that public affairs were "the sole province of CBS News, where trained journalists examine and present all sides." NBC claimed that these commercials "would clearly violate the Fairness Doctrine by opening a discussion on an issue of public importance." ABC claimed that Kaiser Aluminum "commercials employ scare tactics—they imply government is acting as big brother." ABC also stated that it could not accept "commercials saying write to your congressman—commercials should use a positive approach."

Among the arguments used by the networks in rejecting commercials that could be considered controversial were these:

1. The FCC (Federal Communications Commission) Fairness Doctrine prohibits the acceptance of controversial commercials, because the networks might then have to provide free "reply time" to advocates of opposing viewpoints.

Exhibit 1

HOW FREE IS FREE ENTERPRISE?

It's not as free as it used to be.

But it's still too free for some people. Like some in government who are convinced big business is bad just because it's big. They're proposing new laws that would go farther than ever in breaking up private businesses.

They propose this in the face of studies that show "breaking up" industries could *increase*, not decrease, prices to the consumer. And if government control like this can happen to big business, it can happen to any size business.

There's one way to help stop it. That's if people, one by one, stand up and defend the system. You can keep free enterprise from joining the list of a vanishing species. Write, send telegrams, mail letters to Washington. You can keep free enterprise free.

"If we weren't free to control our business from mine to market, we could be out of business."

J. T. Owen is plant manager of our San Leandro Electrical Products facility. In the Bay Area, Kaiser Aluminum & Chemical Corporation employs an average of 1,900 people and has an approximate annual payroll of $67 million.

We make no apologies. We certainly are an example of big business. We produce aluminum from bauxite that was mined by Kaiser Aluminum, refined by Kaiser Aluminum, and cast into ingots by Kaiser Aluminum.

Only by being involved in every step of the process from mine to market can we afford to produce the quality aluminum we require,

exactly when we need it, at a reasonable price our customers can pay. It's a clear case of a bigger company being able to do a better job.

KAISER ALUMINUM & CHEMICAL CORPORATION
KAISER CENTER,
300 LAKESIDE DRIVE, OAKLAND, CA 94643

PLANT CITY NEWSPAPER

This ad is reproduced at approximately one-half original size; each message has been "localized" for the community in which it appears.

Exhibit 2

BUREAUCRAZY.

The red tape it takes to run America has gotten completely out of hand. In 1977, the Commission on Federal Paperwork reported that an estimated $100 *billion* is spent annually by the nation on federal paperwork alone. That's $100 billion of *your* money.

We can't argue over fundamental requirements the government makes for health, safety and environmental controls. But enough is enough.

We've got to do something about excessive red tape, bureaucracy, and over-regulation now. One by one, we've got to speak out against the staggering waste of time, people, and money. Send telegrams, mail letters to Washington. We've gotten out of worse binds than this before.

"Sometimes I think we're in the paper business instead of the refractories business."

Jack Elmer is manager of magnesia operations for the Moss Landing and Natividad plants where Kaiser Aluminum & Chemical Corporation's Refractories Division employs an average of 450 people and has an approximate annual payroll of $10.8 million.

Kaiser Aluminum & Chemical Corporation is suffering from the same red tape all American businesses face. In 1976, in testimony given to the Commission on Federal Paperwork, our company revealed that we spent $4.5 million on federal paperwork alone. And that figure has continued to rise since that time.

We're fighting back, though. Every time we find federal government regulations we think are unfair or unnecessary, we notify the proper authorities. We let them know we're working for our country, our community, our employees and our shareholders. Not for the federal government.

KAISER REFRACTORIES
A DIVISION OF KAISER ALUMINUM & CHEMICAL CORPORATION KAISER CENTER, 300 LAKESIDE DRIVE. OAKLAND, CA 94643

PLANT CITY NEWSPAPER

This ad is reproduced at approximately one-half original size; each message has been "localized" for the community in which it appears.

Exhibit 3

RADIO COMMERCIALS

GENERAL THEME

ANNCR: At Kaiser Aluminum, we believe that only people make things happen. One person *can* make a difference. You.

SONG: VERSE I You've got dreams
You've got things to say
You've got a plan for living
Your own special way
You've got ideas
And whatever you do
Only *you* make the difference
The difference is *you*.

VERSE II You've got rainbows
You've got wings to fly
There's a smile on your face
And a gleam in your eye
You've got a world
And your own point of view
And everyday the difference is you.

ANNCR: At Kaiser Aluminum we know that in everything we do, one person can make a difference.

ECONOMIC IMPACT *

ANNCR: At Kaiser Aluminum we believe that only people make things happen. One person *can* make a difference. You.

SONG: VERSE I only

ANNCR: Here in the Bay Area the people at Kaiser Aluminum are making a difference. They're helping provide America with one of its most energy-saving materials. Aluminum. And in salaries alone, they're contributing over 67 million dollars a year in economic power to the Bay Area. We can strengthen the opportunities for all of us if each of us gets more involved in our country, our community and our work.
One person can make a difference.

SINGERS & MUSIC: Only you make the difference
The difference is you.

TAG: KAISER ALUMINUM

ENERGY

ANNCR: At Kaiser Aluminum, we believe that only people make things happen. One person *can* make a difference. You.

SONG: VERSE I only

ANNCR: Even with a problem as big as the energy crisis you can make a difference. We don't mean just by saving energy, although that helps. We think people should speak up for a strong national energy policy. One that uses *all* available resources, from coal to solar power. But we'll only get it if people, one by one, demand it. Let your elected representatives know where you stand on energy.

SINGERS & MUSIC: Only you make the difference
The difference is you.

TAG: KAISER ALUMINUM

* *This radio commercial has been "localized" for the community in which it is broadcast.*

RED TAPE

ANNCR: At Kaiser Aluminum, we believe that only people make things happen. One person *can* make a difference. You.

SONG VERSE I only

ANNCR: You can make a bigger difference than you might think. Take the problem of government red tape. In 1977, federal paperwork alone cost Americans 100 billion dollars, which we all pay for. Much of that is waste. You can help reduce waste in government and unnecessary regulation. Write your elected representatives and demand change. One person can make a difference.

SINGERS & MUSIC: Only you make the difference
The difference is you.

TAG: KAISER ALUMINUM

FREE ENTERPRISE

ANNCR: At Kaiser Aluminum, we believe that only people make things happen. One person *can* make a difference. You.

SONG: VERSE I only

ANNCR: Will the government regulate our economic lives even more in the future? It's really up to you. If you see free enterprise in trouble . . . If you think America requires a diversity of business, both big and small . . . If you think that our economy will do better with less government interference, then write to your elected representatives and let them know. You can help keep free enterprise free.
One person can make a difference. You.

SINGERS & MUSIC: Only you make the difference
The difference is you.

TAG: KAISER ALUMINUM

INFLATION

ANNCR: At Kaiser Aluminum, we believe that only people make things happen. One person *can* make a difference. You.

SONG: VERSE I only

ANNCR: This country has no bigger problem than inflation. And we're all responsible. But even with a problem this big, one person can make a difference. We can start by making sure that we spend our money wisely. That our elected representatives not spend more than the government takes in. That business and labor abide by price and wage guidelines. Write your elected representatives and demand action.
One person can make a difference.

SINGERS & MUSIC: Only you make the difference
The difference is you.

TAG: KAISER ALUMINUM

2. The public is best served by the networks' coverage of these controversial issues through their news and public affairs programming.
3. If issue advertising were allowed by the networks, those with the most money to spend would control the agenda of public debate.[1]

An official from one network proclaimed, "Where do these guys get off thinking they have a right to express an opinion on these points?" Is it then the networks alone who would have both the "right" and the "power" to decide who has rights to speak and what subjects may be discussed? Kaiser Aluminum decided to pursue the answer to this question. The company noted that Fred Friendly, author and formerly with CBS, once stated: "What the American people don't know can kill them."[2]

Kaiser Aluminum Goes Public with Its Complaints against the Networks

Kaiser Aluminum was not satisfied with this response. Ron Rhody observed:

> The more we thought about it, the unfairness of all this, the more determined we became. We weren't going to let silence indicate acceptance or resignation, but instead of going to the regulatory agency or pleading our case in court, we decided to go directly to the American people.

Under the headline "Can a Corporation Speak Its Mind in Public?" Kaiser Aluminum raised the issue in a full-page ad [Exhibit 4] in the *New York Times, Washington Post, Los Angeles Times, San Francisco Chronicle, Oakland Tribune,* and *Wall Street Journal* in order to bring the matter before the people.

The ads reprinted the entire text of each message rejected by the networks so that people could decide for themselves the extent to which these commercials could be considered "objectionable" or "controversial." The closing lines of the ad copy urged readers who believed that a free exchange of ideas was important to write to their elected representatives or Kaiser Aluminum.

Public response to Kaiser Aluminum, to the television networks, to the FCC, and to members of Congress was overwhelmingly opposed to a system where a corporation's television advertising could sell a product or a service but not an idea. The responses came from people all over America and from all walks of life. Over 96 percent of the responses received by Kaiser Aluminum supported the company's position. In addition, 40 members of Congress responded favorably to Kaiser Aluminum's advertisement. Furthermore, a House Subcommittee on Communications, chaired by Congressman Lionel Van Deerlin of San Diego, held hearings on the issue of denial of access to television in mid-November 1979. Among those who testified was Cornell C. Maier, Kaiser's CEO and chairman of the board.

Kaiser Aluminum's public relations department began responding

Exhibit 4

Can a corporation speak its mind in public?

Not long ago, the Supreme Court ruled that corporations are entitled to the right of free speech.

However, when Kaiser Aluminum & Chemical Corporation tried to exercise this right recently, it was denied by the three major television networks.

Our idea was to produce three commercials drawing attention to issues we felt were of major concern to the people of America. One was about energy. The others dealt with free enterprise and governmental red tape. (The commercials are shown below). We believed at the time that we were exercising our right to speak our mind. We were willing to pay for the air time to run these commercials. And we clearly identified these messages as opinions of our company.

But when we submitted them to the networks, the commercials were rejected. The networks said they would refuse to air them. Not because they were untrue, misleading, or in any way inaccurate. But simply because they were controversial or not acceptable material.

One network cited the "Fairness Doctrine" as a reason for rejecting the commercials. This doctrine was formulated by the Federal Communications Commission (FCC) to insure that a fair balance of opinion is presented on television. We believe, too, that television should present a fair balance of opinion. Even ours.

There is no doubt that television is one of the most powerful media in operation today. And we believe that access to this medium must be kept free and open.

If you believe a free exchange of ideas is as important now as it's ever been, write your elected representatives or write us at Kaiser Aluminum, Room #776 KB, 300 Lakeside Drive, Oakland, California 94643. Let your voice be heard.

Announcer
Is free enterprise an endangered species? How much government regulation is enough? Is business bad just because it's big? Or does a country like ours require a diversity of business—both big and small?

Will excessive control over big business lead to control over all our business?

The answers are up to you.

Whatever your views let your elected representatives know.

People, one by one, need to speak up now. You can help keep free enterprise free.

A message from Kaiser Aluminum.

One person can make a difference.

Announcer
Some people are calling the energy crisis a hoax. Others say that at the rate we're using up our oil reserves we'll be down to our last drop in our children's lifetime.

Whoever's right, one thing is clear. America needs an energy plan for the future *now*. One that uses all resources available from coal and nuclear power to solar.

But we're only going to get it if people, one by one, demand it.

Whatever your views, let your elected representatives know now.

There's not much we can do when the light goes out.

A message from Kaiser Aluminum.

One person can make a difference.

Official Voices (Overlapping)
Applications should be filled out in triplicate . . .
Forms should be returned by the 19th or penalty charges . . .
The Bureau requires all permits to . . .
The Department must be notified . . .
Send one copy to . . .

Announcer
It's red tape. In 1977, America spent $100 billion on federal paperwork alone. And in the end we *all* pay for it.

But if people, one by one, start speaking out, we can begin untangling America's knottiest problem.

A message from Kaiser Aluminum.

One person can make a difference.

KAISER ALUMINUM
& CHEMICAL CORPORATION

SPECIAL ISSUE NEWSPAPER

to inquiries from the press at 2 A.M. on the day the newspaper ads appeared, and the phones rang almost constantly for the next four days. The two major wire services—Associated Press and United Press International—carried stories which appeared in newspapers and were carried on radio stations across the country. In short, the story created quite a splash everywhere, and NBC and ABC both decided to rethink their positions and finally accepted the commercials, whereas CBS still refused to run them.[3]

To reinforce its message, the company also took ads in major national newspapers thanking the readers of those newspapers for their support of Kaiser Aluminum's position [Exhibit 5]. These full-page advertisements appeared on August 2, 1980, in the *Washington Post, Los Angeles Times, New York Times, San Francisco Chronicle, Oakland Tribune,* and *Wall Street Journal,* national edition.

The issues raised by Kaiser Aluminum in its ad "Can a Corporation Speak Its Mind in Public" are indeed quite important, but they are neither as simple nor as straightforward as the ad makes them appear. For example:

1. Are we talking about the right of corporations to speak on public issues, or the right of corporations to force a particular medium to accept its messages, against its will or policy?
2. If it is a question of free exchange of ideas, the inevitable question that follows is what ideas should be discussed, and whose viewpoints should be promoted?
3. When is a message merely "informational" in content, discussing or encouraging the discussion of an issue, and when does it become advocacy advertising—advancing a particular viewpoint directly, by stating it as such, or indirectly, by omitting and downplaying alternative viewpoints?
4. In case there are any ground rules necessary or desirable to promote orderly debate, who should establish those ground rules?

The limited scope of this case and space constraints prevent a serious discussion of how these issues might be best resolved. The problem of airtime scarcity has also been greatly ameliorated because of the tremendous growth of cable TV and the willingness of independent TV stations, including network affiliates, to accept issue-advocacy commercials. For example, it is now possible for a company to put together a package through which it can reach all 50 major markets with advocacy commercials on television.

There is little doubt that Kaiser Aluminum's efforts and those of other companies are having a positive effect in opening up all types of media to advocacy advertising as more and more companies launch similar campaigns. Nevertheless, the fundamental problems still remain, and will continue to remain, even if network access to corporate advocacy commercials becomes more liberal. In many ways the problems could become even more aggravating because issues that are now in the theoretical domain, such as the establishment of ground rules, would become all too real. Each solution would have its own vested interest, and a constituency to push it.

Exhibit 5

Thank you, Post readers, for defending free speech.

Can a corporation speak its mind in public?

Not long ago, the Supreme Court ruled that corporations are entitled to the right of free speech.

However, when Kaiser Aluminum & Chemical Corporation tried to exercise this right recently, it was denied by the three major television networks.

Our idea was to produce three commercials drawing attention to issues we felt were of major concern to the people of America. One was about energy. The others dealt with free enterprise, and governmental red tape. (The commercials are shown below). We believed at the time that we were exercising our right to speak our mind. We were willing to pay for the air time to run these commercials. And we clearly identified these messages as opinions of our company.

But when we submitted them to the networks, the commercials were rejected. The networks said they would refuse to air them. Not because they were untrue, misleading, or in any way inaccurate. But simply because they were controversial or not acceptable material.

One network cited the "Fairness Doctrine" as a reason for rejecting the commercials. This doctrine was formulated by the Federal Communications Commission (FCC) to insure that a fair balance of opinion is presented on television. We believe, too, that television should present a fair balance of opinion. Even ours.

There is no doubt that television is one of the most powerful media in operation today. And we believe that access to this medium must be kept free and open.

If you believe a free exchange of ideas is as important now as it's ever been, write your elected representatives or write us at Kaiser Aluminum, Room #776 KB, 300 Lakeside Drive, Oakland, California 94643. Let your voice be heard.

Announcer
Is free enterprise an endangered species? How much government regulation is enough? Is business bad just because it's big? Or does a country like ours require a diversity of business—both big and small?

Will excessive control over big business lead to control over all our business?

The answers are up to you.

Whatever your views let your elected representatives know.

People, one by one, need to speak up now. You can help keep free enterprise free.

A message from Kaiser Aluminum.
One person can make a difference.

Announcer
Some people are calling the energy crisis a hoax. Others say that at the rate we're using up our oil reserves we'll be down to our last drop in our children's lifetime.

Whoever's right, one thing is clear. America needs an energy plan for the future *now*. One that uses all resources available from coal and nuclear power to solar.

But we're only going to get it if people, one by one, demand it.

Whatever your views, let your elected representatives know now.

There's not much we can do when the light goes out.

A message from Kaiser Aluminum.
One person can make a difference.

Official Voices (Overlapping)
Applications should be filled out in triplicate...
Forms should be returned by the 19th or penalty charges...
The Bureau requires all permits to...
The Department must be notified...
Send one copy to...

Announcer
It's red tape. In 1977, America spent $100 billion on federal paperwork alone. And in the end we *all* pay for it.

But if people, one by one, start speaking out, we can begin untangling America's knottiest problem.

A message from Kaiser Aluminum.
One person can make a difference.

About one month ago in this newspaper we ran the ad you see on the left. We ran it because we had been denied air time by the three major TV networks to run paid commercials about important issues. We felt our right of free speech had been denied, and we wanted to raise the issue with you.

Essentially, the commercials we wanted to run encouraged people to let their elected representatives know their views on key issues.

Frankly, we did not expect the reaction we received. We'd been hearing for so long that the people of America had lost faith in our institutions, that to see hundreds of people take the time to write to us—and their elected representatives—was a startling and eye-opening experience.

It's not often you see average citizens stand up to defend the rights of others   particularly large companies like ours. But you did, and we thank you. Of the many letters we received, 96% supported our effort to get our messages aired.

Not only did people express their belief and faith in free speech, they also clearly expressed their concern about the free exchange of ideas in our society.

Your reaction to our message is being felt right now in Washington. Congressmen and government officials have taken notice of the issue of fair access to television and are discussing its merits.

We realize that the problems facing America are complex. And that there is a wide range of ideas on how to solve them. We know that your views and our views won't always coincide. But we want to express our gratitude to you for defending our right to be heard. We still believe that a free exchange of ideas is the essence of a democratic society. And obviously, so do you.

For several years we've had a guiding principle in our company. It says, "One person can make a difference." Thanks again for making a difference.

Kaiser Aluminum & Chemical Corporation has received over 1200 letters about this issue. The letters have come from all areas of America, from people in all walks of life. If you, too, believe in a free exchange of ideas in the broadcast media, and if you haven't written, please write your elected representatives and let them know. You can make a difference.

KAISER ALUMINUM & CHEMICAL CORPORATION
300 LAKESIDE DRIVE, OAKLAND, CA 94643

KAISER ALUMINUM'S RATIONALE

Kaiser Aluminum's objective for its issue advertising is not so much to discuss the pros and cons of an issue as to raise the issue and let people think about it. This approach is quite different from the one used by SmithKline Beckman and LTV.

According to Rhody:

> We want to draw attention to issues that we think are important to the company, to our shareholders, to our employees, and to the people in the communities in which we operate. We want to invite people to think about those issues. We are trying to create involvement with issues.

The Decision-Making Process

The decision-making process at Kaiser Aluminum for selecting issues is quite informal, although very intensive. It is primarily confined to Rhody and his senior staff in the public relations department. The first step is to poll various regional public affairs vice-presidents to elicit their views on the issues the company ought to be treating in its advertisements. Rhody and two members of his staff would winnow the responses to the five or six issues they considered most important.

Kaiser Aluminum does not engage in systematic environmental scanning or issue tracking. Nor does it undertake any field opinion surveys to measure public attitudes toward various social issues. Instead, management treats issues which it knows to be of concern to its company's operations and the communities where it has its plants. The company deals with those issues as they emerge or as they become full blown.

The smaller list is then presented to the CEO, who chooses three or four for treatment in the ad campaign. Maier, the CEO, is not involved in the day-to-day management of the program, nor does he approve final ad copy. Apart from approving the original program, however, he also retains a veto in dropping an issue from the campaign, and has occasionally exercised his judgment to do so. Kaiser Aluminum is a very unusual company in that its outside directors play a review and analysis role on its advocacy advertising program through the board's Corporate Conduct Committee, which is comprised solely of outside directors.

In the initial stages, there was little internal dissension about the program. However, as the company began to deal with issues that generated high visibility and some controversy, there was a degree of internal questioning on the part of both line and staff managers as to whether or not this was a smart thing for the company to do. Was it smart to associate with ideas which might prove to be controversial? "Those objections were heard, of course," observes Rhody. "However, we continued with the program."

The 1980–81 Campaigns

During 1980, Kaiser Aluminum selected three issues for ad treatment. They were energy conservation, youth jobs, and the vote. The issues selected for treatment in 1981 were minority youth unemployment, energy policy, and productivity. [Illustrative ads are presented in Exhibits 6–9.]

The primary emphasis in media was on television, followed by radio and newspapers. However, Rhody observed that the choice of audience, and therefore the selection of media, depended largely on the issue being treated in the ad copy. For example, in the 1981 program, Kaiser Aluminum was treating three issues: minority youth unemployment, productivity, and energy policy. With the minority youth unemployment issue, it was principally trying to reach businesspeople in key metropolitan areas. The energy policy message was directed to opinion makers in Kaiser Aluminum's plant areas and in Washington, DC. Those were the principal target audiences for the advertisement. Finally, the productivity message was directed at employees and at the general public, including social activists.

The company did not develop any audience profiles to provide a closer match between viewers/readers and the audience it wanted to reach with its messages, except to buy time on those programs that provided some measure of audience fit. With one minor exception, all the media budget in 1981 was allocated to television. The exception was one ad that ran in a limited number of business publications. The company used network-owned and -operated stations in key markets, plus network affiliates, Turner's Cable News Network, and independents.

MEASURING CAMPAIGN EFFECTIVENESS

In October–November 1980, a tracking study was done to evaluate the effectiveness of Kaiser Aluminum's 1980 television issue advertising program. The two-stage tracking study was undertaken by The Research Alliance of San Francisco, and involved telephone interviews of 400 men and women in Los Angeles and Washington, DC, two of the cities exposed to the Kaiser Aluminum campaign. The objective of the study was "to observe the degree to which this [1980] campaign increased awareness of Kaiser Aluminum and Chemical Corporation and of its advertising."

The first wave was conducted between October 1 and October 10, 1980, and the second wave took place between November 3 and November 12, 1980. The study found that consumer belief in the importance of the issues addressed in the Kaiser Aluminum campaign was at an extremely high level prior to the campaign, and the likelihood of considering them "very" or "extremely" important did not increase significantly during the period studied.

Exhibit 6

TELEVISION/"YOUTH EMPLOYMENT"

1. **Announcer:**
   Young people looking for work need all the help they can get.

2. **Announcer:**
   They need our help. And government's too.

3. **Announcer:**
   Write your elected representatives with your views on providing jobs for young people.

4. **Announcer:**
   And do unto others as others did unto you. Start someone out.

5. **Jingle:**
   The difference is you.

6. **Announcer:**
   For more ideas on youth jobs call 800-648-5000.

Exhibit 7

NEWSPAPER "VOTE" ADVERTISEMENT

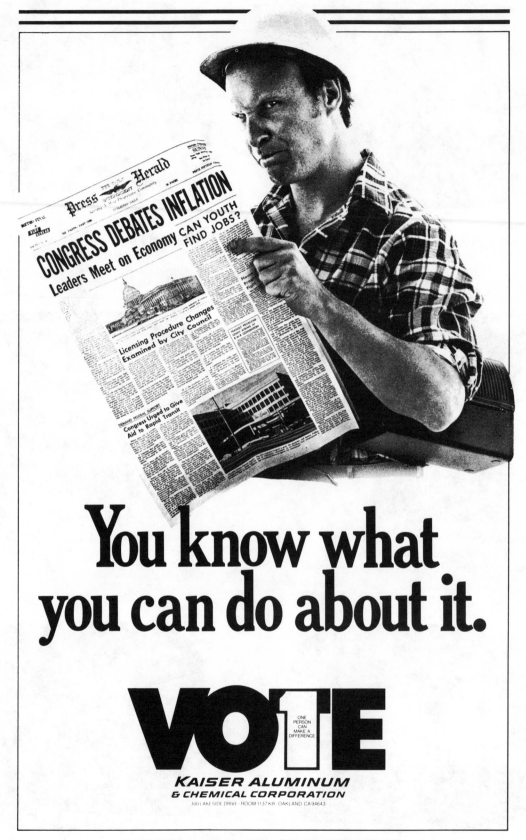

METROPOLITAN AREAS & PLANT CITIES
This is a scaled down version of a full page ad.

Exhibit 8

NEWSPAPER "PRODUCTIVITY" ADVERTISEMENT

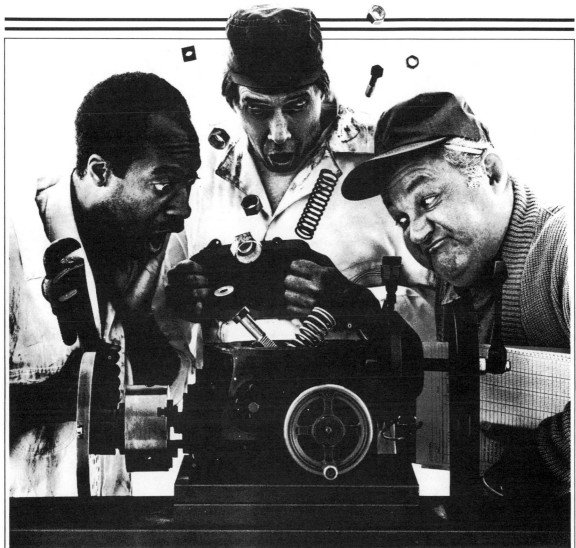

Is America equipped for the future?

Machinery that keeps America going is in danger of running down and taking our economy with it.

How did this ever happen?

America's productivity growth rate used to be the envy of the world. However, in the last decade, the growth of productivity in the U.S. has been significantly lower than in industrial countries like Japan, Germany and France.

Low levels of investment in new plants and equipment have been the major factor in this decline. Existing tax policies coupled with high inflation rates have severely discouraged investment. Excessive and unnecessary government regulation have forced industry to spend much of its available capital in nonproductive investments.

What's to be done?

First, existing tax policies must be revised to promote savings and investment for modernization of the nation's industrial plants and equipment. The tax laws must be revised to permit more rapid capital recovery through accelerated depreciation. Second, excessive and unnecessary government regulation must be eliminated. We've got to get government out of business before it puts business out of business. Third, a new spirit of cooperation between government, labor and business must be established and directed towards increasing the nation's productivity.

Write your elected representatives now and let them know how you stand. We can't get our productivity up with equipment that is running down.

ONE PERSON CAN MAKE A DIFFERENCE

KAISER ALUMINUM & CHEMICAL CORPORATION
300 LAKESIDE DRIVE · ROOM 1137 KB · OAKLAND CA 94643

METROPOLITAN AREAS
This is a scaled down version of a full page ad

Exhibit 9

RADIO COMMERCIALS

VOTE

OPEN ANNCR: At Kaiser Aluminum we believe that wherever you stand on the issues there's one thing you've got to do about it. Vote.

MUSIC: You've got dreams
You've got things to say
You've got a plan for living
Your own special way
You've got ideas and whatever you do
Only you make a difference
The difference is you.

MAN 1: To me it has made a difference and I'll continue to vote.

MAN 2: If you don't go out and vote for these guys you can't squawk about what they do.

MAN 3: What strikes me as stupid is being apathetic!

MAN 4: The people are the ones that made the United States.

WOMAN 1: I feel that I make a difference and as soon as you lose that concept of yourself as an individual who counts, it's all gone.

MAN 5: Sometimes you don't win with them, but they count.

MAN 6: But if you didn't vote, it would be worse. You can bet on that.

MUSIC: Only you make the difference
The difference is you.

ENERGY/SUMMER

OPEN ANNCR: At Kaiser Aluminum, we believe it's time to stop talking about saving energy. It's time to do it.

MUSIC: Song

MAN 1: I'm recycling today bottles and cans.

MAN 2: This is the primary thing that we all ought to be doing. Conserving!

MAN 3: Well, I turned down the thermostat on my water heater.

WOMAN 1: I'm using my air conditioning less, opening up the windows to let more of the fresh air in.

MAN 4: I turned down the heat in my swimming pool and I also joined the carpool. That's two pools.

MAN 5: I ride my bicycle.

WOMAN 2: Ride my moped around.

MAN 6: You ought to be pumping your legs and getting exercise instead of pumping the pump and paying for the gas.

MUSIC: Only you make the difference
The difference is you.

ENERGY/WINTER

OPEN ANNCR: At Kaiser Aluminum, we believe it's time to stop talking about saving energy. It's time to do it.

MUSIC: Song

MAN 1: I'm recycling today bottles and cans.

MAN 2: This is the primary thing that we all ought to be doing. Conserving!

WOMAN 1: I've cut down a lot on my washing. I mean I'm probably doing the same amount, but I'm not doing it as often.

MAN 3: I just hooked up my wood stove yesterday.

WOMAN 2: I could have driven today but I took the bus.

WOMAN 3: I keep my furnace down. I wear a sweater always around the house.

MAN 4: My pipes run outside my house so I put insulation on them to keep them from giving off all their heat to the wind.

WOMAN 4: Keep moving; you won't be so cold.

MUSIC: Only you make the difference
The difference is you.

YOUTH

OPEN ANNCR: At Kaiser Aluminum we believe you can do something to help America's youth unemployment problem.   Start someone out.

MUSIC: Song

MAN 1: We're employers. We decided to help these kids with jobs.

MAN 2: Kids aren't the stereotype you hear so much about. They really do want work. They do want to learn.

WOMAN 1: They had an opportunity to get into the work environment and see how different it actually was from the school environment.

MAN 3: I could see their experiences. I could see their growth.

WOMAN 2: I felt wonderful about it. It's been a long time since I've trained anyone.

MAN 3: Well, you know if you've got a business, I mean, you've just *got* to hire these kids.

MUSIC: Only you make the difference
The difference is you.

"ECONOMIC IMPACT" BAY AREA

OPEN ANNCR: At Kaiser Aluminum we believe only people make things happen. One person can make a difference. You.

MUSIC: Song

DONUT: The people who work at Kaiser Aluminum in the Bay Area are making a difference. How much of a difference? Last year, about $79 million. That's the amount of money we contributed to local economies in salaries and wages alone. It doesn't include taxes and purchases from local businesses. When we do well everybody around here profits from it. One company does make a difference.

MUSIC: Only you make the difference
The difference is you

Among the other major findings of the study were these:

1. Awareness of advertising directed toward these issues was high before the campaign (84 percent, energy conservation; 69 percent, voting rights; and 44 percent, youth employment). Awareness of ads to encourage voting increased significantly overall during the time of the Kaiser Aluminum campaign, as did awareness of youth employment advertising in Los Angeles. The likelihood of associating private corporations with energy conservation declined in Washington during the period studied. While not statistically significant, the likelihood of associating corporations with voting and youth employment advertising was strengthened during the period the Kaiser Aluminum campaign aired.
2. Relative to awareness of advertising by aluminum companies, there were no significant shifts for Kaiser Aluminum during the campaign. Awareness of Alcoa advertising increased significantly in Los Angeles during the period, however.
3. Among those who recalled seeing or hearing Kaiser Aluminum advertising after the exposure of the campaign, relatively few mentioned content that could be identified with the specific advertisements. A handful (2 to 3 percent) associated the content of the specific Kaiser Aluminum ads with Alcoa. However, despite the low content recall, the likelihood of associating advertising by Kaiser Aluminum with the television medium jumped over 20 percentage points in both markets studied.

The study concluded that "All things considered, the campaign's effect on awareness of Kaiser Aluminum or its advertising was minimal." Although there was no statistical evidence, the study advanced the following explanations for the low awareness of Kaiser Aluminum's advertising:

1. The campaign was run during a period when frequent and intense messages concerning social issues were being aimed at consumers from a variety of sources—that period immediately preceding the presidential elections.
2. Other social indicators (such as Yankelovich Monitor and actual voting turnouts), indicate that despite belief in the seriousness of issues such as energy conservation, many consumers had become unwilling to accept responsibility for constructive action to alleviate the problems.
3. It was possible that consumers were weary of the personal sacrifices (such as driving less, turning down thermostats) necessary to make a significant impact on energy conservation, and of the personal cutbacks caused by inflation to the point that they were less receptive to additional messages implying a need for personal involvement, such as "The Difference Is You."

Finally, the study observed that significant upward shifts in awareness of, or concern about, issues that were already at extremely high levels (such as belief in the importance of energy conservation or awareness of major aluminum companies, both of which received scores in the

80 to 90 percent range) were nearly impossible to achieve in short periods of time. "Thus, the relatively minor progress noted for this campaign should *not* necessarily be considered a condemnation of it, but an indication of the difficulty of becoming an agent of social change in a complex and possibly unresponsive climate."

OTHER AVENUES OF REACHING THE PUBLIC AND OPINION MAKERS

A major effort in support of its advocacy advertising program is Kaiser Aluminum's publication of a magazine called *At Issue*. It is directed at a fairly specific, but quite large, audience of educated and informed people. In the publication, the company tries to set out both sides of the issue as fairly as possible, and then present its own position.

Kaiser Aluminum disseminates its issues program through all its internal and external channels. For instance, each year it publishes a major piece on its issues program, including reprints of the storyboards or the ads, and the schedule of where these ads or commercials will air, capped by an explanation of what the company is trying to do and why. This publication is circulated to Kaiser Aluminum employees, customers, and to plant state congressional delegations.

At least once a year, a story dealing with the issues program is published in the shareholders' quarterly report. Shareholders are invited to write and ask for copies of the ads or storyboards.

Issue advertising is also discussed in key corporate speeches delivered by senior executives, which in turn receive further media exposure. The company has no systematic effort to reach editors with the advertising material. Editors, however, are a key contact point for the *At Issue* publication.

ABC'S "20/20" PROGRAM AND THE ALUMINUM WIRE CONTROVERSY

The Incident

On April 3, 1980, ABC's program "20/20" reported a segment entitled "Hot Wire." In this segment, ABC reporter Geraldo Rivera investigated Kaiser Aluminum and Chemical Corporation's marketing of aluminum housing wire. Excerpts from the transcripts of the aired segment are given below:[4]

GERALDO RIVERA: On the day after Christmas, 1978, Dan and Peggy Johnson lost their 15-month-old daughter, Janet, when fire gutted their home in Columbus, Georgia.

FIREMAN: The crib was totally cremated, and the fire was contained to that one particular room. The cause of the fire was an aluminum wiring connection.

ROBERT KELLEY: It's like a time bomb built within your walls.

RIVERA: What government investigator Kelley called a time bomb was marketed to the unsuspecting American public as a safe, inexpensive alternative to traditional copper wiring.

The most critical problems are in construction done between 1965 and 1973. It was during that period that these homes in Fort Worth, Texas, and more than two million others across the country were wired with aluminum. The extent of the problem is indicated by hundreds of sworn affidavits received by the Federal Consumer Protection Safety Commission. The affidavits tell of serious problems, of overheating, and of fires caused as a result of faulty aluminum wiring.

1965 to 1973 was a time of escalating copper prices. And builders and developers flocked to a product that saved them between 50 and 300 dollars per home. The aluminum industry went to great lengths to equate its product with copper. Consider this 1964 Kaiser Aluminum marketing plan obtained by ABC News. It instructs sales personnel to use the approach that aluminum, quote, is just the same as copper.

But aluminum wiring is not just the same as copper. Far from it. When used in electrical work, aluminum is an unforgiving metal, one which must be used only with great care and with specially designed connectors. Our investigation uncovered the fact that between 1965 and '73 that did not happen.

During that period, aluminum was attached to wall plugs with steel screws designed for copper wire. But aluminum and steel have different rates of expansion, and the combination of the two metals can lead to a loose connection. The aluminum oxidizes when it loosens, preventing the electrical current from passing through. Heat builds up, and any flammable material next to an overheating wall receptacle can ignite and start a fire.

We know now that Kaiser Aluminum at least knew their product needed special handling. These confidential documents, for example, were obtained by "20/20." They show that way back in the 1950's, Kaiser Aluminum conducted extensive lab tests on aluminum wire. Their own scientific evidence warned that aluminum wire was very hazardous unless certain procedures were taken to prevent oxidation. But when the company put the product on the market, they failed to adequately warn the public of the hazard. And apparently they later withheld results of their tests from the government.

Here, for example, a Westinghouse engineer is so upset by aluminum wire failures, he told an industry meeting in 1972, quote, I feel it's time we must honestly and sincerely face up to the problem before the United States Government, Congress, Nader, before any federally subsidized agency begins to investigate this area.

So how exactly did the product get on the market in the first place? The National Electric Code, for instance, for eight years allowed the use of aluminum wiring without proper precautions. The code has since been revised.

The drafting of the National Electric Code was admittedly influenced by Kaiser Aluminum's representative on the code-writing panel, a man named R. S. Keith. But was he concerned with product safety or just with company profits?

In this 1967 speech to his sales staff, Mr. Keith told how he regarded the code as a, quote, political instrument, one whose provisions could either be good, i.e., profitable to Kaiser Aluminum, or bad, meaning unprofitable.[5]

Kaiser Aluminum has refused repeated requests for an interview. Mr. Keith has since retired.

Kaiser Aluminum executives had refused to be interviewed for the program *unless* they were given a reasonable amount of time and their comments aired without prior editing. "20/20" did not accept those preconditions.

According to Ronald Rhody, vice-president of Kaiser Aluminum, the corporate executives declined to be interviewed because the interview was viewed as a "trial by television" where the network was the judge and jury, while the interviewee was the accused.

Kaiser Aluminum's Response

"Those accusations are blatantly wrong, and we are not allowing them to go unchallenged," declared Cornell Maier, chairman and chief executive officer of Kaiser Aluminum. Kaiser Aluminum accused ABC of biased reporting and charged that the program had ignored information and expert opinion showing that aluminum wire was safe when used properly.

Immediately after Rivera's report was aired, Kaiser Aluminum demanded that an unedited rebuttal to the segment be shown on "20/20." Kaiser Aluminum also threatened to file a petition of complaint with the Federal Communications Commission (FCC) and sue ABC for libel. On June 2, 1980, Kaiser Aluminum ran a full-page newspaper advertisement in major newspapers protesting what is termed "trial by television" [Exhibit 10].[6]

Kaiser Aluminum requested the House Subcommittee on Communications to hold congressional hearings on the practice of "trial by television." The company contacted various senators and representatives from

Exhibit 10

Trial by Television

The American system of justice is founded on a simple principle: The accused has the right to be fairly heard in his own defense, and to confront and cross examine his accuser.

This principle, more than any other, defines the difference between freedom and tyranny.

Yet today, here in America, charges are aired before tens of millions of people without fair opportunity for the accused to respond.

They call it "investigative" television journalism. We call it "Trial by Television."

Much of investigative television journalism is solid and responsible reporting—but much is not. Many producers of "news magazine" programs too frequently select story segments with their minds already made up about the points they want to make. Then they proceed to select the facts and quotes which support their case. "Interview" opportunities are sometimes provided the "accused." But the edited "interview" format puts the producer (i.e. the accuser) in full control of deciding what portions, and how much of, the accused's defense the public will be allowed to see.

Rarely does this result in balanced and objective coverage.

The television production team becomes the accuser, judge, and jury. With no real recourse for the accused to get a fair hearing in the court of public opinion. Yet the viewing public is led to believe that the coverage is balanced and objective. This is a deceptive and very dangerous practice.

"Trial by Television," like the kangaroo courts and star chambers of old,

needs to be examined. If we decide, as a society, that we are going to try issues, individuals, and institutions on television, then some way must be found to introduce fairness and balance.

Here's what we're doing about it.

Recently, Kaiser Aluminum was the victim of grossly misleading and inaccurate statements on a segment of ABC's "20/20" program. On its "20/20" segment of Thursday, April 3, the announcer accused aluminum house wiring of being unsafe, and Kaiser Aluminum of intentionally marketing an unsafe product. These accusations are blatantly wrong.

Although we were offered an opportunity to be "interviewed," "20/20" reserved the privilege of editing any part of our statement. Any defense we might have made would be subject to their sophisticated editing techniques, and to their commentary. Since it was evident to us that the producers had already formed their opinions, we declined their offer. How can a defense be fair if it is subject to censorship by the accuser?

We have been advised by many to ignore the "20/20" attack on the basis that you can't fight the network, and to prevent further harassment. We will not allow ourselves to be maligned or misrepresented by any group—even television.

Here is what we are doing:
1. We have demanded a satisfactory retraction from ABC-TV.
2. We are asking the Federal Communications Commission, under their "Personal Attack" doctrine, to order ABC-TV to provide us with time and

facilities to present our side of the story to the same size audience in a prime time segment.
3. We have asked Congressman Lionel Van Deerlin (D-California), Chairman of the House Sub-Committee on Communications to consider Congressional hearings to examine the implications of this increasingly insidious and dangerous practice.

Here's what you can do about it.

Unfortunately, not all victims of "Trial by Television" have the resources to defend themselves, as we are trying to do. Their only defense is you.

If you believe the rights of the accused to fairly defend themselves are more important than sensational attempts to increase TV ratings; if you believe the right of the public to get balanced and objective information on issues of importance is as important as it has ever been, please speak out and let your elected representatives know.

America was conceived to prevent tyranny by providing checks on the power of any institution. Today, a new power is dispensing its own brand of justice—television. There's only one check against it. You.

If you are upset by the unfairness of "Trial by Television," write your elected representatives, or us at Kaiser Aluminum, Room 1137KB, Lakeside Drive, Oakland, CA 94643.

KAISER ALUMINUM & CHEMICAL CORPORATION

One person can make a difference

the districts where it had operations, and asked them to urge the chairman of the subcommittee to institute the hearings. It also took steps to initiate a libel suit against ABC, and laid the groundwork for an action before the FCC based on the personal attack rule.[7]

The Repercussion

Kaiser Aluminum's action—legal, legislative, and in the news media—generated tremendous press on the issue, and for once put so much heat on ABC[8] that the network felt obliged to respond.[9]

Media Coverage

Despite its willingness to provide response time, a spokesman for ABC stated: "ABC stands by the story. . . . We just want to be fair. This doesn't restrict us from updating the story." But he declined to elaborate other than for "fairness sake" why the network would air a non-network-produced response, which no network seemed ever to have done before, and which most broadcast journalists viewed as a demoralizing precedent. Usually, if there was a reporting error or unfair treatment that a network believed should be rectified, a network aired a correction or apology.

ABC's willingness to provide response time was not necessarily popular with its reporters and news personnel. Several ABC newsmen said they found their network's move disheartening. "All something like this can do is harm our credibility," a producer said. Another wondered why, if Mr. Rivera's story warranted such extreme action, he apparently wasn't censored by the network news executives.[10]

ABC responded to Kaiser Aluminum's demands by initially agreeing to air a 4-minute unedited videotaped rebuttal on a December 1980 airing of "20/20." Kaiser Aluminum dropped its threat of a libel suit and petition to the FCC. Subsequently, ABC did not air the Kaiser Aluminum rebuttal in December 1980, and kept pushing the air date back. In February 1981, ABC stated it believed that its late-night "Nightline" program would be a "more appropriate" forum for Kaiser Aluminum's rebuttal. Kaiser Aluminum vehemently disagreed with ABC's decision, filed a complaint with the FCC, and initiated a defamation suit charging slander against ABC in California.

Kaiser Aluminum was then asked by ABC to appear on its prime-time news program "Viewpoint," to be inaugurated July 24, 1981. The concept behind "Viewpoint" was to give critics of television news a forum for rebuttal. Kaiser Aluminum accepted the invitation to appear. The program was hosted by anchorman Ted Koppel. The segment opened with an introduction by Ted Koppel, followed by a showing of a shortened version of the "Hot Wire" segment. This was followed by an airing of Kaiser Aluminum's rebuttal film, which included, among others, interviews with housing wire experts. Excerpts from the "Viewpoint" segment dealing with the aluminum wire story follow:[11]

STEVE HUTCHCRAFT: I'm Steve Hutchcraft of Kaiser Aluminum. On April 3rd, ABC's "20/20" devoted a segment to aluminum residential wiring systems. Since that show was aired, a great many people, including many of my fellow employees, have asked questions: Is aluminum wiring really unsafe? Did we, Kaiser Aluminum, really put a product, a hazardous product, in the marketplace? And did we cover that event up?

My answer to these people and to all those questions was no, a very definite no.

GEORGE FLACH: I'm the chief electrical inspector for the City of New Orleans. I've been in this position now for about 25 years.

WOMAN: What's your professional opinion of aluminum wiring?

FLACH: We think that aluminum wiring is just as safe as copper when it's properly installed.

WOMAN: Would you live in a house with aluminum wiring?

FLACH: I have aluminum wiring in my house. You didn't know that.

HUTCHCRAFT: "20/20" also implied that Kaiser Aluminum did not do adequate research-and-development work prior to introducing aluminum branch-circuit-sized wiring to the marketplace. That also is not true. These sizes of aluminum electrical conductors were first developed in the 1950s, and tested for some ten years prior to their introduction to the U.S. market in the mid-1960s.

DR. T. R. PRITCHETT (Kaiser Aluminum VP, metals research): We've tested a number of different types of wiring devices, electrical conductors, including both copper and aluminum. And by making these up with the prescribed methods for the trade, the connections are completely satisfactory.

HUTCHCRAFT: "20/20" also alleged that aluminum connected to steel binding screws and a connecting device gets progressively worse with time, causing a heat buildup when the aluminum wire oxidizes. This was referred to as a ticking time bomb.

Dr. Harry Gatos of the Massachusetts Institute of Technology, and a consultant for Kaiser Aluminum, is one of the world's foremost experts on metallurgy.

DR. GATOS: The statement that aluminum wiring is a ticking time bomb is not only technically unfounded, but also it is misleading and outright irresponsible.

HUTCHCRAFT: "20/20" also accused Kaiser Aluminum of admittedly influencing the National Electric Code. That's just ridiculous.

JOSEPH McPARTLAND (McGraw-Hill publisher): As an electrical engineer who has worked 30 years in this industry, I travel the country continually, analyzing and reporting on electrical work. I've authored over 20 books on electrical design and installation and am the author of the *National Electric Code Handbook*.

I think "20/20's" presentation on aluminum wiring was very unbalanced. It was very distorted. It was very inaccurate. It was extremely prejudicial. It obviously came from the conclusion beforehand that there was something wrong with aluminum wire. They started from the conclusion and then constructed and fabricated a presentation that made their point, in spite of the fact that it was totally unreal.

So that it is really a sorry spectacle to see the type of irreponsible reporting that is done on something on which the verdict is already in. It is a safe product, properly applied, just as any product can be safe only when properly applied.

HUTCHCRAFT: We have no idea why "20/20" chose to single out Kaiser Aluminum. We do know, however, that it is unthinkable that our company would market a product that would put human life in jeopardy.

Following a showing of Kaiser Aluminum's rebuttal film, Ted Koppel turned to a live discussion of the issues involved with ABC's Geraldo Rivera and Kaiser Aluminum's Steve Hutchcraft, both of whom were present at the ABC studios. An excerpted version of the exchange that took place appears below:

HUTCHCRAFT: Ted, it is not correct that we refused to appear on the broadcast. We agreed to appear live on the broadcast so that any comments we make—made—on the broadcast, could not be taken out of context or edited. We were turned down in that request.

KOPPEL: Geraldo, I have to turn to you, then, and ask why that request was not honored. Why could they not appear live?

RIVERA: For us to turn our journalistic responsibility—that is, the preparation of our programs in a fair, impartial, and objective way—over to the people who are the subjects of the stories would be, in my mind, to surrender, to abdicate the responsibility of responsible journalists to people whose interest it is, presumably, to give not only their side of the story, but perhaps not to allow a fair hearing for the other sides. We can't make them the journalists, no more than they can make us the electrical engineers.

KOPPEL: Why would it have been any more unreasonable to do that on "20/20" the first time around than what we're doing right now? I don't think we've abdicated our journalistic responsibility by having Mr. Hutchcraft here with you.

HUTCHCRAFT: That was our point, Ted. We were prepared to do just this type of thing then.

RIVERA: We gave—we gave Kaiser Aluminum several invitations to sit down for a formal interview. If we did an interview with the President of the United States, with the Secretary General of the United Nations, with any chief of state, head of state, anybody, and we were doing a broadcast—would we give Colonel Qaddafi, for instance, the right to edit a program in which he was the subject?

KOPPEL: No. But, Geraldo, forgive me. We're not talking about the right to edit. If I understand Mr. Hutchcraft correctly, what Kaiser Aluminum was asking for was the opportunity to appear live so that there would be no opportunity to edit.

RIVERA: What they wanted was ten minutes of unedited air time to give their specific point of view. . . . Kaiser Aluminum did not want to appear in the studio to respond to what we reported. Kaiser Aluminum wanted to control the content of that investigative piece. Kaiser Aluminum wanted to engineer a piece that reflected their corporation's point of view. For us to cede our responsibility to them, which indeed is what they asked for, regardless of the context they put it in right now, would be for us to abdicate our responsibility as responsible journalists.

HUTCHCRAFT: That is incorrect. As I stated before, we agreed to come on the program live, and enter into a debate very similar to the type of debate that we have here right now. And we were not given the opportunity to do so.

KOPPEL: All right. Let's get to the subject at hand. What Geraldo was charging in his report was that aluminum wiring could be dangerous when it is not properly installed.

In the response it seemed to me that you were not addressing that so much as the notion of aluminum wiring being safe, when it is properly installed.

Isn't that the whole issue here?

HUTCHCRAFT: I think the whole issue here is that electricity is a dangerous commodity. Any electrical wiring system, when either not installed properly or when abused or overloaded, is potentially dangerous. There's in excess of two million electrical fires in people's homes every year in the United States. Only a small handful of those involve aluminum wiring. And I am very happy to say that there has not been one instance in the long time that we have been producing aluminum electrical products that a Kaiser Aluminum electrical product has been found to be a cause of the fire.

I think that's a fantastic safety record, one that I'm proud of, and one that our company is proud of. And I really don't understand what this whole issue is all about.

RIVERA: In 1974 the then-almost-brand-new Federal Consumer Product Safety Commission branded branch-circuit aluminum wiring an imminent consumer hazard. They branded that their number one safety priority. They have recently—well, a test concluded in 1979—commissioned a test done by the prestigious Franklin Institute, a private testing operation. Franklin Institute did that test over a period of one year at a cost of one million dollars. They found that aluminum branch-circuit wiring was 55 times more likely to fail—that is, either overheat or, indeed, result in fire—than copper wiring, the same type of copper wiring.

KOPPEL: But you've heard what Mr. Hutchcraft just said. No fires involving Kaiser Aluminum products. Do you have evidence to contradict that? Because if not, that sounds like a pretty compelling piece of material.

RIVERA: Kaiser Aluminum recently settled a case brought in Long Island in which a parent and child were killed in a tragic residential fire. They settled the case for $300,000.

So, when Mr. Hutchcraft says that the issue has never been resolved by trial, one reason is that Kaiser Aluminum settled before the issue would go to the jury.

I think that there's a great deal of insincerity in his allegation.

HUTCHCRAFT: I think there's absolutely no insincerity in our comment. Kaiser Aluminum is, as I have said before, proud of our safety record on aluminum products—on all of our electrical aluminum products.

What we have missed here tonight is to talk about the issue of trial-by-television, and the fact that the format of the trial-by-television, where the accuser is also the judge, the jury, and the prosecutor, and the only way that the defense can make its point is through the voice of the accuser—this does not lend itself to truth and balance. This is of great concern. It's a concern that the American public should be concerned about. It's a concern that the media should be concerned about.

I would hate to see, and I think it would be a shame, if the American public were to lose confidence in the legitimate TV news, one of the most powerful forces in the country today.

RIVERA: Kaiser Aluminum has painted this as an issue between Kaiser Aluminum on the one hand and "20/20" on the other. That is a very inaccurate reflection of exactly what is going on here. What we were reporting was testimony before the Congress of the United States. What we were reporting was the opinion of the Federal Consumer Product Safety Commission. What we were reporting was the consensus of the electrical contracting, the construction, and the aluminum industries as it exists today.

It's not Kaiser Aluminum against the media. It's Kaiser Aluminum against the facts in this case. They had an opportunity, a fair opportunity to appear on that broadcast, and they chose to reject, to ignore that request, and then react after the broadcast aired.

Epilogue

The reaction of the media to the "Viewpoint" program was best summed up by Ed Bark of the *Dallas Morning News,* who said: "Regardless of who's telling the truth, Kaiser Aluminum certainly was given a fair shot on Viewpoint."[12] Following the airing of "Viewpoint," Kaiser Aluminum declared itself satisfied. Subsequently, the company did not pursue its slander suit and withdrew its FCC complaint.

NOTES

1. *At Issue: Access to Television,* a publication of Kaiser Aluminum & Kaiser Corporation (Oakland, CA, August 1980), p. 18.
2. Ibid.
3. "Denied Entry: The Handicap of Network TV." Remarks by Ronald Rhody, corporate vice-president, Kaiser Aluminum Corporation, at the American Advertising Federation National Convention, Dallas, June 10, 1980.
4. Television audio transcript, aluminum wiring/trial by television segment, ABC-TV's "Viewpoint," 10 P.M., July 24, 1981. Copyright 1981, ABC, Inc.
5. Television audio transcript, aluminum wiring/trial by television segment, ABC-TV's "Viewpoint," 10 P.M., July 24, 1981. Copyright 1981, ABC, Inc.
6. "The Business Campaign Against 'Trial by TV'," *Business Week,* June 2, 1980.
7. "Access to Television Denied," *At Issue,* Kaiser Aluminum and Chemical Corporation, 1980, pp. 6–16.
8. See, for example, " 'Hot Wire' Bias," Editorial Commentary, *Barron's,* February 16, 1981, p. 7.
9. "ABC Agrees to Air a Rebuttal by Kaiser to 20/20 Charges," *Wall Street Journal,* November 3, 1980, p. 39.
10. Ibid.
11. At the time the program was aired, Hutchcraft was a vice-president and general manager of the division in charge of all aluminum products for Kaiser. He has since assumed the presidency of Kaiser Aluminum and Chemical Corporation.
12. Ed Bark, "Koppel Shows Rivera a New 'Viewpoint'," *Dallas Morning News,* July 25, 1981, p. 17C.

Chapter 9

SAVINGS AND LOAN FOUNDATION, INC., WASHINGTON, DC:

ADVOCACY ADVERTISING CAMPAIGN TO SELL THE PUBLIC AND THE U.S. CONGRESS ON ALL SAVERS CERTIFICATES

Starting in 1980, the high interest rates caused serious problems for the thrift industry when people, attracted by large returns from the money market funds of approximately 14 to 18 percent, withdrew their money in droves from the passbook accounts offered by the savings and loan institutions that yielded a paltry 5 1/2 percent annual interest. In just the first five months of 1981, deposits in the savings and loan institutions decreased by $1.4 billion.[1] Trapped between low-interest old mortgage loans and the high cost of new borrowings, the savings and loan industry (S&L) was hemorrhaging with massive financial losses. The industry suffered heavy losses in 1980 and 1981. The financial condition of a large number of thrift institutions had become precarious, and their survival doubtful.

The industry trade group, the Savings and Loan Foundation, Inc.,

Research Assistant: Abbas Alkhafaji.

decided to embark on a new strategy. Instead of merely encouraging people to save, it developed a campaign to persuade Congress to allow it to offer new savings instruments that would be highly competitive with the money market funds, would be very attractive to the public, and would be, at the same time, quite profitable to the S&L industry. The new product was All Savers certificates.

THE SAVINGS AND LOAN FOUNDATION, INC.

The S&L Foundation was started 27 years ago at the recommendation of the Federal Home Loan Bank Board Advisory Committee in an effort to educate the public about the savings and loan business and its advantages to them. It was also felt that it would help educate the government, business, and community leaders regarding the important role the thrift industry plays in the overall economy of this country.

The foundation is a nonprofit corporation, organized by leaders in the savings and loan business. It is operated under the direction of a board of trustees. One trustee is elected by foundation members from each state having $2 billion or more in total member assets in support of the foundation. Six trustees-at-large and state trustees are elected for two-year terms. They serve without compensation. All members of the foundation are also members of FSLIC and the Federal Home Loan Bank System. Membership is restricted solely to FSLIC-insured associations.

Foundation membership is endorsed and recommended by the Federal Home Loan Bank Board and its twelve regional banks. All state organizations and both the United States and the national leagues have, by resolution, endorsed the work of the Savings and Loan Foundation and have strongly recommended membership in the foundation. Membership is based on the assets of institutions. Total assets in support of the Savings and Loan Foundation at the close of business on December 31, 1980, were $334 billion. The foundation's original budget in 1954 was $750,000. In 1981, the budget was $6.6 million. The foundation's operating expenses have been on the decrease; in 1980, 99 cents out of every dollar collected in dues were spent directly in the national advertising program.

ADVERTISING STRATEGY

Until 1979, the S&L Foundation had engaged primarily in institutional advertising campaigns aimed at encouraging consumers to save at savings and loan institutions. A significant change took place in 1980, when specially targeted audiences were reached with specific programs, such as a college savings plan. At the same time, the foundation ran an advertisement advocating an IRA for women whose full-time job was homemaking. The ad was headlined, "Isn't it time to give every woman the right to have her own retirement plan?" and was a combination of subtle advocacy of an idea, together with cultivation of an important public segment by identifying with its needs.

In January 1981, the foundation launched a more aggressive and a purely advocacy campaign, with the avowed purpose of enlisting public support for congressional passage of a program aimed at providing tax benefits to people who save at the thrift institutions, thereby lowering the cost of borrowing for the savings and loan industry and helping it recover from severe financial losses. The 1981 advertising strategy was designed to promote the participation of consumers in the industry campaign. By calling on consumers for assistance and action, the industry hoped to demonstrate that it was on their side on economic issues, and devoted to helping them save an increasing portion of their income.

The plan called for the provision of a forum for the American public to express its opinions. The foundation felt that if it could establish a program that gave the individual a chance to participate in achieving a change, the industry would have accomplished the goal of obtaining the loyalty of the saving public without relying on a rate differential. The 1981 program was designed to make things happen in the marketplace, and thereby to increase its market share of the public's savings. "It all comes down to one word . . . advocacy . . . identifying key issues for savers, taking a position that is in their best interest and speaking up on their behalf."[2]

The first ad in the series appeared in mid-January 1981. Entitled "Isn't It Time to Give a Real Tax Break to Savers?" the ad decried the low savings rate in the United States compared with other industrially advanced countries, notably the United Kingdom, West Germany, and Japan. It advocated that Congress should give savers a real tax break incentive by raising the annual tax-free limit on savings interest to $1,000 for individual filers and $2,000 for joint returns. The ad also included a coupon, which the readers could tear out, fill in, and return to the foundation [Exhibit 1].

By April 1981, different bills were circulating in Congress aimed at encouraging savings and also providing some sort of universal IRA. In keeping with the trend on Capitol Hill, the foundation incorporated the issue of universal IRAs into the second phase of its advocacy campaign. The second ad, similar to the first one in format, now had two questions on the ballots: "Should the first $1,000/$2,000 of interest on savings be tax free?" and "Should everyone be entitled to a tax-deferred retirement account?"

The third phase was launched in May 1981 to mobilize public support for the All Savers Act (H.R. 3456 and S.1279). The ad was entitled, "The Fairest Cut of All" [Exhibit 2]. These bills provided for the issuance of qualified certificates of deposits by various financial institutions, such as cooperative banks and other depository institutions. The certificates would pay interest at a rate not to exceed 70 percent of the yield on one-year Treasury bills. Interest earned on these certificates would be exempt from federal income taxes up to a maximum of $1,000 for a single return and $2,000 for joint returns. Furthermore, as the law was finally passed, it required that 75 percent of all new deposits must be lent to home buyers.

The ad claimed, among other things, that the certificate would give this country a fair chance in its battle against the economic problems that beset it. With its great appeal to savers, the certificate would lure money back into depository institutions and away from unproductive tax shelters. It would also bring back to America much of the money that

Exhibit 1

Isn't it time to give a <u>real</u> tax break to savers?

On the average, Britons save 13% of their disposable income. West Germans save 15%. Japanese, 26%. But Americans save only 5.5%!

A major reason people in other nations save more is that they are given tax incentives by their governments.

The U.S. actually <u>discourages</u> savings, by taxing the interest that is earned.

Isn't it time Congress gave savers a <u>real</u> tax incentive? We think the annual tax-free limit on savings interest should be raised to $1,000 for individuals and $2,000 for joint tax returns.

This would encourage more savings, which would help stabilize the economy and bring inflation under control.

What do you think? Please fill out the ballot, and let us know. If the ballot has already been removed from this page, you can still vote at your nearby Savings and Loan Association.

If we all speak up, Washington <u>will</u> listen.

The Savings & Loan Foundation

© 1981. The Savings and Loan Foundation, Inc., 1111 "E" Street, N.W., Washington, D.C. 20004.

BALLOT

Question: Should the first $1,000-$2,000* of interest on your savings be tax-free?

*$1,000 for individuals, $2,000 for joint tax returns.

☐ **Yes**   ☐ **No**

Please fill out this ballot and drop in the ballot box in your nearby Savings and Loan office, or mail to The Savings and Loan Foundation, Inc., Dept. XX, P.O. Box 461, Washington, D.C. 20044

Name _____

Address _____

City _____ State _____ Zip _____

If we all speak up, Washington <u>will</u> listen.

Exhibit 2

The fairest tax cut of all.

For too long, you've watched the value of your savings erode in the face of rising taxes and inflation. In fact, many of you have been forced to stop saving altogether. And that's not fair.

That's why we're asking Congress to allow a tax-free savings certificate. It would be available from all depository institutions: savings and loans, commercial banks, savings banks and credit unions.

It would be free from federal income tax.
It would be offered in affordable denominations.
It would be insured by a federal agency.
And it would pay a rewarding net return.

<u>F</u>ree from tax. <u>A</u>ffordable. <u>I</u>nsured. <u>R</u>ewarding.
That spells FAIR. That's what we call it. And that's what it is.

The FAIR Certificate is fair to you because it would give you an important tax break as you struggle to save your hard-earned dollars. And it's fair to the country because it would reduce the spending that fuels inflation, while building capital for domestic investment.

What do you think? Please fill out the ballot and let us know. Or vote at your nearby Savings and Loan Association.

If we all speak up, Washington <u>will</u> listen.

The Savings & Loan Foundation

BALLOT

Question: Should Congress allow a FAIR Savings Certificate?

(<u>F</u>ree from tax. <u>A</u>ffordable. <u>I</u>nsured. <u>R</u>ewarding.)

☐ **Yes**   ☐ **No**

Please fill out this ballot and drop in the ballot box in your nearby Savings and Loan office, or mail to FAIR Savings Certificate, c/o Savings and Loans, P.O. Box 461, Washington, D.C. 20044.

Name _____

Address _____

City _____ State _____ Zip _____

If we all speak up, Washington <u>will</u> listen.

©1981. The Savings and Loan Foundation, Inc., Washington, D.C.

has been invested in foreign countries. The certificate would also be an effective weapon against inflation. By encouraging more people to save more of their income, it would help decrease the upward pressure that unrestrained consumer spending puts on prices. And, although it would be tax-exempt, the certificate would actually result in a net increase in federal revenues by prompting growth in business activity and employment. The certificate would benefit almost every sector of the economy, public and private; the business community and the consumer; the wage earner and the unemployed; the investor and the borrower.

The ad asked the Congress to approve this program and urged people to support it by making their views known to their senators and representatives. The program was aimed at both the general public and thought leaders, and was carried out at both national and local levels.

The first two ads were aimed primarily at the general public. Their themes were also adapted to local advertising materials for the foundation, and included glossy proofs, posters, ballots, and envelope inserts. The third ad was directed more toward opinion leaders to inform them of the certificate's economic benefits and encourage their support.

Media Schedule

The media program for the campaign used a national magazine schedule and was designed to create a broad base of support, provide a means to voice that support, maximize ballot responses, and maintain flexibility.

The opinion leader program was designed to educate rapidly a substantial cross section of leaders in business, finance, media, and government. It was planned to use the nation's most influential newspapers to complement rather than duplicate the consumer vehicles, and to be compatible with the "white paper" nature of the message. Among the magazines used were: *Better Homes & Gardens, Money, Ms., National Geographic, Newsweek, People, Reader's Digest, Smithsonian, Southern Business, Southern Living, Sports Illustrated, Sunset, Time*, and *U.S. News & World Report*.

Public Response

According to the foundation executives, the response to the first ad was overwhelming, with an estimated 12,000 ballots being received at the foundation's office from magazine readers each day. An equal number of ballots was also received by various savings and loan associations. The steady trend of votes tallied showed a 99 to 1 vote in favor of an increased tax incentive. The response to other ads, although not as heavy, was also quite impressive.

DEBATE IN CONGRESS

Although the Senate Finance Committee voted to accept the All Savers provision, Senator Robert Dole, chairman of that committee, stated at a news conference on July 5, 1981, that the provision might be changed. He added that they were looking for better ideas on how to spur savings between now and floor time. Senator Dole and others had suggested that the All Savers provision would not generate any new savings, but would simply redirect funds already in the country's savings pool.[3] Congressional staff assistants also indicated that the All Savers certificates would be fine-tuned rather than replaced with some other saving incentive approaches. One of these alternatives would provide more tax relief through greater benefits for contributions to individual retirement accounts or IRAs. A second alternative would allow a federal agency to purchase low-interest mortgages that constituted a financial drag on S&Ls, thus giving them a much-needed infusion of cash. This plan would allow the S&Ls to purchase the mortgages back after interest rates had dropped enough to relieve the current squeeze on S&Ls.[4]

Although the All Saver certificates zipped through the tax writing committees in both the House and the Senate, there was disagreement between the two houses as to the institutions that would benefit from the issuance of these certificates. The House Ways and Means Committee wanted the tax-exempt certificates tied to home loans, which could deny the bills benefits to commercial banks. However, this provision failed because of the strong lobby of the commercial banks, and the final bill allowed all depository-type financial institutions to benefit from the All Savers certificates.[5]

Arguments in Support of All Savers Certificates

The proponents of All Savers made a variety of arguments in support of the new certificates.

1. The most compelling reason for aid was to avoid a crisis of confidence in the entire financial system, which could result from a collapse of the thrift industry. In a worst-case scenario, widespread failures with millions of depositors demanding their money could set off another depression.
2. Even if the worst-case scenario did not come true, the U.S. Treasury would have to make good to millions of depositors under the insurance provisions of deposits, the cost of which would far exceed any other relief measure now being contemplated.
3. Increased borrowings by the Treasury would lead to higher interest rates or an increased money supply (through printing press), thereby contributing to further inflation.
4. If the industry had to liquidate all its assets at the prevailing depressed values, the Treasury's contingent liability, according to one estimate, would exceed $50 billion.[6]
5. The industry also argued that its troubles were not caused by management inefficiency and that it was the victim of government's tight money policies and high interest rates.[7]
6. This approach would allow the industry to compete on a more equal basis with the money market funds.
7. It would encourage more savings, and help the housing and construction industry.

Arguments Against All Savers

Notwithstanding the strong promotional effort by the thrift industry and its support in Congress, the All Savers certificates drew strong criticism from a number of economists, the financial and business press, conservative politicians, municipal governments, and other segments of the public. The criticism ranged all the way from the deceptive nature of the promotional effort to the excessive costs of "bailout" to the taxpayers and the illusory nature of the alleged public benefits.

1. The thrift industry estimated that the certificate would provide a break for people who are in the 30 percent tax bracket. However, this figure was based on the old tax tables, and did not take into account the lower tax rates that were being planned by the Reagan administration during 1982. With the new tax rates, a family of four would have to earn at least $40,000 before the tax-free certificates would even look marginally more attractive than the T-bill rate. Thus it would not help low-income people. At the same time, it would eliminate tax exemptions that benefit all taxpayers.[8]

2. It would cost the Treasury between $4 and $6 billion and is a bail out of the thrift industry because the direct competition of the certificate with tax exempt *short-term* municipal notes and *long-term* bonds would add to the cost of borrowing, requiring cities to increase property taxes.[9]

3. Any assistance to the housing industry would be illusory because the provision was so broadly construed that financial institutions could easily get around it. This has been borne out by the data since the passage of the act.[10]

4. A large part of the funds in All Savers certificates would be diverted from other passbook and fixed-term certificates of deposits, and not from the money market funds. Thus, the industry was unlikely to receive any large infusion of new funds. According to the industry's own estimates, the new certificates would turn a projected industrywide pretax loss of $2.7 billion in 1982 to a modest profit of $440 million. Thus, according to critics, it would be cheaper for the Treasury to give a direct handout to the S&L industry rather than suffer a revenue loss of $4 to $6 billion.[11]

EFFECTIVENESS OF THE CAMPAIGN

The campaign cost approximately $4.5 million over a six-month period and persuaded more than 5.2 million people to respond by sending in opinion "ballots" favoring tax breaks on savings.[12]

The S&L Foundation was quite satisfied with its advocacy campaign and felt that it was very effective. According to Michael Stevenson, president of the foundation: "We feel that, because we're the only ones who went public on this [issue] and pushed for this, it's one in the win column for U.S."[13] "We have achieved our objective in obtaining a new saving instrument that should have tremendous public appeal. . . . These ballots had a tremendous impact, and certainly became the catalyst between the savings and loan business and the public regarding tax incentives for savers."[14]

William O'Connell, executive vice-president of the U.S. League of Savings Associations, stated that this campaign had reached all members of Congress and brought hundreds of savings executives to Capitol Hill. One congressional tax specialist describes the campaign as one of the finest grassroots lobbying jobs done in a long time.[15] This shows how effective the campaign was.[16] However, some people familiar with the workings of Congress, the institution the S&L trade group ultimately wanted to influence, were not as sure. "It is not like five million people who are against abortion. They won't vote against you because of this issue," said an aide for a western congressman. "The guys on Ways and Means don't make (tax) policy based on an ad campaign," he added.[17]

Other people had claimed that the approach to this bill by Congress was not due completely to the success of the S&L campaign; rather, it was due in part to the fears of Congress that without congressional aid, numbers of savings banks and savings associations might fail, and Congress might be blamed.[18]

AFTERMATH—PRIVATE INTEREST AND PUBLIC POLICY

The S&L industry had counted on a tremendous inflow of new funds as a result of All Savers certificates, and the initial sales proved that optimism to be well founded. During the first week, not only did the sales of the tax-exempt certificates meet or exceed expectations, but the surprise was that 25 to 30 percent of All Savers accounts represented new money. A weekend poll conducted by R. H. Bruskin Associates, a New York marketing research firm, indicated that 27 percent of All Savers accounts were being funded with money market fund deposits, while 39 percent came from savings accounts, 8 percent from certificates of deposit, and the rest from other sources. The money market funds, however, disputed these claims, stating that business "has been as good as normal, maybe even a little better."[19]

The euphoria, however, did not last very long. Sales of All Savers certificates were expected to reach $28 billion during the first two weeks, but fell quite short of that target. There was a precipitous decline in the sales rate after the first week, and the program did not prove to be the panacea the thrift industry had hoped for. "On the whole, we're disappointed," said Charlotte Chamberlain, director of policy and economic research for the Federal Home Loan Bank Board. She noted that while sales were strong when the program began, they trailed off significantly after the first week.[20] To encourage people to buy their All Savers from the savings and loan institutions, the foundation ran another ad [Exhibit 3] reminding the public of the role played by the industry in getting the All Savers provision enacted in the Congress.

Certain external factors contributed to this decline. An economist for the U.S. League of Savings Associations predicted that All Savers certificates would total $250 billion by the end of 1982, when authority to issue them expires. But as the interest rate available on the accounts dropped to 8.34 percent from 12.61 percent during the last three months,

Exhibit 3

The FAIR way to earn tax-free interest is at your Savings and Loan.

The All-Savers Certificate is here.

The All-Savers Act, which was passed as part of the President's tax package, makes every American eligible for tax-free savings certificates.

We call it the FAIR way to earn tax-free interest. Here's why:

Free from federal tax. The first $2000 of interest you earn is tax-free on a joint tax return ($1000 for individual returns).

Affordable. The certificates are available for as little as $500.

Insured. They are insured up to $100,000 by the FSLIC, a U.S. Government agency.

Rewarding return. They yield an interest rate equal to 70% of the prevailing yield on 1-year Treasury bills.

Examples of estimated after-tax yields:

If your joint taxable 1982 income is:	Your maximum 1982 tax bracket will be:	All-Savers yield effective during October: 12.61% Equals taxable yield of:
$ 7,601-11,900	16%	15.01%
$11,901-16,000	19%	15.57%
$16,001-20,200	22%	16.17%
$20,201-24,600	25%	16.81%
$24,601-29,900	29%	17.76%
$29,901-35,200	33%	18.82%
$35,201-45,800	39%	20.67%
$45,801-60,000	44%	22.52%
$60,001-85,600	49%	24.73%

Based on estimated 1982 federal rates on net taxable income after deductions and exemptions

The sooner you get one, the better the tax break.

All-Savers Certificates are available at Savings and Loans from now until December 31, 1982.

They mature after 1 year. But you start earning tax-free interest the day you buy one.* You can even convert your present six-month certificates to All-Savers Certificates, with no early withdrawal penalty.

Stop by a Savings and Loan office today and find out how to take full advantage of this new tax break.

Thanks.

This year, we in the Savings and Loan business asked you to vote on these tax breaks for savers.

We thank the more than 5.5 million of you who filled out ballots. 99% of you said, "Yes."

Washington listened.

At Savings and Loans, we're proud to have been able to make your voice heard.

Once again, we thank you for speaking up. And we thank Washington for listening.

*Substantial penalty for early withdrawal.

The Savings & Loan Foundation

If we all speak up, Washington will listen.

© 1981. The Savings and Loan Foundation, Inc., 1111 "E" Street, N.W., Washington, D.C. 20004.

the torrent of All Savers money became a trickle. Home Savings of America, the biggest S&L in the United States, said All Savers deposits plunged to about $6 million in the first 21 days of December from $38 million in November, and $271 million in October. Great Western Savings, the second biggest thrift, experienced a similar fall.

The U.S. League of Savings Associations, a big S&L trade group, contended that the plunge in All Savers activity was just "an aberration" due to the rapid decline in rates. Once all competitive yields "return to a more even keel," a spokesman said, "interest in the 'All Savers' will be rekindled."[21] The situation, however, has not changed, notwithstanding the optimistic pronouncements. The industry losses are expected to continue until 1983.[22] The S&L industry is looking for some "new" instruments to spur depositor interest.

NOTES

1. "All Savers–and All Players," *New York Times,* October 6, 1981, p. A30.
2. The Savings and Loan Foundation, *Marketing and Advertising Bulletin,* December/January, 1981, p. 2.
3. "Tax-Exempt Savings Certificates, Cleared by Congress Panels, Likely Faces Changes," *Wall Street Journal,* July 6, 1981.
4. Ibid.
5. "S&L Industry Backs Subsidy," *Dallas Morning News,* June 30, 1981, p. 13D.
6. Clyde H. Farnsworth, "U.S. Aid for Thrift Units Poses Questions of Need," *New York Times,* July 2, 1981, pp. D1, D6.
7. Ibid., p. D6.
8. Brooks Jackson, "All-Savers Bill Could Create Lots of Losers," *Wall Street Journal,* June 26, 1981, p. 26.
9. Ibid.
10. "All Savers—and All Payers."
11. Jackson, "All-Savers Bill."
12. "S&L Group Takes Some Credit for Its Ad's Effects on Congress," *Wall Street Journal,* June 25, 1981, p. 25.
13. Ibid.
14. Michael C. Stevenson, the president of S&L's, in the foundation's marketing and advertising *Bulletin,* "The Fairest Tax Cut of All Is Here," August/September 1981.
15. "Tax Break for Savings Achievers," *New York Times,* June 29, 1981, p. 19.
16. Ibid.
17. "S&L Group Takes Some Credit for Its Ad's Effect on Congress."
18. "Tax Break for Savings Advances?" *New York Times,* June 29, 1981, p. 19.
19. John Andrew and David J. Blum, "All Savers Sales Are Heavy in First Week, But Effect on Banks, Thrifts Isn't Clear Yet," *Wall Street Journal,* October 8, 1981, p. 10.
20. Karen W. Arenson, "All Savers: No Panacea Yet," *New York Times,* November 4, 1981, p. D1.
21. G. Christian Hill, "Initial Surge in All Savers Deposits Fades as the Rate of Return Declines," *Wall Street Journal,* December 28, 1981, p. 11.
22. "S&L May Be in the Red Until 1983, Official Says," *Wall Street Journal,* December 11, 1981,.p. 56.

Part V CAMPAIGNS USING EXTENSIVE FIELD RESEARCH TO DEVELOP ADVERTISING STRATEGIES AND MEASURE CAMPAIGN EFFECTIVENESS

Chapter 10

CHEMICAL MANUFACTURERS ASSOCIATION, WASHINGTON, DC:

EDUCATIONAL ADVERTISING CAMPAIGN TO CHANGE PUBLIC PERCEPTION AND AWARENESS OF THE CHEMICAL INDUSTRY'S ACTIVITIES AND CONTRIBUTIONS TO AMERICAN SOCIETY

It does not come as a surprise to any informed reader that the chemical industry has had a poor public image and has suffered a lack of public credibility about its commitment to environmental safety. The past decade has witnessed a successive increase in new laws and regulations subjecting the chemical industry to greater restrictions in product development, manufacturing, sales, and waste disposal.

In 1979 the Chemical Manufacturers Association (CMA) convened a special Communications Task Group made up of selected industry communications managers whose objective it was to consider, develop, and revise the CMA communications program to address the industry's credibility problems. They set up a small research subcommittee made

Research Assistants: Abbas Alkhafaji and Josette Quiniou.

up of representatives of companies with survey research expertise to contribute their experience and knowledge.

Research data on public concerns over chemicals and the chemical industry were provided by various companies. Monsanto contributed its proprietary research in its "Chemical Facts of Life" campaign, and Shell put in data from its 1978 cancer study. Other bits and pieces were also contributed. The subcommittee reviewed the data and came to these conclusions:

1. The American public was already convinced that chemicals contributed to the high American living standard. Thus, it felt there was no need to embark on a campaign to urge that position.
2. The American public was nevertheless apprehensive about hazards to their well-being posed by chemicals in the environment. The subcommittee, accordingly, felt this was the subject area a CMA communications campaign might address.

The task force received these conclusions and ultimately accepted them. Accordingly, the theme chosen for the CMA communications program was to increase public recognition that the chemical industry is committed to doing a responsible job to protect the public from the health and safety risks of chemicals.

Once the theme was selected, the task force looked at what syndicated data were telling them. The 1979 Yankelovich Corporate Priorities data, the latest data available at the time, showed that the chemical industry was seen by the following proportions of Americans as doing a poor job in complying with laws and guidelines in the following areas:

Waste disposal	61%
Air pollution	56%
Water pollution	51%
Worker safety	36%
Transportation safety	Data not available
Product safety	32%

These topics therefore were selected as themes for the first year's campaign. A point extensively discussed by the task group was the unique position of CMA in addressing these themes. The task group agreed that acknowledging the potential of environmental pollution by the chemical industry was not something any one chemical company would wish to do. After all these decisions had been made, the 1980 benchmark survey by Cambridge Reports was designed and carried out. The purpose of the benchmark was to establish precampaign data on the target audiences against which campaign effectiveness could be measured. It examined attitudes toward the chemical industry compared to other business sectors. Among the major findings: The public is well aware of and appreciates the benefits of chemicals; *likes* what the chemical industry makes; but is afraid the chemical industry is out to poison them through sloppy and irresponsible operating practices. The public sees chemicals as the greatest threat to the environment and a significant cause of cancer. Fifty percent believe the chemical industry does a poor job of controlling water pollution; 44 percent believe the industry does a poor job of controlling air pollution; 38 percent think the industry does a poor job of observing worker safety rules. More than 50 percent believe there is now more cancer than ten years ago; 47 percent see chemical food additives as a cause of cancer; 44 percent see chemical plant air pollution as a cause of cancer; 42 percent see pesticides as cancer causing; 33 percent see chemical plant water pollution as a cancer cause. Thirty-three percent see the industry as doing especially poorly in providing enough information to consumers; only 15 percent see the chemical industry as socially responsible.

According to one leading advertising professional, "15% of *any* sample are mavericks who like to take the opposite side of any question. So there is a fair chance that *no one* really saw the industry as really responsible."[1] Half the public say they want strong government regulation of the chemical industry. And this is in spite of the public's bias against further government involvement in most other things.

Faced with these findings, industry executives realized that such a negative image had adverse effects on its public image, as well as on relations with government, employees, and the financial community. Inherent in this objective was a desire to reduce the public pressure for restrictive legislation and regulation. Therefore, what was required from the industry was a new approach to help people understand what the industry was doing to protect them from the health and safety risks of chemicals. What was most needed was a dialogue between public and industry to create an acceptable balance between risk and benefits.

With much research data in hand, the CMA launched a Chemical Industry Communications Action Program (ChemCAP), now known as the CMA Communications Program, which was to complement CMA's comprehensive public relations activities. CMA's advocacy advertising is a major element of this program. The objective of the advertising program, like the overall program, is to increase recognition that the chemical industry is committed to doing a responsible job to protect the public from the health and safety risks of chemicals.

A major issue for analysis is, How does the desirability of undertaking industrywide advocacy campaigns compare with the desirability of individual corporations sponsoring their own? Are there specific issues that are best addressed through an industrywide campaign, as opposed to individual corporate campaigns? What are the long-term effects of an industrywide campaign as opposed to those of individual corporate campaigns? Furthermore, is there a danger that industrywide campaigns are likely to deteriorate to the least offensive or controversial level of issue discussion, thereby stifling creativity and making such campaigns bland and boring?

Another question pertains to the use of benchmark studies in selecting issues and media themes. It is always possible to develop benchmark studies that can provide the sponsor with answers that he/she is looking for in determining which issues are critical and, therefore, which issues need to be addressed. A tunnel vision—especially when an industry group is facing public hostility—is likely to ignore the issues that may be underlying public hostility but that are not regarded, or even visualized, by the sponsor as such and are therefore excluded from the study. Second, a poorly conceived study may provide erroneous answers as to copy themes and media approaches and thereby severely limit the effectiveness of a campaign based on such a study.

CMA—ORGANIZATION, STRUCTURE, MEMBERSHIP

The CMA represents the chemical industry in America. Founded in 1872, CMA is the oldest chemical trade organization in the Western hemisphere. The association includes about 200 member companies, most in the United States, with some in Canada. The size of CMA's member companies and the products they make are as varied as chemistry itself. Together, they represent a major portion of the productive capacity of the industry.

The association, with headquarters in Washington, DC, has a permanent staff of approximately 165 persons headed by a full-time president. Its board of directors is composed of major executives of its member companies.

In recent years, CMA's role as the chemical industry's advocate has accelerated, becoming the focal point of many of the association's activities. CMA advocates industry positions in Congress, in the regulatory agencies, and the executive and judicial branches. Equally important, CMA communicates information to the media across the nation.

According to a CMA brochure, the association has been in the forefront in transportation safety, occupational safety, and health and environmental protection. Recently, it has led the way in energy conservation and in solving waste disposal problems.[2] The CMA brochure describes the benefits of the association to its members in the following terms:

> Measured monetarily, CMA activities are estimated to be worth billions of dollars each year. More than $1 billion are saved annually by forestalling inequitable natural gas utility rates; $500 million are saved annually by reducing future increases in freight charges; more than $100 million are saved each year through the development of proper engineering standards. In a recent year CMA saved several billion dollars by deflecting inappropriate environmental and workplace laws, rules and excessive taxes without endangering public health or employee safety.[3]

Structure

CMA's board and executive committees establish policy and define program areas. Responsibility for issue monitoring and development in those areas is assigned to an authorized standing committee. Each committee is usually composed of 15 industry representatives. Under the direction of the association president, the staff is responsible for implementing and communicating policy and helping the committees with their work.

The staff is organized into five function departments: (1) government relations, (2) technical, (3) communication, (4) administration, (5) office of general counsel.

The communications department, which is responsible for public communication, is divided into the communications committee and the communications policy review special committee (now defunct). The communications committee has a major influence on the CMA Communications Program and comprehensive public relations activities. These programs communicate the industry's renewed commitment to doing a responsible job of protecting the public and its employees from the health and safety risks of chemicals. The communications policy review special committee was a board of directors committee which reviewed the overall direction, design, and operations of CMA's communication program. This has become the responsibility of the communications committee.

Decision-Making Process and Program Approval

The first step in developing a communications strategy was to decide on the size and shape of the problem, and to come up with a tailor-made plan for remedial action. A special task force of twelve industry communication experts spent several months developing such a plan. Although CMA's vice-president for public relations participated in all discussions, the plan was developed by the industry. The next step was to persuade other members to accept this proposal.

In May 1979, the thirteen-member executive committee of CMA's forty-five-member board of directors approved the draft plan and appropriated funds for further development. Most important, a copy of the draft plan and a request for comments was sent to executives in member companies who act as contacts with CMA. After receiving member comments, the task force revised the plan and again sent it to all members. At this time too, a public relations consulting agency, a public opinion research firm, and an advertising agency were retained for basic polling, programming, and advertisement development.

Two months later, four regional conferences were conducted across the country to explain the program to industry personnel and to encourage involvement. Different presentations were given to lay out the basics of the plan and explain the importance of member company participation. Target audiences and major markets were pinpointed, and each communication medium was described, along with its role in the overall campaign.

No communication program, no matter how good, will achieve its goals if industry performance is not there to begin with. CMA argued that the industry is already paying heavily because of its poor image. For example, the chemical industry was spending more money than any other industry in cleaning up pollution, and had spent $15.3 billion (most current figure available) to date on pollution control. However, because of its communication gap, no one knew about it. Why not, instead, put some of this money into a program to achieve positive results?

CMA emphasized to its members that the association's communication effort was intimately related to the total industry communication effort, including product advertising by individual firms. The CMA Communications Program would complement programs already in place. It would emphasize issues, and more important, would undertake the otherwise difficult but necessary job of dealing with risks. On their part, individual chemical companies would continue to emphasize products and the benefits of chemicals.

This division of effort was based on the fact that associations, rather than companies, can best discuss industrywide issues, particularly major public issues. Also, an association can act as a lightning rod on controversial issues, taking some of the heat off members.

CMA emphasized to members repeatedly that advertising, while representing the bulk of the program's cost, was one part of a multifaceted program. The other parts of ChemCAP were equally important, and all were constructed to work together to achieve an impact and to meet the program's objective.[4] The association's early efforts to explain the importance of the program to members paid off. In November 1979, the CMA executive committee and the board of directors approved the Communications Program in principle, but it decided that one more across-the-board effort should be made to fully inform the industry on the plan's objectives, scope, and content. Finally, in January 1980, a full year after planning had begun, the board gave approval to the initial $6.1 million two-year package.

The objective of the program was specifically spelled out to members: to broaden public recognition of the chemical industry's commitment to protecting the public from the health and safety risks associated with its products and services. Five areas were identified as topics to be discussed in the program: transportation safety, environmental protection, product safety, worker safety, and hazardous waste disposal. CMA repeatedly emphasized that the members were themselves primarily responsible for the program's success or failure because, notwithstanding the effectiveness of the communications program, it was industry performance that alone could lend credibility to the program's message.

Program Implementation

Board approval was followed by a conference in Washington where people throughout the industry could discuss different ways of implementing the CMA program. The conference underscored several themes: the need for support from chief executive officers, the importance of delegating one person to be in charge of program implementation within a company, a recognition that work on this program would help an employee in his/her career, and the importance of personalizing messages in speeches and letters signed by the chief executive officer.

The CMA board next established a permanent fifteen-member communications committee. James Sites, vice-president for communications, served as the committee's staff executive. Working with the CMA staff, the committee guides program development and implementation. A policy review group, made up of five members of the board (now defunct) was also established.[5] Once the program was developed, its implementation was monitored on a continuing basis, obviating the need for this special committee.

THE ADVERTISING CAMPAIGN

Since the CMA program did not have the resources to cover the entire population, certain key groups of individuals that most intimately affect public attitudes and the public policy formation process became priority target audiences. These included politically active individuals, government representatives, educators, communicators, and "plant neighbors"—those living in areas of major chemical plant concentration. Active individuals were defined as the estimated 14 million people who participated in two or more public actions (such as writing to elected officials, playing leadership roles in local civic or political organizations) other than voting within the past year.

The campaign was developed by the Brouillard Communications Division of the J. Walter Thompson advertising agency. It was designed for the print media and included thought leader magazines and major newspapers in Washington and New York. These were: *Time, Newsweek, U.S. News & World Report, Harper's, Atlantic, Smithsonian, The New Yorker, Psychology Today, Natural History,* the *New York Times,* the *Washington Post,* and *Star.* There have been some adjustments in this media schedule from year to year.

Campaign Budget

The advertising expenditures for 1980–81 were slightly over $3 million. They were reduced to $2.52 million for 1981–82 and $2.25 million for 1982–83.

Copy Themes

The first phase (1980–81) of advertising—a "Scientific American" type campaign—presented the five areas of concern in such a way as to display the chemical industry as one of high technology and scientific innovations. The first ad dealt with the issue of managing chemical wastes. The second dealt with improving chemical product safety [Exhibit 1], and the third discussed the issue of worker safety [Exhibit 2]. Although these ads proved to be persuasive and able to communicate a message, they had a low stopping power. The human interest format was adopted when research by Brouillard Communications showed the personalized advertisements to be more effective.

The second phase (1982) was aimed at showing that chemical industry engineers and scientists are just like other citizens, with normal family concerns; emphasizing that these scientists are responsible citizens and concerned about the environment; and pointing out that they would not be working for the chemical industry if they did not believe the industry was concerned with producing safe products and also protecting the environment. It was felt that a scientist-employee as a spokesperson would have better public credibility than a professional model, well-known public figure, or corporate executive.

Exhibit 1

Improving Chemical Product Safety

What we're doing to minimize risks to people's health and the environment

America's chemical industry invests millions of dollars each year to make our products as safe as we can. For example, we're building new test facilities and using new, highly sophisticated research equipment. When necessary, we're also searching for alternatives. Still, we're not satisfied. Here's how we're trying to do a better job:

1.
Funding an independent test facility

To supplement their own toxicology laboratories, 35 chemical companies have joined to create the Chemical Industry Institute of Toxicology (CIIT), a $14 million research facility at Research Triangle Park, near Raleigh, North Carolina. The purpose: to develop and use more reliable methods to assess the possible effects of chemicals on people and the environment. The institute has total operating independence. It also operates non-profit and is the first facility of its kind in the world.

CIIT's efforts focus on three mutually supportive areas: testing, research and professional training. At present, CIIT is conducting research on the most commonly used chemicals, evaluating them by today's more stringent standards. Information developed by the institute is provided openly and simultaneously to the entire chemical industry, the government and the public. We believe this underscores our entire industry's commitment to making sure our products meet—or exceed—today's exacting health and safety standards.

2.
Increasing on-site research

Seven major chemical companies already have multimillion dollar toxicological laboratories as large as, or larger than, the CIIT facilities. Other chemical companies are opening new research and testing laboratories and adding to existing research facilities. These facilities help companies develop the fullest body of knowledge about their own products should questions ever arise about their proper use, handling characteristics and overall safety.

3.
Finding safer new chemicals and products

When scientific information casts suspicion on the safety of a chemical substance, we search for safer alternatives and develop safeguards. For example, we helped in the development of biodegradable detergents to replace ordinary detergents that created environmental problems. Another example: cellulose acetate film was developed to eliminate the extreme fire hazard that was posed by nitrocellulose film.

4.
Improving detection methods

Steady, sometimes dramatic improvements in scientific measurement techniques and

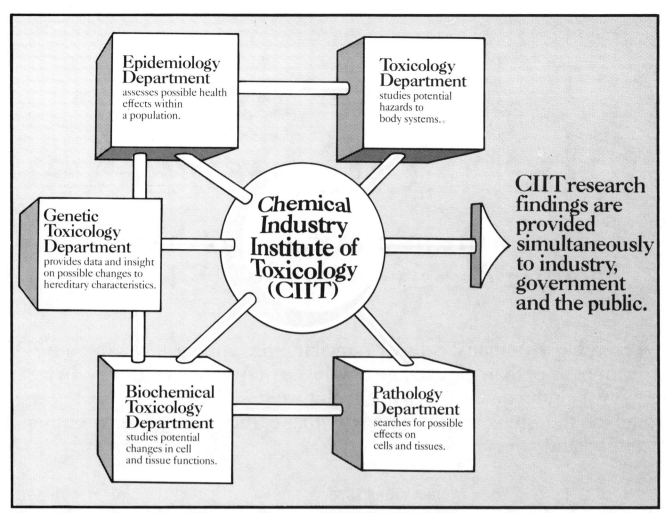

Epidemiology Department assesses possible health effects within a population.

Toxicology Department studies potential hazards to body systems.

Genetic Toxicology Department provides data and insight on possible changes to hereditary characteristics.

Chemical Industry Institute of Toxicology (CIIT)

CIIT research findings are provided simultaneously to industry, government and the public.

Biochemical Toxicology Department studies potential changes in cell and tissue functions.

Pathology Department searches for possible effects on cells and tissues.

The Chemical Industry Institute of Toxicology, an independent research facility funded by members of the chemical industry, conducts research and testing on commonly used chemicals to help protect people's health and the environment.

equipment have brought about a million-fold increase in our ability to analyze chemicals. One instrument, the gas chromatograph-mass spectrometer, for example, helps us detect materials at levels as low as one part per trillion—equal to one grain in an 18-foot layer of sand covering a football field.

5.
Expanding the flow of safety information

Many member companies of the Chemical Manufacturers Association prepare Material Safety Data Sheets on chemicals and chemical products. These sheets, introduced as a voluntary effort by our industry nearly 50 years ago, are designed to give technical people, plant workers and down-stream processors data to help them safely handle chemical substances. The sheets include information on safe handling techniques, appropriate storage and possible hazards, along with health and emergency instructions in case of chemical accidents.

What you've read here is just an overview. For a booklet that tells more about what we're doing to improve chemical product safety, write to: Chemical Manufacturers Association, Dept. ET-08, Box 363, Beltsville, Md. 20705.

America's Chemical Industry

The member companies of the Chemical Manufacturers Association

Exhibit 2

Protecting Chemical Workers

How we're improving one of the best health and safety records in U.S. industry

According to National Safety Council figures, chemical workers are 2.3 times safer than the average employee in American industry. In fact, they are far safer on the job than off. But we're still not satisfied. Here are some of the steps we're taking to make the working environment healthful and safer:

1.
Improving detection techniques

New and more sophisticated devices for monitoring the environment are worn by many workers. Many plants have "area monitoring devices" spotted in strategic locations. Some of these devices change color or sound an alarm to alert workers to even minute traces of contaminants. Others, like the gas chromatograph-mass spectrometer, measure contaminant quantities as low as one part per trillion—equivalent to one second in 32,000 years. Data from these and other measuring devices are analyzed by computer and compared with employee health records to help make sure that exposure is kept at safe levels. (See illustration.)

2.
Upgrading educational programs

Chemical companies are intensifying their safety education programs, especially with videotapes and other visual aid techniques. One company has an 82-page listing of videotape cassettes. It also has an index of safety standards that runs to about 60 pages. And each standard can run as long as 50 pages. The effect of this training goes beyond the plant. Chemical workers learn to "think safety." So they have fewer accidents than the average industrial employee —not only at work, but also on their own time.

3.
Expanding laboratory studies

Throughout the chemical industry, thousands of people are working on new and faster ways to determine the long-term effects of chemicals. It is not an easy job. Doing a study on just one chemical can take over three years and cost more than $1,000,000. To advance this work, 30 chemical com-

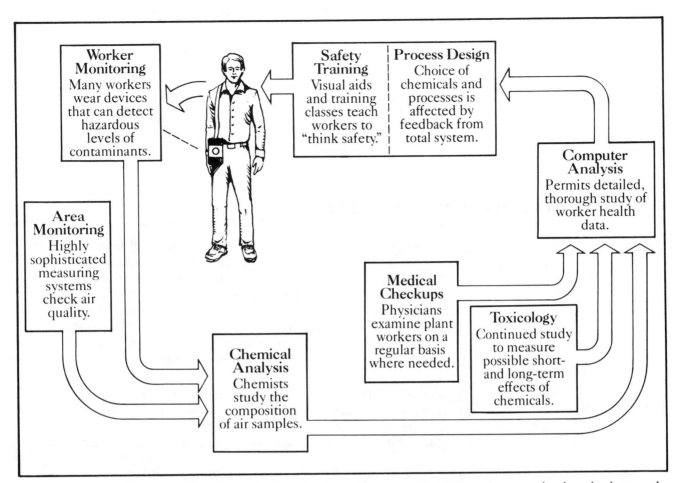

Example of a Worker Safety Protection System: Data from health exams, monitoring devices and laboratory studies are analyzed to identify situations that may require immediate action and to provide information for possible improvements in process design and safety training.

panies have joined to create the Chemical Industry Institute of Toxicology located near Raleigh, North Carolina. The Institute shares its findings with the entire industry, the U.S. Government and the public.

4.
"Engineering out" risks

When tests cast suspicion on the safety of a substance, we often find substitutes. There is a constant search for safer chemicals. If necessary, we may redesign the entire manufacturing process to make it safer.

5.
Monitoring employee health more closely

The number of industrial hygienists has tripled in the past 10 years. And they are only part of the picture. Many chemical companies now use *interdisciplinary* teams to monitor employee health. A typical team consists of industrial hygienists, physicians, toxicologists and engineers. These teams then multiply their effectiveness by using the latest computer technology to process and study the data they collect. The results help chemical companies anticipate and control threats to worker health and safety better than ever before.

For more information, write: Chemical Manufacturers Association, Department BT-05, P.O. Box 363, Beltsville, Maryland 20705.

America's Chemical Industry

The member companies of the Chemical Manufacturers Association

Copies of the two advertisements are reproduced as Exhibits 3 and 4. In both phases, ad insertions were made both in single-page and double-page formats. The copy themes and layouts were designed to show audiences that the chemical industry, in fact, was doing a lot to protect the public from risks associated with chemicals.

MEASURING AD CAMPAIGN EFFECTIVENESS

CMA undertook two tracking studies in 1981 and 1982 to measure the effectiveness of the ad campaign. The studies were conducted by Cambridge Research Associates. Most of the questions asked in the 1981 and 1982 questionnaires were the same as those asked in the 1980 benchmark survey. Interviews were conducted with 900 politically active individuals and 200 "neighbors." The first tracking study to measure the impact of the CMA advertising campaign took place during January–February 1981. Four principal topics were discussed in this survey:

- What is the present image of the chemical industry?
- Have attitudes toward the chemical industry in the target audience (political actives) changed in the last year?
- How aware of the CMA advertising campaign are the target audiences?
- How well is the CMA advertising campaign working?

The 1981 Study

The Image of the Chemical Industry. A majority of people in the study felt that chemical waste was still the major problem related to the chemical industry. At the time of the benchmark survey and the 1981 tracking study, the degree of personal concern over chemical waste had increased dramatically between the two surveys. Overall, the chemical industry continues to be seen as paying too little attention to it.

The Attitude of the Public. Data were analyzed for two separate groups: opinion leaders and politically active individuals, and the chemical industry neighbors. Within the first group, educators were found to be most positive toward the industry, but this group was also less homogeneous. Some members of this group felt that the industry was very concerned about the average person's welfare, whereas others asserted that this was not so, thereby joining the majority of the public.

In measuring the chemical industry's favorability and perceived truthfulness, the industry's position was found "not really good" among the six industries tested, oil, nuclear energy, chemical, retail, banking, and insurance.

Awareness of CMA Advertising Campaign. The tracking study was undertaken by Cambridge Reports. Its major findings were that those who saw the ads found them believable: 85 percent of the "politically

Exhibit 3

"I'm a chemical industry engineer but a concerned father first. I'm working to improve water quality for my kids and yours."

Larry Washington, Manager of Environmental Services for a major chemical company, with daughters Lori and Danielle.

"Clean water is one of our most precious resources," says Larry Washington. "The chemical industry has more than 10,000 specialists working to control pollution and protect the environment.

"One of my responsibilities is to make sure the wastewater discharged from our plant is environmentally acceptable. That means removing suspended solids and using techniques such as carbon adsorption, filtration and biological treatment. It can also mean raising the oxygen content of the water so there's more than enough to support fish in the river.

"I like my job because I know I'm helping the chemical industry improve water quality for my family, yours and for generations to come. We're spending more on pollution control than any other industry. We've already spent $7 billion on protecting the environment, with more than $3.7 billion of that money going just for cleaner water.

"Frequent monitoring is part of our commitment to clean water. We monitor the water as it goes into the river. We monitor the river after our water is mixed with it. At my plant, I know we're doing things right."

For a booklet with more information on how we're protecting people and the environment, write: Chemical Manufacturers Association, Department KY-104, P.O. Box 363, Beltsville, MD 20705.

America's Chemical Industry

The member companies of the Chemical Manufacturers Association

Exhibit 4

"As a chemist who helps decide how industry wastes are managed, my standards are high. As a father, even higher."

Peter Briggs, Senior Advisor, Environmental Analysis, at a major chemical and mining company, with sons Chris and Jonathan.

"I spend most of my time on the job developing progressive company policies to protect the environment. Throughout the chemical industry, there are more than 10,000 specialists like me whose major concern is controlling pollution.

"When I was hired, I was told I was to be the conscience of my company," says Peter Briggs. "I'm concerned about the environment. I want it to be clean for my kids, as well as everybody else's.

"To dispose of chemical wastes, for instance, we use recycling, incineration and other methods, such as building secure landfills with thick, compacted clay linings. Then we check regularly to make sure liquids do not escape.

"In fact, my company has a whole internal Environmental Review Group that works constantly to monitor current operations and improve our standards. They descend on our operations for week-long investigations. Eighteen hours a day, weekends included.

"I know the whole chemical industry is concerned about the environment. We've already spent $7 billion controlling pollution. And our estimates show we'll spend $10 billion more over the next five years on waste disposal alone. So I know I'm not the only one with a conscience."

For a booklet that tells how we're protecting people and the environment, write: Chemical Manufacturers Association, Dept. LM-107, P.O. Box 363, Beltsville, Maryland 20705.

America's Chemical Industry
The member companies of
the Chemical Manufacturers Association

active individuals" and 87 percent of the "neighbors" found them very or somewhat believable. Attitudes of those in the sample who had been exposed to the industry messages improved significantly. Regular readers of *Time* and *Newsweek* (where the industry campaign was running) were significantly more aware than nonreaders of "the Chemical industry's effort to inform the public of its actions to reduce public risks."

There were also some discouraging findings: 60 percent of those interviewed admitted that they were not aware of any industry efforts; of 40 percent of those who claimed awareness of any industry effort to inform them, about one in four—or *10 percent* of the total—claimed to have seen any industry print advertising on what was being done to reduce risk. When asked about the sponsorship of *any* advertising about what is being done to reduce risk, fewer than 10 percent of the politically active individuals named any individual company. And only *1 percent* of the politically active individuals said they were aware of ad sponsorship by America's chemical industry.

Effectiveness of the Campaign. The communications committee of the CMA concluded that attitudes toward the chemical industry had not changed significantly since 1980. There was no significant level of identification of the CMA advertising campaign. (According to CMA, this was not a campaign objective.) There did appear to be somewhat more awareness of messages in the CMA advertisements than of CMA's sponsorship of those messages. *Those aware of CMA messages held more favorable views toward the chemical industry than those who were not aware.* Clearly very little, if anything, was accomplished. One might, however, speculate that the 1981 figures might have been worse if the industry advertising had not taken place, or that the media weight was too low to make a statistically significant impact.

There was only a slight increase in the awareness of CMA communication efforts, but there were some positive results:

• The percentages of chemical industry neighbors and politically active individuals who wanted information about waste disposal has doubled since last year.
• The percentage of people feeling that the chemical industry was concerned rather than unconcerned had grown.
• Worker safety and product safety were seen by the largest percentages of politically active individuals, chemical industry neighbors, and educators as areas where efforts at improvement had been displayed.

John Elliott, former chairman of the board of Ogilvy & Mather, had the following observations to make concerning CMA's advocacy campaign:

> O&M asked Gallup & Robinson to do a computer run of 2,000 corporate advertisements in 1979 and 1980, comparing them on the basis of recall and persuasiveness with the norm for all *product* advertising. It was found that: Giving all product advertising an index of 100, on the basis of recall and persuasiveness, all corporate advertising got a rating of 81, and institutional/advocacy advertising a rating of 62. The index value

of the chemical industry's corporate advertising was 63, compared with the index value of 81 for all corporate advertising.

In Elliott's opinion, by far the most important reason for the slow progress of the chemical industry's campaign was that it was grossly underfunded. He felt that while chemical companies were separately spending millions of dollars in advertising, this effort was largely wasted because it was not well coordinated. He felt that this very modest effort on the part of the chemical industry might be seen on the part of the public as "secretiveness" and as evidence that the industry didn't take the problems seriously and wasn't doing anything about them. Even *more* of the public might come to the conclusion that others (meaning the government) would have to be given the responsibility to fix things. Elliott comments:

> All the hundreds of millions the industry has already spent to control pollution, to reduce risks, won't count a dime if the public isn't aware of it, or if the public sees it as a reaction to laws made necessary by irresponsible engineering and operations.

Elliott also felt that the chemical industry should bring its messages to the *general public,* not just to the so-called politically active individuals and influentials:

> I think there is a myth about thought-leaders. The theory goes that if you get your message to them, they'll lead public opinion. It has been repeated so often that a lot of people accept it. But I can't remember an example of the theory working in advertising. It is the general public—*all* of us—who are besieged daily by front-page stories of spills, leakages, fires, toxic reactions, etc. Elected officials have an inordinate interest in numbers of votes. It is the general public who are the thought-leaders, the influentials who influence the legislators.

The 1982 Study

The second survey revealed that in general the communications objectives of the CMA campaign were being met, in that those who had seen the industry's communications were more likely than those who had not to concur with messages presented in the communications. However, the communications were reaching a limited audience, and current results showed that this audience had not increased over the past year. As a result, overall public attitudes and perceptions of the chemical industry showed little change over recent years, and much of the impact of the communications was "hidden" when evaluated in terms of aggregate results.

The tracking study showed that in many aspects, the CMA communications program had mixed results.

- The ads were reaching a *stagnant* limited audience; there was *no appreciable increase in reach from last year*. It should, however, be kept in mind that the 1981–82 campaign was based on a funding level lower than that of 1980–81.

- The awareness of messages communicating the industry's efforts to reduce the risk of potentially hazardous chemicals had dropped 10 points among persons in all groups except politically active individuals, the main target audience. Among the people who could remember the ads, the reactions to the industry's advertising were positive in terms of both the believability and the importance of those ads. At least seven out of ten persons from all groups sampled stated that the ads were believable rather than not believable. More than eight out of ten politically active individuals who remembered the ads described them as believable.

- One of the more interesting results was that people who had been exposed to the communication campaign held different opinions of the chemical industry than those who had not been exposed. However, as one would expect, responses from individuals in each of the three groups were less likely to show difference of opinion on questions that were not related to the advertising messages. Consequently, there were no differences between the views of people in each of these groups when asked about the general favorability of their opinions on the chemical industry, their impressions of the chemical industry's truthfulness, and their personal levels of concern about each of the issues discussed in the advertising.

The most widespread endorsement of the advertising credibility came from the chemical industry's neighbors. More than nine out of ten persons in this group said the ads were either very or somewhat believable. Last year, reactions to the industry's advertising were equally positive among persons in all groups questioned. In determining the impact of CMA's advertisements, the survey used a conservative and narrow definition of *opportunity of exposure* [Tables 1–3].

Table 1

Changes in Perceptions of the Industry:
Personal Concern for Waste Disposal

	1982		1981	
	Exposed	Unexposed	Exposed	Unexposed
Concerned (very/ somewhat)	98%	94%	96%	94%
Not concerned at all (not very/not at all)	2	6	3	6

Note: This question measures the importance of one of the five designated areas of what the chemical industry is doing to manage chemicals. The response confirms that waste disposal continues to be the most important activity area and that placing the most communications emphasis on this area is warranted. Second, any preexisting difference in the attitudes of exposed and not exposed groups is negligible. This means that such a topic is of major importance to people, whether or not they are likely to be readers of our communications.

Table 2 **Changes in Perceptions of the Industry:**
Industry Effort on Waste Disposal

| | 1982 | | 1981 | |
	Exposed	Unexposed	Exposed	Unexposed
Effort (a lot of/some)	72%	59%	66%	59%
No effort (only a little/hardly any)	27	38	32	35

Note: Those exposed have more favorable opinions as to what the industry may actually be doing to manage hazardous waste disposal.

Table 3 **Changes in Perceptions of the Industry:**
Industry Efforts to Reduce Pollution

| | 1982 | | 1981 | |
	Exposed	Unexposed	Exposed	Unexposed
Effort (a lot of/some)	77%	70%	78%	70%
No effort (only a little/hardly any)	21	27	21	24

Note: The activity area of general air and water pollution is second in importance (after waste disposal) to our sample, again confirming previous hypotheses. For this reason, recommendations were made to put approximately 2/3 of the advertising weight behind waste disposal and approximately 1/4 behind the area of air and water pollution. This chart reflects those proportions of communications effort. Once again, we see a favorable difference between those exposed and not exposed. The differences, however, are less dramatic, as one might expect.

Public opinions and perceptions of the chemical industry often differ between the respondents who were probably exposed and aware of the communications and those who were probably not exposed or unaware of the communications. The most consistent differences between individuals in each of these groups were overperceptions of the chemical industry's concern and the industry's efforts on each of the five issues discussed in the advertisements. Since the advertising focused specifically on the industry's concern about and efforts on each of these issues, these consistent differences of opinion between groups are confirmations that the advertising is having an impact. However, responses from individuals in each of these groups were less likely to show differences of opinion on questions that related less to the advertising messages.

The greatest differences between those who were probably exposed and aware of the communications and those who were not exposed or aware of the communications were overperceptions of the chemical industry's concern about each of the five issues discussed in the advertising. In general, politically active individuals who were probably exposed and aware of the communications were currently 7 to 18 percentage points more likely than their counterparts to believe that the chemical industry was concerned rather than unconcerned about each of the five key issues. In 1982, the widest margin separating individuals in each of these groups was on the issue of chemical waste disposal. In 1981, perceptions of the industry's concern with these issues differed on four of the five issues, the exception being the industry's concern with the transportation of chemicals.

The 1982 results showed equally consistent differences between the perceptions of persons in both groups when asked about the industry efforts at solving the problems with each of the five issues. In 1982, those individuals who were probably exposed and aware of the communications were 6 to 13 percentage points more likely than their counterparts to believe that the chemical industry was making an effort rather than no effort with all five issues. Once again, the greatest difference between individuals in each group was in their perceptions of the industry's effort with waste disposal.

Perceptions of the chemical industry's concern about the average person's welfare also differed between individuals in both groups. The group of individuals with the opportunity for exposure and who were aware of the communications were 9 points more likely than the group who were neither exposed nor aware of the communications to view the chemical industry as concerned rather than not concerned about the average person's welfare.

There was no sizable difference between both groups on *overall* opinions of the chemical industry, however. The absence of a difference between both groups on more general questions about the industry and the consistent differences on questions specifically relating to issues discussed in the communications provides some evidence as to what kind of impact the campaign was having. These findings suggest that those who were exposed to the communications were accepting the specific messages in the campaign. However, this acceptance of the specific messages was not yet being transformed into a general favorability toward the chemical industry.

The Image of the Chemical Industry in Context

Although the communications campaign appears to have had an impact on those exposed to the communications, most of this impact cannot be noticed when we examine the overall attitudes and perceptions of the chemical industry.

Out of a field of six major American industries, the chemical industry continues to receive the fifth most favorable rating overall from politically active individuals. Despite this persistently low ranking of the chemical industry, the actual numbers of favorable and unfavorable ratings given by politically active individuals show a slight improvement over the previous year's ratings. Currently, more than two-fifths (43 percent) of all politically active individuals hold favorable rather than unfavorable opinions of the chemical industry.

The industry neighbors were also most likely to perceive the industry as least concerned about pollution and waste disposal. Perceptions of the chemical industry's concern about both issues had changed little since 1980. For all three years, the fewest chemical industry neighbors (42 percent) felt the industry was concerned about waste disposal, while a moderately larger percentage (52 percent) felt the industry was concerned about air and water pollution.

Perceptions of Industry Effort

Of the five issues, the chemical industry was seen by the fewest politically active individuals (63 percent) as making an effort to reduce the risks associated with waste disposal. For the third year in a row, more than one out of every three politically active individuals felt the industry had made only a little or hardly any effort on waste disposal. Perceptions of the chemical industry's efforts with air and water pollution were more favorable to the industry, however. The efforts with air and water pollution ranked third out of the five issue areas examined. The third largest percentage of politically active individuals (72 percent) stated that the chemical industry was making either a lot of effort or some effort to reduce the risks of air and water pollution.

The percentage of politically active individuals neither exposed nor aware of the communications who believed the chemical industry was making only a little effort or no effort at all with waste disposal had grown slightly, from 35 to 38 percent, over the past year. Meanwhile, those individuals exposed to and aware of the communications believing the industry was making only a little effort or no effort at all had dropped by 5 points, from 32 to 27 percent. What these contrary trends suggest is that those not exposed to the communications are viewing the industry's efforts with waste disposal in increasingly negative terms, while those exposed to the communications are viewing the industry's efforts in increasingly positive terms.

NOTES

1. John Elliott, Jr., former chairman of the board, Ogilvy & Mather, Inc., "Why Don't You Speak for Yourself, John?" Keynote address, "Issue Advertising: How to Make it Work on Television," Sponsored by AAAA, ANA, PRSA, PUCA, TVB, New York, September 15, 1981.
2. *CMA—What It Is, What It Does*. Chemical Manufacturers Association, Washington, DC, October 1981, p. 1.
3. Ibid., p. 2.
4. James N. Sites, "Changing Your Image: The Story of How the Chemical Manufacturers Association Mobilized Its Members to Win Public Support," *Association Management*, March 1981, p. 48.
5. Sites, "Changing Your Image," p. 49.

Chapter 11 | **CANADIAN PETROLEUM ASSOCIATION, CANADA:**

A CAMPAIGN TO CHANGE PUBLIC ATTITUDES TOWARD THE OIL INDUSTRY AND TO INFLUENCE THE CANADIAN GOVERNMENT'S NATIONAL ENERGY POLICY

When the government of Pierre Trudeau announced the formulation of a new National Energy Policy on October 28, 1980, the Canadian Petroleum Association (CPA) found itself confronted with an unprecedented set of problems due to this bellweather shift in the nation's energy policy. Such a radical redirection was likely to affect all aspects of the petroleum industry, from exploration to refining, and was seen as rendering the entire industry infinitely more risky and less profitable. Additionally, the CPA viewed as ominous the nationalistic orientation of the NEP—an orientation that was likely to create a rift between Canadian and foreign (mostly American) companies, and between large and small companies. Thus, the industry felt it had no choice but to present its case to the Canadian public.

CANADA'S NEW NATIONAL ENERGY POLICY (NEP)

The government's goal was to increase Canadian ownership of its oil and gas industry from 35 percent at that time to at least 50 percent by 1990. The greatest foreign ownership was vested in the U.S.-controlled companies. To accomplish its goals, the Canadian government announced a new set of taxes, tax incentives, and grants to Canadian-owned oil and gas companies. The intent of the policy was to provide benefits in direct proportion to the Canadian share of ownership in a company. However, the impact turned out to be quite the reverse. In reality, the tax bite took away more from the Canadian companies because they were concentrated in the upstream operations, crude oil and gas exploration and production. The American multinational oil companies were more integrated and could therefore absorb some of the adverse impacts of the new taxes in their downstream operations, refining and distribution services. In addition, the Canadian government kept the right to take, subject to some compensation, a retroactive 25 percent interest in all oil and gas discovered on federal lands.

The government admitted that the NEP might be discriminatory in the treatment of foreign investors in the oil and gas industry. Unlike foreign investors in other industries that were regulated through the Foreign Investment Review Agency (FERA), which had wide discretion, the treatment of foreign investors under NEP was fixed in law. It should be noted here that Canadian-owned companies were also subject to FERA if they were to sell all or part of their assets to a foreign-owned company.

The energy policy brought opposition not only from the Conservative party, but also from the oil and gas industry. A major criticism of NEP was that it would not help the Canadian petroleum industry. On the contrary, in reaching its aim of nationalization, it would hurt all companies working in the industry. James Deacey of the Canadian Petroleum Association (CPA) states:

> The one nice thing that the NEP has done is that it has hurt everybody. . . . We do not disagree with Canadianization, we disagree with the NEP's concept of Canadianization. It is the method plus timing that gives us problems.

Alan Gregg, president of Decima Research, a leading opinion polling firm, stated:

> This policy is a revenue mission. The government has been having revenue problems even before the election of the Liberal Party. The Conservative Party, which was in power before the liberals, admitted to it. The public reality is the question of where is there a sector where we can grab something to assist us in our revenue problem. Where is there a body of public opinion that will allow that initial overture to be consistent politically and popularly.

Prior to the announcement of the policy, the CPA conducted a public opinion survey in September–October 1980. The findings of the survey showed confusion in the public mind about the energy situation in Canada. CPA therefore felt there was a need for the industry as a whole to start getting involved in this area. Whereas before CPA's involvement in public matters was at a relatively low level, the NEP changed all that, and public affairs became one of its major concerns.

Rowland Frazee, chairman of the Royal Bank of Canada, said in his address to the bank's annual meeting in January 1981:

> It seems abundantly clear by now that it |the NEP| is so seriously flawed as to be a non-starter which should be withdrawn and reconsidered. And in that reconsideration, let all of the key players have reasonable input! We need consensus in energy policy, not tablets from the Mount.

The CPA campaign offers an interesting set of issues for analysis that are generally not found in most other situations where an industry or a corporation is involved in public advocacy of a controversial social issue.

1. In Canada, the government used all the avenues of free communication available to it to publicize its views and persuade the general public to agree to them. Although the Canadian government did not resort to paid political commercials to propagate the NEP, there is a long tradition in Canada for the government's use of paid advertising. What is the rationale and logic for a government engaging in advocacy advertising in a democratic society, as opposed to a merely informational campaign, and what are its sociopolitical implications?
2. The Canadian petroleum industry is dominated by foreign ownership, mostly American. The NEP had a distinctly nationalistic orientation. Under these circumstances, how can an industry association develop a cohesive communications strategy that meets the apparently conflicting needs of its member companies, and at the same time is not viewed as foreign-dominated or antinationalistic?
3. What are some of the organizational and operational problems confronted by such an association that might adversely affect its lobbying, positioning on public policy issues, and public education efforts?
4. What are some of the strategic alternatives available to foreign multinational corporations that engage in public debate and lobbying on issues where their concerns might be viewed as contrary to those of locally owned companies, or policies advocated by the host country government?

In addition to overall strategy, the case also presents some interesting dimensions of tactics that set it apart from other advertising approaches to advocacy campaigns that are more prevalent in the United States.

The design and implementation of CPA campaign strategy was almost identical to advertising campaigns used for product advertising, especially those of packaged consumer goods. The campaign had the heavy involvement of outside agencies, both market research and advertising, in all phases of strategy development and implementation. It relied heavily on field and laboratory research for all aspects of the campaign and used ad techniques designed to measure audience responses similar to those for product advertising associated with new product introductions.

The CPA campaign, therefore, presents a sharp contrast to the alternative approach to advocacy advertising, which argues that selling an abstract and complex idea, and one with strong public policy connotations, is quite different from selling products. The CPA campaign suggests that this type of "selling" can be packaged and moved in essentially the same manner as ordinary products, and by those who are experts in mass merchandising techniques.

THE POLITICAL ENVIRONMENT OF THE NEP

The energy issue became prominent in Canada with the OPEC oil embargo in 1973–74. At that time, Canada was self-sufficient in oil. While it exported oil to the United States from the western provinces, it imported a roughly equal amount to meet the needs of its eastern provinces. This approach was desirable to save on the transportation costs of moving oil from western to eastern Canada.

After the oil embargo, two issues concerned the Canadian government: (1) How much should Canadian consumers pay for domestically produced oil? (2) Who should control Canada's petroleum industry?

The Canadian government chose a policy that would charge the United States the world price for Canadian oil exports, and use the excess money after taxes to subsidize oil imports for eastern Canada. This policy was intended to stabilize domestic oil prices and protect Canadian consumers from rising world oil prices.

However, the policy did not yield the desired effect, because of several factors. First, many of the major Canadian oil companies were shifting their efforts in oil and gas exploration from Canada to the United States, due to the higher net return in the United States. This caused two problems: (1) There was a reduction in oil and gas exploration in Canada. (2) It caused an unstable situation inside Canada due to competing revenue claims from provinces (owners of the resource) and the federal government, which ultimately led to increases in domestic oil prices.

The second problem pertained to the tax incentive plans contained in the energy policy. Prior to the NEP, one of the primary incentives for investing in the oil and gas industry was provided through the income tax system. It allowed producers to defer taxes if profits were reinvested in exploration in Canada. This policy worked in favor of larger companies; smaller companies did not take advantage of the available income tax writeoffs. And yet they had relatively limited opportunities outside Canada and were the ones who were left to do exploration in Canada.

The third area involved the activities of the foreign-owned sector of the oil industry, which was concentrated in Alberta. The foreign ownership, mostly American, in this strategic commodity was very high—approximately 70 to 75 percent. The foreign oil companies were operating in a more advantageous situation as companies compared to the

Canadian-owned companies. In addition to the advantage of size, they were not limited to activities in oil and gas areas alone and were investing in mining, manufacturing, real estate, and other Canadian industries. The federal government of Canada believed that by the turn of the century, there would be a disproportionate amount of wealth concentration in Alberta, controlled by the provincial government.

Oil Policy and Electoral Politics

Energy policy in the oil and gas industry in Canada was directly influenced by the campaign strategies of the ruling Liberal party. In 1974, the Liberal party's leader, Pierre Elliott Trudeau, won the national elections with a large majority. The party had been a strong supporter of social welfare programs and economic nationalism, both of which were designed to appeal to large segments of the Canadian population. However, by 1980 it was losing public confidence because of its inability to improve Canada's economic situation, which was by then beset by high inflation, unemployment, economic slowdown, and rising taxes.

The defeat of the Liberal party in the June 1979 elections brought to power the Conservative party under the leadership of Prime Minister Joe Clark. The victory was, however, very short-lived. Due to a series of blunders in handling the economic situation, the Clark government was defeated on a no-confidence motion in Parliament, and Joe Clark resigned less than nine months after he took office.

The Conservatives had come to power with the promise of lower interest rates and a cut in taxes to stimulate economic growth. And yet the first budget of the new government focused attention on cutting government deficits and spending by imposing an excise tax on oil of 18 cents per gallon, higher energy prices, and failure to provide tax relief for lower-income Canadians. To the public, it appeared a betrayal of trust. The Conservative party had failed to gauge the public mood. The opposition parties, despite their own dismal performance when in power, coalesced in opposition. When the federal budget was presented in Parliament it was defeated, and with it came the end of the Conservative government.

In the 1980 election, energy was again a significant campaign issue. Convinced that its approach to economic issues was right, the Conservative party again advocated an oil self-sufficiency program that would require an excise tax of 18 cents per gallon of gasoline. The excess money was to go into a self-sufficiency fund to be used for direct investment, loans, and loan guarantees aimed at achieving oil self-sufficiency. The Conservative party also proposed to privatize Petro Canada, a government-owned or Crown corporation. Trudeau criticized the Conservative party's proposal as riding on the backs of the poor. His program would establish a blended price for consumers which would be lower than the one advocated by the Conservative party. That program became the cornerstone of the Liberal campaign.

Trudeau, knowing he would win the election with a clear majority, delivered a very strong speech on economic nationalism, thereby setting the general tone for the formulation of the NEP. The Liberal party won the election of 1980. After Trudeau's election, the price of gasoline went up to 43 cents a liter, which was much more than the Conservatives had proposed. The basic element that defeated the Conservatives, apart from a general appearance of incompetence, was the specific issue of energy policy. During their term in office, the Liberals were able to arrive at an energy agreement with Alberta; the Conservatives were not. The Conservatives also attempted several policies regarding Petro Canada, albeit unsuccessfully. Public opinion surveys showed that in the public mind, the government had failed to resolve the two critical issues, federal-provincial relations and energy policy, and that had caused people to switch their votes to the Liberal party.

The Public Relations Effort by the Government of Canada

The government of Canada has always been skillful in the use of advertising. Just prior to NEP, during the spring and early fall of 1980, the government started with a campaign stating that Canada was energy self-sufficient. The entire thrust of the campaign was focused on the profits of the oil companies, mostly multinationals.

Ken Colby, formerly the national political correspondent of the Canadian Broadcasting Company and currently vice-president of government affairs of NORCEN Energy, the second largest Canadian-owned oil company, observed:

> There has been a long history in the Government's use of unpaid mass media and "paid" advertising to promote its policies. It has been, for a long time, a good tool for the Government of Canada to attract the support of the public. One of the examples of media manipulation occurred in 1978 at the time of the Iran revolution and the resultant fear of another oil crisis. When the United States was short of oil, a tanker bound for Halifax carrying oil from the Middle East, and owned by the Exxon Corporation, was diverted to a United States port. Imperial Oil (Exxon's Canadian subsidiary) tried manfully to explain that this was part of the Exxon pool and Canada benefited from the Exxon pool in having a diversity of sources. The oil was more pressing there and it was simply going to be replaced. In reality it was not a diversion of Canadian oil bound for Canada. However, the Federal Government chose to portray it as such. The media portrayed it as a diversion of Canadian oil and the public perception simply persisted that Exxon had taken away Canadian oil to give it to the Americans.
>
> It was 25,000 barrels of oil, a mere drop in the bucket. That's what they were talking about. But it became headlines for a month. It became part of speeches by the Liberals. When the Liberals were in opposition, several Conservative cabinet ministers were taunted in the House of Commons—being called the Minister of Exxon, or the spokesman for big oil. It became a real political football. It is just ludicrous, but it was probably the most dramatic event.
>
> An interesting point to note here is that Imperial Oil tried to respond to this attack with facts and figures and a legalistic argument and an explanation of the Exxon pool. But it is much clearer and more attractive to the public, if you deal in slogans.

The slogan was: "The diversion of Canadian oil by the giant Exxon Corporation of New York." That was it. People don't know what 25,000 barrels of oil is. There is no frame of reference for that. Imperial Oil decided that the only response they could make was to have its CEO Armstrong appear in a meeting with the ministry; let him have a go at that, and hope that the issue would go away. Well, in the Atlantic Provinces of Canada that are captives of foreign oil, it was very much an issue that, coupled with the Conservatives' plan for dismantling Petro Canada, meant that the Tories were virtually wiped out of Atlantic Canada. It was a very very large political issue. Whether Exxon bungled it or not is beside the point. The industry was continually placed in a defensive posture.

An example of the Canadian government engaging in paid political propaganda could be found in the government's (Liberal party) efforts to sell the Canadian public on the sweeping changes in the Canadian Constitution advocated by the ruling Liberal party, but opposed by many of the provinces of western Canada. Ironically, the reasons given by the government for the need for such advertising were similar to those advanced by private users of paid political-advocacy advertising: that the public does not understand this complex issue; that the news media do not explain it adequately; and that therefore we must undertake to educate the public in a controlled and hospitable communication environment. Strange as it may seem, most of the public "education" on this "complex" issue was done through 30-second spot commercials.

THE CANADIAN PETROLEUM ASSOCIATION (CPA)

Members of CPA have been exploring and developing Canada's oil and natural gas resources since the industry's earliest days in western Canada. The industry was drawn together by common needs and interests and just thirteen years ago, following the discovery of oil in Turner Valley, the Alberta Oil Operators Association was formed. As the industry grew and its activities broadened, so did those of its association. The association's name also evolved to reflect its broader role. In 1952, the organization reached the basic form it uses today, and the current name was adopted.

The industry and the association continue to grow as Canada's northern and offshore frontiers are explored and as unconventional resources like the Alberta oil sands are developed. Today CPA has offices and staff in seven provinces. Its major responsibilities include helping to inform the Canadian public about critical energy issues, preparing technical and analytical submissions on behalf of the industry to government agencies, and gathering and disseminating operating, economic, and policy information for members. The active membership of CPA is comprised of companies engaged in Canada's oil and natural gas industries (other than as contractors, suppliers, or marketers), and includes most major pipeline companies. CPA's members produce more than 80 percent of Canada's crude oil and about two-thirds of its natural gas. In addition, some 90 companies that support industry activity in a variety of ways are associate members.

The Decision-Making Process

It was not until after the election of the new Trudeau government that the Canadian Petroleum Association set up a meeting to investigate the issue that would affect the association and the industry. Previously, the oil industry was involved only in advertising its products. The government started with a campaign (not paid commercials) stating that Canada was self-sufficient. The entire thrust of the government campaign was on the profits of the oil companies—mainly multinational oil companies—through the news media. At that time, company profits were going up quite dramatically. The campaign was a careful orchestration of events leading to a restructuring of the industry—NEP.

The CPA realized that it had to do something to respond to the threat of NEP, which it felt was not only injurious to the industry, but also potentially harmful to Canada itself. However, in developing an effective response strategy it faced some unusual problems because of the composition of its membership, and the highly differential effect NEP was going to have on its different member companies. On the issue of NEP, however, the industry found itself quite united, and the emergent industry position vis-à-vis NEP was common in the petroleum industry. There was not a Canadian position versus a U.S. position.

The Campaign Strategy

CPA's campaign had four objectives:

1. A correction in the public's understanding as to who is responsible and who does what in the energy field
2. A statement of what the government is proposing to do under the National Energy Policy
3. A method whereby the public can judge government performance of its stated goals in a different light
4. The offering of a social contract by the industry to the Canadian public

The tone of the campaign throughout would be evenhanded and factual. CPA would avoid being perceived as "moaners, criers, whiners," or earnest advocates, and would strive to be taking the high road, to be nonadversarial and nonaggressive.

In addition, CPA would carry out a full public affairs program, which would include elements of lobbying, a speakers' bureau, and general public affairs activities such as internal and external communications programs, detailed analysis of government activities, and a wide variety of activities to place its case before the Canadian public.

Strategy Implementation

The one unique argument in the meeting of the board of CPA was the choice between going to an advertising agency or, for the first time, creating its own ad agency within the CPA. Because the campaign was a political one, it was believed that no existing Canadian agency expertise was available to undertake such work and do a better job from the point of view of cost and quality control. The project was quite ambitious in scope and potential impact; no other Canadian industry association had undertaken a project of this type or magnitude. Therefore, CPA believed it would be hard to find an agency with the requisite experience, personnel, or ability to do the job.

The other argument against hiring an agency was economic. Any agency would work on a basic markup of 18 percent. The campaign was budgeted at about $11 million. Therefore, it would cost almost $2 million to hire the best agency, while it would cost much less if the association could hire even the best individuals to do the job for it. There was a potential for some significant economies to be achieved if CPA were, in effect, to create its own agency for the implementation of this campaign.

Therefore, it was decided that CPA would create a project team, consisting of the best people in the business, who would respond through an organization chart to the staff, board members, and other interested parties. This process was akin to an established practice among political parties in preparing for elections.

This way there was a guaranty of quality control; the use of the best ad talent in Canada; and significant savings for CPA to use for more media buying. In order to do such a project, there was also a need for cooperation between CPA and other associations, such as the Petroleum Resources Communication Foundation (PRCF), the Independent Petroleum Association of Canada (IPAC), and the Canadian Association of Oilwell Drilling Contractors (CAODC).

CPA Advertising Structure

The functions and operating structure for the proposed advertising campaign were determined as follows:

Program Coordinator. One person would be added to the CPA staff with strong advertising competence whose job would be to act as the "client" on a day-to-day basis with other outside professionals working on the campaign. This would be his sole responsibility, and he would report through the executive director to the steering committee.

Steering Committee. Membership in this group was comprised of the chairman, vice-chairman, public affairs chairman, finance committee chairman, and the executive director, and any other industry association that opted to contribute significantly to the program financially. This committee was to set overall strategy and content for the campaign, give final approval to the creative execution, and evaluate overall performance. However, as the campaign progressed and the members became more comfortable with the work of the CPA staff, this committee was de facto merged into the regular CPA decision-making structure.

Industry Image Study

The first step in creating a supportive public constituency was a public opinion study. The focus of this study was not to answer the question of what people thought of the industry, which was quite apparent, but why the public held such a low opinion of the industry. The survey was conducted by Decima Research of Toronto, a company known for political research. They were the pollsters of the Conservative party of Canada and those of many other provinces. The principal involved was Alan Gregg, a political strategist with strong Conservative party political connections.

The research was conducted during September–October 1980. It was a telephone survey of 1,190 Canadian citizens 18 years of age and older and representative of the Canadian population. The interview lasted approximately 45 to 60 minutes and contained 133 questions.

The findings showed that the public did not have a good image of oil companies because they thought of oil companies as financially dishonest or unfair in setting prices and as socially unaccountable. People did not believe that oil companies were good communicators or good public affairs specialists. The study also showed that people wanted more information about the petroleum industry; the public was confused ("nobody's telling the truth"), and most important, was very likely to adopt a more positive attitude toward the industry if information was made available in a forthright but nonconfrontational style. Research also indicated that a successful information program, aimed at broadening and increasing public knowledge and understanding of the industry, would make future government expansion (at the industry's expense) significantly more difficult than would be the case given a continuation of existing public attitudes and opinion trends. Additionally, it showed that:

> There were certain areas where there was a shared feeling of disbelief and confusion among people. These areas consisted of lack of understanding as to whether it was business or the government who set prices, or which one could run the industry more efficiently, or whether business or government could deliver the product more inexpensively.

Finally, the research indicated that the major means of achieving a shift in public attitudes would be a mass communication program based on a national advertising campaign, with heavy emphasis on television, and aimed at urban populations in the 18–45 age group.

The Communication Strategy

In June 1981, the senior staff of the CPA held a meeting for the purpose of considering the issues and problems confronted by the industry and devising a campaign to change public opinion. It was argued that the federal government was systematically increasing its presence in, and direct control of, the petroleum industry at the expense of virtually all participants in the industry. Through a carefully orchestrated campaign, which appeared designed first to manipulate public opinion and then to respond to the climate of opinion it had thus created, the federal government had engineered a progressively larger role for itself at both political and bureaucratic levels.

The CPA board decided that the problem facing the industry was a political problem, and that the industry had to take steps to change public opinion. The communication problem was squarely rooted in the political problem. As long as the public held a low opinion of the industry, the industry would be defenseless. The attitudes of the public about the industry had to be changed in order to give people greater political power and ability to influence the government in energy policy matters.

What the industry needed was to create between then and the time of the next general election a constituency or a perception of a constituency. It was clear to the board that if the industry did not create a measurable political constituency by the time of the next election (35 to 50 percent of the Canadian population should agree with the oil industry on most of its public policy initiatives), then following the 1984 general election, the industry would cease to exist as a private industry. If not actually nationalized, it would most probably operate as a highly regulated utility. Observed one CPA executive:

> We were determined not to be such an easy picking as we were in the last round. The public *will* know more of what we do and how we do it and why we do it. We cannot count on any political party to leave us alone. I mean, there are many people in the Conservative Party who would take positions on the NEP just as hard or harder than Liberals can. There is no doubt in my mind that no political party would turn back the clock on the NEP.

THE CAMPAIGN

Based on the detailed analysis of the public opinion survey conducted by Decima, CPA's executive committee, at its meeting on December 9, 1980, directed the CPA staff to report on: (a) the specific targets to be achieved through an industry-sponsored advertising program; and (b) the total costs associated with such a program.

Three major premises were a springboard for delineating the campaign:

- The petroleum industry faced a political problem that required a significant change in public opinion between then and the end of 1983.
- Public opinion could be moved, given appropriate "reach" and frequency of messages, and assuming acceptable levels of creativity and "shaping" of messages.
- The data available to the CPA through previous research correctly identified those publics whose opinion could be changed and the messages which were necessary to secure that change.

A mixed media campaign was suggested, with the greatest portion going to TV, but also using magazines, newspapers, radio, and other vehicles as the development of the creative message dictated.

By March 1981, CPA staff, in cooperation with the Decima Research, LTD., and McLaughlan, Mohr and Massey Ltd., advertising agency, developed a basic strategy document that subsequently became the foundation of all actions pertaining to advertising and other public affairs activities. A summary of the document follows.

Announcement of the Campaign

There were two obvious possibilities to consider concerning the level of attention the CPA wanted to attract surrounding the campaign launch. The first was the option of simply buying advertising time and placing ads with no announcement. The second option was for the CPA to release, in some manner, the rationale for the program. The CPA chose the latter option, because:

- It felt that it would be impossible to avoid comment on the program.
- CPA should attempt to be out front, instead of appearing to be reacting to a situation created by others.
- Its communications goals would be furthered by explaining the *need* for information at the start of the program.
- CPA would be able to condition the public, to some degree, to the essence of its message by actively announcing its rationale.
- The free media and the credibility to be gained from the "news" format as opposed to paid advertising were considered important.

Target Audiences and Markets

The focus of the campaign was on the same groups that had caused the Liberal government to be elected. Consequently, CPA had identified the key target groups as all adults above the age of 18, with special emphasis on people 25 to 49 years old, middle-income earners with above-average levels of education. The campaign was timed for the period between March 1981 and December 1984. The weight and placement of the advertising would reflect both the largest target markets and CPA's major problem areas. This ranking was: the provinces of Ontario, Atlantic/Quebec, Manitoba/Saskatchewan/B.C., and Alberta.

The campaign had four phases:

Phase I.   Develop credibility and legitimacy for campaign through factual, low-key messages that address public concerns.

Phase II.   Establish public benefits that derive from industry activities and broaden image of industry.

Phase III.   Move to progressively harder factual information messages at a pace consistent with credibility and the public's willingness to listen, eventually explaining respective roles and responsibilities of government and industry.

Phase IV.   When public's information base is adequate to evaluate our position, state industry's case for change in treatment by government.

Campaign Costs

The total campaign costs for September 1981 through December 1984 amounted to $10,744,400, divided as follows:

Time Period	Total Costs ($ million)	Direct Media	Research/Creative Production/ Administration
Sept. 81–June 82	$3.759	$60.9	$39.1
July 82–June 83	2.890	65.4	34.6
July 83–Dec. 84	1.325	64.2	35.8
Jan. 84–Dec. 84	2.800	60.7	39.3

Media Schedule

For television, a very heavy initial segment was used for the first 10 weeks to give a reach of over 65 percent of the adult population of Ontario with a frequency message of 2.5 times per week. This was to decline but remain reasonably constant for the rest of the year at a level of about 55 percent of the adult population.

The magazine portion of advertising consisted of 10 or more national English and French magazines using, over the course of the year, a total of 77 pages of copy and having reached 89 percent of their readers 15 times. For newspapers, coverage included 49 dailies in 24 markets over the year, placing 9 messages in each. Estimated readership was over 9 million for these dailies.

Major communicators already active were carried over to phase II, thereby reducing creative and production costs. However, media penetration was somewhat lower because of the 15 percent inflation factor in media costs. The entire phase II campaign was comprised almost entirely of 30-second TV ads, with a small amount of secondary media.

For both phases III and IV, the media mix was similar to that employed in phase I.

During the period July–December 1983, the media buy for television was reduced from a nationwide buy to one that covered the target areas: Metro Toronto, the balance of Ontario, French-speaking Quebec, and British Columbia.

The January–December 1984 period saw another change in media scheduling. Because of a smaller budget for media buys, the television commercials were confined to spring and fall periods only. At this stage, there was growing concern that a decreasing level of weight and frequency in exposures would adversely affect public awareness of and attitude toward industry messages.

Other Communication Programs

Other than direct advertising through the media, a number of programs backed up the advertising:

1. *Speakers bureau.* CPA would actively seek appropriate forums for industry spokepersons, prepare speeches, and find opportunities to reinforce those speeches. These activities were like a political campaign.
2. *Lobbying.* Lobbying consisted of communicating with members of the House of Commons, contacting other companies and getting their reaction to NEP, identifying constituencies for these companies' activities, and identifying constituencies of House members to be lobbied.
3. *Public affairs activities.* These included working with companies to develop internal communications and participation plans for employees; developing line-by-line responses to the National Energy Program, including identification of fallacies and accuracies; developing new publications to reflect the overall public affairs strategy; identifying in each member company a National Energy Plan coordinator; and trying to ascertain the level of U.S. parent company reaction.

EXECUTING THE CAMPAIGN

Development of TV Commercials

Because of the long lead times on television production, the development of material for that medium was emphasized. This did not mean, however, that other print media were neglected; it was estimated that they would come on stream very quickly once television development moved ahead. The purpose of the TV advertising was to reach people and communicate better through the development of four separate creative tracks, each delivering essentially the same message, but using different visual techniques.

One more important factor in this matter, "was the choice of spokesmen. It was felt that the person must have a background in the industry, but should not be a chief executive officer of an oil company because people believe that chief executives know all the answers, but would not tell."

An initial set of criteria was established. The selected person should be:

- Identifiably Canadian (although international stature would not hurt)
- Not a familiar advertising face
- Fortyish, masculine, with equal appeal to men and women
- Have a distinctive, authoritative voice that is also friendly

A careful search suggested ten potential candidates. One of these was Ken Colby, who at that time was director of government relations for NORCEN. As a political correspondent for the Canadian Broadcasting Company, he had become a nationally recognized figure and had a highly positive public image. At first Ken was reluctant to accept the assignment, because he might be perceived as a "hired mouthpiece," thereby impugning his integrity and lowering his public credibility. An added concern was the impact it might have on his employer, NORCEN Energy, which had extensive dealings with various federal and provincial government agencies. However, after careful consideration, and with the consent of NORCEN's chief executive, he accepted the assignment.

Television Advertising Problems

The first set of commercials was rejected by the CBC, but the other TV channels accepted it. CPA was concerned that it would not get the opportunity to have its commercials shown on CBC. In Canada, all commercials are submitted to the commercial acceptance departments of the two networks (CBC and CTV), which evaluate them for acceptability based on guidelines approved by the Federal Commission. The networks reject commercials that deal with controversial topics, which are considered part of their news agenda, and have on occasion even rejected commercials sponsored by the Canadian government. However, after some changes, four commercial tracks were accepted for broadcast [Exhibits 1–4]. These were:

Track One—Spokesman on Site: This would be a series of spots with an on-camera announcer delivering the message from such places as a tar sands plant or an offshore oil rig.

Track Two—Family. This would be a series of spots shot in household situations and showing the importance of oil in our everyday lives and for our children.

Track Three—Symbols. This would be a series of spots in which the verbal message would be supported by symbolic devices such as oil barrels.

Track Four—Oil People. This would be a series of commercials in which we actually get to meet people in the oil industry doing all kinds of jobs at all kinds of levels in all kinds of places while the CPA message is being delivered.

Print Ads

The campaign included three print ads. Two were captioned at the bottom with "Energy solutions begin with understanding," while the third captioned "Economic solutions begin with energy."

The first ad was titled "We asked Canadians how they would describe the country's current energy situation. The answer: 'Confusing.'" The message conveyed the notion that the energy situation was not a crisis, but a challenge. It suggested that Canada was not confronted with an imminent energy crisis, but that in the longer run Canadians would have to face the question of security of oil supply. It was possible for Canada to become self-sufficient in the years ahead, but the achievement of that goal would be influenced by decisions made now and in the near future [Exhibit 5].

Exhibit 1

I want to talk to you about energy. In fact, more specifically about oil and gas.

I'm speaking for the Canadian Petroleum Association and its more than 70 member companies who produce around 80% of Canada's oil and gas.

Canadian Petroleum Association
Spokesman/Offshore Rig
Television 60 seconds

We think we're good at our business.

But recently, we discovered something that we haven't been quite so good at... communicating with Canadians.

We conducted a survey to find out how Canadians felt about the whole energy question. You told us you felt confused and frustrated...that you wanted some clear and accurate information.

We share your concern over the current confusion about energy...because decisions being made right now can affect everybody's future.

So from now on, we're going to do our best to help you understand more about the oil and gas aspect of energy.

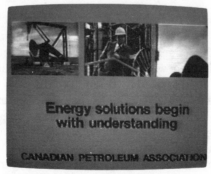

Because we believe energy solutions begin with understanding.

Exhibit 2

Right now, Canadians consume nearly two million barrels of oil each day.

So naturally, people are concerned about...

oil policies, oil prices and oil supplies for the future.

At the Canadian Petroleum Association, we're concerned too.

So we're going to do our best to help you understand about the oil and gas aspect of energy.

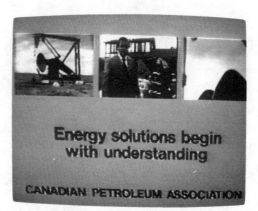

Because we believe energy solutions begin with understanding.

Exhibit 3

A lot of people in Canada are confused about whether or not this country is running out of oil.

Well, they've got good reason to be confused...because the answer is yes...and no.

Yes we are running out of this kind of oil. Oil that's relatively easy and inexpensive to get out of the ground.

But we do have other kinds of oil. In the oil sands, in the Arctic and beneath the ocean floor. Enough oil to last us for several hundred years.

That other kind of oil, however, is difficult to get at and expensive to get out.

Right now, Canada is facing decisions involving hundreds of billions of dollars that will determine when and how much of that other kind of oil will be available for use.

At the Canadian Petroleum Association, we think better energy decisions can be made when everybody understands the facts.

So we're doing our best to help you understand more about the oil and gas aspect of energy. Because we believe energy solutions begin with understanding.

Exhibit 4

"People do not and never will trust the major oil companies"

"I don't believe what the government is telling us."

"No one seems to know how much of the profits should go to the respective governments and how much should go to the oil companies."

"I read the paper every night but I become more confused each time."

At the Canadian Petroleum Association, we're concerned about today's energy confusion because it could affect all of us tomorrow. So we're going to try to tell you more about the oil and gas aspect of energy. We believe energy solutions begin with understanding.

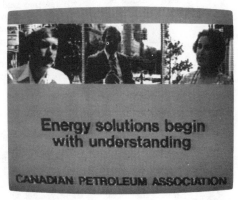

Canadian Petroleum Association

Exhibit 5

We asked Canadians how they would describe the country's current energy situation.

The answer: confusing.

We are the Canadian Petroleum Association. We're made up of more than seventy member companies and together we produce about 80% of Canada's oil and natural gas.

Recently, we commissioned a Canada-wide study to see how people felt about the whole energy question. The results, to put it mildly, were startling.

What people said

The study told us how people feel about the country's current energy situation. It also told us how people feel about oil and gas companies. The answers, frankly, were not entirely flattering.

Canadians told us they found the whole energy question thoroughly confusing. With different kinds of information coming from the federal government, from provincial governments, from the media and from the industry, they said they simply didn't know who to believe.

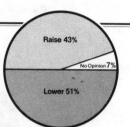

This is the actual study commissioned by the Canadian Petroleum Association. It told us how Canadians feel about energy questions and about the oil and gas industry.

For the Canadian Petroleum Association, the confusion surrounding the country's energy situation presented an obvious challenge. One that could best be met through an information program designed to help people understand more about the oil and gas aspect of energy.

A Rude Awakening

The second part of our study presented a different kind of problem. Canadians told us they thought we were good at finding and producing oil and gas, but not very good at communicating with Canadians. The study suggested that we cared more about profits than about the country. That we favoured the west over other regions of Canada. And that there was some doubt about our honesty and sincerity.

Naturally, we thought some of the opinions revealed by the study were not entirely accurate so we decided to go ahead with an information program. This advertisement and others in newspapers, magazines and television represent a first step in that program. As for honesty and sincerity, we think people will believe us if we do our best to provide accurate and helpful information. It's a program from which we hope everybody will benefit.

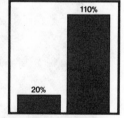

Canadians were almost equally divided on the question of whether to pay more for oil and gas to encourage development or to pay less because we have plenty. Now the new energy agreement has answered that question.

Not a crisis. A challenge.

Right now, Canada is not confronted with an imminent energy crisis. But in the longer term we do face the question of security of oil supply. It is possible for Canada to become oil self sufficient in the years ahead. But achievement of that goal will be influenced by decisions made now and in the near future.

At the Canadian Petroleum Association, we believe oil self sufficiency for Canada is a challenge that must be met because our national security depends on it. But that challenge can only be met when the majority of Canadians agree to the goal and understand the national commitment required of the country.

For that reason, we're going to do our best to help Canadians understand more about the oil and gas aspect of the energy question. That's a commitment we plan to keep. Because we believe energy solutions begin with understanding.

The column on the left shows what percentage of profits most Canadians guess the oil and gas industry reinvests in exploration and development. The column on the right shows the actual percentage of cash flow reinvested by the industry last year.

CANADIAN PETROLEUM ASSOCIATION.
Energy solutions begin with understanding.

The second ad was titled, "We promised on television to help you understand more about the oil and gas aspect of the energy question. We're keeping that promise." The ad argued that the world was experiencing an oil glut, so there appeared to be no likelihood of immediate shortages, but Canada's past experience with revolutions and oil embargos should convince Canadians that they simply could not take things for granted [Exhibit 6].

The third ad was titled, "This is the message the Canadian Petroleum Association is taking to Parliament today." The ad addressed different issues concerning NEP—what the energy security bills were all about, a sober look at the National Energy Program, and the National Energy Program's legacy of loss. The ad concluded with the notice that the CPA was asking the Parliamentary Standing Committee on Energy Legislation to take a new look at the National Energy Program [Exhibit 7].

Media Schedule

The CPA ran its print ads between October 31, 1981, and January 1982. The total number of insertions for the entire campaign was 35 using 20 different publications, as shown in the media schedule [Table 1].

REACTION TO THE CAMPAIGN

Press Reaction

The press had provided extensive coverage of NEP. However, there was no perceptible coverage of the CPA campaign on the part of print or broadcast media. Nor was there any change in the news media coverage of NEP as a consequence of the CPA campaign. Noting the absence of press mention, Ken Colby, a TV veteran, observed: "There is nothing to editorialize about. What we have so far is the oil industry saying that there is confusion on the energy issue, and that this confusion is bad."

Government Reaction

There was no public reaction from the government either. Given the mild, noncontroversial, nonassertive character of the ad copy, this lack of reaction should not be surprising. Moreover, all CPA commercials were shown to the minister of energy before they were aired. Colby comments:

> We had nothing to disturb them [the government] and there was nothing they could object to. I am sure there would have been a strong reaction on the part of the government if we had run a commercial saying that two-thirds of the price of gasoline paid by the people at the gas pump goes to the government as taxes.

Exhibit 6

We promised on television to help you understand more about the oil and gas aspect of the energy question.

We're keeping that promise.

You may have seen some of our messages on television. We're the Canadian Petroleum Association, and our more than seventy member companies produce about 80% of Canada's oil and natural gas.

Offshore oil workers commute to and from the job in big twin-engined helicopters like this. The extra engine and cold water survival suits for the workers are just two of the rigid safety precautions that are part of everyday life on the job.

In a nation-wide study, we asked Canadians how they felt about the country's current energy situation. You said you felt confused and frustrated and that you wanted some clear and accurate information.

We want to do what we can to help clear up some of the confusion surrounding the energy question. So we're working to help you understand more about the oil and gas aspect of energy.

The energy question

The so-called energy question is really made up of many questions. Are we facing immediate shortages? Is Canada in danger or running out of oil and gas? Will conservation solve our problems? Are alternate energy sources readily available to us?

Right now, the world is experiencing an oil glut so there appears to be no likelihood of immediate shortages. But our past experience with revolutions and oil embargos should convince us that we simply can't take things for granted.

Right now, this giant semi-submersible rig is drilling for oil more than two hundred kilometers off the coast of Newfoundland. As high as a thirty-five storey building, the rig has been featured in Ripley's Believe It Or Not.

As to whether or not Canada is running out of oil and gas, the answer is yes and no. Yes we are slowly but surely running out of conventional oil. Oil that is relatively easy to get out of the ground. But we have other kinds of oil. In our oil sands, in the Arctic and beneath the ocean floor. That kind of oil, however, is more difficult to get at and much more expensive to get out.

Will conservation solve our problems? It will certainly help, but given long-term usage projections and a continuing decline in conventional oil production, it is possible for Canada to become self sufficient in oil and gas only with development of new petroleum resources

Alternate energy sources do hold real promise for the future. But that future is probably several generations away. It appears that oil and gas will remain our primary energy sources until well into the next century.

Our energy habits

Currently, petroleum accounts for an estimated 58% of Canada's primary energy requirements. Oil accounts for 40% and natural gas provides 18%.

In 1980, Canada produced about 1.52 million barrels of oil per day. But Canadians consumed 1.87 million barrels per day. The difference was made up by costly imported oil. Our known reserves of natural gas, however, suggest that we will have enough for our own needs plus enough to export for many, many years to come.

Television spokesman Ken Colby stands in front of a pumpjack in Alberta's oil country. The pumpjack extracts conventional oil, the kind of oil that has been a declining resource in Canada for ten years.

A little bit of knowledge

Some people say a little bit of knowledge can be a dangerous thing. At the Canadian Petroleum Association, we believe a little bit of knowledge is an important beginning. Obviously, this advertisement cannot contain enough information to make you an oil and gas expert. But we do hope it has helped you understand more about the oil and gas aspect of the energy question.

CANADIAN PETROLEUM ASSOCIATION.
Energy solutions begin with understanding.

Exhibit 7

This is the message the Canadian Petroleum Association is taking to parliament today.

Today, the Canadian Petroleum Association will be appearing before the Parliamentary Standing Committee on Energy Legislation. The Association plans to present to the Committee a brief outlining the petroleum industry's views on Bill C-104, one of a series of proposed Bills intended to deal with energy security legislation.

What the Energy Security Bills are all about.

The Energy Security Bills represent the last phase of implementation of the National Energy Program. At this time, 18 months after the introduction of the National Energy Program, the Canadian Petroleum Association feels it appropriate to take stock and assess the merits and impact of the N.E.P.

A sober look at the National Energy Program.

The primary stated intentions of the National Energy Program were to ensure oil supply security for Canada and to achieve substantial Canadianization of the petroleum industry. The target for fulfillment of these objectives was set at the year 1990. The Canadian Petroleum Association has long been on record as supporting these laudable objectives.

With the introduction of the National Energy Program, the federal government also claimed the need for a fairer, or larger, share of the revenues generated from Canada's petroleum sector. Again, the Canadian Petroleum Association was on record as supporting a more equitable distribution of revenues.

At the time of the National Energy Program's introduction, the Canadian Petroleum Association expressed concern that the federal government's revenue objectives, and the measures chosen to implement the N.E.P., could prove damaging to both the petroleum industry and the nation's economy. After 18 months, the evidence is overwhelming that this has been the case.

The National Energy Program's legacy of loss.

While the objectives of the National Energy Program are laudable, the consequences resulting from the methods of implementation have been extremely damaging to the petroleum industry in particular, and the nation as a whole. Consider the following:

• The damage inflicted on the petroleum sector has reduced the likelihood of achieving oil supply security by 1990. Meanwhile since the introduction of the N.E.P., Canada's ability to supply its oil needs from domestic production has declined by 12% — a trend which has to be reversed.

• Since the introduction of the N.E.P., more than 15,000 jobs in the oil and gas industry have been lost, plus countless more in related industries in Ontario, Quebec and throughout Canada.

• Governments are heavily taxing both the public and petroleum industry in the name of oil supply security. Typical retail gasoline prices in Toronto, for example, have increased by 34% while net revenue received by producers for each barrel of conventional oil has been halved. Yet we're actually further away from oil supply security.

• Canada's ability to develop its conventional oil reserves has been undermined. Since October 1980, some 334 oil drilling and service rigs have left Canada. The number of wells drilled in 1981 dropped by more than 2,000 from the previous year.

• Non-conventional oil and gas development has also suffered. Land sales, which reflect exploration expectations, dropped by one third from 1980 to 1981. Geophysical activity — the forerunner of exploration drilling — went down as well.

• Canada's oil supply security program is heavily dependent on major energy projects. The Suncor synthetic oil expansion — a pre-N.E.P. project — has been completed. But the Syncrude expansion has been abandoned, Cold Lake has been delayed indefinitely and the future of Alsands is in doubt. At least three other major projects crucial to oil supply security have been suspended or abandoned and development of the major Hibernia offshore discovery is uncertain because of a dispute between governments.

• Canada's economy, as a whole, has been affected too. Some $7.4 billion has flowed out of Canada in acquisition activities prompted by the N.E.P. This outflow has had a negative effect on Canada's balance of payments, weakened our dollar and forced interest rates higher.

Things don't have to be this way.

It has been said that Canada's resource industries can be the engine that drives the nation's economy. This is particularly true of the petroleum sector. And it follows, that a strong, healthy petroleum industry can make a major contribution to economic recovery for Canada.

The need for a healthy petroleum industry has already been recognized in Alberta. And the recent action by government of that province will contribute to the industry's recovery. But the benefits of a healthy petroleum industry go far beyond a single province. They include the recovery and creation of industrial, technical and professional jobs in every province of Canada. The benefits also accrue to the country as a whole in the form of a stronger economy, lower interest rates and ultimately more discretionary income available to stimulate the retail sector of Canada's economy.

Today, the Canadian Petroleum Association is asking the Parliamentary Standing Committee on Energy Legislation to take a new look at the National Energy Program. The Association's stand is consistent with its belief that, in Canada, economic solutions begin with energy.

CANADIAN PETROLEUM ASSOCIATION
Economic solutions begin with energy.

Table 1   **Canadian Petroleum Association 1981–82**
Advertising, October 1981–February 1982,
English Canada, Magazine Campaign

Publication	Scheduled Date	Number of Insertions
Financial Post	Oct. 31	1
Maclean's	Oct. 12, 19/Nov. 2, 16	4
Quest	Nov./Dec.	2
Saturday Night	Nov.	1
Time	Oct. 19/Nov. 2, 16, 23, 30	5
Atlantic Insight	Nov./Dec.	2
Hamilton Magazine	Nov./Dec.	2
Montreal Calendar	Nov./Dec.	2
Ottawa Magazine	Nov./Dec.	2
Toronto Calendar	Nov./Dec.	2
Toronto Life	Nov.	1
Vancouver Calendar	Nov./Dec.	2
Business Beat	Nov./Dec.	1
Harrowsmith	Nov.	1
Racquets Canada	Nov.	1
Ski Canada	Nov.	1
Travelife	Nov. 15	1
Chimo	Nov./Feb.	2
Energy Magazine	Nov.	1
Equinox	Jan.	1

Public Reaction

From the very beginning of the development of a campaign strategy, there was a great deal of controversy among CPA members about the overall thrust of the campaign and its execution. There was a friction between the staff and the voting membership because the latter authorized spending and controlled the budget. Many of them would have liked to have more of an advocacy campaign and less of an image or information campaign. And because of that, there was a great deal of effort from the people who had done the research to convince the supervising committee members to go the long way around in order to be successful.

The staff people who were closely involved in the day-to-day management of the campaign felt that the voting members were not the audience the campaign was targeted at. Alan Gregg commented:

> We have to spend a lot of time saying to these people: "Gentlemen, you're not really the market that we are after. And while you may cast your vote to satisfy your gut reaction, it will not work. If we have to put commercials on the air to please you, then we are looking at entirely the wrong markets and we are probably not going to be very successful."

Ken Colby added:

> It is a general frustration. The industry generally would like to say that people are being screwed around by their government. And it is going to cost us all. It is going to cost us jobs. It is going to cost us exports. So there is a frustration in a campaign that is moving too slowly; that it is too soft. My own intuition is that you are better off moving incrementally rather than coming out with all your guns blazing. During the build-up stage you are establishing credibility. You are establishing spokesmanship. My personal preference would be to go out and hit people over the head. However, I have come to the conclusion that this is probably a safer and ultimately more effective way. Therefore I am committed to it. While the senior executives of companies involved in the CPA might wish in their heart of hearts that we should go out and beat government over the head—they do recognize that they can't. The campaign is going the way it is. They have to do everything that they can to reinforce it.
>
> There will always be public distrust as long as you are making large profits. There is distrust of all institutions. If there is as much distrust of government as of the oil industry, you have won. The idea is simply to put the oil industry back on an equal footing with other institutions. The best that you can hope for is to have a neutral public opinion.

Between 1980 and 1984 there has been a considerable change in attitudes toward business and government interaction. Specifically, Canadians are now much more willing to believe that private industry is more efficient, inexpensive, and trustworthy in ensuring and supplying oil and gas to the public than is government [Exhibit 8]. While the actual percentage of people who chose business has decreased slightly in the past year, this is not picked up as a gain for government. What has occurred instead is an increase in the percentage of people who volunteered "neither."

Furthermore, a majority of Canadians (65 percent) believe that industry in general has a major responsibility for changing government policy, and an additional 26 percent believe it has a minor responsibility. These perceptions of business responsibility are also transferred to a perception by a majority of Canadians that the oil and gas industry specifically has a major responsibility to try to change the government policy affecting it. Any attempt by the industry to change government policy would be viewed as helping either "a great deal" (22 percent) or "a bit" (41 percent), while only 14 percent believe it would hurt. However, fewer people (48 percent) are likely to believe that industry having the final say would help the country either "a great deal" (16 percent) or "a bit" (32 percent), while a core of people believe it would hurt either "a bit" (17 percent) or "a great deal" (13 percent).

The best situation appears to be the oil and gas industry and the government combining to come up with an energy policy; indeed, 84 percent believed it would help the country, and 54 percent of the total population believed it would help "a great deal." CPA studies show that Canadians are most likely to believe that the most benefit to Canada

Exhibit 8

Reliance on Business or Government

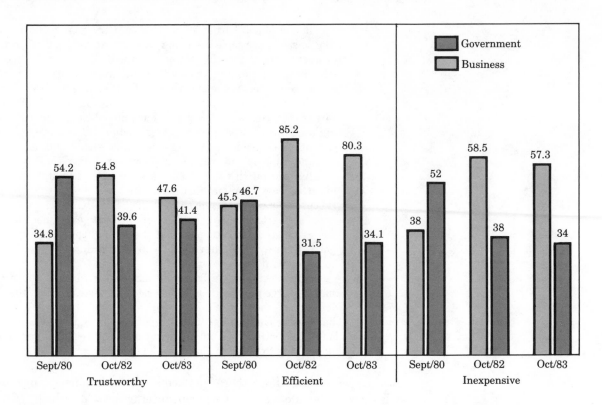

would come from industry and government working together to form an energy policy. Indeed, the result of this joint effort would be of help to the consumer.

Since the inception of the nationwide campaign in 1980, CPA has tracked, through survey research, specific measurable goals that were set up as part of the original strategy. An examination of the goals indicate that improvements in the industry image (phase I) have continued, although there was little change in the 1982–83 period. The largest single change was "managed by Canadians." Moreover, there appear to be incremental changes in the phase II goals of public benefits associated with the industry. There has also been relatively little change in the knowledge issue, which constitutes phase III goals, with a gap continuing to exist in understanding the energy situation. Considerable progress has been made in the area of the public's awareness of the price breakdown vis-à-vis government and industry. Finally, while confidence in the industry goals of phase IV has improved, the public is slightly less confident and, as we saw earlier, slightly more likely to have confidence in neither industry nor government, although the percentage is low [Table 2].

Table 2   **Measurable Goals**

	Sept. 1980	Apr. 1981	Feb. 1982	Oct. 1982	Oct. 1983	Sept. 1980– Oct. 1983 Change	Goal
Phase I							
Honest	32%	46%	55%	57%	54%	22%	60%
Communicate with public	32	39	42	41	40	8	51
Accountable	42	—	61	62	61	19	51
Contribute to Canada	61	71	72	75	73	12	80
Managed by Canadians	27	46	54	58	53	26	60
Trust	—	46	58	58	57	11*	60
Hear of CPA	—	45	51	48	—	—	—
Phase II							
Creates jobs	—	80	81	78	79	−1*	90
Favors one region	39	41	45	47	52	13	60
Industrial growth	—	75	73	70	74	−1*	80
Securing supply	—	63	69	70	73	10*	75
Industry rating (X)	6.17	5.12	5.49	5.53	5.43	−.74	6.25
Phase III							
No one's telling the truth	68	64	66	66	72	4	40
Industry sets price	17	21	19	14	13	−4	5
X% of energy imported	—	38	37	39	—	—	34
X% of profits reinvested	37	34	37	37	34	3	—
Share of price to government	27	28	56	65	69	42	40
Responsibility for situation (government)	—	61	63	64	58	−3*	70
Blame for situation (government)	—	35	40	43	—	—	50
Phase IV							
Trust business	35	39	49	55	48	13	60
Efficient business	46	53	61	65	60	14	60
Inexpensive business	38	44	53	60	57	19	60
Social contract believability	—	26/26	—	—	—	—	40/40
Closer to world price	—	57	48	53	—	—	70
Favor takeover	—	68	—	—	—	—	90

*April 1981–October 1983 percent change reported.
Note: Dashes indicate the question was not asked in that survey.

Decima Research analyzed the measurable goals to discover the relative importance of the attitudinal variable in predicting levels of industry approval. The results indicated that the following variables had the strongest association with overall assessment of the industry:

- Contribution to economic growth
- The way the industry communicates with government
- The industry's ability to get oil and gas to consumers
- The industry's trustworthiness

These factors indicate that public opinion has indeed changed from a concern for the "personality" of the industry in 1980, for its performance expressed through such issues as the price of its products, taxes, and profits in 1982, to current concerns about how the industry can contribute to Canada's economic growth now that the public views the economy as "turning the corner" and how it can cooperate with government and consumers.

Awareness of CPA's Ads

To test the awareness levels and believability of CPA's ads, Decima Research conducted a panel study in Toronto from March to June 1984. Nine hundred people were set up as a control panel in March, and then 300 of that panel were reinterviewed in late June in their homes. The study found recognition levels of the CPA advertisements to be higher than in previous studies, with the highest attributed to "exploration." However, there also appeared to be some falloff in terms of sponsor awareness. Nevertheless, CPA ads had a wider reach than before, with more people saying they saw the advertisements.

The panel survey was designed to assess individual attitude change when people could prove that they recognized the ads in comparison to people who did not recognize the ads. Study results indicated that there was relatively little "net" change in attitudes over the three-month period. Finally, panel results indicated that people who were aware of the CPA sponsorship were more likely to hold either stable pro-industry views or switch to pro-industry opinions.

Chapter 12

BETHLEHEM STEEL CORPORATION, BETHLEHEM, PA:

AN ADVOCACY CAMPAIGN DEFENDING THE STEEL INDUSTRY'S POSITION AGAINST FOREIGN IMPORTS AND RELATED ISSUES

For many years, Bethlehem Steel Corporation had run corporate public relations advertising designed to portray the company as a "good citizen." Then, in 1976, the advertising changed direction, switching from "image to issues"—in other words, to advocacy advertising. Bethlehem Steel thus joined the ranks of a growing number of large U.S. corporations that had embarked on an advocacy or idea-issue campaign in the marketplace of ideas.

THE ADVOCACY CAMPAIGN: INITIAL STEPS

Bethlehem Steel, whose home office is located in Bethlehem, Pennsylvania, is the second-largest steel company in the United States. It has

---

Research Assistant: Jeannie Kee.

traditionally been a public-spirited corporation, as well as something of a maverick within the industry. The corporation's advertising program has several facets: commercial advertising, advertising for recruiting, advertising for its shipbuilding department, and corporate advertising, of which advocacy advertising is an extension. According to Eugene R. Kline, vice-president of public affairs, Bethlehem's corporate advertising campaign in the early 1970s had a "people-oriented thrust":

> It was a very successful series focusing on people within the corporation who were doing good things. We weren't trying to take credit solely for what they were doing, but by showing that our employees were concerned about the society in which they lived, we felt that it also projected Bethlehem Steel as a good citizen.

In 1975, Bethlehem Steel decided to depart from its public relations, or image, advertising approach and to speak out on specific issues it felt were of great importance to the company and therefore the nation. This change in direction did not come from any one corporate official, but emerged as the synergistic effect of several forces: a new "mind set" was developing. The chairman of the corporation, Lewis W. Foy, had exerted an indirect influence on the corporation by becoming, in Kline's words, "much more aware of the need to convey Bethlehem's messages and views to people in Washington and people in leadership positions around the communities in which we live." Foy's personal commitment apparently diffused through the corporation.

The executives in the advertising division and its parent, the public affairs department, felt that there was a need for clarification of the corporation's advertising goals in view of the changing sociopolitical environment. As William A. Latshaw, manager of advertising, states: "If you don't know where you're going, any road will get you there." There was much discussion in the public affairs department of where to go and how. There was a "lack of focus" which executives hoped to remedy by instituting a "quasi-management by objectives" structure for the department. Through discussions with department heads throughout the corporation, six major areas of concern were identified as a prelude to setting priorities in the public affairs area:

1. Capital formation and federal tax reform
2. Energy conservation
3. Pollution and the environment
4. Government overregulation
5. Business concentration
6. Steel imports and foreign trade policy

Once these priorities were identified, the public affairs department "began to seek information with respect to our position to develop a kind of position statement in respect to each of the priorities. Then we directed our division managers to use their tools to lay out a program for fostering the implementation or the completion of the objectives."

Bethlehem's news media division, community affairs division (which handles speaking opportunities), the state government affairs lobbying effort, and the federal government affairs lobbying effort were also converging on these same topics. The people responsible for advertising felt a pressure to direct their efforts toward those who influence and make the laws that have such an impact on the corporation. The new direction in advertising, then, seems to have come about, as Kline states, "because of a recognition, corporate-wide, of the tremendous impact government is having on us. And if we are not going to speak out on those things in one way or another, we're not only letting an opportunity go by, we are being remiss in our responsibility."

In a broad sense, Bethlehem Steel's objectives for its advocacy advertising program were to (1) affect the legislative and executive arenas directly, as well as through opinion leaders; (2) place Bethlehem in a leadership role in the dialogue on national issues; and (3) help the public corporation survive as a legitimate form of business enterprise.

There is no public policy committee within the corporation, although some managers have wondered whether there should be one. "More often than not," the messages presented in the ads are developed by the advertising division, working with appropriate corporate departments.

The Role of Advocacy Advertising in the External Communications Program

Notwithstanding management's obvious satisfaction with its approach to and results from the advertising campaign, there is no "commitment to advocacy for advocacy's sake." If it was felt that Bethlehem could achieve more effectiveness within its financial limits by doing something different, management would do so. The corporation is involved in influencing public opinion and policy in various other ways. For example, some of the managers were involved in a task force, headed by Foy, that resisted the passage of the Humphrey-Hawkins Bill while supporting targeted unemployment programs, particularly with regard to inner-city youth.

The corporation also participates in direct lobbying in Washington and in states where the company has operations. When asked whether corporate officers' being more accessible to the news media would obviate the need for advocacy advertising, Latshaw said, "No" and explained that Bethlehem Steel's executives "are probably more accessible than anybody in the steel industry" through news conferences, interviews, and speeches. However, he stressed the difficulty of any one person's responding instantaneously to inquiries from the news media: "There is no one person who can function as a spokesperson for the corporation to answer the many kinds of questions that come up." Another alternative to advocacy advertising is carried out through a volunteer "speakers bureau" which addresses plant community audiences. A further interface with society is through letters received from the public, which run about 300 a year. Latshaw explained Bethlehem's way of dealing with them:

> We respond to every letter that raises a question, if we feel that the writer is sincerely interested. When we get abusive mail, and a small portion of it is abusive, we don't bother to respond,

because we don't think we are going to be able to change anybody's thought about the issue.

Bethlehem feels that its "mix" of direct and indirect influence on the legislative process is needed. According to Bethlehem's President, Richard F. Schubert:

> There is a limit to how much direct contact you can have which will still have a positive benefit. The legislators also have to feel that someone in their own constituency understands and supports the point of view you are expressing to them. In addition, no matter what you are able to achieve through personal contact, there is a need to tell the broader sector of your corporate audience why you feel the way you do about an issue. Just to contact the people at the end of the path isn't enough. Your plant community people and your other corporate audiences ought to be informed as well.
>
> There is no way that Bethlehem or any other company like it can back off from involvement in the public arena with issues that impact directly on society, and indirectly on the livelihood of the business and its employees. There is just no alternative, and those who suggest that it is possible to retreat into the cloister and let the world go by, don't understand the way it is today.

Evidently, not all large corporations share this view. Although other advertising managers in the industry have expressed a positive, even envious, reaction to Bethlehem's program, they have not been able to persuade their top managements of its efficiency. There is also a feeling among some executives that Bethlehem has "preempted the steel industry's advocacy leadership" and so choose to spend their money in other ways. There is no industrywide, concerted effort—Bethlehem seems to savor its individualistic, somewhat "maverick" character, and its executives do not feel they are "sticking their necks out." They also do not mind if other steel companies benefit from the advertising without sharing the expense, because Bethlehem is benefitting as well.

The Advertising Decision

Selection of specific issues to be addressed in the ad copy is done by the public affairs department. The advertising division of the department is responsible for making the ads timely with respect to legislative events in Washington. When an issue is resolved legislatively, Bethlehem's advertising on that subject is discontinued. At times an ad would be ready to be put into print, only to be made obsolete by congressional action. Latshaw, in discussing "the topicality of specific issues," explained Bethlehem's "bump and run" philosophy: "We get on an issue and we get out, and part of that is related to the legislative timetable. If they are going to be talking about energy, that is when you talk about energy. After that point, there is no further sense going on and discussing energy."

Because Bethlehem uses magazines almost exclusively for print advertising, publishing schedules and closing dates place certain limits in responding to current events. Companies like Mobil Oil, which use newspapers as part of their advertising forum, do not face this difficulty. Magazines require longer deadlines. Therefore, Bethlehem does not attempt to carry on a daily dialogue or give immediate response through its advertising. The corporation does run its advocacy ads in plant community newspapers, in the *New York Times, Washington Post,* and *Wall Street Journal.* Bethlehem's procedure for producing copy itself precludes rapid response or immediacy, since it is a rather time-consuming process. The advertising division prepares a draft of the ad, which is sent to the vice-presidents in charge of various departments that might have an interest in the content of the ad. For example, in a recent case involving steel technology, copies were sent to the heads of the sales, accounting, operations, finance, research, transportation, and engineering departments. Each is asked to review and comment on the ad copy and is given a deadline (in this instance, four days later) by which to return any suggestions to the advertising division, at whose discretion any changes are made. As a further check, the proposed ad is sent to the legal department, and then to the corporate executive to whom the public affairs department reports, who gives final approval.

The advocacy advertising budget as of 1978 was $1.5 million annually. This figure represents media and production costs, but excludes staff salaries and other administrative and overhead expenses. The same staff handles other advertising assignments too, including the entire sales-oriented and college recruiting campaigns. At least on two occasions, funding approval for advocacy campaigns has been separated from the regular budget presentation: "We had to get approval so that we could stagger our ads through the calender year, so we did an advance presentation." The first year's campaign presentation was made to Laurence Fenninger, Jr., then vice-president for public affairs. Subsequent presentations were made to the controller and three vice-chairmen. Latshaw believes an ideal budget for print advertising would be $2.5 million a year.

The format chosen by Bethlehem for its advocacy advertising is an eye-catching black-and-white layout, with an often clever editorial cartoon-type graphic by illustrator John Huenergarth, a bold headline, and smaller-print text. Besides being visually appealing, this sort of layout has another advantage—that of recognition. Latshaw explained that they had toyed with three or four different types of graphics, "none of which worked until it occurred to us that an editorial cartoon approach might lend itself best to what we wanted to say. That format really got you into an editorial concept and created a stronger feeling for advocacy." The concept has been used almost exclusively throughout the campaign. The graphic consistency appears to have created a further benefit in building awareness of Bethlehem's ad campaign: The tracking studies indicate that the standardized approach in format and layout has resulted in "higher levels of recall than might have resulted from the use of visually disparate campaigns over the same time period." This effect was especially notable when, in 1977, Bethlehem ran three two-page ads on the need for a national energy policy, one page of which was a blank "letter" designed to be torn out, completed with the reader's opinion, and sent to the president in one case, and the reader's representative and senator in the other instances. The follow-up study indicated that a large proportion of those who recalled the content of Bethlehem's ads specifically mentioned the physical layout.

Media Selection: Bethlehem's Unusual Approach

In keeping with the advertising division's commitment to management by objectives, the Van Brunt agency and its associate, Richard Manville Research, Inc., were employed to design and carry out surveys on attitudes of readers of certain national periodicals with respect to the six issues of national concern previously isolated by Bethlehem. The magazines were chosen for their demographics—that is, they were read by the people Bethlehem wanted to reach. This approach had a twofold purpose: (1) to provide the most advertising effect for the money spent; and (2) to measure statistically the effectiveness of various ads and the overall campaign.

Bethlehem management did not feel that syndicated data on readership were suitable for its purpose. An attitudinal study was conducted in 1976 in which readers of thirteen national business, cultural, and newsweekly magazines were surveyed. All but one of the publications provided subscribers' lists for developing target audiences. The publications surveyed were *Atlantic, Harper's, The New Yorker, Saturday Review, Smithsonian, Newsweek, Sports Illustrated, Time, U.S. News & World Report, Business Week, Fortune*, and the *Wall Street Journal*.

The measurement began with pilot tests using approximately 100 diverse statements, chosen because they advocated a range of opposing viewpoints on each of the six topics under investigation. Factor analysis was used to examine the correlations among these statements, reducing the data to those few statements that best described the spectrum of attitudes on each issue. The actual survey was then conducted by telephone. Each respondent was asked twenty-five carefully selected questions designed to elicit answers that could be categorized through cluster analysis, on a liberal-to-conservative continuum, on each of the six issues of interest to Bethlehem. The values on the five-point scale ranged from very conservative to very liberal. Though the questions did not mention Bethlehem Steel by name, it was assumed that those people giving "conservative" answers would be in agreement with the corporation's position; the more conservative, the stronger the agreement. The three middle quintiles were considered the "swayables," the ones Bethlehem could and therefore would want to influence. In addition, the primary target audience was defined as "opinion leaders," active politically within their communities, of professional or managerial background, with at least some college education, 25 to 64 years old, earning at least $20,000 annually, and involved in civic and/or political activities in their communities. The criteria had to be met for a person to be included in the survey sample. A secondary audience for the ads included employees, shareholders, customers, and members of plant communities.

Exhibit 1

Graphic Representation of Relative Cost Efficiencies

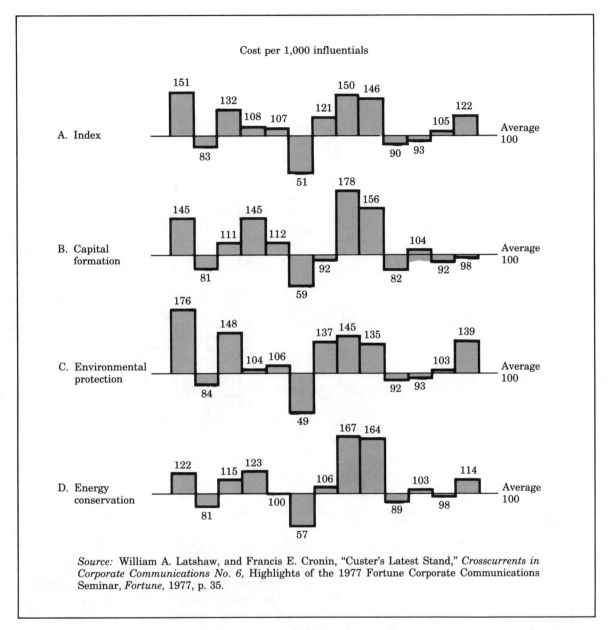

Source: William A. Latshaw, and Francis E. Cronin, "Custer's Latest Stand," *Crosscurrents in Corporate Communications No. 6,* Highlights of the 1977 Fortune Corporate Communications Seminar, *Fortune,* 1977, p. 35.

Combining the space cost of an ad in a given magazine with the attitudes among its readers gives it an efficiency value relative to other magazines for reaching the target audience on a specific topic. The advertiser thereby achieves a logical basis for designing its media schedule [Exhibit 1]. Note that the third magazine from the left, for example, went from an average efficiency of 132 to 111 on capital formation, while the fourth from the left rose in efficiency from 108 to 145; however, on environmental protection that change is reversed, with number 3 becoming more efficient, while number 4 is less so. The attitudinal study

Exhibit 2

Energy Conservation

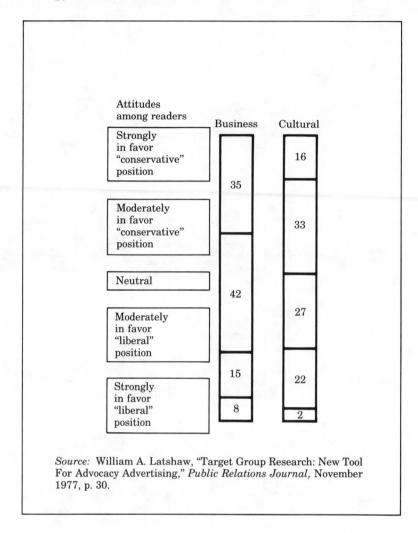

Source: William A. Latshaw, "Target Group Research: New Tool For Advocacy Advertising," *Public Relations Journal,* November 1977, p. 30.

sample consisted of 4,000 readers. When the results were analyzed, it was found that there were significant differences in attitudes among the various publications, and differences in attitudes on various issues within a given magazine [Exhibit 2].

The research group developed a computer program, called the optimal media selection model (OMS), which would take the findings of the survey and data on page costs, discounts, combination costs, and so on for different periodicals and produce an optimal advertising schedule in line with the user's objectives, budget, target audience, and desired frequency of advertising on any one of the six issues. The schedule supplies information on percentage of total target audience reached, mean exposure frequency, and cost-per-thousand/attitudes (cpm/a). This model is quite flexible and thus has possible side applications.

It has changed the way Bethlehem Steel buys its advertising space. Table 1 shows a sample optimal media schedule, with the number of

Table 1 **Sample Optimal Media Schedule (Approximate Budget: $950,000)**

	Capital Formation	Environmental Protection	Energy Conservation	Business Concentration	Government Interference	Foreign Trade
1. Business Publication I	9	13	10	11	7	9
2. Business Publication II	—	—	—	—	—	3
3. Business Publication III	4	6	4	4	4	4
4. Business Publication IV	4	6	4	6	4	4
5. General Interest I	2	—	—	—	—	—
6. General Interest II	9	7	9	8	8	8
7. Literary Cultural I	8	5	8	6	8	7
8. Literary Cultural II	7	6	7	8	8	6
9. Literary Cultural III	10	10	9	10	11	11
10. Newsweekly I	11	11	10	11	11	10
11. Newsweekly II	6	7	7	6	6	7
12. Newsweekly III	7	5	9	7	7	7
13. Newsweekly IV	9	10	9	9	10	10
Percent of total target audience exposed	98.9%	98.1%	98.3%	97.7%	99.1%	97.4%
Mean exposure frequency	9.34	10.07	9.64	9.72	9.17	9.48
Cumulative cpm/a	$500.70	$423.17	$475.80	$418.38	$480.86	$434.61

Source: Bethlehem Steel Corporation, 1976 Media Selection Model Study Richard Manville Research, Inc.

insertions per magazine for each subject. Note that Business Publication I (the actual names of magazines are omitted) can vary from seven to thirteen insertions (pages), depending on the subject. Note also that Business Publication II and General Interest Publication I do not appear in five of the six columns, indicating that the "swayables" who read those magazines can be reached more economically through other periodicals. An important idea in this approach is nonduplication of readership: This schedule is designed to reach a certain *percentage* of the target audience, rather than a specified number of readers, some of whom undoubtedly read more than one ad. The number of insertions is chosen to provide the desired percentage of reach or frequency of exposure. It is believed that the actual campaign reaches approximately 80 percent of the target audience, which consists of about 2 million people.

In May 1976, corporate advertising effectiveness benchmark and follow-up studies were initiated. These studies, which continued through 1978, attempted to measure awareness of Bethlehem as an advertiser, copy point recall, and attitude shifts for each campaign.

As an example of the application of the OMS model, in 1977 the corporation decided to gear its campaign to a more conservative sector. Gene Cronin, production and media director, explains:

> We were looking for a response, and we felt that we would have more opportunity of getting that response from the audience that had viewpoints as close to our own as possible. Therefore when we went into our computer to pull out what we would run, we went in with the top (most conservative) quintile of people, more friendly towards our viewpoint. When you do that, you don't exclude the rest of the circulation. It is just that you are trying to make the most efficient buy. Again, this is a determination on our part that the readers would in fact respond to us. They would be more apt to respond than someone who was neutral or in the "totally against" category.

Bethlehem's management speak of the program with pride. They feel it is a vast improvement over arbitrarily choosing a certain number of insertions in a certain magazine. Latshaw has been quoted as saying: "In our advertising division we tell each other that this survey is unique. There's very little under the sun that's unique, but in our opinion our attitudinal survey is at least 'medium rare'."

ADVOCACY CAMPAIGNS, 1976–1979

The 1976 Campaign

The advocacy campaign began with four ads on capital formation and tax reform [Exhibits 3 and 4] and three ads on pollution control and environment [Exhibits 5 and 6]. The ads began appearing in the media in May, and the campaign ended in October. Reprints of some of the ads were also sent to Bethlehem's workers as part of an "employee economic awareness program."

The ads on tax reform argue for the encouragement of capital formation; that new capital investment is necessary, both through retained earnings and personal savings; and that without new investment, we cannot expand employment. The ads suggest that government take the following measures:

1. A permanent investment tax credit applicable to industrial buildings, fully creditable against income taxes.
2. Amortization of expenditures for pollution control facilities over any period selected by the taxpayer, including immediate writeoff in the year the funds are expended.
3. Replacement of the present depreciation system with a five-year capital recovery system.
4. Elimination of double taxation of corporate income paid out as dividends.

The specific figure advocated in 1976 for investment tax credit was 12 percent, which had been set as an industry position recommended by a committee on taxation of the American Iron and Steel Institute (AISI). By 1978, a temporary credit of 10 percent had been enacted, and Bethlehem urged making this a permanent measure. Latshaw acknowledged that "capital formation" was not a word that "turns people on," yet he felt "it is a very important part of our business," necessitating trying to create an understanding on the part of the reader by tying capital formation to jobs.

Exhibit 3

What will it take to make jobs for your children?

We need to get unemployed people back onto business payrolls—and the sooner the better. Right now, America needs millions of jobs.

But there's also the challenge of a *growing* work force—young people reaching working age, and others entering the job market. *Your* children and ours. That work force will grow by at least 1½ million *every year* from now through 1980.

What will it take to create *new* jobs for them?

Money. The huge sums of money (investment capital) companies need to upgrade and expand their facilities. It's *those* facilities that, when business picks up, maintain jobs and create new ones.

How much money's needed? The average investment to create a *single* new job opportunity in manufacturing is around $25,000 today. It will be at least $35,000 in 1980.

That multiplies out to $37½ *billion* in capital investment *today* to create 1½ million new jobs. By 1980, it will take an investment of $52½ *billion.*

Where will that money come from?

The key to getting the money we need for expansion and improvement of our plants is better earnings*—earnings that can be invested in our operations and that will encourage investors to provide us additional money.

But this alone is not enough because under present Federal tax laws the government would take too much of any additional dollars we can earn. What we need now is Federal tax reform to help lower barriers to capital formation.

* In 1975, Bethlehem's earnings after taxes were only 4.8% of revenues.

Bethlehem

How you can help gear up the American economy

The tax-writing committees of the U.S. Congress are studying the subject of "Capital Formation."

Here are four tax measures which we believe the Congress should enact to encourage industrial expansion and to create jobs: (1) five-year capital recovery system, (2) 12% permanent investment tax credit, (3) write-off of the costs of pollution control facilities in the year they are incurred, (4) eliminate the double taxation of corporate profits paid out as dividends.

If you agree that revisions in present Federal tax laws are needed to provide the additional capital for more and better jobs, we ask you to tell that to your Senators and Congressman.

For a free copy of the folder, *"Project Mainspring—with your help it can wind up the American economy again,"* write: Public Affairs Dept., Room 476-WSJ, Bethlehem Steel Corp., Bethlehem, PA 18016.

Exhibit 4

How can we get Uncle Sam moving forward again?

Of course America's still an economic powerhouse. And of course we still have a sizable lead over most other countries in a lot of respects.

But, for a long period of years, the U.S.A. has been losing its lead, and *fast*. Relative to most other industrial nations we've been lagging in economic growth...lagging in our rate of capital investment... lagging in plant modernization... and lagging in productivity gains.

What will it take to get our nation moving forward again?...to generate the investment capital we need to grow?...to maintain jobs and create new ones?

The key to getting the money we need for expansion and improvement of our plants is better earnings* — earnings that can be invested in our operations and

that will encourage investors to provide us with additional money.

But this alone is not enough because under present Federal tax laws the government would take too much of any additional dollars we can earn. What we need now is Federal tax reform to help lower barriers to capital formation.

*In 1975, Bethlehem's earnings after taxes were only 4.8% of revenues.

Bethlehem

How you can help gear up the American economy

The tax-writing committees of the U.S. Congress are studying the subject of "Capital Formation."

Here are four tax measures which we believe the Congress should enact to encourage industrial expansion and to create jobs: (1) five-year capital recovery system, (2) 12% permanent investment tax credit, (3) write-

off the costs of pollution control facilities in the year they are incurred, and (4) elimination of the double taxation of corporate profits paid out as dividends.

If you agree that revisions in present Federal tax laws are needed to provide the additional capital for more and better jobs, we ask you to tell that to your Senators and Congressman.

For a free copy of the folder "Project Mainspring—with your help it can wind up the American economy again," write: Public Affairs Dept., Room 476-WSJ, Bethlehem Steel Corp., Bethlehem, PA 18016.

Exhibit 5

Some people say we must reach "zero" pollution.
But at what cost? And how fast?

At Bethlehem Steel, we work hard—every day—to control pollution. But the cost is high. We've already spent approximately $400 million to clean up a major portion of the pollutants from the air and water we use. We consider this money well spent.

$600 million more

In an effort to meet existing pollution control laws and regulations, we have many more projects under way or anticipated in the near future. These projects are expected to cost us some $600 million over the next five years.

Where does that leave us?

Depending upon how far regulatory agencies go in stringent interpretation of the present laws and regulations, we may be faced with spending hundreds of millions more to try to remove the last traces of pollution. We do not think that this would be money well spent.

Attempting to remove the last increment of pollution involves new and uncertain technology. The attempt will consume a considerable amount of scarce energy and natural resources. And, in many cases, it will merely transfer pollution problems to the power companies or chemical manufacturers.

Is it time for a rearrangement of priorities?

We are faced as a nation with troublesome alternatives. Do we continue our headlong rush to implement some of the air and water clean-up standards that have yet to be proved necessary—or even sound—or shall we give equal consideration to jobs, our energy requirements, capital needs, and other demands for social priorities?

We believe the national interest now requires that we face up to the dual necessity of preserving our environment while at the same time assuring our economic progress.

Our booklet, "Steelmaking and the Environment," tells more about the problems of pollution and what we're doing to help solve them. For a free copy, write: Public Affairs Dept., Room 476-WSJ, Bethlehem Steel Corp., Bethlehem, PA 18016.

Bethlehem

Exhibit 6

Does this kind of environmental arithmetic add up to you?

So far, Bethlehem Steel has spent about $400 million just to buy and install the hardware to clean up a major portion of the air and water at our various operations.

In the next five years, we project spending at least $600 million more for pollution and environmental health controls.

But as we try to approach perfection, we're faced with increasingly tough technical problems and with skyrocketing costs.

Case in point: In 1959, we placed into operation a baghouse dust collector, which cost approximately $444,000, to collect emissions from an electric furnace shop. It's estimated that this baghouse captures 93.8% of the emissions from that shop.

Then, in 1972, we installed a *second* baghouse at this shop, at a cost of $2,424,000, to further reduce fugitive emissions (those emissions not discharged through a stack). It's estimated these two baghouses capture 99.3% of the total emissions.

Some simple long division shows we spent about $4,700 to capture each 1% of the emissions in the first 93.8%…and about $440,000 to

capture each 1% of the emissions in the next 5.5%! This is one example of the kind of environmental arithmetic we're up against.

What lies ahead? Depending upon how far regulatory agencies go in stringent interpretation of present laws and regulations, we may be faced with spending hundreds of millions more to try to remove the last traces of pollution.

Is it time for a rearrangement of priorities? We are faced as a nation with troublesome alternatives. Do we continue our headlong rush to implement some of the air and water clean-up standards that have yet to be proved necessary— or even sound—or shall we give equal consideration to our energy requirements, to modernization and expansion, and to other priorities?

We believe the national interest now requires that we face up to the dual necessity of preserving our environment while at the same time assuring our economic progress.

Our booklet, "Steelmaking and the Environment," tells more about the problems of pollution and what

we're doing to help solve them. For a free copy, write: Public Affairs Dept., Room 476-WSJ, Bethlehem Steel Corp., Bethlehem, PA 18016.

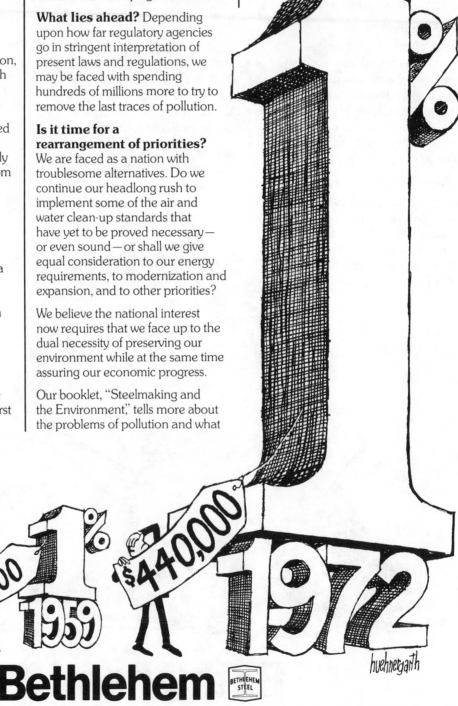

$4,700 1% 1959

$440,000 1972

huehnergarth

Bethlehem

BETHLEHEM STEEL

Those ads dealing with pollution and environmental regulations pointed out that Bethlehem had spent $400 million by 1976 for pollution control, and might have to spend another $600 million over the next five years to comply with existing regulations, as the remaining traces of pollution were increasingly more expensive to capture. The ads argued that the cleanup technologies were often uncertain, used a great deal of energy, and would often transfer the pollution problems to power companies or chemical manufacturers. There were tradeoffs between the environment and the cost of steel, economic progress, and jobs, and the nation should rearrange its priorities on these alternatives. Bethlehem urged these measures:

1. National enforcement of environmental regulations
2. Greater flexibility in compliance timetables
3. Accurate determination of significant sources of pollution, their effect on public health, and the most cost-effective control techniques

It should be noted here that Bethlehem and the steel industry's views on various issues (pollution, imported steel prices) are not necessarily shared by government agencies such as EPA or the Treasury Department. To evaluate the objectivity or balanced presentation of various issues in terms of overall national interest and public policy, the reader should review the viewpoints of the steel industry, industry critics, and various government agencies.

Tracking Studies, October 1976. The first report was an explanation of the benchmark study and the optimal media selection model.

Tracking Studies, November 1976. The second report indicated "the extent of change which may be attributed to the corporate advertising campaign." It was found that a general erosion in awareness of corporate advertising had taken place, with an average decline of 10 percent among fourteen corporations examined. However, against this trend, awareness of Bethlehem Steel's advertising remained unchanged (23 percent), and another steel company's position declined by 7 percent. Bethlehem concluded that "the data illustrated the fact that a continuing advertising effort is necessary to maintain awareness over time. This is especially true during this particular advertising test since it took place during the presidential campaign." Copy point recall showed a "strong increase" on issues mentioned in the ads: 14 to 19 percent (+ 36 percent) in one instance, 4 to 8 percent (+ 100 percent) in another, and 2 percent to 4 percent (+ 100 percent) in a third. It was felt that agreement with Bethlehem's message was a measure of its effectiveness—the extent to which it was convincing. The study found that among those who actually absorbed the advertising message, "agree" rose in the "completely agree" category but dropped in the "agree somewhat" category, with a net increase in agreement of 6 percent, from 71 to 77 percent.

Bethlehem's rating as a "corporate citizen" and related perceptions (responsible foreign trade, energy, and environmental positions) improved "among those aware of Bethlehem's corporate advertising." The campaign also had a polarizing effect on the population, with more of previously "neutral" opinions changing to negative ratings among those aware rather than unaware of the advertising. Bethlehem felt that "making people aware of a company's platform gives them the opportunity not only to agree with it, but to disagree as well." Overall, it was found in terms of general attitudes toward big business that Bethlehem's first advocacy campaign had no attributable influence. The company did not consider this surprising, "since the campaign was in effect for a relatively short time when basic beliefs are established over a lifetime of experience, and thus, are slow to change" [Exhibit 7].

The 1977 Campaign

In 1977, Bethlehem ran three ads on energy and conservation of resources [Exhibits 8 and 9] and a "one-shot" ad in newspapers on deregulation of natural gas. There were three other ads "ready to go" on environment and pollution control, but events in Washington overtook two. As a result, only one ad relating to the environment was run in three major newspapers [Exhibit 10]. By midyear, Bethlehem began a series of three ads on steel imports and foreign trade [Exhibits 11 and 12]; these appeared before the company's announcements of plant closings in September–October, and were run again in the final quarter of the year. Bethlehem also ran a different ad on steel imports in plant community newspapers, with the ad headline customized for each plant location.

The ads on energy stressed the effect on the steel industry and society of rising fuel costs and growing dependence on foreign oil. They suggested that America needed a sane and sensible energy policy which would help to conserve energy; expand coal production and develop new sources of low-sulfur coal; balance energy needs and environmental protection; continue expansion of nuclear power; and encourage research for new sources. The single ad on deregulation of natural gas asserted that the government's temporary deregulation as a solution to an emergency shortage implied that permanent deregulation would be a solution to a continuing shortage. A free market, reflecting actual competitive prices, would encourage investment and result in more gas. Many of these issues are intertwined with other issues addressed by Bethlehem, such as environmental protection and regulatory reform. (The company attempted to make this interrelatedness evident through its jigsaw puzzle approach to its 1978 advertising.)

Bethlehem ran several ads on steel imports in which it pointed out that most foreign steelmakers are owned or subsidized by their governments, thereby removing the profit incentive. Foreign steel thus can be sold below cost in order to continue production, dumping unemployment along with steel in the United States. The ads insisted that Bethlehem is not protectionist, but simply wants competition to be fair, and urged that steel imports be priced at least to cover their full costs of production, delivery, and sale; and advocated prompt temporary relief from the excessive flow of steel imports, and negotiations leading to an effective international agreement on steel trade. Steel, as a world commodity and as an industry, is extremely important to any manufacturing country. Latshaw said: "A country could not stay a first class international power

Exhibit 7

Bethlehem Steel Ad Campaign: Summary of Attitude Shifts

	Benchmark 10/76 %	Environment 11/76 %	PC	Energy 5/77 %	PC	Imports 10/77 %	PC	Imports 1/78 %	PC	Benchmark 5/78 %	PC	Puzzle 9/78 %	PC
Has a responsible program for reinvestment of profits for expansion of facilities													
Agree	52%	79%	27	—	—	—	—	—	—	—	—	—	—
Neutral	41	11	−30	—	—	—	—	—	—	—	—	—	—
Disagree	7	10	3	—	—	—	—	—	—	—	—	—	—
Is concerned with protecting the environment from pollution													
Agree	47%	69%	22	43%	−26	51%	8	56%	5	51%	−5	53%	2
Neutral	40	7	−33	35	28	27	−8	26	−1	24	−2	24	0
Disagree	13	24	11	22	−2	22	0	18	−4	25	7	23	−2
Makes intelligent use of our country's natural resources													
Agree	50%	64%	14	46%	−18	58%	12	56%	−2	53%	−3	55%	2
Neutral	40	13	−27	37	24	27	−10	31	4	31	0	31	0
Disagree	10	23	13	17	−6	15	−2	13	−2	16	3	14	−2
Is a good corporate citizen; doesn't need government to act as a watchdog													
Agree	46%	61%	15	51%	−10	47%	−4	62%	15	47%	−15	50%	3
Neutral	39	8	−31	29	21	25	−4	21	−4	20	1	20	0
Disagree	15	31	16	20	−11	28	8	17	−11	33	16	30	−3
Has a responsible position opposing foreign suppliers selling materials in the U.S. below cost													
Agree	—	—	—	45%	—	51%	6	72%	21	55%	−17	63%	8
Neutral	—	—	—	43	—	33	−10	18	−15	25	7	22	−3
Disagree	—	—	—	12	—	16	4	10	6	20	10	15	−5
Awareness of corporate advertising													
Bethlehem	23%	23%	0	14%	−9	27%	13	39%	12	30%	−9	37%	7
Large Steel Co. A.	48	41	−7	36	−5	23	−13	28	5	30	2	25	−5
Large Aerospace Co.	33	36	3	29	−7	22	−7	24	2	36	12	66	30
Large Steel Co. B	19	15	−4	6	−9	9	3	12	3	5	−7	8	3
Copy point recall													
Environment	14%	19%	5	9%	−10	11%	2	8%	−3	12%	4	7%	−5
Energy	4	2	2	7	5	3	−4	2	−1	2	0	2	0
Regard for mankind	4	8	4	8	0	7	−1	15	8	7	−8	4	−3
Capital formation	2	4	2	3	−1	2	−1	2	0	1	−1	3	2
Imports	1	1	0	2	1	21	19	38	17	13	−25	30	17
Business concentration	1	2	1	0	−2	0	0	0	0	0	0	0	0
Government overregulation	1	1	0	2	1	3	1	2	−1	2	0	2	0
Message agreement on issue													
Agree	71%	77%	6	46%	−31	47%	1	54%	7	49%	−5	49%	0
Neutral	17	17	0	44	27	46	2	41	−5	43	2	43	0
Disagree	12	6	−6	10	4	7	−3	5	−2	8	3	8	0
		(environment)		(energy)		(imports)		(imports)					

PC = percent change (percentage point difference).

without a strong domestic steel industry. Every country of the world, unfortunately, equates the need to have a steel industry with international strength and prestige. It is basic to the economic well-being of a nation."

Some countries, with Japan as a prime example, have made steel a national industry, with government financial support allowing for a much higher debt ratio (almost 83 percent in Japan in 1974) than privately owned companies would consider. Bethlehem's is about 35 percent. The debt ratio results in a high breakeven rate and therefore a need for operating at or near full capacity. Furthermore, in Japan the social system of lifetime employment creates an added pressure for maintaining high levels of operation, even if it means selling Japanese steel overseas at below cost. In competing with this system, Bethlehem feels the need for

Exhibit 8

Time is running out.
Tell President Carter what you think he should do about energy.

We've paid for the page opposite. It contains no message. We leave that for you. Because a message from thousands of voters carries more clout in Washington than a message from us.

It's that simple. We hope thousands of you will write. We hope your messages will help spur action on a national energy policy.

Speak out, America

There's a new administration in Washington. New directions. New ideas. New ears. Let them hear what you have to say.

The cost of energy keeps going up. (That's no surprise to you if you've paid a fuel bill lately.) Domestic oil and gas resources dwindle. Each year America grows *more* dependent on foreign oil, not less.

The Mid-east oil embargo in 1973-74 meant higher prices, gas lines, more unemployment, more inflation. At that time, our country imported 38% of the oil we consumed. Today America imports 42%! And the OPEC nations just raised the price of oil again.

Tell it to the President

America needs a sane and sensible energy policy. And we need it now. The one thing we can't do is wait. Our scarcest resource—time—is running out.

Use the page at right to tell the President you want action now on an energy policy. In your own words and for your own reasons. Then tear it out and send it to President Carter.

What's in it for you?

The same thing that's in it for us. More abundant supplies of energy. Less waste. Increased development of domestic resources. And decreased dependence on foreign fuels.

Take it to the top.

Bethlehem BETHLEHEM STEEL

The President
The White House
Washington, D.C. 20500

Dear Mr. President:

Respectfully,

Exhibit 9

Fuel for the future— will America have enough?
Tell Congress what you think it should do to conserve and develop energy.

The page opposite belongs to you. Use it to spur Congress to enact a much-needed energy policy for our nation.

Tell your Congressman—in your own words and for your own reasons—what you think America must do to develop the energy we need for the future. Energy to keep our lights burning. Our homes heated. Our automobiles running. Our factories working.

Conservation can help

All of us must seek new and better ways to save energy—right now and for years to come. But conservation is no cure-all. If America is to grow, and to become less dependent on foreign fuel, reliable sources of domestic energy must be developed.

Coal and nuclear power are practical answers

America sits squarely on top of one of the largest supplies of coal on earth—enough to last hundreds of years, even if we double or triple present levels of consumption.

As a nation, we should expand coal production and substitute this fuel for dwindling supplies of gas and oil.

Coal, for example, can help replace oil and gas to generate electricity.

Reliance on coal is one answer. Increasing the share of the nation's electric power that comes from nuclear energy is another answer. Without continued expansion of safe, large-scale nuclear power, there's a good chance America will face energy shortages year after year as demand rises.

Tell Washington to act

Your ideas on energy may differ from ours. What matters is that you let Washington know what you think. And that you want action.

Write your Congressman today. Your message—along with the messages of thousands of other voters—won't go unheeded.

Bethlehem BETHLEHEM STEEL

Honorable_____
House of Representatives
Washington, DC 20515

Dear Mr._____:

Sincerely yours,

382

Exhibit 10

"We don't care how clean your addition is, you can't expand your steel plant here."

Will the following fable about Clean Air guidelines become a reality?

SCENE I

1st Environmental Regulator:
What's going on here?

Steelman: I'm going to expand my steel plant here. Our customers in this area need more steel. And the people in this city can use the jobs our expansion will provide.

1st Environmental Regulator:
Sorry about that. The air here doesn't meet the clean air standard yet and you'll be adding more pollution.

Steelman: But our addition would have air and water pollution control equipment designed to meet existing emission standards.

1st Environmental Regulator:
I believe you, but you still can't *expand* your plant here, or build a *new* plant here, either. The air around here is too *dirty*. That means you're stymied, unless you reduce your current level of emissions so there won't be a net increase in emissions in this area.

Steelman: But I'm already doing everything I can to meet existing standards.

1st Environmental Regulator:
Then you've got a couple of choices. You can persuade some other industry in town to reduce its pollution... or you can buy up plants that are putting things in the air and close 'em down. Then you'll be able to add part of the emissions you've eliminated. Got it?

Steelman: But everybody's operating under the same laws. Everybody's already made the big reductions. I'd have to buy up so many old plants I wouldn't have any money left to expand.

1st Environmental Regulator:
Tell you what to do. Why don't you build

a new plant somewhere where the air is cleaner than the regulations require?

Steelman: But that *wouldn't* be where my customers are, but... all right, let's try it.

SCENE II

2nd Environmental Regulator:
Just a minute there. What are you up to?

Steelman: Well, I have this nice new steel mill, see?

2nd Environmental Regulator:
I see, but you can't put it in this area—even though right now the air here is *cleaner* than the regulations require.

Steelman: But with the controls I'll have on my mill the air quality here will still be well above the national clean air standard.

2nd Environmental Regulator:
Doesn't matter. You're too late. The law says only a certain increment of pollution can be added to the air in this area. Another company's already putting up a plant here and they're going to use up that increment. First come, first served.

SCENE III

Steelman: Catch 22. The air's too dirty or the air's too clean. What am I gonna do?

Both Environmental Regulators (in unison): You've got a problem.

* * * * *

That scenario may read like a fable. But we're concerned that the fable may become a reality... if proposals currently being debated by the Congress become law.

The amendments to the Clean Air Act being considered will directly and immediately affect this nation's industrial growth.

At a time when new jobs are urgently needed, less stringent guidelines by the EPA, and legislative remedies to the Clean Air Act, would permit a more balanced approach to industrial development and environmental protection.

Industry needs goals, timetables, and regulatory approaches that are less rigid. And for the sake of business planning, we need them soon.

Bethlehem
Whatever happened to common sense?

Exhibit 11

Is America getting trapped by foreign steel... as we are by foreign oil?

In the oil-crisis winter of 1973-74, another crisis struck—the *steel* crisis. You don't remember America's steel crisis? Well, it was real. And it cost America's steel users a bundle.

The steel trap

Most foreign steelmakers are either owned, subsidized, financed, aided and/or protected in one way or another by their governments. They don't have the same pressure we do to operate profitably or generate capital.

We believe that much of the steel being imported into the U.S. is being "dumped"—that is, sold at prices lower than those charged in the producer's own country, and usually below the foreign steelmaker's full costs of production. Dumping is illegal, but it has been hard to prove.

Here today, gone tomorrow

During periods of slack demand, foreign steelmakers push to maintain high production rates and high employment. They ship excess steel overseas, much of it to the U.S., priced to sell.

That's what happened in the sixties and early seventies. But, suddenly, in '73 and '74, the imported steel was needed "at home." The foreign supply dwindled to a trickle. Domestic mills worked overtime, but our production capacity just wasn't enough. Steel imports had skimmed off increases in the domestic demand for steel and reduced the profitability of the American steel industry.

So they lowered the boom

Foreign producers jacked their prices sky-high. And America's steel users could (1) cut back their manufacturing operations, or (2) pay an exorbitant price for foreign steel—when they could get it! It's estimated that in 1974 alone American steel buyers paid foreign producers $1.6 billion *over* the then current domestic market prices.

Will history repeat itself?

How much should this country rely on imports for its steel supplies? Things were bad in '73-'74, but they could get worse in the future. What could this country expect if we were as dependent on foreign steel as we are on foreign oil?

Free trade, yes! But fair!

Bethlehem Steel and the American steel industry are *not* "protectionist." We are *not* looking for permanent trade barriers against foreign steel coming into our home markets. All we're asking is a chance to compete on fair and equal terms here in our own country.

Washington must help

We urge the U.S. Government to insist on fair trading practices in steel, especially that steel imports be priced to at least cover their full costs of production and sale...to arrange for prompt temporary relief from the current excessive flow of steel imports... and to press for international governmental negotiations leading to an effective international agreement on steel trade.

If you agree with us about the seriousness of this problem, please write your representatives in Washington and tell them so.

Bethlehem

Exhibit 12

Bethlehem Steel is looking for a fight. A <u>fair</u> fight.

Name a foreign steel producer. We'll get in the commercial ring with him and battle it out for America's steel market. And if we both fight by the same rules, we're confident we'll hold our own.

But that isn't the way this "competition" works. When a Japanese or European steelmaker climbs into the ring, his government almost always climbs in with him. That's bending the rules of "free" trade, and we don't think it's fair.

How they fight

Most foreign steelmakers are either owned, subsidized, financed, aided and/or protected in one way or another by their governments. They don't have the same pressure we do to operate profitably or generate capital.

We believe that much of the steel imported into the U.S. is being "dumped"—that is, sold at prices lower than those charged in the producer's own country, and usually below that foreign steelmaker's full costs of production. Dumping is illegal, but it has been hard to prove.

Why they do it

During periods of slack demand at home, foreign steelmakers push to maintain high production rates and high employment. Result: a worldwide glut of

steel…14.3 million tons of steel exported to America in 1976, priced to sell…thousands of American steelworkers laid off or working short hours.

Free trade, yes. But fair!

We're looking for a fight, yes. But a *fair* fight, where all opponents in the international arena are bound by the same rules. Bethlehem Steel and the American steel industry are *not* "protectionist." We are *not* looking for permanent trade barriers against foreign steel coming into our home markets. All we're asking is a chance to compete on fair and equal terms here in our own country.

Washington must help

We urge the U.S. Government to insist on fair trading practices in steel, especially that steel imports be priced to at least cover their full costs of production and sale…to arrange for prompt temporary relief from the current excessive flow of steel imports… and to press for international governmental negotiations leading to an effective international agreement on steel trade.

If you agree with us about the seriousness of this problem, please write your representatives in Washington and tell them so.

A free folder…"Foreign Steel: Unfair Competition?"…explains our answer to that question. Write: Public Affairs Dept., Rm. 476 MT, Bethlehem Steel Corp., Bethlehem, PA 18016.

Bethlehem

governmental action, with the most desirable action being enforcement of the antidumping laws. This is a slow process, though, and could cause ill will abroad, as could import quotas on steel. As an alternative, Bethlehem has supported the "trigger price mechanism," providing for swift penalties against suppliers who undercut a set of minimum import prices based on costs of Japanese producers. Enacted in early 1978, after several months it was seen not to be working effectively to stem the flow of foreign steel into this country; part of the problem was the dollar's slide against the yen, and another part was that the technologically inferior European saw the TPM as a license to dump. Schubert stated: "We really believe that Europeans' cost of production is so much greater than the Japanese that if it weren't for the trigger price mechanism, they wouldn't get a pound of steel in here." As to TPM's inflationary effect, Latshaw explained that *not* having it would be more inflationary because foreign producers would charge higher prices once the American steel industry was unable to supply adequate steel.

Bethlehem President Schubert sees no intellectual inconsistency in asking for more government intervention in certain areas while asking for less in others, "because if it weren't for government interference abroad in terms of state ownership and subsidization, we wouldn't be in the box of having to try to compete against foreign governments. Until that situation is clarified, and we have more free trade in the world steel market, I don't see that, as a temporary measure, there is any alternative, and it really comes from government intervention in the market system."

Tracking Studies, May 1977. This tracking study analyzed the "write-in" advertising effort on the energy issue. It was emphasized that in making comparisons of these new data and those from the previous study, we must bear in mind that different issues were addressed in the ads; different magazines were used; and this latest campaign was geared toward the "most conservative" sector, rather than "influentials" in general.

It was found that awareness of Bethlehem's advertising declined from 23 to 14 percent when compared with an average decline of 7 percent among the other four corporations examined. An increase in overall advocacy advertising by the business community and President Carter's promise of a major revision in U.S. energy policies were "intuitively" felt to have inhibited reader recall of any single advocacy campaign. Copy point recall rose significantly (from 2 to 7 percent, an increase of 250 percent) on the issue of energy conservation, the subject of the latest advertising, with 5 percent specifically mentioning the physical layout of advertisements. The fact that recall on the previous year's issues dropped was felt to provide "vivid evidence of the need for *sustained* advertising to maintain awareness once a satisfactory level is reached," a point made repeatedly throughout all the studies. The level of agreement with the advertising message among those who remembered it was down dramatically (from 77 to 46 percent), but up even more dramatically among those expressing a neutral position (from 17 to 44 percent). Those disagreeing increased somewhat (from 6 to 10 percent). Again it was stressed that these dramatic shifts were probably due to changes made in the tracking study format, question content, and the magazines used for subsequent tracking studies. The perception of Bethlehem as a "corporate citizen" was significantly higher among those aware of the advertising than among those not aware.

Tracking Studies, October 1977. During the advertising campaign dealing with foreign trade, awareness of Bethlehem's advertising was up to its highest level so far (27 percent). Copy point recall on the foreign trade issue rose from 2 to 21 percent, while recall of points from the previous campaign dropped significantly. It was felt that news coverage of advocacy issues may increase awareness of the problem, but decrease the recognition of the source (Bethlehem Steel) that brought the problem to the public's attention.

There was no significant change in agreement with the advertising messages. However, because the number aware of the ads had increased, the absolute number of people in agreement with the company's position had also risen (from 64 to 127 per thousand influential subscribers). Perception of Bethlehem as a "corporate citizen" did not change significantly among those who remembered the ads, but as before, was significantly higher than among those who did not remember them. It was concluded that "the advertising campaigns of the last two years had a very positive influence on influentials' attitudes towards Bethlehem Steel with respect to those topics advertised."

Tracking Studies, January 1978. At the conclusion of the foreign trade advertising, awareness of Bethlehem's corporate advertising had risen significantly, to 39 percent. Copy point recall, apparently due at least in part to the use of a standardized approach in format and layout, had risen to 38 percent on the foreign trade issue, recall of previous issues "remained at a marginal, residual level," again demonstrating "the decay of awareness that is inevitable without continued reinforcement." As before, the absolute number of people in agreement with Bethlehem's position was calculated to have risen to 211 per thousand influentials. Frequent editorial mention of Bethlehem Steel's problems in the news media was thought to have had a "salutory effect" on attitudes toward the company, since "the sympathies of those not aware of the current campaign have reached levels statistically equivalent to those who are aware," and in all cases had risen. Among those aware, perception of Bethlehem as having "a responsible position opposing foreign suppliers selling materials in the U.S. below their own cost" had climbed to 72 percent.

The 1978 Campaign

The 1978 campaign included a series of six ads in a jigsaw puzzle/solution format—one on each of five issues, along with a wrapup ad [Exhibits 13 and 14]. Following this effort, a Bethlehem ad with a headline "You b———— are crybabies" was run in a limited number of magazines in the company's schedule, in which Chairman Lewis Foy responded to some criticisms of the recently completed series of ads [Exhibit 15].

Exhibit 13

Steel must comply with 5,600 Federal agencies. It's a wonder

**Regulatory reform:
part of the solution to the steel industry puzzle.**

regulations from 27 we get anything done.

The Declaration of Independence set forth America's grievances against King George of England. Included was the charge that he had "erected a Multitude of new Offices and sent hither Swarms of Officers to harrass our people..."

That quote still carries a valid warning for all of us about the danger of too much government regulation—not only in our business lives, but in our private lives.

Overregulation by government is no joke.

According to a study recently completed at Washington University in St. Louis, the cost to business for complying with government regulations exceeds $62 billion a year—or about $300 for every man, woman, and child in the U.S. Beyond that, the government itself spends about $3.2 billion a year to administer those regulations.

But no matter who spends those dollars initially, all of us as American consumers and taxpayers eventually pick up the tab.

Our ultimate cost may be paid for in the sacrifice of individual freedom as government intrudes into more and more areas of private and business life.

*Source: Council on Wage and Price Stability

Why we're concerned.

Bethlehem and other domestic steel producers now are required to comply with more than 5,600 regulations from 27 agencies of the U.S. Government.*

These 5,600 Federal regulations pertain only to the *making* of steel. Thousands of other regulations impact upon our mining, transportation, and marketing operations. We also cope with additional thousands of state and local regulations.

The time and money we spend hacking through the regulatory jungle adds needless cost to the making of steel—and that takes money out of everyone's pocketbook.

Must business strangle to death in red tape?

We say no. Some regulation is always needed. But things have gone too far. Today, regulatory *reform* is needed. And needed fast. Business and government should work together to reduce the burden and high cost of red tape—it won't come about by itself. What's needed is the support of all Americans.

If you agree that overregulation by government is a serious problem, make your views known where they count. Write your representatives in Washington and your state capital.

Bethlehem Steel Corporation, Bethlehem, PA 18016.

Bethlehem
In search of solutions.

Exhibit 14

The steel industry puz tough problems in sea

zle:
arch of solutions.

Steel is a basic commodity used by most industries. Thus, the economic health of America's steel industry plays an indispensable role in the well-being of our nation's economy.

Last year, steel's troubles made headlines.

Plant closings and layoffs—triggered by an unprecedented flood of steel imports—focused attention on the plight of the industry.

Since then steel's situation has improved slightly, but our problems are far from solved.

No single solution

Most of the issues confronting Bethlehem and other domestic steelmakers impact on each other to weaken the earnings we need to get moving forward again.

No single solution solves all of the interlocking problems that make up the steel industry puzzle.

If the pieces fall into place

Because steel is essential to the prosperity and national defense of America, we believe the pieces of the puzzle must fall into place. And they will, provided industry and government work together to insure economic health and stability.

Putting it all together

Just as steel's problems have impacted on one another to *diminish* earnings, so workable solutions can interact to *improve* earnings. And better earnings provide the means we need to upgrade productivity, maintain employment, and attract investors.

Consider:

Federal tax policies that generate funds for capital investment can stimulate demand for steel from the construction and capital goods markets.

Vigorous enforcement of America's existing trade laws can prevent foreign producers from "dumping" illegally priced steel that erodes our markets.

Sensible energy policies can help insure adequate supplies of the coal, oil, natural gas, and electric power we need to keep our plants running, our employees working.

Less rigid and less costly environmental mandates by government can free more steel dollars to invest in job- and income-producing facilities—without forsaking environmental goals.

And regulatory reform to eliminate red tape at all levels of government can save tax dollars for everyone.

Write for free booklet

For more information about the problems facing America's steel industry and our recommended solutions, write for our booklet, "In Search of Solutions." Public Affairs Department, Room 476-A, Bethlehem Steel Corporation, Bethlehem, PA 18016.

Bethlehem

Exhibit 15

A reader writes:

"You b_____ are crybabies..."

He also said we "have no guts."

These remarks are one reader's response to an advertisement in our recent corporate advocacy campaign, "In Search of Solutions." The campaign explored many of the problems facing the steel industry.

Other readers implied that we do not always tell the whole truth. One responded by suggesting, in effect, that the solutions to our problems are right under our noses. And a few made comments that aren't printable.

Are we crybabies with no guts? Many readers didn't think so. They wrote in support of our position or asked for more information in order to consider our side of the story.

Those readers who share our concern for a healthy economy apparently got the point of our message: there are no simple, easy solutions to the complex problems affecting the steel industry: en-

Lewis W. Foy, Chairman
Bethlehem Steel Corporation

ergy, pollution control, steel imports, government over-regulation, and tax reform among them. And we're searching hard to find solutions.

Effective communication on controversial issues in-

volves give and take and is rarely achieved instantaneously. For example, a number of misconceptions about the steel industry and its problems emerged in the mail generated by our campaign and in the public press.

Misconception.

The American steel industry is in trouble because it has been slow in adopting new steelmaking technology.

Fact. The subject of an alleged technology "gap" or "lag" in America's steel industry was covered in a report to Congress prepared by the Research Division of the Congressional Research Service, Library of Congress, November 1975. That report concludes: "The United States does not lag significantly behind the rest of the world in the several kinds of technology employed in the steel industry...."

In October 1977, the staff of the Council on Wage and Price Stability stated in its Report to the President on Prices and Costs in the United States Steel Industry: "A comparison of modern efficient plants in Japan and the U.S. shows a substantial Japanese cost advantage because of lower capital construction costs, and lower wage rates, and not because of better technology."

Although we don't always agree with the Council on Wage and Price Stability, this conclusion of its staff is one we're happy to share.

The fact is the American steel industry has spent a whopping $20 billion-plus to modernize and upgrade existing plants over the past ten years alone. As a result, most of our facilities are a lot more modern than some people think. And much of the modern steel technology in use abroad actually evolved from developments right here in the U.S.A.

Misconception.

European and Japanese steelworkers turn out more tons per hour than American steelworkers do.

Fact. In terms of worker productivity, the American steel industry is well out ahead of most of its foreign competitors.

For the year 1976, here's how some of our overseas competitors stacked up when a value of 100 was assigned to the average output per hour of American steelworkers: French steelworkers rated in a range from 61-69, West Germans 81-90, British steelworkers 46-49, and Japanese 108-126.

These productivity ratings are based on data compiled by the U.S. Department of Labor, Bureau of Labor Statistics, Office of Productivity and Technology: "International Comparisons of Productivity and Labor Costs in the Steel Industry...," dated November 1977.

Misconception.

American steelmakers suffer from inefficient management.

Fact. A staff report of the Bureau of Economics to the Federal Trade Commission dated November 1977 says this: "To the extent that an assessment could be made of the technological and financial decisions of the managers of U.S. steel firms, they were found to be efficient. Thus, the data do not appear to support the hypothesis that relatively poor performance by U.S. managers explains the pattern of international steel trade flows."

Misconceptions about America's steel industry continue to abound. Meanwhile, we do what we can to debunk them and move ahead confidently. Today, Bethlehem Steel is lean, technologically advanced, and competitively sound. And we are constantly in search of new ways to work smarter and produce better.

For more information about steel industry problems and our recommended solutions, write for our booklet, "In Search of Solutions." Public Affairs Department, Room 476-A, Bethlehem Steel Corporation, Bethlehem, PA 18016.

Still in search of solutions

Tracking Studies, May 1978. This study was conducted prior to the puzzle/solution campaign of 1978 as a benchmark for that campaign and to measure the residual effects of the 1977 campaign.

After a five-month lapse in advertising, awareness of Bethlehem's corporate advertising efforts had declined to 30 percent. Copy point recall on the foreign trade issue dropped from 38 to 13 percent, although it was still higher than before any advertising was undertaken (11 percent). Although there was no significant change in the proportions of those agreeing with Bethlehem's messages, the absolute number had fallen to 147 per thousand influentials. There was a general decline in pro-Bethlehem sentiment, especially in the "good citizen" and "foreign trade policy" areas.

Tracking Studies, September 1978. At the conclusion of the puzzle/solution campaign, awareness had climbed to 37 percent, nearly equal to the previous high. Copy point recall increased 200 percent (from 1 to 3 percent) in regard to capital formation, and 130 percent (from 13 to 30 percent) on foreign trade, which one ad addressed. There was either no change or a decline on recall of other specific issues.

There was no change in the proportion of those in agreement with Bethlehem's message among those aware of the advertising; however, the absolute number was calculated to have risen to 181 per thousand influentials. There was a modest gain in pro-Bethlehem attitudes and a significant rise in those feeling the company had a responsible position on foreign trade, though all areas remained at levels below those registered at the end of 1977.

The 1979 Campaign

The 1979 campaign included five advertisements, three of which are shown in Exhibits 16–18, advocating a strong domestic steel industry.

The Tracking Studies: An Evaluation

In discussing the tracking studies in terms of their usefulness, descriptions, and relevance of the findings and the amount of changes, the figure Cronin considers most important is the awareness level, upon which all the other measurements are based. He feels the studies are a valid indication of what the advertising is doing.

> We use it as a tool. It's better than anything else we can get our hands on. I use the data as an indicator, and as we get more of the data and I'm able to put it together, I can see trends.
>
> If we had another $100,000 to put into such research, we could probably do better and come up with results which would be more finite. It's the monies you have to work with and what you are looking for. We're looking to see whether, in fact, within the magazines we have chosen, our audience has received our message, is more aware of it, and can come up with copy point recall. And it has.

Exhibit 16

Why does every emerging nation want its own steel industry?

Because just like the mature, industrialized nations of the world, the less-developed countries know the importance of a strong domestic steel industry...to their national economy and to their national defense. Because they don't want to depend on foreign sources for a reliable supply of the world's most useful metal.

What's needed to insure a healthy, growing *American* steel industry? Governmental policies that will allow us to generate the additional funds needed to modernize and expand.

Bethlehem

Bethlehem Steel Corporation, Bethlehem, PA 18016

Exhibit 17

Can you imagine a strong national defense without an adequate supply of steel?

Just how much should America count on overseas sources for steel? What happens if those sources are suddenly cut off—or if they suddenly decide they need their steel at home?

Last year steel imports reached an all-time record of 21.1 million tons. And unless we soon start expanding our domestic steelmaking capacity, that figure could reach 25 to 30 million tons a year by 1985. And America could find itself as dependent on foreign steel as it is on foreign oil.

What's needed to insure an adequate supply of *domestic* steel for America's national economy and national defense? Governmental policies that will allow the American steel industry to generate the additional funds needed to modernize and expand.

Bethlehem

Bethlehem Steel Corporation, Bethlehem, PA 18016

Exhibit 18

Who's going to meet the growing need for steel in this country– and at what price?

If there's one lesson to be learned from America's oil crises, it's this: You can't always depend on foreign sources to supply how much of what you want, when you want it, and at a price you can afford to pay.

Unless we soon start expanding our domestic steelmaking capacity, 25 to 30 million tons of steel imports could be entering the U.S. market annually by 1985. (Compared to 12 million tons in 1975.) And then America could find itself at the mercy of foreign steel producers, as it is at the mercy of foreign oil producers.

What's needed to meet the growing need for steel in this country with *domestic* steel? Governmental policies that will allow the American steel industry to generate the additional funds needed to modernize and expand.

Bethlehem

Bethlehem Steel Corporation, Bethlehem, PA 18016

Some of the variation, Cronin feels, is accounted for by the "mixing of apples and oranges" by surveying different issues. The other "ups and downs" are considered evidence of the necessity for continued advertising to maintain the desired public attitude and awareness. When asked whether this decay indicated lack of education on the part of the public, Latshaw responded that they don't like the word "educate," that they are, rather, trying only to make their readers more aware of Bethlehem's point of view. Cronin explained that after years of negative publicity about corporations, such as payoffs, price increases, and labor problems, attitudes cannot be changed in a short period of time, even the perception of Bethlehem Steel as a good citizen, which was at any rate not the objective of the advertising. These managers point to a continuing residual increase in awareness as evidence that with a continued advertising effort over, say, ten years, a much more substantial change would take place. When asked whether the small incremental increases and high decay rates might show that they shouldn't bother to advertise, Cronin stated:

> We work on the assumption that we better bother—we *have* to bother—we should get involved and do these things. As small or as meager as someone might think the results are, someone has to take the stand and say the things that have to be said, because if we don't, if we just say it's futile and we're not going to win this battle, we're sure enough going to lose.

In discussing the adequacy of the statistical sample, the managers felt their sample size (around 300 interviews for the last five studies with the test group being those aware of Bethlehem's advertising, and the control group being those unaware of it; and all fitting the demographic requirements discussed earlier) was large enough to be valid.

A possible source of feedback on the effectiveness of Bethlehem's advocacy advertising was the letters sent to the White House and legislators as a result of the "write-in" ads, a campaign complicated by a related national energy questionnaire that started coming in soon after the Bethlehem letters. The two were not counted separately. However, in the first two weeks, before the questionnaires began arriving, 5,000 letters (which were projected out to 200,000 letters in all) were received by the White House as the result of one of the ads, which Latshaw claimed "is not bad." As to the impact of these letters on the president or legislators, Latshaw said he "shudders to think what might happen" if they acknowledged being influenced by such campaigns, but that Bethlehem's "people in Washington who contact the Hill" say that the advertising was noted and generally well received and that legislators had heard from their constituents about those issues.

There is a general feeling of satisfaction among the Bethlehem Steel management as to the effectiveness of their corporate advertising. Latshaw summarizes it in this way: "We've measured what we could reasonably measure. We cannot point to a single ad, a year's campaign, or the entire 3-year advocacy program and credit it with the passage of a particular piece of legislation—or its failure to pass. But based on what we are able to measure and what we are told by our associates in Washington and in the state capitals, we believe the series has been a success."

Part VI CAMPAIGNS IN SUPPORT OF PUBLIC POLICY POSITIONS AFFECTING A SPONSOR'S VITAL INTERESTS

CAMPAIGNS OF DIRECT APPEAL

Chapter 13   **LONE STAR INDUSTRIES, INC., GREENWICH, CT:**
A HIGH-VISIBILITY ADVOCACY CAMPAIGN TO STRENGTHEN CORPORATE IDENTITY

On November 3, 1980, on the eve of presidential elections, Lone Star Industries, Inc., the Greenwich, Connecticut, based producer of cement, joined a select list of major U.S. corporations by launching an issue advertising campaign. The first full-page advertisement appeared in national newspapers under the banner "The workhorse is willing—but what a load!" The top half of the page showed a cartoon workhorse called "American Industry" burdened down with heavy loads of "over environmentalism," "over taxation," and "over regulation." The brief copy exhorted the nation toward the reindustrialization of America by reducing environmental, regulatory, and tax restraints on American industry. It also stated that the foundation of reindustrialization must be the construction industry—which depends heavily on cement [Exhibit 1].

THE CORPORATION

Lone Star was incorporated in 1919 as International Cement Corporation. In 1935, its name changed to Lone Star Cement Corporation, and

---

Research Assistant: Josette Quiniou.

Exhibit 1

The workhorse is willing— but what a load!

The reindustrialization of America is a top-priority goal for the 80's.

Unless we turn around our sagging economy, how will we sustain our standard of living?

How will we pay for our social programs, which cost more than our defense budget?

The foundation? Cement.

Rebuilding America's basic industry and economy means construction, which means cement.

But the cement shortages of 1973 and 1978 will soon return, because America's relatively small, highly-segmented cement industry cannot afford the $6 billion needed for its own reindustrialization, at today's inflated costs.

Give the horse a chance — and some nourishment.

Government can help. It can lighten the paperwork, remove red tape, ease the burden of taxes, regulations and environmental demands...allow industry to use more of its earnings to finance plant renewal and expansion.

With a lighter load, American industry can step a lot faster.

James E. Stewart

James E. Stewart, Chairman of the Board and Chief Executive Officer
Lone Star Industries, Inc. One Greenwich Plaza, Greenwich, Connecticut 06830.
For more about the cement industry's challenges and dynamics in the 1980's,
write for our Annual Report.

LONESTAR

Number One in Cement... Serving America's Great Builders

in 1971 it became Lone Star Industries, Inc. The headquarters are located in Greenwich, Connecticut.

Lone Star is the largest producer of cement in the United States and the Western Hemisphere, the country's largest source of ready-mixed concrete and sand and gravel aggregates, and one of the nation's major sources of crushed stone aggregates and concrete products.

In 1980 Lone Star and its affiliates operated thirteen domestic cement plants in the United States. (In 1982 Lone Star purchased Marquette Company from Gulf & Western Industries, adding six more U.S. cement plants.) The company also operates three wholly-owned cement plants in South America, two in Argentina and one in Uruguay, and has a 48 percent interest in a company currently operating five cement plants in Brazil.

Lone Star's mix of products makes it highly capital-intensive, and cost-sensitive to rising standards of air quality at federal, state, and local levels. Compliance with these requirements has required expenditures totaling more than $40 million to date, and the cost of additional programs for abatement of air, water, and noise pollution that Lone Star may undertake in the future has been estimated to be $26 million for existing facilities over the next five years.

The manufacture of cement is also highly energy-intensive, with energy in the form of kiln fuel and electric power accounting for approximately 37 percent of manufacturing costs. As the cost of oil and gas has increased dramatically in recent years, Lone Star has been converting plants using natural gas to coal as rapidly as practicable. By the end of 1981, approximately 90 percent of Lone Star's domestic plants used coal. In addition, Lone Star has been taking other steps to reduce overall energy usage by adopting energy-saving technology.

The cement industry is highly cyclical; sensitive to general economic conditions, and very price-competitive. The company's operations are subject to fluctuations in government spending for highway construction, water resources, sewage systems, airports, mass transit, and other projects, as well as fluctuations arising from general business conditions, increases or decreases in housing starts, industrial and commercial construction, the tightening or easing of credit, interest rates, and other factors. While sales by the company directly to federal, state, and local government agencies are not significant, customers of the company are engaged in government contract construction business to an important extent.

James E. Stewart, 60 years old, is chairman and chief executive officer of Lone Star Industries, Inc.

Under favorable conditions, the company is highly profitable. During the period 1971–1980, sales grew at an annual rate of 23 percent, with a peak in the period of 1977–78 and a decline in the period 1979–1981. The trend of net income closely follows the trend in revenues during the decade, except in 1975 and more recently in 1980, when the income was 18 percent lower than the previous year, despite higher revenues. One of the major expense items is interest payments, which grew 42 percent in 1980 and 75 percent in 1981 over the respective previous year.

Rationale For Advocacy Campaign

Prior to the current campaign, the company had confined its corporate advertising to financial and corporate image campaigns. Its first corporate institutional ad campaign started in 1975 with the theme "In the Right Place at the Right Time." It was a typical Wall Street-oriented corporate communication. Later, another campaign in news magazines with the theme of "Great American Builders" began to suggest that the nation was not building as courageously as it used to. In the Fall of 1980, the corporate advertising program came up for reevaluation. The top management did not consider those campaigns sufficiently effective, and when no conventional substitutes were found acceptable, it was decided to undertake a reassessment of the corporate institutional advertising.

The company felt that its prosperity and that of its customers and the entire U.S. economy depended on reindustrialization and economic revitalization, and ultimately on reduced interest rates. Therefore, it decided that it should develop an efficient communication program to inform people of the problems connected with reindustrialization and similar issues at the national level. In an article in the December, 1980 issue of *Lonestar Journal,* the in-house magazine, the company stated that the purpose behind the public issue ads was to encourage the public to speak out for "common sense in government."

A major problem area for Lone Star, moreover, was a lack of strong identity among the nation's investment community, opinion leaders and governments. There was considerable public confusion in Lone Star's name with other companies having similar designations. Public opinion surveys conducted by the Opinion Research Corporation and Benson & Benson indicated that the financial community and general public had a relatively low level of awareness about Lone Star Industries, Inc., and its activities. Therefore, the company sought to establish a stronger identity for itself among people of influence and a reputation as a "forward thinking and outspoken corporate leader."[1]

Decision-Making Process

According to Theodore Price, director of advertising and creative services for Lone Star Industries: "The decision to engage in advocacy advertising essentially was made by James E. Stewart, the Chairman and Chief Executive Officer." Price, then creative director and a speechwriter for Stewart, but with prior advertising experience, had been called on to develop an advertising recommendation. He was not given any particular specifications, but since he knew the CEO's thinking and convictions, it was felt he could "come up with a campaign internally that would reflect Mr. Stewart's leadership, and the company's direction." It was also his own conviction that the advertising needed more visibility, and more impact. The creative planning and the decision to go ahead were completed within the space of about two weeks.

IMPLEMENTING THE AD CAMPAIGN STRATEGY

The Target Audience

The target audience was defined primarily as Wall Street, Washington, Lone Star's customers, and other business leaders. Beyond that, any additional audience of influential people that could be attracted was considered a positive factor. In placing the ads on the business pages, the goal was not primarily to reach a broad public, but to have Lone Star's leadership better identified by Wall Street, business leaders, Congress, and the administration. The company felt that this approach would enable it to get the recognition and reception it needed in its communications with, and presentations before, the financial and the legislative and regulatory communities.

Selection of Issues and Copy Themes

The company did not use any systematic approach to identify various issues or institutionalize the process of issue selection. Comments Price:

> One reason is that we are a smaller, less diversified company than some of the major conglomerates that have public issue analysis departments. Nor do we have a large economics department to undertake detailed evaluation of national economic issues. Our objective is primarily to call attention to important issues and problems that are not getting enough attention and action in Washington.

The initial approach to choice of themes was to rough out two or three ideas at a time and submit them to Stewart, who would choose one for implementation. Price stated that the objective was to shoot for eight to ten good ads a year, out of perhaps fifty ideas considered. "It's not always easy to get a big idea on schedule." This strategy takes the pressure off deadlines and provides flexibility in implementation.

The ad campaign has concentrated on two major issues:

1. A strong advocacy for America to reindustrialize and for the removal of regulatory barriers to accomplish this goal.
2. A strong protest against the rigid high interest policy of the Federal Reserve Board as contrary to public interest.

These issues were implemented through the following copy themes:

1. "The workhorse is willing." This was the lead-off advertisement of the campaign and ran on November 3, 1980, the day before Election Day. It pleads the industry's cause and protests against the major obstacles blocking faster progress. Three problems are identified and attacked: over environmentalism, over taxation, and over regulation.
2. "How America became a colony again." This ad appeared later that month, on the day before Thanksgiving. It explains, according to

the text of the ad, that the United States has become the Thanksgiving turkey by importing manufactured goods and exporting its natural resources. It argues that U.S. money was used in the postwar period to rebuild the war-torn foreign cities and industries, while American factories were allowed to run down. Capital investment now is required in the United States to rebuild our major industries [Exhibit 2].

3. "You can't ring a big bell with a small hammer." This ad ran in December 1980. It shows American industry trying to ring the bell of reindustrialization, armed only with a small hammer of capital. It contends that America's profit system really works, and we should let it work again. It argues for greater capital formation to restore the productivity of American industry (this was the first drawing by Jack Davis, the former *Mad* magazine cartoonist, who did several of the subsequent ads.)

4. "Poison Warning." At the end of December 1980, as the prime rate jumped to another peak, the skull and crossbones ad was conceived and drawn up within one day to protest the interest rate "flip-flops."[2] The message is labeled "Poison Warning." The Federal Reserve Board's interest rate policy is "driving the economy of the U.S. into self-destruction." Readers are asked to send their own feelings on the matter to Paul Volcker, Federal Reserve chairman, and to their representative in Congress [Exhibit 3].

5. "The President Can't Do It Alone." On Inauguration Day 1981, this ad encouraged farmers, consumers, government employees, Congress, labor, and business to work together and help President Regan get the American economy "out of the mud." The copy concludes, "O.K. Everybody out and push. The free rides are over" [Exhibit 4].

6. "To the Members of the 97th Congress." When the company felt in February 1981 that Congress was dragging its feet, this ad exhorted cooperation with the president to get the economy moving; otherwise, voters were liable to turn them out of office [Exhibit 5].

7. "They Flew a Brave Flag." This April 1981 ad stressed the American colonists' spirit of freedom, self-reliance, and independence. "They flew a brave flag . . . and we must recreate that spirit today." The ad features the "Don't Tread on Me" flag that had been shown in two earlier ads, and offers a miniature desk flag to the reader for one dollar.

8. "Jaws." This very eye-catching June 1981 ad concentrated once again on the Fed's interest rate policy as hurting the construction industry. A huge shark, labeled "Federal Reserve" and with "High Interest Rates" teeth, is shown as having eaten the skeletons of 1980 and 1981 housing. Just above, a swimmer labeled "1982 Housing" is watching in horror.

9. "Congratulations, Doctor." This ad, presented in the fall of 1981, states that even though the Fed policy succeeded in curing inflation, high interest rates were still stifling the economy. The headline summarized the controversy by saying, "Congratulations, Doctor! It was a good operation on inflation . . . too bad the patient died." Again, readers are requested to write their feelings to the Fed [Exhibit 6].

Exhibit 2

How America became a colony again

And what to do to regain our independence now

Look at it this way: we ship natural resources and food to other nations—and we buy their manufactured goods, like television sets and automobiles.

We send our troops abroad in times of war, we cough up the money to rebuild war-torn foreign cities and factories, we let our own factories run down, and our reward is the contempt of the world.

Our citizens suffer high unemployment, high inflation, high taxes, and still go out and buy foreign goods.

If that isn't being a good colony to the rest of the world, what is? We are politically free, but economically we're in shackles.

Isn't it time to declare our economic independence again?

That will mean looking to our own productivity, encouraging capital investment here at home, and rebuilding our basic industries.

It will mean putting our money and our citizens back to work again for America.

It will mean flying our Colonial flag again, the one that tells the world, "Don't Tread on Me."

We did it once before, when we got mad enough.

James E. Stewart

James E. Stewart, Chairman of the Board and Chief Executive Officer
Lone Star Industries, Inc., One Greenwich Plaza, Greenwich, Connecticut 06830.
For more about the cement industry's challenges and dynamics in the 1980's, write for our Annual Report.

Number One in Cement... Serving America's Great Builders

Exhibit 3

The interest rate policy of the Federal Reserve System
is driving the economy of the United States into <u>self-destruction</u>.

You can help!

Write or wire your feelings to:

The Honorable Paul A. Volcker
Chairman
Board of Governors
Federal Reserve System
Washington, D.C. 20551

And to your Congressman. Send us a copy if you can.

<u>Speak up</u>—if you don't, nobody else will.

You're not too big or small to count!

James E. Stewart

James E. Stewart, Chairman of the Board and Chief Executive Officer
Lone Star Industries, Inc., One Greenwich Plaza, Greenwich, Connecticut 06830.

LONESTAR

Number One in Cement... Serving America's Great Builders

Exhibit 4

The President can't do it alone

Our economy is stuck in the mud.

We've been spinning our wheels—with high taxes, higher interest rates, big government, over-regulation, social insecurity, foreign give-aways—and we just keep digging ourselves in deeper.

Our new President can get us unstuck—but he certainly can't do it alone.

Americans are known for get-up-and-go . . . self-reliance . . . independence.

We haven't exercised those muscles lately; now we must.

O.K. Everybody out and push.

The free rides are over !

James E. Stewart

James E. Stewart, Chairman of the Board and Chief Executive Officer
Lone Star Industries, Inc., One Greenwich Plaza, Greenwich, Connecticut 06830
Reprints on request; write Dept. A. Permission granted to reproduce.

LONESTAR
Number One in Cement . . . Serving America's Great Builders.

Exhibit 5

To the Members of the 97th Congress!

Want to get re-elected?

DON'T PULL
THIS NATION APART

Your Voters
are watching!

James E. Stewart, Chairman of the Board and Chief Executive Officer
Lone Star Industries, Inc., One Greenwich Plaza, Greenwich, Connecticut 06830
Reprints on request. Write Dept. B. Permission granted to reproduce.

LONESTAR
Number One in Cement . . . Serving America's Great Builders.

410

Exhibit 6

Congratulations, Doctor!

It was a good operation on inflation...
too bad the patient died

Maybe the high interest rate policy of the Federal Reserve will cure inflation— but the rates are killing the economy.

Sensible balance is needed. Our national goals can't be achieved without a strong economy.

Write your feelings about interest rates to your Congressman, and to The Honorable Paul A. Volcker, Chairman, Board of Governors, Federal Reserve System, Washington, D.C. 20551. Send us a copy if you can.

Your voice counts. Make sure it is heard.

James E. Stewart

James E. Stewart, Chairman of the Board and Chief Executive Officer
Lone Star Industries, Inc., One Greenwich Plaza, Greenwich, Connecticut 06830
Reprints on request to Dept. D.   Permission granted to reproduce.

LONESTAR

Number One in Cement . . . Serving America's Great Builders.

10. "Blood Shortage." This ad ran in February 1982, and followed the same pattern as "Jaws" and "Congratulations, Doctor." It emphasizes how both industry and people are hurt by the high interest policy. "Too much money goes into interest expense and not enough into new cars, new homes, new factories that create jobs, and needed public works." For the fourth time, Lone Star asked its readers to write to Paul Volcker [Exhibit 7].

11. "West of the Potomac." In May 1982, Lone Star ran two more blasts at the Fed's high interest rate policy, which had permitted only a slight pullback in rates. This first message protested the failure of Congress to reach a budget consensus and to solve the basic economic problems. "It's tough out here" is the theme—"The economic fire of a depression is burning here, while you, the firemen, are arguing how the blaze should be fought."

12. "Good News." Two weeks later, this Jack Davis cartoon showed a Fed spokesman telling the good news about inflation to the skeletons of agriculture, industry, labor, and construction—all of which had apparently died of inaction and boredom waiting for interest rates to come down. The spokesman complains, "Hey, You're Not Listening!!!" Both this and the preceding ads also exhort the reader to write to Volcker and Congress [Exhibit 8].

Copy Design and Execution

Each advertisement is made up as a full page, with a large political cartoon, a strong headline, and a short message signed by Lone Star's CEO, James E. Stewart. The messages are invariably emotional or exhortational in character, with a clear and straightforward content, and avoid lengthy editorializing or complex issue analysis.

No outside advertising agency was used, the ads being conceived in-house for speed and timeliness. Outside art direction and illustration were employed, with mechanical preparation and placement by the company's public relations firm.

Media Selection

Advertisements were placed in various leading daily newspapers, such as the *Wall Street Journal* (all editions), the *New York Times,* and the *Washington Post,* and leading conservative newspapers in eighteen other major cities that are Lone Star's primary markets. *Forbes* was the only magazine, and was included to gain extra investor impact. Total circulation was about 8 million readers per ad. The first six ads ran at the rate of about one per month. Deteriorating economic conditions slowed the frequency a little for the subsequent ads; a total of twelve ads were run within an eighteen month period.

Newspapers were selected as the primary and virtually sole medium for several reasons, the company says:

1. Every decision-maker in the worlds of business, economics, finance,

Exhibit 7

Blood Shortage

Too much of our economic blood is being sucked away by the high interest rate policy of the Federal Reserve.

Too much money goes into interest expense —and not enough into new cars, new homes, new factories that create jobs, and needed public works.

Like you, we support the fight against inflation—but not by destroying the economy with high, erratic interest rates.

Tell your Congressman what **you** think of high interest rates. Send a copy to The Honorable Paul A. Volcker, Chairman, Board of Governors, Federal Reserve System, Washington, D.C. 20551—send us a copy if you can.

Do it now—you are not too big or too small to count.

James E. Stewart, Chairman of the Board and Chief Executive Officer
Lone Star Industries, Inc., One Greenwich Plaza, Greenwich, Connecticut 06830
Reprints on request; write Dept. E.   Permission granted to reproduce.

LONESTAR

Number One in Cement . . . Serving America's Great Builders.

Exhibit 8

and government absolutely must (in the company's opinion) read one or more good newspapers every day—at least page 1 and the financial news—"even if that means letting the magazines pile up on the bedside table."

2. Following this reasoning to a reverse process of media selection, it was felt that anyone who did not read a newspaper was probably not a key influential or decision-maker, and not a part of the target audience.

3. The larger full-page ad size provided in standard-sized newspapers gives the ads greater visibility and impact. "In view of the limited reaction to our previous corporate campaigns, we felt that if we were going to get through to important people, we were going to have to knock them off their chairs."

4. Lack of full-page advertising competition on the business pages added to the opportunity for visibility and impact on the target audience.

5. The timeliness of the ad messages would be enhanced by their appearance adjacent to the day's economic news.

For the future, the corporation is willing to consider TV to get even greater visibility in Lone Star's markets—possibly spots on the local late evening news to reach the older, more affluent, and better-educated male audience at its peak. Nevertheless, there is awareness and concern for the anti-advocacy standards that TV generally imposes, which may require a tempering of the messages to make them acceptable, or even a whole new approach.

ANALYSIS OF THE AD CAMPAIGN

On the face of it, Lone Star's advocacy campaign might appear to have some internal contradictions in terms of choice of themes, execution of ad copy, and selection of media. For example, a tight money policy is generally considered important to fight inflation and an integral part of President Reagan's economic program. Therefore, it might seem strange to support President Reagan's economic policies and at the same time criticize Paul Volcker and the Federal Reserve Board for its tight money policy and the higher interest rates that go with such a policy.

Two, the company wants to reach influential people in the financial community, in the legislative bodies, and in the administration. The company's choice of media reflects this preference. This target audience is supposedly better informed and more rational than the average American citizen, and yet the company is trying to reach them with simplistic and emotionally charged cartoon messages with very little effort to inform in depth.

Lone Star's Theodore Price does not find these approaches to be mutually contradictory. In terms of the twin themes of support for Reagan's economic program and opposition to the Federal Reserve Board's high interest rate policies, Price explains: "We do not present complex, highbrow theories. These are the gut reactions to what's happening. We say, 'The President can't do it alone,' and he needs to be supported. But that ad really is saying that the free rides are over and everybody's got to get out and push. We are implying that too much money has been given away by the government and that there should be better accountability. We don't think that's in conflict with another ad that says interest rates are too high, because that's another problem. The President hasn't said we need high interest rates per se, that I have read. If interest rates can be moderated and stabilized, within his economic recovery program, that would be ideal. We think the Fed should try much harder to do that."

There is also another explanation. Lone Star wants to show its customers—the construction industry—that it is aware of their problems and wants to help them, and the ads are an expression of the company's concern for the plight of the construction industry. "We are speaking on behalf of our customers, and we have made sure of that," explains Price. "Every new ad is sent to them with a letter seeking their reaction and support. And it's been amazing, the support that we've received. The fact is, our customers are sitting on their hands waiting for jobs to come along. There is no money for construction, because investors won't pay the high interest rates. If our customers don't work, and we don't ship them products, then we don't make money. It is a very practical marketing argument as well as an economic argument. We help our customers by expressing this point of view we share about high interest rates. It is almost as though we were speaking for an association of customers, who have given us tremendous support."

Lone Star is not alone in its criticism of the Fed's high interest policies. Many other businessmen have echoed similar views. According to Emery:[3] "This idea of escalating interest rates, by curbing the money supply, is causing further damage to the economy. When a business can't borrow money to expand, then the federal government ends up suffering, since it does not get more taxes." Wallace, of Bangor Punta, doubts that keeping tabs on the money supply or interest rates will work unless the effort is conducted jointly with a decrease in spending.

Lone Star hoped that by encouraging people to write to Volcker and their representatives to express their feelings, it might cause the Fed chairman to balance his judgment a little bit, more than if there were no opposition at all.

Price agrees that the ads are simplified, and even highly exaggerated cartoon statements. He based this approach on three considerations:

1. To attract interest and communicate clearly
2. To appeal to the emotional responses of even sophisticated people
3. To develop a strong identity for Lone Star

The use of political cartoons, with very simple and direct headlines, expresses ideas clearly to many more people, the company maintains. "You can get 50 percent or more of your circulation audience to see and understand your message—not just 5 percent or 25 percent. It is a matter of using available techniques of getting our point across quickly, understandably, and perhaps emotionally. We don't propose detailed legislative solutions to these issues. We are expressing a need, not a technical solution."

Lone Star executives point out that the large number of unsolicited response letters from thousands of sophisticated and intelligent people prove that many readers follow the ads, agree with them, and write to Congress and to the company about them enthusiastically. "They understand that we are also trying to reach a broad mass of people," says Price. "I have to say that intellectuals are not necessarily our audience. Our audience is the influential people, the doers and leaders, who are writing us letters saying, 'Great, keep up the good work. We may win this battle yet.'"

Campaign Costs and Ad Budget

The budget for the advocacy advertising program has been about $1 million a year and includes space, production, and merchandising mailings. This amount is equal to Lone Star's expenditures on corporate institutional advertising over the last five years, prior to the change in its advertising policy. Since Lone Star produces heavy construction products, well known to the commercial buyers in each area, product advertising is almost nonexistent.

Lone Star treats its advocacy advertising expenditures as normal business expenses on its tax returns. A company spokesman states: "We have no problem with this because it is primarily a marketing device. We advocate no particular legislation. Our commercial objective is a stronger corporate image and a leadership identity among customers, investors and legislators/regulators. In the letters we receive we are constantly urged to continue because we do plead our customers' cause— i.e., we must have lower interest rates in order for the construction industry to survive."

Evaluation of Campaign Effectiveness

Lone Star believes that its campaign has been highly successful and cites examples of thousands of unsolicited letters received by the company— many of them from important customers and other key influentials. It has never been established, however, what the relevant criteria are for evaluating the success of advocacy advertising.

One of the main objectives of the campaign was to improve Lone Star's identity and leadership image in the financial and investing community. Public opinion surveys conducted in 1975, 1977, and 1978 had shown that Lone Star had a low identification factor among its target audiences. The impact of the company's new ad campaign on its audiences has yet to be tested scientifically.

There are, however, other measures of evaluating community response that might provide a good proxy measurement. The readership data for various ads is one measure. Lone Star has not been able to obtain many tests of its ad readership. One of the problems has been that few readership-measuring services cover newspapers, and the infrequent survey dates seldom coincide with the ad insertion dates. The "Poison Warning" ad did have a Starch survey and it was measured as one of the three best-read ads in the *Wall Street Journal* in the last ten years. This may be partly due to the "scare approach" applied in that ad [Table 1]. Price does not think that all the ads rated that high, but he believes that advertising professionals would agree that the campaign should do very well because of the cartoons and other high-readership techniques employed.

The company's evaluation of campaign effectiveness is also found in three other measures:

1. Unsolicited response from the readers
2. News media publicity
3. Additional free ad placements

The reader response to Lone Star ads was impressive [Table 2]. The company was indeed taken by surprise, since it rarely received letters from readers. In addition, "The company sent out over 17,000 of those flags for $1.00 each. Although we absorbed $1.50 per mailing in the process, for postage and handling, nobody minded."

It is not easy, however, to put any qualitative measure on the reader response rate. An unsolicited letter is strong evidence of the writer's intensity of interest in the subject. Nevertheless, what do 1,500 letters mean in relation to 1.8 million estimated readership per ad? Is it the extreme fringe who would love to express itself or blow off steam, or is it a true reflection of the large, otherwise silent majority?

Since conventional methods of evaluating product advertising are somewhat inappropriate for use with advocacy advertising, there may be an important need to develop a system for more carefully evaluating and classifying unsolicited letters, so that objective norms can be derived. Lone Star's own response to these thoughts is to agree in principle, except for the time, cost, and judgment involved in the evaluation. Company management is reported highly enthusiastic over the support received from specific customers, business leaders, and sales personnel, to the point of near disinterest in outside research. The company is also very proud of a letter President Reagan wrote to Lone Star Chairman and CEO Stewart. The letter expressed Reagan's gratitude for Lone Star's "The President Can't Do It Alone" advertisement in support of his economic program.

In addition to the action from readers directed toward the Fed or Congress, there have been a large number of requests for ad reprints — at least 10,000 reprints of each ad have been mailed by the company. Another measure of the effectiveness of the ad campaign is the attention given it by the news media. Most of the ads have been widely reproduced and commented on in the national media. The "Poison Warning" and "Jaws" ads were reprinted in *Time* magazine, the *New York Daily News,* and other newspapers with supportive articles. *The New York Post* also referred to the "Congress" ad in an article saying that President Reagan's budget is not encountering much opposition in Congress, because members of Congress are afraid of appearing negative or blocking progress. The *Post* specifically mentioned the Lone Star ad as having attracted considerable attention on the Hill.[4] Similar comment appeared in a page 1 story in the *Washington Post,* and literally hundreds of clippings have been received from regional and local media around the country. Few advertising campaigns can boast of such attention from the editorial side.

Table 1   **Highest "Read Most" One-Page Ads: Wall Street Journal, 1970 Through December 1980**

	Noted	Seen-Associated	Read Most
February 14, 1974 Gulf Oil Corporation	69%	62%	36%
April 26, 1979 United Technologies Corporation	67	53	40
February 12, 1980 United Technologies Corporation	72	63	39
December 17, 1980 Lone Star Industries, Inc.	68	61	36
Total number of one-page ads, 1970–1980		2,808	

Table 2   **Reader Response to Lone Star Ads**

Ad Headline	Response Solicited	Approximate Number of Letters Received
How America became a colony again	No	200
Poison Warning	Yes (copy of letter to Volcker)	1,500
President Can't Do It Alone	No	1,000
Don't Pull This Nation Apart	No	800
Don't Tread on Me	Flags offered for $1	5,000 (17,000 flags ordered)
Jaws	No (only a letter to Volcker)	300
Congratulations, Doctor	No (only a letter to Volcker)	400
Blood Shortage	Yes (copy of letter to Volcker)	400
West of the Potomac	Yes (copy of letter to Volcker)	(incomplete, c. 300)
Good News	Yes (copy of letter to Volcker)	(incomplete, c. 300)

Finally, a number of businesspeople and Lone Star customers also reprinted various ads in their in-house magazines and local newspapers, at their own expense. These free insertions were encouraged by a small line in each ad saying, "Permission granted to reproduce." The resulting ad tear sheets have come from good-sized dailies, small-town weeklies, financial newsletters, political organs, and other publications. Again, this extension of the campaign at no cost to the advertiser is considered an unprecedented benefit, and a valid indication of successful impact.

NOTES

1. *Mining Congress Journal,* March 1981, p. 3.
2. Mary Beth O'Boyle, "Lone Star Industries Speaks for America," *Rock Products,* April 1981, pp. 139–141.
3. Comments from "Area Executives Counting on Economic Recovery," *Business and Economic Review,* Stamford (CT) *Advocate,* February 3, 1981, pp. 1–2.
4. Niles Lathem, "Inside Washington," *New York Post,* March 21, 1981.

Chapter 14

EDISON ELECTRIC INSTITUTE, WASHINGTON, DC:

USE OF ADVOCACY ADVERTISING AS AN INTEGRAL PART OF THE PUBLIC RELATIONS AND COMMUNICATIONS EFFORT

In fall 1981, Edison Electric Institute, Washington, DC, the trade association of the investor-owned electric utility industry, launched a public relations program to make people more aware of the critical importance of a financially strong electric utility industry to the nation's economic well-being.

The decade of the 1970s had been very hard on the investor-owned electric utilities. The OPEC oil shock and the consequent spiraling inflation, high interest rates, and weak stock prices all led to a skyrocketing increase in the cost of generating and delivering electricity. At the same time, some elements of the general public, suffering from inflation and high prices for almost everything, were extremely hostile to electric rate increases. As a result, utilities were finding it increasingly difficult to get rate increases. Moreover, under intensive political pressure, the utility regulators were not allowing rate increases to keep pace with utilities' rising costs. Many utilities had undertaken to build power plants in the 1960s, anticipating an annual 7 percent rate of growth in elec-

---

Research Assistant: Mohamed Nabil Allam.

tricity consumption. However, due to a variety of reasons, the cost of building and completing such plants increased many times over the original estimates. These factors combined to cause a tremendous drain on the utility industry's resources without generating any compensating revenues.

When public opinion started to become antagonistic in terms of legislation and regulation at the national and state level, the utilities expanded EEI, relocated it in Washington, and embarked upon a pro-active, aggressive program to advance the industry's interests.

By the end of the 1970s, the investor-owned utilities were not generating enough revenues to keep up with plant modernization from internal funds, and were not profitable enough to attract further capital from the financial markets through the sale of debt and equities at competitive rates. The cost of attracting the necessary dollars to complete essential construction programs grew and grew. By 1981, the industry was in dire financial straits, leading many informed observers to conclude that the stability of the nation's energy delivery system was threatened. Under these cloudy circumstances, and in a highly charged political environment, the industry launched a communication program to take its case to the public.

This campaign was novel in a number of ways as to its underlying assumptions about the communication process, the role of issue advertising, and the strategy for executing a public communication program.

The financial viability campaign was conceived as a comprehensive and aggressive public relations strategy. Although advocacy advertising played an important role in this strategy, it was nevertheless viewed as one part of the overall public relations campaign. This approach is quite different from most other advocacy campaigns, where issue advertising is at the core of a company's communications strategy. All other communications elements are built around this advertising to extend its reach and take advantage of the momentum created by it.

The primary responsibility for conceiving and executing EEI's campaign rested with Kalman B. Druck, public relations counsel, and Ruder, Finn and Rotman (a public relations firm), under the close direction of industry committees. This is quite unlike most other advocacy campaigns that have been created by either in-house corporate staff or advertising agencies. Therefore, it offers an excellent opportunity to evaluate the relative merits of campaign execution by an industry organization that defines the problem differently, brings a different outlook to the concept of public communications, and seeks solutions that are likely to be quite different from those advocated by an individual company or by advertising agencies whose main forte lies in product advertising.

Even under normal conditions, measuring the direct effect of advocacy advertising is quite difficult. The contributory role of advocacy advertising is generally discernible in circumstances where it is used intensively, over a relatively short period of time, and for a narrowly defined objective, for example, enactment or repeal of a particular law. How might one measure the impact of such advertising where it is informational in character, does not call for any specific action on the part of the receiver, and is but a part of a larger public relations effort?

The most unusual and, in many ways, the most controversial aspect of the campaign is the definition of its objective. According to Druck, who was the chief architect of the campaign, and a counselor to EEI:

> The target audience for our campaign is 9–15 million Americans who influence public opinion and political action. Our objective was to articulate the public interest in strong, financially healthy electric utilities. This would provide a political climate in which rate decisions would be better understood and more acceptable, especially to the influential segments of the population.
>
> We specifically gave great weight to the long-range interests of the states by recognizing that the ability of a state to attract industry depends heavily on having healthy utilities.

How rational and cost-effective is this approach for reaching and persuading a target group? How convincing and logical are the assumptions about the communications process that underlie such a strategy?

EDISON ELECTRIC INSTITUTE—BACKGROUND

Edison Electric Institute (EEI) is the association of America's some 200 investor-owned electric utilities. Its members provide over 77 percent of the country's electricity, serving over three-quarters of the U.S. population. EEI provides the principal forum where investor-owned electric utility people exchange information on developments in their business and maintain liaison between the industry and government. Its officers act as spokesmen for investor-owned electric utility companies on subjects of national interest.

Since 1933, one of EEI's basic objectives has been the "advancement in the public service of the art of producing, transmitting, and distributing electricity, and the promotion of scientific research in such fields." EEI gathers data and statistics relating to the electric industry, and makes them available to member companies, the public, and government representatives.

EEI's dues from member companies are currently at an annual level of about $18 million. Some 72 million ultimate customers are served by these companies. Thus, the per customer average of EEI dues amounts to about 25 cents annually.

EEI provides a broad spectrum of services to its member companies. For example:

- EEI sponsors utility management training programs so that member companies can coordinate problem-solving activities. For example, it maintains a Mutual Assistance Agreement Plan, which provides immediate assistance to utilities in emergency situations by indicating which personnel from neighboring utilities can provide help.
- EEI coordinates information gathering and analysis about necessary industry-related federal legislation and regulation.
- EEI was instrumental in developing the Nuclear Mutual Insurance Group—now independent of EEI—which provides a resource pool to meet insurance requirements and reduce insurance premiums.
- EEI assists member companies in the implementation of new ac-

counting rules and enables utilities to coordinate their participation in the development of new rates. It shares analyses of tax law applications with its member utilities.

Antecedents to the Financial Viability Campaign

EEI has a long but sporadic history of using advocacy advertising. Some individual utilities have been engaged in sustained advocacy campaigns that deal with issues of importance to the industry and individual companies. The most notable examples are American Electric Power, Commonwealth Edison, and Consolidated Edison. During the past five years, EEI's efforts have been on an ad hoc basis where a particular situation dictated the need for immediate and controlled response through the insertion of one or more advertisements in leading national magazines and newspapers such as the *New York Times,* the *Washington Post,* and the *Wall Street Journal.*

Most of this advertising is oriented toward Washington. For example, EEI was very active in its opposition to the bill for railroad deregulation. According to Trey Taylor, who at that time was EEI's director of advertising:

> The whole idea of deregulating railroads was to prevent the government from further subsidizing the railroads. The truth of the matter is that the deregulation would only allow the rich railroads to get richer, and the poor ones to get poorer. The reason the rich can get richer is that many of them have what's called captive shippers. Coal, for example, delivered to the utilities would be a captive shipment. The industry's concern about the deregulation was that without a cap or a ceiling on the railroads' profits, all the costs of hauling coal would be passed on directly to their customers. So, we raised some yellow flags that were very effective in making a compromise in having a trigger mechanism to question the profitability of hauling coal. That's where our advocacy campaign paid off. It was a very tangible question.
>
> We've done ads, for example, on the Clean Air Act. It was not our intention to tamper with the Clean Air Act itself, but there were some amendments proposed in 1977 to the act that would have been very expensive to meet without commensurate benefits to the public. For example, if pipelines have to be buried nationally at certain depths to keep them from freezing, it costs the companies in the South a lot of money. However, the ground very rarely freezes in the South. Our concern with these amendments was to make them more regional in order to make them relevant and probably less costly.

Decision-Making Process

The institute's major policy decisions are made at two levels:

1. The policy committee is comprised of fifteen chief executive officers

of the member companies and sets the direction that is implemented by EEI, as approved by the EEI board of directors.

2. All aspects of EEI's operational activities are coordinated by the EEI staff in cooperation with their counterparts in the member companies, and under the direction of appropriate advisory committees with representatives elected from the member companies.

The communications executive advisory committee is responsible for developing and approving public relations and advertising programs for the institute. It is made up of senior officers in communications from fifteen different utilities, with one-third rotating each year. Members serve a three-year term. In January 1980, EEI's communication division was given the assignment to develop a campaign that would emphasize the continuing and growing need for electricity. An ad campaign was created that would talk about what the electric power industry was doing in research and development, and in conservation. The copy theme was that despite the industry's best efforts in conservation, there was still a need to build more power plants. The campaign was developed by the N. W. Ayer advertising agency and launched in November 1980. Unfortunately, December 1980 was probably one of the worst fiscal months that the industry had in its history.

The chief executive officers of the member companies met in their annual conference in January 1981. Their response to this campaign was very negative. The consensus was that the need to build more power plants was the wrong issue, and that it was the wrong campaign. According to Taylor, the CEOs felt that they couldn't even think of building more power plants. Their financial troubles were so severe that they were having problems merely surviving. That is when financial health for the electric utilities was identified as the all-important issue. "The CEOs were so critical of the campaign and so concerned about the direction of our efforts, that they even wanted us to fire N. W. Ayer, our ad agency."

Accordingly, in July 1981, the communications executive advisory committee invited a number of agencies to make presentations dealing with the problem of financial viability. The committee members perceived the pressure from their CEOs for a change in direction and felt that if they didn't take immediate action, the CEOs would take it into their own hands and do it themselves.

One of the firms making the presentation was Harshe-Rotman and Druck. Kal Druck, who had been a principal in the firm, had sold his interest and was acting as a consultant to HRD. He played the leading role in preparing and making the presentation. According to an HRD spokesperson:

> Kal has had a long and intensive background in national programs involving federal and state regulation of business. Specifically, for ten years he had directed an HRD program for the United States Independent Telephone Association. He had also worked closely with the Michigan Consolidated Gas Company on its financial/regulatory problems. Kal had been and still is, without question, one of the guiding forces of the public relations business.

HRD was awarded the account. An interesting aside to the story is that the runner-up agency in the selection process was another public relations firm, Ruder & Finn. In January 1982 HRD and R&F merged to become Ruder Finn & Rotman. The EEI program was by then already underway. By the time of the merger of HRD and R&F, Kal Druck had become a direct consultant to the Edison Electric Institute, rather than through the agency itself.

FINANCIAL VIABILITY CAMPAIGN

Strategy

The most distinguishing characteristic of the RFR strategy was its emphasis on a total communications approach. The advocacy advertising campaign was integrated with the full range of communications devices from publicity to special events. Nevertheless, print advertising was the centerpiece of the overall campaign strategy. According to Shirley Kaiden, RFR senior vice-president and account manager in charge of the EEI campaign: "Although the credibility of publicity and other PR efforts overall is usually higher than paid advertising for reaching the general public, a major advertising campaign has a visibility and frequency that tells the public: 'We really think this is important and there is a full case that we want to present to you.'"

Each element of the communication mix was selected for its ability to support the case for electricity. Kaiden observes:

> The entire campaign focused on what needs to be done to maintain an adequate supply of electricity *at the best possible price to the consumer over the long term*. The point being that the short-range political expediency of keeping rates artificially low is not only bad for the electric utilities' financial health, but costs the consumer more in the long run. Beyond the residential consumer, the country's industrial and economic infrastructure absolutely require adequate, reliable electricity at reasonable cost. Essentially, we were telling people about the need to have higher rates now so that rates won't have to be higher than necessary later.

Kal Druck makes three points about his approach to the financial viability campaign:

1. The objectives of the campaign must be perceived as deserving public support, and there must be a clearly thought out model of how the public opinion process works.
2. Whereas the individual electric utility had always been considered a local institution, the need for adequate electric energy is a national problem and should be so perceived.
3. The utmost credibility would be achieved by having the most credible third party spokespeople presenting the case. Therefore, the campaign features messages from prominent leaders of the subgroups comprising the most important influentials.

The essence of a successful public communication process is that it starts with a clearly defined set of objectives that are translated into actionable themes, which are transmitted to the targeted audiences through appropriate communication elements.

Target Audience

H. J. Young, EEI's senior vice-president, defined the target audience in terms of "a series of concentric circles moving outward from the people to whom regulators listen, to the people who influence them, to the people who they might hear from and those they would not normally hear from, like large industrial customers."

Another important audience for the campaign was the investment and financial community. Observes Kaiden:

> You have to understand that this issue had to be identified as a problem with broad public ramifications. Until the first ad ran in October 1981, there was very little public discussion about the electric utility's financial problems.
>
> For the most part, the regulators did know the industry had a problem. The other people who knew the industry had a problem were the financial community. That was reflected in downgrading of bond ratings, low stock prices and premium interest rates that utilities had to pay for bonds against comparably rated industrial bonds.
>
> Normally, when you are trying to make Wall Street feel better about your securities, you do not go public with a message that says "Guess what? We are in deep financial trouble." We were able to turn what could be a terribly negative message, as far as the investment community was concerned, into a positive. Analysts cited the program as evidence the industry was being more aggressive in seeking rate relief to improve its financial health. This is one aspect of this entire program that I think we as an agency are proudest of.

The electric utility industry is the country's most capital-intensive industry. It requires almost $3 of capital invested for every $1 of revenue. The industry uses more capital a year than any other part of the economy except the federal government itself. Therefore, in telling the financial viability story, it was concerned about the possible negative impact on the investment community, even though the *long-range* benefits to the companies and their investors could be considerable.

The company that has an issue coming to market tomorrow, next week, or next month cannot afford to have investors scared away. They have to balance the short-term impact versus the long-term benefits of such a program.

The core audience consisted of approximately 250 utility commissioners and their staff of about a thousand people. According to Kal Druck:

> We understand that an overwhelming majority of the commissioners were well aware of the financial problems of their utilities. However, there were a few on public record as unal-

terably opposed to any rate increases. By and large most commissioners are professionals with a thorough understanding of the industry and its problems.

We therefore set out to create a supportive political environment. This is why our target audience was not the broad general public, but rather the clearly identified political influentials. We did not seek to reach commissioners directly with a special message, nor did we intend to persuade individuals to take any overt action regarding utility regulation. We simply intended to provide important viewpoints and facts to emphasize the public interest, short-range and long-range, in a financially healthy electric utility industry.

The first outer core from the regulators is "social actives" or "activists." This group, estimated to be about 2 million people, is comprised of those persons who have engaged in one or more community-related or political activities, ranging from writing to elected officials to running for a political office. Other opinion leader groups included are: the financial community, capital suppliers, the news media, leaders of activist groups (labor, religious, special interest), government officials (federal and state), allied industry leaders, and member company managements.

In order to reach these groups, the best available approach was to buy select media space that covered people who were upper-scale Americans with the following characteristics: adult; age 25 to 64; professional or managerial position; attended or graduated from college; have written an editor, visited a public official, or addressed a public meeting. According to the Simmons advertising research organization, 9,021,000 Americans fall into this classification.

COMMUNICATION ELEMENTS

Print Advertising

The use of print advertising provided the surest means available to EEI to deliver its message under the most controlled circumstances: Print allowed selectively targeted advertising to specific audiences. Readership levels do not vary from issue to issue, thus ensuring uniform audience levels. It offers the opportunity to select editorial format, which will provide a complementary environment for the subject and lend prestige to the advertising.

Advertising was scheduled in both national and local media. National print (primarily magazines) provided a foundation for the generic advertising message. Relatively long issue life offered the advantage of repeated exposure to the ad and the opportunity for advertising to be studied at leisure. Nationally oriented daily and Sunday newspapers were used to fine-tune the ad message to the needs of individual markets. Druck stated: "Print advertising gave us an urgency and immediacy and a controlled visibility that we couldn't get any other way. We could buy exactly the media that we wanted to, reach exactly the audience that we wanted and on a schedule that we wanted. And we could control the message."

In developing its copy themes, EEI did not undertake any specific field or focus group research. Instead, it relied on personal discussions with individual regulators and their staffs, and experience with the problems faced by the electric utility industry.

EEI undertakes regular nationwide opinion surveys that elicit people's views on various issues of interest to the industry. The data from these surveys provided important inputs into the choice of copy themes and the manner of their execution, including media selection.

All advertising messages focused on the public interest in a financially healthy electric utility industry. Emphasis was given to those actions necessary to sustain the industry's ability to meet its obligation to serve, and to keep costs to users as low as possible over the long term.

An important element that tied the target audience to print advertising, together with copy themes, choice of spokespersons, and media vehicles, was EEI's expectation of its advertising effort. EEI felt that most successful issue advertising aims forcefully and persuasively to call attention to a problem and provide solid background on which the reader can build a foundation of understanding. Rarely does advertising of this kind elicit tremendous direct response. But by calling attention to the problem and providing useful information on why the solution of the problem is important to the reader, it paves the way for follow-up action generated by other means (publicity speeches, audiovisuals, printed materials, and special events).

The nature of the target audience for this campaign was "actives" and "activists." Therefore, it was assumed that these ads would generate requests for more information and stimulate debate and discussion of the issue among important opinion leaders. The campaign was designed to create a synergistic effect with the total communications program to enhance the impact of both efforts.

Third-Party Spokespersons

All advertising messages were signed by credible third parties stating the industry's case on the need for financially viable utilities in terms of the national interest. These spokespersons were quoted both in the advertising and in the public relations program. They were selected from the "actives" and "influentials" in a variety of fields (finance, economics, education, labor, politics, industry, consumer) to address the issue from as many perspectives as possible.

The use of third-party authorities was based on two criteria:

1. Business and industry credibility in the United States was particularly low at the time in the case of electric utilities.
2. It was felt that demonstrating the concerns of people who were experts in some area in which electric utilities played a role and who at the same time had no ax to grind were very important to the credibility of the programs. This was an *industry-created* campaign. It is therefore not surprising that the burden of proof must fall on the sponsor and that its concerns, as expressed in advertising, go beyond narrow self-interest and encompass a broader public interest.

Table 1   **List of Authors Used in the EEI Campaign**

Dr. John M. Albertine, president, the American Business Conference

Alvin L. Alm, director, Energy Security Program, Kennedy School of Government, Harvard University, and former assistant administrator for planning and management in the U.S. Environmental Protection Agency

Warren M. Anderson, chairman of the board, Union Carbide Corporation

Charles J. Cicchetti, former chairman, Wisconsin Public Service Commission, and professor of economics and environmental studies at the University of Wisconsin, Madison

Maurice Fulton, chairman of the board, The Faritus Company

Robert A. Georgine, president, Building and Construction Trades Department, AFL-CIO

Claire V. Hansen, president and chief executive officer, Duff and Phelps

Eugene M. Lerner, professor of finance, Northwestern University Graduate School of Management

Senator Clarence M. Mitchell III, senator from Maryland and president, National Black Caucus of State Legislators

David Packard, chairman of the board, Hewlett-Packard Company

Sanford I. Weill, chief executive officer of Shearson American Express, Inc., and chairman of the executive committee of its parent company, American Express

A list of third-party experts used as spokespersons in the campaign is given in Table 1. The suggestion for third-party spokespeople came from a variety of sources, including EEI staff, EEI member utilities, and the agency. The objective was to find people of stature and with expertise, and then match them with the campaign needs in terms of availability, willingness to participate, and credibility with the influential audiences.

The preparation of the copy itself varied according to the spokesperson, but all of the ads expressed the thoughts and the concerns of the people who signed them. In most cases, the spokesperson did the first draft. In a few cases, agency executives went out and interviewed the spokesperson and prepared the first draft. Shirley Kaiden, the agency executive in charge of the campaign, maintained close supervision of the project and worked directly with all the authors. In each case, ad copy was reviewed and approved by a subcommittee of the EEI policy committee.

Publicity

Announcement of the financial viability advertising program itself was to provide a publicity hook to tell the story of the electric industry and its needs. Those who wrote and broadcast about business, government, and national affairs were given a complete package describing the EEI campaign and its significance to the country and to individual electricity users.

As stated earlier, public relations—including press relations—were an integral part of the campaign. It was recognized that generating additional press coverage would not be easy. The industry needed to take its case not only to the public, but to the media as well.

The plans called for preparing mat articles and editorials for publication by newspapers and magazines. These materials were carefully prepared to ensure that facts could be amply documented not only by industry experts, but also by third-party spokespeople, whether they were authors of ads or other authorities.

The campaign created "events" by having spokespeople give speeches throughout the country that could be used as news hooks for the story. Industry and government reports were carefully monitored and used as a basis for news releases to present the case in newspapers and magazines. A broad variety of formats and outlets were used; they ranged from straight press releases to recorded news clips featuring ad spokespeople for radio use. Specific articles were targeted to very specific audiences, such as the article by-lined by bond ratings expert Claire Hansen in *Financier* magazine.

Editors of major news, business, and trade publications and the producers of major network TV and radio news and interview programs were targeted for personal visits. Special efforts were put into arranging for "Wall Street Week" on PBS to interview representatives of EEI.

An important ingredient in this publicity program was the trade press. Major media that covered the electric utility industry, fuels, energy, and the economy were included in the press briefings and supplied with additional and individually tailored story ideas and material.

IMPLEMENTATION OF THE FINANCIAL VIABILITY COMMUNICATIONS PROGRAM

Campaign Costs

From its inception in November 1981 to April 1983, total campaign costs amounted to approximately $2.5 million. These expenditures were allocated between advocacy advertising and other elements of the communication programs roughly at a ratio of 2:1.

Advocacy Campaign

An important point to observe here is EEI's approach to the development of advertisements, their media placement, and how the two fitted into the overall campaign objectives. EEI's campaign breaks some of the rules of effective advertising strategy and reflects a public relations approach quite different from the one generally followed by advertising agencies.

The first rule broken was the one that states that ad copy should be "short and snappy." Kal Druck, however, believed that the length of the copy reflected both the complexity and the seriousness of the issue. The implication was that if the spokesperson had that much to say on the subject, it must be worth talking about. Readership scores per se were not a concern. Said Druck: "We expected good readership by the ultimate targets, but we were not seeking particularly high scores among the general public. We were pleasantly surprised when the first flight of ads received high Starch rankings."

Other aspects of the layout also reflected this strategy. The first wave of ads were editorial in format, very serious in tone and featuring a photograph of the spokesperson in a very strong posture. This conservative layout was intended, again, to convey the seriousness of the issue. Said Druck: "Layouts for the second phase of the program were more 'slick,' but we don't know if the accompanying decline in readership scores resulted from the increased 'addy' look of the insertions or if, by that time, most people felt that they had learned as much as they needed to know about the issue."

The second broken rule had to do with frequency of use of each ad. A general advertising principle is that repetition of the same ad in the same media over a period of time builds familiarity for the audience and recognition of the ad's basic message. (It also tends to build profits for the ad agency, because there are fewer development and production costs charged against commissions). It was decided to run each ad only once in each publication, and to work the schedule so that, when possible, one spokesperson would be appearing in the daily newspapers while another appeared in the newsweeklies and still another appeared in the monthlies. Again, the objective was not so much to build readership as to make it very clear that the issue was a matter of concern to a wide *variety* of authoritative people.

The advocacy campaign was launched in November 1981 with a two-page advertisement in the *Wall Street Journal*. It was entitled "It's Time to Bring America's Hidden Energy Problem into the Open." In this ad, Charles J. Cicchetti emphasized a number of financial and political problems that he believed to be the result of restrictive regulatory policies and procedures. He argued that unless action is taken, the future may well include power rationing, blackouts, and brownouts [Exhibit 1].

The second ad in the series was entitled "Electric Utilities in Jeopardy Mean a Nation in Jeopardy." In this advertisement, Alvin L. Alm addressed the idea that some of the effects of short-sighted utility regulation would be felt soon, while others would be passed on to our children. He concluded that restoring the financial integrity of investor-owned electric utilities is crucial if this nation is to have a strong economy and a healthy society [Exhibit 2].

Both ads included a statement to the effect that spokespersons advocating these viewpoints were not paid by EEI, but presented their opinions because they believed these issues should be understood more widely and acted upon. EEI also invited readers' comments.

The major theme of the 1982 advertisements was the adverse effect of regulation on consumers, stockholders, small savers, workers, industry, and the general public. The messages were delivered by spokespersons from diverse fields of activity including academia, finance, the stock market, industry, and labor. The advertisements presented detailed and well-documented arguments in support of the case for the electric utility industry. Exhibits 3–9 are illustrative of this approach.

One of the more interesting advertisements in the 1982 series featured Robert A. Georgine, president of the Building and Construction Trades Department, AFL-CIO. Headlined "American Workers Need Healthy Electric Utilities," the advertisement stated that not only did today's jobs rely on electricity, but, more important, economic growth—the source of tomorrow's jobs—depended on continued supplies of electricity at a reasonable cost [Exhibit 11]. In making his case for support of the utility industry, Georgine asserted that:

- Utilities must be able to compete with other industries in the market to raise vast sums of money.
- National security will be threatened by dependence on energy supplied by a foreign country.
- As a nation we must compete with other countries for industrial development. Other nations attract new industry through provision of low-cost electricity. We should make sure that the policies and practices of some regulatory agencies do not sap the financial strength of electric utilities.

The year 1983 marked a major shift in the direction of the campaign. Instead of arguing against overregulation, these ads emphasized the positive aspect of the role of electric energy in America's economic recovery and future growth. The first ad was entitled "Let's Not Short-circuit America's Growth Companies." In this ad, John Albertine addressed the idea that a healthy electric utility industry is essential to an overall economic environment within which growth companies can flourish [Exhibit 10]. The advertisement by Warren M. Anderson was entitled "Will We Have the Power to Sustain Economic Recovery?" In "Power Is the Key to America's Future," David Packard stated that regulators at the federal and state level made the decisions that determined rates of return and power-plant licensing procedures. "However, they alone cannot be expected to correct the problems with the regulatory process. Government, in the long run, reflects the attitudes of the people. It is up to all of us—business, industry, politicians and consumers—to demonstrate our support for policies that will enable us as a nation to exercise sound options for the future."

Publicity Support

During the first year of the campaign (November 1981–October 1982), RFR, in cooperation with EEI, organized a number of activities to generate additional publicity and media support. Among these activities were the following:

- The original campaign press release, "Electric Industry to Campaign for Fair and Reasonable Rate Regulation," released November 12, 1981; resulted in coverage by AP, UPI, the *Washington Post, San Francisco Chronicle, Desert News, Capital Times* (Madison, Wisconsin), the *Milwaukee Journal,* Jack O'Dwyer's *Newsletter, P.R. News, Advertising Age* Ad Week, *Electrical Week,* Energy Users Report (BNA), *Industrial Marketing, Environmental Action,* and *Channels of Communication.*

Exhibit 1

A message from one of the nation's leading authorities on utility regulation.

IT'S TIME TO BRING ENERGY PROBLEM

By Charles J. Cicchetti
Former Chairman, Wisconsin Public Service Commission

Charles J. Cicchetti was formerly Director of the Wisconsin Energy Office and Chairman of the Wisconsin Public Service Commission. In 1980 he resumed his position as Professor of Economics and Environmental Studies at the University of Wisconsin-Madison. He is also a partner in the Madison Consulting Group.

Professor Cicchetti served with Resources for the Future in Washington, D.C. from 1969 to 1972. He has served as a consultant on electricity, natural gas, telephone and postal pricing and on oil and conservation policy, and has appeared as an expert witness before many state and federal agencies. He is a frequent contributor to journals devoted to economics and energy and has co-authored several books on energy policy.

This country's "energy delivery system" — its investor-owned electric utility industry — is in trouble, and a dramatic change in state regulatory policies is needed urgently nationwide.

This is one of a series of messages about the investor-owned electric utility industry — the system that delivers 77% of the nation's electricity. Sponsor of the series is the Edison Electric Institute, representing some 200 investor-owned electric utilities. The self-interest of the individual companies in this series is obvious, but we believe there is a broader public interest at stake.

We have therefore asked prominent authorities outside the electric utility industry to present their views. They are not paid for these messages, but set them forth because they believe these are issues that should be understood more widely and acted upon. The Edison Electric Institute welcomes your views and comments.

As one concerned about energy problems, increasingly I am disturbed that a major part of our nation's energy supply system — the investor-owned electric utility industry — has a pressing need for relief. Moreover, very few people apparently are aware of this critical situation.

I have seen all sides of the energy issue: as an intervenor for consumers and environmentalists, a state utility regulator, and now a university professor of economics and consultant on energy problems. During the past ten years, I have watched the electric utilities go from blue-chip investments to companies beset with financial difficulties. As a nation we face disastrous deterioration of our industrial strength and our living standards — unless this trend is reversed.

The ultimate losers will be: (1) consumers who will pay even higher prices; (2) taxpayers who will pay more as industry moves away to other states or foreign countries; and (3) people facing unemployment in a shrinking economy. In short, all of us.

Consider the following financial and political problems:

- Electric utilities have become political scapegoats.
- Rates of return have been kept so low that stockholders are often subsidizing consumers.
- Modernization or replacement of aging plants, many fueled by costly petroleum products, has become prohibitively expensive.
- Electric utilities have been forced to retrench to such an extent that some are even encouraging large customers to disconnect.

Relationship of Regulatory Climate To Utility Bond Ratings

(December 31, 1980)

States Regarded By Bond Rating Services As:

"Favorable"

"Acceptable"

"Unfavorable"

NO. OF UTILITIES   0   20   40   60

"Enlightened regulation is the key to the future. It is imperative that all regulators respond realistically to present needs and respond quickly."

All of this has resulted largely from restrictive regulatory policies and pro-

Edison Electric Institute

AMERICA'S HIDDEN INTO THE OPEN

cedures. These have prevented many power companies from earning sufficient returns to attract capital needed to sustain their vital role in the national economy. Unless action is taken, the future may well include power rationing, blackouts and brownouts.

Ironically, electric bills today are probably higher than they should be because of regulators' well-intentioned attempts

Electric Utility Senior
Debt Rating Changes by Moody's
1971-1981

Year	Number of Ratings	
	Lowered	Increased
1971	3	1
1972	3	1
1973	2	3
1974	25	1
1975	15	2
1976	9	0
1977	2	3
1978	4	1
1979	6	3
1980	13	1
1981 (August 31)	4	1

Source: White Weld & Co., Salomon Brothers

"Downgrading of utility creditworthiness has been epidemic. In the last four years more than three times as many issues have been downgraded as were upgraded."

to keep rates artificially low. To compensate in part for increased fuel costs and record interest rates, regulators have held down utility earnings. Earnings are required to compensate stockholders for their investment, to assure bondholders of the safety of their capital, and for reinvestment in the company. As a result of reduced earnings, the credit ratings of electric utilities have weakened, and interest burdens have increased. Conversion to other, less expensive fuels has become more difficult and costly.

Regulatory practices that would enable utilities to earn a *fair* return would not mean a return to the expansionist philosophy of the early 1970s. Nor would they mean a huge jump in consumers' electric bills.

Consider that, if on an industry-wide basis, utility return on stockholder equity were increased from 12% to 18% (some fifty percent additional income) overall consumer bills would increase by less than five percent. With acceptable returns utilities could make those sound investments which ultimately would result in lower electricity costs. Examples include investments in conversion from oil to coal, nuclear and other fuels; in transmission and distribution grid maintenance; in intercon-

nection improvement; and in meeting new local growth requirements.

Merely to provide adequate new plants and equipment for the rest of this decade, utilities will have to spend an estimated $365,000,000,000 — that's billions of dollars. At least 20% of this will require more stock to be sold.

That simply can't happen under current conditions!

Today, the actual rate of return on equity achieved by utilities, on average, is well below that offered by other, less risky investments.

Electric utility stocks are selling at approximately 20% below average book value and, when new shares are sold below book, new stock issues actually confiscate the capital of existing stockholders. Financial rating services now regard electric utility bonds as very risky and the utility companies must therefore pay higher interest rates.

While average rate of return on equity allowed by state utility regulators so far in 1981 has edged up to about 15%, their actual case-by-case rate decisions and delays have not permitted utilities to earn much more than 11%. This rate is too low. It is often less than the inflation rate, and the interest on utility bonds, which is now about 17%.

Downgrading of utility creditworthiness has been epidemic. In the last four years, more than three times as many companies have been downgraded as were upgraded. Some securities are rated so low that certain institutions, by law, may not purchase them.

Where $1 Of Revenue Went	Electric Operations	1973	1980
Fuel		23¢	37¢
Taxes		16	12
Materials, supplies, others		12	11
Salaries and wages		12	11
Depreciation and amortization		10	7
Interest and preferred dividends		14	13
Dividends to common stockholders		8	7
Retained in business		5	2
Total		**$1.00**	**$1.00**

"To compensate in part for increased fuel costs and record interest rates, regulators have held down utility earnings."

As a result of many state utility commissions following the path of least resistance, the utility industry has been denied the rates of return that are necessary to build new plants that will either lower prices or supply necessary energy. Such proposed plants are being postponed indefinitely. Thus, we have arrived at the moment of truth.

In those states with a reasonable regulatory environment, there are signs of resurgence of utility health. Where political expediency has supplanted economic reality as the basis for rate decisions, the situation is critical. What has to be done?

1. **Regulatory commissions should follow the lead of those states that are now permitting an adequate rate of return on equity — "adequate" meaning at least 17%, and perhaps 19% or more, based on real earnings, not accounting devices.**
2. **Commissions should expedite rate proceedings, reduce regulatory lag, and allow interim rates, so that inordinate delays do not invalidate decisions by the time they are handed down.**
3. **Commissions should permit automatic rate adjustments for inflation, higher wage costs, higher capital costs and other factors that are beyond the control of utility management.**
4. **Commissions should grant rapid increases for major expenditures such as new equipment or new plants and permit cost recovery during construction.**
5. **Commissions should be careful to reward, not unintentionally penalize, innovative ratemaking, conservation, productivity increases and other constructive actions.**

I don't think it is overly melodramatic to characterize this moment as one of great opportunity or great peril for state utility regulation. Present consumer anger over prices will seem mild when compared with general public anger if electric power shortages are allowed to develop in the future. Enlightened regulation is the key to the future. It is imperative that all regulators respond realistically to present needs and respond quickly.

The electric utility system is the core of this nation's industrial strength and social fabric. It is time that thoughtful people throughout the country realize the national stake in the system's health and strength. Procrastination will be more costly, and many good options will be lost. If political expedience and inertia continue to rule the day, the ratepayer and the nation will be worse off.

The association of electric companies
1111 19th Street, N.W., Room 716, Washington, D.C. 20036

Charles J. Cicchetti

Exhibit 2

America's Hidden Energy Crisis

ELECTRIC UTILITIES IN JEOPARDY MEAN A NATION IN JEOPARDY

By Alvin L. Alm

**Director, Energy Security Program,
Kennedy School of Government, Harvard University**

Alvin L. Alm has been involved in analysis and direction of U.S. energy policies for many years. He served on the White House Energy Policy and Planning staff in 1977 and was Assistant Secretary for Policy and Evaluation in the U.S. Department of Energy 1977-1979. Previously, he was Assistant Administrator for Planning and Management in the U.S. Environmental Protection Agency.

The investor-owned electric utility industry is in financial trouble. State public utility commissions, reacting to public anger over rising electricity rates, have squeezed utility earnings and returns to investors so that capital improvements have been delayed or denied.

Some of the effects of short-sighted utility regulation will be felt soon, others will be passed on to our children. All are reasons for urgent national concern now:

1. Cutting utility earnings or curtailing capital investment will eventually cost the public more money.

Lower credit ratings and equity values resulting from eroding earnings increase interest costs which are eventually borne by the consumer. Deferral of needed capital investments will only shift costs to the future.

2. Continued deferral of capacity investments may lead to serious reliability problems in some areas, including brown-outs and black-outs.

Demand growth remains high in some regions. In some low-growth areas, demand forecasts may be unusually conservative and demand may accelerate because of changing economic factors. With so much of our economic future tied to electricity-intensive high technology industries,

it is vital that we have sufficient capacity to keep the electric system dependable. If necessary investments are not made, electric utilities could follow the same downward spiral of services that railroads have experienced.

3. Substantially higher rates or less reliable service could drive industry, jobs and taxes right out of the country.

A number of foreign countries are now courting new manufacturing industries with the lure of cheap and dependable electricity. An undependable electric system might prod many U.S. firms to embrace these offers.

4. Lack of capital to reduce oil use adds to higher inflation, balance of payment outflows and decreased national security.

Many electric utility capital requests to finance projects to "back out" oil are denied because they would initially raise electric rates. With our current level of vulnerability, continued use of oil for baseload generation makes no sense.

Given these compelling reasons, can we rescue our investor-owned electric utility industry without government bail-outs and fast enough to avoid chaos? It seems to me that progress along the following lines is essential:

Utilities must be able to earn a rate of return comparable to equivalent investments.

Returns that are considerably below low-risk money market funds or utility bonds, and even lower actual cash earnings, are sapping utilities' strength and causing capital costs to increase.

Utilities should be rewarded for cost-savings improvements.

These improvements would include reducing capacity additions and oil use — the two most significant reasons for rate increases.

Public utility commissions must permit company managements to be more innovative.

Utilities must be able to meet future needs through measures that make sense in their service areas, including conservation, rate reform, cogeneration, small-power technologies as well as more efficient generating facilities.

Restoring the financial integrity of investor-owned electric utilities is crucial if this nation is to have a strong economy and a healthy society. An industry that is financially strapped, heavily in debt and enervated from constant battles with state regulatory commissions is in no shape to meet urgent national needs. Through reasonable regulation, state commissioners will serve not only the interests of the people of their individual states but also of the nation as a whole.

Alvin L. Alm

Alvin L. Alm

This is one of a series of messages sponsored by the Edison Electric Institute, representing the investor-owned utilities that deliver 77% of the nation's electricity.

Participating independent authorities are not paid for these messages, but present them because they believe the issue is of critical national significance. EEI welcomes your comments.

Edison Electric Institute
The association of electric companies
1111 19th Street, N.W., Room 716, Washington, D.C. 20036

U.S. News & World Report "Blue Chip" — 12/28, 1/4/82
Nations Business — 1/1/82
Time "B" — 1/4/82

Newsweek "Executive" — 1/11/82
Smithsonian — 2/1/82
Psychology Today — 2/1/82

The Wall Street Journal — 12/7/81
The Washington Post — 12/13/81
The New York Times — 12/13/81

Exhibit 3

A message from one of the nation's leading authorities on utility finance . . .

ELECTRICITY USERS WILL PAY FOR ADVERSE REGULATION

By Eugene M. Lerner
Professor of Finance, Northwestern University Graduate School of Management

During nearly 30 years in education, Eugene M. Lerner has provided expert testimony before legislative committees and regulatory agencies on national and state levels, has authored or contributed to 28 books, and has written more than 50 articles for leading financial, economic and management publications.

Tomorrow's electricity consumer probably will pay higher than necessary costs for poorer service — the inevitable result of the shortsighted regulation of electric utilities that prevails in many states.

Consumer ultimately pays

Future costs and quality of service depend upon the ability of electric utilities to finance new facilities and equipment now. To attract the capital required, utilities must be able to earn sufficient amounts to provide a fair return to investors after actual operating costs have been defrayed.

Unfortunately, the returns permitted by most state regulatory commissions today are below those offered by competitive, relatively safer investments. Actual returns are even lower. As a result, many utilities have had to cut back efforts to increase efficiency, convert to lower cost fuel, and develop new generating technology. When they do undertake such programs, they often must pay premium rates for funds. In either case, the consumer ultimately will pay.

In some states, regulators *are* taking action to protect the long-term interests of the community at large. At this time, there are nine states that, in my opinion, have a more reasonable regulatory climate than generally prevails. Their constructive regulatory policies include:

- **basing allowed returns on the rate base that will generate service when the rates become effective, not on some historical rate base;**

- **permitting the utility to apply tax benefits to equipment replacement and system expansion;**

- **including construction work in progress in the rate base, rather than delaying recovery of current financing costs;**

- **automatic rate adjustments for increased costs of some raw materials, instead of holding lengthy and expensive hearings;**

- **prompt rate decisions;**

- **setting allowed returns at levels comparable with those offered by competitive investments.**

My analysis shows that utilities in these states, because they are allowed to be financially healthy, can retain a significant portion of their earnings for reinvestment in the system while maintaining dividend payments to stockholders at adequate levels. Consequently, they not only can attract equity investors, but also offer greater safety to bondholders. Therefore, they can obtain funds on more favorable terms.

Financing costs significant

Financing costs are a significant factor in the rates utilities must charge their customers. Sooner or later, the consumer must pay the higher financing costs that financially weak utilities incur. An alternative is to delay necessary improvements, which will mean still higher costs in the future and possible deterioration of service.

As an important result of more favorable regulation, utility managements are able to make operating and investment decisions based on long-term public need, rather than on short-term financial exigencies. The nation as a whole is the beneficiary.

Eugene M. Lerner

This is one of a series of messages sponsored by the Edison Electric Institute, representing the investor-owned utilities that deliver 77% of the nation's electricity.

Participating independent authorities are not paid for these messages, but present them because they believe the issue is of critical national significance. EEI welcomes your comments.

Edison Electric Institute
The association of electric companies
1111 19th Street, N.W., Room 716, Washington, D.C. 20036

Nations Business — 3/1/82
Time "B"   — 3/29/82
U.S. News & World Report "Blue Chip" — 3/29/82

Newsweek "Executive" — 3/22/82
Smithsonian — 4/1/82
Psychology Today — 4/1/82

Exhibit 4

A message from one of the nation's leading authorities on utility securities . . .

ADVERSE REGULATION HINDERS UTILITIES IN CAPITAL MARKETS

By Claire V. Hansen, C.F.A.

President and Chief Executive Officer, Duff and Phelps, Inc.

Claire V. Hansen, president of Duff and Phelps, Inc., is a recognized authority on valuation and a certified financial analyst.
For more than 50 years, Duff and Phelps has provided investment research and financial analysis to institutions and corporations. The firm has long been a leader in utility investment research, tracking more than 200 utility companies across the country. In addition, Duff and Phelps issues credit ratings on fixed income securities and commercial paper.

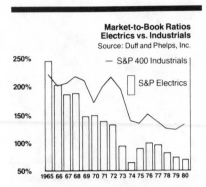

Electric utilities are the nation's most capital intensive businesses. They constantly face vigorous competition for the investment dollars required to maintain a healthy and reliable energy delivery system.

To compete effectively for capital, utilities must be able to earn rates of return that compensate for the additional risks of an inflationary environment. In many states, restrictive and erratic regulation has increased investor risk while holding returns below those offered by such investments as money market funds, savings certificates and some government securities.

In evaluating utility securities, a major consideration is whether the governing regulatory commission permits the company to earn a sufficient return on equity to:

1) **provide adequate funds to meet rising debt service requirements;**
2) **sustain dividends at levels that at least keep pace with inflation;**
3) **accumulate internal cash to reinvest in the system.**

For the average electric utility company we track, the ratio of pre-tax earnings to debt interest payments has dropped by more than one-third since 1970. In the same period, while average reported dividends have increased 60%, dividends after adjustments for inflation actually decreased by 30%.

Consequently, credit ratings have deteriorated, and most utilities must pay premium interest rates on bonds to compensate for increased investor risk. To raise equity capital, companies often must sell stock at prices below book value. As a result, the ownership of those who have already invested in the company is diluted.

The impact of regulation on utility creditworthiness becomes evident when bond ratings are correlated with regulatory environment. Of the 13 companies that have our highest ratings (D&P #1 or #2), all have operations in states we consider to have reasonable regulation (see "How D&P Rates the Regulators").

Utilities in states where reasonable rates are permitted have higher credit ratings. Therefore, they can raise funds at lower cost to the consumer for plant and equipment modernization, conversion to lower cost fuels, new technology development, transmission grid maintenance, and meeting basic local growth requirements. Denial of reasonable earnings will inevitably result in degradation of service — including possible power rationing and brownouts — and even greater escalation of costs to consumers over the long term.

When establishing allowable rates of return, regulators must balance their efforts to keep down immediate consumer costs against the even more important responsibility to assure adequate power supplies for the future.

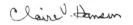

Claire V. Hansen

How D&P Rates the Regulators

In addition to rating utility company securities, Duff and Phelps rates state regulatory commissions. It looks for:

1) **decisions based on realistic projections of sales, expenses and investments, rather than on out-of-date historical data;**
2) **permissible rates of return on equity that are competitive in financial markets;**
3) **prompt rate decisions.**

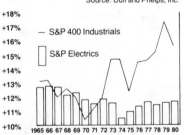

This is one of a series of messages sponsored by the Edison Electric Institute, representing the investor-owned utilities that deliver 77% of the nation's electricity.

Participating independent authorities are not paid for these messages, but present them because they believe the issue is of critical national significance. EEI welcomes your comments.

Edison Electric Institute
The association of electric companies
1111 19th Street, N.W., Room 716, Washington, D.C. 20036

Nations Business — 2/1/82
Time "B"   — 3/1/82
U.S. News & World Report "Blue Chip" — 3/1/82
Newsweek "Executive" — 2/22/82

Smithsonian — 3/1/82
Psychology Today — 3/1/82
Survey of Wall St. Research — 1/82 - 2/82
The Wall Street Journal — 1/14/82

The New York Times — 1/17/82
The Washington Post — 1/17/82
The Arizona Republic/
    The Phoenix Gazette — 1/14/82

HEALTHY UTILITIES CRUCIAL TO NATION'S SMALL SAVERS

By Sanford I. Weill
Chairman, Shearson/American Express Inc.

"Sandy" Weill is chief executive officer of Shearson /American Express Inc. and chairman of the executive committee of its parent company, American Express Company. The nation's fastest growing major financial services firm, Shearson /American Express serves more than 600,000 active investors around the world.

From my perspective, the financial health of the investor-owned electric utility industry is crucial to America.

Business and industry are dependent upon adequate, reliable power at the lowest possible price. Without it, the companies in which our clients invest could not prosper.

Emerging industries could not grow, and basic industries would disintegrate. Essential programs to rebuild the nation's industrial plant and increase productivity would be doomed.

$340 Billion Needed

Electric utilities will have to spend about $340 billion in the remainder of this decade to increase the efficiency of existing facilities, reduce dependence on petroleum fuels and build the minimum capacity required to meet tomorrow's power needs.

At least half that capital will have to come from outside investors. For utilities, probably more than any other kind of business, that means being able to attract the savings of individuals.

Small savers traditionally have invested in utility stocks to preserve capital, to obtain dividend income that at least kept pace with inflation, and to build equity in a stable and essential institution.

Utilities benefited not only from the use of funds invested directly by shareholders, but from increased borrowing capability that a strong equity ownership base provided. As a result, the industry could build the world's most reliable energy delivery system.

However, during the 1970s, economic conditions and the failure of state regulatory commissions to respond adequately to those conditions had a serious effect on utilities and their shareholders.

Regulatory commissions, trying to insulate consumers from the full impact of inflation, kept authorized utility returns below those of competitive investments, such as money market funds and government securities.

Individuals seeking to preserve their savings by investing in utility stocks instead saw their capital eroded. Dividend payments, after adjustment for inflation, have actually declined.

Consumers Subsidized By Shareholders

In effect, utility shareholders were subsidizing consumers of electricity, and the securities markets responded accordingly.

To attract new capital, utilities have been forced to issue stock at prices below book value, causing dilution of the equity ownership of existing shareholders. The portion of utility earnings required to pay dividends has climbed precipitously, leaving less to be reinvested in the system.

Current low market prices, in relation to book value, make some utility stocks attractive today, particularly those of companies in states where the regulatory environment apparently is becoming more reasonable. Action at the Federal level which enables shareholders to defer taxes on reinvested dividends provides an additional incentive.

But a great deal still must be accomplished to overcome the negative impact of the regulatory policies of the last decade.

Returns Must Be Competitive

Not only must authorized returns be high enough to compete with other investments, but the regulatory climate must enable utilities to earn those returns. Rate proceedings must be speeded up, and the proportion of cash earnings to non-cash credits included in returns must be increased. Mechanisms must be put into place that permit utilities to recover current financing costs for construction projects.

When utilities can attract new savings without diminishing the investment of existing shareholders, they in turn can make the capital investments necessary to assure adequate, reasonably priced power in the future.

Sanford I. Weill

Sanford I. Weill

This is one of a series of messages sponsored by the Edison Electric Institute, representing the investor-owned utilities that deliver 77% of the nation's electricity.

Participating independent authorities are not paid for these messages, but present them because they believe the issue is of critical national significance. EEI welcomes your comments.

Edison Electric Institute
The association of electric companies
1111 19th Street, N.W., Room 716, Washington, D.C. 20036

Nations Business — 4/1/82
Time "B"   — 4/26/82
U.S. News & World Report "Blue Chip" — 4/26/82

Newsweek "Executive" — 4/19/82
Smithsonian — 5/1/82
Psychology Today — 5/1/82

The Wall Street Journal — 3/11/82
The New York Times — 3/14/82
The Washington Post — 3/14/82

Exhibit 6

POWER IS THE KEY TO AMERICA'S FUTURE

By
David Packard
Chairman of the Board, Hewlett-Packard Company

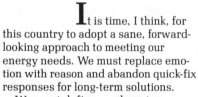

It is time, I think, for this country to adopt a sane, forward-looking approach to meeting our energy needs. We must replace emotion with reason and abandon quick-fix responses for long-term solutions.

We must define our long-term energy goals and set about making the commitments and investments that are essential to achieving those goals. No area is in need of greater attention than the nation's electricity supply.

Basic and New Industry

Electricity is a key factor in any long-range energy policy. Our basic industries are becoming increasingly electrified. Our new, high technology industries are all electronic based. Not only will our use of electricity increase substantially with a step-up in industrial activity, increased electricity use and supply are essential to the nation's sustained economic recovery.

> **If we continue in the current trend, not only will sufficiency of supply be threatened, but cost to consumers will be higher than need be.**

The link between growth in electricity use and growth in Gross National Product has been established over many years. This linkage has remained even as we have become more energy conscious and have reduced the overall energy content of manufactured products.

In many industries, electricity is replacing other energy forms that are less efficient at the point of use or are subject to the whims of foreign suppliers. This trend undoubtedly will—indeed, must—continue.

At the same time, our means of generating electricity must be made more efficient and secure. In recent years, electric utilities have made great strides in displacing imported oil as a fuel for generating power.

But much remains to be accomplished. Electric utilities are still the largest stationary users of oil in the nation.

Danger of Complacency

We must resist being lulled into false complacency by declines in energy use and the resulting appearance of excess supplies that have accompanied economic recession. Any such cushion of supply will be quickly eliminated by restoration of economic vigor.

Right now, new power plants must be planned and commitments made for construction up to 14 years before they can be put into service. Decisions made today will determine whether we will be able to power American industry reliably and economically in the decades ahead. Today's decisions will determine job opportunities for the generation now growing to adulthood, our ability to compete for world markets with

National Journal–April 30   Newsweek "Executive"–May 16
Time "Business"–May 23   US News "Blue Chip"–May 23

David Packard is chairman of the board and co-founder of Hewlett-Packard Company, a leading manufacturer of computers and other information processing equipment. He also served as United States Deputy Secretary of Defense.

nations that are still developing economically, and the basic security of the country as we head toward the 21st century.

Unfortunately, most of the decisions being made today are weighted toward not building for the future.

New Construction Risky

Utility managements, responsible for preserving the savings of those who have invested in their companies, cannot risk building for tomorrow when they are unable to earn competitive returns on plants in place today. They are being forced to operate on the basis of short-term survival after a century of being America's most long-term oriented industry.

Solutions to the utility industry's financial problems and the nation's long-term energy problems coincide:

1. Rates charged for electric power must reflect the actual cost of providing service and provide a rea-

sonable return to shareholders.
2. The licensing and regulatory process must be streamlined so that new generating plants can be brought into service more quickly.

Combined, these steps will assure the nation sufficient power at lower cost in the future. If we continue in the current trend, not only will sufficiency of supply be threatened, but costs to consumers will be higher than need be.

Everyone Responsible

Who is responsible for developing those solutions? While regulators at the federal and state level make the final decisions that determine rates of return and power plant licensing procedures, we cannot expect that they alone can correct problems with the regulatory process.

Government, in the long run, reflects the attitudes of the people. It is up to all of us—business, industry, politicians and consumers—to demon-

strate our support for policies that will enable us as a nation to exercise sound options for the future.

David Packard

David Packard

This message is sponsored by the Edison Electric Institute, which represents the investor-owned utilities that deliver 77% of the nation's electricity.

Participating independent authorities are not paid for these messages. They believe a healthy electric industry is of critical national importance. EEI welcomes your comments.

Edison Electric Institute
The association of electric companies
1111 19th Street. N.W.. Room 716. Washington. D.C. 20036 •

Exhibit 7

Will We Have The Power To Sustain Economic Recovery?

By
Warren M. Anderson
Chairman of the Board, Union Carbide Corporation

Electricity—in adequate supply and at reasonable cost—is essential to a sustained economic recovery for America.

Electricity's reliability and efficiency are helping to spawn new industrial processes and products in the energy-conscious industrial sector. In the chemical industry alone, use of purchased electricity increased 23 percent between 1972 and 1980. In all U.S. industry, electricity's share of total industrial energy consumption rose from 23 percent to 33 percent in the same period.

Electrification Will Accelerate

This electrification of industry will accelerate as the economy begins to recover.

If our nation is to avoid short-circuiting economic revitalization, we must take the steps necessary to assure the long-term recovery of

66The industry must be able to undertake programs that mean the lowest possible costs for all consumers in the future.99

the electric system. That calls for rates for all classes of customers that reflect the actual cost of providing service. Keeping rates artificially low now means higher costs for everyone in the long run and threatens the financial integrity of the systems.

We must avoid the temptation to let the increased cost of providing electricity be borne disproportionately by industrial customers. By requiring industry to pay more than a fair share, we further undermine the nation's overall economic well-being.

Cost-of-service pricing, which includes a fair return to utility shareholders, will enable utility managements to sustain the quality of

supply at the least cost over the long-term.

It is ironic that, as American industry in general is being criticized for supposedly sacrificing long-term goals in favor of short-term results, we may be forcing the foundation of our industrial future to do just that.

Utilities Look Ahead

Electric utilities have tended to take the long-range view. That farsightedness over the past century has built for America the most efficient, reliable and economical power supply system in the world. In recent years, the industry's planning horizons have been extended even further as lead times for new plant construction and new technology have steadily increased.

Right now, the electric utility industry should be increasing its investments in programs to modernize and increase efficiency in existing plants, further reduce de-

National Journal — April 9
Newsweek "Executive" — April 18
Time "Business" — April 25
U.S. News "Blue Chip" — April 25

Warren M. Anderson is chairman of the board and chief executive officer of Union Carbide Corporation, one of America's largest diversified industrial and consumer products companies. Union Carbide, with 143 U.S. locations, has been a pioneer in the development of industrial energy conservation techniques and in the electrification of manufacturing processes.

pendence on imported fuels, and develop new capacity to meet the needs of an expanding economy.

Energy Problems Not Over

The recent easing of demand for electricity, combined with increased supplies of petroleum products, do not signal an end to America's energy problems. Both conditions are in large measure caused by severe recession. A strong upturn in industrial activity will quickly reverse these conditions.

Yet financial constraints are forcing many utilities to defer or cancel needed investments. The approximately $164 billion in capital expenditures projected for the next five years is the bare minimum required to keep the system intact. This amount could be difficult for a financially weak industry to raise.

The financial condition of the electric utility industry has apparently improved somewhat recently. Some state regulatory commissions have authorized rates of return on equity investment that more closely reflect the cost of capital. Inflation and interest rates have dropped, and the general stock market recovery has brought utility share prices closer to the asset values they represent. Within the industry, cost-cutting programs have been effective.

But much remains to be done.

Improving Productivity

The industry must be able to undertake programs that mean the lowest possible costs for all consumers in the future. There must be an overhaul of the regulatory system that now causes inordinate delays in building more efficient generating plants.

The resulting increase in overall energy efficiency and self-sufficiency will in turn lead to improved productivity and a more competitive position for American industry in world markets.

Everyone will benefit from greater employment opportunities, a stronger tax base and a more secure America.

Warren Anderson

Warren M. Anderson

This message is sponsored by the Edison Electric Institute, which represents the investor-owned utilities that deliver 77% of the nation's electricity.

Participating independent authorities are not paid for these messages. They believe a healthy electric industry is of critical national importance. EEI welcomes your comments.

Edison Electric Institute
The association of electric companies
1111 19th Street. N.W., Room 716. Washington, D.C. 20036

State Legislatures — May 1
Forbes — May 9
Harvard — May/June, 1983
Columbia Journalism Review — May/June, 1983

Exhibit 8

A message from one of the nation's leading authorities on industrial development...

INDUSTRY MUST HAVE DEPENDABLE ELECTRICITY

By Maurice Fulton
Chairman of the Board, The Fantus Company

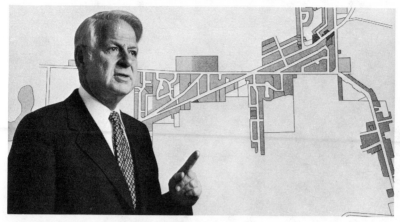

The Fantus Company, a subsidiary of Dun & Bradstreet Corporation, is the oldest and largest firm specializing in facilities location, regional economic development and industry feasibility studies.

In the search for suitable industrial locations, the availability and reliability of electric power possibly is becoming the single most critical factor considered.

Other essential requisites — labor and transportation — can be attracted to a particular site if necessary. But power must exist — in sufficient, dependable supply — before we even begin evaluation of all the other characteristics of a community that may or may not make it an appropriate environment for industrial expansion or new development.

This is true not only for studies we undertake for clients with unusually large power requirements, but also for those who simply need moderate amounts of power on a steady, predictable basis. Increasingly, that is every manufacturer in America.

More and more, factories depend on computers, precision electronic tools and automated machinery. Interruptions or reductions in electricity supply are disruptive and expensive.

Adequate Supplies Critical

Therefore, we cannot risk siting a plant where power supplies are at all questionable. And we must be assured of adequate supplies well into the future.

A new plant or a major expansion represents a substantial long term investment. Our clients must be confident that necessary resources will be available for the life of the facility.

Utilities Need Capital

The ability of America's electric utilities to make the investments necessary today to assure adequate supplies tomorrow is critical to the industrial revitalization of the country. New generating facilities can require ten years or more to be brought on stream. In the meantime, existing facilities are becoming out of date and increasingly expensive to operate.

But utilities cannot invest in new generation, transmission and distribution facilities — or even adequately maintain existing facilities — if they cannot attract investment capital. To do that, they must be permitted to earn sufficient amounts to assure their financial health and provide returns competitive with other potential investments. In many cases, shortsighted regulatory policies are sapping the financial strength of utilities so that they are having difficulty raising capital at reasonable cost.

Consequently, programs for new capacity, conversion to cheaper, dependable fuel supplies and replacement of obsolete facilities have been postponed or abandoned.

The inevitable result will be less reliable service, probably at higher-than-necessary rates, which industry cannot tolerate for long.

DOE Warns of Power Shortfall

A report issued recently by the U.S. Department of Energy warns:

"...continued utility financial problems, against a background of modest demand growth, may cause a long-term shortfall in electricity supply. If powerplants continue to be cancelled and deferred as they have been recently, supply sufficiency could be at risk in much of the country as early as 1990."

From the point of view of industrial development, the electricity supply problem may be closer at hand than the next decade.

With alarming frequency, utilities are telling us that they cannot economically handle the increased demand a major industrial development represents today, much less provide assurance of adequate supplies into the 21st century.

The eventual cost to the communities served by these utilities — in lost employment, erosion of tax base, stagnant economic activity — will far outweigh the cost of restoring America's electricity system to financial health.

Maurice Fulton

This is one of a series of messages sponsored by the Edison Electric Institute, representing the investor-owned utilities that deliver 77% of the nation's electricity.

Participating independent authorities are not paid for these messages, but present them because they believe the issue is of critical national significance. EEI welcomes your comments.

Edison Electric Institute
The association of electric companies
1111 19th Street, N.W., Room 716, Washington, D.C. 20036

Nations Business — 7/1/82
Time "B"   — 7/19/82
U.S. News & World Report "Blue Chip" — 7/19/82

Newsweek "Executive" — 7/12/82
Smithsonian — 8/1/82
Psychology Today — 8/1/82
Industry Week — 6/28/82

The Wall Street Journal — 6/10/82
The New York Times — 6/13/82
The Washington Post — 6/13/82

EVERYONE PAYS FOR ADVERSE UTILITY REGULATION

By Senator Clarence M. Mitchell, III,
Senate of Maryland and President, National Black Caucus of State Legislators

Sen. Mitchell, Majority Whip of the Maryland Senate, is in his second term as president of the National Black Caucus of State Legislators.

The National Black Caucus of State Legislators believes every American should be concerned about the financial health of the nation's electric utility industry.

The past century's economic growth, through which we attained the world's highest standard of living, was powered, literally, by electricity. Economic revitalization — indeed, economic survival — in the future is dependent upon the availability of reliable, reasonably priced electricity for our factories, businesses and homes.

To assure that availability, electric utilities must commit billions of dollars today. They must modernize existing facilities and replace inefficient, obsolete plants. They must displace high cost petroleum-based fuels, and they must build sufficient new capacity to meet tomorrow's needs.

Bills Artificially Low

State regulatory commissions are not acting in the long-term interest of consumers — or the nation as a whole — when they attempt to keep bills artificially low by sapping the financial strength and investment attractiveness of the utilities in their jurisdictions.

None of us wants to pay more than necessary for an essential service. By paying less than the fair price for the service now, we guarantee that, at best, we will pay more for electricity in the future.

A recent study by the Department of Energy projects that, if utilities are unable to make needed investments, by the mid-1990 s, electricity prices in some states will be as much as 24% higher than they would be otherwise.

Utilities Vital to Industry

The electric utility industry makes other industries possible. If our communities do not have reliable, abundant power, industries will move elsewhere, taking jobs, tax revenues and social stability with them.

To keep our electric system and our industrial base competitive, utilities will have to spend about $340 billion in the rest of this decade. The major portion of that amount will have to come from outside investors, primarily the savings of individuals and the pools of money that comprise workers' pension funds and insurance programs.

Utilities can attract investment only if their earnings are sufficient to assure reasonable safety of the capital and returns that are competitive with investments such as government securities and money market funds.

Some state regulatory agencies, which establish the maximum amounts electric utilities can earn on the capital invested in them, have not permitted returns to keep pace with inflation or other kinds of investments. Extensive delays in rate proceedings and other adverse regulatory policies have prevented utilities from earning even the amounts authorized by the regulators.

Caucus Aware of Problem

The 337 members of NBCSL are concerned with those issues, national and local, which relate to the quality of life of the people we represent. The dilemma of public utilities and utility regulation will be the subject of public forums conducted by our Energy Committee, which will prepare a resolution for the consideration of the entire Caucus. The result is expected to be a realistic legislative policy which recognizes industry needs.

There are some signs that, at both the State and Federal level, recognition of the need to restore financial health to the electric utility industry is growing. But we still have a long way to go.

If the electric power industry falters, the nation's economy falters, diminishing our ability to compete in world markets, our employment opportunities and even our national security.

Clarence M. Mitchell

Clarence M. Mitchell, III

This is one of a series of messages sponsored by the Edison Electric Institute, representing the investor-owned utilities that deliver 77% of the nation's electricity.

Participating independent authorities are not paid for these messages, but present them because they believe the issue is of critical national significance. EEI welcomes your comments.

Edison Electric Institute
The association of electric companies
1111 19th Street, N.W., Room 716, Washington, D.C. 20036

Nations Business — 5/1/82
Time "B"   — 5/24/82
U.S. News & World Report "Blue Chip" — 5/10/82

Newsweek "Executive" — 5/17/82
Smithsonian — 6/1/82
Psychology Today — 6/1/82
Ebony — 6/1/82

The Wall Street Journal — 4/12/82
The New York Times — 4/18/82
The Washington Post — 4/18/82

Exhibit 10

Let's Not Short-Circuit America's Growth Companies

by
Dr. John M. Albertine
President, American Business Conference

America's growth companies hold a key to the nation's economic revitalization. They are the creators of jobs, the developers of new technologies, the source of productivity improvement, the successful competitors in international markets.

They depend on a healthy electric utility system.

POWER FOR GROWTH

Growth companies are efficient users of energy. Their products and services increasingly are electronic- or electricity-based. Their manufacturing processes are computer controlled and electronically automated. They must have dependable, adequate electric supplies.

Perhaps more important, a healthy electric utility industry is essential to an overall economic environment within which growth companies flourish.

Therefore, these companies are concerned about the long-term prospects of the electric utility industry.

They know that investment in new facilities to increase efficiency and productivity makes sound economic sense for all business and particularly for producers of energy. But today's electric utility industry is finding it difficult to make needed investment. Essential construction programs are being cancelled or deferred due to the precarious financial condition of the industry.

According to the Department of Energy, as well as studies commissioned by the industry itself, the result at best will be a higher than necessary cost for electricity in the future.

"..a healthy electric utility industry is essential to an overall economic environment within which growth companies flourish. "

Power shortages could begin developing before the end of this decade.

UTILITIES MUST INVEST

Diminished industrial activity and conservation efforts have slowed demand growth for power considerably in recent years. In a rejuvenated economy, though, electricity will account for a larger share of industrial energy use, and demand should go up accordingly.

Even if demand growth remains relatively low, utilities must invest in new facilities to:

• reduce the nation's dependence on unreliable and expensive imported fuel;

• replace aging, inefficient facilities;

• improve transmission capability;

• meet the supply and reliability re-

Time "Business" — 3/14/83   Newsweek "Executive" — 3/21/83
U.S. News "Blue Chip" — 3/14/83   Industry Week — 3/7/83

Dr. John M. Albertine is president of The American Business Conference, an organization limited to chief executives of 100 U.S. corporations that have grown at least 15% annually for the past five years. Its member companies have revenues between $25 million and $1 billion and represent a broad range of manufacturing and service businesses.

quirements of an increasingly electrified economy.

If utilities cannot make these investments, the cost to the nation will be immeasurable. Utility capital requirements for essential facilities are estimated at $320 billion for the remainder of the decade. At least half of that amount will have to come from outside investors.

ADEQUATE RETURNS NEEDED

Tax-deferred dividend reinvestment programs, declining interest rates and the general stock market rally have helped improve the investment attractiveness of utilities. The prime beneficiaries, though, are utilities that are not building. Investors recognize that, in the current economic and political environment, utilities may be prevented from earning adequate

returns on new facilities.

Those companies with major construction programs for the most part must pay premium interest rates to bond holders and other lenders or issue stock at prices below book value. Consequently, utility managements, in order to protect the investment of their current shareholders and to assure their ability to meet obligations to current lenders, must cut back on investments for the future.

What is the solution?

All of us—American business, consumers, regulators, legislators and the utilities—must participate in efforts to restore the utility industry to financial health and to assure long-term power supplies. That means consumers must recognize that the cost of providing electricity, as with all other energy sources, has risen and must be borne by the ultimate user.

BENEFITS FOR ALL

Those of us in business and government must support efforts to assure utilities an adequate return on their investments.

All of us will benefit in the long run.

John M. Albertine

John M. Albertine

This message is sponsored by the Edison Electric Institute, which represents the investor-owned utilities that deliver 77% of the nation's electricity.

Participating independent authorities are not paid for these messages. They believe a healthy electric industry is of critical national importance. EEI welcomes your comments.

Edison Electric Institute
The association of electric companies
1111 19th Street, N.W., Room 716, Washington, D.C. 20036

INC.—4/1/83   State Legislatures—4/1/83
Nation's Business—4/1/83   National Journal—2/19/83

Exhibit 11

A message from one of the nation's leading authorities on jobs...

AMERICAN WORKERS NEED HEALTHY ELECTRIC UTILITIES

By Robert A. Georgine
President, Building and Construction Trades Department, AFL-CIO

No one has a greater stake in the financial health of the nation's electric utility industry than Americans who work for a living.

There is scarcely a job today that is not somehow dependent upon electricity. More important, economic growth — the source of tomorrow's jobs — requires continued dependable supplies of electricity at reasonable cost.

Huge Investment Needed

Electric utilities must spend well over $300 billion in the remaining years of this decade if they are to convert from high-cost petroleum fuels, replace aging, inefficient plants and meet national demand growth.

I am told that a substantial portion of that enormous sum apparently will have to be provided by outside investors — individual savers and pools of money which often represent workers' pension and insurance programs. To attract that much and that kind of investment, utilities obviously must be able to compete with other potential investments.

This means care must be exercised to assure that the regulatory policies and practices of some states or agencies do not sap the financial strength of electric utilities.

Utilities must be financially strong in order to make the investment necessary to power the industrial revitalization the United States needs if we are to produce the jobs that are absolutely essential to bring about our immediate economic recovery and subsequent growth.

Industry Requires Power

Industry strongly considers the availability and dependability of electricity in its decisions to locate new or to expand existing plants. Communities which cannot assure reliable, abundant power over the long term, therefore, will lose jobs and tax revenues. Indeed, we are already seeing some signs of this on a regional basis.

We as a nation must compete with other countries for industrial development.

The lure of low-cost, dependable power abroad is a strong one, particularly for electricity-intensive industries with international markets. These industries are, for the most part, the basic ones that provide vast employment opportunities and are tremendously important to our national security.

National Security Threat

Nor should our national security be threatened by a dependence on energy supplied principally by a foreign country or group of countries.

In addition, high-growth industries, such as electronic data processing and information services, rely on constant, reliable supplies of electricity.

Neither the industries nor the individuals of our nation can long sustain the dislocation brought about by brownouts, blackouts or power rationing that would result from insufficient or unreliable generating capacity.

There is a direct relationship among sufficient power, meaningful employment and job opportunities, as well as between developing our own sources of energy and assuring our independence.

Robert A. Georgine

Robert A. Georgine

This is one of a series of messages sponsored by the Edison Electric Institute, representing the investor-owned utilities that deliver 77% of the nation's electricity.

Participating independent authorities are not paid for these messages, but present them because they believe the issue is of critical national significance. EEI welcomes your comments.

Edison Electric Institute
The association of electric companies
1111 19th Street, N.W., Room 716, Washington, D.C. 20036

The Wall Street Journal — 5/3/82
The New York Times — 5/16/82
The Washington Post — 5/16/82
Nations Business — 6/1/82
Time "B"   — 6/21/82
U.S. News & World Report "Blue Chip" — 6/21/82
Newsweek "Executive" — 6/14/82

- Two media briefing luncheons about the financial viability campaign held at EEI in November for the Washington press and the industry resulted in a story in the *Washington Post.*
- National press briefings were conducted with Scripps-Howard Newspapers, Newhouse Newspapers, and Hearst Newspapers.
- Press briefings resulted in stories in the *Wall Street Journal* (three), *Cincinnati Enquirer, Baltimore Sun,* and *Birmingham Post Herald.* A *Los Angeles Times* article generated from information provided by RFR appeared in ten local papers in Florida, Ohio, Texas, Arizona, and Wisconsin. A four-part series by Terry Atlas of the *Chicago Tribune* was picked up by six newspapers in Utah, Pennsylvania, California, Oklahoma, Connecticut, and Minnesota.
- Press releases issued on each ad's author generated a number of stories.
- An article by Charles Cicchetti was placed in *Public Utilities Fortnightly.* Mat page articles entitled "Fact and Figures" and "What's in It for You" were written and distributed through the North American Press Syndicate to 2,800 weeklies and 1,000 dailies. By August 1982, clips had appeared in over 90 publications.
- Two Radio Actualities apiece were produced on ad authors Cicchetti, Hansen, Lerner, Mitchell, Georgine, and Fulton and distributed to 1,700 AP, UPI and radio stations nationwide. An additional actuality was produced by Cicchetti and distributed to 80 black-owned radio stations nationwide the day he addressed the National Conference of Black Mayors (April 23, 1982). The radio feed was accepted by 61 of the 80 stations.
- An omnibus financial viability speech with slides for use by EEI and industry spokespeople was developed by RF&R. All EEI member companies received the speech, which was distributed directly by EEI, and offered access to the slide show. A number of companies used the slide show.

During the first year of the campaign (November 1981–October 1982), RFR in cooperation with EEI organized a number of efforts to generate additional publicity and media support for the financial viability campaign. Among other things:

- There was general support for the campaign among the member companies.
- The companies had been using audiovisual materials in conjunction with their own programs. Quite a few said they would like to see more EEI broadcast materials, but the topic itself evoked mixed comments. "Any radio material that goes straight from EEI to the local station is good because it precludes any perceived bias our company's signature might raise," commented one utility executive.
- Several individual companies created local ad programs based specifically on EEI's financial viability campaign.

In the January to May 1983 period, a number of press and broadcast media interviews were arranged. These included:

- UPI interview with Douglas C. Bauer, EEI senior vice-president for economics and finance, resulted in more than 80 stories in 35 states.
- Ad spokesperson Charles Cicchetti appeared for a half-hour live interview on PBS's "Late Night Show."
- EEI Director of Fossil Fuels Charles Linderman was interviewed by *National Black Network* and was heard on 200 NBN stations nationwide.
- EEI Director of Rate Regulation David Owens was interviewed on *RKO Radio's #2 Network,* with 298 facilities.
- Media briefings continued during this period and resulted in a number of news stories in *Time, Newsweek, U.S. News & World Report, National Journal, Forbes, Fortune, Dun's Business Review, Wall Street Journal, Barron's Business Week, USA Today, Christian Science Monitor, Washington Times, Industry Week,* and with United Press International and Associated Press.

Media Education

One of the earliest discoveries in implementing EEI's financial viability campaign was the tremendous gaps in reporters' and editors' knowledge about such subjects as electric utility rates, fuel costs, financial markets, and future growth.

On the media education, Shirley Kaiden, RFR creative supervisor for the campaign, commented:

> This was a very complex issue and we found that the level of understanding among the media was incredibly low. For example, in one of our press conferences, a prominent reporter from the *Washington Post* expressed his frustration by saying that he did not understand much of this material and did not know how he was going to explain it to his readers. Therefore, on the national level, we launched an all-out effort to brief key reporters and editors on the financial state of the industry. On the local level, the agency, with member company approval, used its five domestic offices to conduct basic educational briefings with local media in 15 states and the District of Columbia.

EVALUATION OF CAMPAIGN EFFECTIVENESS

Measuring the results of a public relations program is not always easy, at least in the short run. However, given the sizable commitment of resources, an attempt must be made. The most direct measure of the campaign's effectiveness would be to see how it achieved its purported objective—that is, whether there was a perceptible difference in rate increases granted to the nation's electric utilities compared to what might have been the case in the absence of such a campaign. This criterion, however, is unachievable. The process by which various factors influence rate-making decisions is very complex. Nor can it be measured to isolate the effect of one variable, the EEI communication program.

The next best criterion would be to measure the effectiveness of the program in terms of its perceived influence on various target audiences. This criterion is output-oriented. The relationship between program output and objective achievement, however, is not direct and is at best surmised.

EEI officials and RFR executives responsible for the campaign appear quite satisfied with the results. According to H. J. Young, EEI senior vice-president:

> The measurement of opinions in national attitude surveys that we made before, during and after the program by audience segment indicated to us that the program was doing the kind of job that we wanted it to do.

Kal Druck commented:

> The readership surveys showed that we reached a lot of our target audience.
>
> The next question is: What are we reaching them with? Here the use of third party spokesmen becomes important. We went back to our selected spokesmen who are identified with that audience. A former utility commissioner, a labor leader, a big industrialist understands the reasoning that says that you've got to have a healthy electricity industry in order to be attractive to industry, in order to be viable in terms of the state economy, and in order to be beneficial to all the people. It's not an easy argument to make. The average consumer advocate is really not interested in going around that tree.

The Starch scores show that EEI's financial viability ads did consistently well in the *Wall Street Journal* and *Psychology Today*. The high scores are a strong indication of the attractiveness of the ads and the message content to the readers. The scores do not, however, provide enough information on certain other aspects of the ads that are important to the campaign. For example: To what extent were the ads believed by the readers, and how effective were they in *increasing* their understanding of the issues? It would also be desirable to have additional information as to how long these ads or their contents are remembered. Is there any relationship between people's increased understanding of the financial needs of the electric utilities and their willingness to accept higher electricity rates?

In another survey, more than three-fourths of a representative sample of state public utility commissioners surveyed for EEI by Cambridge Reports said they had seen the ads, and 75 percent said that they found such ads "very" or "somewhat" believable. The program also generated attention in the news media.

The media attention, however, was slow in coming and caused some agency concern. Shirley Kaiden of RFR comments:

> While we acknowledged the need for media education on this complex issue—and, in fact, built that into the original pro-

gram—no one anticipated the enormous information gap that existed or how hard our task was going to be.

Indeed, during the first twelve months alone, the agency conducted over a hundred one-on-one media briefings or interviews and distributed over 2,000 information kits. In addition, the agency issued one press release each month based primarily on research study results that supported the campaign's objectives.

Speaking engagements provided another important opportunity for focusing media attention on the issue. Over twenty speaking engagements were scheduled before such groups as the New York Rotary, the Houston Rotary, the Milwaukee Kiwanis, The Conference Board, the Economics Club of Orlando, the National Conference of Black Mayors, and The Executives Club of Chicago.

The media briefings and other publicity efforts finally paid off as stories began to appear in both national and regional publications. At the national level, the financial viability issue was discussed in the *Washington Post*, the *New York Times*, the *Los Angeles Times*, the *Chicago Sun Times*, the *San Francisco Chronicle*, the *Herald Examiner*, the *Journal of Commerce*, the *Christian Science Monitor* (three-part series), *Newsweek*, *Business Week*, and *Industry Week*.

Although the advertising part of the campaign ended in June 1983, the publicity campaign has continued. As for the agency, Kaiden says:

> We as an agency are very proud of the program and the results that have accrued to date.
>
> The program helped clear the way for a more conducive regulatory climate by opening a dialogue between EEI and the National Association of Regulatory Utility Commissioners (NARUC). While the dialogue is often stormy, it nonetheless continues to provide regulators with a better understanding of their responsibilities to both consumers and to the industry itself in assuring America of adequate supplies of electric power at reasonable prices.
>
> We think that over the long term the results of the financial viability campaign will continue to build and that the industry will get the appreciation and the support it needs to continue to provide America with the best energy delivery system in the world.

Finally, it should be noted that an annual attitudinal survey conducted for EEI in 1984 indicated a significant increase between 1981 and 1984 in the percentage of consumers who say their opinion of their electric company is either very or somewhat favorable. During those years, the survey showed a marked decrease in the number of Americans who think their local electric company makes too much profit.

A comparison between these activities and those of the original plan, however, shows that the publicity element of the program fell somewhat short of its planned targets. There were no major articles in *Business Week*, appearances on network television, or on public television programs. RFR executives recognized the slow progress of the public relations campaign. Kaiden comments:

This program is only about 18 months old. It is easier to do the advertising. We had the first ad running in about six weeks of the start of the campaign. It takes longer to develop a staff and the whole process for publicity. And publicity is much more limited and it's much harder to do because the media are not particularly receptive to good news.

I would say that we have done 100% of what we should be doing in advocacy advertising. I would not say that it would be productive to double the expenditure in advertising. We're using the media we need to use on a monthly frequency to reach the audience that we have targeted. I would say that in publicity, we are maybe 5 to 10% of what I would like to see us reach.

Chapter 15   # AMERICAN FEDERATION OF STATE, COUNTY, AND MUNICIPAL EMPLOYEES (AFSCME), WASHINGTON, DC:

AN ADVOCACY CAMPAIGN AGAINST REAGANOMICS

Soon after winning the election, President Reagan launched a new economic program, dubbed Reaganomics, aimed at changing the direction of the U.S. economy away from governmental intervention and toward greater reliance on the market system, individual initiative, and private savings and investment. The program called for a marked reduction in social entitlement programs, and a reduction in taxes for both individuals and corporations. The programs scheduled for major cuts included: food stamps, aid to families with dependent children (AFDC), tightening of eligibility criteria for Medicare and Medicaid, school lunch, student loans, and a cutback in increases in social security benefits.

This program generated a great deal of controversy in Congress, especially among liberal Democrats, among urban constituencies, and among the poor, all of whom feared Reaganomics would help the rich and the large corporations at the expense of the poor and the minorities. The country's conservative mood, together with the personal popularity of President Reagan and his tremendous media appeal, created such an

---

Research Assistant: Minoo Mortazavi.

irresistible force that all opposition to the program was drowned in an avalanche of publicity created by the White House, conservative political elements, and the business community.

Against such apparently overwhelming odds, AFSCME decided to launch its ad campaign against Reaganomics and President Reagan's budget proposals. The need for the campaign was best expressed by the late Jerry Wurf, the president of AFSCME, who felt that Reagan's proposal was unfair in all its dimensions, and singled out working families of moderate income for the greatest sacrifice. Moreover, it was obvious that President Reagan's policies would severely hurt unions like AFSCME, since they called for a major reduction in federal programs that would result in drastic reduction in public employees at all levels of government, the constituency served by AFSCME. According to Phil Sparks, director of public affairs of AFSCME, "Our union is a union of public sector workers. We don't deal with U.S. Steel at the bargaining table, we deal with the U.S. taxpayer. Our credibility and our standing with the taxpayer translates into better wages and working conditions, and our ability to organize. We see a direct relationship between our public image and our ability to function."

AFSCME—BACKGROUND

AFSCME is the fastest-growing union in the AFL-CIO. It has 1.4 million public employees throughout the United States, and they include employees of state, county, and municipal governments; school districts; public hospitals; and nonprofit agencies. Members work in blue-collar, clerical, professional, and paraprofessional jobs. White-collar employees account for one-third of the membership.

AFSCME began as a number of separate locals organized by a group of Wisconsin state employees in the early 1930s. In 1936, AFSCME was chartered by the American Federation of Labor (AFL). Today AFSCME is organized into more than 2,800 local unions, most of them affiliated with one of 70 district councils. AFSCME's late president, Jerry Wurf, was a vice-president of AFL-CIO. The president, the secretary-treasurer, and 25 vice-presidents make up AFSCME's international executive board, which meets quarterly to set policies.

AFSCME is the founder of the Coalition of American Public Employees (CAPE). It is composed of four public employee organizations with a combined membership of more than 4 million workers. CAPE works to secure equity for all men and women employed in the public sector. AFSCME is a politically active union. Its work is unusual in organized labor, because it is one of the very few unions so involved in political education campaigns through the advertising medium.

AFSCME started its educational campaign in the early 1970s. Its first campaign was against the B-1 bomber. Through advertisements placed in newspapers and leading opinion magazines, the campaign suggested that heavy defense expenditures on such weapon systems as the B-1 bomber are misdirected because they cause a reduction in funding for public education, highway maintenance, and the revitalization of cities and urban areas. One advertisement was headlined "One of these could educate every kid in Cincinnati," and showed a picture of a B-1 bomber. The copy cited a Brookings Institution study suggesting that no significant military advantages were to be gained by deploying a new penetrating bomber such as the B-1. It said that AFSCME supported a strong national defense, but was against spending $100 billion on the B-1 program [Exhibit 1]. The campaign ran for about twelve to eighteen months and cost approximately $100,000. Subsequent advocacy advertisements covered other public issues, such as false budget cuts by government and its consequences, inhuman suffering, and lack of adequate public funding for mental health and human services programs [Exhibits 2–5].

At the time of launching its campaign, AFSCME offered its ad to other unions who wanted to buy the air time; sponsorship of the ad would change depending on who bought the air time. As a result, the ad was run in cooperation with AFSCME and other labor unions. The AFL-CIO was one of those who wanted to buy air time to run AFSCME's social security advertising.

RATIONALE FOR THE ADVOCACY CAMPAIGN

AFSCME was the first opposition group to start advocacy campaigning against Reaganomics. The union felt that there was a clear need to inform the American public about the problems inherent in Reagan's proposals, and to communicate to the public the adverse social consequences that would follow if these proposals were enacted. Philip Sparks, director of public affairs for AFSCME, states: "We have learned the hard way that it is not enough to be right on an issue, you have to present the issue in the right manner."

Decision-Making Process

There are no formal voting procedures to ascertain the views of rank and file members to undertake such activities; the decision to launch the ad campaign was made by AFSCME's president in consultation with the executive board. According to a union spokesman, "The President and the executive board of our union are given wide discretion in terms of expenditures of union treasury money. Those two groups jointly proposed, initiated, and approved the original campaigns in the early '70s as well as the present campaigns."

Appropriation of Funds

The campaigns were financed from the union treasury, and the funding came out of membership dues. According to a union spokesman, this was an educational campaign; it was not directed toward any particular candidate, but against specific, and in most cases national, policies and programs. Therefore, it fell outside the jurisdiction of the Federal Election Commission. No political action funds, which are raised in an entirely different manner, were used.

Exhibit 1

"One of these could educate every kid in Cincinnati."

"One brand-new B-1 bomber costs $87 million.

Enough to wipe out the cost of public education in Cincinnati. With enough left over to fund the libraries in the District of Columbia.

A single B-1 could pay for fire protection in Los Angeles for one year. Or finance the entire budget for the city of Atlanta.

Or pay all yearly expenses for streets, parks, and sanitation for Indianapolis, St. Louis, Pittsburgh, Hartford, and Milwaukee. *Combined.*

But what about the military benefits of the B-1?

According to a host of experts, there aren't any.

A Brookings Institution study found: 'No significant military advantages [are] to be gained by deploying a new penetrating bomber such as the B-1.'

Yet, two weeks ago, Congress voted full speed ahead on the most expensive weapon in U.S. history—a 244-plane system that could cost $100 billion.

Our union wants to stop the B-1 funding.

And we urge the Democratic Convention to join us.

We support a military strong enough to deter any aggressor foolish or venal enough to attack us.

But what good is it to be able to destroy Moscow ten times over if our own cities die in the meantime?"

—**Jerry Wurf,** President
American Federation of State,
County and Municipal Employees

 **AFSCME**
the union that cares

American Federation of State, County, and Municipal Employees, 1625 L Street, N.W., Washington, D.C. 20036 Jerry Wurf, President William Lucy, Secretary-Treasurer.

In New York City, AFSCME Is The Parent Organization of The 105,000 Municipal Employees Who Belong To District Council 37, AFSCME: And 10,000 Members of District Council 1707, The Community And Social Agency Employee Union.

Exhibit 2

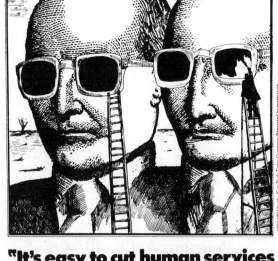

"It's easy to cut human services if you don't see human suffering."

"Too many public officials are trying to cure budget problems in state and local government by cutting human services. And by closing their eyes to a lot of human problems we see every day.

Like the 70-year-old widow who has nowhere to live when the state shuts down the nursing home. Or the working mother who's forced onto welfare when the daycare center closes.

Or even the retarded kids who sit in locked rooms because there's no one to care for them.

But human suffering won't go away by ignoring it. Or by blaming the people who work in nursing homes, daycare centers, or mental hospitals.

Our union represents these workers, so we know what the politicians are ignoring. Our goal is to open your eyes."

"The business of government is people."

—Jerry Wurf, President

 **AFSCME** *in the public service*

American Federation of State, County and Municipal Employees
1625 L Street, NW, Washington, D.C. 20036

"Some budget slashers are missing the point."

"Budget cutting in state and local governments is politically popular. Unfortunately, it's not always financially smart.

Take New York for example. Without much thought, the state proposed to shut down 135 day care centers, serving 7,500 working families, in hopes of saving $20 million.

In fact, a Columbia School of Public Health study calculated that this 'saving' would have created $18.8 million in spending by other government agencies, both state and federal.

As the union representing state and local government workers, we see these kinds of blind budget decisions being made in every state, every day.

We know legitimate budget cuts are hard enough to live with. But false cuts are intolerable."

"The business of government is people."

—Jerry Wurf, President

 **AFSCME** *in the public service*

American Federation of State, County and Municipal Employees
1625 L Street, NW, Washington, D.C. 20036

EXECUTION OF CAMPAIGN STRATEGY

AFSCME campaign strategy had four distinct features:

1. Extensive use of public opinion polls prior to campaign launch to determine not only the issues to be advertised, but also the copy themes to be utilized.
2. Employment of an outside agency to plan and implement the campaign.
3. Use of television as the primary medium.
4. Postcampaign public opinion polls to measure the effectiveness of the campaign.

Precampaign Public Opinion Survey

In the spring of 1981, prior to launching the campaign, AFSCME asked Fingerhut and Granada's, a Washington-based firm, to conduct a public opinion survey. This survey was based on 1,500 respondents and was developed to provide a statistically accurate representation of the U.S. population. The primary objectives of the survey were (1) To test the public's knowledge of the budget and tax cuts. (2) To ascertain public reaction to the specifics of both the tax and the budget cuts.

The data showed that there was a clear misunderstanding as to the depth and the magnitude of both the tax and the budget cuts, and that specific programs the president was proposing to cut had attracted and continued to attract widespread support. Based on these findings, the union concluded that it was not going to be enough—in terms of the message to be conveyed in those 60 short seconds in the ad—just to make assertions that the president was cutting back on social programs, or that the president was giving money to the rich, while he wasn't doing much for working people. The poll indicated that specific details were going to be needed in the advertisements to document the union's assertions.

The campaign strategy benefitted from the poll in two ways: (1) It identified specific programs that had high approval ratings. (2) It helped the union develop a message that included information on specific programs and their public impact which the union wanted to impart to viewers. AFSCME feels that it probably wouldn't have known either of those things if it had not done the polls.

1981 Campaign

Based on the information generated from the survey, AFSCME developed two campaigns with the assistance of the J. Walter Thompson advertising agency. Actual production was done by the agency. The ad concept was developed by the public affairs and political affairs departments working with agency writers. Production and logistics were done by the agency people. The agency was also responsible for buying air time.

According to Philip Sparks:

In terms of the advocacy campaign, we were interested in states that were urban, and traditionally democratic, with a high concentration of labor union members. Our message in both the spring and the fall campaign was: The administration was proposing things which the Congress had opposed. President Reagan had been quite successful in pressuring Congress into passing his program; and people should let Congress know about how they felt about the Reagan program. We were not out to hew a middle of the road line in terms of our ads. We were trying to energize traditional Democratic voters, and labor union members, and get them to counterbalance the pressures that were being put on Congress by the administration.

The first series of commercials and print ads was launched in the spring, the second was launched in the fall of the same year.

The Spring 1981 Campaign. AFSCME's public opinion poll had clearly indicated that Reagan's overall budget had strong public support which was not going to be diminished by the union's campaign. Therefore, the first round of commercials was not designed to win the battle of the budget, but rather to try to make people aware of the details of the program, and to have second thoughts. It was hoped that once the program was implemented, those doubts would probably become suspicions, and would translate into opposition to further cuts. The spring campaign was the beginning of a long educational program "to tell the other side of the story." According to a union spokesman: "We felt we were absolutely right and on target in what we were doing. Once the cuts go into effect in October 1981, people will realize that it is going to be more than just the welfare cheaters who are going to suffer from the program."

The main copy theme of the spring campaign was "Let Them Eat Cake!" Commercials talked about the budget and tax cuts. One commercial showed an immense cake, the "Republican Economic Policy." It indicated that, according to the new administration, putting our economic house in order was a piece of cake. Budget cuts plus tax cuts, that was it. It also showed that because of the way in which the cuts were made, it was the workers and breadwinners who suffered. The answer of the administration was to let them eat cake if they did not have enough money to support their families. The commercial asserted that the new administration took care of economic problems by increasing unemployment, cutting the budget for Medicaid, school lunches, and college loans, and the appropriations for the health and safety agencies.

In terms of the tax cut, the commercial showed a loaf of bread being given to the rich, while a crumb fell to the working poor. It stated that a family of four earning $15,000 a year would receive only $185 from Uncle Sam, if the Reagan proposal was enacted, while a person making $100,000 would get back $3,300 from the government. It asked viewers to write to their congressmen [Exhibit 3].

The Fall 1981 Campaign. In the second round, the campaign was much more focused on one particular issue, social security. This ad featured the social security tax cuts, and the message was "Social security is a contract, not a handout!"

461

Exhibit 3

According to the new administration, putting our economic house in order is a piece of cake

Budget cuts and tax cuts, that's the ticket. If workers run out of unemployment benefits? Tough. If the breadwinner can't find a job? Let him eat cake.

Then lop off medicaid, school lunches, college loans. If middle-income people suffer? Let them eat cake.

Now let's give them a tax cut. For a family of four making $100,000 dollars, we'll return $3,300. But, for a family of four earning $15,000, we'll give them back all of $185. Whoops, we forgot the social security tax increase and inflation.

Coming from an administration that says its on the side of the American worker, that doesn't leave much on the plate.

If you agree, contact your congressman. The American Federation of State, County and Municipal Employees.

Exhibit 4

Don't Do It, Mr. President.

President Reagan still wants to cut Social Security.

We can't afford to let him do it.

Social Security is *not* a handout. It's a contract between the United States Government and the American people — a contract we've earned through lifetimes of hard work.

The Administration and many Republicans want to break that contract. If they do, millions of Americans who paid into Social Security for years — and who have planned their retirement on it — are going to be hurt.

President Reagan wants to cut benefits by more than one-third for over 70 percent of those who retire next year. The worker who retires at age 62 could lose up to $160 a month; by 1986 the loss for an early retiree would more than double. Benefits would also be reduced for families, disabled persons, and workers retiring at 65.

President Reagan's cruelest cut will hurt those of us who must retire early. Over 70 percent of all early retirees don't have a choice. Some are in poor health. Others have lost their jobs. And many more workers, counting on the government's word, have made irreversible decisions to retire.

Right now, the axe is about to fall on the minimum Social Security benefit of $122 a month. This cut will directly hurt more than 1.5 million Americans, many of them women over 70.

President Reagan says he's cutting Social Security to save it. His strategy is to make people believe the system will go bankrupt if benefits aren't cut drastically. That's not true. The cuts

President Reagan proposes aren't needed. Even worse, they'd come out of the modest $7,000 the average retired couple on Social Security gets per year. That's not much to live on.

Sure, our Social Security system has problems, caused by high unemployment and inflation. But there are ways to solve them without breaking government's promises to working Americans.

The immediate problem lies within just one of the three Social Security trust funds. The other two trust funds are financially healthy. Simple bookkeeping changes would allow them to make temporary loans to the one fund that needs help.

For a longer-term solution, we should fund Social Security from general tax revenues. Just about every other country does.

Improvements like these would *strengthen* Social Security. They wouldn't undermine it, as President Reagan's plan would do.

Together, we can stop these unfair cuts. Send a letter or mailgram, or call, your U.S. Senators and Representative. Tell them you want the federal government to keep its word. Tell them you've paid into Social Security and want it to be there when you need it.

The Administration and its friends in Congress want to cut Social Security fast, so write or call today. Don't let them take away what we've earned. And don't settle for a compromise that merely pushes back the cuts to a later date. Remember . . .

Social Security is a Contract, Not a Handout!

AFSCME.
American Federation of State,
County, and Municipal Employees

International Union
United Automobile, Aerospace,
and Agricultural Implement Workers of America

UAW

463

The ad indicated that American workers have contracted with government to pay each year for their retirement. Now the government wants to cut one-third of this money. But it is money earned, not a handout. It encourages the American people to fight for their rights by writing to their congressmen to prevent such a proposal from being passed [Exhibit 4].

EFFECTIVENESS OF THE CAMPAIGN

The purpose of the first round of the campaign was to make people aware of the details of the program, so that they would start to have second thoughts. According to the postcampaign polling done by the union, it showed that the campaign was quite successful for its purpose, and that it had an impact on people even if it was transitory. It showed that overall support for the Reagan economic program had dropped by 15 to 20 points among people who had seen the ad a number of times.

Although there was no postpolling on the second ad, which was focused on the problem of social security, the feedback from House Democrats showed that the campaign generated a substantial amount of mail in opposition to the Reagan social security program, at a very critical time—when the administration was deciding whether it was going to go ahead with the program or back off. As Sparks puts it, "Our ad was adding fuel to the fire. . . . I do not have any doubt at all that our second ad played a major role in the Republican back down on social security."

The purpose of the ad was to educate people about the problems with the budget proposals. And the polling that was done afterward showed significant success in this regard. However, there was a secondary purpose for this ad campaign, and that was to translate the education into opposition for further cuts in the following proposals. This was a longer-term commitment, and its effects were going to be seen later on.

COMPARATIVE ADVOCACY ADVERTISING

Chapter 16

ASSOCIATION OF AMERICAN RAILROADS, WASHINGTON, DC:

COMPARATIVE ADVOCACY ADVERTISING CAMPAIGN AIMED AT CORRECTING PUBLIC MISPERCEPTIONS OF AMERICAN RAILROADS AGAINST COMPETITIVE ALTERNATIVE TRANSPORTATION MODES

Since 1977 the Association of American Railroads (AAR) has been engaged in an astute advertising campaign that contains a mixture of institutional image, product-service, and issue-advocacy elements. The campaign has a three-pronged objective: to correct the public perception of American railroads as technologically outmoded and suffering from poor and inefficient management; to promote the public perception of railroads as an efficient form of transportation compared with other competitive transportation modes; and to suggest that railroads have been

---

Research Assistant: Mohamed Nabil Allam.

overregulated, causing them to become less productive and less competitive, which is contrary to public interest.

This is a highly unusual campaign and, along with the campaign by the American Trucking Association, one of the two advocacy campaigns that engages in comparative advertising. There are other advocacy campaigns, notably that of LTV Corporation, where alternative viewpoints on a given issue are presented in a single advertisement. The AAR campaign, however, deals with alternative viewpoints with specific reference to a particular industry with which it competes in the marketplace for public acceptance and consumer loyalty.

Another interesting feature of this campaign has to do with the extensive use of market research at every step of the development of the campaign strategy—from audience research to selection of issues, pre- and posttesting of ad copy, tracking studies, and measurement of campaign effectiveness. This campaign comes closest to following the kind of plan typically used for product advertising, and has heavy involvement by an ad agency. Thus this case provides a good source of illustrative material to examine the unique creative needs of advocacy campaigns; the need for substantive knowledge of the complex subject matter and expertise in its treatment; and the extent to which ad agencies are equipped to handle such campaigns, given their primary experience in product-related advertising.

ASSOCIATION OF AMERICAN RAILROADS (AAR)

The Association of American Railroads (AAR) was established in 1934 as an umbrella organization for the railroad industry, consolidating a number of smaller, more specialized groups. AAR serves as the representative of its members in political matters that require joint handling to better enable the railroads to influence national transportation policy as set by Congress. One of AAR's most important functions is to work with committees made up of representatives of member railroads on matters affecting the progress of the industry as a whole. AAR also represents the railroads in appropriate cases before the courts, administrative tribunals, congressional committees, and other governmental bodies.

At the beginning of 1981, AAR membership consisted of 39 U.S. Class I line-haul railroads; 13 U.S. Class II line-haul railroads; 85 U.S. Class III line-haul and switching and terminal railroads; 1 leased-line railroad; 5 Canadian lines; and 5 Mexican lines. In addition to the full members, there were 82 associate members—railroads and switching and terminal companies that participate in the activities of certain departments of the AAR, but without voting rights. Altogether, AAR member railroads account for 92 percent of the rail mileage and 97 percent of the business of all railroads in North America.[1]

Antecedents to the Advocacy Advertising Campaign

AAR had not engaged in any significant institutional advertising since

1972. However, in early 1977 several railroad executives urged the industry association to increase its public relations and advertising activities in order to develop better understanding among the general public, opinion leaders, and government officials of the freight railroads' ability to play an increasingly larger role in hauling freight with minimum fuel consumption.

Awareness of these inherent strengths was deemed essential if the railroads were to be afforded enhanced opportunities for freight transportation in an environment of heightened national concern for energy conservation and deregulation. It was felt that the American public must acquire an accurate perception of the railroad industry's service capacity and inherent fuel economy if the industry was to receive public support for its positions with regard to the Locks and Dam 26 controversy[2] and in state and federal confrontations involving legislation to permit heavier, wider, and longer trucks on the nation's highways.

Issues for Analysis

AAR shares certain common characteristics with other corporate industry campaigns in that it seeks greater public understanding and support for its position while decrying excessive government regulation of its activities. However, it has two elements not commonly found in other campaigns: (1) While most industries suffer a lack of public confidence, the railroad industry works under the added disadvantage of its management being perceived by the public as inefficient and technologically backward. (2) Unlike any other industry, railroads must fight other transportation modes—trucking, barge lines—for public claims made for the efficiency and social good pertaining to their respective industries, which ultimately put railroads at a disadvantage.

Such a campaign thus raises important issues of strategy and tactics for the advertiser, and for the quality of information transmitted to the public. In particular:

1. Is advocacy advertising a suitable mode for comparative advertising? In a sense, most advocacy advertising has a specific or implied adversary, but in the majority of such cases the adversary is passive; the government agency attacked, for example, does not respond directly to its accuser. Instead, the response function, if any, is taken up by the news media. The situation is quite different when opposition to the advertiser's position is taken up by an adversary that can also claim persecution by big government and the ill effects of uninformed public opinion.

   The evidence is inconclusive as to the effectiveness of comparative advertising for brands and products. Studies show that, in general, the advertiser does not gain any long-term competitive advantage in terms of market share or consumer loyalty. There is also some evidence that such advertising tends to confuse customers and creates distrust for all advertisers' products. To what extent would these conditions apply to advocacy advertising? It could be argued that the public stands to benefit from a more specific and informed discussion of issues because competition among the sponsors would force it. Conversely, competitive point–counterpoint argument might turn such a campaign into a discussion of successively finer technical points, thereby risking loss of public interest.

2. The agenda for such a campaign is often determined by the advertiser, who emphasizes the flaws in the opponent's position. The opponent responds in kind. The inevitable result is that all campaigns end up accentuating the negatives, and thereby reinforcing, at least to some extent, the public's previously held negative beliefs. Furthermore, the advertiser seldom gets an opportunity to present its positive message in a controlled environment.

3. Is comparative advocacy advertising more appropriate for individual companies than an entire industry? No industry is perfect. If charges and countercharges are directed at an entire industry, all companies, regardless of the relevance of these charges, get tarred. Conversely, there is the advantage of presenting a united front against common adversaries.

4. What role does market research play when an advocacy campaign assumes a competitive character? It has been argued that since issue advertising, in general, leads public opinion rather than follows it, a creative approach to issue discussion is more important than measuring what different people believe about certain issues. However, where advocacy advertising becomes more direct and responds to specific charges and countercharges, a precise measure of public opinion may be more relevant to the sponsor for developing specific ad copy.

The Nature and Scope of the Industry's Competitive and Regulatory Problems

According to AAR, America's freight-hauling railroads suffer from a number of competitive disadvantages caused by a regulatory bias against the railroads and unfair subsidization, on the part of the government, of their competitors. For example:

1. Railroads allege that while the rights-of-way for railroad competitors are highly subsidized, private sector freight railroads have to spend more than $1 billion a year for rights-of-way construction, and some $5 billion a year for maintenance. Additionally, the freight railroads pay some $180 million annually in ad valorem taxes on those rights-of-way, a tax fully escaped by barge and heavy truck operators because their rights-of-way are publicly owned.[3] Stated differently, while the annual inland commercial barge rights-of-way subsidy (according to the United States General Accounting Office) is equal to about 42 cents of every revenue dollar earned by the inland barges, the freight railroads themselves spend about 25 cents of each of their revenue dollars on rights-of-way construction and maintenance.

2. Heavy trucks are currently subsidized by automobile owners, light truck owners, and even general taxpayers. The Federal Highway Administration (FHWA), in its second progress report on the Federal Highway Cost Allocation Study, confirmed that automobiles and light trucks had traditionally paid user charges far out of proportion to their

cost responsibility. FHWA recommended increasing heavy truck user charges by 81 percent, and stated that even with such an increase, heavy trucks would still be underpaying their cost responsibility by 10 percent.[4]

3. AAR also believed there was a misperception surrounding the railroad industry and its role in society. Jim Kyser, AAR's director of advertising, observed:

> This misperception has come about through a combination of many unfortunate factors that have occurred over a long period of years. There were serious financial problems with some of the major railroads: Rock Island, Milwaukee Road, Penn Central, etc. that gained nationwide notoriety.
>
> There was a period of time in the early 1970s when there were a series of serious train accidents that were very newsworthy. Passenger service had been continually deteriorating since World War II and had raised people's awareness of the poor condition of the railroads' physical plant.
>
> Our industry attributes much of this to the fact of unrealistic ICC regulation, high restrictive economic regulation that created many of the problems for the roads. An inadequate return on investment capital that was available to carry out necessary maintenance, purchase rolling stock, and make all the other changes.
>
> All these unfortunate factors combined to create the general public perception that the railroads were going down the drain. Although over the years, we have had a large number of very efficient and very profitable freight railroads, the public in general was, and to a large extent still is, unable to differentiate between freight railroads and passenger service.

4. The effect of massive subsidies to barge and heavy truck competitors since World War II had been devastating to the freight railroads. AAR considered that much of the recent financial distress of the railroads was a direct result of federal subsidies to competing modes. Furthermore, the post-1975 federal aid to freight railroads in the Northwest and Midwest, according to AAR, might have been avoided had trucks and barges not previously been the recipients of billions of dollars in unrecompensed subsidies.

According to the U.S. Department of Transportation, between World War II and 1975 alone, federal aid to highways amounted to almost $82 billion; to the inland commercial barge industry, it was more than $10 billion; and to the freight railroads, it was about $859 million.[5] As a result, the freight railroads were unable to compete against heavily subsidized trucks and barges. They ranked last among 73 industries in terms of rate of return on equity, and a full 10.9 percent behind trucking companies.[6]

AAR believed that at the national level, such unnecessary subsidies for transportation rights-of-way has led to market inefficiencies. Specifically, AAR alleged that this policy caused:

• Overbuilding of highways and barge rights-of-way, largely for speculative purposes, because users did not have to face private sector financial discipline.

- Maintenance needs that exceeded the public's willingness and ability to pay. Many public works projects wore out ahead of their design life. A prime example was the premature pavement deterioration of interstate, state, and local highways.
- An inability of nonsubsidized modes to compete with heavily subsidized modes. Several railroads were forced to seek federal assistance, and the threat of nationalization of the entire private sector railroad system had become a distinct possibility.

America's freight railroads did not believe that the solution to the railroads' financial ills was to equalize and perpetuate the unnecessary subsidies. They advocated an elimination of all such subsidies.

AAR'S ADVOCACY CAMPAIGN

Campaign Objectives

AAR, in consultation with individual railroad companies, delineated three basic objectives for the expanded external communications program:

1. Develop a better public understanding of the importance of highly modernized freight railroads in the nation's overall energy and transportation policies.
2. Fight the ever-increasing taxpayer subsidization of railroads' competitors that had placed the freight-hauling railroads at a competitive disadvantage.
3. Correct the ICC regulatory bias against the railroads that adversely affects their efficient operation.

Organization and Decision-Making Process

The AAR board directed the executive committee to take immediate action to develop an advertising program meeting the specified objectives of the campaign. This committee is comprised of the chief public relations executives of the Class I member railroads represented on the AAR board of directors. In its instructions to the executive committee, the AAR board of directors specified that the proposed advertising program should be limited to the print media and be a supplement to the advertising programs of member railroads.

Campaign Budget—Costs

An important factor in determining the target audience for the AAR advertising was the cost consideration in reaching various-size audiences with a national advertising campaign. In considering the medium best suited for broad national reach, television would have been the obvious choice, but costs were prohibitive for the type of programming and time periods that would be necessary for the AAR campaign to be effective. The industry would not permit the expenditure of from $4 to $6 million to support an intensive television advertising campaign. According to Jim Kyser, AAR's director of advertising, "These considerations have remained unchanged over the years, and we are still not into the electronic media." The campaign cost approximately $1.4 million in 1978, $1.5 million in 1979, and some $2 million per year during the 1980–1982 period.

Execution of the Campaign, 1977–1982

The tactical approach to implementing the campaign strategy showed five different stages in the overall campaign, with each successive stage building on the gains from the previous stage. The five stages were:

- The pilot campaign (1977)
- Myth-fact surprise campaign (1978)
- The maturing process campaign (1979)
- Advertising continuity campaign (1980)
- The 1981–1982 campaign (1981–82)

In terms of process, each stage had three phases: generating market intelligence or understanding public's preconceived notions; developing and implementing an advertising strategy utilizing research data; and evaluating the effectiveness of the strategy.

The campaigns placed heavy emphasis on research and attempted to be very "scientific." It was a conservative and cautious approach; advertising dollars and messages were finely tuned to targeted audiences for maximum effect. This type of positioning is the hallmark of product advertising. It is somewhat timid in approach. It minimizes challenging previously held beliefs, and instead provides palatable doses of what previous research shows people want.

Research in other cases has shown that this type of strategy may be less than totally effective when applied to issue advertising. Prior convictions on issues, in general, are more strongly held than attitudes toward products, and they are not easily changed. Dislodging of previously held beliefs has been successful with a combination of creative copy (providing new ideas, unbiased authoritative or expert opinion) and a high degree of source credibility. Even where a more cautious product type of approach has been effective, its impact has had a high decay rate, with readers reverting to their original views shortly after a campaign is discontinued. These campaigns may have a lower rate of learning and retention, and result in a negligible change in long-term beliefs.

Since the AAR campaign has all the ingredients of a typical product-type advertising campaign, its experience should add significantly to our knowledge of the relative merits of using such an approach.

THE PILOT CAMPAIGN, 1977

The first step was to undertake a benchmark public opinion survey. It was conducted by William R. Hamilton & Staff of Washington, DC. The Hamilton organization had previously conducted public opinion and attitude research for the AAR and was thoroughly familiar with railroad problems, terminology, and operations.

The survey was conducted on the basis of personal, in-home interviews with 1,520 Americans 18 years of age and older and 410 community leaders during May 1977. The sample represented the composition of the U.S. population according to important socioeconomic and demographic characteristics. The maximum sampling error was ±3 percent for the general population, and slightly higher for community leaders.

The primary focus of this initial research was to investigate the American public's view of railroads and railroad management. For the community leaders, an added objective was to evaluate the potential effectiveness of various railroad advertising messages. The survey's major findings are summarized below.

General Public

In 1977, 76 percent of the American public considered the railroads to be extremely or very essential to the country, compared to an average of 81 percent over the past seven years. In a similar vein, 28 percent of the people assigned "extremely" essential value to the railroads, compared with 37 percent in 1973–74.

There was also a slight increase in the percentage of Americans who felt other forms of transportation could completely or largely take over the freight-hauling services of railroads, if they had to shut down (32 percent in 1977, compared to 24 percent in 1974). At the same time, 60 percent saw it as difficult or impossible to fill a freight-hauling void should the railroads shut down.

The American outlook toward railroad freight hauling in the future was good. More than half (53 percent) regarded railroads as the form of transportation that could best handle future demands for freight hauling. Less than a third (29 percent) named trucks as the answer for the future, and only 3 percent named barges.

Generally speaking, attitudes had not changed regarding suggested courses of action to deal with the railroads' financial problems. Nearly three-fifths (56 percent) suggested government assistance (slightly below the average for the past seven years), while one in five opted for nationalization.

Railroad management was rated lower than the management of other industries tested in the survey. Trucking management received the highest rating (66 percent positive, 14 percent negative), followed by airlines, telephone companies, and steel manufacturers. However, trucks were rated lower on safety than railroads and received only average marks on the dimension of frugal versus wasteful.

Other measures of the railroad management, using word pair descriptions, showed the following: Railroads received positive marks for "safety" and to a lesser extent on the dimensions of being "skilled" and "concerned." They were negatively viewed for being "dull," "rigid," and "old-fashioned," and to a lesser degree "undependable," "wasteful," and "backward."

Target Audience

The 1977 study showed that upper-income groups, community leaders, and activists were more critical of railroads and railroad management than was the general public.[7] It was therefore decided to concentrate advertising efforts on reaching these groups. To match the audience characteristics with available syndicated magazine research, the target audience was defined as professional-managerial adults with individual employment incomes of $25,000 or more. The secondary target audience of social activists was defined as adults who, during the past year, had written to an elected official, addressed a public meeting, or taken an active part in a local civic issue.[8] In none of the four demographics was age or sex considered a factor.

Community Leaders

Two separate messages were tested in the course of the survey to measure possible impact on the community leaders' attitudes toward the railroads. Each message was presented to a random half of the total sample. Message 1 pointed out the unused capacity of the railroads in this time of energy conservation. Message 2 stressed the handicap the railroads suffer because of government regulations and subsidies to railroad competitors.

In general, neither message had a highly significant positive impact on attitudes toward management or the railroads in general. Overall, however, message 1 appeared to have a slightly more favorable impact on community leaders. Both messages had approximately the same impact in terms of making leaders feel more favorable toward railroads— 38 and 37 percent, respectively.

Leaders were also asked about the future need for railroads before and after being presented with the messages. The results showed that neither message positively affected their attitudes regarding the railroads as essential. With the same pre- and post-message test, however, a 9 percent increase (from 51 to 60 percent) resulted in a number of leaders who chose the railroads as the ones who could best handle future demand for freight hauling after reading message 1.

Although neither message appeared to have a dramatic effect on attitudes toward the railroads, message 2 appeared actually to increase negative feelings toward management, albeit only to a small degree. Overall, message 1 had slightly more appeal, causing respondents to see railroads in a more positive light with regard to the future of freight hauling. Message 2 had a "sour grapes" effect, reinforcing the negative image of railroads, especially among community leaders.[9]

Execution of the Pilot Campaign

Based on the research, it was decided that the thrust of the campaign would be a positive one concerning capacity, fuel efficiency, service, and new technologies. Attempts to explain the negative effects of govern-ment regulation and subsidies in relation to railroad performance would not be believable and would run the risk of increasing the public's negative perceptions of the railroad industry.

The AAR board of directors approved the recommendation of the executive committee directing that the primary media to be used would be newspapers with selective circulations—the *Wall Street Journal, Chicago Tribune, Washington Post, Los Angeles Times* and *Washington Star; Business Week* magazine, and media trade publications such as *Editor & Publisher, Broadcasting,* and *The Quill.* A funding level of $400,000 was approved for the remainder of 1977.

Ad Copy

Four black-and-white advertisements were developed for the pilot program with insertions to begin during September. The messages were designed to emphasize recent innovations in rail service and underscored the importance of railroads in a fuel-conscious, energy-sensitive society. The theme was "Today's Railroads—America's Great Untapped Resource." The first three advertisements were of the typical institutional public relations variety. They emphasized railroads' modernization efforts ("Railroads aren't just resting on their advantages") and fuel economy ("Today's railroads get more miles to the gallon"). The third ad was geared to the overall capacity of the railroad industry ("Today's railroads, America's great untapped resource"). The fourth advertisement was an omnibus treatment stressing recent innovations and progress in all three areas—fuel efficiency, coal-hauling capacity, and industry capacity.

Effectiveness: The Focused Group Evaluation Research

It was necessary to undertake an evaluation of the pilot campaign before launching the full-year campaign. Three focus-group interview sessions were conducted by the research firm of Peter Honig Associates, Inc., during December 1977[10] in Minneapolis, Los Angeles, and Atlanta, with a total of 30 participants. In Minneapolis and Atlanta, men over 21 years of age who were considered to be "activists" or opinion leaders, and who earned $25,000 per year or more, comprised the groups. In Los Angeles, a cross-section of men and women over 21 years of age participated. All participants were screened to eliminate anyone associated with the railroad, trucking, or airline industries.

The discussion focused on attitudes and opinions about railroads as freight carriers, their management, and a comparison of the rail freight system with other forms of transportation. Other areas of concern were reaction to the AAR pilot advertising program, railroad advertising in general, and in what media it was carried. The results indicated that although the railroads were perceived to have an excellent future because of the energy crisis, they suffered from a negative image. Specifically, personnel managing the railroads were perceived to be very conservative, apathetic, and noncompetitive. The railroads were perceived to be ideal for hauling commodities and heavy goods that did not have to be at their destination at a specific time. Although railroads were perceived to be fuel-efficient and less expensive to use per ton mile than were trucks, the savings gained by using rail for shipping most goods was not considered to be worthwhile. Additional image problems faced by the railroads included a perception that methods of handling freight, controlling shipments, and other operations were not up to date; that freight shipped via rail was subject to more damage than freight shipped via trucks; and that because of the routing required, railroads were considered to have relatively little flexibility in terms of being able to expedite shipments.

On the positive side, railroads were perceived to be extremely important to the national economy, and given the nature of the energy crisis, they would continue to be of even greater importance in the future. Piggybacking of truck shipments and the increased importance of moving large amounts of coal were features of the rail freight system that were perceived to have major positive potential for the future.

AAR's pilot campaign was not perceived to be effective. The basic messages were considered to be meaningful, but the ads had minimal impact because they were not noticed enough. Additionally, they were perceived to be too verbose and seemed to turn off readers before they had a chance to get the message. According to James Kyser, the use of four-color printing was recommended to help overcome the dull, old-fashioned image of railroads.

THE SECOND STAGE—MYTH-FACT-SURPRISE CAMPAIGN (1978)

Based on the research conducted by the Hamilton and Honig organizations in 1977, a new campaign strategy was developed. In future campaigns, emphasis was to be placed on developing a better public understanding of the railroads' ability to haul increasing amounts of freight (particularly coal) in the future with less fuel, less environmental damage, less need for additional rights-of-way; and railroad accomplishments in terms of improved services, equipment innovations, modern technology, and progressive management.[11]

Key points that offered the most appeal to the public were to serve as guidelines for copy preparation. Today's railroads are essential transportation. They use modern technology, offer innovative services, and are leaders in developing new equipment to meet the needs of their customers. They are fuel-efficient and environmentally safe, and they provide safe, economical freight transportation. They are led by capable, progressive management; have unused capacity for vastly increased service; and are capable of meeting the current and future transportation challenges of modern America.

Using the guidelines of specific advertising objectives and key communications points, multiple creative approaches were reviewed by the executive committee, AAR executives, and Bozell and Jacobs, Inc., and gave birth to the "Myth-Fact-Surprise" format.

Ad Copy and Graphics

The ad copy was designed to speak to the major issues confronting the railroads by offering a bold statement with which the majority of readers would agree—the myth—and then dispelling the myth with irrefutable facts that would support the railroad position and viewpoint. The "Myth-Fact-Surprise" format provided the opportunity to address an almost unlimited range of subjects. It would work well in either color or black and white, and would be adaptable to magazines or newspapers.

A major creative consideration was the use of the "reverse" format (white type with a black background) for the magazine advertisements. However, due to inherent problems in newspaper reproduction and the relative low quality of newsprint as compared to the paper stock used in magazines, the reverse format was discarded for newspaper advertisements. For newspapers, AAR advertisements would be the traditional black type on a white background. In all other ways, they would be identical to the magazine advertisements, using a bold "Myth" line to state a common misperception relative to the railroad industry, countering the "Myth" line with an equally bold "Fact" line, and providing body copy to substantiate the "Fact" line with detailed information. The "Surprise" line at the end of the copy would say: "Surprise—We've been working on the railroad," thereby reinforcing the "Fact" message in the body of the advertisement.

The vertical photograph illustrated the subject of the advertisement. Inasmuch as the AAR advertisements were viewed as integral elements of the overall industry communications program, "they were designed to look like advertising in order to attract the reader, but presented the information in the body copy in an editorial manner that would be compelling, interesting, and believable." It was the belief of the advertising agency and AAR that these advertisements combined the best of both the advertising and the public relations approaches.

Four advertisements appeared in the "Myth-Fact-Surprise" format in 1978. The first addressed innovation and modern technology, using a photograph of a modern railroad yard control tower. The perceived myth was "Railroads are old-fashioned and outdated," and the purported fact was "Today's railroads are bringing space age technology down to earth." [Exhibit 1]. The second advertisement in the series talked about railroad fuel economy and featured a striking photograph of a one-gallon fuel can. Piggybacking of truck trailers and other innovative railroad services were the subject of the third advertisement in the series [Exhibit 2]. The final 1978 advertisement talked about modern technology innovation and capacity in railroad operations, and was illustrated with a striking photograph of a railroad yard at sunset. The stated myth was "Trains still go 'Clickety-Clack,'" while the purported fact was "Modern, welded track is quiet and smooth."

Since the focus group research in December 1977 had shown that use of color in advertising would be a positive factor in overcoming the negative image of being old-fashioned, dull, and overly conservative, the first and fourth advertisements in the series were run in four color as well as black and white during the course of the year.

Exhibit 1

Myth:
Railroads are old-fashioned and outdated.

Fact:

Today's railroads are bringing space-age technology down to earth.

The tower at left is not part of a space installation—it's the nerve center of a major railroad yard. Automated yards are only one of the many places in which computers are being put to use in today's railroad industry. Other computers keep track of two million freight cars and thousands of locomotives across the country, and help get better use of equipment by forecasting demand and controlling operations.

We are also using imaginative new services, such as "bridge" operations (combined rail-water movements of international cargo); special lightweight coal cars; enclosed cars for moving new automobiles; and sleek low-profile cars to take more trucks and containers off the highways.

What all this means is increased railroad capacity—the ability to carry more tons of freight more miles than ever before while using about half as many trains as were needed 30 years ago.

This unused capacity is important because the Department of Transportation expects the need for rail freight transportation to double by the end of this century.

Railroads will be ready for it with a system that will save both fuel and money. They're getting ready for it today.

Association of American Railroads, American Railroads Building, Washington, D.C. 20036.

Surprise:
We've been working on the railroad.

Exhibit 2

Myth:

Truck traffic can move only on the highways.

Fact:

More than two million truckloads moved by railway last year.

Piggybacking—the movement of truck trailers or containers by rail—is the fastest-growing part of the railroad business. It set a new record in 1977 and it's now our second-largest source of traffic—next to coal.

The piggyback concept has come of age. Better yet, it has generated a wealth of innovations and improvements. Containerized cargo destined for foreign countries now moves across America by rail. New designs in flatcars are saving fuel and increasing loads. Truck trailers that actually ride either roads or rails with two separate sets of wheels are being tested.

This is good news for the railroads, but it's better news for the consumer and the nation. Many piggyback trains move their cargo with about half the fuel that would be required by trucks to move the same goods.

Usually there's a cost saving in piggyback shipments, too, with the advantage of fast, long-distance travel and expedited door-to-door delivery service.

Because these truckloads travel on the railroads, not the highways, the motoring public enjoys a greater degree of safety and less congestion, while damage to the highway system is reduced.

Not all trucks can move by train, but thousands more are doing so every year. And the ones that do aren't leaving potholes in your favorite road.

Association of American Railroads, American Railroads Building, Washington, D.C. 20036

Surprise:

We've been working on the railroad.

Cost and Media Plan

Because of the budget constraints, the 1978 advertising program continued to appear in selected national magazines, four major newspapers, and trade publications reaching editorial personnel in the print and broadcast media.

Specific publications were selected based on how well various magazines performed against selected demographics. A subjective evaluation resulted in a short list of 17 possible publications from an original list of 119 magazines. Each of the 17 publications' performance was measured against the desired demographics, and rankings determined. Finally, each demographic factor was weighted, and a composite weighted ranking was developed. From these weighted rankings, a media plan of national magazines was developed that would generate the best reach and frequency levels against the target audiences.

As a result, advertising insertions in 1978 were scheduled in *Time, Newsweek, U.S. News & World Report, Business Week, Scientific American,* and *National Geographic.* Due to the nature of the publication, the *Wall Street Journal* was considered as a magazine, and insertions were scheduled in it. In the newspaper category, regular insertions in the Op-Ed position were scheduled in the *New York Times* and *Washington Star,* and in the business section of the *Washington Post. Broadcasting, Editor & Publisher,* and *The Quill* were the publications selected to reach media editorial personnel.

Overall, the media plan resulted in 84 advertising insertions, with AAR advertisements reaching 89 percent of the P/M IEI (P/M = professional managerial; IEI = individual earned income) $25,000+ audience and 73 percent of the activist audience. Frequency against the primary target audience was 12, and 8 against the activist audience. This was accomplished with a budget of $1.3 million.

Effectiveness of the 1978 Campaign

During the course of the year, 1,066 responses that could be specifically traced to AAR advertising were received by the Office of Information and Public Affairs. In previous years, only some 200 to 300 letters were received annually seeking information about the railroad industry.

Inasmuch as public responses were deemed to be an unscientific and relatively unreliable measure of the recall or acceptance of AAR advertising, research was again conducted by the Hamilton organization in August 1978. The study consisted of 387 personal interviews with upper-income residents of four urban-suburban areas: Montgomery County, Maryland; Westchester County, New York; Milwaukee, Wisconsin; and Kansas City, Missouri. The study was conducted against a target group of individuals with salaries of $25,000 or more annually to assess the potential impact of the 1978 AAR print media campaign.[12]

The major findings of the research were as follows:

1. The upper-income groups continued to rate the railroad industry negatively by three to one, and much lower than trucking, airlines,

telephone, and steel. Poor management was still the reason most often given for the railroads' plight. The perception that railroads needed government assistance to operate was lower in this group than it was a year before. Additionally, there had been a drop from 62 to 52 percent in the choice of government assistance as the alternative to nationalization of the railroads.

2. Of these upper-income respondents, 42 percent voluntarily recalled having seen advertising for railroads in the past three months. About a third of all those interviewed recalled seeing one or more of the four AAR ads when they were prompted by being shown copies of these advertisements.

3. More than half of the target group responded that they would be likely to look at and read through the ad if they saw it in a publication. The same was true of the opinion leader subgroup. Over 70 percent of the respondents felt the ads' messages were clear. It was obvious that the vast majority had read the ads, understood the overall message, and also learned some specifics about the railroad industry.

4. The first reaction of the target group about the four ads was that the railroads were trying to modernize and upgrade their services and equipment. The ads were viewed as credible; the myths tended to attract readership. The statement of each myth, followed by a simple, direct fact, added immensely to the clarity and quick receipt of the message. Only the "Tower" ad appeared to evoke any feeling of unsubstantiated claims.

5. The graphics appeared to have added to the noteworthiness and clarity of most ads. Color definitely seemed to have added in terms of people's willingness to read the ad. It was, however, unclear whether increased use of four color would justify the 50 percent increase in the media costs. The Hamilton Organization suggested that as much color should be used as possible because black and white did not fit as well with the concept of modernization and new technology.

This conclusion is in sharp contrast to some other advocacy campaigns, notably those of LTV, Dresser Industries, and W. R. Grace, which ran exclusively in black and white. From all accounts these campaigns were highly successful in attracting attention, readership, recall, and persuadability. However, none of these companies or their industries suffered from a public image of outdated technology and backward management. Furthermore, the issues covered in those campaigns were already among major topics of public debate and had attracted considerable new media attention.

The overall sample rated the railroad industry 69 percent negatively to 23 percent positively. When asked after seeing the ads, 54 percent responded positively, and only 23 percent continued to volunteer negative comments.

THE THIRD STAGE—THE MATURING PROCESS (1979)

The 1979 campaign was evolutionary in character and built on the experiences of the previous year. The "Myth-Fact-Surprise" format was retained. One important change was the use of photographs taken specifically for particular advertisements. To overcome as much as possible the negative effects of the reversed type, a continuing effort was made to keep body copy to as few words as possible, while still presenting a strong, positive railroad story.

Another change was elimination of the "Surprise" line used during 1978, "Surprise: We've been working on the railroad," one of the copy lines being used by AMTRAK. Such a change was important, because the perceived decline in passenger service was a continuing "top of the head" reason for rating railroads negatively.[13] The new "Surprise" lines related to the subject of the advertisement, supported the "Fact" line, and tied the positive elements of the advertisement (Fact = body copy = Surprise) together. It was also felt that even if readers did not read through all the body copy, seeing the illustration and reading the "Myth-Fact-Surprise" lines would expose them to the main points of the advertisement. This concept began to be referred to by the agency and AAR advertising personnel as "The 10-second commercial." Also, to reinforce the separation between freight and passenger railroads and service, the modifier "freight" began to be used wherever possible in conjunction with the word "railroads."

Emphasis on Fuel Conservation

In June 1979, in response to the energy crunch, emphasis was placed on railroad fuel efficiency and energy conservation efforts. The advertisement featured a dramatic use of two colors. The ad copy stated: "Myth: Railroads waste a lot of energy; Fact: America's freight railroads are in the forefront of energy conservation."

AAR also developed a special brochure about railroad fuel efficiency and energy conservation. The brochure cover used a graphic rendition of the photograph used in the advertisement. This was an initial attempt to integrate more effectively and to coordinate advertising and public relations activities. These brochures were used not only as responses to requests for more information generated by the advertisement and disseminated to the news media, but as handouts at public meetings, following speeches, and at exhibits and open house activities.

Ad Copy and Format

As 1979 drew to close, the first in a series of hard-hitting advertisements addressing matters of public policy and industry concern appeared. This was the start of the comparative advertising campaign. The 1979 program included four advertisements. The first and the third ads addressed the issue of modernization ("MYTH—Railroads run on legends and old tracks." "FACT—America's freight railroads spent a record $10 billion in capital improvements and maintenance in 1978.") The third was "MYTH—Railroads waste a lot of energy." "FACT—America's freight railroads are in the forefront of energy conservation."

The second advertisement discussed the innovations in freight hauling by America's railroads and was entitled: "MYTH—Railroads haven't kept up with the times." "FACT—Railroad innovations are changing the way America moves freight" [Exhibit 3]. The fourth and last ad in 1979 was entitled the "Rail Alternative." It confronted the trucking industry, and pointed out the damage being done to the nation's highway system by big trucks. The ad stated that despite the user taxes paid by the trucking industry, big trucks were having their rights-of-ways subsidized by drivers of passenger cars and light trucks. The advertisement also used a two-color, stylized graphic rendition of a piggyback train to illustrate the story.

Campaign Costs

The 1979 campaign cost $1.5 million, which was an 11 percent increase over 1978.

Effectiveness of the 1979 Campaign

An interesting innovation in the 1979 campaign was to add an "action" line in the ad copy. This was done both to get a measure of reader interest in the ad message and also to furnish more information.

The 1978 campaign had drawn a significant number of public responses. Consequently, in 1979 AAR began a two-way communication with readers by offering additional and more detailed information about the subject of individual advertisements. The information offer was buried at the end of the body copy and required respondents to write a postcard or letter, affix the necessary postage, and mail the request. There was no coupon and no 800 number to call. It was thought that this would deter the coupon-clipper and casual browser and provide responses from readers who were sincerely interested in the information being offered—a "quality" response. The results were 6,012 advertising responses during the year, compared with a little over 1,000 in 1978.

Hamilton was commissioned to conduct a biannual national opinion survey as part of the continuing research program to track national public opinion and attitudes toward America's freight railroads. The survey was undertaken among 1,500 Americans aged 18 and older, projectable to the U.S. population. The sample of 378 community leaders was drawn from the public sample meeting the criteria, with an oversampling to produce the total needed. All community leaders resided in households with an annual income in excess of $30,000 and were active in at least one category of civic and community affairs or political involvement.

The key findings of the 1979 research[14] were as follows:

1. The public and community leaders felt that financial difficulties extended to at least half of the nation's freight railroads. The chief

Exhibit 3

Myth:
Railroads haven't kept up with the times.

Fact:
Railroad innovations
are changing the way
America moves freight.

"Piggybacking"—carrying truck trailers and containers on railroad flatcars—is one of the most innovative concepts in modern railroading. It conserves fuel, reduces highway congestion and often means lower costs for shippers.

"Railbridge" evolved from the piggyback concept. These services move overseas cargo in containers by rail between U.S. seaports on opposite coasts, or between a seaport and an inland city. Railbridge rates are competitive and save time and fuel over the all-water routes.

"Slingshot" trains are another recent variation on the piggybacking theme. These short piggyback trains operate on fast, flexible schedules and compete with trucks in dense traffic corridors. Less highway congestion, fast service and substantial cost savings that shippers can pass on to customers are the results.

To add a new dimension to piggybacking, experiments are underway to develop special truck trailers equipped with two separate sets of wheels—one set for highways and one set for rails. Success could mean even greater handling efficiency and fuel savings.

And, to encourage more efficient use of rail equipment, shipper groups that move fresh produce in piggybacked trailers can earn special reduced rates by guaranteeing a return load for the trailer.

Railroad piggybacking—with its variations and advantages—is one of many bright spots in the rail transportation picture.

For more facts about today's innovative freight railroads, write: Service, Association of American Railroads Building, Washington, D.C. 20036.

Surprise:
America's freight railroads
apply new technologies to
reduce costs and save energy.

cause of these financial problems was considered to be poor management. Community leaders held both poor management and outdated labor practices to be the principal causes of financial problems for the railroads.

2. The public remained convinced that the best course of action, if the financial problems were to continue, would be to continue government financial and other assistance. Leaders also held this view, but slightly less than the public did.

3. The performance rating of railroad management as a whole continued its downward trend among both the public and community leaders, primarily due to overwhelmingly negative ratings of passenger railroad management. The overall poor image of railroad management was so broadbased that there were few geographic or socioeconomic differences in the public's assessment of the industry.

4. Freight railroads were perceived to have a clear-cut advantage over trucks with regard to fuel efficiency. Freight railroads were also seen, especially by community leaders, as being in the most advantageous position to serve the growing needs of freight hauling in the next decade.

5. The condition of tracks was still considered dilapidated by both leaders and the public, which perpetuated some concern about railroad safety, despite a relative advantage in perception of trains versus trucks as the safer mode.

6. Understanding of federal regulation of the railroads was fuzzy at that time. Regulation by the ICC was construed by the public to be advantageous to the railroads. Partially for this reason, the public supported continued ICC regulation of freight railroad rates and routes by a margin of 43 to 31 percent.

7. Community leaders recalled from memory advertising for both railroad and trucking industries to a very similar degree. This was despite the fact that AAR outspent ATA by a substantial margin.[15]

THE FOURTH STAGE—ADVERTISING CONTINUITY (1980)

During 1980, the continuity effect of advertising began to take effect, resulting in a rise in cumulative impressions, each impression reinforcing the reaction to previous advertisements, and making each successive advertisement easier to relate and identify for the target audiences. Major changes in the advertising program centered around media plans and publications. *Scientific American* was dropped from the media schedule. And because of high out-of-pocket cost, the five insertions scheduled for the national edition of *Time* were reduced to five insertions in the less costly demographic edition, *Time* B. To compensate for these losses in reach, five insertions were scheduled in the *Smithsonian* and *The New Yorker,* both of which ranked well against target audiences.

A new element was added to the campaign strategy in 1980 through a separate media schedule designed to build reach and frequency with the community leader and activist audiences: 42 additional advertising insertions were scheduled for "thought leader" publications. *Harper's, Atlantic, Harvard Business Review, The Washington Monthly, World Press*

Review, Technology Review, and *National Review* each were scheduled for four insertions during the course of the year, and *The Christian Science Monitor* was programmed for ten insertions. The audiences represented by these publications were considered particularly important in view of the more aggressive direction of AAR advertising toward issues of industry and public policy concern.

It would appear on the surface that the copy strategy designed for other audience groups would be inappropriate for the needs of the opinion leader–activist readers. The current strategy was based on short copy with a simple message, accompanied by bold headlines and large pictures to catch attention. Other research in advocacy advertising had shown that thought leader groups tended to be better informed, and receptive to reading long, complex messages. Therefore, overly simplistic messages are likely to have low credibility with these groups.

There were 174 advertising insertions by the AAR during 1980. These advertisements reached 88 percent of the primary target audience with a frequency of 11.5, and 71.7 percent of the community leader–activist audience with a frequency of 8.1.[16]

Ad Copy

The primary advocacy message of the 1980 campaign was the need for deregulation of freight-carrying railroads: "MYTH—Government regulation benefits railroads." "FACT—America's freight railroads are hampered by government regulations, and that puts the squeeze on everyone" [Exhibit 4]. Another advertisement on deregulation was a major departure from the Myth-Fact format and was aimed at the U.S. Congress, urging it to take action on The Rail Act of 1980. This advertisement ran only once in each of the two Washington newspapers.

The comparative advocacy message was continued through another advertisement comparing railroad piggybacking to highway freight trucking: "MYTH—Truck trailers on the public highways move freight most efficiently." "FACT—Freight railroads save highways, tax dollars, and energy by piggybacking truck trailers." The message of this advertisement was similar in content to some other advertisements that had run the previous year.

Another departure from the long-term campaign strategy took place in the form of a corrective advertisement. Under the headline "An Open Letter to Mr. Roone Arledge President ABC News," the advertisement took the network to task for misleading and erroneous reporting of facts on railroad safety in its June 5, 1980, "20/20" program [Exhibit 5]. This advertisement appeared in media trade publications for a brief period.

Evaluation of 1980 Campaign Effectiveness

All 1980 advertisements were coded by subject and publication in which they appeared to track advertising responses and provide an additional indicator of the effectiveness of the publications in the advertising schedule; 9,174 responses were received and analyzed. Publications were then

Exhibit 4

Myth:
Government regulation benefits railroads.

Fact:
America's freight railroads
are hampered
by government regulations,
and that puts the squeeze
on everyone.

Today's freight railroads are subject to rules and regulations that date from horse-and-buggy days. Heavy-handed strictures that don't apply to most other businesses or even the railroads' direct competitors—the largely unregulated truck and barge industries.

While competition is virtually free to raise or lower prices to meet changing market conditions, railroads are not. America's freight railroads can't change their freight rates, drop unprofitable lines, add new services, or even initiate innovative pricing that could save consumers money—without first getting government approval. And that's a process which can involve excessive delays.

Doesn't make much sense in these tight-money times, does it? But it's a fact. And as long as non-polluting, energy-efficient freight railroads are denied the right to compete equally for business in the free market, the consumer will continue to pay the extra freight—in terms of added dollars or poorer service, or both.

For more information, write: Regulation, Dept.Z1, Association of American Railroads, American Railroads Building, Washington, D.C. 20036.

Surprise:
In freight transportation,
the market is the best regulator.

486

Exhibit 5

AN OPEN LETTER TO MR. ROONE ARLEDGE PRESIDENT ABC NEWS

Dear Mr. Arledge:

After viewing the "20/20" segment on rail safety on June 5, I concluded that "20/20" bears about as much relationship to real journalism as "Charlie's Angels" does to real police work.

Having briefed ABC's producer on the well-documented facts of rail safety, particularly concerning the rail movement of hazardous materials, only to have those facts all but ignored, I must comment on the lack of professionalism displayed in the "20/20" broadcast. With its conspicuously biased report, "20/20" has done significant harm to the reputation of the railroad industry in general and to the individual railroads depicted so inaccurately on this program.

We were informed by the producer before any filming took place that "20/20" was working on the thesis that railroad track is deteriorating, that increasing amounts of hazardous materials are being shipped by rail, and that catastrophic accidents "are waiting to happen." In response to our demonstration that this premise was invalid, "20/20" made several offhanded comments that things were getting better, and proceeded to use ten-year-old film clips in an effort to prove that the predetermined story line was accurate. The resulting broadcast showed reckless disregard for the truth.

Railroads aren't perfect. But the facts, which are available to anyone willing to check them, clearly establish that railroads are the safest way of shipping anything overland. Last year, freight trains moved 70% of all hazardous materials transported within the United States. Yet trains were involved in _only 9%_ of all accidents related to the shipping of such materials. Of the remaining 91% of hazardous materials accidents, 75% of all injuries and 80% of all fatalities occurred on public highways and involved motor vehicles. And as "20/20" knew, but ignored, there were _no_ fatalities last year in rail accidents involving hazardous materials.

Railroad safety has been improving steadily. Last year was the railroads' safest since record keeping began more than one hundred years ago. This is why I am particularly concerned about the distortions and bias of the "20/20" report.

Because I am as much a journalist as a public relations practitioner, I believe the best interests of my industry and the public are served by a full and open discussion of matters of public concern. In that belief, I have always cooperated with reputable members of news organizations. Even after my confrontation with "20/20," I still intend to assist reputable reporters and writers. I hope ABC News will provide some of them.

Sincerely,

Lawrence H. Kaufman
Vice President
Information and Public Affairs

ASSOCIATION OF

AMERICAN RAILROADS

OFFICE OF INFORMATION AND PUBLIC AFFAIRS
1920 L STREET, N.W. · WASHINGTON, D.C. 20036 · 202/293-4160

For facts about the safe transportation of hazardous materials or any information about America's freight railroads, write to: Association of American Railroads, Dept. 20 B, American Railroads Building, Washington, D.C. 20036

ranked based on this indexed response-rate analysis. Realistic comparisons could thus be made between such publications as *National Geographic,* with a circulation of 10.5 million, and *Editor & Publisher,* with a circulation of 27,300. The response-rate analysis, combined with quarterly positioning reports prepared by Bozell & Jacobs, Inc., and Starch Readership Report scores were used as additional tools in evaluating the effectiveness of various publications on the advertising schedule.[17]

THE FIFTH STAGE—1981–82 CAMPAIGN

In 1981, budget restraints forced curtailment of plans to expand advertising activities to achieve increased frequency against both primary and secondary target audiences and to venture into the areas of network radio and spot radio. A reduced level of advertising activity was experienced as compared to 1980, with only 128 advertising insertions scheduled, compared to 174 the previous year. Although curtailment of advertising activities did not seriously affect reach and frequency levels against the primary target audience, considerable loss of impact was experienced against the community leader–activist audience. This was due primarily to the elimination of the separate opinion leader program element instituted in 1980. Limited dollar savings from this series of advertising insertions were applied against advertising schedules in national magazines, editorial trade publications, and New York and Washington newspapers to compensate for steadily rising media costs. To further reduce media costs, the size of the thirteen insertions in the *Wall Street Journal* was reduced from 880 to 800 agate lines.

Creative execution did not vary during the early months of 1981 from the previous year and a half; AAR continued to speak out against prevalent myths with compelling visuals and strong copy. The advertising confrontation between the railroads and competing modes of transportation continued with development of an advertisement addressing the subject of public subsidies for trucks and barges and the resulting negative effect on competition [Exhibit 6]. Other advertisements during 1981 addressed the issues of railroad safety and nineteenth-century land grants; no energy ads were developed in 1981.

The safety advertisement was illustrated by a photograph of a locomotive on a track being examined through a magnifying glass to support the "Fact" line, "A close look shows America's freight railroads are the safest form of general transportation." The land grant advertisement was illustrated with a photograph of the actual golden spike, driven in on May 10, 1869, to mark the completion of the transcontinental railroad.

Public Response to 1981 Campaign

The rate of public response to AAR advertisements for 1981 was down to 63 percent from the level attained in 1980; slightly fewer than 6,000 responses were received in 1981. The Hamilton organization undertook another biannual public opinion survey,[18] based on 1,504 telephone in-

Exhibit 6

Myth:

All freight carriers compete on an equal basis.

Fact:

Public subsidies for trucks and barges throw competition out of balance.

You, as an individual, pay part of the cost for everything shipped by truck or barge—whether you use it or not.

The public roads and highways—the rights-of-way for heavy trucks—are built and maintained primarily by money collected from drivers of passenger cars and light trucks. If a product travels by barge, it moves through locks and dams and over waterways built and maintained almost entirely with your tax dollars.

Nearly all of America's freight railroads build, maintain and pay taxes on their track and rights-of-way, and these costs are paid from dollars earned by the railroads. As a result, it costs the railroads 34¢ out of every dollar of revenue for track and rights-of-way, compared to the 5¢ paid by trucks and the .003¢ paid by barges, neither of which amounts to a fair share of costs.

All transportation has received government assistance at one time or another. The freight railroads, however, have reimbursed the government for most prior aid. Much of the current aid to some railroads is in the form of loans to be repaid with interest. On the other hand, trucks and barges have long received outright subsidies.

All forms of freight transportation should pay their full costs of doing business. When they do, the American people will receive the most economical transportation services—and a needless burden will be lifted from the motorist and taxpayer.

For more information, write: Competition, Dept. 1, Association of American Railroads, American Railroads Building, Washington, D.C. 20036.

Surprise:

Rights-of-way costs are heavy for America's freight railroads; motorists and taxpayers carry most of the burden for highways and waterways.

RIGHTS OF WAY COST

terviews during June 1981. The major findings of the survey were as follows:

1. Although the American public continued to believe that railroads were essential to the country, the railroad industry in general, and freight railroads in particular, continued to suffer in terms of adverse public image regarding management, the state of equipment and tracks, and financial well-being. About twice as many people selected a negative (58 percent) as a positive (27 percent) rating of management, increasing to a 75 percent negative–18 percent positive ratio among community leaders.

2. Of the respondents, 44 percent agreed that railroad management had improved over the past few years, a level that has remained virtually unchanged since 1977. An almost equal number (42 percent) disagreed with this viewpoint. This was a deterioration from the previous two surveys (1977 and 1979). Negative assessment appeared to be solidifying. Compared to railroads, all other industries tested for management competence had a higher positive rating. Over 60 percent of the respondents rated airline, telephone, and trucking industry managements as excellent or good.

3. Approximately 70 percent of the people considered the railroad industry to be dilapidated and out-of-date, and over 40 percent disagreed that the condition of tracks and equipment had improved over the past five years.

4. Almost half (48 percent) of the public and a clear majority (56 percent) of community leaders continued to believe that most or all of the country's freight railroads were in financial difficulties. Among the reasons, the public more often chose poor management (33 percent) than insufficient share of government transportation funds (19 percent), outdated labor practices (18 percent), or out-of-date regulations (16 percent). If convinced the railroad industry was in serious financial trouble, a majority (52 percent) believed that government should provide financial assistance and an additional 25 percent favored nationalization. Findings in 1981 differed from past results, when on average, more than 60 percent favored government assistance.

5. As many named railroads as named trucks and barges combined as the most fuel efficient, being in the best position to handle expected increases in freight to be hauled over the next ten years, and as instituting the most technological innovation. And more chose railroads than either trucks or barges as having the best overall safety record in hauling freight.

6. Public opinion research was finding that the mood of the country in 1981 was leaning toward more free enterprise and less government control and regulation. Within this atmosphere there appeared to be a continued perception among many that government favored or "holds up" railroads. A plurality (43 percent) considered freight railroads having an advantage over trucks or barges due to the government assistance received, while only 18 percent thought rail was at a disadvantage. However, by a three to one margin, Americans believed that less (66 percent) rather than more (22 percent) government control of the railroads would benefit them as consumers.

7. Slightly over one in ten Americans (11 percent) were aware that they had seen advertising for freight railroads recently, increasing to two in five community leaders (21 percent). While few people named AAR as a sponsor, the highest recall was found among the upscale segments of the population that included AAR's target audience. Those who recalled advertising were more likely than the general public to hold certain viewpoints expounded in industry advertising, indicating that the advertising had affected public opinion in those areas.

8. Those aware of advertising were just as likely as the general public to believe government assistance was a handout rather than a loan, and more likely to continue to rate railroad management negatively. Since the profile of people aware of freight railroad advertising was very similar to the profile of those with the strongest criticisms of railroad management, it was not surprising that even recognition of "steps in the right direction" would not yield a positive assessment of management overall.

Almost two-fifths of the American public (and over two-thirds of the community leaders) said they were familiar with issue or advocacy advertisements sponsored by companies or industry groups, especially those of oil companies. Among this group, a majority (53 percent) considered this advertising to be either uninformative or unbelievable. Only one-fourth admitted that such advertising had altered their opinion toward an issue. In summary, people who were conscious of their exposure to issue-advocacy advertising appeared generally supportive of the right of industry to advertise its viewpoints and even felt that such advertising had some merit as a useful way to gain information on issues.

The 1982 Campaign

The 1982 campaign continued with the themes developed in previous years. However, there was greater emphasis on the institutional-image component of the program. In addition to the land grant ad, two other copy themes emphasized the benefits of deregulation: "New freedoms. New ideas. New benefits for everyone. New horizons for America's freight railroads" [Exhibit 7]; and "Resource," a coal-oriented ad, which addressed the role of the freight railroads, referred to as "an important national resource," in transporting coal, "an important natural resource."

THE 1983–1984 CAMPAIGN

The most recent phase of the campaign, introduced in June 1983, was marked by some radical changes in design and execution. The comparative approach was dropped, and elements of advocacy were sharply downplayed. Instead, the advertisements emphasized positive aspects of freight railroads. Ad copy was considerably shortened, with greater space devoted to graphics and layout. The ads became four-color, more "happy" and "artsy," and closer cousins to traditional corporate institutional rather than advocacy or issue-oriented advertising [Exhibit 8].

Exhibit 7

New freedoms. New ideas. New benefits for everyone.

New horizons for America's freight railroads.

America's freight railroads are being freed from overregulation and the real winner is the public—the consumers of rail-delivered goods.

With less government interference since the passage of the 1980 Staggers Rail Act, railroads are better able to compete in the marketplace. Using options long available to other businesses, railroads are developing innovative marketing programs that are making rail shipment much more efficient and cost-effective.

For example, now that they can sign long-term contracts, railroads are offering price and service incentives in return for guaranteed volume. And, with the deregulation of piggyback (the movement of truck trailers and containers on rail flatcars), railroads now are free to change rates when necessary to meet competition, putting more traffic on the rails—and less on the highways.

Reduced regulation has given railroaders the opportunities and the freedom to manage more efficiently. Railroads and those who ship freight by railroad benefit. And so do the final customers for goods shipped by rail—the public.

For more information, write: "It's Working," Dept. RP, Association of American Railroads, 1920 L St., N.W., Washington, D.C. 20036.

Freight Trains. America's most vital moving force.

Exhibit 8

Mary DeSapio
First Vice President
Lehman Brothers Kuhn Loeb
May 1981

"For possibly the first time in two generations, one can make a sound, long-term case for investing in rail equities."

Wall Street's enthusiasm for railroad equities remains unabated since that statement was made. Despite an uncooperative economy, railroad equities have tripled in market value. Obviously, America's freight railroads are a growth industry. Last year, trains handled almost twice as much traffic as their nearest competitors. They moved it efficiently, inexpensively, reliably. This growing efficiency is the result of a massive program of capital improvement. Over the last three years, freight railroads spent an average $3.1 billion a year on new equipment, improved track and expanding technology. America's freight railroads are investing for today and tomorrow—and increasing their share of the transportation market along the way. The railroad renaissance is welcome news—because railroads keep America running.
For more information, write: Renaissance, Dept. 000, Association of American Railroads, 1920 L Street, N.W., Washington, D.C. 20036.

ASSOCIATION
OF AMERICAN
RAILROADS

FREIGHT RAILROADS ARE ON THE MOVE.

The new campaign was not accompanied by a larger advertising budget. The ad expenditures were targeted at $1.7 million and $1.6 million for 1983 and 1984, respectively. Accordingly, a further narrowing of the target audience became necessary, and a greatly constricted media schedule resulted. The current target audience for AAR advertising is professional-managerial with individual earned incomes of over $40,000 annually, working in one of fourteen specified industries (advertising, agriculture/forestry, communications, construction, education, finance/banking, government/public administration, insurance, law, manufacturing, mining/minerals, public utilities, publishing/printing, transportation), *and* who participated in one or more of these five public activities: wrote an editor of a newspaper or magazine, worked for a political party or candidate, ran for public office, wrote an article or book for publication, and served on a corporate board of directors. The total number of insertions in 1983 dropped to 107, appearing in *Business Week, Forbes,* the *New York Times,* the *Wall Street Journal, The Christian Science Monitor, Broadcasting, Editor & Publisher, Columbia Journalism Review, Washington Journalism Review,* and *The Quill.* Reach was 87 percent, and frequency was 18.1 against the primary target audience.

For 1984, 98 insertions were scheduled in the *Wall Street Journal,* the *New York Times, Business Week, Forbes,* and *Barron's,* with a very "modest" schedule in *Traffic Management, Distribution, Handling & Shipping Management,* and *Railway Age.* No regular insertions were scheduled for any of the communications trade publications, as had been the case in previous years. AAR estimates a reach of 90 percent and a frequency of 20.8 against a target audience of 2.07 million.

NOTES

1. Association of American Railroads, 1981 Annual Report, p. 4.
2. Locks and Dam 26 is on the upper Mississippi River. Here the U.S. Army Corps of Engineers and public money were used to enhance and improve the inland waterway so that it would become major competition for the parallel railroads. Association of American Railroads, 1981 Annual Report, p. 4.
3. Frank N. Wilner, *User Charges and Transportation Efficiency,* Association of American Railroads, Washington, DC, September 1981, p. 4.
4. *Report by the Secretary of Transportation, Second Progress Report on the Federal Highway Cost Allocation Study,* January 1981.
5. Ibid., Figure 29, p. III-25.
6. *Citicorp Monthly Economic Letter,* April 1980.
7. William R. Hamilton and Staff, "Attitudes toward America's Railroads: The Public and Community Leaders," research report prepared for the Association of American Railroads, Washington, DC, May 1977, p. 7.
8. Bozell & Jacobs, Inc., "1978 Communications Program for the Association of American Railroads," communications plan prepared for the Association of American Railroads, New York, December 1977.
9. "Attitudes toward America's Railroads," pp. iii–vii.
10. Peter Honig Associates, "Focused Group Interview: The Image of Railroads Relative to Their Role in Carrying Freight," unpublished research report, New York, December 1977, p. 1.

11. Richard E. Briggs, "Memorandum to AAR Board of Directors," Washington, DC, December 5, 1977.
12. William R. Hamilton and Staff, "An Evaluation of the AAR's Print Media Advertising Campaign," research report prepared for the Association of American Railroads, Washington, DC, August 1978, p. i.
13. William R. Hamilton and Staff, "Attitudes toward the Railroad Industry: Survey of Trends, Issues and Advertising Awareness among the Public and Community Leaders," research report prepared for the Association of American Railroads, Washington, DC, October 1979.
14. William R. Hamilton and Staff, "Attitudes toward the Railroad Industry: Survey of Trends, Issues and Advertising Awareness," pp. iv–v.
15. See the case study on American Trucking Association's advocacy advertising campaign.
16. James G. Kyser, "MYTH-FACT-SURPRISE, The Association of American Railroads Advertising Campaign to Change Public Perceptions of America's Freight Railroads," unpublished research, 1981, p. 38.
17. Ibid., p. 38.
18. William R. Hamilton and Staff, "A Survey of Americans' Opinions of the Railroad Industry," research report prepared for the Association of American Railroads, Washington, DC, June 1981.

Chapter 17   # AMERICAN TRUCKING
ASSOCIATION, WASHINGTON, DC:

A COMPARATIVE ADVOCACY
CAMPAIGN AIMED AT CORRECTING
PUBLIC MISPERCEPTIONS CAUSED
BY A COMPETITIVE
TRANSPORTATION MODE

The American Trucking Association (ATA) has had a long running battle with the American Railroad Association about the latter's claim that the trucking industry has had an unfair competitive advantage because it pays comparatively lower overall taxes, does not have to build or maintain its own right of way, and is subjected to less government regulation.

For a number of years, the battle was fought in the political and regulatory arena through lobbying for changes in laws and regulations that allegedly gave competitive advantage to one or the other group. However, as railroads began to be deregulated, they became more aggressive in trying to reclaim lost markets. And one of the methods they used was to garner public support for their claims of unfair competition.

In many ways, the ATA campaign was a direct response to the advocacy campaign by the American Association of Railroads (AAR), which

Research Assistants: Mohamed Nabil Allam and Alan Rosenberg.

had been using public forums and paid commercial messages to present its case.

THE RATIONALE FOR THE ATA CAMPAIGN

The trucking industry as represented by ATA was concerned about the adverse impact of the continuing public relations and advocacy advertising effort by the AAR. ATA had already noticed a number of editorials in respected news media that generally echoed public policy positions advocated by the railroads and treated as "facts" some of the data and interpretations provided by the railroads that pertained to the relative tax and regulatory advantages enjoyed by the trucking industry.

On March 3, 1981, an editorial in the *New York Times* appeared with the headline "Trucks Should Pay Their Way":

> As most drivers are painfully aware, the once-proud Interstate Highway System has become an obstacle course of pot holes and crumbling bridges. It needs a major rebuilding effort costing tens of billions. It's not clear, though, who will foot the bill. Congress will no doubt look first to the Federal fuel tax. The 4-cent-a-gallon levy hasn't been raised since 1959. But a larger part of the burden should be borne by the heaviest users: heavy trucks. . . . According to the Transportation Department, autos pay a far higher percentage of highway costs than can reasonably be attributed to them. A fair tax change would shift some of the burden to big tractor-trailers. . . . The American economy is no longer so blessed. Dollars collected and spent unproductively on highways are, well, unproductive.

Another editorial under the headline "Heavy Trucks Should Pay for Their Wear and Tear of Highways" appeared on March 29, 1981. The *Times* stated, among other things, that in response to the earlier editorial (March 3), the American Trucking Association claimed that the trucking industry was paying its "fair share" to the highway trust fund and that no supporting evidence of any kind had been produced to substantiate contrary claims. The editorial went on to state:

> Unfortunately the ATA stands alone in these convictions. According to the Federal Highway Administration and the General Accounting Office much of the Interstate System has reached design life far ahead of its time because its enormous popularity and use were underestimated, particularly the growth of the long distance trucking industry.
>
> The Congressional Budget Office, GAO, FHWA and others have indicated that any shift to rehabilitation from construction would probably result in higher allocation of highway costs to trucks. The concept of imposing new or more stringent heavy-vehicle use taxes on trucks clearly faces a politically hostile climate in this time of budget reductions and tax cuts. But we have a $76 billion investment in the Interstate highway system alone, which is daily undermined as necessary rehabilitation is deferred for lack of funds. This is one area where it is clearly uneconomical not to spend, for damage can only get worse and prices only go up. If trucks don't pay their own way, it will

either be paid for them by already overburdened lightweight vehicles or it won't be paid at all.

The last editorial appeared on July 5, 1981, under the headline "Highway: Let the User Pay." The *Times* summarized the issues as follows:

> The problem would not be so serious were it just a matter of a few big trucks. But there has been a distinct historical shift to the use of big trucks over the years so that the percentage of vehicles that impose a net cost on the system is rising.
>
> This is certainly one of the major reasons why restoration needs are outpacing the supplementary state funds that are supported by state taxes and used for maintenance needs. The economically most efficient way to restore the balance between maintenance fund availability and maintenance needs is to reduce the needs rather than raise the fund. This is because the high maintenance needs are caused in the first place by the failure of the big trucks to cover the costs of their actions and consequently this deprives society of a way to tell whether they place a high enough value on their action to cover the social costs involved.

AMERICAN TRUCKING ASSOCIATION (ATA)

The basic structure of the American Trucking Association may be likened to a tripod, with the state trucking associations, national headquarters, and the national conferences serving as the three legs supporting the trucking industry. A number of state associations were in existence before the founding of ATA in 1933, and prior to that there were local organizations in some of the larger metropolitan areas. Today, there are 51 state associations, each virtually autonomous and at the same time an integral part of ATA. State affiliates have their own governing bodies, bylaws, dues structures, and programs, but ATA's board of directors has established basic criteria for membership of affiliates in the national body. This was done to ensure that in order for ATA to be the sole spokesman for the trucking industry, it must be truly representative of that industry. For example, ATA insists that membership in all state affiliates "be open to all classes and types of motor carriers of property, with equitable and adequate representation and voice for all."

Because the size and extent of the trucking industry varies from state to state, so does the size of the various state associations. Offices of state associations range from quite small staffs up to those with nearly a hundred employees. While motor carriers pledge financial resources directly to ATA, their membership in ATA technically is held only through their affiliated state associations.

The ATA national conferences came into being shortly after the founding of the parent organization. They were established to deal with problems and matters of particular interest to the various branches of the motor carrier industry. Today, there are thirteen conferences, all created by ATA.

The trucking industry consists generally of two classes of operators, for-hire and private. For-hire truck operators transport goods for others for a fee. Private truck operators transport their own goods in their own trucks. Most interstate for-hire truck operators are of two general kinds, common carriers and contract carriers. There are two basic kinds of common carriers, regular route and irregular route carriers.

The goal of ATA, as stated in the certificate of incorporation, has remained the same: The education, improvement and advancement of the interests of those engaged in the industry.

CAMPAIGN STRATEGY

The overriding objective of ATA's campaign was to counteract the allegedly false and misleading charges being made by AAR in its publicity campaign. ATA believed that the railroad industry's campaign was designed primarily to reduce the trucking industry's competitiveness, thereby allowing the railroads to charge even higher prices than their prevailing rates.

ATA felt that it must correct any misapprehension caused by the railroad industry concerning some critical issues, such as damaging the highway system, trucking subsidization, safety, and fuel efficiency. This objective made ATA's campaign largely reactive in character; the agenda was determined by what AAR did. A further limitation on developing a totally independent strategy was ATA's modest financial resources when compared with those of the railroad industry. John McGill, ATA's managing director for public affairs, comments:

> We have never responded directly or with such vigor to their (AAR's) attacks in the past. We just felt that our business is hauling freight over the highways and their business is hauling freight over the rails, which they do very well, and we leave it at that.
>
> If you do not discern a clear strategy or a campaign in what we are doing, it is because we do not have the financial resources for advertising as the rails do. Therefore we must develop different approaches to do more with less. We make greater use of such things as brochures, news releases, speakers and speeches.

Prior to the current campaign, ATA had pursued a positive approach in its ads. The association emphasized what it did and how it served the public. Even when it came to issues of public policy, the effort was focused on what can be done rather than talking "against" competitors.

Based on its analysis of AAR's charges, ATA decided to concentrate on four issues: new highway financing, damage to highways by heavy trucks, payment for highway repairs, and allocation of highway costs among different groups of users. A brief summary of AAR's assertions and ATA's counterassertions is given below. These points and counterpoints provide the core of ATA's campaign themes. More detailed versions of these themes were presented in booklets that were widely distributed to the press, influentials, and the general public.

AAR: Almost three-fourths of the interstate highway system is obsolete.

ATA: The AAR is using the term obsolete to describe many miles of highway in need of only minor repairs.

AAR: Automobiles pay an unfair share of taxes to maintain the nation's highways.

ATA: Trucks pay a fair share of highway taxes—indeed, heavy trucks, which account for 1 percent of highway use, pay 25 percent of highway taxes.

AAR: Roads were built to carry a maximum of 50,000 pounds. Current heavy trucks exceed this by almost 50 percent.

ATA: Gross weight is not a true measure of highway wear; axle weight is a true measure, and trucks do not overstep this measure.

AAR: 80 percent of all highway damage is attributable to heavy trucks.

ATA: This allegation pertains only to roads that are already weak and underdesigned.

AAR: Fuel taxes fall disproportionately on motorists.

ATA: Trucks pay the "overwhelming" proportion of fuel taxes.

AAR: Motor vehicle travel will increase 30 to 50 percent over the next 15 to 20 years; truck travel will increase 100 percent in that time. This will subject our roads to much greater damage.

ATA: ATA agrees that truck travel will increase by this amount—this is proof of the desirability of trucks for the nation's economy. There is, however, no proof that such damage will result.

IMPLEMENTING THE CAMPAIGN STRATEGY

The first step in ATA's strategy was to develop material for public dissemination that responded to specific AAR claims concerning the relative overall superiority and cost effectiveness of railroads. A cornerstone of that strategy was to label the AAR campaign the "Big Lie."

The "Big Lie"

The first shot in the campaign was fired on June 18, 1981, with a public statement by Bennett Whitlock, president of ATA:

> The railroad industry has launched a massive lobbying, public relations, and advertising campaign aimed at recovering their long-lost competitive advantage vis-à-vis the trucking industry.
>
> Their thinly disguised purpose is being pursued at both the state and federal levels and has two objectives:
> 1. the imposition of unreasonable taxes upon truck owners and operators, and
> 2. artificially restricting the productivity of the trucking industry.

> The railroads are relying upon the so-called "Big Lie" technique: you make a statement sufficiently outrageous, publicize it, repeat it often enough, and people will come to believe it. . . .

The implementation of the "Big Lie" strategy called for a combination of different tools of mass communication, including special studies, press kits, contacts with news editors, legislators, and members of Congress, and paid advertising. The campaign was to be carried out not only by ATA, but by all member carriers through their own advertising and public relations efforts. The communication style was to be aggressive and assertive. Notwithstanding the new aggressive stance, ATA's John McGill maintained:

> Our ads are designed for a specific audience and we feel we are reaching them. One can get a lot of attention just by running pretty ads. Our ads do not tell people to take a position, they simply try to present our side of the issue, which we feel is not getting the right exposure in the news media. We are trying to correct misapprehensions.

In consultation with industry leaders, ATA developed and circulated a list of eight topics that were to be emphasized in the campaign. ATA also outlined possible copy messages that could be used in addressing those topics. These were: role of highways, improved productivity, safety, energy conservation, sophistication, total transportation, financing, and special equipment.

Print Campaign

In 1981 ATA ran two ads. The first one addressed the idea that railroads are not competitive with the trucking industry. The ad carried the headline: "Shoemaker (And Railroad Executive)—Stick to Your Last!" The ad, which was a single insertion in the *Wall Street Journal,* suggests that railroads believe they can gain a competitive advantage by raising the taxes on trucks. Trucks, however, offer efficient, flexible, door-to-door service. Rails cannot match truck service for volume. The ad emphasizes that the American consumer should not be fooled by the rail campaign and concluded that to relieve the American taxpayer of a burden, the railroad industry should be paying federal taxes on its fuel and equipment, just as the trucking industry does [Exhibit 1].

The second ad used an issue-answer format and appeared in the *Washington Journalism Review.* It focused on the alleged attempts by the railroad industry to fool members of the news media with false and misleading statements about the nation's trucking industry, and asserted that the journalists were a lot smarter and were not going to be fooled by the railroad industry [Exhibit 2].

Exhibit 1

Shoemaker (And Railroad Executive): Stick to Your Last!

Despite years of Federal handouts and special treatment by Congress, the railroads are not competitive with the trucking industry.

So, they have returned to their same old shopworn charges, their same low tactics, with the same old goal: if you can't compete in the marketplace, then tax your competitor to death and artificially restrict his productivity.

The railroads apparently believe they can gain a competitive advantage if they can increase taxes on trucks, while at the same time imposing out-of-date truck size and weight limits. If they are successful, the result will be higher transportation rates and less efficient service. The obvious loser is the American consumer.

No question about it—rails move heavy bulk commodities efficiently and economically. This is good freight for the railroads. But trucks offer efficient, flexible, door-to-door service to every community in the nation. That's why trucks receive 57 percent of the total intercity transportation revenue.

Rails simply cannot match truck service for the large volume of freight that trucks move efficiently, dependably, and economically. And the rails know this.

The rails' only hope of recapturing some of this freight now moving by truck is to push up the trucking industry's cost of doing business. This in turn would push up truck rates. At some point, the rails apparently reason, shippers would either be willing or forced to shift their freight to less efficient rail transportation.

The American consumer should not be fooled by the rail campaign, which is being carried on by extensive (and expensive) advertising, public relations and lobbying at both the state and Federal levels. The railroads pose as public spirited corporate citizens who are trying to protect the nation's highway investment. That is a farce. Their campaign can only result in raising everyone's cost of doing business . . . and everyone's cost of living.

The railroads accuse other modes of transportation of being subsidized. In a statement on the floor of the U.S. House of Representatives on June 30, 1980, Rep. James J. Florio of New Jersey, Chairman of the Subcommittee on Transportation and Commerce, pointed out that more than $11 billion had been spent in Federal rail subsidies over the previous five years. Billions more taxpayers' dollars have been spent since.

To relieve the American taxpayer of this burden, the railroad industry should be paying federal taxes on its fuel and equipment, just as the trucking industry does.

In 1979, over-the-road trucks paid $1.8 billion into the Highway Trust Fund to maintain a highway system that benefits all Americans. This constitutes 25.1 percent of the receipts of the Highway Trust Fund, though over-the-road trucks comprise only 1.1 percent of all vehicles.

It is time for the railroad industry to pay Federal taxes on its fuel and equipment. It is time for the American taxpayer to get a break.

And it is time for the railroad executives to stick to railroads and quit trying to be highway engineers and highway tax experts.

American Trucking Associations, Inc.
1616 P Street, N.W.
Washington, D.C. 20036

Exhibit 2

ISSUE:

The railroads are attempting to manipulate the news media through propaganda targeted against America's trucking industry.

ANSWER:

The nation's journalists are a lot smarter than the rail industry thinks they are.

Railroads have always been good at blaming their problems on someone else. First they claimed they were over-regulated and couldn't make a buck. Now, rails have the deregulation they fought so hard for and they're still complaining that things are unfair.

Their latest complaint is that trucks are "subsidized" because they use public highways to move the nation's freight.

What a phoney issue! Trucks pay for their use of the highways through state and federal taxes. And the trucking industry pays its fair share of these taxes.

The railroads deal in vague terms, complaining that all motorists suffer by having to pay a portion of the cost for roads that trucks also use.

But the facts are far from vague!

It's a fact that heavy trucks account for only one percent of vehicle registrations, yet they pay 25 percent of all federal highway taxes collected in the United States.

Trucks of all sizes make up 20 percent of the vehicles on the road but pay 50 percent of the federal taxes that support the nation's highway system. In plain dollars and cents, the owner of a typical car pays $33 into the Federal Highway Trust Fund, while the owner of an over-the-road tractor trailer pays 54 times that much— $1,782. When state taxes are added, trucks pay annual taxes of $4,572 compared to $127 for autos.

The $33 that a car owner pays came from the federal fuel and tire taxes. Heavy trucks pay these taxes also, but, in addition, trucks pay excise taxes on new trucks and trailers, parts and accessories, and a special truck weight tax.

It should be clear that trucks don't get a free ride. But what about the railroads? At least one U.S. Congressman estimated the federal subsidy to railroads at $11 BILLION during the past five years alone. Now, *that's* subsidy!

The next time the railroads (or any other group) sound off about who is being "subsidized," think twice about their motives and challenge what you hear.

We will be happy to tell you what the facts really are!

News Service Department
American Trucking Associations, Inc.
1616 P Street, N.W.
Washington, D.C. 20036
(202) 797-5237

Washington Journalism Review, May; *Quill*, June; *Columbia Journalism Review*, July-August.

ATA also ran two small special news featurettes called "Fancy That" and "Facts and Figures" that addressed the idea that road transportation (and trucks) are energy-efficient both in absolute terms and also when compared with the rails. Exhibit 3 is illustrative of the ads run by ATA member companies and deals with the topics of the highway trust fund and highway cost sharing.

EFFECTIVENESS OF THE CAMPAIGN

It is difficult to isolate the impact of the campaign. There was not enough frequency for individual ATA ads, and many other ads were placed by the member companies. Moreover, the advertising effort was only a small part of the overall campaign, whose important elements were those of special reports distributed to opinion leaders in major areas. Therefore, measures of campaign effectiveness have to be indirect, focused on changes in public attitudes and opinion about the trucking industry.

The ATA campaign, however, did attract the attention of the advertising industry and was the subject of a major article by Alfred Edelson that ran in *Advertising Age* on July 6, 1981, and was entitled: "Two Transportation Associations Go Head to Head in Advocacy Ads Intended to Influence Anyone Who Will Listen."

Findings of Public Opinion Survey

A public opinion survey was jointly shared by Monsanto and ATA and conducted by Market Facts. It was based on phone interviews of 1,002 licensed drivers, age 18 and older between March 31 and April 19, 1981. The objectives were to ascertain public attitudes toward the trucking industry and public perception of truck operators, manufacturers, and truck drivers on key topics. Major findings of the survey are summarized below:

1. *Industry Ratings in Holding Down Inflation*. None of the industries measured received a positive majority rating, but the trucking industry didn't fare too badly. The positive ratings were: Telephone industry, 42 percent; airline industry, 34 percent; trucking industry, 31 percent; railroad industry, 22 percent; electric power, 22 percent; and automobile industry, 14 percent.

2. *Attitudes toward and Perceptions of the Trucking Industry*. Fully 61 percent of the public offered at least one positive impression of the trucking industry, while 43 percent offered at least one negative impression; 14 percent of the respondents have no positive views of the industry, and 32 percent have no negative impressions. By a margin of two to one, a majority of the public regards truck owners and operators as concerned with the public interest. Sixty-three percent of the public now agrees that trucks pay their fair share of highway costs, up sharply from the 45 percent who felt this way in 1962 in a similar Market Facts study; 18 percent disagree, and 19 percent are not sure. But in another part of the interview, after being told how much cars and trucks pay in annual highway use taxes,

Exhibit 3

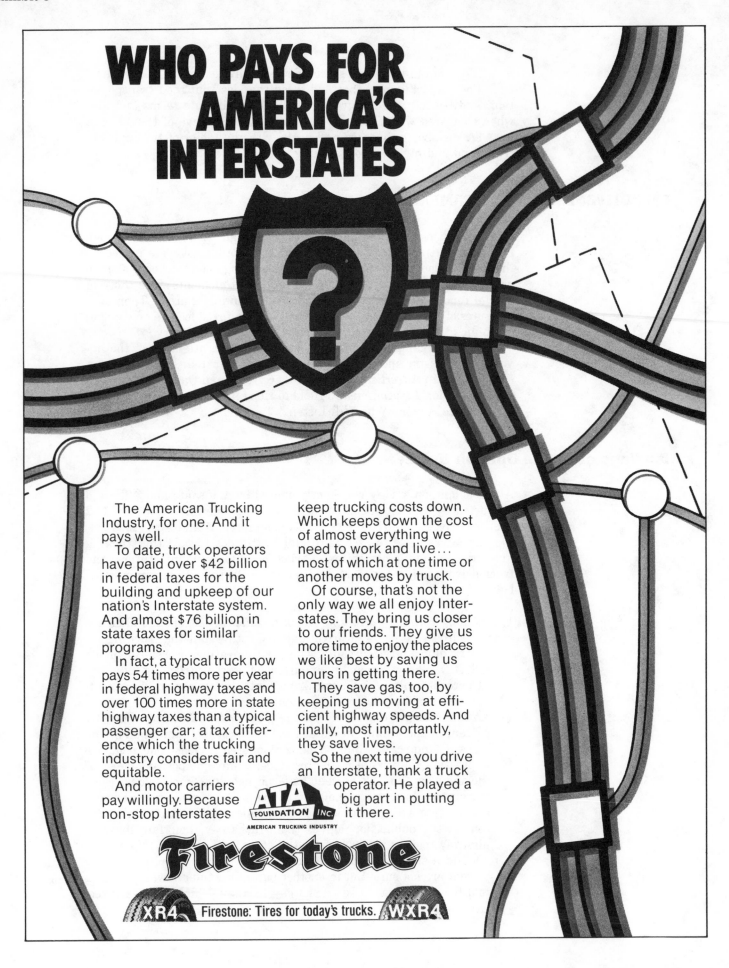

WHO PAYS FOR AMERICA'S INTERSTATES

The American Trucking Industry, for one. And it pays well.

To date, truck operators have paid over $42 billion in federal taxes for the building and upkeep of our nation's Interstate system. And almost $76 billion in state taxes for similar programs.

In fact, a typical truck now pays 54 times more per year in federal highway taxes and over 100 times more in state highway taxes than a typical passenger car; a tax difference which the trucking industry considers fair and equitable.

And motor carriers pay willingly. Because non-stop Interstates keep trucking costs down. Which keeps down the cost of almost everything we need to work and live... most of which at one time or another moves by truck.

Of course, that's not the only way we all enjoy Interstates. They bring us closer to our friends. They give us more time to enjoy the places we like best by saving us hours in getting there.

They save gas, too, by keeping us moving at efficient highway speeds. And finally, most importantly, they save lives.

So the next time you drive an Interstate, thank a truck operator. He played a big part in putting it there.

ATA FOUNDATION INC.
AMERICAN TRUCKING INDUSTRY

Firestone

XR4   Firestone: Tires for today's trucks.   WXR4

the response was as follows: 23 percent thought trucks paid more than their share, 62 percent thought the amount paid by trucks was just right, 10 percent reported trucks paid less than their share, and only 6 percent were not sure.

3. *Safety and Driver Courtesy.* Forty-seven percent of the public sees the industry as making some progress over the past five years in improving driver safety records, while 23 percent reported the industry has made a lot of progress. In volunteering general information, 56 percent of the respondents state that truckdrivers are courteous, helpful, and safe, and 14 percent mention their driving experience and professionalism. In a comparative safety evaluation of truck drivers and automobile drivers, 68 percent of the sample stated that truckdrivers were better than automobile drivers, 24 percent said they were about the same, and 4 percent said they were worse. As for the 55 MPH speed limit, this is one aspect of the survey where truckdrivers received bad marks. Only 10 percent said they were about the same, and 44 percent said they were worse than automobile drivers.

4. *Experiences with Truck-Related Problems on the Highway.* Motorists were asked to identify problems they encountered on their last trip on the highway from a list read to them by the interviewer. When asked which of these problems they considered major or minor when encountered, the order of annoyance or "aggravation index" was: 27 percent, splash and spray; 27 percent, tailgating; 17 percent, lane changing; 16 percent, speeding; 14 percent, turbulence and sway; 13 percent, driving side-by-side; and 12 percent too fast down hill.

5. *Attitudes toward Trucking Industry Policy Issues.* Almost two-thirds of the public believes that trucks pay just about the right amount in highway use taxes, and about a quarter believe that trucks pay more than their share. Of the 52 percent who were able to offer a substantive estimate of the amount paid by the typical over-the-road truck in highway use taxes, 39 percent based their estimate on a sign they saw on a truck, 32 percent indicated their estimate was based on nothing factual, 3 percent claimed to have gotten it from an ad appearing in a newspaper, and 25 percent said they got it from a wide variety of sources, including magazines, television, and word of mouth from friends and co-workers.

A majority of the respondents were receptive to different truck configurations if it would improve fuel conservation and reduce air pollution. The public generally disagrees (68 to 18 percent) that larger trucks are safer, easier to handle, sway less, or turn more easily. However, by a 50 to 38 percent majority, the public agrees that "larger trucks ought to be encouraged since they can haul freight with a fuel savings of up to 30 percent." This argument was more widely accepted by those in lower age groups, as well as those in upper income levels.

The majority of the respondents favored federal rather than state control over weight limits or were in favor of uniform national load limits (56 to 38 percent), with just 6 percent undecided.

Part VII   CAMPAIGNS BY STATE-OWNED AND QUASI-GOVERNMENT AGENCIES

Chapter 18   **BRITISH RAILWAYS BOARD,
UNITED KINGDOM:**

**AN ADVOCACY CAMPAIGN BY
A STATE-OWNED ENTERPRISE
TO BRING PRESSURE ON
THE BRITISH GOVERNMENT
FOR INCREASED INVESTMENT
IN BRITISH RAILWAYS**

In June 1980 the British Railways Board (BR), a state-owned monopoly, launched an advocacy advertising campaign designed to bring pressure on the government to increase the level of capital investment in the railways. This was done at a time when the country was suffering a high level of inflation, budget deficits, and an unfavorable balance of trade and payments with the world. The industry in general was mired in excessive unutilized capacity, outmoded plants, and low labor productivity. The situation would have been worse but for the revenues from the North Sea oil.

In the public debate, a large part of the blame for this national malaise was being placed on the government's spending on social programs

Research Assistant: Mahmoud Elfekey.

and ever-increasing subsidization of state-owned but money-losing enterprises like the National Coal Board (the coal monopoly), British Steel (the steel monopoly), British Airways (the national airline), and British Leyland (the state-owned auto company). Britain has a long history of taking over money-losing private enterprises with a view to rationalizing their structure, modernizing their plant and equipment, and above all protecting jobs. However, job protection, when coupled with restrictive work rules, industrial strife, and strong trade unions, inevitably came into conflict with the drive for modernization and improved productivity, and resulted in further red ink and even bigger government subsidies. This unhappy situation brought the Conservative government of Margaret Thatcher into power on the promise of a strong stand against the unions, a reduction in the size of state-owned enterprises, and cutbacks in state subsidies.

The sociopolitical environment for the campaign could not have been more inhospitable for BR. On the one hand, it had to fight its traditional constituency of employees and workers in its effort to improve productivity, for which it needed the support of the Conservative party and a favorable public opinion. On the other hand, it also had to oppose the same Conservative elements to seek a greater share of the government's resources for a state-owned monopoly, a policy that ran counter to both the philosophy and the party platform of the victorious Conservative party.

ISSUES FOR ANALYSIS

That the campaign largely succeeded in its broad objective is a testament to a thoughtful strategy well executed. The success of the strategy, however, has brought into sharp focus some broad issues of public policy that must be faced. In particular:

1. By what rationale, if any, should a state-owned enterprise speak out against the public policies and programs of a democratically elected government? Clearly, all government agencies are expected to engage in internal dialogue and lobbying to seek their "fair" share of government budgets. However, this is in-house debate, and once compromises have been reached, they become part of the government's agenda. From every perspective, British Rail's advocacy campaign was political in character. Under these circumstances, should a state-owned entity, whose management is not elected by the people, engage in a direct political campaign? Where would its mandate come from? Would it make a difference if, for example, as in the United States, these agencies were not part of the executive branch, but independently established entities like the Federal Trade Commission, or those having a separate charter like the TVA?

2. To the extent that a state-owned enterprise engages in political rhetoric and grassroots lobbying, who does it speak for? Moreover, what criteria of public accountability might be considered appropriate to evaluate its legitimacy? The management of such an enterprise clearly does not speak for its stockholders (the government). Does it speak

for the corporate entity, for itself, or for its other traditional constituencies—employees, suppliers, consumers, and so on? Can the management of such an enterprise claim a public constituency separate and independent of a democratically elected government, of which it is a part?

3. In case the programs advocated by a state-owned enterprise are likely to adversely affect other government-sponsored programs or agencies, the government can, in theory, provide the public with information about alternatives or opposing viewpoints. However, should this not happen, how does the public receive information to balance that provided by the advertiser? Does the state have an obligation to provide such information?

4. An associated question would be the financial interests of a privately owned enterprise or industry that might be adversely affected by the success of the advocacy campaign of a state-owned enterpriser in changing competitive conditions in the marketplace.

5. A monopoly operates with a specific franchise from the state and the public. It carries a special burden of serving the public interest in return for privileges accrued to it under its monopoly powers. In the United States, there are regulations about public advocacy or grassroots lobbying by such regulated entities as power utilities to ensure that the private monopolies do not abuse their powers by passing on the expense of such campaigns to consumers in higher rates or charges. No such constraints, however, seem to exist on BR, which is not only a state-owned enterprise, but also a monopoly in the sense that there is no other national railroad company. Should there be a process by which private parties are provided equal access, without serious financial burden, to reach the public and respond to claims made by private or public monopolies?

BRITISH RAILWAYS BOARD—THE CORPORATION

British Railways Board (BR) was organized in 1962 under the Transport Act and given the task of breaking even in its operations within six years. The government was to cover its deficits in the interim period. This target has never been achieved, and the date has been moved back every year. The government eventually recognized that passenger service, although unprofitable, was socially necessary and must be supported with state subsidies. This is called "the contract" with government for which BR receives a public subsidy.

BR is a transport conglomerate with interests in passenger service, freight hauling, shipping, engineering and construction, hotels and other property management, and advertising services on its various modes of transportation. It is a major national business consisting of some twenty million passenger miles, 169 million tons of freight, and jointly with its partners, a group of interrelated businesses. Despite tremendous success in reducing overall deficits, it was expected to lose about £26.5 million in 1981, down from £79 million in 1980. However, if interest charges are excluded, BR actually generated a surplus from continuous operations of £25.5 million in 1981, compared with a deficit of £26.3 million in 1980.

BR must maintain a delicate balance between the commercial railways and the social railways. For the former, it must depend on the government—its stockholder and banker—to support it in lean times, to allow it to retain part of internally generated revenues, and also to provide additional capital for expansion and growth. For the latter, it must persuade the government to pay reasonable charges to cover the cost of other unprofitable, but socially necessary, passenger and commuter services. BR ranks somewhat in the middle of the spectrum of all state-owned enterprises in terms of its public image. Public opinion polls show that British Gas is viewed as the most efficiently run of all the state-owned enterprises in Britain, while British Leyland is perceived to be the least efficient and is lowest in public popularity.

Need for New Investment

Investment in BR since 1945 has not followed a consistent pattern based on corporate needs, but has reflected the changing priorities and political exigencies of successive governments. In the immediate postwar years, government policy was directed toward building up export trade, and the railways were neglected. There followed a period of some ten years when a very high level of investment was made available on the basis of the 1955 modernization plan. According to BR:

> Since 1956, the allocations given by the government have been considerably less than the level needed to renew the assets required for the present scale of railway activity. The position has improved somewhat over the last few years, and the gap is now only about £80.0 million per year against a total annual requirement of around £340.0 million needed to keep BR as a going concern in a "steady state" future.[1]

BR asserts, however, that it will be necessary to spend £120 million a year, considerably more than the "steady state" level, for a number of years in the 1980s and 1990s on the replacement and modernization of locomotives and rolling stock track and signaling equipment. This peak replacement period will have to be extended over about ten or fifteen years because of, among other things, the inability of the railway supply industry to meet such a heavy demand.

Organizational Structure

BR is managed by a fifteen-member board comprised of eight inside and seven outside members. All the outside members are part-time members. Therefore, the numbers notwithstanding, real decision-making power rests with the inside members. Sir Peter Parker is chairman of the board.

Grant Woodruff, director of public affairs, manages the corporate communications program, with an annual budget of over £20 million. This includes all product and corporate advertising, employee communications, press relations, and other aspects of public relations. He is one of the very few staff executives who reports directly to Sir Peter Parker.

Antecedents to the Advocacy Campaign

For a number of years, BR had engaged in a conventional institutional image-building campaign. However, it was not yielding good results. According to Woodruff, who moved to his job from within BR in early 1978, the campaign lacked both a clear strategy and an identification of specific publics. Moreover, according to Woodruff, "Sir Peter had felt, quite rightly, that we weren't getting our message properly to the people in the corridors of power."

The company's advertising effort was being managed by three different agencies covering different parts of its business, none of which talked to the other, with the result that the advertising effort was quite fragmented. At the same time, BR was facing two major problems:

1. Investments had been handicapped for many years by inadequate financial structures that were devised by government as a means of controlling expenditure by the public sector, with little regard for the needs of British Rail as a commercial organization.
2. BR felt it needed a far greater commitment to electrification than the 21 percent of the network currently electrified. This was a low proportion when compared with any other European country, and grossly inadequate if the railways were to play their proper role in the economic and social development of the UK over the next quarter of a century.

BR considered that its prosperity and that of its customers and the entire economy depended on getting realistic levels of support and investment by the government. Therefore, it decided that it should develop a comprehensive and coordinated communications program to inform people of the problems that faced the railways connected with the central government.

The work on the new campaign started in November 1979. As a first step, BR decided to consolidate all its advertising business in one agancy. After competitive presentations, Allen, Brady & Marsh Ltd. (ABM) was chosen to handle the account.

THE ADVOCACY CAMPAIGN—FIRST PHASE (1980–1981)

BR's Rationale

Because BR was a national industry owned by the state, it had to approach the matter of increasing its investment carefully to avoid any conflict with the government's other policies.

The political realities were constantly in the minds of the BR and its ad agency executives. According to David Hall, ABM account executive:

> A lot of marginal seats are in commuterland. This is something I get nervous of being specific about. But we have always been aware that it is a political campaign. It places a lever on the people making the decisions.

For both BR and ABM the campaign involved a continuous balancing act—how to exert pressure without alienating those whose support was needed.

BR thus recognized the political character of its campaign. However, it felt perfectly justified in undertaking such a campaign. The company offered an explanation.

BR makes a distinction between a state-owned company engaged in commercial activities and a government department organized to perform a government function. "We are not part of the government. We are a national industry that has its shareholder in the government—the shareholder is also the banker," observes Woodruff. "We have a public charter. It is vitally important for us to swing public opinion—of which the government in power is only a part—in favor of railways. There would be an enormous conflict if we were a government department because in that case we would exist to perform a government function assigned to us."

Woodruff conceded that there would be times when the interests of the corporation would run counter to the policies of the government. However, to the extent that these corporate interests were within the scope of its charter, he would advocate an active lobbying effort both within the government and in the public forum. He states:

> We knew that there would be conflict. We started off knowing that. However, in spite of the conflict this is something that we had to do. We felt we ought to do. We had hoped that there would be a larger transport cake, but if this wasn't going to be the case, we wanted a larger share of the existing transport cake. . . . And it had been very successful. Just because it had never been done before, there was no reason why we shouldn't do it.

Notwithstanding the importance of the issue both as a principle and as an operational concept, it appears that it did not generate any serious debate either in Parliament or in the news media, or for that matter within BR itself.

Decision-Making Process

Role of the Board Chairman. Although BR is a state-owned corporation, with a governing board selected by the government that contains political appointees, the decision-making process for launching the advocacy campaign was quite similar to that found in most U.S. corporations where the CEO played a decisive role. If anything, BR decision-making was even more centralized, and the extent of Sir Peter's involvement more intense and personal, than was the case of any of the U.S. private corporate campaigns.

The initiative for the campaign came from Woodruff at the instigation of Sir Peter Parker, who immediately authorized its implementation. There were no formal meetings of the board, or any effort to seek board approval. The decision was treated primarily as an advertising (operational) decision, for which Sir Peter had the authority to give a go ahead.

One indication of the program's importance can be seen in the amount of time and attention given it by the board chairman: "All advertisements, including every word of copy, were vetted by BR Chairman, Sir Peter Parker. Some were altered or even cancelled at the last minute, sometimes because of changes in the political climate."

An analysis of the decision-making process within BR compared with the one followed by major U.S. corporations showed that there were no discernible differences between the two types of organizations, even when the issue involved was political in nature. Regardless of the merits of the case, it would appear that the public accountability obligation of a state-owned organization, and a monopoly at that, was not any broader than that perceived by the top managements of stockholder-owned companies in the United States. In both cases CEOs made the decision as a corporate decision, as good for the organization, and without seeking even symbolic approval from the owners' representatives, the board of directors.

This may be an organizationally efficient process. It may also suggest that large organizations have certain structural characteristics which create an internal momentum providing very large degrees of discretion to the CEOs. The fact that such a company is owned by private stockholders or the state does not appear to affect significantly its obligation of public accountability. As Woodruff aptly points out:

> We argue that we are a business organization which has a contract with the government for the provision of certain socially desirable services. We have a contract to provide those services. We have been running at a loss for the last 18 months because of the recession in Britain, but until then we were making a profit. That profit incorporated a contract with the railways to provide those services which on their own could not be profitably provided. As businessmen we would close the commuter railways into London. We would also close the passenger services in the rural areas. The government wants these services to remain. This being the case, we are asking the government to specify what it wants and we will undertake to provide these services under a contract and at a specified cost. That's the way it works. We are a self-sustaining business organization. Therefore, the conflict that you [the author] are suggesting doesn't really arise.

Role of the Advertising Agency. Another distinctive feature of the BR campaign was the extensive involvement of the ad agency, ABM, in all phases of the campaign. After detailed briefing from Woodruff, agency staff helped in the development of the original concept, strategy formulation, selection of target audiences, the development of ad copy, placement of advertisements, and tracking and evaluation studies.

Objectives of the Campaign

Following intensive discussion between BR executives and ABM representatives, three objectives were identified for the campaign:

1. To create a positive climate of opinion that would secure public recognition of the need for higher priority to be given to the railways as an essential and desirable subject for increased financial backing from the community.
2. To illuminate and stimulate the debate about financing the railways.
3. To change the image of the railways from a somewhat unappreciated and misunderstood national industry to a picture of a modern, well-led, well-managed, efficient and popular customer-oriented business.

Target Audiences

The target audience was primarily opinion leaders, especially articulate, active commuters likely to influence the situation. According to Woodruff, "We found that there were four other groups that we hadn't properly identified. The members of parliament (MPs), and all the pressure groups that go with them, our own staff, the trade unions and Trade Union Congress associated with us, and the suppliers of services and material." Opinion leaders, therefore, included politicians, especially MPs, local authority leaders, heads of industry, the media, and senior civil servants. Beyond that, any additional audience of influential people that could be attracted was considered a positive factor: "Because we are a national corporation, one of our publics is the nation as a whole."

Within this broad group, BR also recognized a specific subset in London commuters. According to Woodruff:

> They [the commuters] are not only our most dissatisfied customers, but are also extremely important as opinion formers, constituting a serious political pressure group in the Southeast. Our objective in addressing commuters was to make them aware that the economics of operating the commuter network are such that British Rail alone cannot solve the problems. The financing of the network needs to be reviewed by all those involved—the government, those who use the commuter services and those who benefit from them, as well as British Rail.

Copy Design and Execution

The copy design and execution were determined jointly by a committee of senior BR and ABM executives having two attributes: advertising skill and political astuteness. The tone of the messages was to be "confident, successful, and authoritative."

It was decided that ad copy would emphasize a need and a strategy. The ads must make the readers aware of the problems that existed between the railways as a state corporation and the state and the nation.

The primary need of the railways was more investment, and this became the theme that tied all BR messages together.

> We have argued that investment was vital for the future of an efficient modern railways system. And it was in the investment

area that we were having the greatest difficulties in achieving authorization from our government, because as our stockholders and bankers, the government must approve our investment decisions, even where the funds for such investments were internally generated.

The advertisements were positioned to indicate that BR trains had a great future and were worth greater financial support than they were getting. The slogan adopted was "This is the age of the train—so make sure you look after your railways." Every corporate ad also carried the following paragraph:

> This is one of a series of advertisements designed to increase public awareness of the position of the railways in the national transport system and also in the life of the community as a whole. While the facts and figures contained in these advertisements are known and appreciated by those directly concerned in shaping the future, an industry as much in the limelight as ours has a duty to address itself to a wider audience, which needs to be well informed, if it is to play its part in helping to form public opinion.

British Railways featured this paragraph on the basis of justifying the expenditure on advertising for corporate purposes, ensuring that its messages received a thorough public airing, and defusing any potential negative or defensive reaction on the part of readers.

The layout of advertising copy, with bold graphics and slick artwork, accompanied by short, crisp copy, again illustrated the influence of an ad agency with a product orientation, and is quite similar to ads for advocacy campaigns in the United States where ad agencies played an important or dominant role.

The message is almost exclusively one-sided, with information content presented in simple terms. The copy avoids the conditions or qualifications that are inevitable in the treatment of a complex subject. No effort is made to educate the public on the "issue" itself, except in the context of BR's position and the policy advocated by the corporation. Thus the copy style is at once both pure advocacy and soft sales pitch. One might therefore raise the legitimate question of how alternative perspectives on these issues might be brought to the public to help people make informed judgments.

Selection of Issues and Copy Themes

The first phase of the campaign, with four advertisements, was designed to create great public awareness of the financial needs of British Railways.

1. "How Long Can We Go on Running the Most Cost Effective Railways in Europe?" This was the lead-off advertisement of the campaign and ran on July 7, 1980. In this ad the company deliberately set out to surprise people who tended to disparage British Rail. Seizing the reader's

attention with this challenging headline, the company advertisement proceeded to tell readers that BR's cost effectiveness represented a very real marketing achievement. However, there was a price for BR's success—the company received a lower level of capital expenditure from the state than any of its European counterparts [Exhibit 1].

2. "Electrification." This second ad ran July 14, 1980. In it, the company set out the basic justification for further electrification of the railways, which would result in greatly reduced fuel consumption, lower costs, and greater reliability. The ad title was "More of Our Financial Resources Could be Used to Save Our Natural Ones." The company rationalized the cost of electrification by stressing the future savings that will result from achieving large-scale electrification now.

3. "Motorway Comparison." The third ad, which ran July 28, 1980, was certainly the most provocative one. With the title of "This is no time to undervalue our railway," the ad compared the cost of one mile of motorway with the cost of four high-speed trains. The real point was to emphasize that the different methods of investment appraisal were used to evalute road and rail projects at the Department of Transport worked to the detriment of the railways [Exhibit 2].

4. "The Trouble with a Chinese Deal Is That an Hour Later You're Hungry Again." This ad, which ran on July 28, 1980, was part of BR's campaign to extol it's achievements in export trade. The essential message was that British Rail's expertise was renowned the world over, but inadequate investment in the company network left the potential for engineering exports to be unfulfilled because the company's home industry was too small.

The unusual nature of the advertisements, at least in the British context, and the special character of the sponsor as a state-owned enterprise, created quite a stir in the British press. Although it did not raise the inherent philosophical questions, such as those raised in Canada when the Canadian government undertook advocacy advertising in support of the reform of the Canadian Constitution, it nevertheless raised issues of the specificity, comparability, and accuracy of individual ad messages.

For example, the corporate motorway advertisement immediately gave rise to the following exchange between MPs in the House of Commons after it appeared.

> MR. ROBERT ADLEY [Conservative, Christchurch and Lymington]: If we are, as we do, to ask British Rail to tell us whether they make profits or losses, is it not odd that we never seem to ask ourselves how much profit or loss we are making on the M1 or the M6?

> MR. NORMAN FOWLER [Secretary of State for Transport, Conservative, Sutton Coldfield]: The comparison between road and rail is something we are trying to make progress on.

> MR. ROBERT McCRINDLE [Conservative, Brentwood and Ongar]: Has he seen the advertisement by British Railways that we should scrap the M25 and therefore be able to meet the cost of a number of the Advanced Passenger Trains?

Exhibit 1

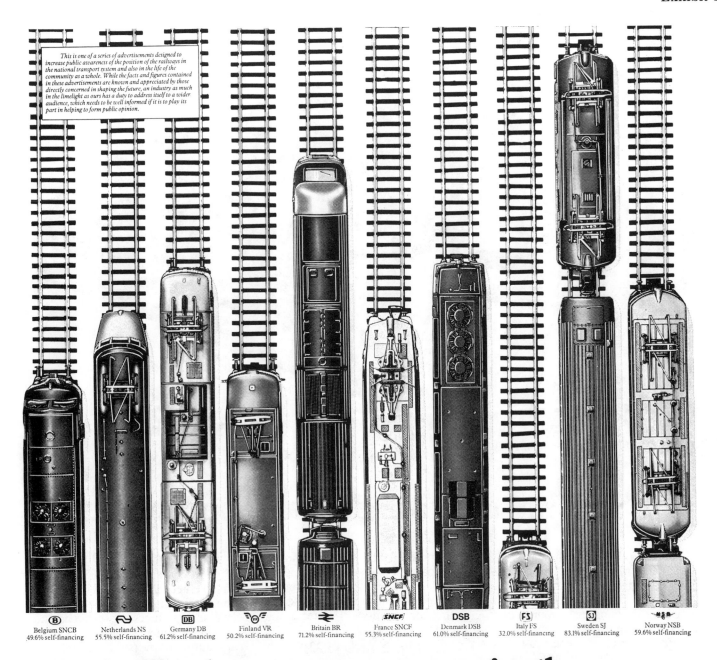

This is one of a series of advertisements designed to increase public awareness of the position of the railways in the national transport system and also in the life of the community as a whole. While the facts and figures contained in these advertisements are known and appreciated by those directly concerned in shaping the future, an industry as much in the limelight as ours has a duty to address itself to a wider audience, which needs to be well informed if it is to play its part in helping to form public opinion.

| ⒷBelgium SNCB 49.6% self-financing | Netherlands NS 55.5% self-financing | DBGermany DB 61.2% self-financing | VRFinland VR 50.2% self-financing | Britain BR 71.2% self-financing | SNCFFrance SNCF 55.3% self-financing | DSBDenmark DSB 61.0% self-financing | FSItaly FS 32.0% self-financing | SJSweden SJ 83.1% self-financing | Norway NSB 59.6% self-financing |

How long can we go on running the most cost-effective major railway in Europe?

COST EFFECTIVE?

No railway in Western Europe is *wholly* self-financing.

However, in Britain *71.2%* of our costs (based on 1977 data) are covered by fares and charges – the highest net contribution to the cost of running a major railway in Western Europe.

Only Sweden, with a relatively small rail network, has a higher self-financing ratio than our own.

A MARKETING ACHIEVEMENT

Here in Britain, where fares are comparatively high, more people are travelling by train than would be expected.

Passenger sales mileage in 1979 was the highest recorded in Britain since 1961, when the network was 30% bigger, and there were less than half as many cars on the road.

The reasons are varied, but, in part:

We have a more extensive range of alternative fares – Awayday; Weekend Return; Senior Citizen, Student and Family Railcards; and the rates vary between routes according to market conditions and quality.

No other railway has adopted market pricing to this extent.

Our continued growth is, therefore, a measure of our commercial ingenuity.

THE PRICE OF SUCCESS

A recent study of European railways, based on 1977 data, showed that, apart from Sweden,* the relative contribution *our* community makes to the cost of rail travel is *the lowest*.

This level of contribution was pegged in 1975 and since then, in real terms, *it has declined*.

Most crucially, the level of investment – (see chart) that is, expenditure on renovation, replacement and improvement for the future – is *also* the lowest in Europe. The repercussions are obvious, as too many of our customers know.

Capital Expenditure by Railways (£ per train kilometre)

BR	SJ	DB	SNCB	NS	SNCF	DSB	NSB	FS	VR
0.264	0.410	0.332	0.368	0.789	0.812	0.823	1.061	1.423	1.992

Unfortunately, today we are running the railway very hard just to stand still.

To replace worn out assets, our current investment levels need to be raised by 30%. Without this extra investment, the consequences will be severe.

THE TIME OF THE TRAIN HAS COME AGAIN

In a world beset by energy shortages, the prospects for the railways have never been brighter. It would be a pity if short-term problems were allowed to eclipse the prospects for rail.

With a far-sighted approach towards finance and investment, Britain can and will go on running the most cost-effective major railway in Europe for as long as the railways run.

*THE SWEDISH EXPERIENCE. Since the collection of data in 1977, the situation of the railways in Sweden has changed drastically. A massive injection of national funds has precipitated a reappraisal of investment plans and the fares structure. The experiment has really only just started but the first signs are that the railways have increased their relative importance in the transport network.

This is the age of the train ⇌

Exhibit 2

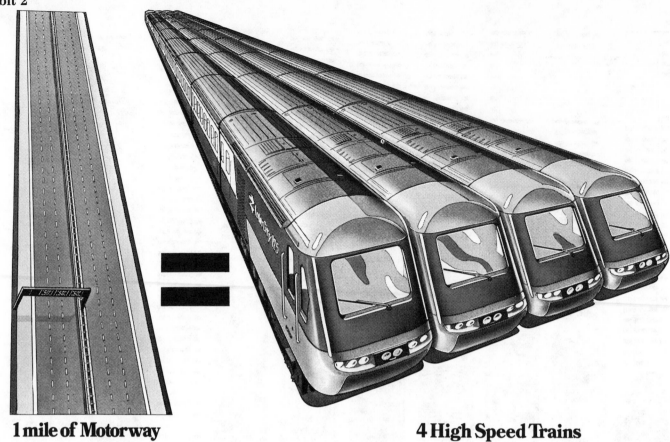

1 mile of Motorway   **4 High Speed Trains**

This is no time to undervalue our railway.

For many years British Rail's investment programmes have been under heavy financial pressure.

Consequently, we've learned how to make limited financial resources go rather further than most.

For instance, the average cost per mile of the sections of the new M25 motorway under construction on 1st February 1980 was £8.4m., allowing for overheads. For this sum we could provide 4 High Speed Trains or electrify 28 miles of route.

In an era of energy shortages and high inflation, this sort of value for money is crucially important.

THE CAR, THE TRAIN, THE FUTURE

Road and rail are intrinsically linked and mutually dependent.

Indeed, modern railway station design is quite overtly geared to providing for the car.

But when money is tight, and both road and rail projects are under consideration, a balance should be achieved, with all projects assessed on their relative merits and subjected to the same kind of tests.

APPLES AND PEARS

Currently, road projects are appraised by a method that takes into consideration the social benefits delivered to travellers–such as the expected time saving, the increased safety and the greater convenience.

These benefits are quantified and included in calculating the return on investment.

On the other hand, rail projects normally have to be justified in purely financial terms.

Social benefits cannot be included in these analyses, although it is usually the case that such benefits heavily outweigh the crude financial returns.

THE ROOT PROBLEM

So long as British Rail's investment criteria are specified in purely financial terms, the allocation of national resources between road and rail development schemes is bound to cause controversy.

MAXIMISING THE POTENTIAL

Financial resources are scarce. They must be allocated so as to provide maximum benefit to the transport system as a whole.

Today, the potential for rail has never been greater. That's why, in weighing the alternatives, this is certainly no time to undervalue the railway.

This is one of a series of advertisements designed to increase public awareness of the position of the railways in the national transport system and also in the life of the community as a whole. While the facts and figures contained in these advertisements are known and appreciated by those directly concerned in shaping the future, an industry as much in the limelight as ours has a duty to address itself to a wider audience, which needs to be well informed if it is to play its part in helping to form public opinion.

This is the age of the train ⇌

> Yet my commuter constituents who bear the whole of the fares and taxes to sustain British Rail and are looking forward to the completion of the M25, consider that public money should not be spent in this way to oppose what is, after all, the Government's policy.

> MR. FOWLER: I agree with him. I do not think this is a particularly distinguished piece of advertising on British Railways' part. I do not think there is any justification for expensive and barren knocking matches between road and rail.

The European comparisons advertisement also gave rise to much discussion. For example, on December 19, 1980, in the House of Commons, the following exchange took place:

> MR. CHRISTOPHER DRUCE [Conservative, Lewisham]: Does the Minister agree that British Rail is one of the least subsidised rail systems in Europe and that if we are to have the standard of the systems in other countries that simply means more public investment, not less.

> KENNETH CLARKE [Under Secretary of State for Transport, Conservative, Rushcliffe]: European comparisons are freely made in this area but they are difficult to make with any accuracy . . . having said that I accept that British Rail is one of the more successful of the European systems in making contributions from its own revenue towards its operating costs.

Then on Radio 4 on January 2 Sir Peter Parker was engaged in a discussion with Norman Fowler and Roy Watts, chief executive of British Airways, on Barry Norman's show, "Going Places." Sir Peter remarked that he had been delighted to learn that in the House the other day Kenneth Clark had said that British Rail was probably the most cost-effective railway in Europe, to which Norman Fowler replied: "I actually don't think too much of all the European comparisons. . . . They can provide a certain amount, but I don't think anyone would seriously doubt that British Rail probably provides the best cost-effective service as far as the public is concerned."

Proceeding from the success of the first phase in creating heightened awareness of the issues surrounding investment in the railways, BR launched the second phase of its corporate campaign, which continued until June 1981. In this phase, the company built on the positive climate created by the first phase to push for investment decisions from the government. Three different tasks were identified:

1. To make use of positive success stories about British Rail in order to project a picture of a modern, well-led business.
2. To preempt negative comments along certain predictable lines of attack.
3. To continue to press explicitly for investment using arguments relating closely to current economic and political issues in the UK.

There were five advertisements in this phase.

1. "Can You Win If You Come in Third?" dealt with the subject of productivity. The company again used European comparisons to show that British Rail was third in productivity and beaten only by two small networks, Holland and Sweden. In the ad, BR detailed many important improvements made during the 1970s which were frequently ignored or overlooked by its critics. The ad asserted that British Railways was determined to remove any cause for criticism in this area, and when this had been done there would no longer be any valid excuse for withholding new investment.

2. "In theory, a monopoly has no competition" dealt with another familiar line of attack on British Railways and ran in June 1981. As a monopoly, British Railways was protected from the rigors of normal competitive commercial activity and therefore allegedly wallowed in idleness and inefficiency. The ad pointed out that British Railways faced intense competition in all aspects of its business, like any ordinary commercial enterprise, but did not enjoy their financial freedom [Exhibit 3].

3. "It's really a big plus!" This ad, which ran on January 19, 1981, focused on the fact that in a year of severe economic recession, BR was able by skillful marketing to maintain its volume at almost the same level as 1979—which had, in fact, been its most successful year for almost two decades.

4. "Why the railways need a drop of Britain's oil" dealt with the issue of investment and ran on June 22, 1981. It suggested that North Sea oil revenues should be used constructively to invest in important national projects and that British Railways was one of them [Exhibit 4].

5. "When the economy thaws, investing in the railways could be just the tip" again dealt with the issue of investment, and ran on June 29, 1981. The ad highlighted the economic benefits which accrue to the community as a whole when government invests in major projects for national industries in a mixed economy.

Media Selection and Schedule—Corporate Campaign

The advertisements were concentrated in quality dailies and Sundays, which were the obvious forum for discussing issues of national importance, and provided direct and immediate access to all opinion leaders, not the least of which were the media themselves. To this were added political magazines.[3] These are highly cost-effective means of adding frequency among the important groups of politicians and civil servants.

The first phase of the corporate campaign was scheduled to run in July 1980. It was four full-page ads and ran in quality press (9 newspapers, dailies and Sundays) and in the political press (5 magazines) at the same time.[2]

Exhibit 3

In theory, a monopoly has no competition...

It's true that British Rail operates the only national railway system in the country. By definition, that should make us a monopoly.

By implication, we should therefore enjoy a cosy existence, sheltered from competition, insensitive to customers' needs, complacent and unadventurous.

Nothing could be further from the truth.

COMPETITION IN EVERY SECTOR

On the passenger side intense competition comes from over 15 million private and company cars owned in this country. Owners who use their cars on business benefit from tax relief. And company car owners (of which Britain has more than anywhere else in Europe) usually have only to find marginal costs, like petrol, out of their own pockets. Not surprisingly, the incentive to use the car is considerable.

Air services provide vigorous competition for British Rail's Inter-City trains.

With the passing of the 1980 Transport Act, long-distance coaches now compete for our business much more actively than before.

In the freight sector, competition is similarly intense. We don't benefit, as road hauliers do, from the UK licensing laws – for example, there is no "quantity" licensing, as in Germany and France, to limit the amount of freight to travel by road. What's more, only now is taxation of

heavy goods vehicles being increased to make the competitive framework fairer.

FINANCIAL BURDENS – WHAT ABOUT FINANCIAL FLEXIBILITY?

We have a statutory obligation to run services which are socially necessary but financially unviable. This is known as the Public Service Obligation – the basis of the annual "contract" between the Government and British Rail. In real terms this has not increased since 1975 – leaving Britain with the least supported major railway in Europe.

If British Rail does not use up the whole of the contract payment in any year the residue cannot be "credited" to the next year.

Monopolies generally enjoy more financial flexibility – and muscle – than other business. But not British Rail. Instead British Rail is restricted by the rules and conventions which apply throughout the UK public sector where, for example, each industry has its External Financing Limit. This represents the maximum sum in terms of "outside finance" that any public sector industry can call on each year. If the economic recession makes it impossible for British Rail to keep within its External Financing Limit, the excess will be deducted from the next year's Limit.

THE SERIOUS IMPLICATIONS

The direct consequence of financial inflexi-

bility is on investment. British Rail's investment per train/Km is lower than that of any other major railway in Western Europe. The railway network needs 30 per cent extra investment just to maintain the present standard of service.

If Britain wants a worthwhile railway system in future, people will have to appreciate the importance of railways, as they have done in other countries.

Investment in the railways is a sound and sensible use of money. This so-called monopoly *can* behave adventurously, *can* stand up to competition and *can* justify its role in the economy.

Do not forget that in 1979 British Rail's recorded passenger miles were actually higher than in 1961, when the rail network was thirty per cent larger and there were only half as many cars on the road.

This is one of a series of advertisements designed to increase public awareness of the position of the railways in the national transport system and also in the life of the community as a whole. Whilst the facts and figures contained in these advertisements are known and appreciated by those directly concerned in shaping the future, an industry as much in the limelight as ours has a duty to address itself to a wider audience, which needs to be well informed if it is to play its part in helping to form public opinion.

So much for theory.

This is the age of the train ⮀

Exhibit 4

Why the railways need a drop of Britain's oil.

To conserve world energy supplies, it is crucially important that all countries optimise their transport systems.

It is clear that other countries attach a greater priority to the development of their transport systems than does Britain. 1977 figures show that West Germany devoted 1.3% of GDP to rail and road investment, France 1.2%, and Italy 1% while the UK devoted 0.8%. Yet both West Germany and France already had superior road and rail networks.

Why should there be this difference in priorities?

One explanation perhaps is energy resources – they have no oil of their own and Britain does. Time, for once, has been on our side.

In the financial year 1979/80, government revenue (royalties and tax) from North Sea Oil was £2.32 billion. Official estimates of June 1980 expected 1984 revenue to be about £6.5 billion.

Wealth on this scale needs to be made the most of. One of the benefits it could bring is to free the railways from the rust of neglect.

OIL FOR NEW JOINTS AND OLD

Much of British Rail's equipment originated from the 1956 Modernisation Plan – a strategic decision to update the railways with a massive injection of money, the equivalent of £7.2 billion today. This equipment is now nearing the end of its serviceable life. We are rapidly reaching the point where 'mend and make do' is not only not enough, it can be harmful. Without extra money, by 1990, 3,000 miles of track will be unusable, many of our signal installations will be more than 50 years old, and the condition of rolling stock will have deteriorated much further.

An injection of investment would not only provide much needed renewals to make the railways run more smoothly, a major electrification programme could *even* conserve oil.

LUBRICATING THE ECONOMY

Greater investment for British Rail would, in turn, provide a shot in the arm for British Rail's suppliers, the majority being in the private sector. They would benefit from increased orders for rail equipment. These companies are of great importance to Britain's economy. They employ thousands of people and could employ more.

Railways are once again in expansion throughout the world. With our widely acknowledged rail expertise, there is a growing export potential for Britain. A thriving home market generated by a long term commitment to railway investment can only strengthen our capacity to export.

TIME TO TURN ON THE PUMP

Having our own oil, there is nothing strange in advocating that we should follow the example of countries who don't.

The point is, of course, that we must ensure that the North Sea's benefits are put to good use – before they begin to run out.

Surely one of the best uses of oil revenue today is the provision of a better transport system for tomorrow.

So when the oil does begin to run out, at least it will have helped to free the wheels for a better railway.

This is one of a series of advertisements designed to increase public awareness of the position of the railways in the national transport system and also in the life of the community as a whole. Whilst the facts and figures contained in these advertisements are known and appreciated by those directly concerned in shaping the future, an industry as much in the limelight as ours has a duty to address itself to a wider audience, which needs to be well informed if it is to play its part in helping to form public opinion.

This is the age of the train ⇌

The Commuter Campaign October—November 1980

Commuters are of special interest to British Rail. They are not only the most dissatisfied customers, but are also extremely important as opinion leaders, constituting a serious political pressure group in the Southeast. In October 1980, British Railways felt it was necessary to address the issue of operating the commuter network to the commuters and to make them aware of the problem of investment. This was important from the viewpoint of BR, especially after the government, early in 1980, had asked the Monopolies and Mergers Commission to investigate British Railways' running of the commuter services in London and the Southeast. The commission was to report during October 1980, and the company knew the issue would be prominent. BR therefore timed the commuter campaign to appear just before the report was issued, welcoming the opportunity to debate the issues in public.

In the commuter campaign advertisements, BR positioned itself as a caring organization, concerned about the commuter's lot. However, it needed the help of the commuters to make things better. The slogan, "This Is the Age of the Train," was also used to connect the commuter campaign with the corporate campaign.

The commuter campaign consisted of a series of quite provocative messages that debated key issues affecting the commuters and British Railways.

1. "Commuters have been up against it long enough" was the first ad in the campaign and ran on October 6, 1980. Empathizing with the commuter, the ad copy goes on to say: "Have you ever felt that complaining about your daily journey is like banging your head against a wall. Maybe it was. But the wall is now coming down." BR stated that it was expressing its views about how it saw the problem in a series of statements. As part of the BR effort to serve commuters, BR offered a booklet called "Toward a Commuter Charter," available by writing to BR [Exhibit 5].
2. "Could we reach the point of no return?" ran on October 6, 1980. The ad clearly set out the sobering facts about the state of the network in the southern region. The cause was shortage of money. Commuters were encouraged to express their views through their elected representative or a consumer group or the media.
3. "Where does the money go?" was the third ad, and it ran on October 13, 1980. The ad explained how British Railways spent its investments to increase safety, reliability, and handling efficiency.
4. "How We Took the Spaghetti out of Our Junction" was the fourth ad in the series, and ran on October 13, 1980. In this ad, British Railways took the opportunity to proclaim one of its great successes, the story of developing London Bridge, one of British Railways major achievements during the 1970s and a major bottleneck in the commuter network.
5. "Who Benefits?" was the last ad in the commuter campaign and ran on October 20, 1980. The ad asks "who pays," and "who benefits." BR argues for additional investment in British Railways and the benefits that it would accrue to British society [Exhibit 6].

Exhibit 5

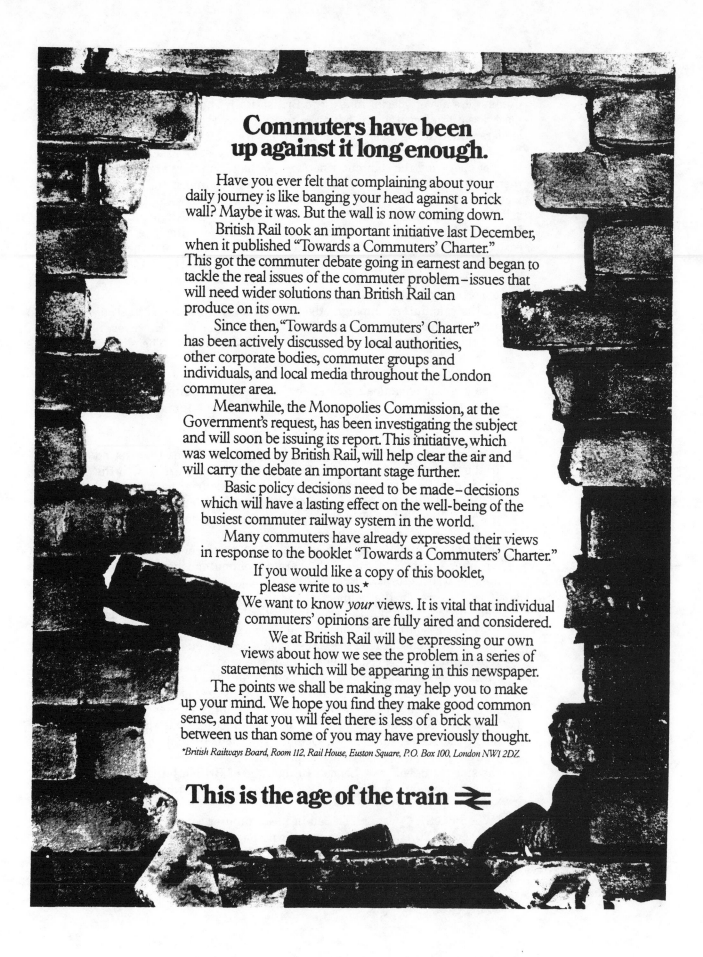

Commuters have been up against it long enough.

Have you ever felt that complaining about your daily journey is like banging your head against a brick wall? Maybe it was. But the wall is now coming down.

British Rail took an important initiative last December, when it published "Towards a Commuters' Charter." This got the commuter debate going in earnest and began to tackle the real issues of the commuter problem – issues that will need wider solutions than British Rail can produce on its own.

Since then, "Towards a Commuters' Charter" has been actively discussed by local authorities, other corporate bodies, commuter groups and individuals, and local media throughout the London commuter area.

Meanwhile, the Monopolies Commission, at the Government's request, has been investigating the subject and will soon be issuing its report. This initiative, which was welcomed by British Rail, will help clear the air and will carry the debate an important stage further.

Basic policy decisions need to be made – decisions which will have a lasting effect on the well-being of the busiest commuter railway system in the world.

Many commuters have already expressed their views in response to the booklet "Towards a Commuters' Charter."

If you would like a copy of this booklet, please write to us.*

We want to know *your* views. It is vital that individual commuters' opinions are fully aired and considered.

We at British Rail will be expressing our own views about how we see the problem in a series of statements which will be appearing in this newspaper.

The points we shall be making may help you to make up your mind. We hope you find they make good common sense, and that you will feel there is less of a brick wall between us than some of you may have previously thought.

*British Railways Board, Room 112, Rail House, Euston Square, P.O. Box 100, London NW1 2DZ.

This is the age of the train ⇌

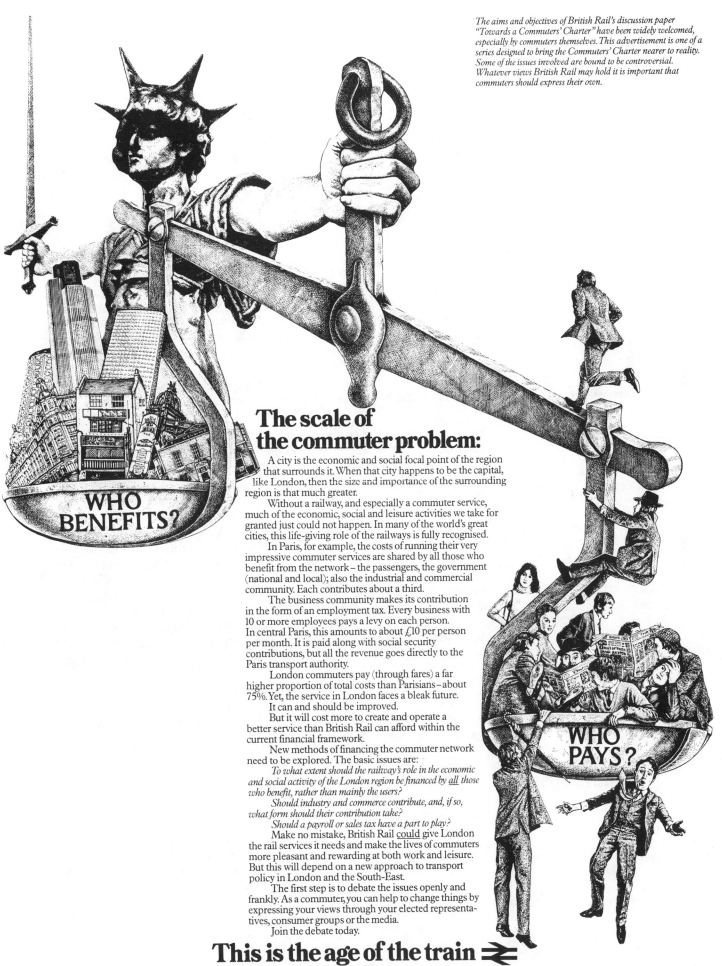

Exhibit 6

The aims and objectives of British Rail's discussion paper "Towards a Commuters' Charter" have been widely welcomed, especially by commuters themselves. This advertisement is one of a series designed to bring the Commuters' Charter nearer to reality. Some of the issues involved are bound to be controversial. Whatever views British Rail may hold it is important that commuters should express their own.

The scale of the commuter problem:

A city is the economic and social focal point of the region that surrounds it. When that city happens to be the capital, like London, then the size and importance of the surrounding region is that much greater.

Without a railway, and especially a commuter service, much of the economic, social and leisure activities we take for granted just could not happen. In many of the world's great cities, this life-giving role of the railways is fully recognised.

In Paris, for example, the costs of running their very impressive commuter services are shared by all those who benefit from the network – the passengers, the government (national and local); also the industrial and commercial community. Each contributes about a third.

The business community makes its contribution in the form of an employment tax. Every business with 10 or more employees pays a levy on each person. In central Paris, this amounts to about £10 per person per month. It is paid along with social security contributions, but all the revenue goes directly to the Paris transport authority.

London commuters pay (through fares) a far higher proportion of total costs than Parisians – about 75%. Yet, the service in London faces a bleak future.

It can and should be improved.

But it will cost more to create and operate a better service than British Rail can afford within the current financial framework.

New methods of financing the commuter network need to be explored. The basic issues are:

To what extent should the railway's role in the economic and social activity of the London region be financed by all those who benefit, rather than mainly the users?

Should industry and commerce contribute, and, if so, what form should their contribution take?

Should a payroll or sales tax have a part to play?

Make no mistake, British Rail could give London the rail services it needs and make the lives of commuters more pleasant and rewarding at both work and leisure. But this will depend on a new approach to transport policy in London and the South-East.

The first step is to debate the issues openly and frankly. As a commuter, you can help to change things by expressing your views through your elected representatives, consumer groups or the media.

Join the debate today.

This is the age of the train ⇌

Then, on November 17, 1980, after the report of the MMC was released, the company issued another ad. The thrust of "Judge for yourself" was not to defend the company against criticism in the report but to show up and ridicule certain members of the press. These journalists were known to be anti-British Railways and had not bothered to read the report very carefully. The ad contained a reprint of the summary of the report's conclusion, which stated that British Railways was already taking steps that would lead to substantial improvement in its performance [Exhibit 7].

Campaign Costs

The corporate and commuter campaign cost about £0.5 million a year, a modest amount even from the British perspective. This represented 3 percent of BR's total public affairs and corporate communications budget. BR does not expect to exceed this level in future advocacy advertising efforts.

Supportive Activities, Corporate Campaign

British Railways issued three important documents in the latter part of 1980 and in early 1981 to support and enhance the impact of its advertising: British Railways' Corporate Plan 1981–85, the Review of Main Line Electrification and Rail Policy. The corporate plan (an annually published five-year rolling plan) set out the broad background factors affecting planning for British Railways and highlighted the constraints government financial policy was placing on investment. For the first time ever, the company made this document available in full to the media. The Review of Main Line Electrification was a complex consideration of five alternative proposals for different scales of electrification. Financial analyses highlighted the wisdom of broad-scale electrification, with a real rate of return of 11 percent. The Rail Policy document set out the long-range strategic options for the railways—a severely reduced network or a commitment to a major program of investment from 1983 onward in order to create the modern and efficient railway system Britain needed.

BR also engaged in intensive communications through in-house publications to inform its employees and workers of its efforts to improve productivity, increase investment, and maintain British Railways as a viable and robust enterprise.

ACHIEVEMENT OF CAMPAIGN OBJECTIVES

British Railways believes that its campaign, including the commuter campaign, has been successful and has achieved its objectives. The success could be measured along three dimensions: (1) achievement of its investment objectives; (2) creation of favorable press coverage, and (3) changes in public opinion as evidenced through tracking studies.

Exhibit 7

Who's right about the Monopolies and Mergers Commission Report on Commuter Services?

But we have heard this excuse before. Public money has been poured into the railways, though to little effect, ever since the war.

The root cause of the present awful services is not Government stinginess but, as the Monopolies Commission's report on the commuter services of London and the South-East points out, restrictive labour practices and inefficient management.

One wonders, do Sir Peter the other British way gr...

Daily Mail, Friday, October 3, 1980

commuter ... got a more sensible an ... than it deserved. The Commission was asked to report simply on costs, efficiency and monopoly. It has replied that while the service could certainly be improved through better management, and might be made to yield more revenue, such steps as it has identified will not solve the problems of a service which it says is under-capitalised, under-paid, under-manned, and demoralised by lack of clear objectives.

The 'social railway'

The Commission gets to the heart of the problem when it defines the commuter network as "the social railway." Railways are almost as necessary ... ctioning of ...

The task of Government is to decide how far commuter services should be supported by those who do not use them, but nevertheless benefit from their existence—road users, employers, retail and entertainment, businesses, and society at large. Only within a realistic financial framework can the commuter services be expected to maximise their returns and plan for the future.

Unfortun ... he C ...

Financial Times Friday October 3 1980

These are two contrasting views. To enable you to make up your own mind, we have reprinted the summary of the Report's conclusions below. We have underlined some of the major points—those we find especially significant.

Judge for yourself.

... the possibility of s... ... outcome of the discussions now starting with ... unions of the Board's productivity proposals.

13.5. We have made a number of recommendations for the improvement of the Board's performance. We believe that if these recommendations are adopted the public interest will be better served than it is today. We have found, however, that the Board are already taking steps which should lead to a substantial improvement of their performance. This they are doing in each of the major areas which we have investigated—the quality of the service provided, productivity and the efficient use of resources, the adjustment of services to match demand and the planning of investment. These efforts should be supplemented in accordance with our recommendations; but in our judgement, it cannot now be said that the Board are pursuing a course of conduct which operates against the public interest.

13.6. We conclude this report with three observations. The first concerns the commuter's aspiration. Stated in the simplest terms, this is for an adequate service and a punctual train providing a seat in a reasonably clean coach. This is modest enough; but to satisfy it on a railway system as complex and as highly utilized as that in London and its surroundings is not a simple matter. There are direct connections between the level of service which can be provided and the price which is paid for it, and between the frequency of the service and its reliability. The Board's relations with the public would be better, we believe, if these connections were better understood. We have made a recommendation with this in view (paragraph 12.39).

13.7. Our second observation concerns the effect of the financial constraints under which the Board work. On the one hand, they have brought a new awareness at all levels of management of the need to operate the social railway with due regard for economy. The concept of what the business can afford is being built into investment appraisals. The pace of strategic planning has quickened. Management seems to be approaching the problem of labour productivity both more systematically and with greater resolve than has sometimes appeared in the past. On the other hand, arbitrary cuts have sometimes been made in response to a particular crisis and on occasions have subsequently been restored. Station maintenance and refurbishment are being neglected and the ultimate cost is likely to escalate as a result. The rate of track renewal is being reduced and if this continues quality of service will eventually suffer.

13.8. We make these two observations conscious of our conclusion that to some extent the Board's costs could be reduced without reduction of the quality of service and the quality of service could be improved without increase of costs. However, there is obviously a limit to what can be done in this way. Our final observation therefore concerns the future. The problem of the interrelation of service, costs and charges cannot be tackled satisfactorily unless the business is being conducted with a clear objective. The 1974 direction however useful it may have been in the past, is no longer adequate for this purpose. We found uncertainty both at the Headquarters of the Board and in the Regions about the extent of the limitation which it places on management's discretion. Such uncertainty may easily lead to inaction. It is urgently necessary that the Government should redefine the objective which the Board are to be expected to achieve in operating the social railway in L & SE. The Government's decision about this will presumably be reached after consultation with the Board. We hope that these consultations may extend also to our recommendations, so that there may be clear understanding between the Government and the Board of the programme for implementing them.

J G LE QUESNE (Chairman)

C J M HARDIE

H L G GIBSON

R L MARSHALL

T M RYBCZYNSKI

S SADLER

J GILL (Secretary)
28 August 1980

Giving his initial reaction, Sir Peter Parker, Chairman of British Rail said: "I welcome the Report because it goes to the very root of the problem, to urge a re-definition of our objectives in operating London and South-East services...This Report does make plain that there must be a clearer focus on the needs of the commuter, there must be an act of national will to build up resources to serve London and the South-East."

British Rail has already made its case perfectly clear in the booklet 'Towards a Commuters' Charter,' which raised the crucial issues:

To what extent should the railway's role in the economic and social activity of the London region be financed by all those who benefit, rather than mainly the users?

Should industry and commerce contribute, and, if so, what form should their contribution take?

Should a payroll or sales tax have a part to play?

The most important thing, however, is that you make up your own minds—and express your views. Join the debate today.

This is the age of the train ⇌

On June 18, 1981, the secretary of state for transport announced a government commitment to electrification, asking BR to submit a ten-year plan for the commencement of work. This was a very important step forward for the railways. The British Monopolies and Mergers Commission Report, published in November 1980, commented on the British Railways campaign as it pertained to the running of commuter services in London and the Southeast. After analyzing the effects of the financial constraints under which the British Railways board was operating, the report concluded that "in our judgement, it cannot now be said that the board is pursuing a course of conduct which operates against the public interest."[3]

One of the most interesting measures of the effect of the campaign, as stated by the company, was the vast increase in the number of questions asked in the House of Commons about British Railways. On January 28, 1981, when the second phase of the corporate campaign was running, "there were 32 written questions for the Secretary of State to answer and half of them related specifically to levels of investment in the railways."

Creation of Favorable Press Coverage

Corporate campaign achievement is perhaps best encapsulated in these statements or comments in the media.

The political editor of the *Financial Times* wrote about the concern of some ministers about BR investment and stated that: "Conservative back-benchers, who have been critical of recent relaxation of spending by the nationalized industries, were critical last night. Mr. Fowler, the Secretary of State for Transport, is likely to face anxious questioning next week when he is to make a detailed statement to parliament."[4]

On June 15, 1981, Frances Gibb stated that "British Rail is confident that it is likely to be the large-scale £700 million option, despite prediction in the past few days that misgivings about productivity performance of the railways would result in only minor electrification in East Anglia."[5]

The *New Standard,* once very hostile to British Rail, in an editorial on December 31, 1980, urged Mrs. Thatcher "to allow British Rail money it needs to invest and keep its passengers, even if that goes against the [Government's] general doctrine."

Hugo Young, political editor of the *Sunday Times,* on May 10, 1981, stated: "Major investment programmes . . . would have good effects through the economy. More electrification for BR is the fashionable front-runner."

This idea was echoed by the *New Standard* on May 11, 1981: "There is wide acceptance, from the cabinet down, that it is worth spending every penny we can afford on major capital investment for the future which add to the prosperity of the whole country. BR's electrification plans are a classic example." And a leading article in the *Times* on May 29, 1981, concluded: "The choice is not between investing in the railways or letting them stumble along as they are. Standards will decline sharply in a very few years unless there is heavy expenditure. The chances of gaining a satisfactory return on the investment are good so long as productivity really does improve. BR's renewal program is just the kind of addition to the country's wealth-producing public services that is required at a time of slump."

Changes in Public Opinion

To evaluate the effectiveness of individual advertisements, BR engaged Research Bureau, Ltd., to undertake a field study. The qualitative research was undertaken during September–November 1981 and consisted of 20 individual in-depth interviews among opinion leaders selected from a contact sample of 100 people drawn from the target group. These 20 people were divided among various occupational groups. The composition of the final sample was: senior managers, private industry, 6; members of Parliament, 4; news/press representatives, 4; senior personnel, nationalized industries, 2; advisory/professional associations, chief executives, 2; academic research, 1; publishing, 1. Nondirective interviewing techniques were employed to explore comprehension and reactions to the advertisement's content and treatment, and all interviews were taped.

The research was designed to look at the reactions of target groups to the campaign as a whole, and to each of the four ads (European comparison, motorway comparison, electrification, and export performance). More specifically, it sought to:

- Assess awareness and perceptions of the campaign and its individual components
- Examine the intelligibility of the advertisements
- Gauge the credibility, relevance, and level of acceptance of the British Rail presentation of the case among the target audience
- Evaluate reactions to the treatment values of the four campaign elements

The results of the research are briefly summarized below:

1. *Stated aims of the campaign.* A number of respondents did wonder what the objectives of such a campaign were, and who the target audience was. On the one hand they considered the ads too complicated and political for the "man in the street," while on the other hand they felt they were lacking in detail and hard facts if they were to be interesting and useful for "opinion formers." It was also felt that people in the latter group would be unlikely to spend the time reading advertisements like these, and if they needed this type of information they would look elsewhere for it.
2. *This Is the Age of the Train.* As a slogan for British Rail, "This Is the Age of the Train" was thought to work well. Certainly the majority of the sample had heard the phrase before, and the idea of using the same theme across all British Rail advertising was well received. However, until they were questioned about its meaning, few people had considered the phrase as being anything more than

a clever piece of advertising. At this level it was successful—it was catchy and easy to remember.

3. *Level of awareness.* Even though interviewing was conducted some time after the corporate campaign had been in the press, the level of awareness of the individual advertisements was disappointingly low. When they were prompted, similar proportions of the contact sample—about a third—said they recalled seeing the European comparison and motorway comparison in the newspapers, very few remembered the other two advertisements—electrification and export performance. This poor recall seems to be in part due to the way these opinion leaders read newspapers. While it is necessary for them to be knowledgeable about current events, the time they can dedicate to newspaper reading is limited, and they therefore tend to be highly selective in the articles they read, concentrating mainly on news items and editorial comment, and often intentionally avoiding advertisements.

4. *General knowledge of the subject.* One important point that emerged from this research was that people had little knowledge about how British Rail's income was derived, or on what it was actually spent. What knowledge there was tended to be confused, and it was thought that a number of misunderstandings occurred because of it, some of them detrimental to British Rail's image. For example, the majority of the sample assumed that British Rail competed with the rest of the public sector for its funds and that if it was to receive further government assistance, it was likely to be at the expense of other "worthy causes" such as the National Health Service or education. There was only minor awareness of the Transport Fund and the fact that British Rail's subsidy comes out of this. On the expenditure side, little was known about the amount of money needed simply to maintain existing standards, or about the large amount of British Rail's spending that was invisible to travelers.

5. *Consistency of the campaign.* Although the four advertisements were designed to make up the first phase of the corporate campaign, respondents felt that the last of these was not consistent with the others, for several reasons. While the first three were concerned with increasing investment in British Rail, export performance seemed to be more of a public relations or image-building exercise. Also, whereas the style of the others was fairly straightforward and serious, it was felt that in the export performance ad, British Rail had adopted a rather flippant approach which made the organization appear to be slightly complacent about it achievements. While it was thought that there was room for a less sophisticated version of this advertisement, designed to improve the general public's image of British Rail, for opinion leaders this lighthearted treatment was considered to be out of place.

The small size of the sample and the unstructured questionnaire make the findings of this study highly suspect in terms of reliability and as a guide for further action. Nor should one put a great deal of faith in the researchers' analytical comments and conclusions. Nevertheless, certain observations are in order:

1. The campaign was initiated without paying adequate attention to developing an understanding of the target audiences and how best to communicate with them.

2. It should not have come as any surprise to the company or its agency that the so-called opinion leaders, the upper income-education-occupation group, pay comparatively less attention to advertisements in their daily newspapers, especially to elicit information about complex issues of public controversy. This is why a product-type ad with high graphic and pictorial content has not been generally successful in attracting readers to advocacy messages. Tracking studies in the United States consistently show that long copy, which is full of facts and figures, and a straight editorial no-nonsense format have been most successful in generating high levels of attention, comprehension, and recall of ad messages.

3. This was not necessarily a poor campaign. Perhaps the very fact of the campaign created enough excitement among those people who watch and follow each other that it forced the issue onto the front burner and generated desirable government action.

Conclusion

The government announced its commitment to electrification in June 1981. There followed somewhat of a hiatus in the debate about the railways. November 1981, however, saw the subject creeping back into the headlines, culminating in the railway finance debate in the House of Commons on Tuesday, November 24, 1981.

It was therefore an appropriate time for the British Rails to take the initiative once more by reminding a wider audience about the issues involved. On the morning of the debate, the "Iceberg" advertisement appeared in the *Times* [Exhibit 8]. This ad had first appeared as part of the second phase of the corporate campaign. It was rapidly followed by the "monopoly" advertisement, with another advertisement, "Could we reach the point of no return?" scheduled to follow soon after [Exhibit 9]. This ad was part of the original commuter campaign and dealt with the problems of running the commuter network. It was also the only advertisement in the entire campaign that urged readers to contact their elected representatives to give the representatives their views.

Exhibit 8

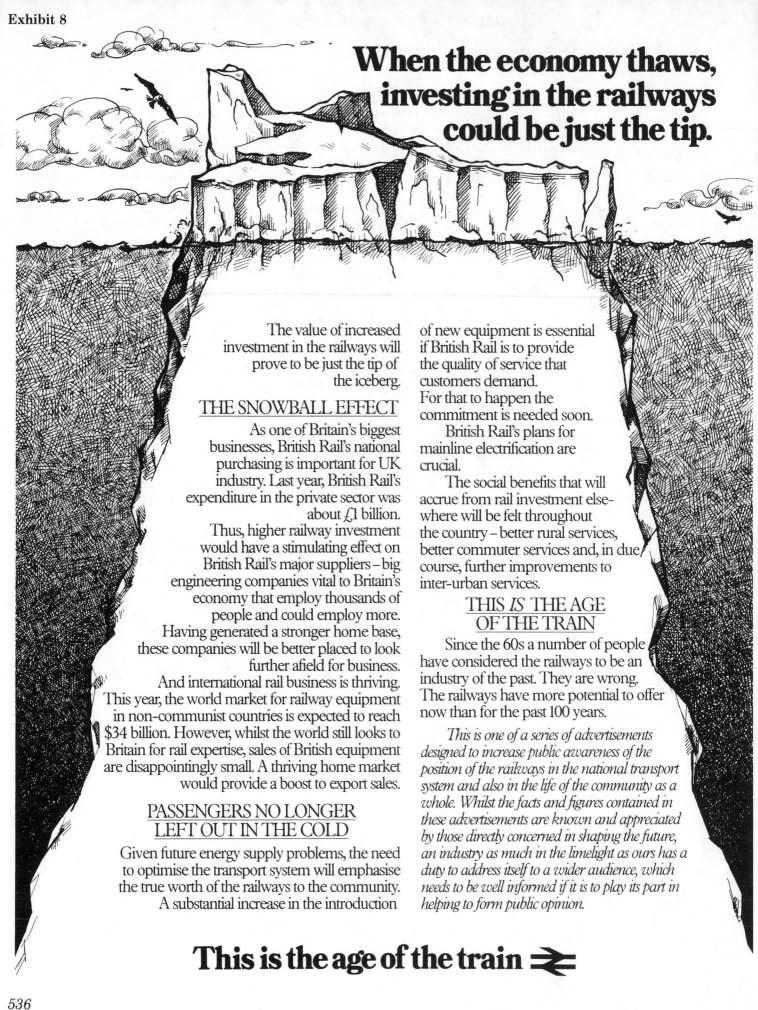

When the economy thaws, investing in the railways could be just the tip.

The value of increased investment in the railways will prove to be just the tip of the iceberg.

THE SNOWBALL EFFECT

As one of Britain's biggest businesses, British Rail's national purchasing is important for UK industry. Last year, British Rail's expenditure in the private sector was about £1 billion.

Thus, higher railway investment would have a stimulating effect on British Rail's major suppliers – big engineering companies vital to Britain's economy that employ thousands of people and could employ more.

Having generated a stronger home base, these companies will be better placed to look further afield for business.

And international rail business is thriving. This year, the world market for railway equipment in non-communist countries is expected to reach $34 billion. However, whilst the world still looks to Britain for rail expertise, sales of British equipment are disappointingly small. A thriving home market would provide a boost to export sales.

PASSENGERS NO LONGER LEFT OUT IN THE COLD

Given future energy supply problems, the need to optimise the transport system will emphasise the true worth of the railways to the community. A substantial increase in the introduction of new equipment is essential if British Rail is to provide the quality of service that customers demand.

For that to happen the commitment is needed soon.

British Rail's plans for mainline electrification are crucial.

The social benefits that will accrue from rail investment elsewhere will be felt throughout the country – better rural services, better commuter services and, in due course, further improvements to inter-urban services.

THIS *IS* THE AGE OF THE TRAIN

Since the 60s a number of people have considered the railways to be an industry of the past. They are wrong. The railways have more potential to offer now than for the past 100 years.

This is one of a series of advertisements designed to increase public awareness of the position of the railways in the national transport system and also in the life of the community as a whole. Whilst the facts and figures contained in these advertisements are known and appreciated by those directly concerned in shaping the future, an industry as much in the limelight as ours has a duty to address itself to a wider audience, which needs to be well informed if it is to play its part in helping to form public opinion.

This is the age of the train ⇒

Exhibit 9

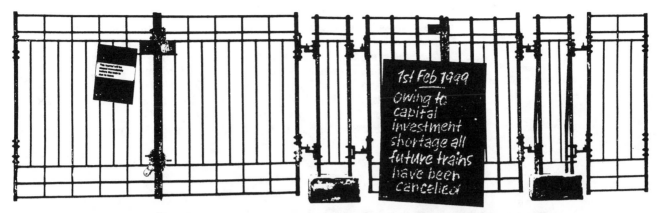

Could we reach the point of no return?

Imagine it is Monday morning, 1st February 1999. London is in danger of grinding to a halt.

Many roads into the capital are blocked. Thousands of commuters are stuck in traffic jams.

Some even feel reluctant to attempt the journey. The more conscientious get to work on foot.

The commuter service looks moribund. It seems too late to resuscitate it.

This vision of the future could be a real possibility.

WHAT IS DAMAGING THE RAILWAY?

Let's examine the railway's financial system. There are two sorts of costs. The direct costs of operating the trains, and the indirect costs of maintaining the network.

Both have to be paid for. But all over the world, railways have

lived within these cash limits ever since.

Costs are being forced upwards all the time. Even allowing for considerable productivity gains, it is forecast that direct costs of operating commuter services will increase by about 45% in real terms by 1993. The revenue contribution for covering indirect costs will fall to one quarter of its present level.

Worse, the financial outlook is so bad on inner zone services (those up to 20 miles from Central London) that in the immediate future, it will become impossible to cover even direct costs.

FEAST AND FAMINE

Even the briefest examination of investment in the commuter network over the last few decades shows the glaring contrast between the 1950's and recent years. In the

bished. The introduction of new trains has dwindled to minimal proportions. Only one third of the inadequate investment funds likely to be available to London and the South East over the next ten years will be deployed on essential new equipment. The rest will be used for patching up, which is no solution to the real problem.

HOPES FOR RECOVERY

The railway can have a bright future, providing it can overcome the problems of the past.

Given the extreme shortage of money for investment, progress has still been made.

By 1978, the considerable improvements to the Great Northern services from Kings Cross and Moorgate had been completed.

1979 saw the final re-equipping of the London Bridge Complex, now more convenient and pleasant for passengers and more efficient in operation. London and the South East also benefitted from 200 new coaches, with a similar number planned for each year after.

1980's comprehensive programme, including electrification, modern signalling, improved track, better stations and new trains, will change the face of the Bedford – St. Pancras/Moorgate route. Improvements to the approaches to Victoria are already well under way. And rolling stock on the Kent Coast routes and services out of Liverpool St. will be given a new lease of life.

THE STANDARDS YOU WANT

Here are the standards we want to be able to achieve throughout the commuter network:

- The target rate of cancellation to be less than 1%.

- At least 95% of departures should be on time and at least 95% of arrivals should be within five minutes of the stated time.
- Seats for all passengers on longer trips. At least 70% seated on short journeys.
- All trains to be exterior-washed regularly, swept out after each return trip; seats to be brushed and toilets cleaned daily. Walls and floors to be washed at least monthly and graffiti to be cleared currently.
- The standards of heating, ventilation and riding to be improved.
- The facilities, cleanliness and information services of stations to be improved.
- Better information links with the media.

FACING REALITY

So what is the biggest problem facing rail commuter services?

The answer is shortage of money. Not enough to keep fares from rising faster than inflation. Not enough to prevent services from deteriorating.

The hardships and turmoil you have read about at the beginning of this advertisement lie in the future – perhaps.

A bad dream, maybe, but it could become a reality.

The issues involved concern the economic and social role of the railways in the whole region. It is a role that needs to be discussed by all involved; the issues are too broad for British Rail to resolve by itself.

As a commuter, you can help to change things, but only by expressing your views through your elected representatives, consumer groups and the media. Join the debate today.

Because by looking after today, we can ensure a better tomorrow.

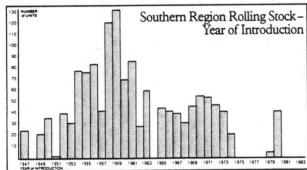

Southern Region Rolling Stock – Year of Introduction

suffered from the same problem – they have needed financial support from their governments. British Rail's self-financing ratio is higher than all the major railways in the rest of Western Europe. The real level of support for passenger services was fixed in 1975 and British Rail has

Fifties, new trains were built, new track laid and new signalling equipment installed. A veritable feast for the ailing post-war railway.

And then, famine. Most of that ageing equipment is still inevitably in service today. Instead of being replaced, it is having to be refur-

This is the age of the train ⇌

NOTES

1. *Facts and Figures,* 2nd ed. (London: British Railway Board, 1980), p. 12.
2. Quality press included: *Daily Telegraph, Financial Times, Times, Guardian, Sunday Times, Observer,* and *Sunday Telegraph;* political press included: *New Stateman, Spectator, Tribune, New Society,* and *New Scientist;* commuter London evenings included: *Evening Standard* and *Evening News.*
3. See the advertisement "Judge for Yourself" [Exhibit 7].
4. Julian Haviland, political editor, "Cabinet Critics Force Thatcher to Back Railway Electrification," *Financial Times,* June 1, 1981.
5. Frances Gibb, "BR Confident of 700 Million Pound Go-Ahead," *Financial Times,* June 15, 1981.

Chapter 19

NATIONAL MARITIME COUNCIL, WASHINGTON, DC:

ADVOCACY ADVERTISING BY A GOVERNMENT-AFFILIATED PRIVATE TRADE ORGANIZATION USING TAXPAYER-SUPPORTED RESOURCES

In March 1977, the National Maritime Council (NMC), assisted by the United States Maritime Administration (MarAd), began a national media advertising campaign, "Don't Give Up the Ships." The ads ran in *U.S. News & World Report, Business Week, Time, Newsweek, Fortune,* the *Wall Street Journal,* and the *Columbia Journalism Review.* The campaign continued into 1978 and expanded to include a public relations campaign developed by Rafshoon Communications Company. Rafshoon and his agency had long been associated with President Carter. He was media consultant to Carter during the 1976 election campaign and developed many of the ads used in that campaign. The NMC campaigns were designed to stimulate public concern about the state of the American merchant marine and generate a public climate supportive of legislative efforts to revitalize the U.S. shipping industry.[1]

This case study was coauthored with Professor Carl L. Swanson, School of Business, North Texas State University.

The 1977 and 1978 advertising campaigns and the 1978 public relations campaign were investigated in 1978 by the Commerce, Consumer and Monetary Affairs Subcommittee of the House of Representatives Committee on Government Operations, chaired by Congressman Benjamin S. Rosenthal. The subcommittee's investigation initially focused on the tax treatment accorded expenditures by members of the NMC for the 1977 and 1978 ad campaigns. The charge was that the campaigns fell squarely within the grassroots lobbying section of the Tax Code and that improper tax deductions for advertising costs had been taken by members of the NMC. The investigation expanded to encompass the relationship between MarAd and NMC and the legality and propriety of taxpayer-supported MarAd activities in support of NMC and the public relations campaigns of 1977 and 1978.[2]

The "Don't Give Up the Ships" ad campaigns became the center of controversy. The 1977 campaign was defended as a joint government-business-labor effort to overcome the public's perception that the U.S. merchant marine was no longer a viable means of transportation for import and export and foreign commerce. Critics labeled the 1977 campaign as "blatant propaganda on pending legislation," which "clearly attempts to influence segments of the general public with respect to legislative matters" (H, p. 2). The MarAd/NMC relationship was described as "incestuous," "blatantly improper," and "demonstrated an utter disregard for conflict-of-interest requirements and considerations" (R, pp. 31, 33).

The subcommittee investigation was concerned with two narrow issues. Was the purpose of NMC/MarAd campaigns informational, only to create a favorable climate of public support for an American Merchant marine, or was the 1977 ad campaign, in particular, a covert form of grassroots lobbying whose purpose was to generate congressional support for cargo preference legislation then pending before Congress? Was MarAd's involvement in and support of NMC advertising activities authorized under its statutory authority, or did such activities constitute a misappropriation of public funds, subjecting MarAd staff to charges of criminal misconduct?

The involvement of NMC and through it, MarAd, a government agency, also raises significant issues of public policy. An important issue is the use of public funds by federal agencies and the executive branch to engage in paid partisan propaganda advocating a position designed to influence specific legislation. Such a course of action, if allowed in any form, would clearly endanger open public debate and subvert the flow of information on public issues on which informed public choices must depend. The NMC ad campaign illustrates this problem. Advocates of the NMC campaign contended that the only purpose of the campaign was to create favorable public opinion toward federal support of the U.S. merchant marine fleet. If the public was indeed ignorant of the needs of the U.S. merchant marine, why was there no attempt to inform the public and present both sides of the controversy surrounding the use of federal subsidies in the maritime industry? This should have been the logical course of action for a federally supported program and a federal agency. The objective of MarAd should have been "educational" in character, and not "advocacy" with a view to influencing legislation in a specific direction.

THE ADVERTISERS

The Maritime Administration

The public policy of the United States regarding maritime matters and the U.S. merchant marine is set forth in the declaration of policy of Section 101 of the Merchant Marine Act of 1936, as amended:

> It is necessary for the national defense and development of its foreign and domestic commerce that the United States shall have a merchant marine (a) sufficient to carry its domestic water-borne commerce and a substantial portion of the water-borne export and import foreign commerce of the United States and to provide shipping service essential for maintaining the flow of such domestic and foreign water-borne commerce at all times. . . . It is hereby declared to be the policy of the United States to foster the development and encourage the maintenance of such a merchant marine. [H, p. 153].

Primary responsibility for the implementation of this policy is vested in the secretary of commerce. Under the provisions of section 201 of Reorganization Plan No. 7, a major portion of the secretary's responsibilities are delegated to the assistant secretary of commerce for maritime affairs and to the Maritime Administration (H, p. 154).

Subsections 212(b) (1) and 212(d) of the 1936 act authorize and direct the secretary of commerce:

> (b) to study and cooperate with vessel owners in devising means by which—
>
>> (1) the importers and exporters of the United States can be induced to give preference to vessels under United States registry. . . .
>
> (d) to establish and maintain liaison with such other boards, commissions, independent establishments, and departments of the United States Government, and with such representative trade organizations throughout the United States as may be concerned, directly or indirectly, with any movement of commodities in the water-borne export and import foreign commerce of the United States, for the purpose of securing preference to vessels of United States registry in the shipment of such commodities. [H, pp. 134–155]

MarAd administers programs to aid in the development, promotion, and operation of the U.S. merchant marine. MarAd, among other things,

> (1) administers Federal subsidy programs whereby it pays certain construction and operating cost differentials for ships constructed in U.S. shipyards and operating under the U.S. flag.
> (2) administers the construction, chartering, acquisition, and disposal of merchant ships to meet national defense needs and ensure compliance with the statutory requirements of the Merchant Marine Act. [R, pp. 6–12]

The Merchant Marine Act of 1970 was enacted into law, with only two dissenting votes, in response to the decline of the U.S. flag fleet since World War II. The share of cargo carried on U.S. ships had dwindled and was continuing downward. Obsolescence was engulfing the American merchant fleet. Frequent strikes and work stoppages plagued the shipping industry. The Senate Commerce Committee *Report* on the 1970 legislation noted the need for stability in the industry. The 1970 legislation emphasized market development and broadened the direct and indirect financial assistance programs available to the maritime industry (R, p. 7).

MarAd, under section 603(b) of the 1970 act, through its Maritime Subsidiary Board, is authorized to pay operating-differential subsidies. During fiscal years 1975 through the first half of the 1978 fiscal year, MarAd awarded to ship operators a total of $977 million in such subsidy payments. MarAd is also authorized to pay construction-differential subsidies, and during that same fiscal period awarded a total of $300 million. As of March 1978, Maritime Administration guarantees under the ship financing guarantee program totaled over $1.66 billion. The 1970 act also created a capital construction fund program which, as of December 31, 1977, totaled $97.7 million. The assistant secretary of commerce for maritime affairs serves as maritime administrator and chairman of the Maritime Subsidy Board (R, pp. 7–8).

The National Maritime Commission (NMC)

The NMC is a direct result of the 1970 act. Under the stimulus of the 1970 legislation, MarAd's newly formed Office of Market Development (OMD) initiated a major program to establish direct personal contact with exporters, importers, and other organizations controlling or influencing the routing of cargo.

One of OMD's first projects was to establish a nonprofit organization which would bring together all elements of the shipping industry under an umbrella organization, in which MarAd would play a major role, to develop and maintain programs aimed at improving the public image of U.S. merchant ships through advertising and similar promotional activities. Under the auspices of Andrew Gibson, assistant secretary for maritime affairs in 1971, industry leaders were invited in the spring of 1971 to form such an organization. The first meeting of MNC was held on June 30, 1971, and NMC became operational on December 16, 1971, with its incorporation in the District of Columbia (H, pp. 92–94, 274).

The original membership of the board of governors of NMC consisted of 12 U.S. flag liner companies, 7 shipbuilding or repair companies, 5 representatives of maritime-related labor unions, one representative of MarAd, and one trade association representative. The board consisted in 1977 of 37 member organizations, including the assistant secretary of commerce for maritime affairs (also maritime administrator and chairman of the Maritime Subsidy Board). Membership in the council is open to citizens of the United States who own or operate U.S. flag vessels, shipyards, maritime trade associations, maritime labor unions, and appropriate departments and agencies of the federal government (H, p. 265).

Until July 25, 1978, MarAd was a member of NMC, though it did not pay any dues or assessments. The assistant secretary of commerce for maritime affairs served on the board of governors, the director of MarAd's Office of Market Development (OMD) served as executive secretary, and OMD staff operated as the executive secretariat to NMC. As such, OMD performed various tasks and services generally considered to be of a secretarial nature—handling of correspondence, notification of and preparation for programs and meetings, management of NMC social events, billings and collections of regular and special assessments, maintenance of mailing lists, reporting of activities and meetings, maintenance of general files and assistance to NMC committees, as well as providing the necessary continuity for activities undertaken by NMC. In addition, MarAd personnel devised an official NMC seal, created an NMC press kit, issued NMC press releases, and published a quarterly newsletter. Though NMC paid for stamps, stationery, a post office box, etc., MarAd staff time was provided free of charge at a cost of approximately $200,000 annually. MarAd employees were active in discussion, planning, and implementation of virtually all phases of NMC's policies, activities, and programs, including the NMC advertising campaigns. Meeting space was provided NMC in the Department of Commerce Building in Washington, DC (H, p. 157; R, pp. 10–12).

THE DON'T GIVE UP THE SHIPS ADVERTISING CAMPAIGNS

The Burson-Marsteller Attitudinal Study

In 1976, NMC funded a study of the U.S. merchant marine industry and institution to determine attitudes, level of interest, knowledge, opinions and positions of decision-makers and influentials who affect the shipping industry. Conducted by Burson-Marsteller, the executive summary, dated March 18, 1976, stated:

> There is confusion in government officials' minds over the role of the Merchant Marine and whether it is an industry or an official institution like the Reserve or National Guard. This blurs the image of the Merchant Marine, causing a decision-maker to doubt the need for the institution—since he doesn't understand its national security function—and to doubt the need to subsidize the industry—since he doesn't see its services as essential to the nation. [H, p. 406]
>
> We found more apathy and skepticism than outright antagonism. This attitude was due to confusion and ignorance—a lack of basic knowledge about the industry. [H, p. 407]

The Burson-Marsteller Report recommended the industry communicate with its present and potential allies to give them a more solid factual basis for their support, turn reluctant friends into active advocates wherever possible, and change the atmosphere within which political decisions concerning its future are made by creating more positive industry news in the media decision-makers read and watch. To those who will accept it, the industry and its allies must drive home the following positions:

- The merchant marine is as vital to national defense as the National Guard or any other reserve force.
- The merchant marine is essential to national trading interests.
- Foreign merchant marines are seen by their governments as political and military tools and are protected, so the U.S. merchant marine also needs and warrants protection.
- The merchant marine is an integral part of our total transportation and commerce system.

The proposed communication targets, in order of priority, were:

- Key decision-makers in the administration and on the Hill
- The media, with particular emphasis on national media in Washington
- *The grass roots, but tailored to the decision-makers' constituencies so that there is political feedback* [emphasis added]

The report recommended that an intensive and comprehensive Washington media campaign be mounted to create favorable news in the Washington-based national media (H, pp. 407–408).

James R. Barker, chairman of the NMC board of governors and chairman of Moore-McCormack Resources, Inc., would testify on July 21, 1978, that the Burson-Marsteller Report was the genesis of the 1977 and 1978 "Don't Give Up the Ships" advertising campaign.

> With respect to the National Maritime Council's advertising program for 1977 and 1978, the Council was seeking legitimate means to determine what best could be done to revitalize the United States merchant marine. Toward this end the Council contracted with Burson-Marsteller to conduct an evaluation of the public image of the United States merchant marine. That study was completed in February of 1976 and noted inaccurate public perceptions such as, "The United States merchant fleet is made up of old, dirty ships." "American ships are manned by tough, irresponsible adventurers." "The industry is unreliable." "Ocean shipping is dying out because it takes too long."
> These perceptions were all the more appalling because they were totally inaccurate. . . .
> Based upon the finding of Burson-Marsteller, recommendations were made to the Council with respect to a program to improve the public identity of the United States merchant marine. The Council determined that one of the best answers to solving this public image problem was to engage in a national advertising campaign designed to dispel misconceptions.
> In March of 1977, the Council began its national media campaign "Don't Give Up the Ships." . . .
> I believe that the advertising copy of both the 1977 and 1978 campaigns was designed to stimulate the interest of the American importer and exporter to utilize the United States merchant marine—that was its purpose. [H, p. 276]

Selection of Van Sant Dugdale as the Advertising Agency

Van Sant Dugdale & Co. learned through *Business Week* that NMC was seeking an advertising agency to prepare and implement a national media advertising campaign. The agency submitted a written presentation on September 1, 1976, based upon data furnished by the executive secretary of NMC which included the Burson-Marsteller Report. In December 1976, the board of NMC selected Van Sant Dugdale to be the agency for the media campaign (H, p. 15).

Van Sant Dugdale proposed a media campaign directed to two audiences: (1) Congress and its staff; the executive branch, with emphasis on DOD and OMB; and the resident Washington media community. (2) Senior management and directors of large American corporations. The agency's Perspective, Creative Strategy, and Media Recommendation Report recommended that:

> Because the industry is so subject to the policies set out, laws enacted and budgets allocated in Washington, it is necessary to insure that the positive NMC story is told effectively in Washington. Certainly the Congress and its staff personnel must be made aware of the value of a healthy U.S. Merchant Marine. The existing subsidy program must be protected. The Program should additionally work to foster a new climate. *One that would see legislation passed requiring that a quota of various cargoes be carried in U.S. flag vessels.* [Emphasis added; H, pp. 35–36]

The Campaign Strategy

Van Sant Dugdale's creative strategy was to build the NMC story around a short, memorable theme, "Don't Give Up the Ships"—a theme that captured the principle of NMC advertising, that America must not resign itself to being a third-rate maritime power. Using that theme as an umbrella, print advertisements would be placed in selected publications and run on selected TV programs. The advertisements were designed to reach two target audiences. The primary target audience was the small but powerful group in the federal establishment numbering about 3,000 to 3,500 persons that has a direct and forceful influence on the well-being of the merchant marine. The secondary target was businesses that use U.S. shipping for foreign commerce.

The following publications and advertising expenditures [Table 1] were recommended for 1977 and 1978 (H, pp. 16, 40–43, 77).

The Washington editions of *U.S. News & World Report, Time, Newsweek,* reinforced by spots adjacent to "Face the Nation" (CBS) and "Issues and Answers" (ABC) were selected to reach the primary target. The three newsweeklies were selected because they also reach every member of Congress and the executive branch. Because these readers are important to the magazines themselves, Congress, cabinet members and high government officials receive complimentary copies. The two TV talk shows were chosen in the belief that these programs, even though they have low ratings, have great appeal among the primary target audience.

Table 1

Publication/Television	1977	1978
U.S. News (National)	$94,920	$150,660
U.S. News (Wash./Balt.)	13,255	15,925
Time (Wash.)	23,530	23,530
Newsweek (Wash.)	20,085	20,930
Columbia Journalism Review	5,625	3,750
Fortune	71,520	—
Business Week	81,550	104,850
Wall Street Journal (Eastern)	36,361	184,242
Face the Nation (Sunday)	4,550	—
Issues & Answers (Sunday)	7,800	11,700
Production costs/contingency fees	11,150	58,500
Van Sant Dugdale agency costs	57,000	85,000
Rafshoon Communications agency costs	—	90,000
	$427,346	$749,087

To reach the leaders in both broadcast and print journalism, ads would be placed in the *Columbia Journalism Review,* with a circulation of 35,000. To reach the corporate executive, Van Sant Dugdale recommended two of the nation's best-edited and prestigious business magazines, *Forbes* and *Fortune,* as well as the *Wall Street Journal's* Eastern Edition. The general business community would be reached through *Business Week* and the national edition of *U.S. News & World Report* (H, pp. 40–42).

The 1977 campaign featured six advertisements, five of which urged readers to contact their representatives. (Exhibits 1–3 are illustrative of this campaign.) Table 2 is a capsule summary of 17 advertisements published by NMC during 1977 and 1978. Three of the 1977 ads ran in January and February 1978. The 1978 campaign featured eight advertisements, none of which urged readers to write their representative. (Exhibits 4–6 are illustrative of this campaign.)

Table 2

Title of Advertisement (Abbreviated)	Number of Times Published in Various Media	Nature of Communication Regarding Congress
1977		
This message is brought to you (upside-down flag)	21	Tell your Congressman how you feel
It isn't often that labor (hands)	18	Tell your Congressman how you feel
When American flag ships (money)	7	No message
If you want a stronger America (flag ship)	6	You can still tell your Congressman how you feel
One if by land (ships)	9	Then share your thinking with your Congressman
Almost every ship in the world (cargo/smokestack)	8	Talk to your Congressman
1978		
Almost every ship in the world (cargo/smokestack)	3	Talk to your Congressman
One if by land (ships)	7	Then share your thinking with your Congressman
This message is brought to you (upside-down flag)	3	Tell your Congressman how you feel
If you want a stronger America (flag ship)	14	No message
Beware of a bear in sheep's clothing (bear)	10	No message
We've had smooth sailing for six years (ship w/outrigger)	9	No message
RO/RO your boat (money ship)	8	No message
Survival of the fittest (waves/hands)	8	No message
Do you know one way to measure (shipyard cranes)	8	No message
Can you name another industry (dog and cat)	8	No message
How much should an American merchant (ship's wheel)	6	No message

Exhibit 1

This message is brought to you by your Merchant Marine.

Actually, this "signal of distress," applied to our merchant marine, is an understatement. The position of our U.S. cargo ships in today's international marketplace is not merely distressing; it is potentially dangerous to our country politically, militarily, and economically.

Do we sound like alarmists? Consider this. After World War II, we had over 4800 U.S. flag merchant ships; today we have 577. Compare that 577 to Liberia's 2600, Russia's 2400, Japan's 2000. Today our commercial merchant fleet is tenth in size and we're eighth in merchant ship construction. Today, while Russian flag ships carry 50% of Russia's foreign trade and Japanese ships carry 39% of Japan's foreign trade, U.S. flag ships carry less than 6% of ours. (In dry bulk, less than 2%!)

If we do not build up our merchant fleet, it means losing a vital link in our intermodal transportation system. It means more dependence on foreign shipowners and their standards of care for our environment. It means less protection from unfair freight rates and practices. It means a weakened defense arm and the loss of our nation's shipbuilding capability in case of emergency. It means economic losses affecting our balance of payments, tax contribution and employment situation.

From the viewpoint of national interest, these are all good reasons to ship on U.S. flag ships. But what of the individual shipper? Does he get any direct benefit? Yes. Today, despite the erosion of our fleet, unions, management and government have been working together through the National Maritime Council to help a new-generation industry achieve its highest level of labor stability and reliable service. Technological innovations have increased U.S. capability and efficiency, and U.S. crews are among the most highly trained and productive in the world. In addition, general cargo shippers

know that U.S. flag ship rates are fully competitive with those of most foreign flag ships. You can see why it pays to ship American.

What to do? Tell your Congressmen how you feel about the American merchant marine. If you export or import, specify that your cargo goes on American flag ships. If you'd like to learn more, send for our booklet on U.S. Flag Shipping. Write National Maritime Council, Box 7345, Washington, D.C. 20044.

National Maritime Council
Management, labor and government working together for a strong, stable U.S. flag shipping industry.

DON'T GIVE UP THE SHIPS

Exhibit 2

It isn't often that Labor, Management and the Government can agree.

They do in the National Maritime Council. As a matter of fact, the Council is a unique instance of U.S. flag steamship companies, shipbuilders, labor unions and government working together. It is unique in that, since its formation in 1971, it has fostered among other things a remarkable spirit of cooperation among all elements in maintaining labor stability and reliable service in the U.S. flag cargo fleet.

Today the U.S. flag shipping industry is efficient, highly trained and technologically advanced, with freight rates comparable to most foreign shipping.

Notice we didn't say strong? While our merchant marine has been building amity within the industry, streamlining our operation and upgrading itself as a transportation system, our size and importance in the world market have eroded to a dangerous degree.

Today our post-World War II fleet of over 4800 U.S. flag merchant ships has diminished to 577. (Compare that to Russia's 2400 and Japan's 2000, for example.) Today U.S. flag ships carry less than 6% of U.S. foreign trade. (Thanks to the support of their nations, Russian ships carry 50% of USSR foreign trade; Japan, 39% of theirs; Greece, 45% of theirs.) Our share must be increased and our merchant marine strengthened if we are to continue building our intermodal transportation system, if we are to count on our merchant fleet in times of emergency, if we are to depend on its economic contribution in terms of balance of payments, increased employment and dollar-return to the American economy.

Tell your Congressmen how you feel about a stronger American merchant marine. If you export or import, specify that your cargo goes on American flag ships. If you'd like to know more, send for our booklet on U.S. Flag Shipping. Write National Maritime Council, Box 7345, Washington, D.C. 20044.

National Maritime Council

Management, labor and government working together for a strong, stable U.S. flag shipping industry.

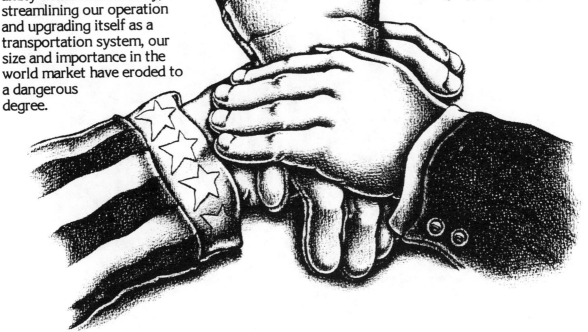

DON'T GIVE UP THE SHIPS

Exhibit 3

Almost every ship in the world carries American cargo. It's too bad more of them don't carry the American flag.

It's more than "too bad"...it should frighten you when you think of the future well-being of the country.

Since World War II, the fleet of U.S. flag merchant ships has dwindled from over 4800 to 577. In that same period, the number of Russian ships has expanded to four times the number of ours. Today, while other major nations have about 50% of their foreign trade carried on their own cargo ships, the U.S. has less than 6%.

How does this low level of participation affect our future well-being? As our merchant fleet loses strength, we lose stature in the international trade community. We lose leverage in the discussion of international freight rates. We lose a vital defense arm in case of emergency. We lose economically,

too, in our balance of payments, in number of jobs, and in taxes that a stronger merchant marine would generate.

There's no need to lose. Today U.S. cargo ships offer labor stability and efficient service, backed by highly trained crews and technological innovations and, as general cargo shippers know, at rates competitive with most foreign flag ships. What we need to do is **utilize** these modern-day advantages of the U.S. merchant fleet and rebuild it to its rightful position among world fleets.

Talk to your Congressmen. If

you'd like to know more, send for our booklet on U.S. Flag Shipping. Write National Maritime Council, Box 7345, Washington, D.C. 20044.

National Maritime Council
Management, labor and government working together for a strong, stable U.S. flag shipping industry.

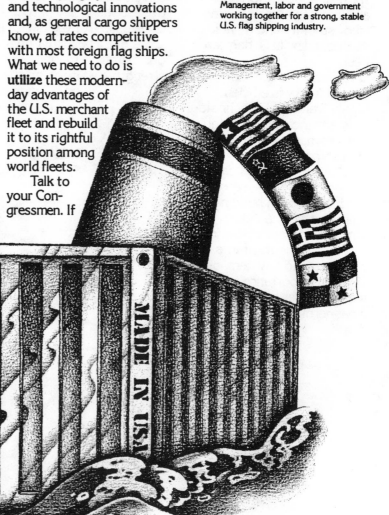

DON'T GIVE UP THE SHIPS

Exhibit 4

If you want a stronger America, there isn't any choice.

The choice <u>has</u> to be U.S. flag shipping, if you're concerned with the future well-being of our country.

Since World War II, the fleet of U.S. flag cargo ships has dwindled from over 4800 to 577. In that same period, the number of Russian ships has expanded to four times the number of ours. Today, while other major nations have about 50% of their foreign trade carried on their own cargo ships, the U.S. has less than 6%.

How does this low level of participation affect our future well-being? As our merchant fleet loses strength, we lose stature in the international shipping community. We lose leverage in the discussion of international freight rates. We lose a vital defense arm in case of emergency. We lose economically, too, in our balance of payments, in number of American jobs, and in taxes that a stronger U.S. flag merchant marine would generate.

There's no need to lose. Today U.S. cargo ships offer labor stability and efficient service, operated by highly trained crews and technological innovations and, as general cargo shippers know, at rates competitive with most foreign flag ships. What we need to do is utilize these modern-day advantages of the U.S. merchant fleet to rebuild it to its rightful position among world fleets.

If you'd like to know more, send for our booklet on U.S. Flag Shipping. Write National Maritime Council, Dept. A, Box 7345, Washington, D.C. 20044.

National Maritime Council

Management and labor working together for a strong, stable U.S. flag shipping industry.

DON'T GIVE UP THE SHIPS

Exhibit 5

Beware of a bear in sheep's clothing

The fast way to Washington, Jackson, Jefferson & Lincoln

Balt-Atlantic ad, appearing in *Containerisation International*

If you happen to have seen the advertising of Soviet shipping lines during the past year, you've come to a logical conclusion: Russians like American things. American freight. American dollars.

Are we biased in believing that their use of American presidents is deliberately deceptive? Are we biased in believing that such deception poses a threat to our economic and political welfare?

Some facts. Russia's Tenth Five-Year Plan, like those before it, calls for an expansion of the Soviet merchant marine. One of their acknowledged goals is to provide capacity for military cargoes and assist in the expansion of Soviet policy throughout the world. To this end, the Russian government gladly subsidizes its merchant fleet and often cuts shipping rates, offsetting financial loss by political gain.

Is the plan working? Twenty years ago, Russia's merchant fleet capacity was 20th in world ranking. Today, it's eighth. In 1977, Russia's merchant fleet boasted four times the number of ships in America's fleet, and their order for ships that year alone was more than one-third of our entire fleet. In 1970, Russian merchant ships called on American ports 13 times; in 1976, they made 1371 American port calls. Between 1971 and 1976, just in American ports, Russian merchant ships increased their cargo tonnage participation by nearly 22 times.

Their maritime

expansion is working. But here's what you can do about it. Help to develop a strong American merchant marine. As a shipper, before you ship goods anywhere, check out the shipping line. If it's under the Soviet flag, ask yourself if you want to continue becoming dependent on Russian merchant ships. Or, doesn't it make sense to ship on American flag ships? If the Russians are right in believing that a strong merchant marine is vital to their political goals, then a strong American flag fleet is vital for our safety.

If you'd like to know more, send for our booklet on U.S. Flag Shipping. Write National Maritime Council, Dept. E, Box 7345, Washington, D.C. 20044.

National Maritime Council

Management and labor working together for a strong, stable U.S. flag shipping industry.

DON'T GIVE UP THE SHIPS

552

Exhibit 6

Survival of the fittest

The "cruel sea" is not merely a figure of speech; it is a fact of life to those who live with it. Another fact of life: the ships most fit are the best able to survive.

American flag ships are among the fittest in the world. How do we earn that distinction? Through care—care in the three major areas of construction, equipment and crew. The standards for the construction and maintenance of American flag ships are the most stringent in the world; they are the responsibility of the Coast Guard and that responsibility is strictly exercised. Standards for equipment are equally stringent, and the gear and electronics on American flag ships are the best that technology can provide. Although our emphasis on tech-

nological innovations amuses some of our foreign friends, we've found it pays off here.

Perhaps our strongest point is the capability of American crews. To start with, their common use of one language facilitates quick communication. (Sound strange? Some accident investigators found that crews on foreign flag ships spoke <u>five</u> different languages and often didn't understand each other.) And American crew members are well-trained, thanks to the high quality of our merchant marine academies and union/management schools. In addition, every rated seaman on an

American flag ship carries a U.S. Coast Guard document, certifying he is qualified for his specialty. Those papers are carefully checked and a seaman is assigned only to a job for which he's rated. No papers, no job.

We said that American flag ships are among the fittest because of care. The care that goes into American flag shipping reflects an American tradition of another kind of caring—for the individual and his environment.

If you'd like to know more, send for our booklet on U.S. Flag Shipping. Write National Maritime Council, Dept. A, Box 7345, Washington, D.C. 20044.

National Maritime Council
Management and labor working together for a strong, stable U.S. flag shipping industry.

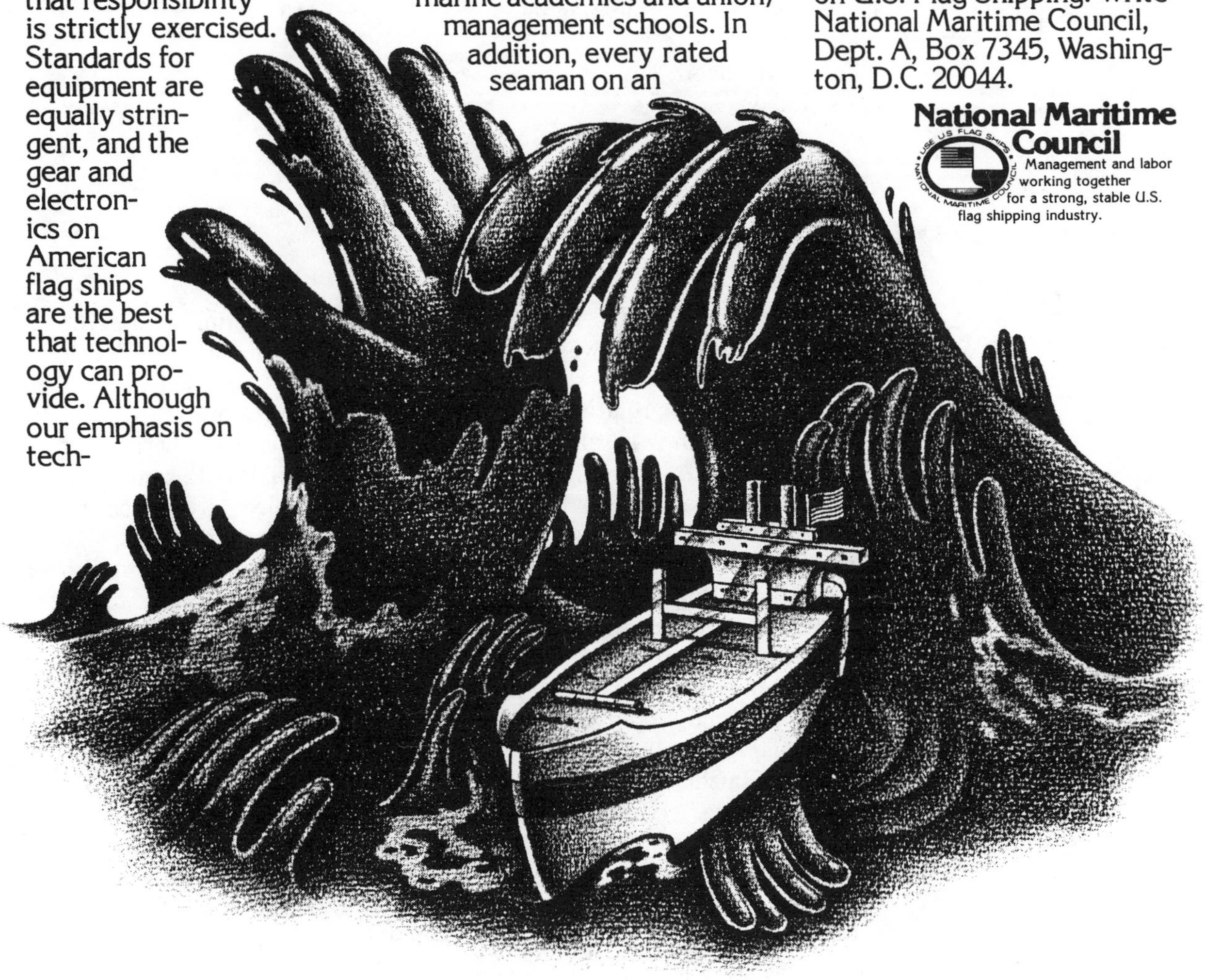

DON'T GIVE UP THE SHIPS

Media Survey of the 1977 Campaign

The advertising agency ran a media survey of the 1977 advertising campaign. It estimated that the number of magazine copies in which ads appeared reached approximately 125 million, and that the total number of readers exceeded 333 million. Based on independent research reports, the agency further estimated the following readership:

- Readers who noted the ads: 35 percent or 100 million
- Readers who identified with the ads: 20 percent or 67 million
- Readers who read most of the ads: 8 percent or 27 million

Reader response in 1977, as reflected in written requests to NMC for further information on U.S. flag shipping, was:

General public	1,263
Businesses	982
Educational institutions	154
Investment professionals	149
Media	121
Government	56
Labor	26
	2,751

The Public Relations Campaign

In late July or early August 1977, Rafshoon Communications, headquartered in Atlanta, was invited to make a presentation to NMC for a long-term public relations program. On November 1, 1977, NMC signed a one-year public relations contract with Rafshoon Communications (H, p. 74). Rafshoon was selected, according to NMC officials, because of its familiarity with maritime problems. Members of the Rosenthal committee, however, suggested that Rafshoon was selected because it was intimately acquainted with the then pending cargo preference legislation, having served as public relations consultant to President Carter who, during his bid for the presidential nomination in 1976, supported the cargo preference legislation.

Rafshoon's proposal for public education and media relations program contended that ". . . the media and, through them, the general public and many opinion leaders, view the American shipping industry with suspicion often bordering on outright hostility" (H, p. 411). NMC engaged Rafshoon to counteract and modify what was believed to be "unfair reporting" (H, p. 412). Since NMC "shares many of the concerns expressed by supporters of cargo preference legislation," Rafshoon's background in maritime matters and its experience in media relations was considered valuable in assisting NMC "to enrich public understanding and acceptance of the need for a strong U.S. flag merchant marine" (H, p. 415).

Rafshoon's objectives were: (1) To educate and inform opinion leaders and decision-makers; (2) to develop methods of exploiting interest created by and positions enunciated in current NMC advertising. The proposed public relations targets were, in order of priority: members of Congress, the administration, the Washington media, major U.S. corporation executives, traffic managers, interested government agencies, and other business, union, and association personnel. PR strategy included periodic news conferences, particularly with Washington-based media; preparation of fact kits, speech boards, a new film, and newsletters; and the development of a speakers bureau and seminars. Estimated budget was projected as $125,000 (H, p. 420).

Total Campaign Costs

The Rosenthal subcommittee investigation determined that NMC spent approximately $1,000,000 on the "Don't Give Up the Ships" advertising and related public relations campaigns. This cost was paid through special assessments of NMC members. The committee's concern focused on the executive secretariat services performed by MarAd staff, all federal employees, which the committee estimated cost the American taxpayer approximately $200,000 annually. The NMC members who notified the subcommittee that they had taken or intended to take tax deductions for the payments in support of the 1977 and 1978 campaigns were: American Export Lines; American President Lines; American Ship Building Co; Avondale Shipyards; Bethlehem Steel Corp.; Central Gulf Lines, Inc.; Crowley Maritime Corp.; Delta Steamship Lines, Inc.; Farrell Lines; Ingalls Shipbuilding; Lykes Corp.; Maryland Shipbuilding and Drydock Co.; Moore-McCormack Lines, Inc.; Moore-McCormack Resources, Inc.; National Steel and Shipbuilding Co.; Newport News Shipbuilding and Dry Dock Co.; Norfolk Shipbuilding and Dry Dock Co.; Pacific Far East Line, Inc.; Prudential Lines, Inc; Sea-Land Service, Inc.; States Steamship Co.; Todd Shipyards Corp.; United States Lines, Inc.; and Waterman Steamship Corp.

THE SUBCOMMITTEE INVESTIGATION

In August 1977, the subcommittee began an investigation of the Internal Revenue Service's enforcement and administration of tax laws relating to lobbying, particularly section 162(e) (2) of the Tax Code. This section prohibits deductions from gross income "of any amount paid or incurred (whether by way of contribution, gift, or otherwise—). . . . in connection with any attempt to influence the general public, or segments thereof with respect to legislative matters, elections or referendums." NMC reported that it did not engage in lobbying activities. The subcommittee, however, obtained copies of the "Don't Give Up the Ships" advertising, which the subcommittee felt possessed the characteristics of a grassroots lobbying effort.

As the investigation proceeded, the focus of the inquiry shifted to the "intimate" relationship between NMC and MarAd evidenced by the performance of executive secretariat functions for NMC by MarAd personnel and the presence of the assistant secretary of commerce for maritime affairs on the NMC board of governors.

Hearings were held by the subcommittee on the NMC advertising campaign and the NMC/MarAd relationship on July 20 and 21, 1978, and focused on three separate but related issues:

1. Was the "Don't Give Up the Ships" campaign a grassroots lobbying activity?
2. Did the relationship between NMC and MarAd create a conflict of interest for MarAd staff?
3. Did MarAd staff activities violate the federal statute prohibiting the use of federal funds for grassroots lobbying?

The Issue of Grassroots Lobbying

The question of whether the "Don't Give Up the Ships" campaign was a covert form of grassroots lobbying was the first target of the subcommittee inquiry. Officials of NMC and MarAd denied that the ads were designed to influence pending legislation. The following question and answer exchange between Representative Elliott H. Levitas and Raymond J. Sachs, executive vice-president of Van Sant Dugdale & Co., illustrates this difference of opinion:

> MR. LEVITAS: Let me see if I can simplify it for my thinking. One of the reasons that Government leaders were to be influenced directly or indirectly by these ads was assumedly because of the role to be played by Government in making it strong.

> MR. SACHS: Yes.

> MR. LEVITAS: It so happened that during 1977 a major piece of legislation to this end; namely, the cargo preference bill, was pending in the Congress.

> MR. SACHS: That is correct.

> MR. LEVITAS: To my knowledge . . . the only major piece of legislation pending in Congress that year was the cargo preference bill which the advocates said would make the merchant marine stronger. I would find it a dereliction on the part of your agency, which obviously does a good job because your ads are very effective, not to see the linkage between this campaign and that legislation

> MR. SACHS: I am not going to deny linkage or the potential effect. All I am saying is that the task or main objective of this advertising was not to get the cargo preference bill passed. . . . I cannot imagine that people in this period seeing this advertising and being urged to contact their Congressmen were not talking in some cases about specific legislation, but that was not a primary intent of the advertising. [H, pp. 29–30]

Sachs' denial of the linkage between the 1977 ad campaign and the cargo preference legislation then pending in Congress was complicated by his agency's "Perspective," which stated:

> The program should additionally work to foster a new climate. One that would see legislation passed requiring that a quota of various cargoes be carried in U.S. flag ships. [H, p. 19]

When questioned regarding the purpose of the campaign as stated in the Perspective, Raymond Sachs contended that the Perspective was a "selling document" and that when the agency was notified of its selection the agency was told that this objective was not consistent with the function of NMC. Sachs invited the subcommittee's attention to handwritten notes in the margin of the Perspective that stated: "Council does not officially take position on legislation" (H, p. 20). Consequently, the subsequent clarification of the role of NMC would act as "a correction to [Sachs'] understanding of what [his] role would be" (H, p. 20).

The advertising agency, NMC members, and MarAd staff would draw a distinction on when an advertisement became grassroots lobbying which the subcommittee members found unacceptable. The distinction was succinctly stated by Sachs:

> . . . it was my understanding that as long as specific legislation was not addressed in an advertisement and as long as we were not asking people to comment on specific actions or set of actions, then we were performing an information program which is distinct from a lobbying function. . . . We did not direct the reader to endorse any position. We did not ask them to favor existing or proposed legislation. We did not ask them to support any specific action or set of actions. [H, pp. 16, 18]

The subcommittee's refusal to accept this distinction can be seen in the following exchange between Sachs and Congressman Robert F. Drinan:

> MR. DRINAN: . . . Here is a sentence from your ad: "Tell your Congressman how you feel about a stronger American merchant marine." . . . How is a Congressman supposed to make it stronger unless he makes more laws that favor it or more subsidies? What other inference possibly could be drawn? It says, "a stronger merchant marine." How do we make it stronger? . . . I am just asking you what inferences can be drawn from that particular mandate to the American people.
>
> MR. SACHS: It is not a mandate. If I said to them, "Tell your Congressmen—"
>
> MR. DRINAN: It is a mandate.
>
> MR. SACHS: If I said, "Tell your Congressmen if you believe in a stronger U.S. merchant marine," that is a mandate. "Tell your Congressmen how you feel about a stronger merchant marine" is not a mandate.

MR. DRINAN: With all due respect, that is absurd. [H, p. 26]

Lewis C. Paine, director of the MarAd Office of Market Development and executive secretary of NMC, testified that he laid down instructions that there would be no discussion of any legislation in the advertisement at any time. His reasons were twofold: One, the NMC was not a lobbying organization and did not take positions on legislative issues. Two, the government was involved in the executive secretariat of NMC (H, pp. 143–144). Robert J. Blackwell, assistant secretary of commerce for maritime affairs, argued that the theme of the campaign was not consistent with the inferences being drawn by the subcommittee. He contended that if the ads were directed to the cargo preference legislation, the theme would have been on inadequacy and a need for a government handout. On the contrary, the theme was upbeat, saying that the U.S. flag fleet was reliable, competitive, and could do the job (H, p. 150).

The issue was clear-cut. NMC and MarAd staff contended that if no mention was made of specific legislation, the communication did not constitute grassroots lobbying. A legal opinion rendered by the American Law Division of the Library of Congress on June 19, 1978, supported the subcommittee's position. While case law was sparse on the issue, a U.S. district court opinion in 1976 indicated that the question centered around whether the use of funds was likely to induce persons to contact their congressional representatives. Thus a pamphlet published by a federal agency that did not mention any specific legislation "nor urge or request readers to communicate with Members of Congress" did not violate 18 U.S.C. 1913 prohibiting the use of appropriated funds in grassroots lobbying (H, pp. 358, 359).

The subcommittee's findings and conclusions were that: "The National Maritime Council's 'Don't Give Up the Ships' advertising campaign in 1977 was designed to influence and had the effect of influencing the public or segments of the public to communicate with Congress on a legislative matter [the cargo preference bill]" (R, p. 4). On the other hand, the 1978 ads, which did not mention any specific legislation nor urge readers to write to Congress, did not constitute grassroots lobbying.

The Issue of the MarAd and NMC Relationship

The subcommittee expanded its original grassroots lobbying inquiry to encompass the issue of whether Section 212 of the Merchant Marine Act of 1936, which authorizes the Maritime Administration to maintain liaison with private trade groups, permits the type of intimate association the Maritime Administration had with the National Maritime Council (H, p. 3). Robert J. Blackwell, assistant secretary of commerce for maritime affairs, would testify on July 21, 1978, that:

> MarAd's participation in the initial organization of the NMC activities are based upon our clear statutory authority in section 212(b) (1) and (2) of the Merchant Marine Act of 1936. [H, p. 94]

This position was supported by James R. Barker, chairman of the board of governors of NMC. He testified that the NMC was established to further national maritime policy, that a strong U.S. merchant marine was necessary to the national defense and commerce of the United States. A former staff member of MarAd would tell the subcommittee on July 20, 1978, that "This is the only occasion in which the symbiotic relationship of a Government agency and private industry was so clearly spelled out. It may happen in other areas, under the table or covertly or in other ways. Here you actually had a marriage formalized with documents saying the Government and private business are right in bed together" (H, p. 13).

The subcommittee's investigation focused on an opinion by the General Counsel's Office for the Department of Commerce. A July 24, 1972, memorandum stated:

> 4. There is a potentially serious conflict of interest and/or a professional ethical problem regarding:
>   (a) MarAd attorneys furnishing legal advice to the corporation;
>   (b) MarAd CPA's furnishing accounting advice to the corporation;
>   (c) MarAd Employees serving as officers of the corporation. [H, p. 4]

The recommendation was that outside legal counsel and accountants be retained, that MarAd employees be removed from positions of official responsibility in NMC, and that the assistant secretary should determine whether he wants to remain on the board of directors because of the potential legal liability imposed upon directors.

The subcommittee was to view this memorandum as a warning of a potentially serious and "adverse legal" relationship between MarAd and NMC (R, p. 3). MarAd staff would contend that the general counsel recommendations were based on policy considerations. The assistant secretary for maritime affairs contended that MarAd's presence on the board of NMC would serve as a moderating influence over NMC actions that might be embarrassing to the executive branch. Furthermore, if NMC took a position that was contrary to the official government position, MarAd could cast a negative vote and formally dissociate itself from the action (H, pp. 108–110).

The subcommittee requested an advisory legal opinion from the Congressional Research Service of the Library of Congress, American Law Division. In an opinion dated May 18, 1978, the division concluded that:

> . . . although in other regulatory agency situations, "undue familiarity of an employee" with government contractors, "serving two conflicting interests," or "divided loyalties" of employees who have close associations or business contacts or arrangements with government contractors or other regulated organizations, may lead to adverse actions and dismissals under (federal conflict of interest) standards. . . . a different result may be argued in the case of the Federal Maritime Administration officers and employees because of Congress' specific au-

thority to "cooperate," "collaborate," and "maintain and establish liaison" with representatives of private industry. [H, p. 353]

Despite this legal opinion, the subcommittee would find that the MarAd/NMC relationship was established over the "strong objections" of the Commerce Department general counsel staff and was "a blatantly improper one from its inception in 1971 and demonstrated an utter disregard for conflict-of-interest requirements and considerations" (R, p. 3).

The Issue of Misuse of Appropriated Funds

A general prohibition is placed upon all officers and employees of the United States involving the use of appropriated funds to "lobby" Congress. The subcommittee found that MarAd employees performed secretariat functions for NMC amounting to approximately $200,000 annually. The subcommittee further found that MarAd staff, particularly the executive secretary of MarAd, who also served as director of the Office of Market Development, was prominent in the selection of the advertising and public relations agencies and in establishing the policies for the 1977 and 1978 advertising campaigns of NMC. The subcommittee contended that these activities would be illegal under Section 1913.

The legal staff of the Library of Congress, in an opinion dated June 19, 1978, concluded that MarAd sponsorship of the "Don't Give Up the Ships" advertising was the type of conduct and activity with which the prohibitions on appropriated funds were intended to deal. While government officials are not prohibited from all public expression of support or opposition to legislation, use of federal funds to finance or aid in publishing an advertisement which is part of a publicity campaign intended to garner public support on a legislative issue or *to stimulate communications to members of Congress* is the type of prohibited conduct contemplated by Section 1913 (emphasis added; H, pp. 359–360).

The subcommittee's findings that MarAd, through the time of its employees and the furnishing of government facilities, expended appropriated funds for a grassroots lobbying purpose in possible violation of 18 U.S.C. §1913, was a natural result of the previous finding that the 1977 advertising campaign by NMC was a grassroots lobbying activity. Once the facts established that NMC was engaged in grassroots lobbying, any involvement by MarAd staff in that advertising activity raised questions of Section 1913 violations.

The Issue of Maritime Subsidies

One issue which the committee did not explore was the merit of the ad campaign's support for cargo preference legislation and the need for such legislation. This did not prevent some members of the committee from questioning the need for maritime subsidies. In response to Blackwell's defense of the NMC advertising campaign as a method of carrying out the congressional mandate given MarAd in the 1970 legislation, one congressman responded:

> Why doesn't the Federal Government . . . do the same thing
> for applegrowers, and for bus manufacturers, and for the chair-
> makers of America? . . . *Maybe we have to go back to revise the
> basic statutory law that another subcommittee of the Congress
> wrote.* [H, p. 127; emphasis added]

The committee's reluctance was largely due to its awareness that
such an inquiry fell properly within the domain of another congressional
committee, the Subcommittee on Merchant Marine of the Committee on
Merchant Marine and Fisheries. That committee had evaluated and approved the maritime subsidy program as a result of hearings held during
June–November 1975. However, the support of maritime experts for
subsidies was not unanimous. Gerald Jantscher of the Brookings Institution; J. Robert Vastine, deputy assistant secretary for trade, Department of the Treasury; and the General Accounting Office, in testimony
during the 1975 hearings, proposed a reconstruction of the maritime
subsidy program.[3]

They argued that the only reason for subsidies was the national security needs of the country. Economically, the subsidy program could
not be justified. They dismissed the three economic arguments usually
offered: (1) higher quality of services offered by U.S. flag ships, (2) favorable impacts on employment and output, and (3) favorable balance
of payment effects. Contrary to U.S. maritime industry contentions, current studies suggest that foreign flag ships provide as good a service as
American flag ships. More important, the objection of many maritime
experts to the cargo preference legislation is the unavailability of U.S.
flag ships to meet the needs of American shippers and the resulting
hardship (MMR, p. 68). The impact of government payments on shipbuilding and ship operating industries was considered minuscule, since
the operating subsidy program supports only 18,000 workers at a cost
of $250 million—about $14,000 a year per worker (MMR, p. 69). Finally,
the unfavorable impact on the balance of payments was estimated to be
about $700 million, or 7 percent of the total U.S. export trade. Deputy
Assistant Secretary Vastine described the magnitude of this impact as
"quite small" (MMR, p. 71).

The critics of the subsidy system agreed that the U.S. merchant marine was not adequate to meet the defense needs of the nation, but blamed
the problem on "the absence of specific defense objectives for the subsidized shipbuilding industry." Among their recommendations was the
less expensive purchase-and-put-in-reserve of *foreign-built* shipping to
be placed in the National Defense Reserve Fleet (emphasis added; MMR,
pp. 82–83).

THE AFTERMATH

On September 27, 1978, the House Committee of Government Operations approved and adopted a subcommittee report which was transmitted to the Speaker of the House of Representatives on October 2, 1978.
The subcommittee report recommended:

1. A strict arm's-length relationship between MarAd and all private maritime interests
2. Written guidelines governing future conduct of MarAd employees in joint MarAd-industry activities
3. A departmental reorganization of the promotional and subsidy functions of MarAd
4. Appropriate action by the attorney general with respect to possible violations of 18 U.S.C. §1913
5. Appropriate action by the comptroller general to recover funds improperly or unlawfully expended by MarAd in support of the NMC "Don't Give Up the Ships" advertising campaign
6. Assurances by MarAd and the Department of Commerce that federal funds would not be used to engage in grassroots lobbying (R, pp. 5–6)

On July 25, 1978, four days after completion of the July 20–21, 1978 hearings before the subcommittee, the Secretary of Commerce, Juanita Kreps, terminated the formal ties established in 1971 between MarAd and NMC. Secretary Kreps noted that while the basis of both MarAd and NMC was to maintain a strong, viable U.S. merchant fleet, "it has been demonstrated that MarAd and the council can effectively contribute to this effort by independent actions" (R, p. 36).

The secretary noted that U.S. flag penetration of the general cargo (liner) market on U.S. foreign trade routes had risen from about 22 to 30 percent, and there had not been a single major U.S. seafaring strike. She noted with approval that "The innovative marketing programs conducted by MarAd's staff under the direction of Assistant Secretary Robert J. Blackwell have contributed substantially to this improvement. His accomplishments are well recognized throughout the Government and the industry, and he deserves a great deal of credit for the progress made by the U.S. merchant marine in this decade" (R, pp. 36–37).

NOTES

1. *Hearings before a Subcommittee of the Committee on Government Operations, House of Representatives, 95th Congress, 2d Session, Part 2, Problems in the Relationship Between the Commerce Department's Maritime Administration and the National Maritime Council, a Private Trade Organization; Tax Treatment of National Maritime Council Expenditures for the "Don't Give Up the Ships" Advertising and Public Relations Campaigns,* July 20, 21, 1978. References to this citation in the text will be made as (H, p.).
2. *Report on Problems in the Relationship Between the Commerce Department's Maritime Administration and the National Maritime Council, a Private Trade Organization—Thirty-second Report by the Committee on Government Operations,* 95th Congress, 2d Session, transmitted October 2, 1978 to the Speaker of the House of Representatives. References to this citation in the text will be made as (R, p.).
3. *Hearings before the Subcommittee on Merchant Marine of the Committee on Merchant Marine and Fisheries,* House of Representatives, 94th Congress, 1st Session on National Security/Economic Benefits, June 5, 11, 19, July 9, 23, August 1, 1975; Construction Subsidy Program, Sept. 5, 10, 23, November 5, 11, 1975; Serial No. 94-15. References to this citation in the text will be made as (MMR, p.).

INDEX

INDEX